Lotus Notes 4.5 and the Internet 6 in 1

by Jane Calabria with Sue Plumley

A Division of Macmillan Computer Publishing
201 West 103rd Street, Indianapolis, Indiana 46290 USA

To My Guy

 For information, address Que Corporation, 201 West 103rd Street, Indianapolis, IN 46290. You can reach Que's direct sales line by calling 1-800-428-5331.

Library of Congress Catalog Card Number: 96-70771

International Standard Book Number: 0-7897-0975-9

99 98 97 8 7 6 5 4 3 2

Interpretation of the printing code: the rightmost double-digit number is the year of the book's first printing; the rightmost single-digit number is the number of the book's printing. For example, a printing code of 97-1 shows that this copy of the book was printed during the first printing of the book in 1997.

Printed in the United States of America

Publisher
Roland Elgey

Publishing Director
Lynn E. Zingraf

Editorial Services Director
Elizabeth Keaffaber

Managing Editor
Michael Cunningham

Director of Marketing
Lynn E. Zingraf

Acquisitions Editor
Martha O'Sullivan

Technical Specialist
Nadeem Muhammed

Product Development Specialist
John Gosney

Technical Editor
Debbie Lynd

Production Editor
Tom Lamoureux

Book Designer
Barbara Kordesh

Cover Designer
Dan Armstrong

Production Team
Michael Beaty
Erin Danielson
Maribeth Echard

Indexer
Kevin Fulcher

About the Authors

Jane Calabria has contributed to several other Que books on Lotus Notes and is also the author of the *10 Minute Guide to Lotus Notes Mail 4.5* and the *10 Minute Guide to Lotus Notes 4.5 Web Navigator.* She and her husband, Rob Kirkland, are both Certified Lotus Instructors who specialize in teaching and consulting in Lotus Notes and Lotus Internet products. They are also contributing authors to Cate Richards' *Special Edition Using Lotus Notes and Domino 4.5* and they are currently working on the soon-to-be-released *Domino 4.5 Developers Guide.* Jane is heard weekly in the Philadelphia area on KYW News Radio 1060 AM, giving reports on computing and computer news as "JC on PCs." Her reports are also found on AOL.

Sue Plumley has trained staff and employees of local companies, large corporations, and federal agencies in the use of various Microsoft applications, Microsoft Office, and other software programs, as well as offering support. She has taught the use of various software applications at Beckley College in West Virginia, and she has written and contributed to over 30 books for Que and its sister imprints.

Acknowledgments

To Dorothy Burke, whose contributions throughout this book are too many to count, and whose friendship I cherish. Thanks to Martha O'Sullivan for the opportunities she provides, and the guidance and experience she freely shares. Special thanks to John Gosney and Tom Lamoureux, who stayed focused and dedicated through exhaustive rewrites during beta releases and who kept the vision focused. And to the highly charged "Que East team: Christina Rockey, George Heake, Filza Protopova, Joan Olsen, Duncan, and Domino, the famous race horse"!

Trademarks

We'd Like to Hear from You!

As part of our continuing effort to produce books of the highest possible quality, Que would like to hear your comments. To stay competitive, we *really* want you, as a computer book reader and user, to let us know what you like or dislike most about this book or other Que products.

You can mail comments, ideas, or suggestions for improving future editions to the address below, or send us a fax at (317) 581-4663. For the online inclined, Macmillan Computer Publishing has a forum on CompuServe (type **GO QUEBOOKS** at any prompt) through which our staff and authors are available for questions and comments. The address of our Internet site is **http://www.quecorp.com** (World Wide Web).

In addition to exploring our forum, please feel free to contact me personally to discuss your opinions of this book: I'm **104436,2300** on CompuServe, and I'm **jgosney@que.mcp.com** on the Internet.

Although we cannot provide general technical support, we're happy to help you resolve problems you encounter related to our books, disks, or other products. If you need such assistance, please contact our Tech Support department at 800-545-5914 ext. 3833.

To order other Que or Macmillan Computer Publishing books or products, please call our Customer Service department at 800-835-3202 ext. 666.

Thanks in advance—your comments will help us to continue publishing the best books available on computer topics in today's market.

John Gosney
Product Development Specialist
Que Corporation
201 W. 103rd Street
Indianapolis, Indiana 46290
USA

Contents

Part III: Application Development 275

Part VI: Domino.Action 549

Welcome to *Lotus Notes 4.5 and the Internet 6 in 1*

Lotus Notes and the Internet make an obvious marriage. Each has something to offer the other. Both are versatile information repositories. Both exist to enable users to communicate and work together more effectively. Lotus Notes has been *the* ace groupware product, but has developed a reputation for being proprietary and expensive. The Internet and the World Wide Web were cheap but unruly and lacked the slick interface and control of an integrated product. Extending Notes security and document management to the Internet and pulling Internet information into Notes documents would be like harnessing the world's knowledge base. Toward that end, Lotus introduces Release 4.5.

Release 4.5 of Notes comes with some new capabilities, functionality, and names. The capabilities include the HTTP server, which dynamically delivers Notes databases to the Web; the Personal and Server Web Navigators, which retrieve pages from Web servers and convert them into Notes documents; and Domino.Action, which builds a Notes Web site in a day.

New names include the new server software now called "Domino 4.5, Powered by Notes." The Notes client remains "Lotus Notes," but now it is version 4.5. These names will initiate some readjusting for those of us who have habitually called the product "Notes." Please keep that in mind as you read through this book, and forgive me if the new names were missed here or there. It's a bit of an awkward transition for me. Finding a proper title for the book was also tricky. I opted for "Lotus Notes" because this book deals primarily with the Notes client; that is to say, most of the skills learned in this book apply to work performed with the client software.

With version 4.5 of Lotus Notes, Lotus changed the name of their software to Domino, while keeping their client software name as Lotus Notes. Throughout this book, we may universally refer to both the client and server software as Notes or Lotus Notes. Only when it becomes crucial to differentiate between client and server software do we call the server software "Domino."

We have all been affected by the Internet. I believe the Internet is about to be affected by Domino 4.5. For those of you who are new to Lotus Notes, new to this version of Notes, or new to the marriage of Notes and the Internet, this book is designed to help you "catch up" quickly.

Who Should Use This Book

Lotus Notes 4.5 and the Internet 6 in 1 is for anyone who:

- Has upgraded or is considering upgrading to Domino 4.5.
- Needs to assess the new capabilities of this version of Notes.
- Wants to learn about Lotus Notes and the Internet features of Notes.
- Needs a jump start to learning the basics of Lotus Notes.
- Wants to develop or fine-tune Notes applications for Domino 4.5 and the Internet.
- Wants to learn how to build a Domino 4.5 Web site in a day with Domino.Action.
- Is considering Lotus Notes as a business solution.
- Is a Notes application developer who needs to assess their database compatibility for Domino 4.5.

How This Book Is Organized

Lotus Notes 4.5 and the Internet 6 in 1 has lessons ranging from the basics to some more advanced features. You can work through the book lesson by lesson, building upon your skills, or you can use the book as a quick reference when you want to perform a new task.

If you are new to Notes, you will learn the basic concepts and the navigation of the product. If you're upgrading from a previous version of Notes, you'll learn how to use some of the new features of Domino 4.5, such as calendaring and scheduling. If you have been a Notes user, you will learn the basics of application development. And if you are new to the Domino 4.5 server, you will learn the basics of developing Notes applications for the Web and for configuring and running Domino.Action to build a Web site.

Icons and Conventions Used in This Book

TIP **Tip** icons point out hints and shortcuts for using the program more efficiently.

Term icons mark explanations of new terms.

Caution icons identify information that can help you avoid trouble—or help you get out of trouble you're already in.

Commands, buttons, and hotspots that you need to select, or click with your mouse, will appear in **bold;** as in, "select the **Save** button in the dialog box."

Text that appears on-screen will appear in `monospace font`. Also, field names, Window titles, and titles of dialog boxes will have the first letter uppercased, as in Window, Field, Dialog box, and so on. Sometimes you might be directed to use a combination of keyboard characters, such as "select **Ctrl+K**." This means that you should hold down the Ctrl key and the K key simultaneously.

Lotus Notes 4.5

Navigating Notes

In this lesson, you learn to start and exit Notes, identify elements on the Notes workspace, and use the mouse and keyboard.

Starting Notes

You start Notes from the Windows 95 desktop. After starting Notes, you can leave it on-screen, or you can minimize the Notes window so it's easy to access anytime during your workday.

To start Lotus Notes, follow these steps:

1. From the Windows 95 desktop, select the Start button.
2. Choose **Programs**, **Lotus Applications**, **Notes**. (If Notes is not in the Lotus Applications folder, it will be in whichever folder you specified during installation.) The Choose Location dialog box appears unless your Notes program is automatically set up for network operation.

TIP For the most part, starting, exiting, and otherwise using Notes on NT will be the same as on Windows 95.

3. Choose from the following options in the Current Location list:

   Home (Modem) Use this option when you're not connected by cable to the network and you plan to use a modem and telephone lines instead to connect to the network.

Island (Disconnected) Use this option when you plan to work in Notes but you don't plan to connect to the network during the session.

Office (Network) Use this option when you're connected to the network with cables.

Travel (Modem) Use this option when you're not connected by cable to the network and you plan to use a modem and phone line to connect instead. (The major difference between the Travel and Home locations is in how you set phone numbers and dialing options.)

This book assumes you're connecting using the Office (Network) option; however, most procedures and tasks are similar no matter which location option you choose. The Notes window appears (see Figure 1.1).

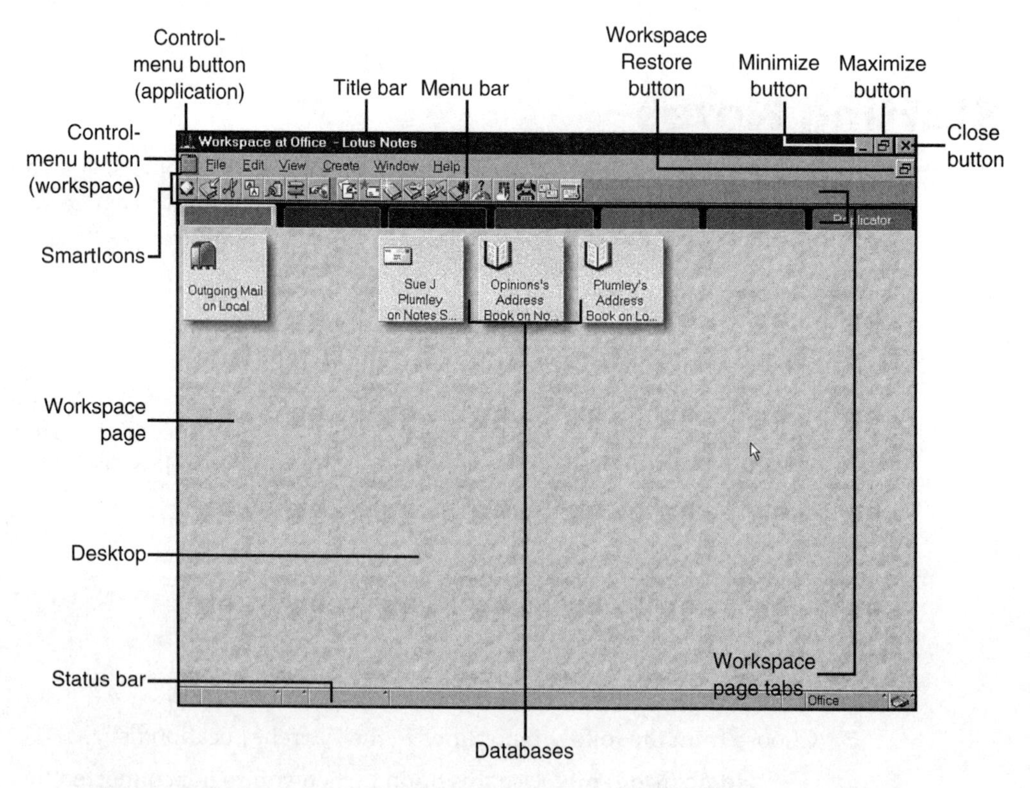

Figure 1.1 The Lotus Notes main window.

Understanding the Notes Workspace

Think of a workspace as a file cabinet drawer that holds all the data you need to complete your work at the office. Other workspace "drawers" hold the data you need when traveling, when at home, or when disconnected from the network completely. The data within a workspace consists of information databases, mail, documents you create, and documents you copy from the network, as well as various other articles you might collect to complete your work.

Each item you see in the Notes workspace has a function that helps you navigate the Notes window and complete your work efficiently. Table 1.1 describes the elements of the Notes window.

Table 1.1 Notes Window Elements

Element	*Description*
Control-menu button	Provides such commands as Move (application), Size, Minimize, and Close, with which you control the application window.
Control-menu button	Provides such commands as Move (workspace), Size, Minimize, and Close, with which you control the workspace window.
Maximize button	Enlarges the Notes window to cover the Windows 95 desktop; when the window is maximized, the Maximize button changes to a Restore button that you can click to return the window to its previous size.
Minimize button	Reduces the Notes window to a button on the taskbar; to restore the window to its original size, click the button on the taskbar.
Workspace Restore	Returns the maximized workspace button window to its previous size; when the workspace window is restored, you can display other workspace windows in the application window.
Close (X) button	Closes the Notes program.
Title bar	Contains the name of the current workspace and the program's name; also displays a description of selected menu commands.
Menu bar	Contains the menus you use to perform tasks in Notes.

continues

Table 1.1 Continued

Element	*Description*
SmartIcons	Enable you to perform tasks quickly by clicking the mouse on an icon in the SmartIcon bar.
Workspace page tabs	Enable you to change pages within the workspace; click a page tab to change to that page.
Workspace page	Holds databases and other information you want to store.
Databases	Contain collections of documents relating to the same topic; double-click a database to open it.
Mouse pointer	Enables you to access menus and perform tasks.
Status bar	Presents information about the selected item.

Workspace Pages Each workspace contains six pages you can use to organize databases. Databases contain documents and data that you create, import, copy, or otherwise access from the network.

Using the Mouse

You use the mouse to perform many actions in Lotus Notes. You can use the mouse to select items, open databases and other files, or move items, for example. After you select an item, you can perform another task on that item, such as copying, moving, or deleting it. Performing actions with a mouse is a matter of pointing, clicking, and double-clicking.

Selecting with the mouse involves two steps: pointing and clicking. To *point* to an object (an icon or a menu, for example), move the mouse across your desk or mouse pad until the on-screen mouse pointer touches the object. You can pick up the mouse and reposition it if you run out of room on your desk.

To *click*, position the mouse pointer on the object you want to select, and then press and release the left mouse button. Clicking an object selects it; the selected object becomes highlighted. A selected button (on the taskbar, for example) looks as if it's pressed in. When a button looks raised, it's deselected.

To *double-click* an item, you point to the item and press and release the left mouse button twice quickly. Double-clicking is often a shortcut to performing a task. For example, you can open a database by double-clicking its icon.

You can also use the mouse to move an object (usually a window, dialog box, or database) to a new position on-screen. You do this by clicking and dragging the object. To *drag* an object to a new location on-screen, point to the object, press and hold the left mouse button, move the mouse to the new location, and then release the mouse button. The object moves with the mouse pointer as you drag it.

You can point to an item—a workspace page or a database icon, for example—and click the right mouse button to display a shortcut menu. The shortcut menu usually has common commands relating to that particular item. This mouse operation is called *right-clicking*.

You also can perform certain actions, such as selecting multiple items or copying items, by performing two additional mouse operations. *Shift+click* means to press and hold the Shift key while clicking the left mouse button; *Ctrl+click* means to press and hold the Ctrl key while clicking the left mouse button. The result of either of these actions depends upon where you are in Lotus Notes.

Using the Keyboard

You can use the keyboard to move around in Lotus Notes and to access many, but not all, of its features. For example, you can access menus with the keyboard, but you cannot access SmartIcons.

TIP **Shortcuts** If you have a choice when working with Notes, use the mouse the majority of the time, and use the keyboard mostly for shortcuts, as described throughout this book.

To open a menu with the keyboard, press the **Alt** key and then press the underlined letter in the menu. For example, to open the File menu, press **Alt+F**. The menu drops down.

To select a command from the menu, press the underlined letter in the command. Alternatively, after you open a menu you can use the up and down arrow keys to move to a command and then press **Enter** to select the highlighted command. See Lesson 3, "Getting Started with Notes," for more information about menus, commands, and dialog boxes.

Within dialog boxes, press the **Tab** key to move from option to option, or press **Alt** plus the underlined letter to select an option. Press **Enter** when an option is selected to activate that option. You can press **Enter** when a dialog box's OK button is active to accept all changes you've made and close the dialog box, or you can press the **Esc** key to cancel changes and close the dialog box.

Finally, you can access any window's Control menu by using the keyboard. Press **Alt+Spacebar** to open the application's Control menu. To access the workspace page Control menu, press **Alt+F** to open the File menu and then use the left arrow to move to the Control menu.

TIP **Cancel a Menu** To cancel a menu, press the **Esc** key twice.

Exiting Notes

When you're finished with Notes, you can close the program in a couple of different ways. To close Notes, do one of the following:

- Choose **File**, **Exit Notes**.
- Double-click the application's Control-menu button.
- Click the application's Control-menu button and choose **Close** from the menu.
- Press **Alt+F4**.
- Click the **Close** (X) button at the right end of the Notes title bar.

In this lesson, you learned how to start and exit Notes, how to use the mouse, and how to select commands by using the keyboard. In the next lesson, you'll learn some more basic Lotus Notes concepts.

Understanding Domino Concepts

In this lesson, you learn some of Domino's capabilities, ways you can use Domino in your work, and terminology that describes Domino's components and procedures.

Understanding Domino's Capabilities

Lotus Domino is a *client/server* platform that enables you to access, share, and manage information over a network. The network could consist of five or ten computers in your office building cabled together or 30,000 computers across the United States connected to each other in various ways.

A Lotus Domino network is made up of at least one server and one or more clients, or workstations. A *server* is a powerful computer set aside to communicate with other computers and supply those computers with whatever they need to complete their work. A *client* is the computer that accesses the server and uses its resources.

Resources Any shared data or hardware, such as files, printers, CD-ROM drives, and so on.

For example, a server might supply a workstation with files, programs, and backup options. In addition, a Lotus Domino server supplies each workstation with a mailbox and a place to store information that everyone can share.

You can communicate with others on the network by sending and receiving mail messages or through online group discussions. You can collaborate with your coworkers by sharing such documents as text files, spreadsheets, graphics, and tables that you use in your work every day.

Communicating over the Network

Someone working at a workstation can create e-mail (electronic mail) messages, or memos, that he or she can send to anyone else on the network using Lotus Domino. The message travels across the network to the Lotus Domino server and remains in the specified mailboxes until the owners of the mailboxes open and read their mail. The recipients can then reply to the message.

Another form of communication over the network is the discussion group. A *discussion group* can consist of two or more people connected to the network. When you join a discussion group, you type messages on-screen in Lotus Notes, while others in the discussion group read your message and reply. You get immediate feedback from your messages, just as you would over the phone.

Sharing Information over the Network

You also can use Notes to share *documents* over the network. These might include reports, letters, or tables of data. The Domino server contains many *databases*, collections of documents you can tap into and read, or even store on your computer.

Generally, a company will use the server to store many documents that its employees may need for work (such as instructions, regulations, and guidelines). Additionally, anyone connected to the network can create a document database and add it to those on the server for you and others to access. You can even create document databases yourself and add them to those already on the server.

How Do You Fit In?

When using Lotus Notes, you can work either on the local drive or on the network drive. When you work on the *local* drive, you are working with the files, databases, or messages stored on your computer's hard drive. When you work on the *network* drive, you are accessing files and such stored on the server. Which you choose depends on your current project.

Local versus Network The local drive refers to your workstation's hard drive (usually C). The network drive refers to a drive you connect to through the LAN (local area network) or WAN (wide area network); it might be drive F, G, or H, for example.

Lotus Domino gives you the choice of Local or Network depending on the task you're about to perform. For example, when you open a database, you must tell Domino whether the database is on your local drive or on the network.

Working on Local

You can choose to work on your local drive whether or not you're connected to the network. For instance, you might be at home or on the road using your laptop, in which case you're not physically connected to the network. Or you might be physically connected, but using files and databases on your hard drive instead of the network resources.

The advantages to working on local are that you get quicker data access times, you don't have to hassle with network traffic, and you can work away from the office. However, you have to use more of your hard drive's disk space, your data selections are limited, and you are unable to interact with coworkers through mail or discussion groups.

Working Alone? You can create mail while working locally and then connect to the network to send the mail. While you're connected to the network, you can also access other databases and discussion groups. (See Lesson 25 for more information on remote access to Domino.)

Working on the Network

When you work on the network, you can access files, send and receive mail, or join a discussion group while attached to the network drive. You might choose the network drive so you can access certain files and then add them to your local drive for quick and easy access at any time. Or you might just want to work in the files directly on the network.

Network Access When you choose to access a database that's stored on the network drive, you can only use that database while connected to the network. If you disconnect from the network, the database is no longer available to you.

You'll find several advantages to using the network drive. First, you have access to a larger selection of data and information. In addition, you have direct mail connections with coworkers, and you can receive immediate feedback through discussion groups. Of course, there are also disadvantages to using the network drive. For example, network traffic may cause slower access times, and you might run into long wait times when trying to access certain sought-after information.

Understanding Domino and Notes Terminology

If you're used to working on a *stand-alone* computer (one that's not attached to a network), you may want to read over this section for clarification of some terms.

As you just learned, Lotus Domino works as a client/server application. Your computer is the client that accesses the Notes server for purposes of e-mail, discussion groups, and information sharing. Depending on the type of network you're attached to, you might hear the following terms used in reference to networks and Domino in addition to those already discussed in this lesson.

Network Your workstation is attached to a network that enables you to share files, printers, and applications, as well as Lotus Domino. The network might be Windows NT, OS/2, Novell, or some other network type.

File Server Your network most likely uses at least one file server. A file server is a powerful computer that holds all data and applications shared over the network, all information about each user on the network, and so on.

System Administrator Your system administrator is the person who manages the network file servers and resources, sets passwords and securities, and troubleshoots problems with the network.

Domino Network The Domino network is an additional network set up on Windows NT, OS/2, or some other network.

Domino Server A computer specified as a server to handle Notes traffic (such as mail and databases) using specific application software from Lotus. Very large organizations may have more than one Domino server.

Domino Administrator A Domino administrator is the person who manages and organizes Notes users and Domino servers. This person sets security for Domino, troubleshoots Domino problems, and so on.

Workgroup A group of workstations on a network identified by a workgroup name. The system administrator creates and uses workgroups to make viewing and organizing workstations on the network easier.

Domain In Windows NT networks, a collection of computers, users, or workgroups gathered within a network or over several networks. Domains enable the system administrator to assign rights and permissions to a group, which is much easier than assigning them to each individual separately.

Protocol The language your computer uses to communicate over the network. The workstation must use the protocol the server uses. Additionally, Lotus Domino servers and clients use the same protocol as the network.

Permissions and Rights Privileges assigned to each user or workstation, thereby providing access to the server(s) and resources on the network.

User ID Every Notes user has a unique ID used to store his or her access privileges to the Domino server. You can password-protect your User ID so that no one else can use it; see your Domino administrator for more information.

Password You generally must use a password to attach, or *log on*, to any network. (The operating system usually supplies a dialog box or screen prompt when you turn your computer on.) Also, you may need a password to access certain tasks or procedures in Lotus Notes. If you are prompted to give a password and you do not know what that password is, check with your Domino administrator.

In this lesson, you learned some of the tasks you can accomplish using Domino and Notes, how Notes and you fit into a network structure, and some common networking terms you may need in order to work in Notes. In the next lesson, you'll learn to use menus, commands, InfoBoxes, dialog boxes, SmartIcons, views, and the Status bar.

Getting Started with Notes

In this lesson, you learn to use Notes menus and commands, SmartIcons, workspace pages, the Status bar, and views.

Opening Menus and Selecting Commands

As do most Windows applications, Notes supplies *pull-down menus* that contain the commands you use to work in Notes. Each menu contains a list of commands that relate to the operation of Notes. For example, the Edit menu contains such commands as Cut, Copy, Paste, and Clear. In addition, some menus change depending on the task you're performing; for example, Notes adds the Actions menu to the menu bar when you open a database.

Pull-Down Menu A menu that includes a list of related commands or actions. You pull the menu down by activating it with the mouse or the keyboard.

To open a menu by using the mouse, click the menu name in the menu bar. To open a menu by using the keyboard, press the **Alt** key, and then press the underlined letter in the menu name. (For example, to open the File menu, you can press **Alt+F**.) Either way, the menu drops down to display a list of related commands (see Figure 3.1).

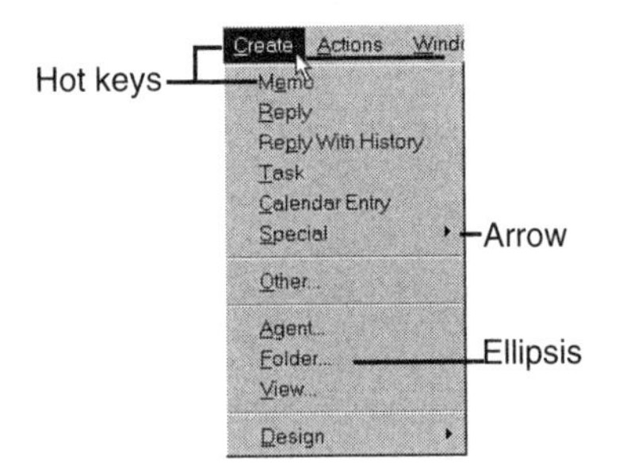

Figure 3.1 Pull-down menus contain the commands you use to work in Notes.

To select a command by using the mouse, simply click it. To activate a command by using the keyboard, press the *hot key* of the command you want. If selecting a command leads to a secondary menu, click a command in the secondary menu or press its hot key to activate it.

Hot Key The underlined letter in a menu name, command, or other option that you press (often in combination with the **Alt** key) to activate that option. Also referred to as the *accelerator key*.

Menus can contain a number of elements along with the commands. For example, some commands have hot keys you can use to access them from the keyboard, and some have keyboard shortcuts with which you can bypass the menu altogether. In addition, certain symbols might appear in a menu to give you an indication as to what will happen when you activate the command. Table 3.1 describes the command indicators you might see in a menu.

Table 3.1 Command Indicators

Element	*Description*
Arrow	Indicates that another menu, called a secondary or cascading menu, will appear when you select that command.
Ellipsis	Indicates that a dialog or InfoBox will appear when you select that command.
Hot key	Marks the letter key you press to activate the menu or command by using the keyboard.
Check mark	Indicates that an option or command is selected or active.

continues

Table 3.1 Continued

Element	*Description*
Shortcut	Provides a keyboard shortcut you can use to activate the command without accessing the menu; you cannot use the shortcut if the menu is open.
Dimmed command	Indicates that the command cannot be accessed at the current time. (For example, you cannot tell Notes to delete unless you've selected something for it to delete; so if nothing is selected, the Delete command is not available.)

Cancel a Menu To cancel a menu, point to any blank area of the workspace and click once. Alternatively, you can press the **Esc** key twice.

Using Dialog Boxes and InfoBoxes

Often, selecting a menu command causes Notes to display a dialog box or InfoBox. You can use dialog boxes and InfoBoxes to set more options and make specific choices related to the menu command. Each type of box contains certain elements you need to understand in order to use it.

Dialog Boxes

Figure 3.2 shows the Open Database dialog box. It contains most of the elements common to Notes dialog boxes. Table 3.2 describes those elements and tells you how to use them.

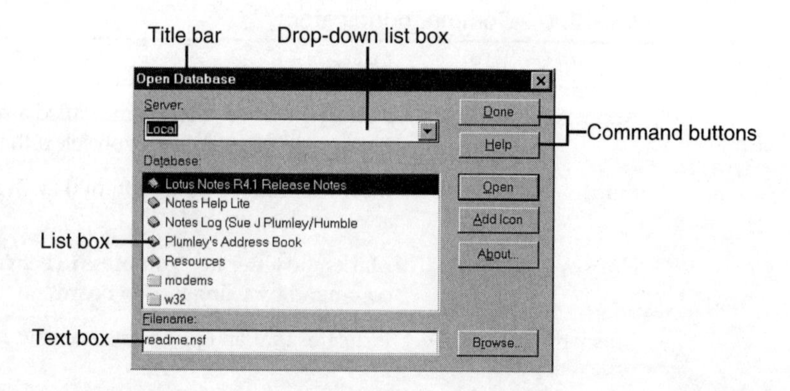

Figure 3.2 Use dialog boxes to make additional choices related to the selected menu command.

Table 3.2 Dialog Box Elements

Element	*Description*
Title bar	Indicates the name of the dialog box (such as the Open Database dialog box).
Drop-down list box	Displays one option from a list; click the arrow to the right of the box, and the box drops down to display the entire list.
List box	Displays a list of options so you can see more than one choice at a time.
Scroll bar	Enables you to display additional items in a window or list box; click the up or down arrow to see more.
Text box	Enables you to enter a selection by typing it in the box.
Command button	Completes the commands or leads to another related dialog box containing more options.
Close (X) button	Closes the dialog box without (Windows 95) saving changes.
Check boxes	Enable you to select or deselect options individually; when the option is selected, a check mark appears in a small square box beside the option.
Check list	Enables you to select one or more items from a displayed list of options; click an option to select or deselect it, and a check mark appears beside it or disappears (respectively).

To use a dialog box, you make your selections as described in Table 3.2, and then choose a command button. The following list describes the functions of the most common command buttons:

- *OK* or *Done* accepts and puts into effect the selections you've made in the dialog box, and then closes the dialog box.
- *Cancel* cancels the changes you've made in the dialog box and closes it (as does the Close (X) button at the right end of the title bar).
- *Browse* (or any other button with an ellipsis following the button's name) displays another dialog box.
- *Open* (or any other button with only a command on it) performs that command.
- *Help* displays information about the dialog box and its options.

I Can't Get Rid of the Dialog Box Once you've opened a dialog box, you must cancel or accept the changes you've made and close that dialog box before you can continue with your work in Notes. Use the command buttons or the Close (X) button in Windows 95 to close the dialog box.

InfoBoxes

An InfoBox also presents options related to the menu command. However, you work with an InfoBox in a different way than you do a dialog box. An InfoBox displays only the properties of a specific item, such as a workspace or a database. *Properties* are types of information about an item such as its name, location, settings, design, size, and so on. When you make a selection in an InfoBox, it takes effect immediately—even though the InfoBox remains on-screen as you work.

InfoBoxes contain *tabs* that offer various types of options about the subject. Figure 3.3 shows the Properties for Database InfoBox.

Tabs A tab in an InfoBox is similar to a tab in a drawer full of file folders. Select a tab to see information related to the tab's title.

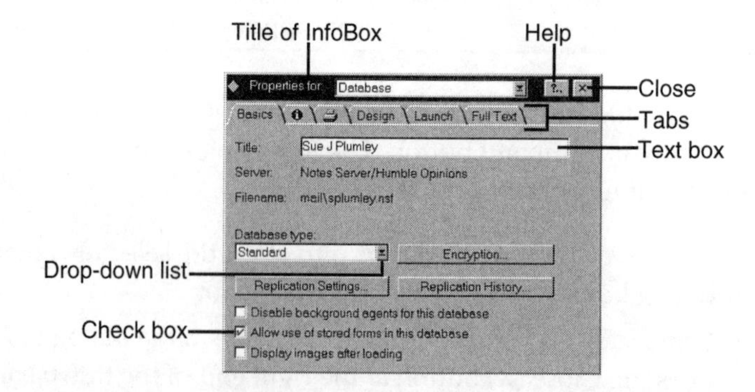

Figure 3.3 Use an InfoBox to change properties, or definitions, of selected items.

InfoBoxes have many of the same elements that dialog boxes have: drop-down lists, list boxes, text boxes, and check boxes, for example. However, InfoBoxes also contain the additional elements described in Table 3.3.

Table 3.3 InfoBox Elements

Element	*Description*
Title of InfoBox	All InfoBox titles begin with "Properties for." You select the element for which you want to change the properties in the drop-down list in the title bar. You can change the properties of a database or a workspace.
Tabs	Named flaps that represent pages of options related to the selected element.
Help	Click the Help button and then click any item in the InfoBox to view an explanation or definition of the item.

A Properties for InfoBox remains on-screen until you close it by clicking its Close (X) button. However, changes you make in the box take effect immediately; you don't have to okay them. If an open InfoBox is in your way, you can move it around on the screen by clicking the title bar and dragging it to a new position.

TIP **Collapse and Expand** Double-click an InfoBox's title bar to *collapse* it. Collapsing hides all but the title bar and the tabs and frees up space on the workspace. Double-click the title bar again to expand the InfoBox back to its original view and size.

Using SmartIcon Shortcuts

As do other Lotus applications, Lotus Notes includes SmartIcons you can use to perform common tasks quickly. Notes supplies specific SmartIcons depending on your task and your location in the Notes program. When in Workspace view, for example, the SmartIcons offer shortcuts for saving files, editing tasks, creating mail, and so on. On the other hand, when you're viewing an open database, the SmartIcons offer shortcuts for viewing documents and lists and for searching for specific text.

Notes includes more than 150 SmartIcons you can use as shortcuts. Notes arranges many of the icons in sets that are useful for performing specific actions, such as formatting or editing a document. To change the SmartIcon set that's displayed, choose **File**, **Tools**, **SmartIcons**. In Show, make sure the Context Icons check box is selected (if a check mark doesn't appear in the check box, click the option) and choose **OK**.

To find out what a SmartIcon represents, hold the mouse pointer over the icon, and a bubble or description appears containing the name of the menu command for which the icon is a shortcut. Figure 3.4 shows a description for the SmartIcon that represents the Create, Mail, Memo command. To activate a SmartIcon, simply click it.

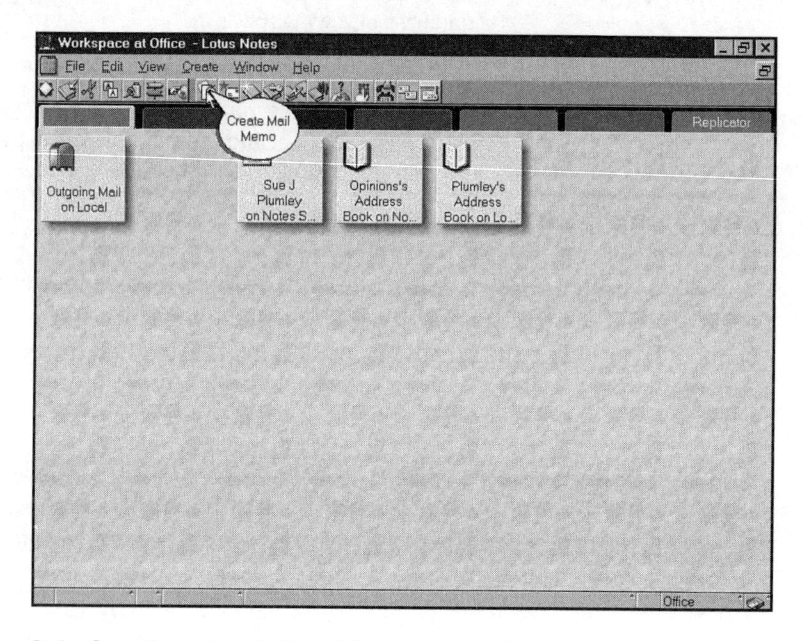

Figure 3.4 SmartIcon descriptions tell you what the icons do.

TIP **Modify SmartIcons** You can customize SmartIcons by choosing File, Tools, SmartIcons. For more information, see Lesson 23.

Using Workspace Pages

Workspace pages are similar to file folders in that each page has a tab and an area in which you can place *databases*. Your Notes desktop contains six workspace pages, and you use the tabs to move from one page to another. To customize your workspace, you can name the tabs and organize the pages any way you want.

Database A collection of information represented by an icon on the workspace. In Notes, that information might be addresses, incoming or outgoing mail, spreadsheet documents, or word processing documents, among other things.

By default, the first page of the workspace contains items related to mail—address books and your mailbox, for example. You can move or remove these items, or you can add other items to the workspace pages.

- To move to another page in your workspace, click the page's tab.
- To move a database icon around on the displayed page, click and drag the icon. A hand appears in place of the mouse pointer, and the database icon moves with it. When you reach the desired location, release the mouse button.
- To select a database icon on the workspace page, click the icon.

You can right-click a blank area of the workspace to display a shortcut menu of commands related to the workspace. Choose **Workspace Properties** from the shortcut menu to view information about the workspace. See Lesson 9 for more information about workspace pages; see Lesson 10 for more information about databases.

Using Views

When you open any database, Notes displays the contents of the database in a list. This list is called a *view*. Each line in the database represents one document, person, mail message, or other item. The line gives you information about each entry, such as name, address, subject, date, or other data. No two database lists look exactly alike, and the elements displayed within the view depend upon which database you're viewing.

Explanation Pages Many databases open up to display an explanation page that gives you information about the database. For more information, see Lesson 10.

Figure 3.5 shows a mailbox view. From the mailbox, you send, receive, forward, delete, read, and answer messages (see Lesson 4). After you've opened a database to view its contents, you can return to the workspace by choosing **File, Close**.

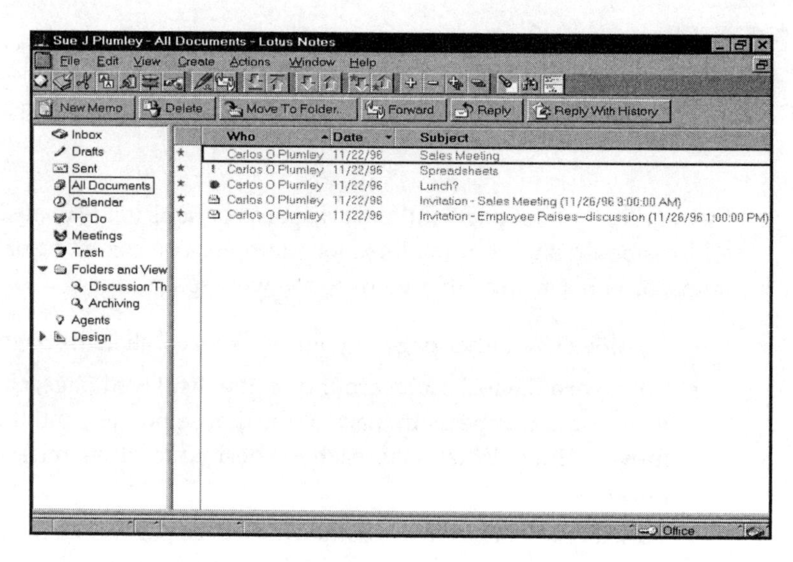

Figure 3.5 A view lists the various elements in the database.

Getting Information from the Status Bar

The *Status bar* is the bar across the bottom of the Notes window that displays messages, icons, and other information you'll use as you work in Notes. The Status bar is divided into sections. Some of those sections display messages, and others lead to a *pop-up box* or *pop-up menu*. Figure 3.6 shows the Status bar with the recent messages displayed in a pop-up box.

Pop-Up Box or Menu A list of commands or items that appears when you click on certain Status bar buttons. A pop-up box displays such items as messages; a pop-up menu displays a list of selections.

As you can see in Figure 3.6, each section of the Status bar is a button with a specific function. Table 3.4 explains the Status bar buttons and their functions.

Table 3.4 Status Bar Buttons

Button	*Description*
Accessing network	Automatically displays a lightning bolt when Notes is accessing the network; the button is blank when Notes is working from the local disk.

Button	*Description*
Change font	Displays a pop-up menu of fonts from which you can select a font to assign to text in a document.
Change text size	Displays a pop-up menu of type sizes you can assign to text in a document.
Change paragraph style	Displays a pop-up menu of paragraph styles (preformatted headings, subheads, and so on) you can apply to text in a document.
View recent messages	Displays a pop-up box containing messages about Notes' activities.
View your access level	Displays a dialog box that shows your status—or level of access—to open the database.
Switch between locations	Displays a pop-up menu that shows your current location (Office, Home, Island, or Travel) and enables you to select another.
Perform mail tasks	Displays a pop-up menu from which you can choose to create, send, read, and/or receive mail.

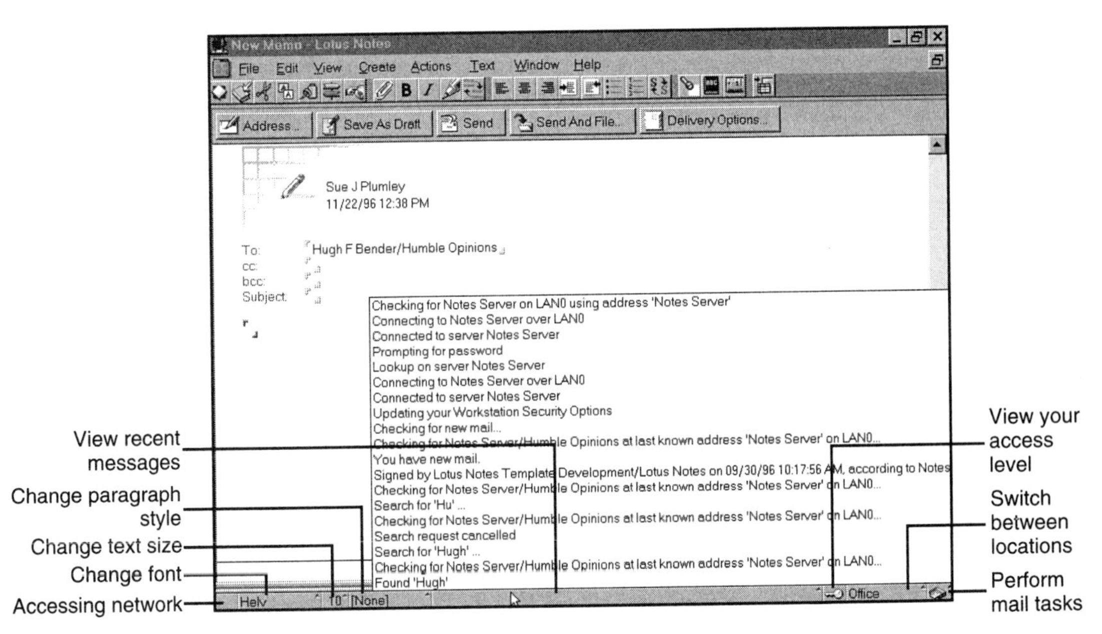

Figure 3.6 Use the Status bar for shortcuts and information.

CAUTION

No Button Labels? If your Status bar buttons do not display labels, don't worry. Labels only appear in some of the buttons when you're in a view that (for example) uses fonts or styles. Likewise, even if the message button does not show a label, Notes always displays a list of messages when you click it.

In this lesson, you learned to use menus and commands, dialog boxes and InfoBoxes, workspace pages, and the Status bar. In the next lesson, you'll learn to read incoming mail.

Reading Incoming Mail

In this lesson, you learn to open your mailbox, select a message, read the message, answer mail, and close the message.

Opening Your Mailbox

When you have new mail, Notes displays a message in the Status bar to notify you. Your mailbox is a *database* stored on the server and accessed via the network.

Database A collection of related documents that you can access.

Your mailbox is usually on the first workspace page, and you can open it and read the mail whenever you want. To open your mailbox, follow these steps:

1. Move to the workspace page containing your mailbox by clicking the page's tab. Your mailbox appears as a box with your name and an envelope on it (see Figure 4.1).

TIP **Is It Selected?** When your mailbox is selected, it looks like the button is pressed in.

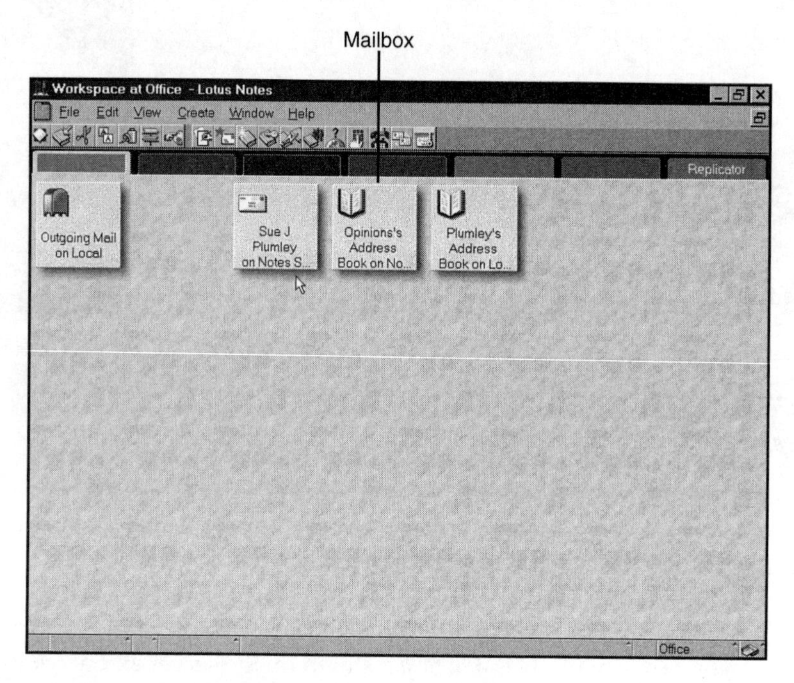

Figure 4.1 Your mailbox appears on the workspace.

2. Double-click your mailbox to open it, or right-click it and select **Open** from the shortcut menu that appears. An informational page set up by your Notes administrator might appear (see Figure 4.2).
3. If necessary, choose **File**, **Close** to close the informational page and display the mailbox view. Figure 4.3 shows my mailbox in the Inbox view.

CAUTION

No Mail? If you do not see mail, but you know you have mail waiting, click **Inbox** in the navigation pane of the mailbox.

The mailbox consists of two panes and an action, or tool button bar. The active view pane (on the right) displays your mail messages. You can see who sent the message, the date he or she sent it, and the subject he or she assigned to it.

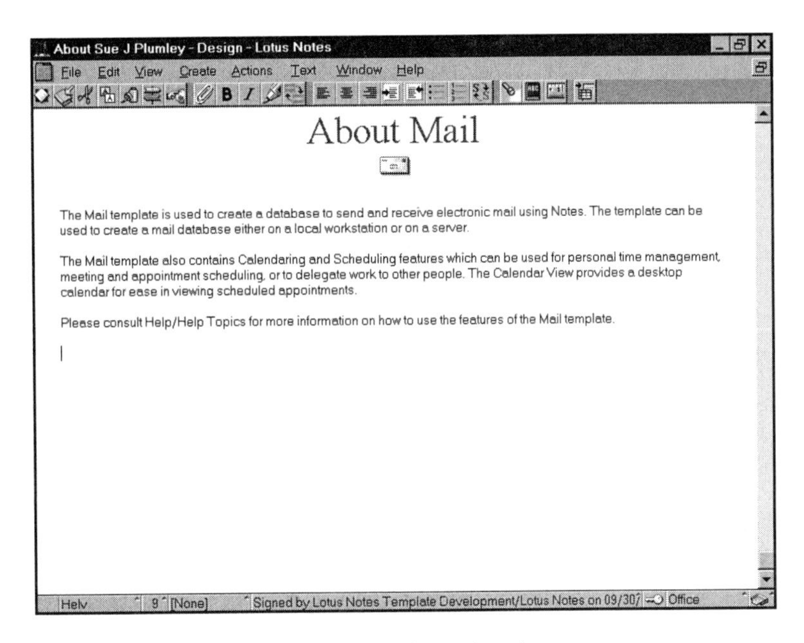

Figure 4.2 Many databases display an informational page.

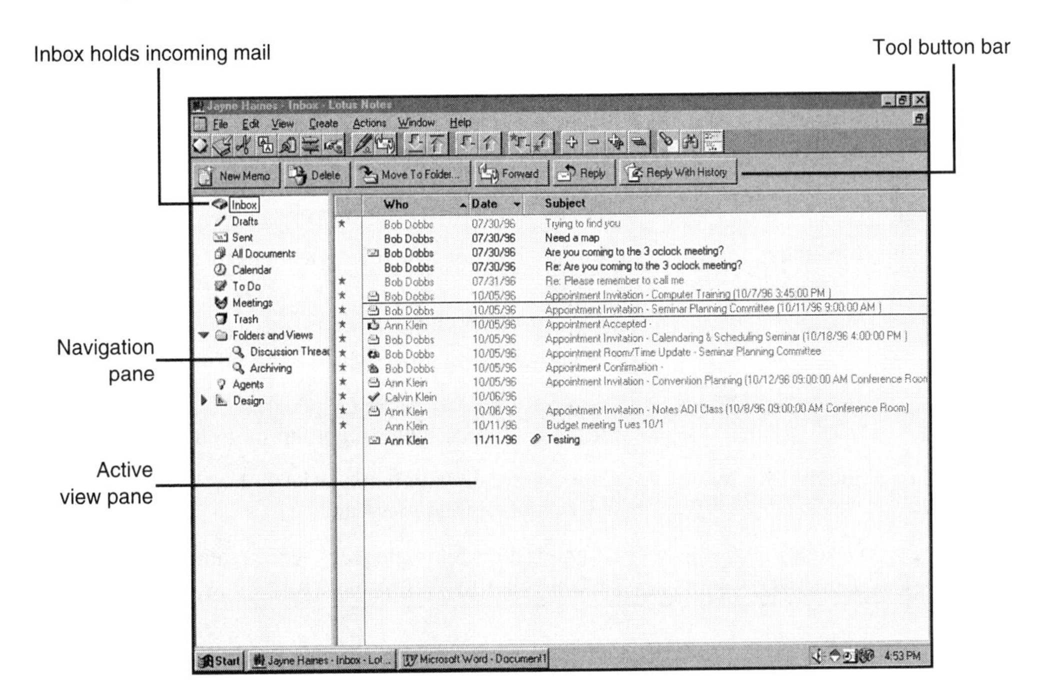

Figure 4.3 Notes displays your mail messages in the Inbox view.

The tool button bar contains command buttons that perform tasks related to the procedure. For example, when you're looking at your incoming messages, you can click one of these buttons to delete a message or reply to a message. The tool buttons change depending on which view you're in.

The navigation pane (on the left) lists the views you can use to manage your mail at different stages. Table 4.1 describes the views listed in the left pane of the mailbox.

Table 4.1 Mailbox Views

View	*Description*
Inbox	Stores mail that has been sent to you.
Drafts	Stores mail messages you're working on but have not sent yet; also contains any mail you create but choose to save as a draft.
Sent	Stores copies of messages you have sent (if you choose to keep a copy of the messages).
All Documents	Displays all messages, including those you've sent, received, saved in folders, and so on.
Calendar	Displays appointments and meetings you create and those created by meeting invitations e-mailed to you.
To Do	Displays the tasks you've created, who assigned the task, the due date, and to whom the task is assigned; also shows priority assignments of 1, 2, or 3.
Meetings	Displays a list of scheduled meetings by date, time, and subject.
Trash	Holds deleted messages until you empty the trash or remove the message from the trash.
Folders and Views	Provides access to folders in which you can save various messages, discussions, and other important mail you receive.
Agents	Contains preset, automatic tasks such as backups and deletion of expired messages.
Design	Offers various templates for use in creating documents. (See Lesson 15 for more information.)

TIP **Down Arrows** The down arrows in the navigation pane (beside Folders and Views and Design) reveal or hide additional items relating to the topic. Click the arrow to show related topics; and then click the item again to hide the topics.

Selecting a Message

Before you can read, delete, print, or otherwise manipulate a mail message, you must first select it. One message is already selected when you open your mailbox. The selected message has a rectangle (usually black) around the name, date, and subject of the message. That rectangle functions as a *selection bar*.

To select a different message in the list, click the message, or use the up and down arrows to move to it. To select multiple messages, press and hold the **Shift** key and click the messages. A check mark appears to the left of each selected message.

Reading Your Mail

You can select any message in your Inbox to read at any time. To read a mail message, double-click the message, or right-click it and choose **Open** from the shortcut menu. Figure 4.4 shows an open mail message.

Every mail message, or memo, contains the following elements:

- **Heading** The heading includes the name of the person who sent the message, and the date and time he or she sent it. In addition, if you're on a Windows NT network, you might see the domain name, company name, or other information, beside the sender's name.
- **To** The To line shows the name of the person to whom the message is being sent. Again, the domain name might be included.
- **cc** The cc (carbon copy) line displays a list of any others who received a copy of the message.
- **Subject** The subject describes the topic of the message, as defined by the sender of the message.

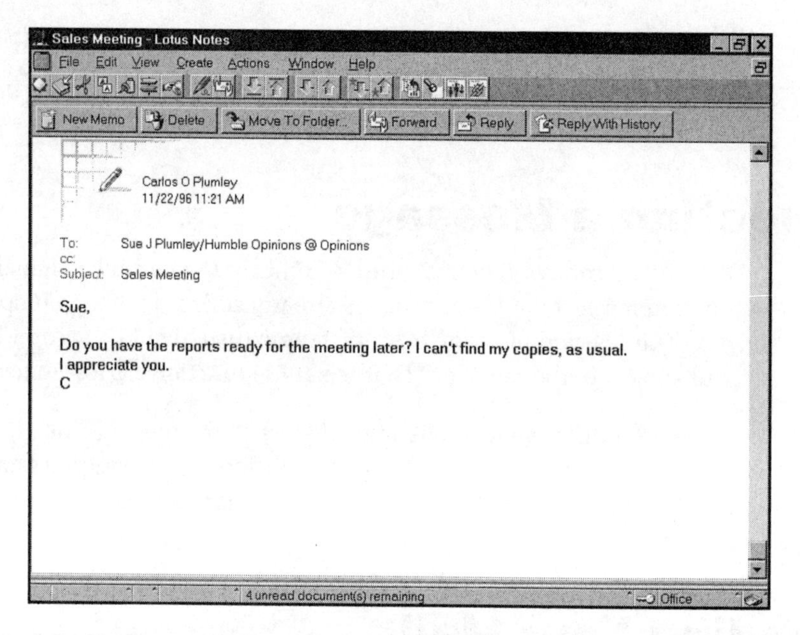

Figure 4.4 The open message fills the workspace.

The rest of the message is the body, which is made up mostly of text but also can contain graphics (pictures), tables, and other items. A message can be as short as a word or two, or as long as 21,000 paragraphs. The length of the message is limited, of course, by your computer's memory. If you cannot view all of a message on-screen at once, use the vertical scroll bar or the Page Up, Page Down, and arrow keys to view more of the message.

TIP **Shortcuts** You can press **Ctrl+End** to go to the end of a long message or **Ctrl+Home** to go to the beginning of a message.

Answering Mail

After you've read your mail, you can choose from various options. Often, you will want to reply to your mail message. To reply to a mail message, follow these steps:

1. With the mail message open, click the **Reply** tool button. The New Reply window appears (see Figure 4.5).

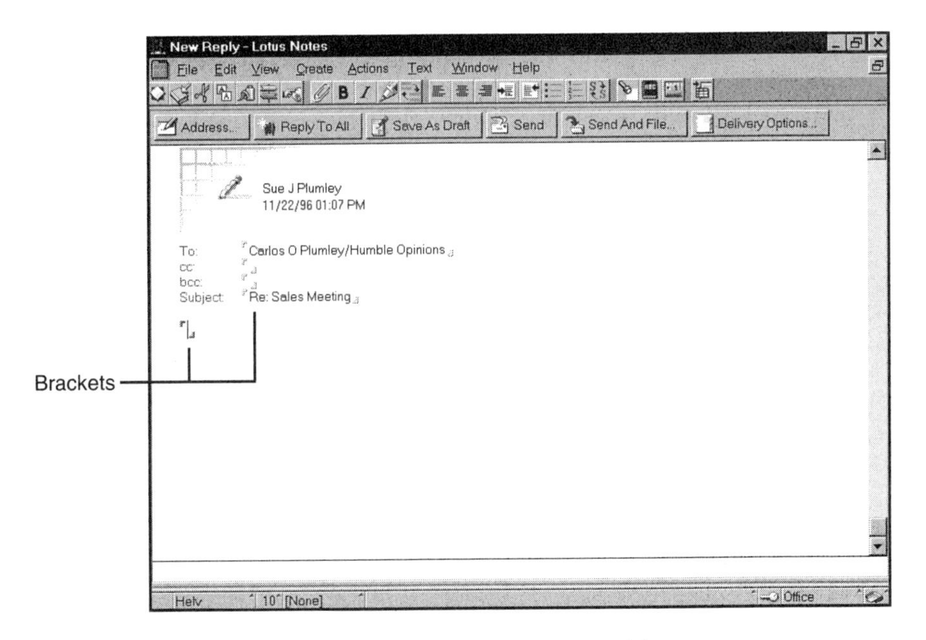

Figure 4.5 Notes fills in the recipient's name and address.

2. To send a carbon copy of the message to another party, click between the brackets after cc and enter the name(s).

   To send a blind carbon copy, enter the name of the party in the brackets after bcc. (A blind carbon copy is sent to someone without the primary recipient knowing it.)

3. Position the insertion point between the brackets in the message body and begin typing the message.

4. (Optional) Click the **Reply With History** tool button to have Notes attach a copy of the original message to the reply.

5. When you're ready, click the **Send** button to send your reply. For more information about creating and sending your own mail, see Lesson 6.

Closing a Message and the Mailbox

When you reply to or forward a message, Notes closes the message automatically when you select Send (however, you still have to close the original message). If you choose not to reply to the message at this time, you must close it to return to the mailbox.

To close the message without performing any additional tasks, choose **File**, **Close**. Notes returns to the mailbox, and you can read other messages or exit the mailbox. To exit the mailbox, choose **File**, **Close**.

TIP **Delete the Message** If you're sure you do not need the message, click the **Delete** tool button to delete it.

In this lesson, you learned to open and close your mailbox and work with your mail messages displayed there. In the next lesson, you'll learn to manage mail from the mailbox view while performing such tasks as printing and deleting messages and saving messages in a folder.

Managing Incoming Mail

In this lesson, you learn to print, delete, and forward messages, and to save a message to a folder.

Printing Mail

When you're viewing your mail in the Inbox, you can perform a variety of tasks on selected mail using the commands on the shortcut menu. For example, you can print a message without opening it. To print a mail message, follow these steps:

1. In the Inbox, select the message you want to print and right-click the message. The shortcut menu appears (see Figure 5.1).
2. Choose the **Print** command, and the File Print dialog box shown in Figure 5.2 appears. Table 5.1 describes this dialog box's options in detail.
3. Set the print options to meet your needs, and then click **OK** to print the message.

Table 5.1 Common Printing Options

Option	*Description*
Printer	Select this button if the printer listed in the box is not the correct one. In the Print Setup dialog box that appears, choose the printer you want to use.
Print range	Select All to print all pages of the message, or select From and To and enter the page numbers for the range you want to print in the text boxes.

continued

Table 5.1 Continued

Option	*Description*
Draft quality	Select this option if you don't need a letter-quality copy (dark text and nice-looking graphics). Draft quality enables the printer to print more quickly.
Graphics scaled to 100%	Select this option if there are pictures in the message and you want them to appear full-sized on the printout.
Copies	Enter the number of copies of the message you want to print.
Print View	Select this option to print a copy of the Inbox view with a list of your messages.
Print selected documents	Choose this option to print the selected message(s) in the Inbox view.

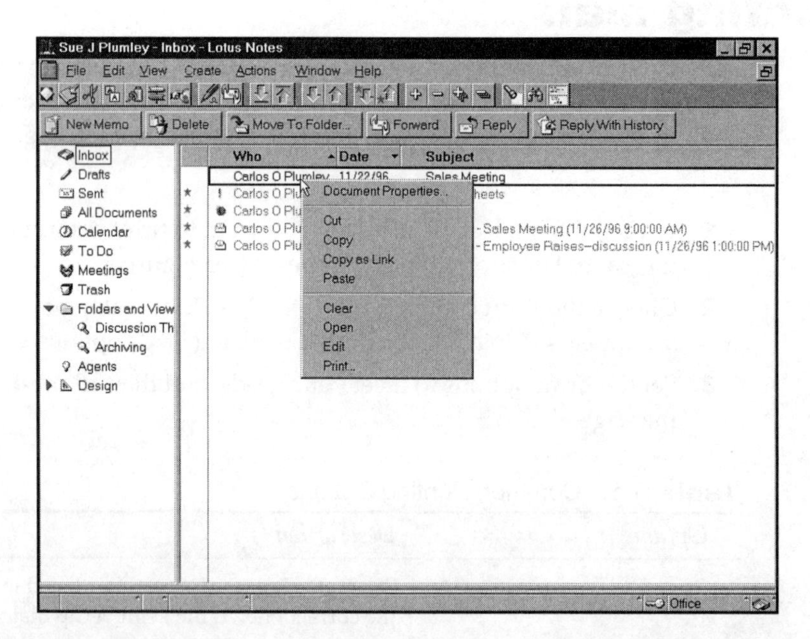

Figure 5.1 Use the shortcut menu to print a message from the Inbox.

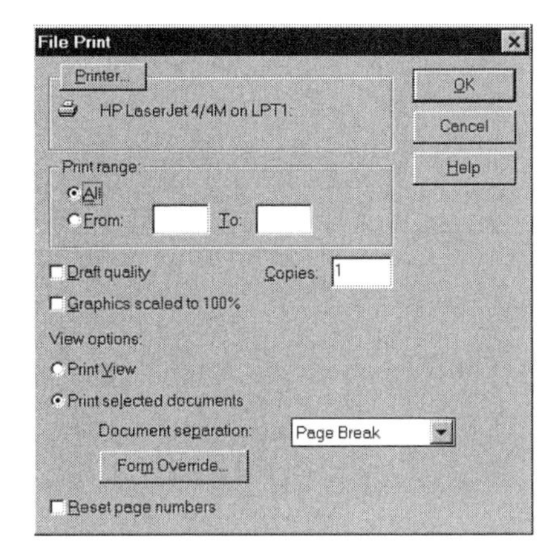

Figure 5.2 Set print options in the File Print dialog box.

TIP **Print Multiple Messages** You can print two or more messages at the same time by holding the **Shift** key while clicking each message; a check mark appears to the left of the selected messages. Then right-click any selected message and choose Print. Finally, in the File Print dialog box, make sure you select the Print Selected Documents option.

Deleting Mail

You can delete one or more messages in the Inbox by selecting the messages and marking them for deletion. A message marked for deletion remains in the Inbox until you empty the trash or until you exit the Notes program. The following steps walk you through deleting a message, in case you don't want to wait until you exit Notes:

1. Select the message(s) you want to delete and click the **Delete** tool button. When you click the Delete tool button, a trash can icon appears to the left of the selected message, marking that message for the trash.
2. To empty the trash, click **Trash** in the navigation pane. You'll see the message you marked for deletion in the view pane as shown in Figure 5.3.

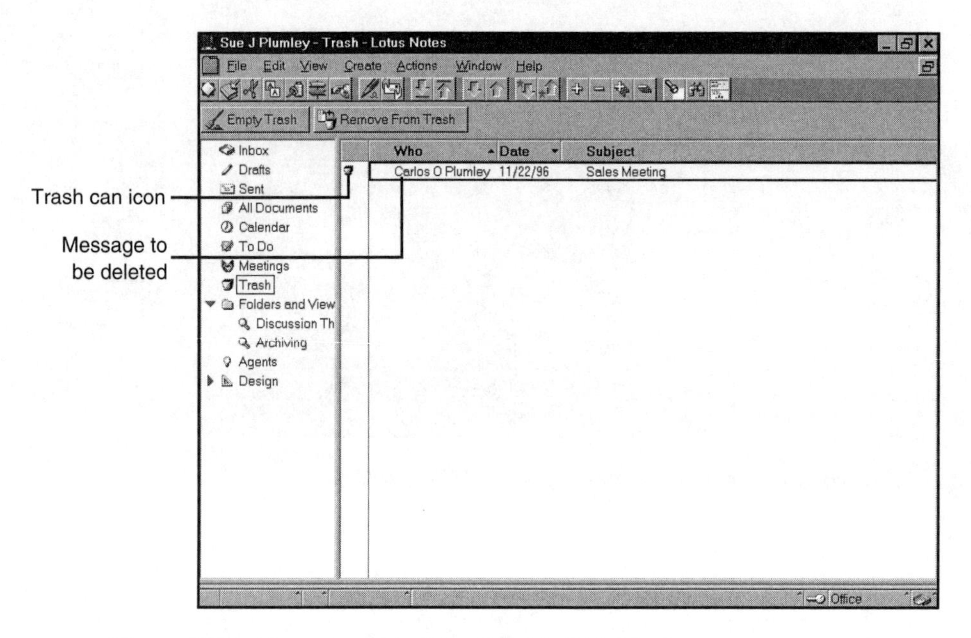

Figure 5.3 Message marked for deletion in Trash view.

3. To delete the message, click the **Empty Trash** tool button. A confirmation message appears; click **Yes** to delete the message.
4. To return to the Inbox, click **Inbox** on the left side of the mailbox pane.

CAUTION

Change Your Mind? If you decide you don't want to delete a message shown in Trash view, select it and click the **Remove From Trash** tool button.

Saving Mail in a Folder

If you want to save a mail message, you can assign it to an existing folder. (However, you cannot save messages to the Folders and Views folder in the navigation pane.) If you don't like the choice of existing folders, you can create your own folders in which to save your mail. To save mail in a folder, follow these steps:

1. In the Inbox, select the mail message you want to save.
2. Click the **Move To Folder** tool button. The Move To Folder dialog box appears.

3. Select **Folders and Views** and then click the **Create New Folder** button.
4. In the Create Folder dialog box that appears, enter a name for the new folder and click **OK**. Notes closes the Create Folder dialog box and returns to the Move To Folder dialog box, which now includes the name of the new folder.
5. Select the new folder and click the **Move** button. The dialog box closes, and Notes moves the message to the newly created folder.

TIP **New Folder** The newly added folder immediately appears in the navigation pane under Folders and Views. You can open it at any time by clicking it; its contents appear in the view pane (on the right side of the window).

Forwarding Mail

You can forward any mail message to another party, and you can even add your own comments or reply to it. To pass a message on to someone else, you click the **Forward Mail** button. The New Memo window appears (see Figure 5.4).

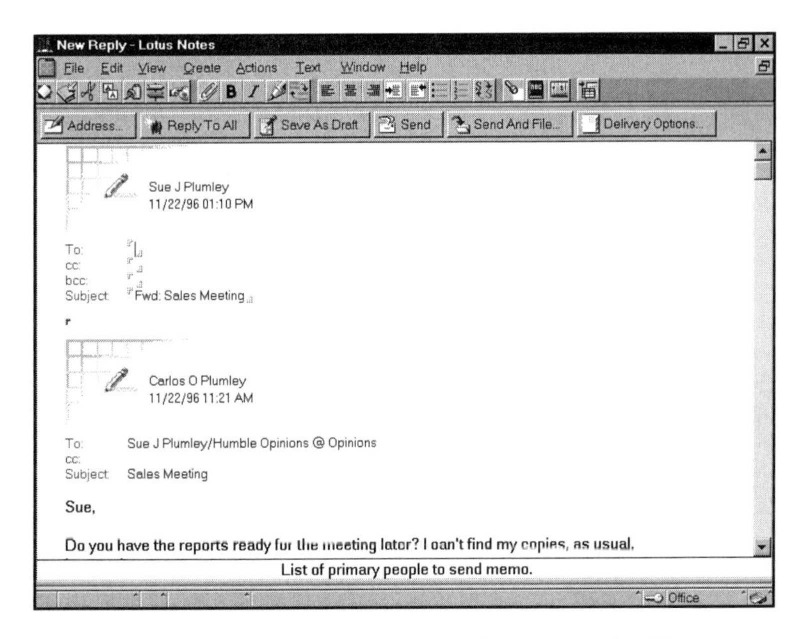

Figure 5.4 You can forward the message to another party and add your own comments.

The existing message moves down on the page to make room for the forwarding information. Enter the party's name and any other information you want. Then add your comments above the **Forwarded by** line and the horizontal blank line. Click the **Send** tool button to send the message.

In this lesson, you learned to print, delete, and forward mail, as well as to save mail in a folder for future reference. In the next lesson, you'll learn to create, address, and send your own mail messages.

Creating and Sending Mail

In this lesson, you learn to create mail, address mail, and send your mail messages.

Creating Mail

The most common type of mail message is the memo. Even though the message looks like a memo (it includes To, CC, and Subject lines), you are not limited in terms of the length of the mail message or the items you can include in a mail message. (For more information on mail, see Lessons 4 and 5.)

Open your mailbox, and then follow these steps to create a mail message.

1. In your mailbox database, choose the **New Memo** tool button. A blank memo like the one in Figure 6.1 appears. Notes automatically fills in your name, the date, and the time.

TIP **Quick Memo** You can quickly create a memo from your workspace by choosing the **Create**, **Memo** menu command. Create the memo and click **Send**, and Notes returns to the workspace.

2. Click in the **To** brackets and enter the name(s) of the person(s) to whom you want to send the memo. As you type a name, Notes searches your company's address book and your personal address book for the letters you've typed. If it finds a match, Notes fills in the name for you.

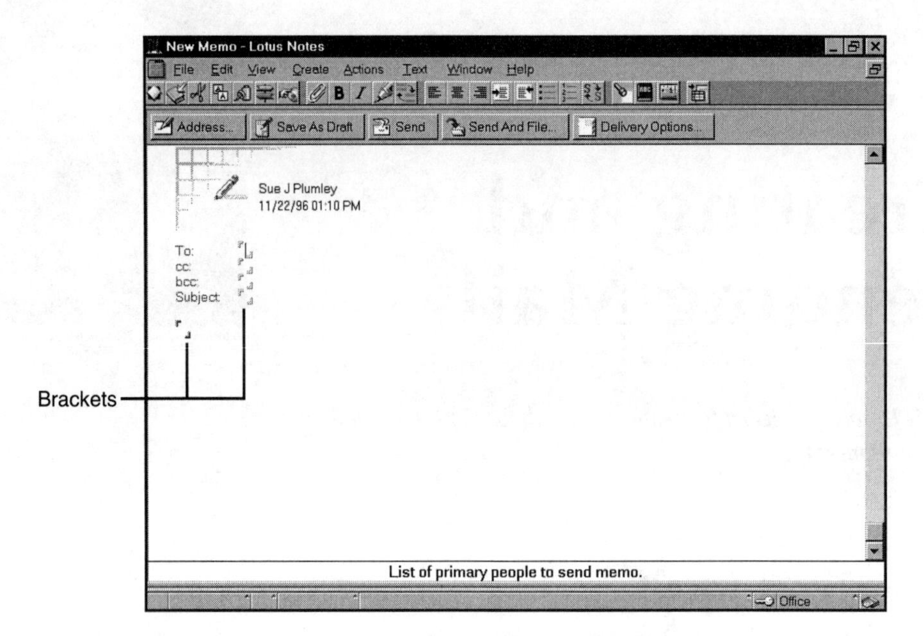

Figure 6.1 You start out with a blank memo.

3. (Optional) Click in the **cc** (carbon copy) brackets or press the **Tab** key, and then enter the name(s) of the person(s) to whom you want to send a copy of the message. Again, Notes fills in names for you if it finds the first letters you enter in either address book.
4. (Optional) Click in the **bcc** brackets and enter the name(s) of the person(s) to whom you want to send a blind carbon copy.
5. In the Subject brackets, enter a word or phrase to use as a title for your message.
6. In the brackets below the Subject line, enter the message you want to send. When entering the message, follow these guidelines:

   Press **Enter** only when you want to start a new paragraph.

   Use the Delete and Backspace keys to edit text as you type.

Address Book Notes provides address books you can use when sending mail. Your company's address book is stored on the Domino server and contains the names of all those people attached to the network to whom you can send messages. See the section "Using the Address Book" later in this lesson for details.

When creating a message, you can use the mailbox's SmartIcons or menu commands to add emphasis to and change the format of text in your memo. (To brush up on using SmartIcons, flip back to Lesson 3.) For example, try some of these ideas, using either the appropriate menu commands or the SmartIcons pictured:

  You can cut and paste text within the memo as you would in any word processing document. Simply select the text, choose Edit, Cut, position the insertion point in the desired location, and choose Edit, Paste.

 Select any text you want to emphasize and click the Bold SmartIcon or the Italic SmartIcon. (You'll learn more about formatting text in Lesson 17.)

 Print the memo by choosing File, Print and selecting the appropriate options in the File Print dialog box (see Lesson 5 for more information).

 Check the spelling by choosing Edit, Check Spelling. (Lesson 20 covers the details of using the Spell Checker.)

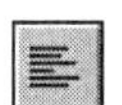  Align selected text by clicking one of the Text Align SmartIcons. (If you're not sure which SmartIcon is which, use the Help description bubbles that you learned about in Lesson 3.)

  Indent selected text by clicking one of the Text Indent SmartIcons. (Again, if you're not sure which SmartIcon is which, use the Help description bubbles.)

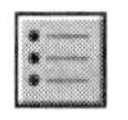 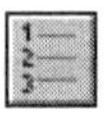 Change a list into a bulleted list or a numbered list (respectively) by selecting the text and clicking the appropriate SmartIcon.

TIP **Selecting Text** Before you can delete, format, or otherwise manipulate text, you must select it. To do so, place the insertion point to the left of the text you want to select. Then click and drag the mouse over the text to be included, and the text becomes highlighted.

Sending Mail

When you finish creating your mail message and are ready to send it, you can simply click the **Send** tool button. Notes sends the mail to the recipient's mailbox. By default, Notes saves a copy of your message in the Sent view.

To send mail and file a copy, follow these steps:

1. Choose the **Send And File** tool button, and the Folders dialog box appears (see Figure 6.2). From here, you can file the message in an existing folder (proceed to step 2), or you can create a new folder (skip down to step 3). However, you cannot store the message in the Folders and Views entry.

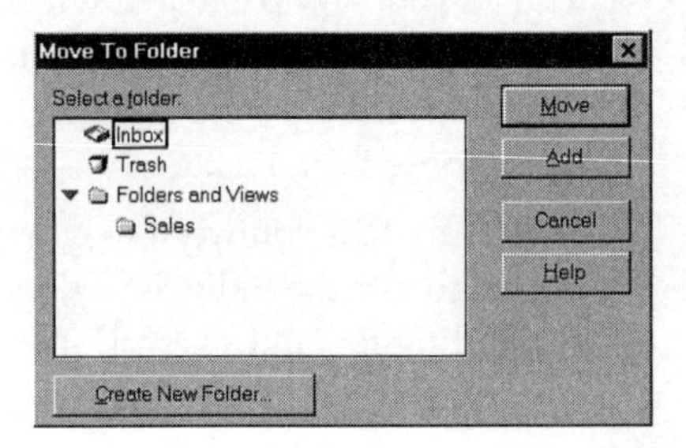

Figure 6.2 Save your messages in a folder for future reference.

2. To store the message in an existing folder, select the folder from the list and click **OK**. Notes saves the message to that folder, and you're done.
3. To create a folder, click the **Create New Folder** button. The Create Folder dialog box1 shown in Figure 6.3 appears.

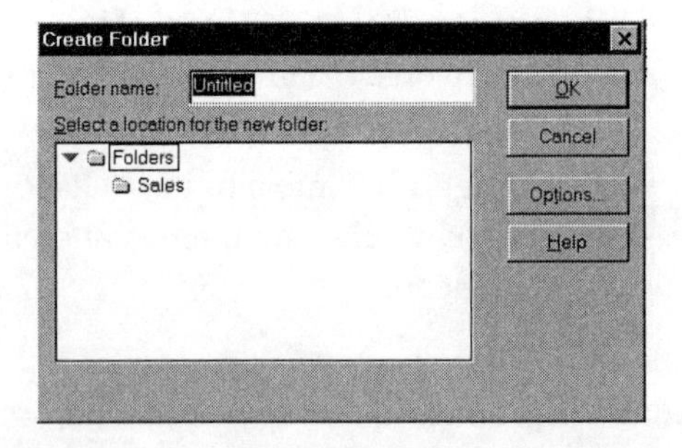

Figure 6.3 Select a location and enter a name for the new folder.

4. In the Folder name text box, enter a name for the new folder.
5. In the Select a location for the new folder list, choose the folder in which you want to place the new folder.
6. Click **OK**. Notes creates the folder and adds it to the Folders list in the Folders dialog box.

7. Select the newly created folder and click **OK** to store the mail message. Notes returns to the mailbox or workspace.

CAUTION

Two Folders Selected? If you accidentally select two or more folders in the Folders dialog box, click any selected folder to deselect it. If Notes prompts you for a password, enter your password to complete the procedure. (If you do not know the appropriate password, see your Notes administrator.)

Using the Address Book

Your Domino administrator most likely maintains a company address book that you can use to quickly and easily find and address your mail. You may also have your own personal address book you can use. Address books usually appear on the first workspace page. Like your mailbox, the address book is a button with an icon, but its icon has a picture of an open book. The following steps teach you how to use the address book.

1. Open a new memo by clicking the **New Memo** tool button. Notes displays a blank memo with your personal heading.
2. Click the **Address** tool button, and the Mail Address dialog box appears (see Figure 6.4).

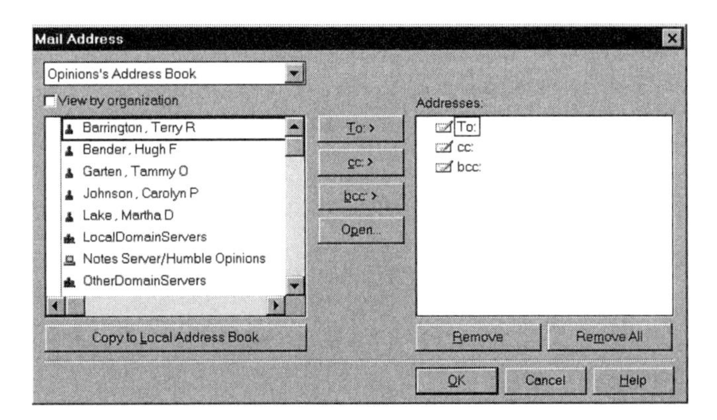

Figure 6.4 Use the address book to see who's available in your company or domain.

3. Open the drop-down list in the upper-left corner and choose the address book you want to look through (your company's address book, your personal book, or another domain's book, for example). Which books appear in the list depends on how your Domino administrator configured your mailbox.
4. In the list of addresses, select one recipient by clicking his or her name. To select multiple recipients, click to the left of the desired names to display a check mark.
5. After selecting the recipient(s), choose one of the following buttons:

   To Addresses the message to the selected recipients.

   cc Sends a carbon copy to each selected recipient.

   bcc Sends a blind carbon copy to each selected recipient.

6. Click **OK** to close the dialog box. Notes lists the selected names in the memo. Complete the memo, and then send it or send and file it.

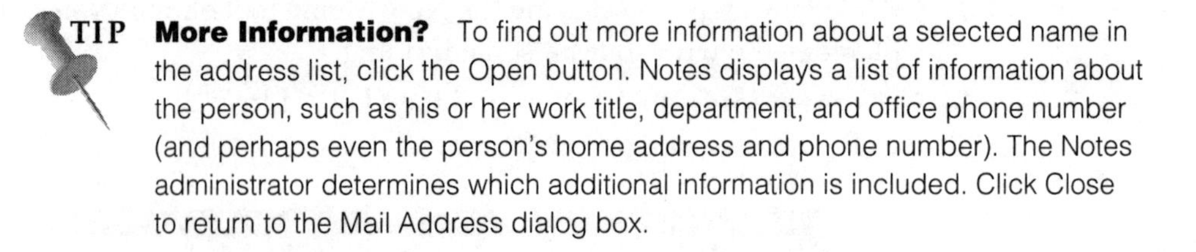

TIP **More Information?** To find out more information about a selected name in the address list, click the Open button. Notes displays a list of information about the person, such as his or her work title, department, and office phone number (and perhaps even the person's home address and phone number). The Notes administrator determines which additional information is included. Click Close to return to the Mail Address dialog box.

In this lesson, you learned to send mail, file your mail for future reference, and use the address book. In the next lesson, you'll learn to change mail options.

Setting Mail Options

In this lesson, you learn how to choose various delivery options, as well as how to change the type of mail message you're sending.

Choosing Delivery Options

Notes lets you control the details of how and when it delivers your mail messages. You can choose delivery options to request a delivery report or to set a priority level for your mail, for example. You must set delivery options before you send your mail message. Table 7.1 describes the available delivery options.

Table 7.1 Delivery Options

Option	*Description*
Importance	Tags the message with an importance level (Normal, High, or Low) that the recipient can see.
Mood stamp	Provides additional messages you can add to your memo. Select a mood, and Notes adds a graphic and/or text (such as "Thank You," "Good Job," "FYI," or "Joke") to your memo.
Delivery report	Tells Notes to place a report in your mailbox that indicates how the delivery of your message went. You can have Notes confirm the delivery, trace the path of the delivery, report only on failure of the delivery, or not report at all.
Delivery priority	Marks the message as Normal, High, or Low priority. Priority governs how quickly the mail is delivered across the network.

continues

Table 7.1 Continued

Option	*Description*
Sign	Adds a unique code to your message that identifies you as the sender.
Encrypt	Encodes the message so that no one but the intended recipient can read it.
Return receipt	Places a receipt in your mailbox that tells you the time and date the recipient received the message.
Prevent copying	Prevents the recipient from copying your message.

To set delivery options, follow these steps:

1. In your mailbox, open and create a new memo. Then click the **Delivery Options** tool button. The Delivery Options dialog box appears (see Figure 7.1).

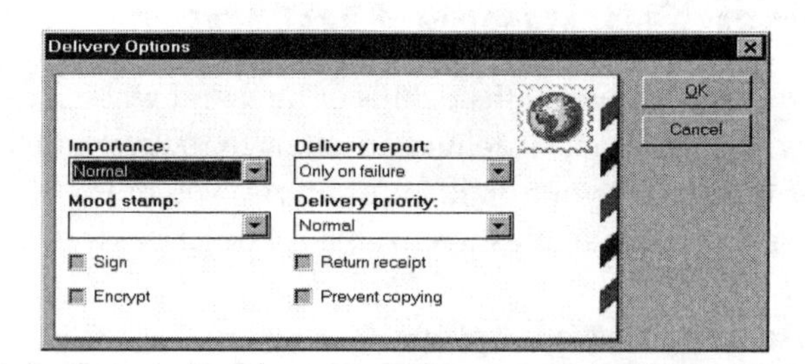

Figure 7.1 You control how and when your mail is delivered.

2. Open the **Importance**, **Mood stamp**, **Delivery report**, and **Delivery priority** drop-down list boxes and make your selection for each option. (Refer to Table 7.1 for details.)
3. Select or deselect the **Sign**, **Encrypt**, **Return receipt**, and **Prevent copying** check boxes as necessary. (These options are also described in Table 7.1.)
4. Click **OK** to set the delivery options. Then send your memo as usual.

Sending Other Mail Types

The most common type of mail message is the memo, but you can send other types of mail as well. For example, you can send invitations for meetings, you can send phone messages, and you can even send task assignments. The difference between the mail types is the format of the message.

Sending a Phone Message

The phone message memo offers an easy, timesaving method of sending someone his or her phone messages. If, for example, you take a colleague's messages while she's out of the office or in a meeting, you can enter them in Notes as you take them and then send them to her via mail. To send a phone message, follow these steps:

1. In your mailbox, choose **Create**, **Special**, **Phone Message**. The phone message memo appears (see Figure 7.2).

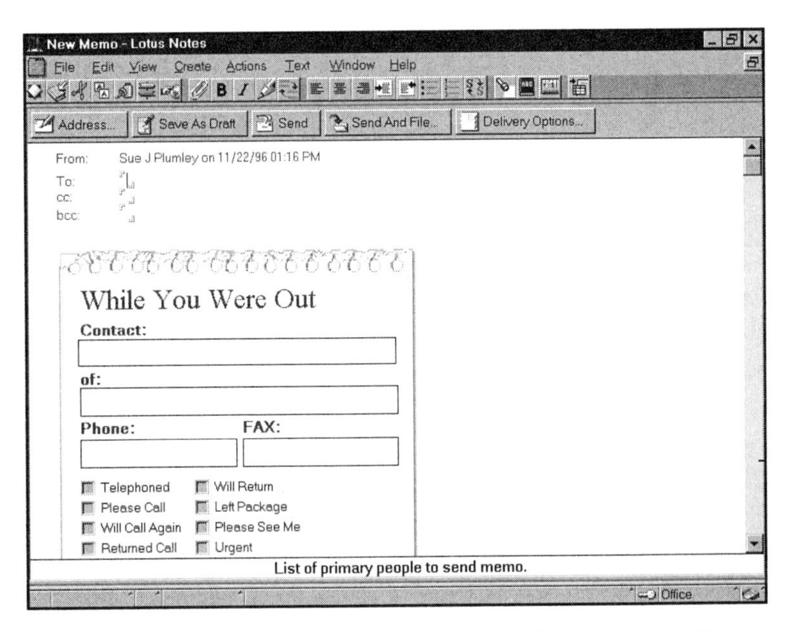

Figure 7.2 Take a phone message in Notes and send the person a mail message memo.

2. Enter the heading information as usual. Type the phone message information in the text boxes.
3. Send the phone message as you would any mail message.

Assigning a Task

Tasks are similar to items you place on a To Do list. You can create a task list to display in your To Do view (see Figure 7.3). To help you keep track of your task list, Notes enables you to choose a task, and then update it, delete it, or mark it as completed using the tool bar buttons in To Do view.

You also can choose to assign tasks to others in your organization. To assign a task, follow these steps:

1. In your mailbox, choose **Create, Task**. The Task memo appears (see Figure 7.4).
2. Enter a subject in the Task text box, and enter a date and priority, if you want.

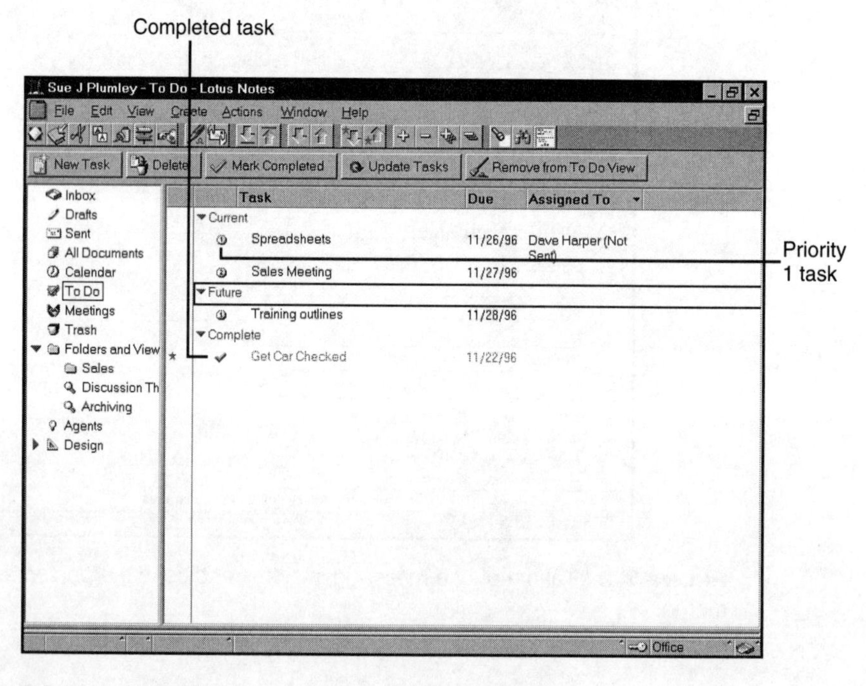

Figure 7.3 Use Notes' Task List to organize your duties.

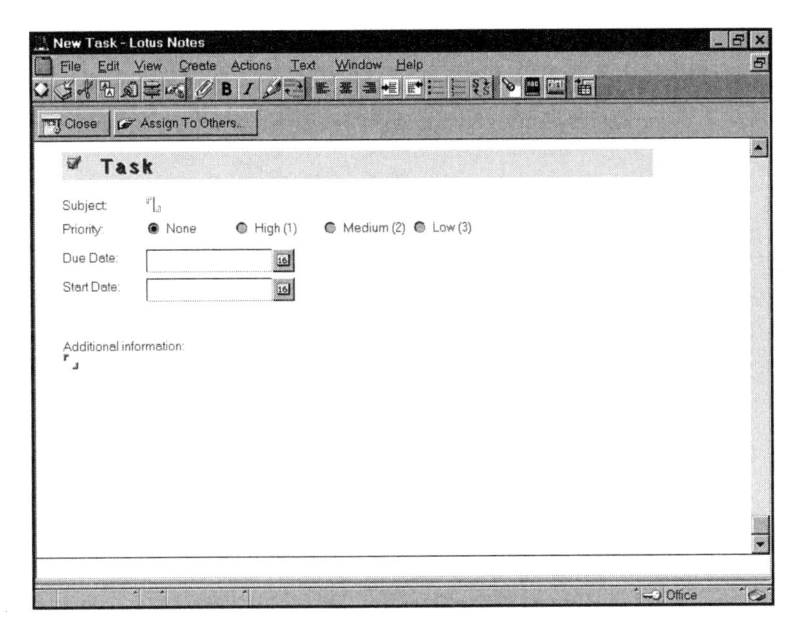

Figure 7.4 Assign a task to yourself or to others.

CAUTION

No Date? If you enter a date but do not deselect the No Date check box, no date will appear in the Task list.

3. (Optional) Enter a description of the task in the brackets below **Additional information**.
4. To assign the task to your own task list, click the **Assign Now** tool button. Notes adds the task to your list and returns to your mailbox in To Do view. The first time you assign a task to your own task list, a message appears telling you the task was saved in your To Do view.
5. To assign the task to someone else, click the **Assign To Others** tool button. The Assign To and CC fields appear below the Task Request graphic, and the toolbar buttons change to Address, Assign Now, and Delivery Options.

   To have the task appear in your calendar, click the **Display Task On My Calendar** button.

Fields In a memo or other mail message, the areas with brackets that you fill in are called "fields." Some fields, such as the To field, contain certain instructions from Notes that help you fill the field. For more information about fields, see Lesson 16.

6. Complete the message, and then send it by clicking the Assign Now tool button.

In this lesson, you learned to set delivery options and to create an invitation, a phone message, and a task. In the next lesson, you'll learn such advanced mail tasks as attaching and importing files.

Using Advanced Mail Features

In this lesson, you learn to organize your mail, attach a file to a mail message, and import and export files using mail.

Organizing Mail

When working with Notes, you might be inclined to accumulate messages that you want to keep as reminders. However, accumulated messages take up valuable disk space and make it hard for you to find important items in your mailbox. To help you keep your mailbox cleaned up and to optimize your hard disk space, Notes offers these areas, or views, in which you can organize and store your messages.

- **Inbox, Drafts, Sent, and All Documents** Use these views to store both incoming and outgoing mail. For more information, see Lesson 4.
- **Trash** Place mail messages you no longer want to keep in the Trash view and then delete them from your hard disk by emptying the trash (see Lesson 5).
- **Folders** Create your own folders in which to store messages you need to keep. For example, you might create a general Sales folder, and create a folder within it for each product or service you sell. Then you can place mail messages about each product or service in their own folders so you can quickly and easily find them. (See Lesson 5 for details.)

Figure 8.1 shows the open mailbox, with the previously described views listed in the navigation pane.

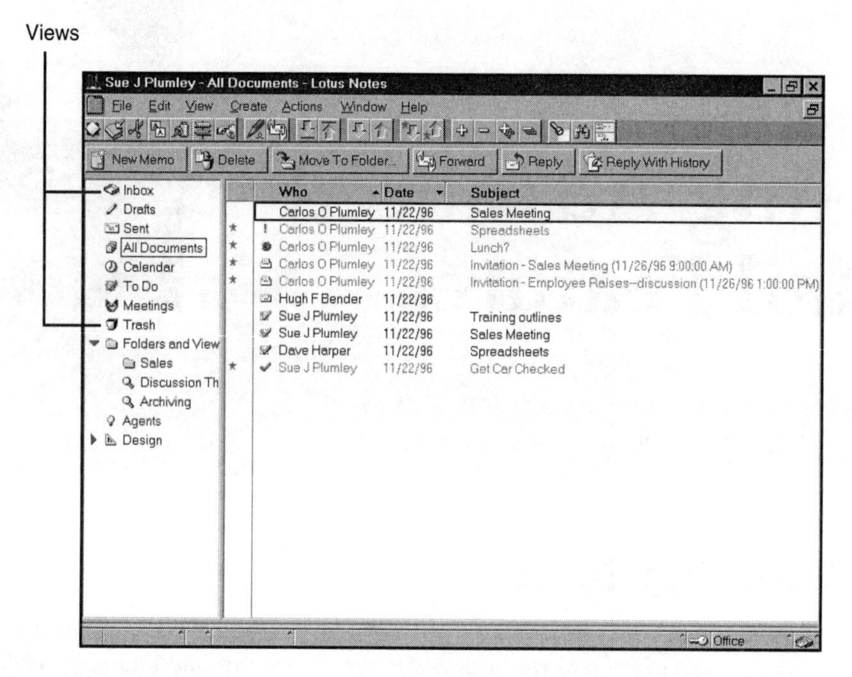

Figure 8.1 Use the views in the Notes mailbox to organize your mail.

Storing mail messages in certain places makes it easier for you to locate them. In addition to doing that, follow these guidelines to prevent excess files from accumulating on your hard disk. Overall, these practices conserve disk space and make managing and organizing those files you keep easier and more efficient.

- When you receive a message, deal with it immediately. You might want to delete the message after you read it, reply to the message and then delete it, or store the message in a permanent place.
- Don't save copies of the messages you send unless you really need the information in the message. Saved outgoing messages take up disk space, too.
- If you must save outgoing messages, you might consider saving a printed copy instead of the copy on disk.
- Every month or so, review the messages in the Inbox, Sent, Drafts, and other views of the mailbox, and delete any messages you no longer need.

Attaching Files

You can send, or attach, files—word processing documents, spreadsheets, programs, data files, and so on—with a mail message to anyone on the Notes network. To attach a file to a message, follow these steps:

1. In your mailbox, create a new memo as described in Lesson 6. Enter the addressing information and any message you want to send.
2. With your insertion point within the body text brackets, choose **File, Attach**. The Create Attachment(s) dialog box appears (see Figure 8.2).

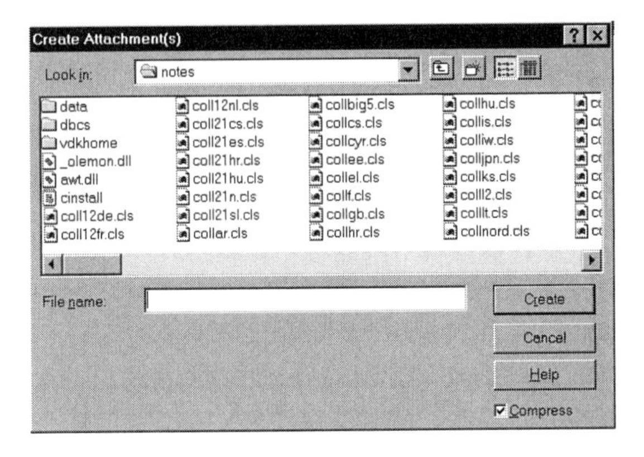

Figure 8.2 Choose the file you want to attach to a mail message.

3. In the **Look in** drop-down list, select the drive and directory containing the file you want to attach. (You can attach any file from your local drive, from a floppy drive, or from the network drive.)
4. Select the file from the list, or type the file name in the File name text box.
5. (Optional) Choose the **Compress** check box if you want Notes to compress the file.

Compress the File? If you choose to compress the attached file, the file is packed, or reduced in size, to speed up the transfer over the network. The recipient of the compressed file won't know the difference; Notes decompresses the file automatically when the recipient opens it.

6. Choose **Create**. An icon representing the file and the file's name appears in your memo (see Figure 8.3).
7. When you're finished with the message, send it as you normally would.

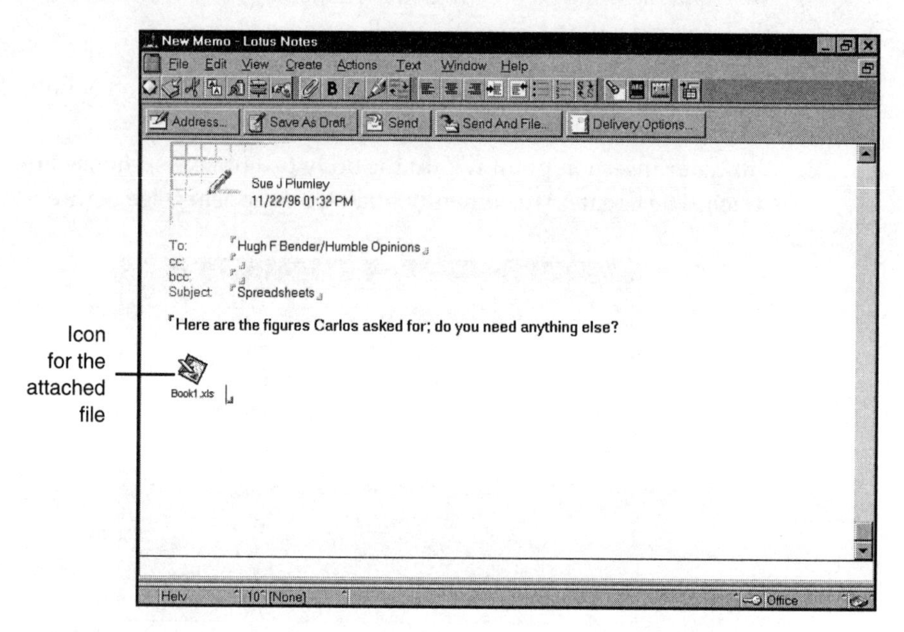

Figure 8.3 Attach one or multiple files to a memo, invitation, or other mail message.

In the mailbox, mail messages that contain attached files have a paper clip beside their subjects. Open such a message as you would any other, and you see that it contains an icon for the attached file. To read an attached file, double-click the file's icon. The Properties for Attachment InfoBox appears (see Figure 8.4). Click the Information tab—with the lowercase i on it—and click one of the buttons described in the following list.

- **View** Select this button to display the file in the File Viewer. The File Viewer does not enable you to edit the document in any way, and you can't view all file types. View may try to launch the program associated with the file type, or it may display an error. Choose **File**, **Close** to exit the File Viewer and return to the memo in Notes.
- **Launch** Choose this button to *launch*, or start, the program with which the file was created. You can edit, format, or otherwise manipulate the file, using this option. Click the application's **Close** button to return to Notes.

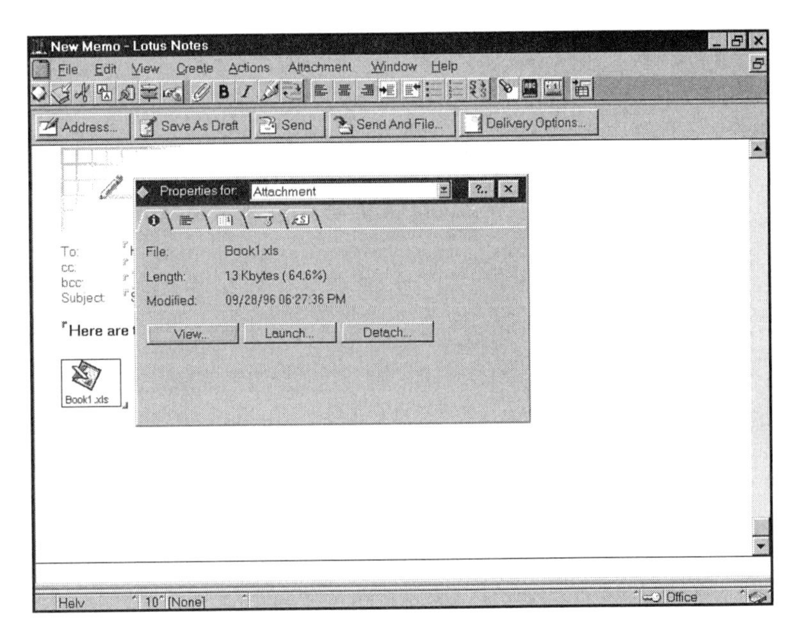

Figure 8.4 Use the InfoBox to control the attached file's properties.

- **Detach** Choose Detach to display the Save Attachment dialog box, where you choose a folder in which to store the file. You can save the file on your local drive or on the network drive, and you can save the file with the same name or a new name. Click the **Detach** button in the Save Attachment dialog box to complete the process.

Launch To start, or execute, a program. When you open Notes, for example, you're launching the program.

To close the InfoBox, click the **Close** (X) button; to open an InfoBox, right-click the attached file's icon and select **Attachment Properties**. To learn more about InfoBoxes, see Lesson 3. To learn more about the other tabs in the InfoBox, see Lesson 17.

Don't Worry If you want to get rid of an attached file, click its icon and then press the **Delete** key.

Importing Files

You *import* a file by opening another application's file in Notes. When you do, the imported file becomes a part of Notes, taking on all characteristics and formatting of the Notes document. You might import a file if your reader doesn't have the necessary software to launch an attached file, or if the reader only needs the text or data and doesn't need to format or alter the data in its original program.

Import versus Attach When you attach a file, that file remains in its original format (say, WordPad, 1-2-3, or Word for Windows, for example) and the file moves with the mail message to which you attach it. When you import a file (from WordPad or 1-2-3, for example), you convert the text so it works in Notes. The text becomes part of your mail message.

Table 8.1 lists the most common types of files you can import to Lotus Notes. For a more complete list, look in the Files of Type drop-down list in the Import dialog box.

Table 8.1 File Types Notes Can Import

File Type	*Description*
Lotus 1-2-3, Symphony	Spreadsheet files
Ami Pro Document	Word processing files
ASCII Text	Text files
BMP, GIF, JPEG, PCX, and TIFF Images	Picture files
Excel 4, 5	Spreadsheet files (change to 1-2-3 before importing)
Word for Windows 6, 7	Word processing files

Follow these steps to import a file into your mail message:

1. In your mailbox, start or open the memo into which you want to import the text.
2. Position the insertion point within the brackets in the location where you want to insert the imported text.
3. Choose **File, Import**. The Import dialog box appears (see Figure 8.5).

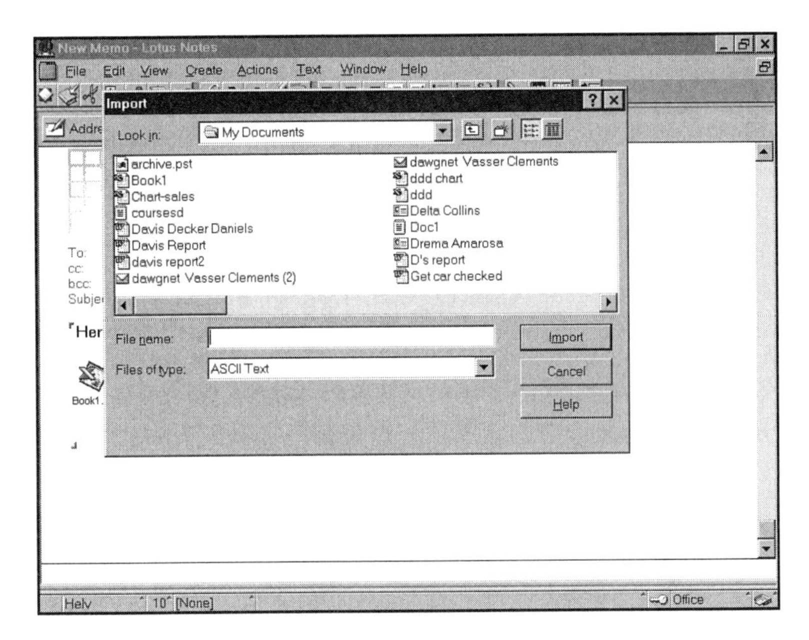

Figure 8.5 Select the file you want to import to the mail message.

4. In the **Look in** drop-down list, choose the folder in which the file resides.
5. In the list of files, select the file you want to import.
6. In the Files of type drop-down list, select the type of file you're importing.
7. Click the **Import** button, and Notes imports the file to the message.

CAUTION

Won't Accept File Type? If Notes displays a message saying the file type is not supported, you might need to go back into the original application and save the file in a different format, such as ASCII text. See the application's documentation for more information.

Notes imports the text into the message. You can now select the text, edit the text, or otherwise manipulate the text before you send the memo.

Exporting Files

You can *export* any of your mail message files for use in another application. If you open the message before you export it, Notes offers more export options, such as WordPerfect and Ami Pro.

Export To convert a file to another file format, such as a format you can use in a word processing or spreadsheet application.

Table 8.2 lists the file types to which you can convert a Notes file for use in another application.

Table 8.2 File Types to Which Notes Can Convert

File Type	*Description*
ASCII Text	Straight text
Ami Pro	Word processing file
CGM and TIFF	Picture files
Word for Windows 6, 7	Word processing files
WordPerfect 6.0, 6.1	Word processing files

CAUTION

It Doesn't Work You can use these file types only when reading or editing a memo.

To export a file from Notes, follow these steps:

1. In your mailbox, select the file you want to export and choose **File**, **Export**. The Export dialog box appears (see Figure 8.6).
2. In the Save in drop-down list, choose a folder in which to save the exported file.
3. In the File name text box, enter a name for the exported file.
4. In the Save as type drop-down list, choose a file type to save the exported file as.
5. Choose **Export**. The file type Export dialog box appears.
6. When prompted, enter options depending on the selected file type.

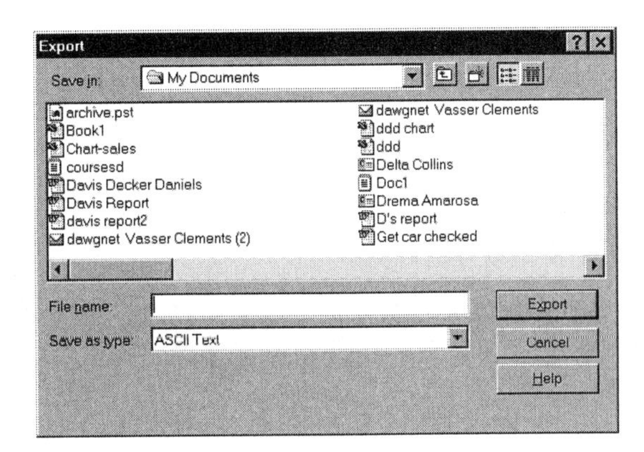

Figure 8.6 Choose a location and file name for the exported text file.

7. When you finish setting the options, click **OK** in the Export dialog box. Notes exports a copy of the file to the location you selected. You can open the exported file(s) in an application that uses the designated file types.

In this lesson, you learned to organize your mail, attach files to mail messages, and import and export files to Notes. In the next lesson, you'll learn to manage workspace pages.

Managing Workspace Pages

In this lesson, you learn to label page tabs, arrange workspace pages, locate database files, and add a database to a page.

Labeling Page Tabs

Notes provides six workspace pages you can use to store and organize your work in Notes, plus one page titled *Replicator*. You can label, or name, the workspace pages to suit you and your way of working.

Replicator The Replicator page contains tools you use to work remotely with Notes (when you're using a modem to attach to the network, for example). For more information on remote access to Notes, see Lesson 25.

The following steps walk you through labeling page tabs.

1. Select the page tab you want to label and double-click the tab. The Properties for Workspace InfoBox appears (see Figure 9.1).
2. In the Tabs page of the Properties InfoBox, position the insertion point in the Workspace page name text box and enter a name.

What's in a Name? A workspace page name can contain as many as 32 characters, including letters, numbers, spaces, and other keyboard characters.

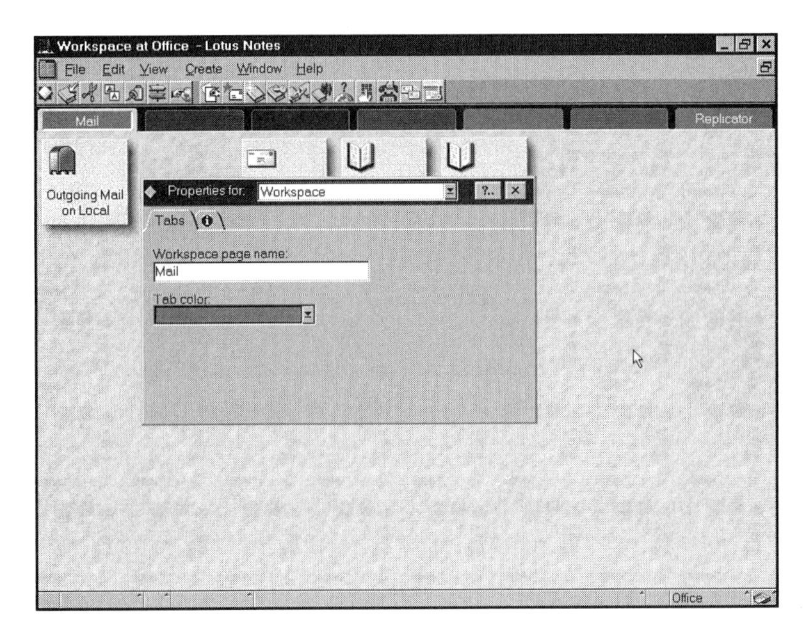

Figure 9.1 Use the Properties for Workspace InfoBox to name or rename a workspace page tab.

3. Press **Enter** to assign the page name. To close the InfoBox, click the **Close** (X) button.

TIP **Color** You can click the **Tab color** drop-down arrow in the Properties for Workspace InfoBox and select a different color for the page tab, if you want.

Arranging Icons on the Workspace Page

Thus far in working with Notes, you've used your mailbox, your company's address book, and perhaps your personal address book to create and send mail throughout your network. On the workspace page, icons represent each of these items. You can move the icons around on your workspace pages to better organize your workspace, and you can move icons from page to page. In addition, you can use the same methods to move other *databases* you access, copy, and create on your workspace.

Databases Databases contain documents; your address book is a database, for example. For more information about databases, see Lesson 10.

To move an icon on the same page, click and drag the icon to a new location. The mouse cursor changes to a hand while the mouse button is pressed in, and it changes back to a pointer when you release the button.

CAUTION

Overlap Icons If you drag one icon over the top of another, the two icons switch places.

To move an icon to another workspace page, click and drag the icon until the mouse pointer (a hand) is over the top of the page tab to which you want to move the icon. When you release the mouse button, the icon appears in the selected workspace page.

Adding a Database to a Page

You can add a database to any of your workspace pages from either the server or your local drive. When you add a database, you're simply adding reference documents you can use in Notes. One database you might add, for example, may contain Help files. Another database might contain company files you need for a specific job.

To add a database to a page, follow these steps:

1. In your workspace, choose the page tab to which you want to add the database. Label the tab if you want.
2. Choose **File**, **Database**, **Open**. The Open Database dialog box appears (see Figure 9.2).
3. In the Server drop-down list, choose one of the following:

   Local Select this option to add a database from your own local drive.

   Other Select this option to view a list of available servers or computers from which you can choose. The Choose Other Server dialog box appears with a list of servers. Select one and click **OK**.

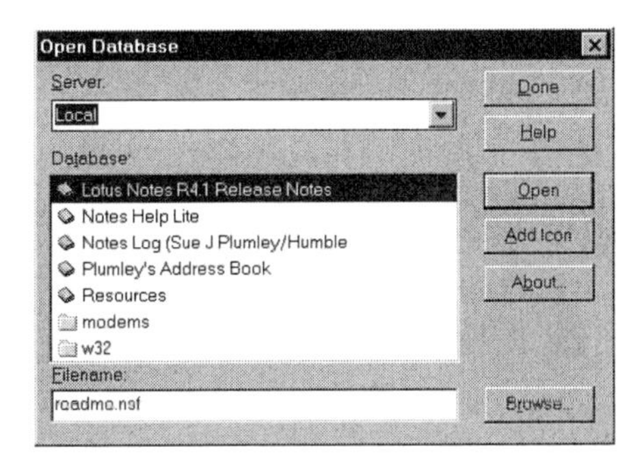

Figure 9.2 Add materials and documents to your workspace for easy access.

4. In the Database list, select the database you want to add to your workspace page.
5. If you cannot find the database you want in the Database list, click the **Browse** button. The Choose a Notes Database or Template File dialog box appears. Look through the available resources until you find the drive and folder that contain the database file you want to add. When you find the database, select it and click the **Select** button to return to the Open Database dialog box.
6. Click one of the following command buttons:

   Done Closes the Open Database dialog box without adding a database to your workspace.

   Help Displays Help information on adding a database to your workspace.

   Open Adds the database to your workspace and opens the database for you.

   Add Icon Adds the database icon to your workspace and returns to the Open Database dialog box so you can select another database.

   About Displays a preview window with the database showing so you can see if it's what you want. Click **Close** when you finish viewing the database to return to the Open Database dialog box.

7. If you're finished with the Open Database dialog box and it's still open, click **Done**. The database icon appears on your workspace page.

Can't Find a Database? Select one of the command buttons described in step 6 to complete the process.

Removing a Database from a Page

You can remove any database icon from the page. Removing the icon does not delete the database, so you can add the deleted database to your workspace page again at any time.

To delete a database icon from a page, right-click the icon to display the shortcut menu. Choose **Remove from workspace**, and the Lotus Notes confirmation dialog box appears. Click **Yes** to remove the icon, or click **No** to cancel the command.

In this lesson, you learned how to name workspace page tabs, arrange icons, add a database icon, and remove a database icon. In the next lesson, you'll learn to open and close a database as well as to understand a database.

Using Databases

In this lesson, you'll gain an understanding of what a database is and how to use the database view, and you'll learn to open and close a database.

Understanding Databases

In addition to using Notes for mailing messages to your coworkers, you can use Notes to share and access documents of various types. You might want to access your company's handbook, a colleague's sales reports, information on a new client or service, advertising letters, or any other important data you may need in order to complete your work.

A Notes database is not the same as what you would typically consider a database. You're probably used to the type of database you create with Access, Approach, or Q&A, in which you use fields to define such information as names, addresses, products, numbers, and prices. In Notes, however, related documents are stored in databases. The documents in a database can contain text, graphics, pictures, and other types of data. One Notes database you're already familiar with is your mailbox—a collection of documents you've received and sent.

Think of a database as a file folder; related documents are stored within the file folder. The creator of the database designates the types and designs of documents that are stored in the database. For example, advertising letters may be stored in one database, and quarterly sales figures may be stored in another.

Think of a workspace page as a file cabinet drawer containing several related databases or file folders. Use your six workspace pages to organize and manage different types of databases. You might use one page, for instance, for customer records and another page for product information.

You can access databases from your local drive and store them in your workspace pages. Two Notes databases already on your drive are the Help Lite files and your personal address book. You also can create and store your own databases on your local drive. You'll learn how to create your own databases and documents in Lesson 15.

Another feature enables you to access databases from any server available to you on your network. Your Domino server contains many default databases, including Help files and your company's address book. In addition, your supervisor, your Domino administrator, and perhaps some of your colleagues can add databases that you can access. If you're attached to other domains or Notes servers, you also may be able to access databases stored on those networks.

These are a few of the types of databases you may encounter:

- **Information Services** Current or updated data about your company, new products, procedures, services, employees, and policies.
- **Document Libraries** Forms, reports, memos, and other document types you would normally find on paper are stored electronically in a document library database.
- **Discussion Databases** Online written discussions between you and your colleagues in which you share ideas, solve problems, and discuss current events (or whatever else you want). For more information, see Lesson 13.

If you're used to working in a word processing or spreadsheet program, you're used to saving one document as a file. In Notes, however, the entire database—including all of its documents—is saved as a file. A database full of documents is like a word processing file full of paragraphs. So when you want to copy or delete a document from a database, for example, you have to copy or delete all documents in the database because they are all part of the saved file.

Opening a Database

All databases display similar elements and views. Depending on the type of database you open, you'll see general views (such as All Documents, Folders and Views, and so on) and specific views that apply only to the database. For example, a document library database may contain such views as My Favorite Documents, Archive Logs, and Review Stats.

To open a database already on your workspace page, double-click the database's icon. Alternatively, you can right-click the database icon and choose **Open**.

New Database For information about adding a new database to your workspace, see Lesson 9.

Viewing the About Document

The first time you open many databases, an About document appears. The About document displays information about the database you're about to view, and it appears only the first time you access a database. The About document is created by the person who created the database. For example, suppose your department head creates a database full of departmental forms such as expense reports, referral forms, and timesheets. She might then create an About document that describes each form and explains when you can use it.

When you create your own database in Lesson 15, you'll also create an About document. Figure 10.1 shows the About document for a database about new training services that was created for the Humble Opinions company.

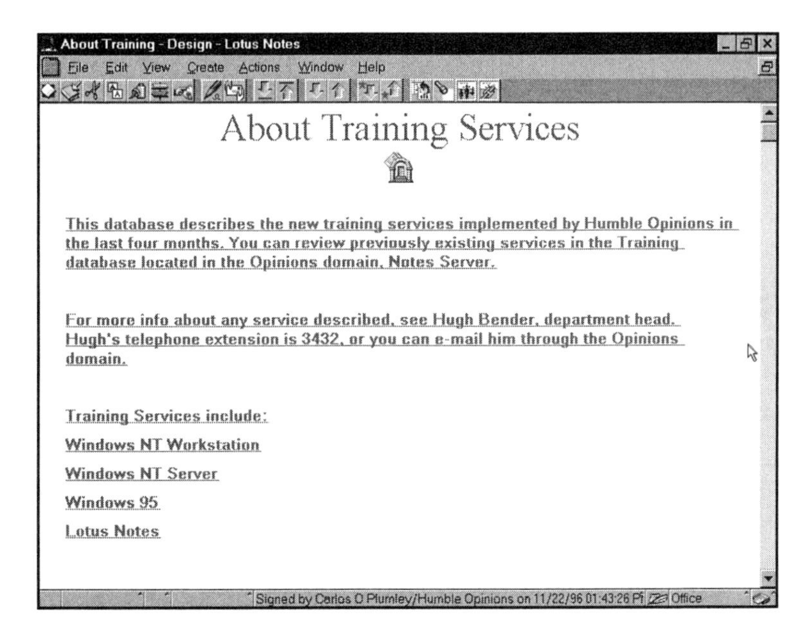

Figure 10.1 Read the About document for more information about the database you opened.

When you've finished viewing the About document, choose **File, Close** to close it and open the database.

Oops You can access the About document again at any time. Simply open the database and choose **Help, About This Database**. The About document appears. Choose **File, Close** to close the document again when you're done.

Viewing the Database

When you close the About document, the database appears (see Figure 10.2). You'll recognize many elements of the database window because it is similar to your mailbox window. All databases contain similar elements.

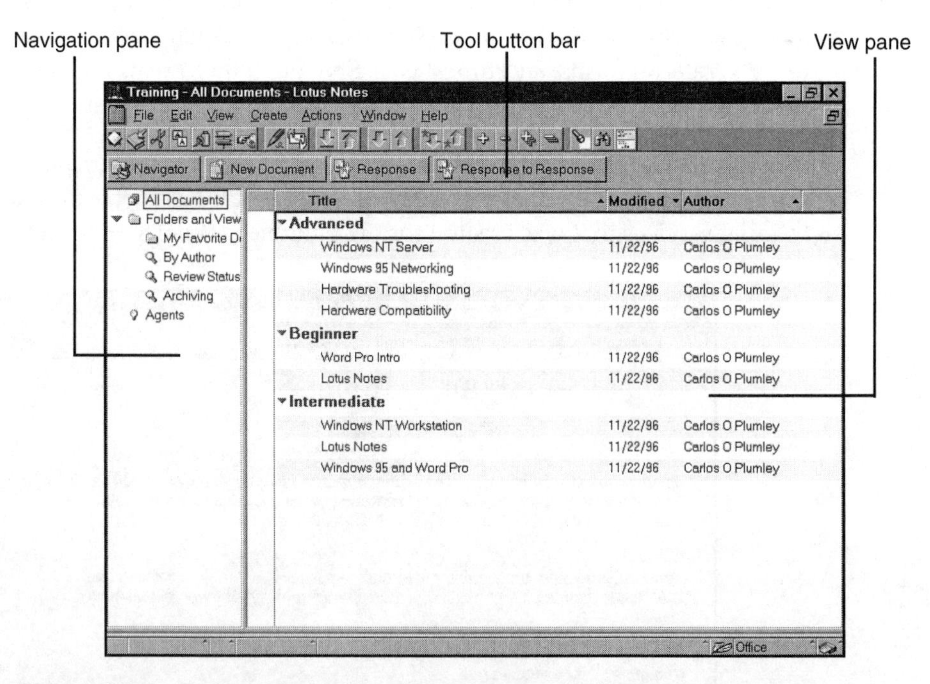

Figure 10.2 Each database contains some unique views and elements.

When working in a database, just as in your mailbox database, you select a view in the navigation pane by clicking once on that view. A right arrow beside a view means you can display more related topics by clicking that arrow. When all views are displayed, the arrow changes to a down arrow, which you can click to hide the related views. Click once on any view to select it. A rectangular outline appears around a selected view, and the items in the view pane change.

In the view pane, a right arrow beside a *category* represents hidden document titles. You must click the arrow beside the category to display the document titles. Click the arrow a second time to hide the related topics. For more information about viewing a database, see Lesson 11.

Category In a database, a category describes the documents filed within that particular database. You cannot open the category like a document, but you can expand or collapse it by clicking the arrow beside it. When it is expanded, the titles of the documents within the category appear.

Closing a Database

When you're finished with a database, close it by choosing **File**, **Close** or by pressing **Ctrl+W**. If you've added documents or made any changes to the existing database, Notes will prompt you to save. Click **Yes** to save your changes; click **No** to abandon the changes; click **Cancel** to return to the database.

CAUTION

Don't Close If you don't want to close the database but you need to do something else in Notes, such as work in your mailbox or view your workspace, you can leave the database open. To switch to the workspace, choose **Window**, **Workspace at Office**. To switch to another open database, choose **Window** and the name of that database.

In this lesson, you learned to open and close a database and to work in the database window. In the next lesson, you'll learn about database templates, and you'll learn how to view and manipulate documents in the document window.

Working with a Database

In this lesson, you learn about database templates and how to view documents in the view pane, mark documents, and print documents.

Understanding Templates

Each database in Domino is based on a *template* of some sort. The template governs how the database looks when you open it. Although all databases have a navigation pane and a view pane, the template supplies tool button bars and various views in the database. Therefore, when you use a template, you can have several different databases that all display the same elements.

Template A formatted design for a database that governs how the documents and the database view look. Each template displays different views, tool button bars, and options. In addition to the templates supplied by Domino, your Domino administrator may create his or her own templates to use with company documents.

Figure 11.1 displays a document library database for a company called Humble Opinions. The tool buttons represent actions you can take while in this particular database. Likewise, the views in the navigation pane (on the left side of the screen) show various collections of the documents in the database.

Figure 11.2 shows a database based on the room reservations template, which is used for reserving company meeting rooms at specific times. The tool buttons and navigation pane are different from those in the template shown in Figure 11.1.

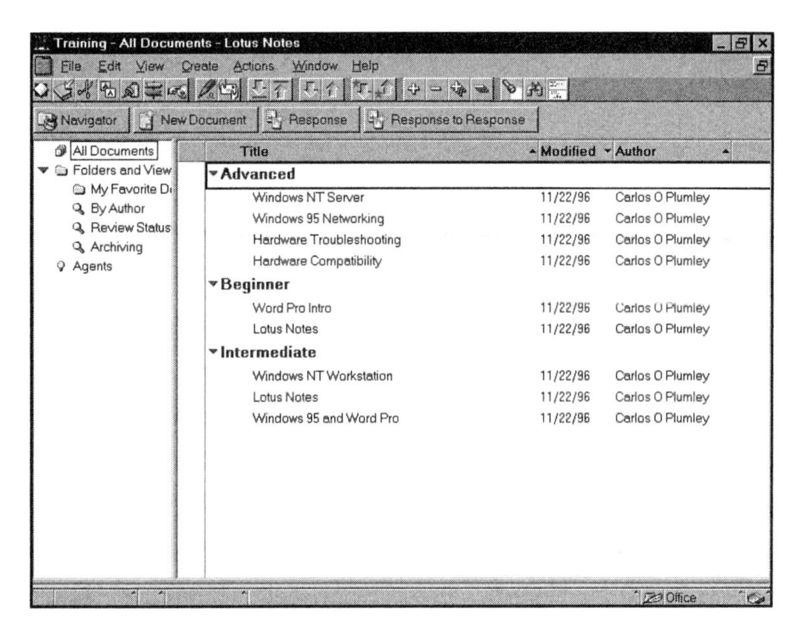

Figure 11.1 A document library displays the documents, views, and tools available in this database.

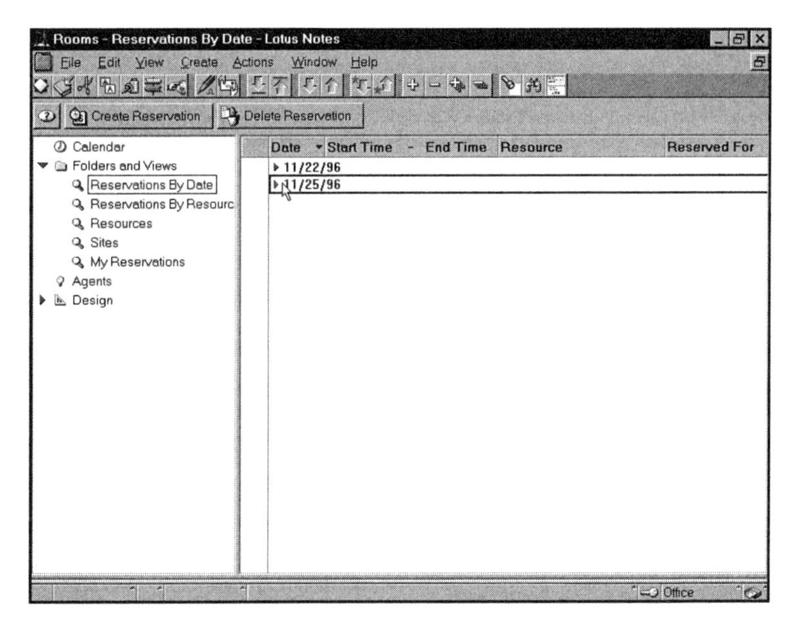

Figure 11.2 Each database offers different views and tool buttons.

TIP **Help** If you open a database and you're not sure how to view or use it, choose **Help**, **Using This Database** for instructions about using the database. Choose **File**, **Close** to close the Help window when you're done.

Viewing Documents in the View Pane

Most Domino databases offer similar tools for accessing help when viewing the documents in the database. In the view pane (on the right), a set of buttons describe what you see on-screen—for example, the Title, Modification Date, Resource, and Time. Depending on the database type, you can rearrange, or sort, the documents in the view pane using these buttons.

To arrange documents in the view pane of a database, follow these steps:

1. Click the **Title** button in the view pane. The document titles appear in alphabetical order, as shown in Figure 11.3. (The database in the figure is based on a Journal template—one in which you can record personal or professional information.)
2. Click the **Modified** button in the view pane to arrange the entries by the modification or creation dates, from most recent to least recent.
3. (Optional) If your database lists the name of the last person to modify each document, click the **Modified By** button to alphabetize the files by those names.

TIP **Don't Miss Any** Some databases display documents by categories, dates, or locations only. You can choose the **View**, **Expand All** menu command to make sure you see all documents in the database.

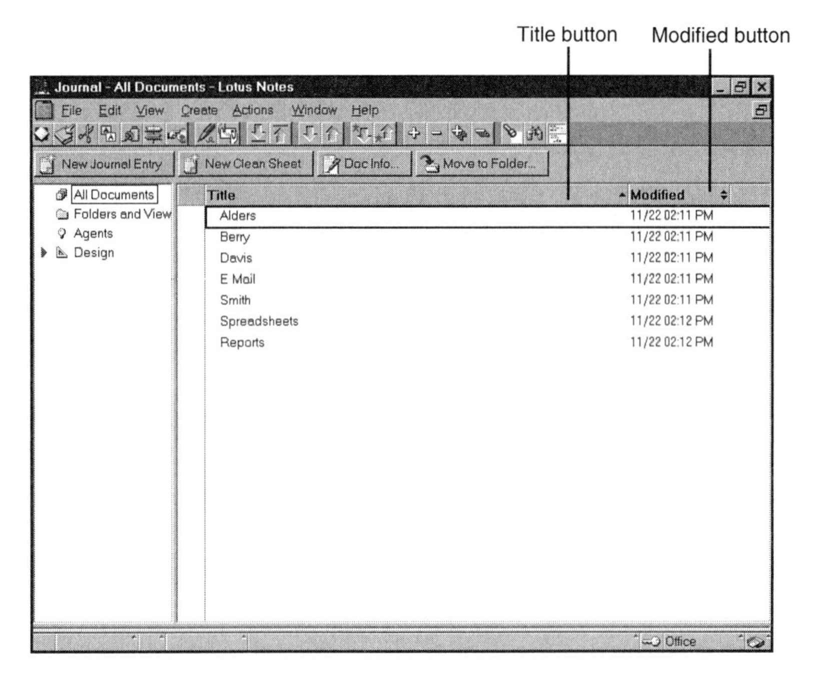

Figure 11.3 List documents in alphabetical order so you can easily find the one you want.

Manipulating Documents

You can print, cut, edit, or otherwise manipulate many documents in a database, depending on the type of database and whether you have access control to edit or cut documents from it. (See Lesson 12 for more information about access control.) Before you can perform some actions (such as printing), you must select, or *mark*, the document(s) you want to work with. You select documents in the view pane before you open any document.

Mark a Document Marking is a method of designating a document for the next action, such as deleting, editing, or copying. Marking is the same as selecting.

TIP **Open a Document** Open a document by double-clicking the document's title in the database. You'll learn more about opening a document in Lesson 14.

Marking Documents

You mark the document or documents on which you want to perform an action. To mark a document, click in the column to the left of the document title. A check mark appears beside the marked document, as shown in Figure 11.4. To remove the mark from a document, simply click the check mark.

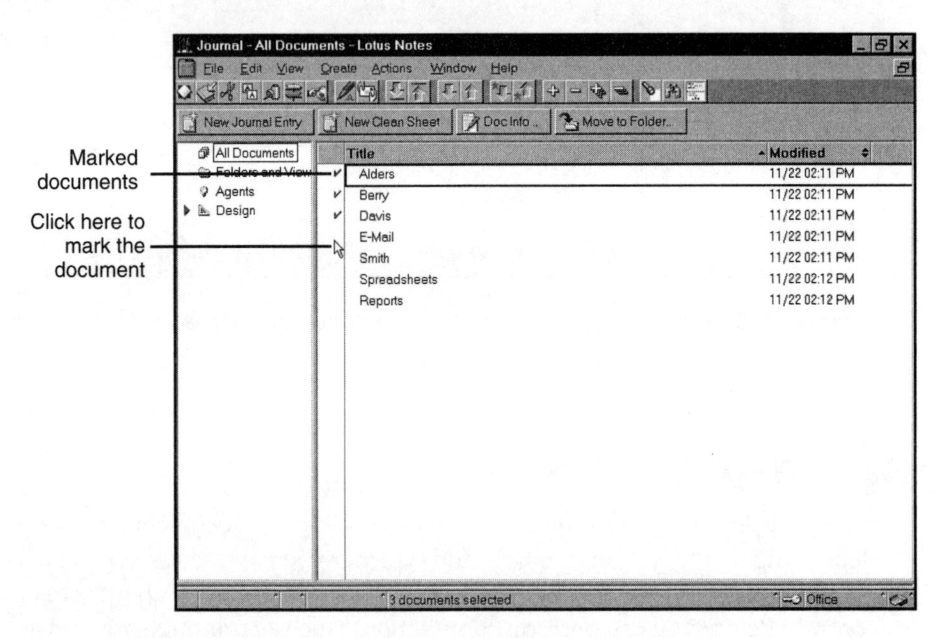

Figure 11.4 Mark documents on which you want to perform an action.

Printing Marked Documents

You can print the documents you've marked without opening them. To print marked documents, follow these steps:

1. Mark the documents you want to print. Then right-click one of the marked documents, and the shortcut menu appears.

2. Choose **Print**. The File Print dialog box appears (see Figure 11.5).

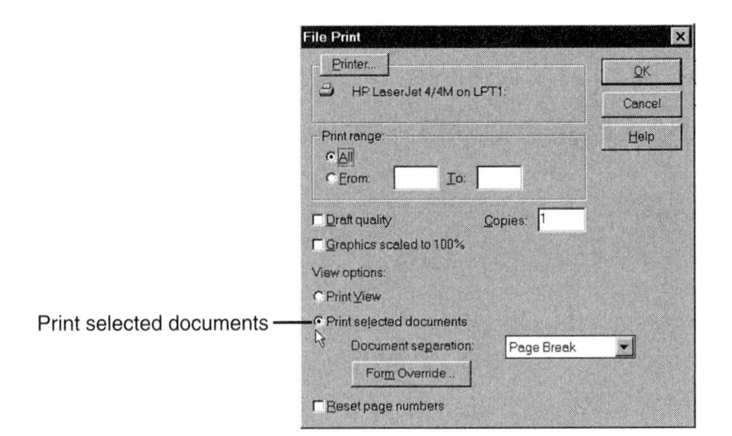

Figure 11.5 Tell Notes to print only the marked documents.

3. Choose **Print selected documents** and choose a Document separation mark from that drop-down list. Choosing this option is the same as placing a page break between the documents. (For more information about printing a document, see Lesson 5.)
4. Click **OK** to print the selected documents.

Copy a Document? The only way to copy a specific document from a database is to right-click the document and choose **Copy** from the shortcut menu. You can then paste the document into another database. You also can copy an entire database of documents (see Lesson 12).

In this lesson, you learned about database templates and how to view and manipulate documents in the view pane. In the next lesson, you'll learn to copy, scan, and remove a database.

Managing Databases

In this lesson, you learn about access rights. You also learn to scan a database for unread documents, read those documents, and remove a database.

Understanding Access Rights

Domino enables you to perform certain tasks in a database—such as editing, deleting, and copying—only if you have rights to do so. Either the creator of a database or the database manager decides and assigns access rights to the users of the database. Some people may be allowed to create documents for the database, and others may be allowed only to read documents from the database.

The manager of a database assigns rights to various people through the *access control list*. The manager can assign any of seven user access levels, each of which brings with it certain privileges. The following list describes each user access level in an access control list:

- **Manager** The manager has the right to perform any and all functions within the database, including assigning access rights to others on the network and deleting the database.
- **Designer** The designer can create, modify, and delete documents, as well as create and modify forms and views.
- **Editor** The editor can create, modify, and delete documents in a database, including documents created by others.
- **Author** The author can create and read documents. An author can modify his or her own documents, but he or she can only read others' documents.

- **Reader** A reader can only read documents in the database.
- **Depositor** A depositor can only add items to a database.
- **No Access** Prevents the user from performing operations within a document or accessing the document at all.

Forms and Views Designing and creating forms and views is part of designing your own database, which is beyond the scope of this book. To learn more about designing your own database, pick up Que's *Special Edition Using Lotus Notes*. On the other hand, creating a database and documents is covered in Lesson 15.

Your access rights may vary from one database to another. To find out your access rights in any database, click the **Access** button on the Status bar (the third button from the right). The Status bar's message area displays your access level, as shown in Figure 12.1. In addition, the Groups and Roles dialog box appears, in which you can view your access level. Click **Done** to close the dialog box.

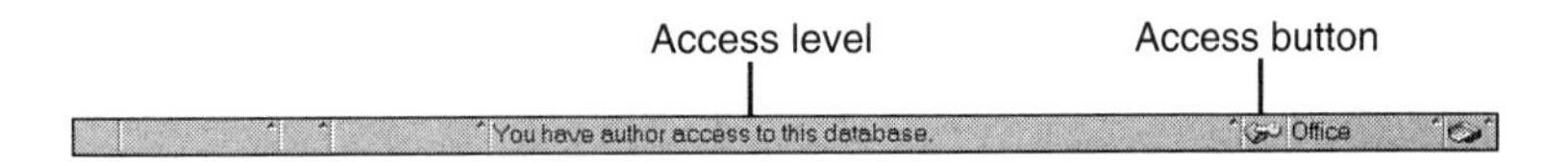

Figure 12.1 The Status bar shows your level of access rights.

As you work with databases and documents, remember that you may not have the access you need to perform all procedures you want to perform.

Copying a Database

You can copy a database from your local drive to another folder or drive, or from a server to your local drive. You might want to copy a database for easier access or availability, for example. To copy a database to another location, follow these steps:

1. In the open database, choose **File**, **Database**, **New Copy**. The Copy Database dialog box appears (see Figure 12.2).
2. In the Server drop-down list, choose either **Local** or the server to which you want to copy the database.
3. In the Title text box, use the original title or enter another name for the database.

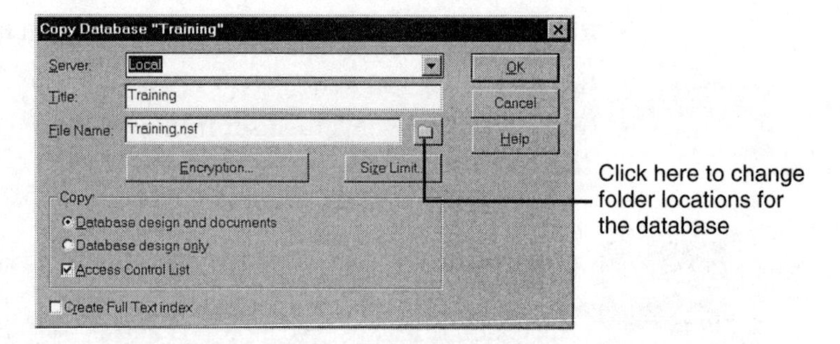

Figure 12.2 You can copy a database and all of its documents, but not just one or two documents from a database.

4. In the File Name text box, use the default file name or enter a new one. If necessary, click the folder icon to change locations. Notes displays the Choose a folder dialog box shown in Figure 12.3.
5. Choose a drive and folder in which to place the copied database and click **OK**.
6. Click **OK** again in the Copy Database dialog box, and Notes copies the database. Notes also adds a database icon for the copied database to the active workspace page.

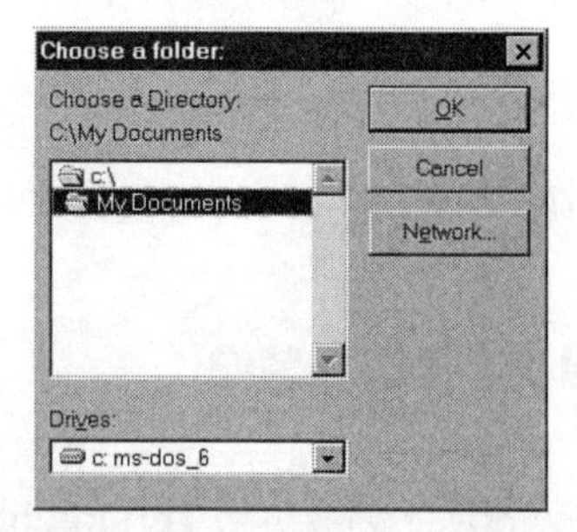

Figure 12.3 Copy the file to your local drive for your own personal use.

Move the Icon If you want, you can move the copied database icon from one workspace page to another by clicking and dragging the icon to any page tab in your workspace.

Scanning a Database

If your company uses many databases in which documents are added and updated daily, you may want to use the Notes scan feature to locate documents you have not yet read. This saves you from having to wade through each database every day.

Identifying the Databases

Before you can scan databases, you must identify those databases to Notes. Make sure no databases are selected, and then follow these steps:

1. In your workspace, choose **Edit**, **Unread Marks**, **Scan Unread**. The Scan Unread dialog box appears (see Figure 12.4).
2. Click the **Choose Preferred** button. The Scan Unread Preferred Setup dialog box appears (see Figure 12.5).

Figure 12.4 Choose which databases you want to scan for new or updated documents.

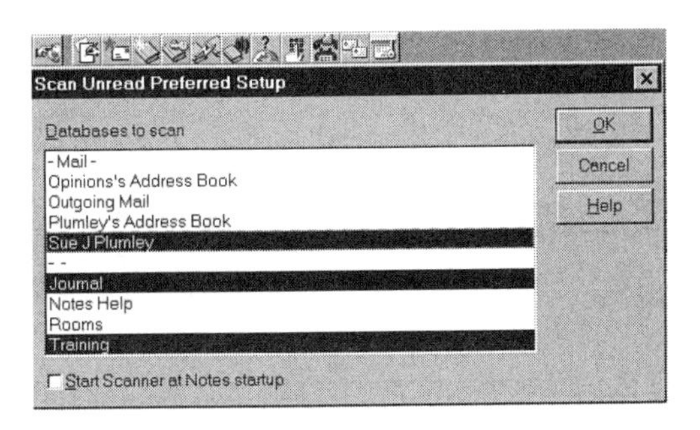

Figure 12.5 Scan those databases you use the most.

3. Select the databases you want to scan. Notes automatically scans any database with a hyphen in front of it.

4. (Optional) Choose the **Start Scanner at Notes startup** check box if you want Notes to scan automatically each time you start the program.
5. Click **OK** to return to the Scan Unread dialog box. Choose **Done**.

Scanning and Reading

You can scan one database or multiple databases for new additions. Follow these steps to scan the database.

1. In the workspace page, choose **View, Show Unread**. A box appears in each database icon showing the number of unread documents in that database (see Figure 12.6).

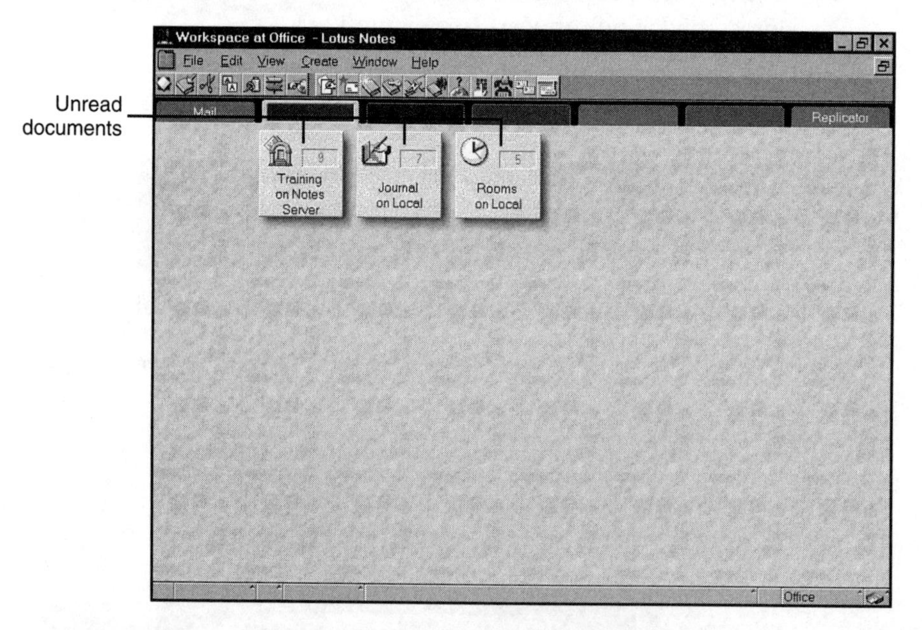

Figure 12.6 Each icon shows the number of unread documents.

2. To refresh the scanned view at any time, choose **View, Refresh Unread Count**.
3. To read unread documents in a database, select the database and choose **Edit, Unread Marks, Scan Unread**. The first document appears for you to read.

SmartIcon Shortcuts Use the Navigate Next Unread and Navigate Previous Unread SmartIcons as shortcuts for browsing through unread documents.

4. Close that document, and the next unread document appears.
5. Repeat step 4 until Notes has displayed all unread documents in the database.

Removing a Database

You can remove any database from a workspace page. To do so, right-click the database to reveal the shortcut menu, choose **Remove from Workspace**, and choose **Yes** in the confirmation dialog box. Notes removes the database icon, but the database data remains on the local or network drive.

To remove a database from your local drive, open the Windows Explorer, select the database file you want to remove (look for NSF extensions), and press the **Delete** key. Confirm the deletion, and then close the Windows Explorer.

When using NT 4 with Domino databases, you must have permission to use the server. If you have trouble accessing any database on the server, see your Domino or system administrator.

In this lesson, you learned about access control. In addition, you learned how to copy a database, scan a database for unread documents, read those documents, and remove a database from a workspace page. In the next lesson, you'll learn how to join a discussion group.

Joining a Discussion Group

In this lesson, you'll learn to join a discussion group, post a message, answer a message, and exit the group.

Joining the Group

A *discussion group* is a database shared among those in your workgroup and is usually focused on one topic, such as an advertising campaign, a new product line, or some other special interest. Think of a discussion group as an informal meeting place where you can share your ideas on the subject at hand.

When you join a discussion group, you add your comments, questions, theories, and so on to those of your coworkers. All discussion is stored in a database that you can open and read like any other. To join a discussion group, follow these steps:

1. In your Notes workspace, choose **File**, **Database**, **Open**. The Open Database dialog box appears (see Figure 13.1).
2. In the Server drop-down list, choose the server on which the discussion group database resides. If you're not sure where the database is located, use the **Browse** button to access the network. (You can also ask your Domino administrator if you cannot find the database.)
3. In the Database list, select the discussion group database. Ask your Notes administrator for the name of the database if you're unsure.
4. Click the **Add Icon** button.

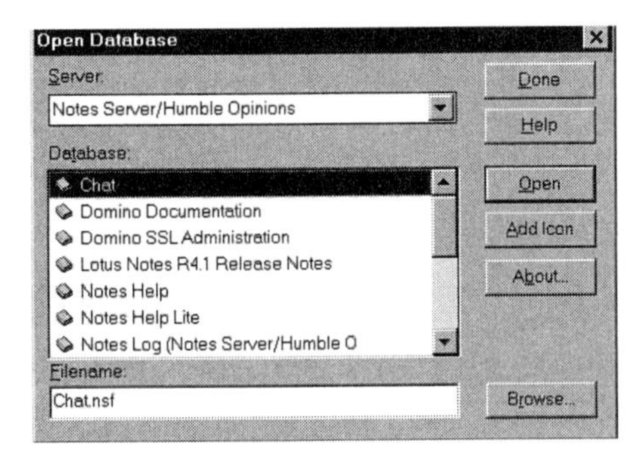

Figure 13.1 The Open Database dialog box gives you access to discussion groups.

5. Choose **Done**. Notes adds the database to your workspace.
6. To open the discussion group database, double-click its icon on your workspace. Notes opens the database. Figure 13.2 shows an example discussion group database.

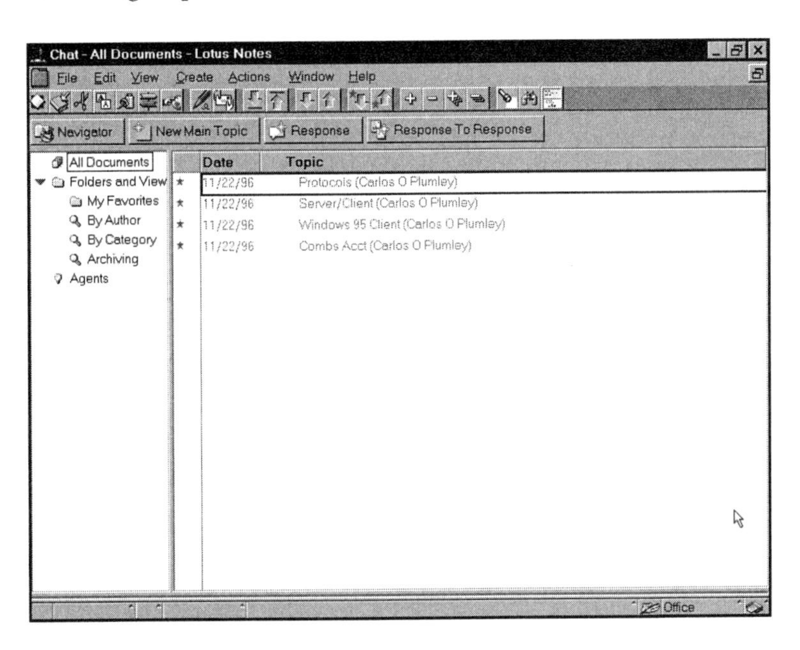

Figure 13.2 A discussion database lists main topics for discussion.

Viewing the Discussion Window

The navigation pane (on the left side of the discussion database window) provides several views you can use to find and organize messages. The default view is the All Documents view shown in Figure 13.2. The All Documents view displays all messages in the database listed by date, topic, and author. You can rearrange the topics by clicking the Date button in the document pane. By default, Notes sorts the messages from the most recent to the oldest dates. If the items in your navigation pane look different from those in the figure, click the Navigator button on the tool button bar.

The second view, My Favorite Documents, looks just like the All Documents view. The difference between My Favorite Documents and All Documents is that My Favorite Documents view displays fewer messages because you save only the messages you want. If you run across an important or particularly interesting message in the All Documents view, you can click and drag it to the My Favorite Documents icon in the view pane. Notes copies the message for you to keep.

In the third view, By Author, Notes displays a list of all documents by one author directly under that person's name. The date and the topic of the message are also displayed.

The fourth view is By Category. All messages stored in the database are created within a specific category, or section. To view the categories, click the By Category icon.

TIP **Icons in the Navigation Pane** Some databases enable you to display the views by icon instead of by standard folders. To change the look of the view pane, click the **Navigator** tool button. To change back to the default view, click the Standard Folders button.

Posting a Message

You can join a discussion group by opening the database and reading messages from those in the group, or you can compose your own messages to add to the discussion. To post a new message to a discussion group, follow these steps:

1. In the discussion database, click the New Main Topic tool button. The New Topic window appears (see Figure 13.3).

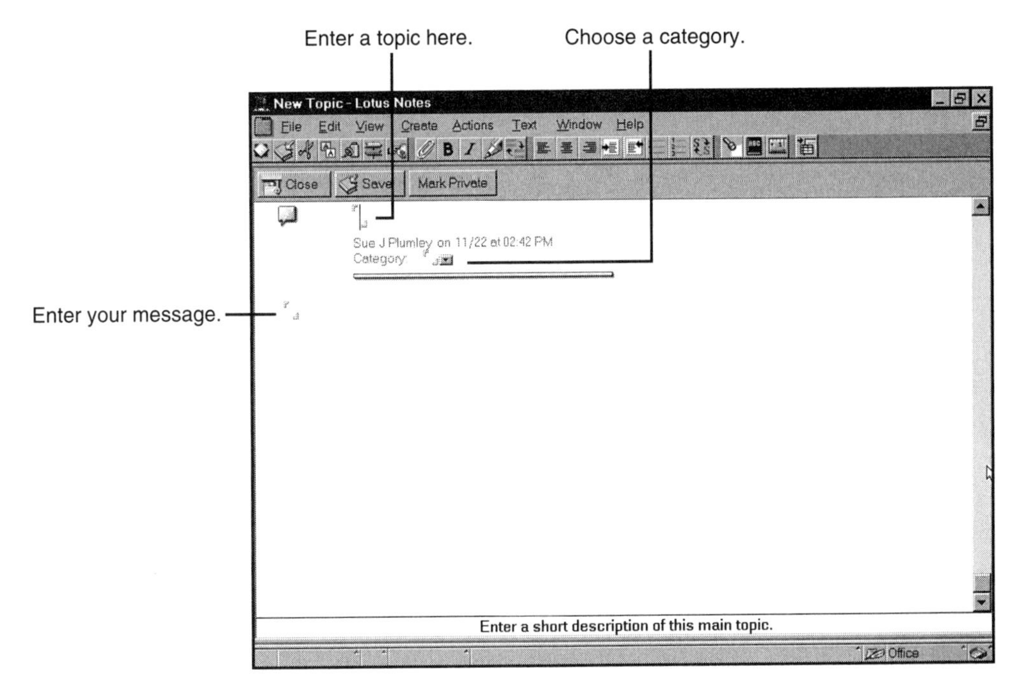

Figure 13.3 Create your own messages to add to the discussion.

2. Enter a topic in the first set of brackets. The topic is the name of your message, and it is what Notes displays in the database window.
3. Click the down arrow next to Category to choose the category in which your message fits. The Select Keywords dialog box appears, with General selected by default (see Figure 13.4). A document may fit into one, two, three, or more categories at the same time.
4. In the Keywords list, click the keyword for the category to which you want to assign your message. Notes displays a check mark beside it. You can click a selected category to deselect it and remove the check mark. When you're satisfied with your choice, click **OK**.

TIP **Add a Keyword** If you want to add a keyword to make it a category, enter it in the New Keywords text box in the Select Keywords dialog box. Press **Enter** to add the category and close the dialog box.

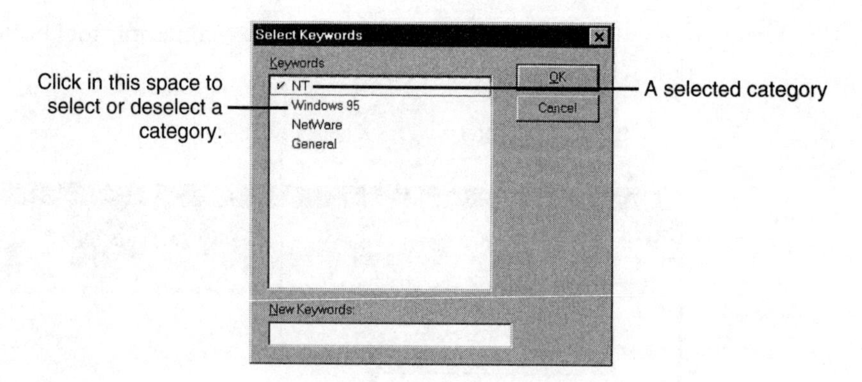

Figure 13.4 Choose the category under which you want your message listed.

5. Position the insertion point between the text brackets and enter your message.
6. When you finish entering the message, click the Save tool button.
7. Click the Close tool button to return to the discussion group database.

Reading and Replying to a Message

In addition to creating messages, you'll want to read the messages from others and reply to them. You can respond to a message from the message itself or from the database window. Follow these steps to read and respond to a message.

1. From the database window, double-click any message you want to read. Notes opens the message, displaying the topic, author, date, and category at the top (see Figure 13.5).
2. To respond to the message, choose the Response tool button. The New Response window shown in Figure 13.6 appears.
3. Enter your topic and your message in the New Response window.
4. (Optional) If you need to refer to the original message, click the Parent Preview button on the tool button bar. The screen splits in half so you can see both the original message and your response.
5. When you finish the response, click Save and then Close.
6. Close the original message to return to the discussion database window.

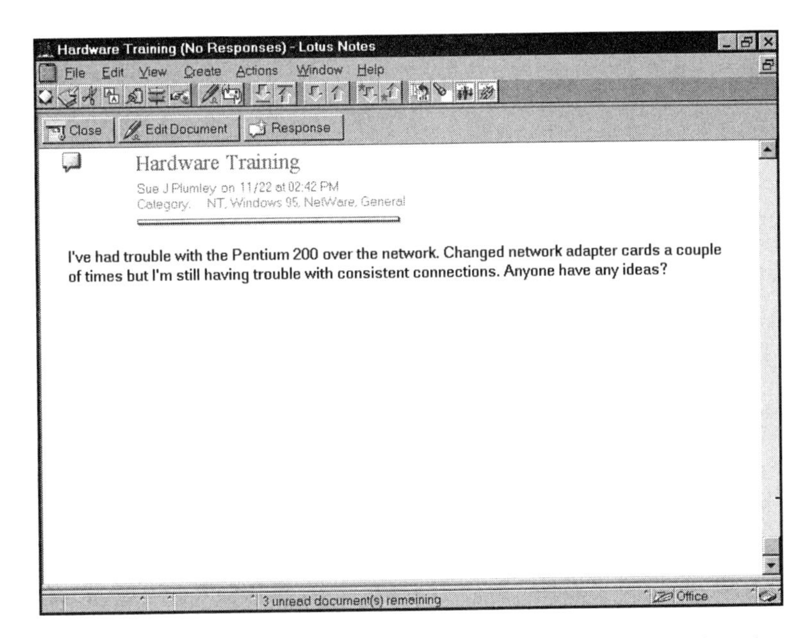

Figure 13.5 Open a message and read it, and then respond to it or close it.

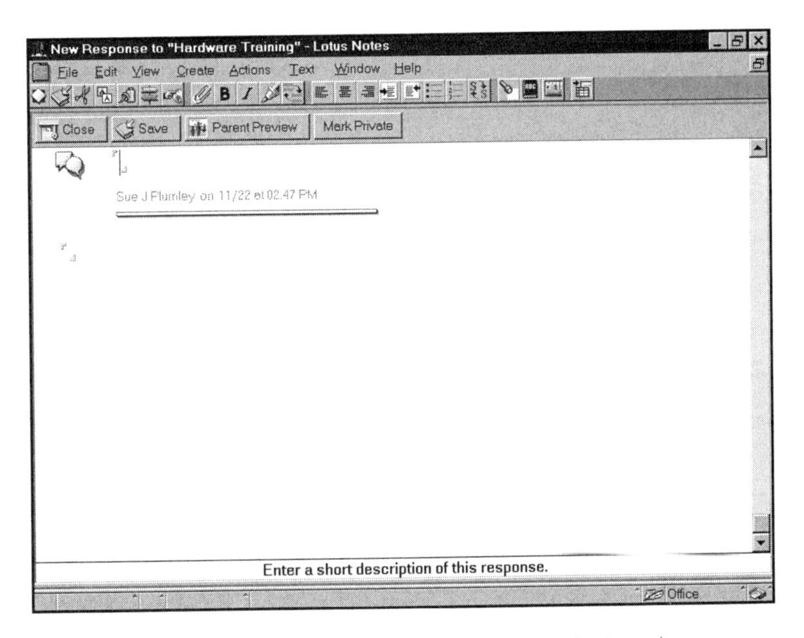

Figure 13.6 Enter a message in response to the one you just read.

CAUTION

You've Got a Reply! In the discussion database window, responses appear directly below the original message and in a different color. In addition, Notes displays the number of responses you've received to your messages beside your name.

TIP

Response to a Response? In the database window, you can respond to a message without opening it. Simply select the message and choose the Response tool button to display the New Response window. Click the Response to Response button to reply to a message that's a response to an original.

Exiting the Group

You close the discussion group database as you would any other database. Choose **File**, **Close** to return to the workspace. If you have created messages but have not saved them, Notes displays a confirmation dialog box prompting you to save. Choose **Yes** to save the messages you've created.

In this lesson, you learned to join a discussion group, post a message, answer a message, and exit the group. In the next lesson, you'll learn to work with documents within databases by opening them, marking them, and moving around in the documents.

Working with Documents

In this lesson, you learn to open a document, move from document to document, mark a document as read, and exit a document.

Opening a Document

Select the document you want to open from the document window of any database. To open a document, double-click it, or right-click it and choose **Open** from the shortcut menu. Figure 14.1 shows an open document from a library database named "Training."

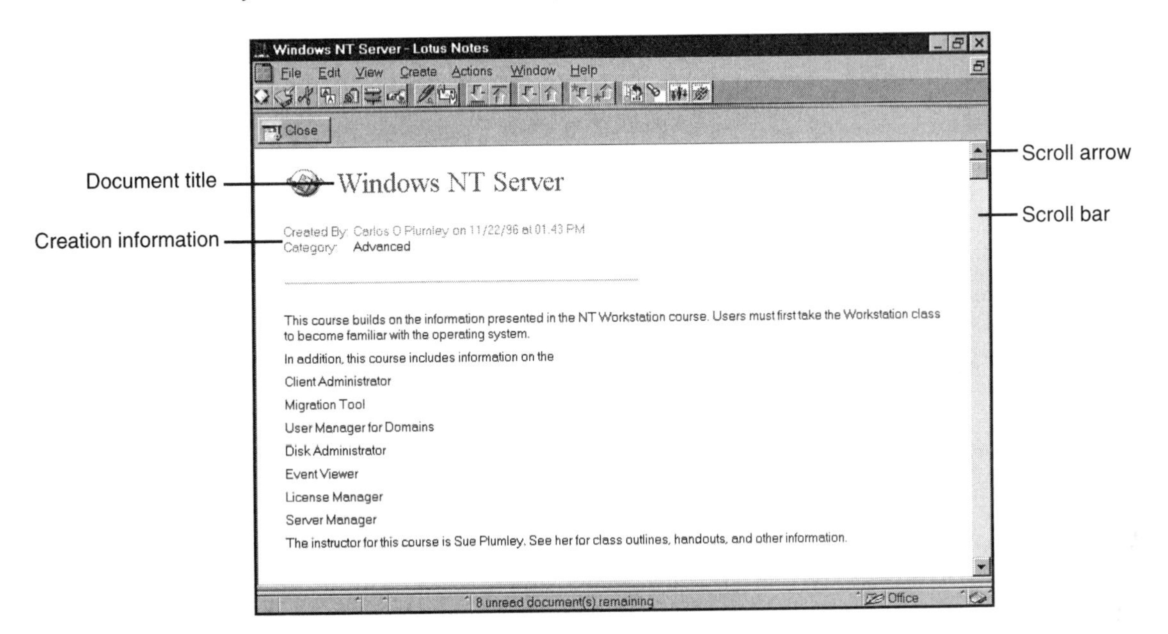

Figure 14.1 Open a document to read the data in it.

In the open document, you can use the scroll bar to view any of the document that's not displayed in the window. Click the scroll arrows to move up or down in the document one line at a time.

TIP **Shortcuts** You can also move around in a document by pressing the Page Up and Page Down keys.

Moving from Document to Document

You can move to the next or previous document in a database without closing the current document and returning to the database. To do so, you use the SmartIcons in the document window. The following list shows those SmartIcons and explains their functions.

Use the Navigate Next icon to move to the next document listed in the database.

The Navigate Previous icon moves you to the previous document in the database.

Use the Navigate Next Unread icon to move to the next unread document in the database.

The Navigate Previous Unread icon moves you to an unread document previous to the current one.

If the database does not contain a document that matches your request (if there is not a next unread document, for example), Notes returns to the database view. See the next section for more information about marking documents as read or unread.

Marking a Document as Read

Many databases will contain so many documents that it's difficult to keep track of the ones you've read. Notes provides a way for you to mark the documents you've read so you don't waste time opening them again. You can also use marking options to help you organize and manage the documents in a database.

In order to see marked documents, you must be in the database view window. A red star appears beside each unread document; no mark at all indicates that you've read (or at least opened) that document. Figure 14.2 shows six unread documents.

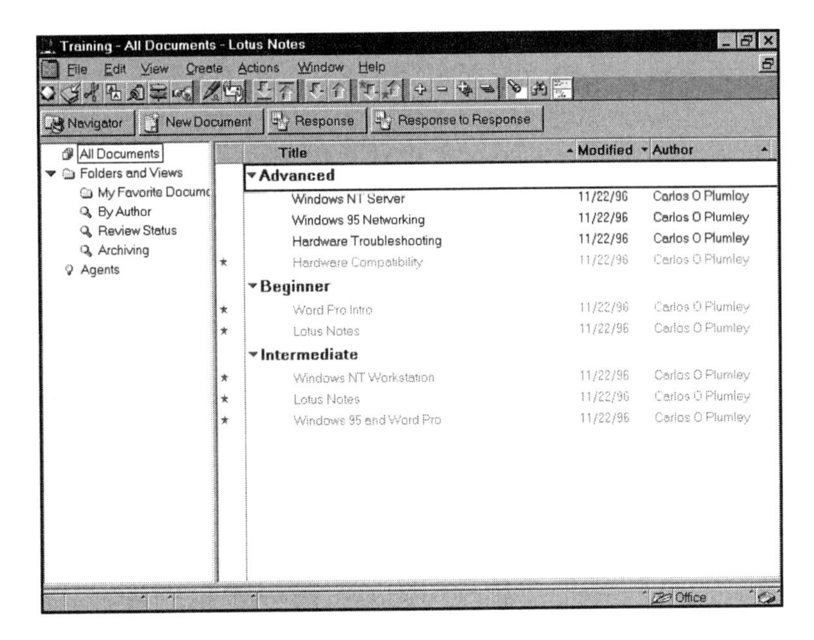

Figure 14.2 A red star marks each unread document.

To mark documents in the database view, choose **Edit**, **Unread Marks**, and then choose one of the following marking options:

Mark Selected Read Marks any documents you select as read; unread documents remain unmarked and easy to find.

Mark All Read Marks all documents in a database as read; this makes it easy to find new documents added to the database.

Mark Selected Unread Marks selected documents as unread, which is useful if you need to be reminded to reread important documents in a database.

Mark All Unread Marks all documents in the database as unread.

CAUTION

Scan Unread You can choose **Edit**, **Unread Marks**, **Scan Unread** to quickly view only the unread documents in a database. See Lesson 12 to learn more about scanning.

Editing a Document

Sometimes you will need to edit the documents in a database. You can add or delete text or graphics in a document, and you can *format* the documents. The following steps walk you through the basics of editing a document. For information about formatting documents, see Lesson 17.

Format To change certain visual characteristics of a document. This might include changing fonts or type sizes, making text bold or italic, or aligning the text on the page.

Editing Others' Documents You cannot edit others' documents unless you have permission to do so. If you cannot edit a document, see your Notes administrator.

1. In the database, open the document you want to edit.
2. Right-click anywhere within the document and choose **Edit** from the shortcut menu, or simply double-click in the text area of the document. Brackets appear, marking areas in which you can make changes (see Figure 14.3).

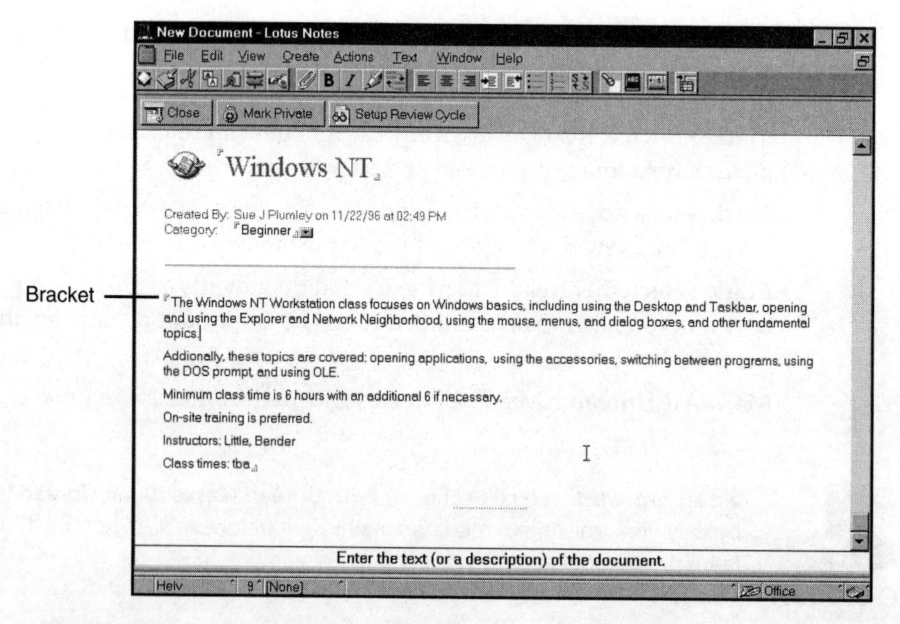

Figure 14.3 Edit a document by positioning the insertion point between the brackets.

3. Enter or edit the text within brackets.
4. When you finish editing, choose **File**, **Save**.

Exiting a Document

When you're finished reading a document, you should close it. Multiple open documents clutter your Notes work area and can slow down your computer's reaction time. To close, or exit, a document, choose **File**, **Close** or click the **Close** tool button.

TIP **Save Before Closing** If you forgot to save changes you made to the document, Notes prompts you to save before it closes the document. Click **Yes** to save the changes, click **No** to close without saving the changes, or click **Cancel** to return to the document.

In this lesson, you learned to open and exit a document, to move among documents in a database, and to mark a document as read. In the next lesson, you will learn to create a document in a database.

Creating a Database and Documents

In this lesson, you learn to create a database, create documents, and delete a document.

Creating a Database

You can create your own database in which to store documents for your personal use on your local drive, or for use on the network. As creator of the database, you can choose the document types that go into the database, and you can compose any or all of the documents in your database. To create a database, follow these steps:

1. In your workspace, choose **File, Database, New**. The New Database dialog box appears (see Figure 15.1).
2. In the Server drop-down list, choose the local drive or the network drive to which you want to save the database.
3. In the Title text box, enter a name for the database. Notes automatically fills in the File Name text box as you enter the title.
4. In the list at the bottom of the dialog box, choose a template on which to base your new database. (Table 15.1 describes some of the available templates.) Click the **Template Server** button to view templates the Notes administrator may have created for your use.
5. Click **OK**. Notes creates an icon on the current workspace and opens the new database for you.

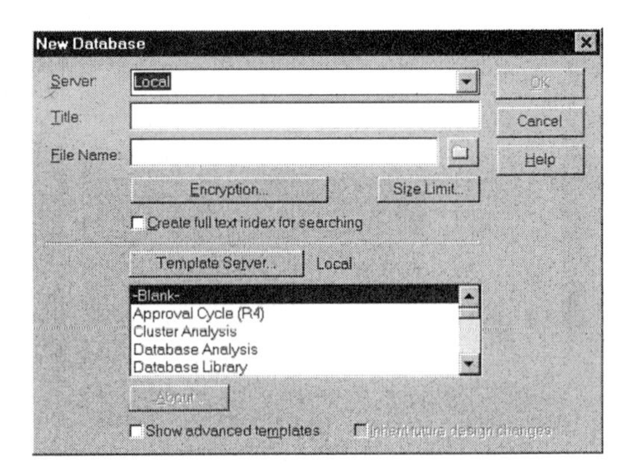

Figure 15.1 Create your own databases and documents.

Need More Template Choices? You can click the **Show advanced templates** check box in the New Database dialog box to access more templates from which you can choose.

Table 15.1 Common Database Templates

Template	*Description*
Blank	Creates an empty database you can use to create anything from documents to views to the design of the template. (I do not recommend that you choose this unless you're experienced with creating databases.)
Discussion	Creates a database you can use for discussion groups for specific groups of people—such as instructors, salespeople, or advertising agents. (See Lesson 13 for details on discussion groups.)
Document Library	Creates a database in which you can store reference documents such as handouts, financial statements, or product descriptions. This is for access by a workgroup.
Personal Address Book	Creates a personal address book for your local drive.
Personal Journal	Creates a database that contains documents in which you can enter any data you want, including notes, To Do lists, and other topics of interest.

Template	*Description*
Resource Reservations	Creates a database in which workgroups can reserve and schedule the use of such company resources as meeting rooms, company cars, and office equipment.

TIP **Need Help?** To learn more about any template, click the **About** button in the New Database dialog box to view the About document on the selected database. Choose **Close** when you finish with the About document.

Creating an About Document

When you first create a database from a template, the About document appears. The About document describes the database template and its uses and provides other relative information about it. Figure 15.2 shows an example of an About document.

You can leave the information in an About document as it is, or you can edit the document and enter your own information. When creating an About document, you might want to enter such information as:

- Descriptions of the documents
- The names of groups or users who can edit or access the documents
- Guidelines to follow when using the documents
- The name and e-mail address or phone number of someone who can help users with the database

To create your own About document, follow these steps:

1. In the About document that appears when the database opens, right-click anywhere in the document and choose **Edit**.
2. Click anywhere in the document and enter, edit, or delete the text.
3. When you finish making changes, choose **File**, **Save** to save your changes to the About document.
4. Choose **File**, **Close** to view the new database.

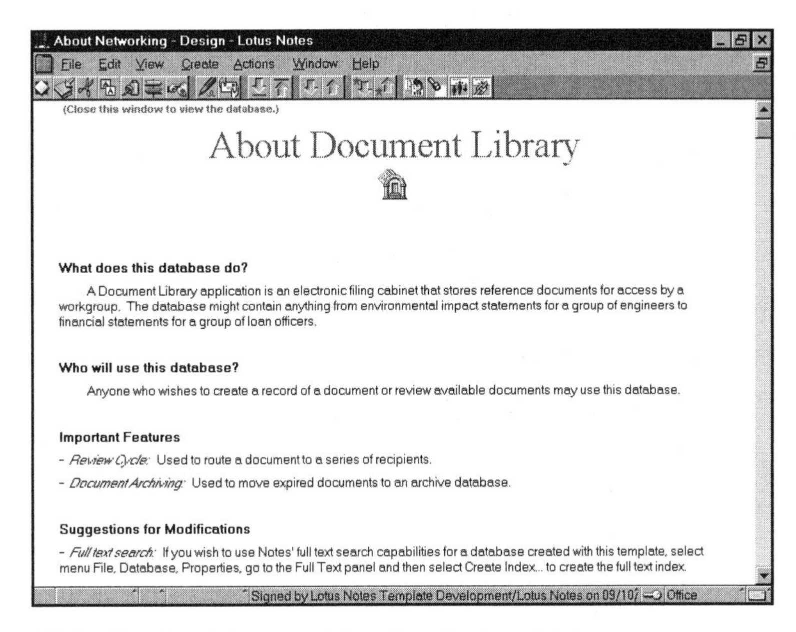

Figure 15.2 The About document describes the template's uses.

Composing a Document

You might need to create a document for your own database or for a database you've accessed over the network. For example, you might create reports or articles in your own database that you want to share with your coworkers, or your company may require you to submit status reports or other information to a *public* database.

Public Database A database that is accessible to anyone on the network. Some databases may be marked as private or completely inaccessible, and others may have limits set by the network or Notes administrators that enable only certain groups to access them. In a similar way, you can create a private folder in a database and limit access to that folder and the documents it contains, and you can encrypt certain documents within a database. However, those topics are beyond the scope of this book. For more information, see Que's *Special Edition Using Lotus Notes*.

Whether you're adding a document to an existing database or creating your own database documents, the procedure is the same. Follow these steps to create a document.

1. In the database view, choose the location for the new document from the view pane. You might choose to place the document in the All Documents view or in a specific folder, for example.
2. Click the **New Document** button on the tool button bar. A new document like the one in Figure 15.3 appears.

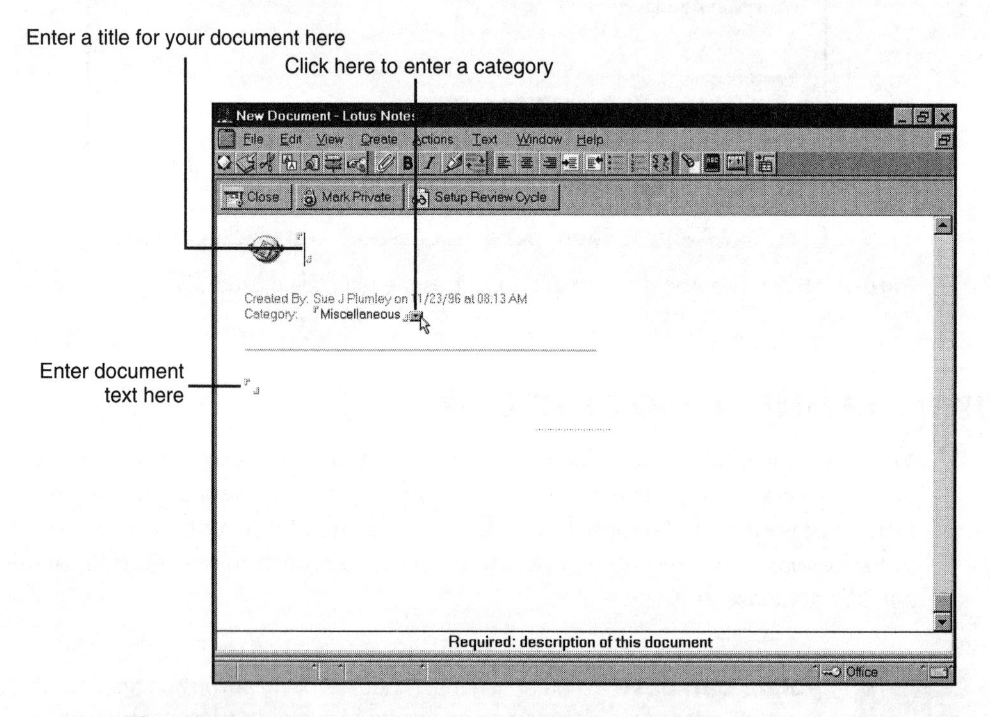

Figure 15.3 Enter your own document title and text.

TIP **Sound Familiar?** The process of creating a new document may sound familiar to you because it's similar to creating a message in a discussion group database (which you learned about in Lesson 13). You also can import and export data in a database document just as you would with mail (see Lesson 8).

3. In the first set of brackets, enter the title for the document. This title will appear in the document window of the database view.
4. For the category, you can leave Miscellaneous as the selection, or you can click the down arrow to reveal the Select Keywords dialog box (see Figure 15.4).

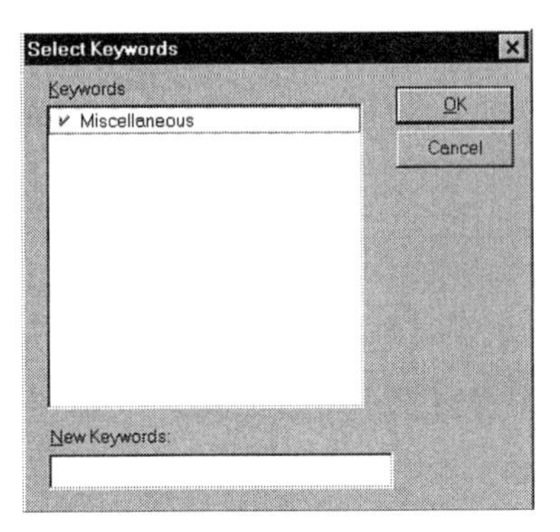

Figure 15.4 Select a keyword to use as the category, or enter a new keyword.

Categories Categories are main topics into which you organize your documents. Some example categories might be Quarter 1 and Quarter 2, or Expenses and Income. Categories appear in the database view with the associated documents listed below them.

5. In the **Keywords** list, click a category. A check mark appears beside it to show that it's selected. To deselect a marked keyword, click it, and the check mark disappears.

   If there are no categories, or if you do not see a category you want to use, enter the name of a new category in the **New Keywords** text box.
6. Choose **OK** to apply the keyword.
7. Click inside the third set of brackets and enter the document text.

Formatting a Document For more information about formatting—applying fonts, text characteristics, and so on—see Lesson 17.

Saving a Document

When you're finished creating a document, you must save it to the database. To save a document, choose **File**, **Save**. You can then close the document by clicking the **Close** button in the tool button bar. When you close the document, Notes returns to the database view.

Oops! If you try to close the document without saving it, Notes prompts you to save your changes. Click **Yes** to save the document, click **No** to abandon the changes, or click **Cancel** to return to the document.

Deleting a Document

If you no longer need a particular document, you can delete it from the database view. Simply right-click the document and choose **Cut** from the shortcut menu that appears. The document disappears from the database, but it's not completely gone. Notes moves the document you cut to the Clipboard, which means you can paste it back into your database for as long as it remains on the Clipboard. A cut or copied document remains on the Clipboard until you cut or copy another item. To retrieve the cut document, choose **Edit**, **Paste**.

In this lesson, you learned to create a database, compose a document, save a document, and delete a document. In the next lesson, you will learn to work with text fields.

Editing Text Fields

In this lesson, you learn about text fields. You also learn how to move around in a document, select text, and move and copy text in a document.

Understanding Text Fields

When you enter text into a mail memo, a discussion group message, or a document, you enter the text between the brackets on the page. These brackets define the *text field*. A text field is simply an area in which you can enter text, graphics, or other items (such as an attached file). Depending on the document and the database template, you may see one or several fields. In some documents, a text field is preceded by a few words that explain the type of text you're to enter in the field. Figure 16.1 shows three types of fields: a text field, a rich text field, and a keyword field.

The following list describes the common fields and elements you'll find in Notes' database documents. Note that not all documents contain all of these elements.

- **Text Fields** Fields in which you can enter words and sentences, usually titles or topics.
- **Rich Text Fields** Fields in which you can enter text, import text, import graphics such as .PCX or .TIFF files, and attach files. The rich text fields usually make up the body of the document. (For more information about importing and attaching, see Lesson 8.)
- **Keyword Fields** Fields in which you can enter only specific words, such as categories, dates, or phone numbers. Depending on the database design, you may be allowed to enter your own keywords as well.

- **Time/Date Fields** Most often, these fields are automatically filled by Notes using your computer's clock. You may not be allowed to edit some time/date fields.
- **Number Fields** Fields that can contain only numbers, such as currency or quantities.
- **Document Author Field** A field that contains the document author's name. You cannot change the contents of this field.

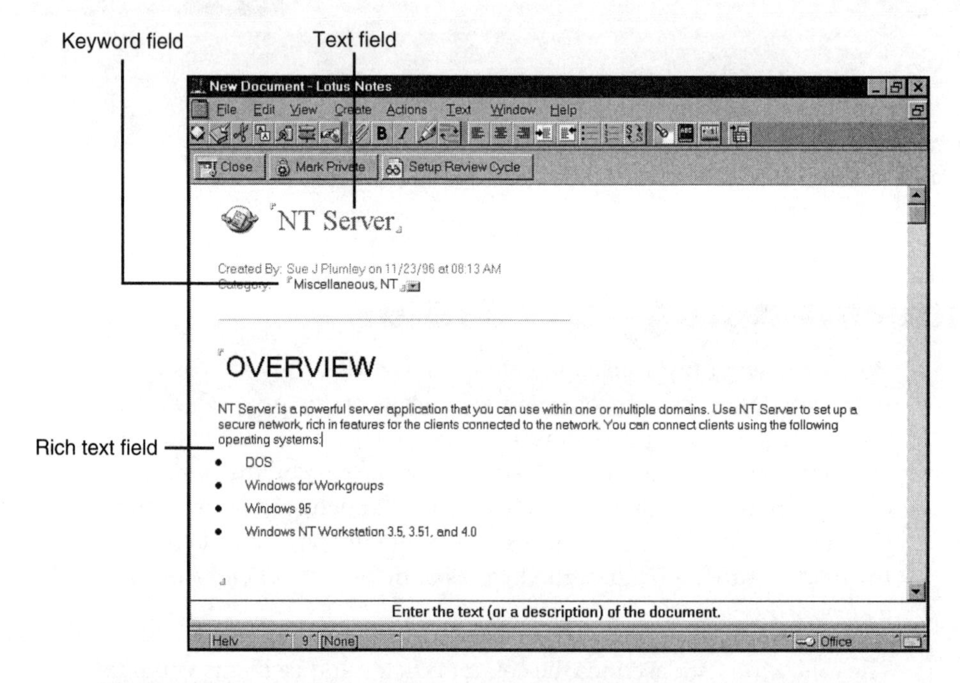

Figure 16.1 Use fields to enter text and graphics into a document.

Using Fields You cannot type anywhere in a Notes document that does not contain brackets. You must click within the brackets to add or edit text.

Moving in a Document

You can move around in a document by using the scroll bars and mouse or by using the keyboard. You'll probably learn to use a combination of the two methods to get around in a document quickly and efficiently.

To use the mouse to move around a document, you use scroll bars. Lotus Notes displays a scroll bar along the right side and bottom of the document window when the document is too large to fit in the window. Within the scroll bar is the scroll box. The scroll box indicates the relative location of your insertion point within the document. Figure 16.2 shows a window with a scroll bar.

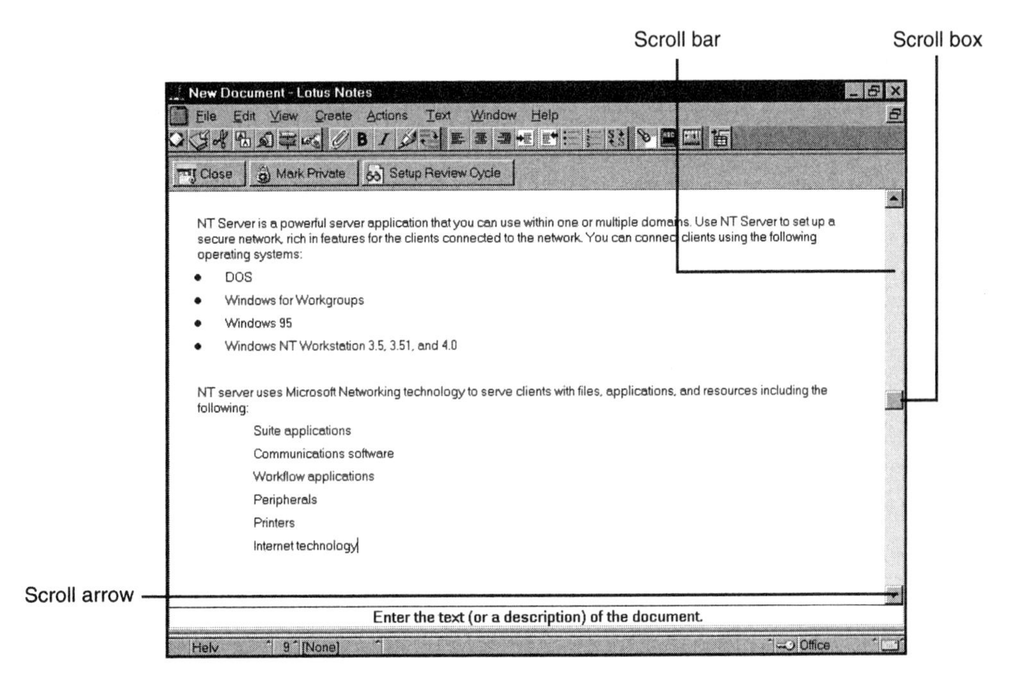

Figure 16.2 Use the scroll bar to quickly move around in a document.

When you scroll to any area in the document, you must click in that location before you can select, edit, or create text in that area. If you do not click to reposition the insertion point, the insertion point remains in its previous location. Use the following methods to scroll through a document:

- Click the up or down scroll arrow to move one line up or down in a document.
- Click the scroll box and drag it along the scroll bar to move up or down in a document more quickly.
- Click anywhere in the scroll bar to move to another location in the document.

As I mentioned earlier, you can also move around the document using your keyboard. Table 16.1 lists some keyboard shortcuts you can use.

Table 16.1 Keyboard Shortcuts for Moving in a Document

Shortcut	*Result*
Tab key	Moves the insertion point from field to field (unless you're in a rich text field and then it inserts a tab).
Arrow keys	Moves the insertion point from character to character, line of text to line; when you reach the end of a field, the down or right arrow moves you to the next field.
Page Up/Page Down	Moves the insertion point one screen at a time in the document.
Home	Moves the insertion point to the beginning of the current line of text.
End	Moves the insertion point to the end of the current line of text.
Ctrl+Home	Moves the insertion point to the beginning of the document (the first text field).
Ctrl+End	Moves the insertion point to the end of the document.

Selecting Text

Before you can copy, move, delete, or format text in a document, you must select it. The quickest and easiest method of selecting text in a document is to click and drag the mouse I-beam across the text you want to select. When text is selected, it appears in reverse video as shown in Figure 16.3.

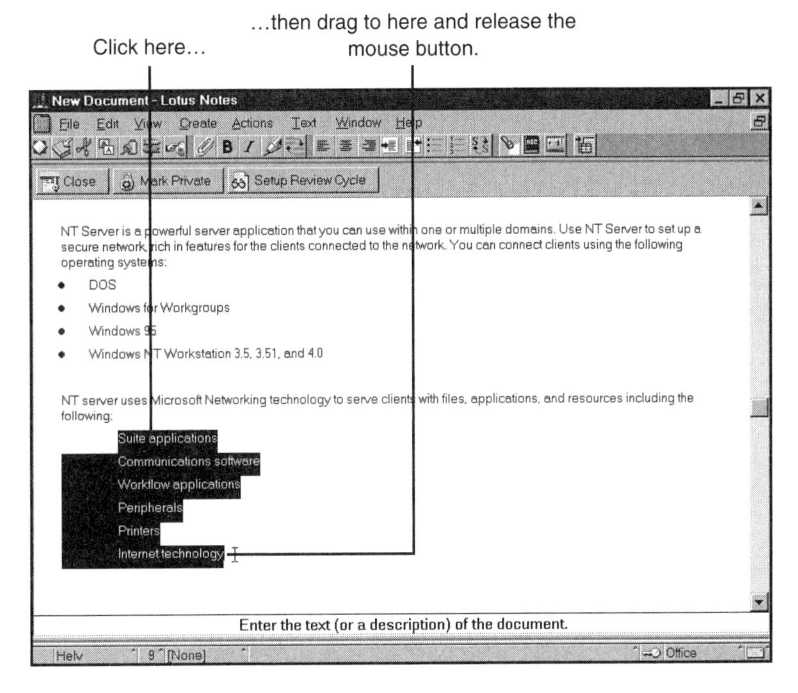

Figure 16.3 Click and drag the mouse to quickly select text.

Deselect Text If you selected too much text or you didn't mean to select text at all, click the mouse anywhere in the document to deselect the text. Alternatively, you can press the right or left arrow on the keyboard.

Shortcut Double-click any single word to select just that one word.

Moving and Copying Text

You can move text from one part of the document to another or from one document to another. You also can copy text between documents or within the same document. Follow these steps to copy or move text.

3. Select the text you want to move or copy.
4. Choose **Edit**, **Cut** if you want to move the text, or choose **Edit**, **Copy** if you want to make a duplicate of the text. Notes moves or copies the text to the Clipboard.
5. Reposition the cursor where you want to place the text (it can be in the same document or in another document).

TIP **Window Menu** If you want to place the cut or copied text in another document, use the Window menu to switch back to the database or to another open document.

4. Choose **Edit**, **Paste**, and the copied or cut text appears at the insertion point.

TIP **Shortcuts** If you prefer to work from the keyboard, press **Ctrl+X** to cut text, **Ctrl+C** to copy text, and **Ctrl+V** to paste text.

Undoing Changes

You often can undo editing or formatting changes you've made to a document. Undoing a change cancels the effects and returns the document to its previous state. For example, if you cut some text and you didn't mean to, you can undo that action. Notes simply puts the text back in its original location. To undo changes, choose **Edit**, **Undo** or press **Ctrl+Z**.

You must choose to undo an action before you perform another. Because Notes can remember only one action at a time, each new action replaces the last one.

CAUTION

Can't Undo Not all changes and edits can be undone. If the Undo command is dimmed, you cannot undo your previous command.

In this lesson, you learned to use text fields, move around in a document, select text, move and copy text, and undo actions. In the next lesson, you'll learn to format text and pages by changing fonts, setting alignment, and using page breaks.

Formatting Text and Pages

In this lesson, you learn to change fonts, set spacing and alignment, use page breaks, and add headers and footers to a document.

Character Formatting

In Notes, you can change character formatting in any of the documents you create. Using character formatting, you can make your documents more interesting and attractive or you can emphasize important text. Character formatting includes working with all of the following characteristics:

- **Font** Apply a typeface to text in the document. For example, you can make a title stand out by assigning it a font different from that of all other text. And you can set the tone of the document or make body text easier to read simply by choosing certain fonts.
- **Type Size** Apply a size (say, 24-point size) to the text so titles are large and easy to read, and less important text is smaller (10-point, for example).
- **Attributes** Apply emphasis to text by making it bold or italic.
- **Styles** Apply preformatted characteristics (such as bulleted text or headlines) for quick and easy formatting.

Figure 17.1 shows a document that contains examples of each character formatting trait.

Font / Typeface A font is a style of type applied to text; Times New Roman, Courier, and Helvetica are common fonts.

Point A measurement of type; there are 72 points in an inch. Body text is generally 10- or 12-point, and headlines or titles are usually 14-, 18-, or 24-point.

Bulleted Text Text, usually in list form, that is preceded by a small black dot, an arrow, a check mark, or another item that makes the text stand out.

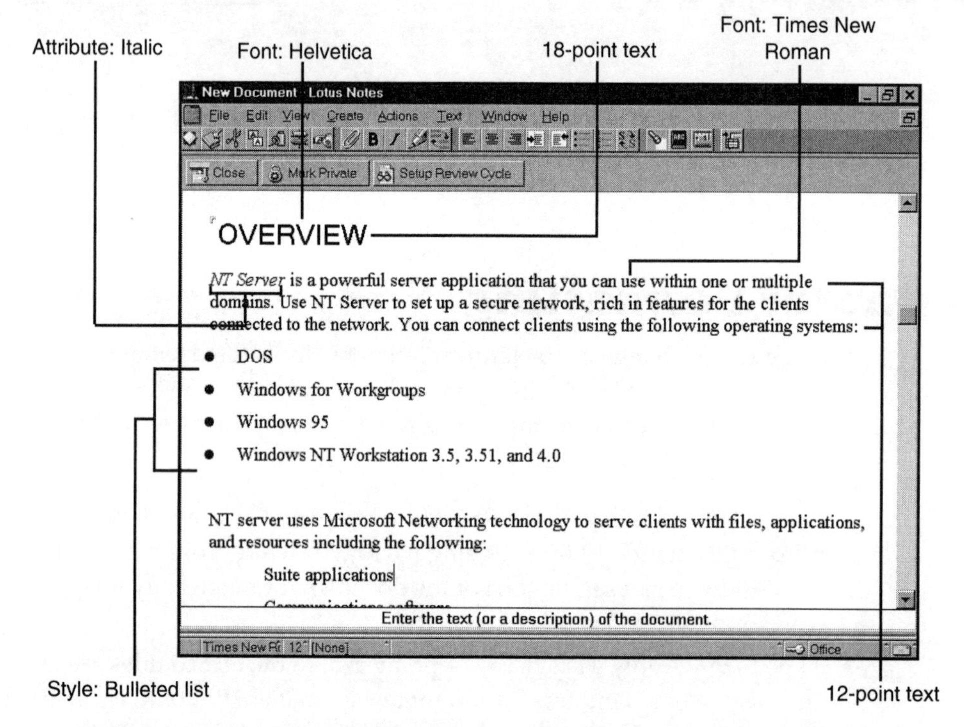

Figure 17.1 Make your documents more attractive with character formatting.

Formatting Text

To format text, follow these steps:

1. Select the text you want to format (as explained in Lesson 16).
2. Use the following methods to apply any text formatting you want:

Font On the Status bar, click the Font button. A pop-up menu appears, listing the fonts that are available on your system. Select the font you want to use.

Size On the Status bar, click the Type Size button and choose the point size you want from the pop-up menu shown in Figure 17.2.

Style Click the Style button and choose the style you want to assign to the selected text.

Attributes Click the Bold or Italic SmartIcon to apply the corresponding attribute.

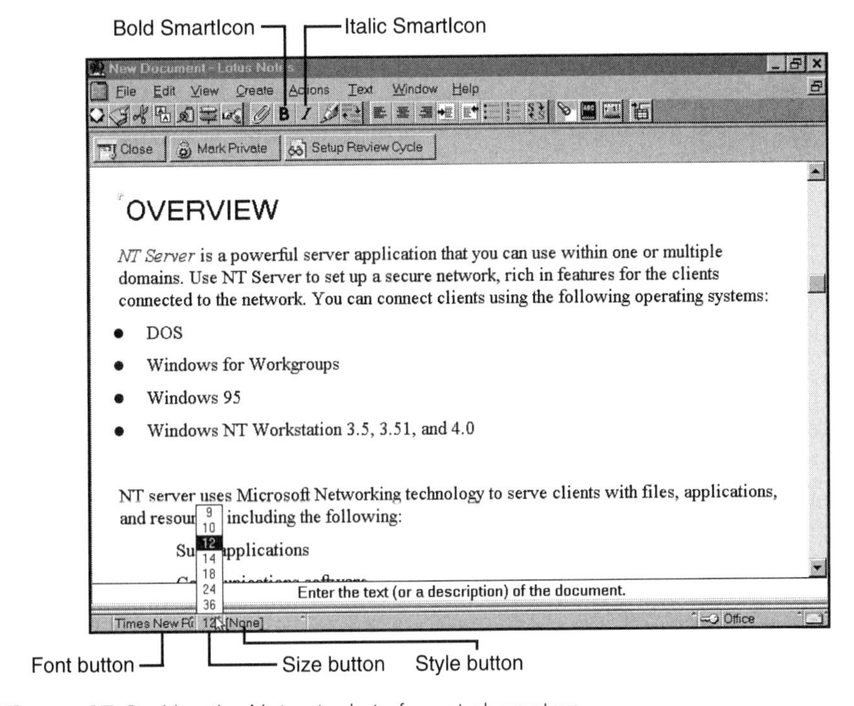

Figure 17.2 Use the Notes tools to format characters.

TIP **Alternative Method** You also can set font, type size, and attributes by using the Font tab in the Properties for Text InfoBox. To display the InfoBox, right-click the text and choose **Text Properties** from the shortcut menu. The Font tab is the first tab (the one showing when you open the InfoBox). To learn more about the Properties InfoBox, see the next section.

Setting Spacing and Alignment

You can adjust the spacing between lines of text in a document and the alignment of text in a document by using the Properties for Text InfoBox. To display the InfoBox, right-click the text you want to align and choose **Text Properties**. The Properties for InfoBox appears. To use the spacing and alignment features (shown in Figure 17.3), click the second tab in the InfoBox. For more information about InfoBoxes, refer to Lesson 3.

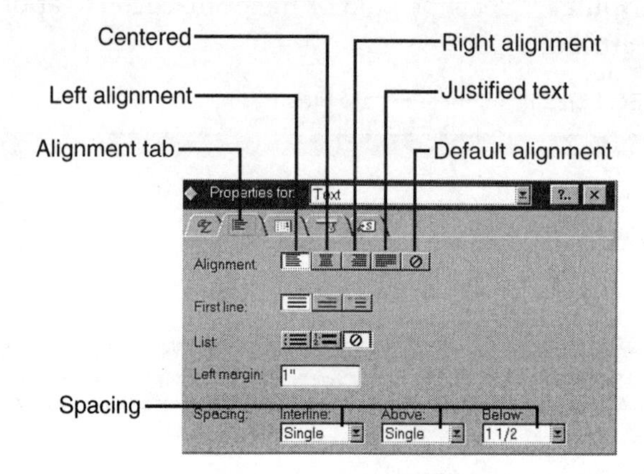

Figure 17.3 The Properties for InfoBox provides tools for governing how text in a paragraph looks.

To set alignment, select the text and click the appropriate alignment button. Left-aligned text has a flush left edge and a ragged right edge. Center-aligned text is arranged so that the distance from the left and right margins to the edge of the text is the same. Right-aligned text is text with a flush right edge and a ragged left. Justified text is text with flush left and right edges.

To set spacing, select the text and then choose from one of the following:

- **Interline** Determines the space between the lines of text in a paragraph.
- **Above** Determines extra space added above a paragraph.
- **Below** Determines extra space added below a paragraph.
- **Single, 1 1/2**, or **double** Sets the spacing for the selected paragraph.

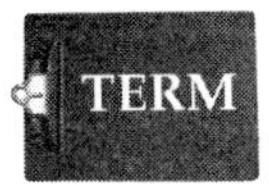

Paragraph In Notes, a paragraph is defined as a line with a hard paragraph return (which you create by pressing Enter) at the end of it. A paragraph may contain several sentences, several words, or one word or letter, or it may even be a blank line.

Using Page Breaks

Notes automatically breaks pages for you, but you might not always like where the page break falls. You can insert page breaks to organize the pages in your document to suit yourself.

Can't See Breaks? If you cannot see the page breaks that Notes creates, choose **View**, **Show**, **Page Breaks**.

To insert a page break, follow these steps:

1. Position the insertion point where you want a page break.
2. Choose **Create**, **Page Break**. Notes displays a thin black line across the page to show the page break (see Figure 17.4).

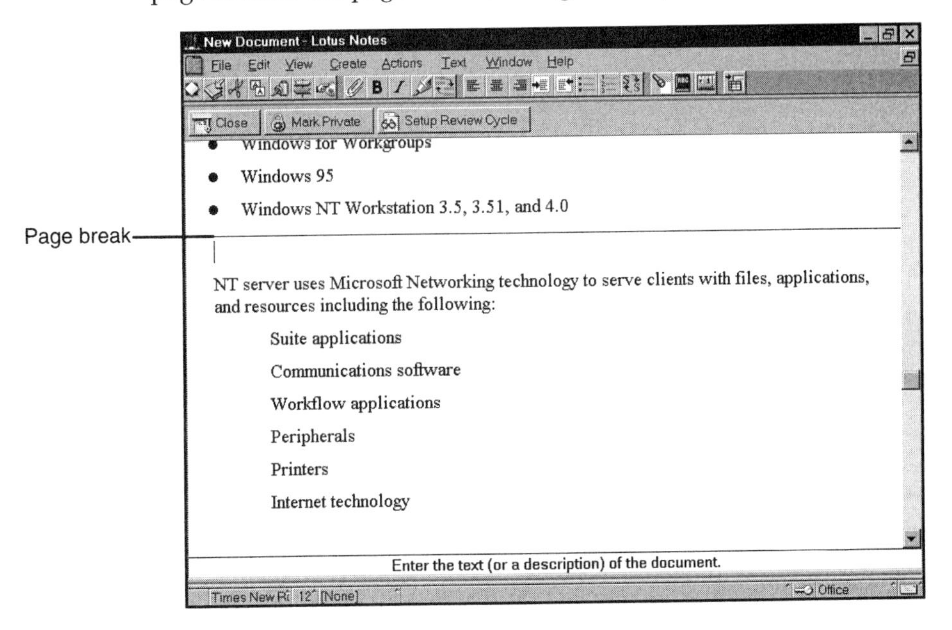

Figure 17.4 Separate pages for organization and printing purposes.

Adding Headers and Footers

You use the Properties for Document InfoBox to insert page *headers* or *footers*. Headers and footers appear on the document only when it's printed.

Headers and Footers A header appears in the top margin of every page of the document, and a footer appears in the bottom margin of every page. Headers and footers often include such information as the creation date, author, title, page number, or company name. You can include any information you want to add to the document.

Follow these steps to add a header and/or a footer to your Notes document:

1. In the document, right-click the page and choose **Document Properties** from the shortcut menu.

No Document Properties? If Document Properties does not appear on the shortcut menu but Text Properties does, choose **Text Properties**. When the InfoBox opens, click the drop-down arrow in the title bar and choose **Document**.

2. Select the printer tab in the InfoBox (see Figure 17.5).

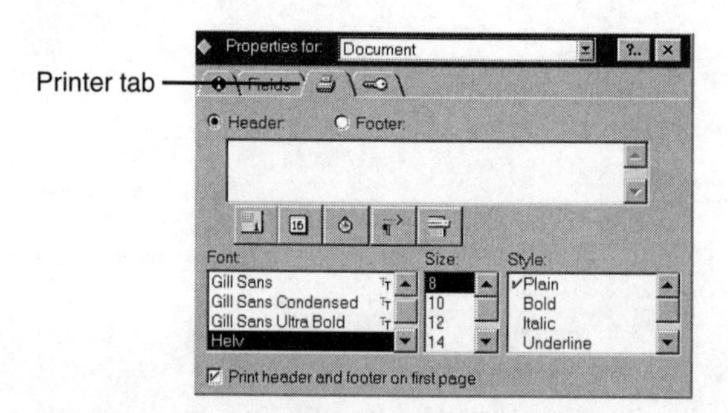

Figure 17.5 Header and footer options appear on the printer tab because they appear only in a printed document.

3. Choose **Header** or **Footer**. (You can always enter one and then come back and choose the other if you want to use both a header and a footer in your document.)

4. In the text box, enter any text you want in the header or footer, or click an icon below the text box to insert one of the following items:

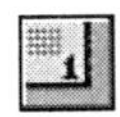

Page Number Inserts a symbol representing the page number; Notes replaces the symbol with the correct page number when the document is printed.

Date Inserts a field that displays the date of the day you print the document.

Time Inserts a field that displays the time you print the document.

Tab Sets a right tab in the header or footer.

Title Adds the document title to the header or footer.

5. In the Font, Size, and Style list boxes, choose the formatting for the header or footer.
6. (Optional) Choose the **Print header and footer on first page** check box.
7. Close the InfoBox and then save the document.
8. To view the header or footer, print the document by choosing **File**, **Print** and clicking **OK** in the File Print dialog box. Figure 17.6 shows a header printed on the first page of a document. The date and the document title appear in the header.

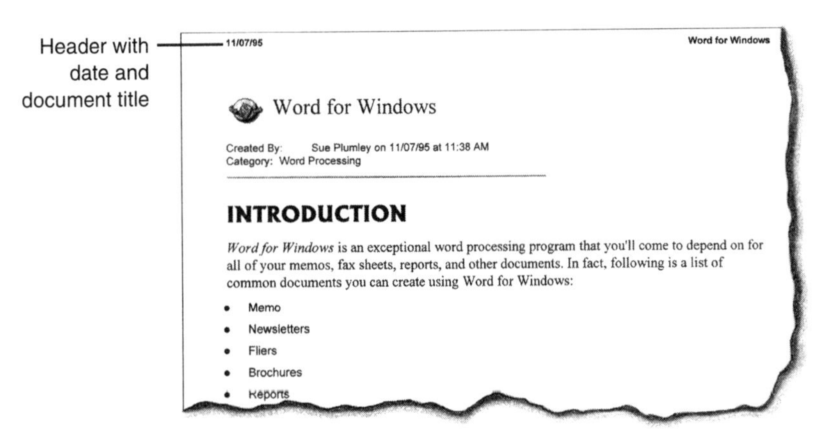

11/07/95 Word for Windows

Word for Windows

Created By: Sue Plumley on 11/07/95 at 11:38 AM
Category: Word Processing

INTRODUCTION

Word for Windows is an exceptional word processing program that you'll come to depend on for all of your memos, fax sheets, reports, and other documents. In fact, following is a list of common documents you can create using Word for Windows:

- Memo
- Newsletters
- Fliers
- Brochures
- Reports

Figure 17.6 Insert any information you want in the header or footer of a document.

In this lesson, you learned to change font characteristics, set spacing and alignment, use page breaks, and create headers and footers in a document. In the next lesson, you'll learn to create, edit, and format tables.

Using Tables

In this lesson, you learn to create, edit, and format tables in your documents.

Creating Tables

You can create tables to organize the data in a document. After you create a table in Notes, you enter data into cells, which are the intersections of the table's columns and rows. The data in a table might be words, phrases, or numbers.

Table One or more organized lists of data presented in columns and rows. A table can only appear in a rich text field (see Lesson 16).

To create a table, follow these steps:

1. In the document, position the insertion point in a rich text field and choose **Create, Table**. The Create Table dialog box appears (see Figure 18.1).

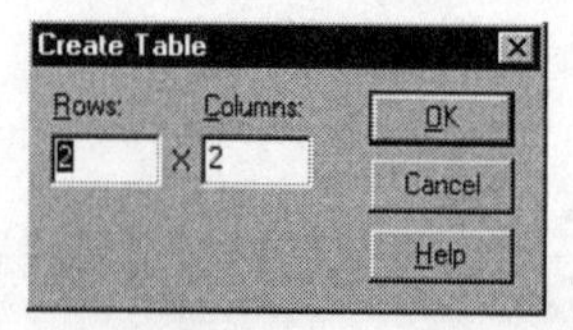

Figure 18.1 Enter the number of rows and columns.

2. In Rows, enter the number of rows you want in your table. In Columns, enter the number of columns. (You can change these numbers later if necessary.)

3. Click **OK** to create the table. In your document, Notes inserts a grid with the number of columns and rows you specified. In addition, it adds the Table menu to your menu bar, as shown in Figure 18.2.

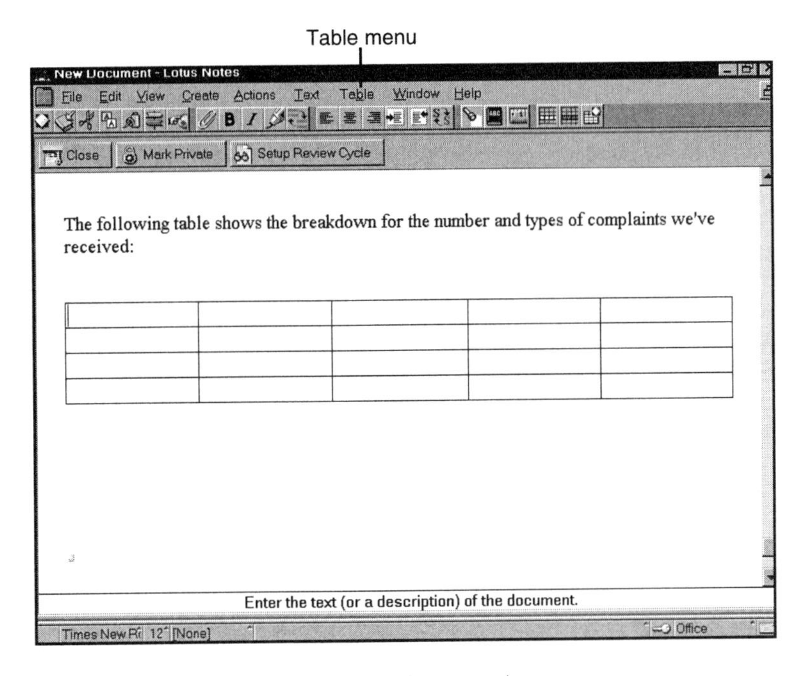

Figure 18.2 A table grid helps you organize your data.

Entering Data in a Table

To enter data in a table, you place your insertion point in any cell and begin typing. If you continue to type past the end of the cell, Notes wraps the text within the cell as you type, adjusting the cell height to accommodate the text. Use the Backspace and Delete keys to edit the text in the table, just as you would any other text in a document.

To move around a table, you can click in any cell you want to move to. If you prefer, you can also use any of the following keyboard keys:

- **Tab** Moves the insertion point to the next cell to the right. At the end of a row, the insertion point moves to the first cell in the next row.
- **Shift+Tab** Moves the insertion point to the previous cell.

- **Arrow keys** If the cells are empty, the left and right arrow keys move the insertion point to the next cell in that direction. If the cells contain data, the left and right arrow keys move through the data one character at a time and then to the next cell. The up and down arrow keys always move from row to row.

TIP **Selecting Table Text** You select text in a table just as you would any text in a document—by dragging the mouse across the text.

Editing Tables

You can edit the table, and you can edit the text within a table. You edit text in a table as you would any text. For example, you can select the text and then delete it, you can insert new text, and you can copy and paste the text.

Another important feature enables you to edit the table itself by adding and deleting rows and columns. To add rows or columns, follow these steps:

1. Position the insertion point in the row above which you want to insert a new row, or in the column immediately to the right of where you want to insert a new column.
2. Choose **Table, Insert Row** or **Insert Column**. Notes inserts the row or column in the table. Figure 18.3 shows a table with an added row and column.

CAUTION **Add More Rows?** You can even add more than one row at a time. To do so, position the insertion point and choose **Table**, **Insert Special**. Enter the number of rows or columns you want to add to the table, choose **Row** or **Column**, and choose **Insert**.

The following steps show you how to delete a row or column:

1. Position the insertion point in the row or column you want to delete.
2. Choose **Table, Delete Selected Row[s]** or **Delete Selected Column[s]**. A confirmation dialog box appears.
3. Click **Yes** to delete the row or column.

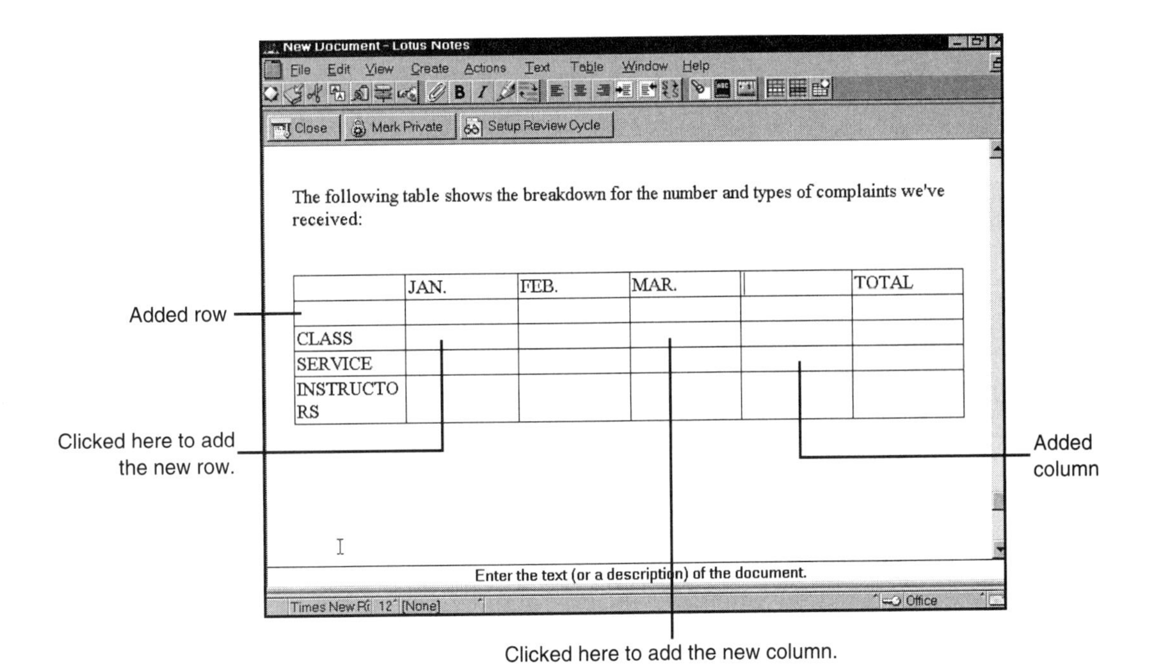

Figure 18.3 Notes inserts the row or column in front of the insertion point.

TIP **Delete More** To delete more than one row or column, choose **Table**, **Delete Special**. Then enter the number of rows or columns, choose **Row** or **Column**, and click the **Delete** button. Click **Yes** to confirm the deletion.

To quickly add one row or column at the end of the table, choose **Table, Append Row** or **Append Column**. Or you can simply place your insertion point in the last cell in the table (the intersection of the last column and the last row) and press the **Tab** key.

Formatting Tables

After you enter your data, you can format both the text within a table and the table itself. To format text in a table, select the text and apply formatting by using the Text menu commands or the Status bar buttons. (Lesson 17 covers formatting text in a document.)

By default, the table itself is formatted with a single line outlining the table and separating the columns and rows. To modify that, you can select certain cells or the entire table, and you can remove all borders or add a double border.

To format the table, follow these steps:

1. Double-click the table to put it in edit mode. Then right-click in the table and choose **Table Properties** from the shortcut menu. The Properties for Table InfoBox appears (see Figure 18.4).

Edit Mode Edit mode means the document is ready to accept text.

2. Select the cells to which you want to apply a border.
3. Select the type of border you want to apply to the selected cells. Extruded and embossed add a bit of variety to the standard border.

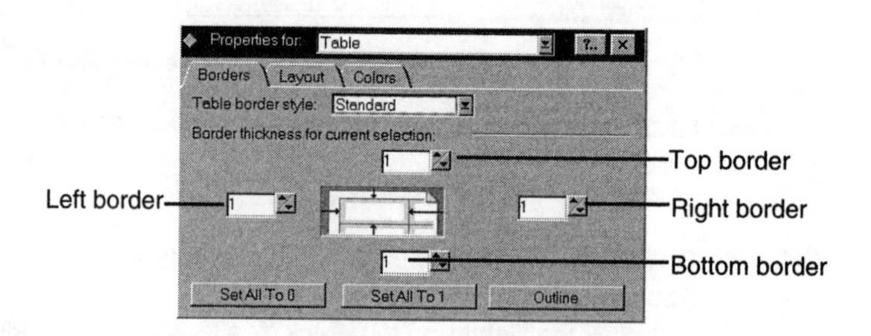

Figure 18.4 Use the Table Properties InfoBox to apply cell borders.

Figure 18.5 shows a table with a standard border applied to the entire table.

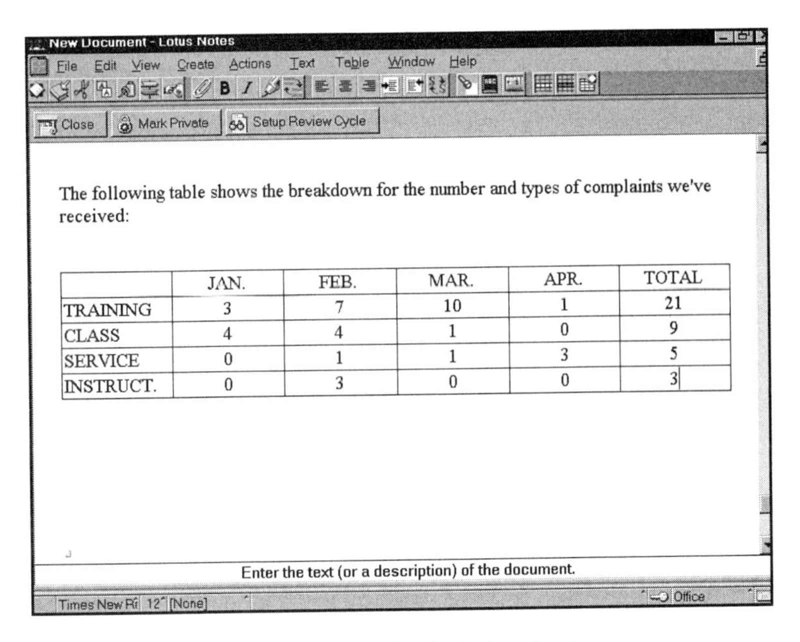

	JAN.	FEB.	MAR.	APR.	TOTAL
TRAINING	3	7	10	1	21
CLASS	4	4	1	0	9
SERVICE	0	1	1	3	5
INSTRUCT.	0	3	0	0	3

Figure 18.5 Apply a heavy outline to make the table stand out.

In this lesson, you learned to create a table, enter text in the table cells, edit data, and format the table and its cells. In the next lesson, you will learn to find and replace text in a document. After reading the next lesson, you will also be able to find specific text in a database.

Finding and Replacing Text

In this lesson, you learn to find text in a document, replace that text, and find text in a database.

Finding Text in a Document

You can easily find words or phrases in a document in Notes. You might want to find specific text in order to read about a topic, to refer to the page on which it appears, or to replace that text with new text.

To find specific text in a document, follow these steps:

1. With the document in edit mode, choose **Edit**, **Find/Replace**. The Find and Replace dialog box appears (see Figure 19.1).

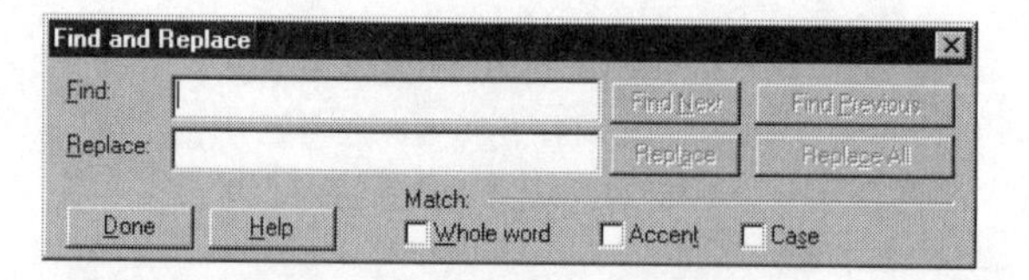

Figure 19.1 You can find all occurrences of a word or phrase in your document.

2. In the **Find** text box, enter the text you want to find. The entry can consist of up to 45 characters and spaces, depending on the characters you enter and whether or not you use capital letters.
3. (Optional) In the Match area of the dialog box, choose any of the following options:

   Whole Word Finds the character string you entered only when a space precedes and follows the word. For example, if you enter "the" and do not choose Whole Word, Notes finds such words as "their," "there," "other."

Accent Tells Notes to include diacritical accent marks (such as those that are used in foreign languages).

Case Searches for the character string that matches the case exactly, such as with names of programs or people.

4. Click the **Find Next** button to find the next occurrence of the word in the text. Choose the **Find Previous** button to find the previous occurrence of the word. If it finds a match, Notes highlights the word in the text and leaves the Find and Replace dialog box open.
5. If you just wanted to locate the word, click the **Done** button to close the dialog box so you can work in the document. If you want to replace the found word, move on to the next section. Figure 19.2 shows the Find and Replace dialog box, as well as the highlighted word that Notes found in the document.

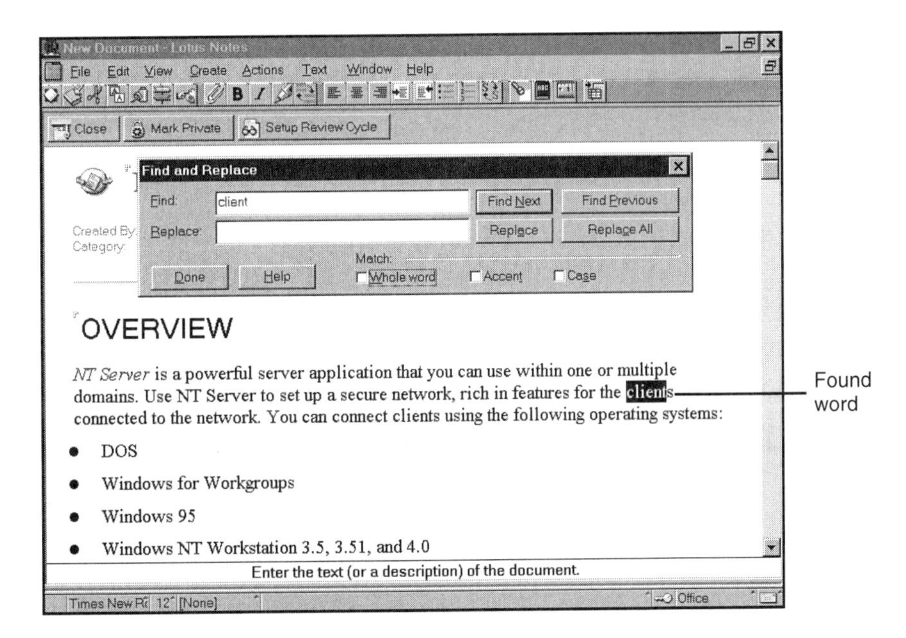

Figure 19.2 You can find words anywhere in the document.

TIP **Shortcut** Press **Ctrl+G** to find the word or phrase again without opening the Find and Replace dialog box. Notes remembers what you entered in the Find and Replace dialog box the last time, and it finds that text again.

Replacing Found Text

After you find text, you can replace it quickly and effortlessly using the Find and Replace dialog box. Follow these steps to replace the found text:

1. In edit mode, choose **Edit, Find/Replace**. The Find and Replace dialog box appears.
2. In the **Find** text box, enter the text you want to locate.
3. (Optional) In the **Replace** text box, enter the text you want to substitute for the found text.
4. Choose any options you want to apply.
5. Click the **Find Next** or **Find Previous** button to move to the first occurrence of the word or phrase in the respective direction. If Notes finds a match, it highlights the text.
6. (Optional) Click the **Replace** button to replace the highlighted text that Notes found with the text you typed in the Replace text box. Or if you're sure you want to replace all occurrences, click the **Replace All** button to replace them all automatically.
7. (Optional) Click **Find Next** or **Find Previous** to skip this occurrence and find the next occurrence of the specified text.
8. When you finish with the Find and Replace dialog box, click **Done**.

CAUTION

Careful! Before you choose to Replace All in the Find and Replace dialog box, save your document in case something goes wrong. If you make a mistake, close the document without saving it. Then open it and try again.

Finding Text in a Database

Notes even enables you to search through any database of documents for specific words or phrases without opening each document. Instead of using the Find command, you use the Search bar. Notes searches the entire database and lists all documents containing the specified word or phrase.

To search through an entire database, follow these steps:

1. In database view, choose **View, Search Bar**. The Search bar appears below the SmartIcon bar in your database.

2. Enter a word or phrase in the Search for text box.
3. Click the **Search** button. Notes lists all the documents that contain the word or phrase, with a check mark beside each one (see Figure 19.3).
4. Click the **Reset** button to start a new search and display all of the documents in the database.

You can also set search criteria when you use the Search bar. To do so, click the button at the right end of the Search bar. The pop-up menu shown in Figure 19.4 appears.

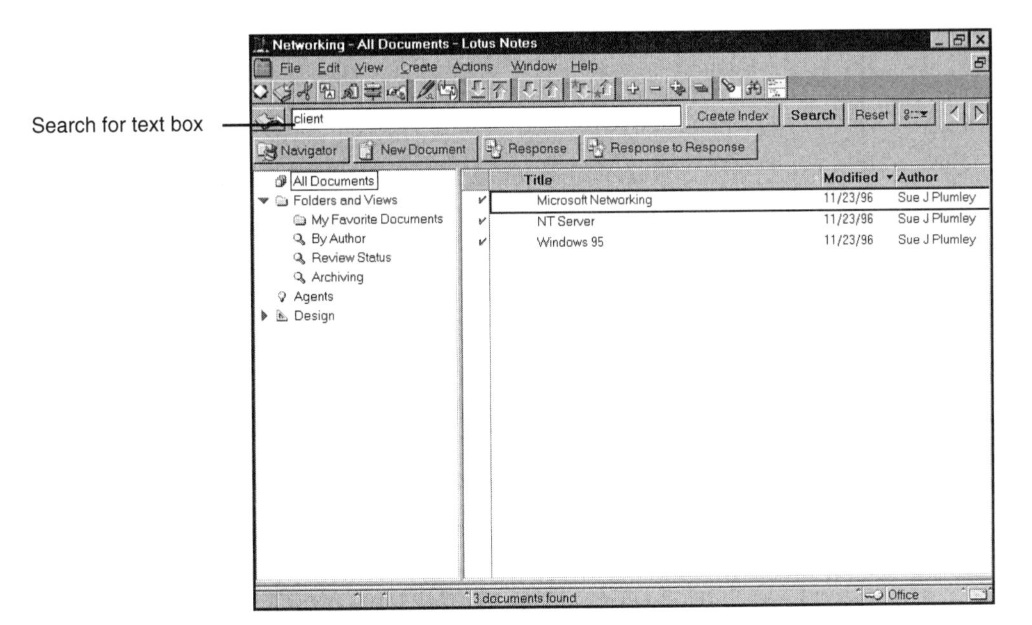

Figure 19.3 Notes lists the documents that contain the search text.

In the pop-up menu, select any of the following search criteria:

- **Include Word Variants** Includes such variants as plurals in the search. For example, if you enter the word "network," Notes finds "networks," "networking," and so on.
- **Use Thesaurus** Includes synonyms in the search string; for example, if you're searching for the word "test" and you choose to Use Thesaurus, Notes searches for other words such as "quiz."
- **Sort by Relevance** Lists the documents with the most occurrences of the word first.

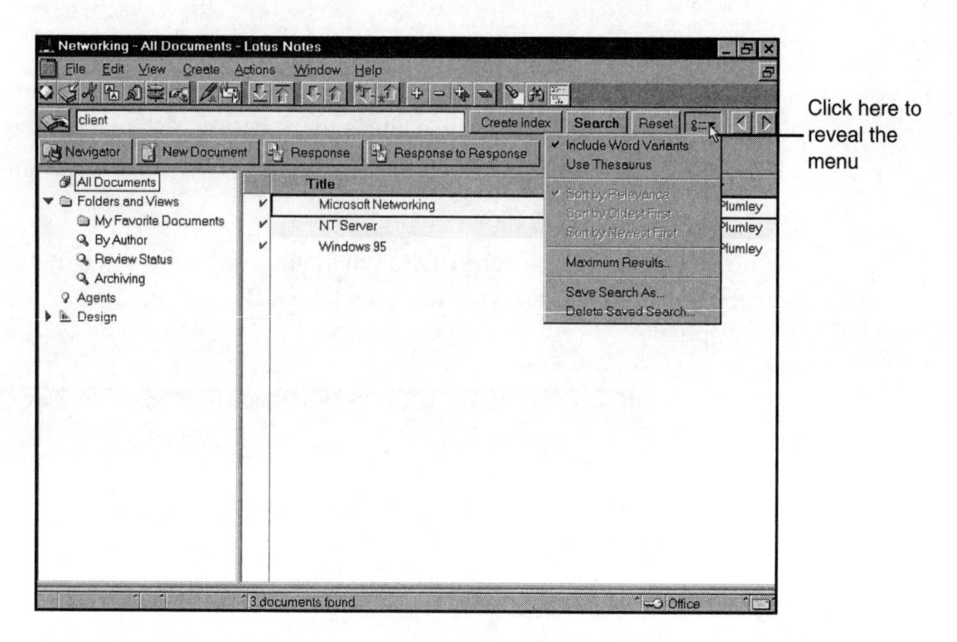

Figure 19.4 Set search criteria using the Search bar pop-up menu.

- **Sort by Oldest First** and **Sort by Newest First** Sorts the documents by date.
- **Maximum Results** Displays the Maximum Results dialog box in which you enter the maximum number of finds you want Notes to display; the default is 250 documents.
- **Save Search As** Displays the Save Search As dialog box in which you can name the search so that you can use it again with other databases. Once you save a search, its name appears at the bottom of the Search bar pop-up menu. Select the name to automatically carry out the search.
- **Delete Saved Search** Displays the Delete Saved Search dialog box from which you select saved searches and delete those you no longer use.

In this lesson, you learned to find and replace text within a document and to search for text in a database. In the next lesson, you learn to use the spelling checker, doclinks, and pop-ups.

Using Advanced Editing Techniques

In this lesson, you learn to check your spelling, reference other pages with doclinks, and add information for the reader in pop-ups.

Checking Spelling

Notes provides a spelling checker that you can use to make sure your documents are presentable to others on the network. To check your spelling, follow these steps:

1. With your document in edit mode, choose **Edit**, **Check Spelling**. Notes begins the spelling check. If Notes finds a questionable word, it highlights the word and displays the Spell Check dialog box shown in Figure 20.1.

TIP **You're in Luck!** If Notes does not find any misspellings, it displays a message that says `No Misspellings Found`. Click **OK** to continue editing your document.

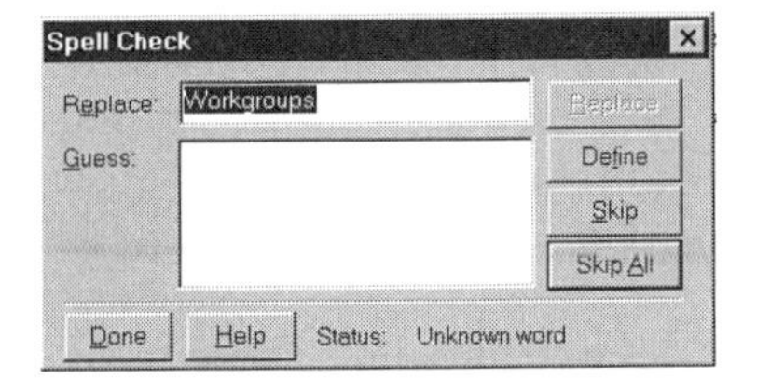

Figure 20.1 Notes displays any questionable words or spellings.

2. In the Spell Check dialog box, use one of the following techniques to tell Notes what to do about the word in question:

   Type the correct spelling in the Replace text box and click **Replace**.

   Select the correct spelling from the Guess list box and click **Replace**.

   Click the **Define** button to add the word to the dictionary so Notes doesn't question the spelling again.

   Click the **Skip** button to ignore this particular occurrence of the word.

   Click **Skip All** to ignore all occurrences of this word in this document.

   Click Done to quit the spelling checker.

3. If you choose any of the previous options except Done, Notes carries out your command and continues to check the spelling. Repeat step 2 for each word Notes stops on.
4. When Notes completes the spelling check, it displays the message shown in Figure 20.2. Click **OK** to close the spelling checker.

Figure 20.2 Notes tells you when it finishes the spelling checker.

Referencing Documents

Sometimes you'll find that several of your documents contain related information and the reader would benefit from viewing both documents. You can include a reference, or *doclink*, to one document within another document. Then by double-clicking the doclink, the reader can open and view the second document. You can add doclinks to documents within the same database or in different databases.

To reference a document, follow these steps:

1. Place the insertion point in the document *to* which you want to refer the reader.

2. Choose **Edit, Copy As Link**. Choose the type of link you want to copy and Notes copies the text to the Clipboard.

Link The word "link" comes from the longer "hyperlink," a term used in programming before Windows. Both terms refer to a live connection between two or more documents. When documents have a live connection and the text in the source document changes, the linked text in the destination document is automatically updated to reflect the change.

3. Open the document in which you want to create the doclink.

Document Switch To switch to another document, open the **Window** menu, choose the name of the database, and open the second document. (Or you can select the name of the document from the Window menu if the document is already open.)

4. In edit mode, position the insertion point where you want to add the doclink and choose **Edit, Paste**. Notes inserts the doclink icon, a small page with the corner turned down (see Figure 20.3).
5. (Optional) If necessary, add text to tell the reader how to open the doclink.

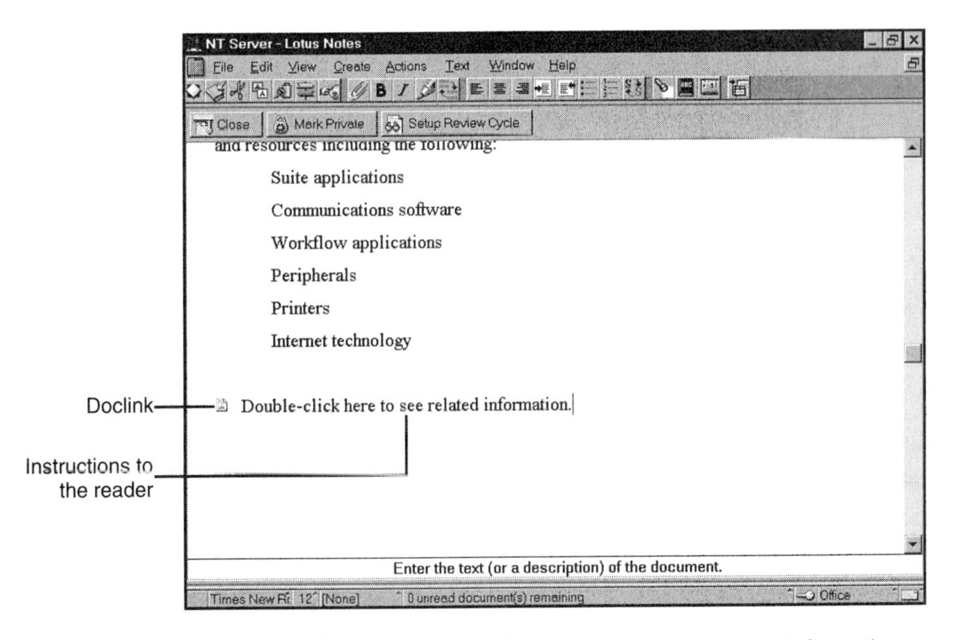

Figure 20.3 A doclink gives the reader quick access to related information.

Delete Doclink You can delete a doclink by positioning the insertion point in front of the document icon and pressing the **Delete** key. You cannot undo a doclink deletion, but you can paste the link again.

To open a doclink within a document, just double-click the doclink icon. The second document opens immediately. When you finish reading it, choose File, Close to return to the original document.

Adding Definitions and Explanations

Suppose you've placed a proposal document in a network database, and you want to provide an explanation of a process you mentioned that you don't know if everyone on the network will know about. You can add extra information—such as a definition or an explanation of text—to a document by using what Notes calls a *pop-up*. Pop-ups are brief messages that appear when the reader clicks on a marked area of text. Figure 20.4 shows a text pop-up in a document.

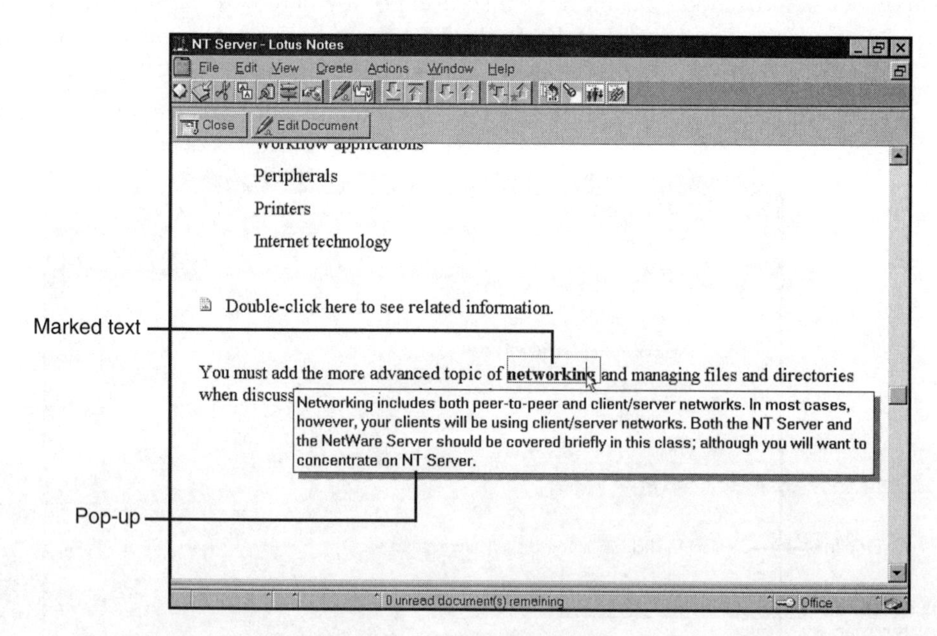

Figure 20.4 Add information and interest to your documents with pop-ups.

Follow these steps to add a pop-up to your document:

1. In edit mode, select the text you want to define or explain.

2. Choose **Create, Hotspot, Text Popup**. The Properties for HotSpot Popup InfoBox appears (see Figure 20.5).
3. In the **Popup text** box, enter the text that you want Notes to display when the reader clicks the marked text. (The text can exceed the window's size limit.)

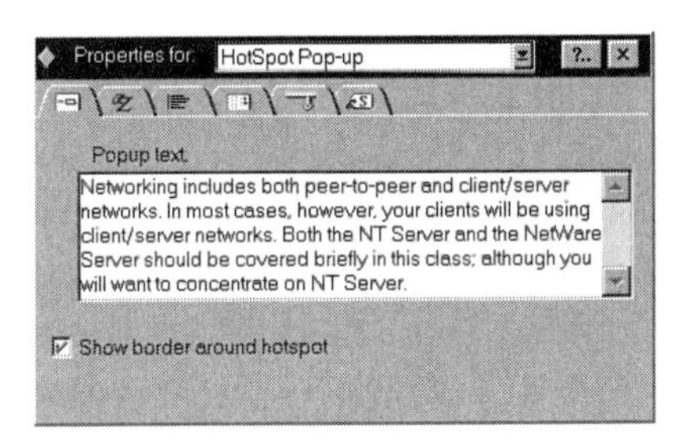

Figure 20.5 Enter a description or explanation.

4. (Optional) If you want to mark the selected text, select the **Font** tab (the second tab in the InfoBox), and you'll see the options shown in Figure 20.6. Choose a different font, size, style, or color.

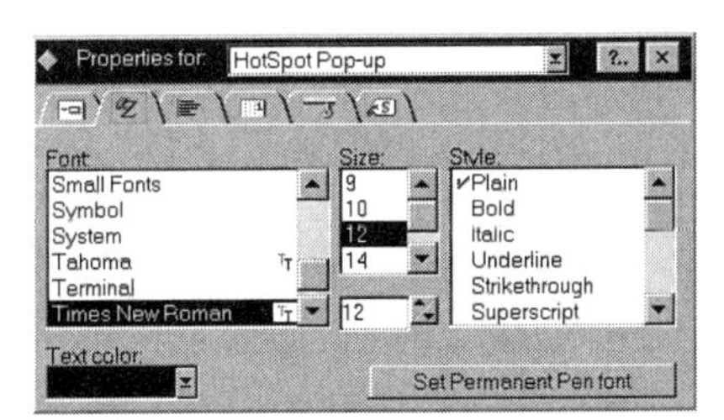

Figure 20.6 Change the selected text to make it stand out.

5. When you are done, close the InfoBox by clicking the **Close** (X) button. To view the pop-up, you must save the document, close it, and then reopen it so that it's not in edit mode.

To view a pop-up, the reader clicks the marked text. The pop-up remains on-screen as long as the reader holds the mouse button.

In this lesson, you learned to check your spelling, create a doclink reference, and add a text pop-up to a document. In the next lesson, you will learn to manage document groups.

Configuring for Calendaring and Scheduling

In this lesson, you learn to set options for your calendar profile, choose who may view your calendar, and change view options.

What Is Calendaring and Scheduling?

You use calendaring and scheduling to keep track of appointments, check the calendar of other Notes users, and invite coworkers to meetings and appointments. The calendar, which is part of your mail database, enables you to do the following:

- Schedule appointments on your own calendar
- Schedule meetings and invite others to those meetings
- Enter repeating appointments, such as a weekly or monthly meeting
- View the free time of mail users who may use Notes mail, Office Vision, or cc:Mail
- View your appointments by the day, week, or month

Calendar Views

You can view your calendar and the information it contains in two different views (see Figures 21.1 and 21.2).

- **Calendar View** This view displays appointments and meeting information in a two-day, one-week, two-week, or one-month format.

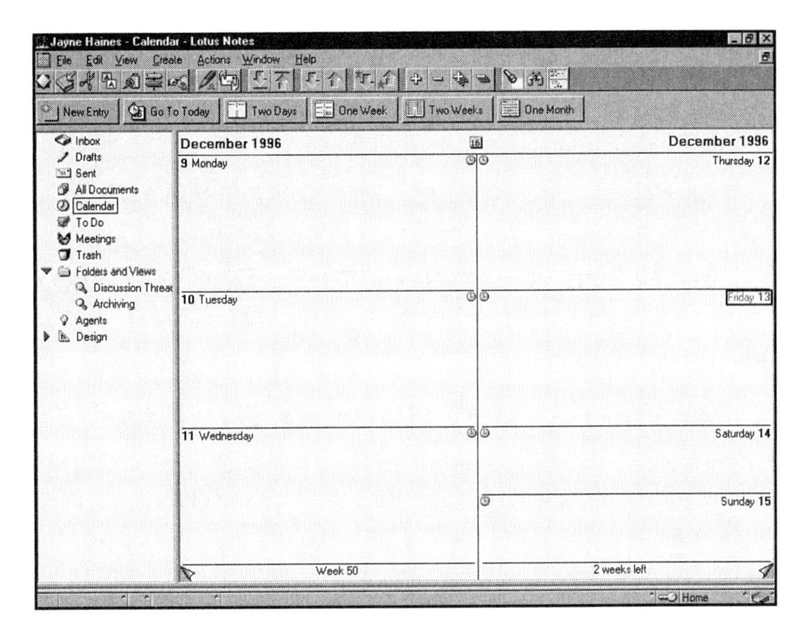

Figure 21.1 View your appointments by the week.

- **Meetings View** This view lists meeting invitations and meetings you have accepted by date and meeting time.

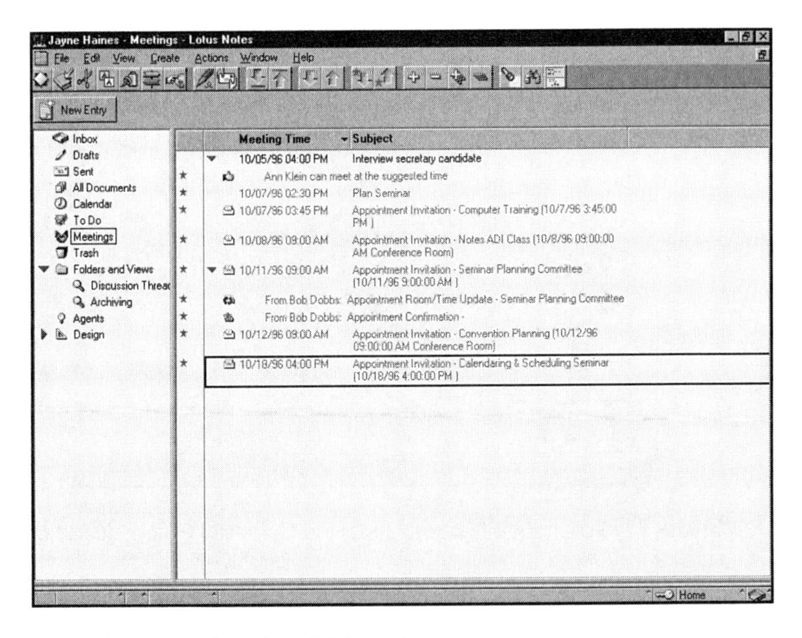

Figure 21.2 View meetings in a list format.

Setting Options

You use two documents contained in your mail database to administer your calendaring and scheduling functions:

- **The Calendar Profile** lets you set defaults for the appointment alarm and free times.
- **The Delegation Profile** enables you to choose who can read your calendar, open your mail, send mail on your behalf, and delete mail in your mail database.

Setting the Calendar Profile

Your Notes Adminstrator might have completed your Calendar Profile document for you; however, if she didn't, you can set the profile yourself. If you click the calendar view and receive a message that your Profile must be set, implement the following steps. You also can use the following steps to confirm the settings in your profile. Figure 21.3 shows the Calendar Profile document with the default settings.

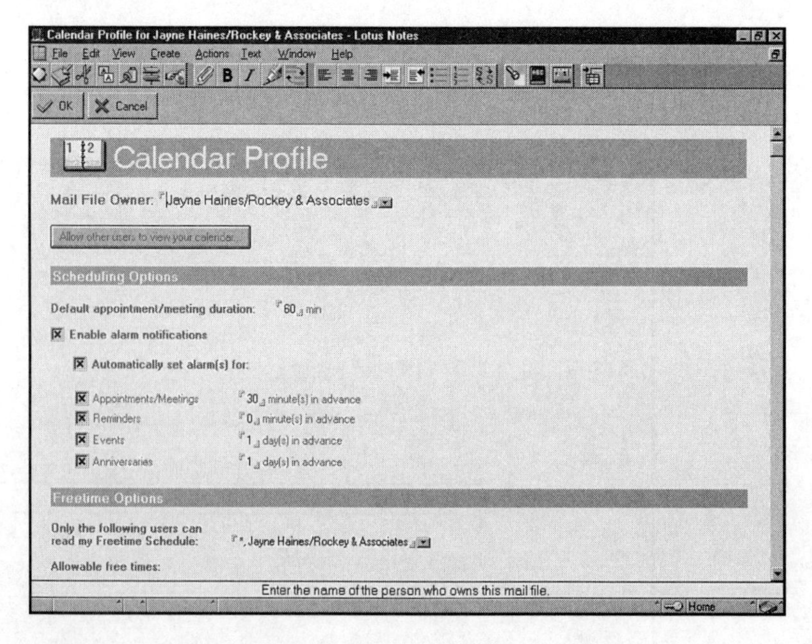

Figure 21.3 Change the defaults in the Calendar Profile document.

To configure your Calendar Profile, follow these steps:

1. Open your mail database.
2. Choose **Actions**, **Calendar Tools**, **Calendar Profile** from the menu. Confirm that your name appears in the Calendar Owner field of the document.
3. If you want to enable others to view your calendar, you can click the text **Click Here to Allow Other Users to View Your Calendar**. This will open the Delegation Profile, which is covered in the next section, "Setting the Delegation Profile."
4. In Scheduling Options, enter a time limit as a default for appointment durations. You also can check the Enable the Alarm Daemon check box if you want Notes to warn you prior to any meetings or appointments.

Daemon Pronounced "demon," a program that automatically runs in the background, collecting information, or performing operating system administration tasks.

5. In Freetime Options, enter the names of the people you want to have access to your calendar by clicking in the **Freetime Schedule** field; alternatively, you can click the down arrow beside the option and choose names from your address book.
6. Use the list of Allowable Free Times to set the days and hours available to others to view.
7. You can set Notes to add meeting invitations to your calendar automatically. Click the **Advanced Calendar Options** and click the **Meetings** check box in **Autoprocessing Options**. You can also choose to remove invitations from your inbox after you respond to them.
8. In the **Calendar Entry Options** area of the document, set options for conflict checking and default viewing settings.
9. Choose the **OK** button on the Action Bar to save the settings and close the document. You can also choose the **Cancel** button to cancel all changes you made to the document and close it.

Setting the Delegation Profile

The Delegation Profile lets you specify the people who may read your mail and view your calendar. You can also specify that the designated people can send messages and replies on your behalf or can delete any of your mail documents. Figure 21.4 shows the Delegation Profile document. You can open the

Delegation Profile by clicking the text **Click here to allow other users to view your calendar** in the Calendar Profile document.

Delete My Mail? Reply to My Messages? No Way! Be careful when you enable others to send mail on your behalf or to delete your mail from your mail file. These privileges should be reserved for only those you trust implicitly.

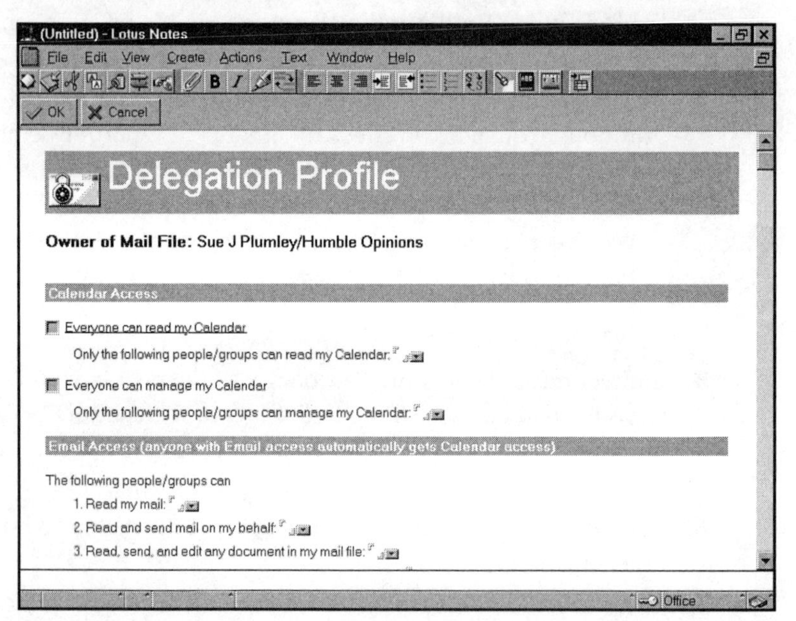

Figure 21.4 The Delegation Profile enables you to specify who may access your mail and calendar.

To edit the Delegation Profile document, follow these steps:

1. Open your mail database.
2. Open the **Actions, Calendar Tools** menu and choose **Calendar Profile**.
3. Click **Click Here to Allow Other Users to View Your Calendar**. The Delegation Profile document appears.
4. In **Calendar Access**, choose either or both of the following options:

    Everyone Can Read My Calendar Enables others to view your calendar but not make changes or additions to it.

Everyone Can Manage My Calendar Enables specified people to add, delete, and edit your calendar entries.

You can enter the names of the people to whom you grant permission to view your mail database, or you can click the down arrow and choose names from the address book.

5. In Email Access, choose or enter the people to whom you want to give access to your mail for each of the following options:

   Read My Mail Gives the designated people the right to only read your mail messages.

   Read and Send Mail on My Behalf Enables the designated people to read all of your mail and to reply or send new messages with your name as the sender.

   Read, Send, and Edit Any Document in My Mail File Gives the right to read and send mail, as well as to edit messages, attachments, imported documents, and so on, in your mail file.

   Delete Mail Use this option in conjunction with the two previous options, enabling the designated user to delete any of your mail messages.

CAUTION

E-mail Access Means Calendar Access Notice that if you grant a person or group access to your e-mail, you're also granting them access to your calendar, because your calendar is in your mail database.

6. Click the **OK** button in the action bar to save the changes and close the document; click the **Cancel** button to cancel the changes and close the document. Click **OK** again to close the Calendar Profile document.

Changing View Options

The Calendar is one view in your mail database, just like Inbox, Drafts, To Do, Meetings, and other views. To view the calendar, open your mail database and click the **Calendar**. Figure 21.5 shows a one-week view of a calendar.

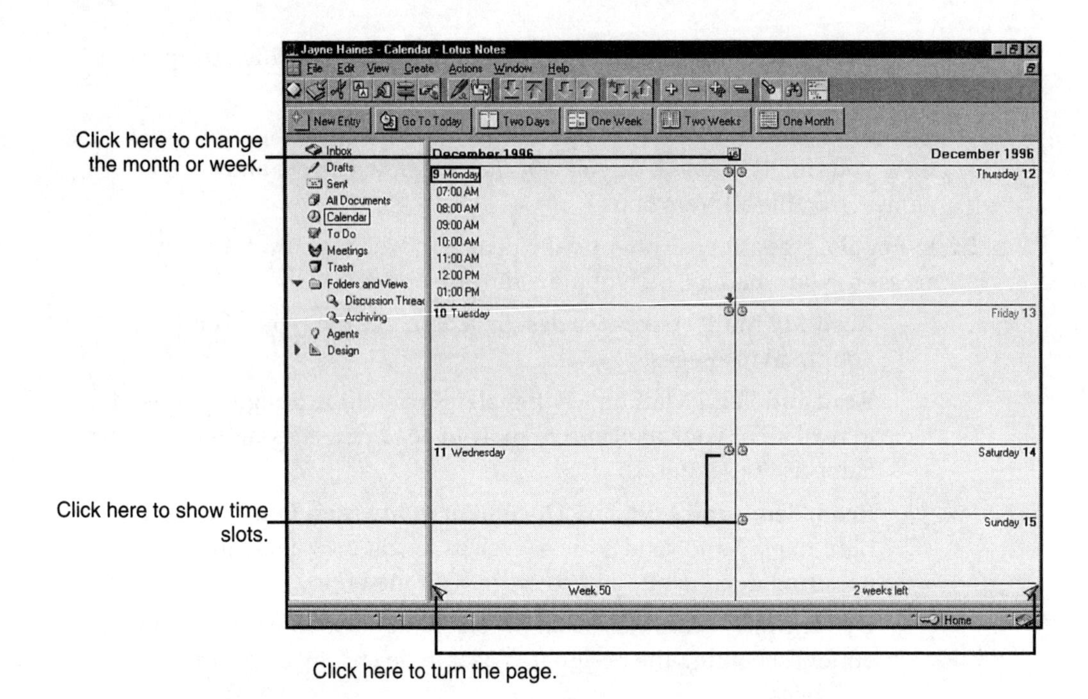

Figure 21.5 Enter appointments and meetings in your calendar.

Do the following to change the view of the calendar:

- To turn a page in the calendar, click the curl at the bottom of the page.
- Click the small clock icon in the corner of any day to display the time slots. Alternatively, choose **View**, **Calendar**, **Show Time Slots**.
- Click the date icon in the middle of the calendar's title bar to change the month, week, or day.
- Click one of the following buttons, in the action bar, to change the Calendar's view: **Go To Today**, **Two Days**, **One Week**, **Two Weeks**, or **One Month**.
- Choose **View**, **Calendar**, and **Go To**; enter a specific date in the text box and choose **OK**.
- You also can view meetings from your mail database. Choose the **Meetings** view to see appointments listed by time, date, and subject.

In this lesson, you learned to set options for your calendar profile, choose who may view your calendar, and change view options. In the next lesson, you will learn how to use the calendar.

Using the Calendar

In this lesson, you learn to make calendar entries, invite people to meetings, and to respond to invitations.

Making Calendar Entries

When you make a calendar entry, you're creating an appointment, event, reminder, or other item that will appear in your calendar. The calendar entry appears on the specified date and at the time you defined. Besides the date and time, you can enter other details about the entry, as described in the following list:

- **Entry type**—Choose from the following as an entry type: **Appointment**, **Invitation**, **Event**, **Reminder**, or **Anniversary**.

Appointment Schedule any appointment you want by entering a brief or long description, date, and time, and set options for public viewing.

Invitation Use an invitation when you want to schedule a meeting to which you invite others. You enter a description, time, date, and then enter or choose the people you want to invite.

Event An event usually lasts one or more full days, as opposed to the hour setting used in a standard appointment. You also can add a brief or detailed description and a date.

Reminder A reminder is similar to an appointment: You enter a description, date, and time to enter into your calendar.

Anniversary An anniversary usually occurs once a week, month, or year and will be entered into your calendar as a recurring appointment. Enter a description and date for the anniversary.

- **Date**—Enter the date of the calendar entry; or click the **month** button to view the month and select a date.
- **Time**—Set the duration of the calendar entry by setting a beginning and ending time in the Time text box; some appointment types enable you to enter a beginning time only. You can, alternatively, click the clock button to view the time scale; drag the indicators up or down on the scale to set the time and duration of the appointment. Time doesn't appear in an Anniversary or an Event.
- **Brief description**—Enter a brief description of the entry, such as a person's name or the topic of the meeting.
- **Detailed description**—Enter names, places, topics, or any other text in this field to create a detailed description of the calendar entry.
- **Room**—Enter the room in which the meeting will take place; this is available only with the Invitation calendar entry.
- **Not for Public Viewing**—Click this check box if you do not want others to see the appointment in your calendar.
- **Pencil In**—Click this check box to show the appointment or meeting is tentative.

Figure 22.1 shows the New Appointment document for an invitation. Many of the fields and options change when you choose a different calendar entry type.

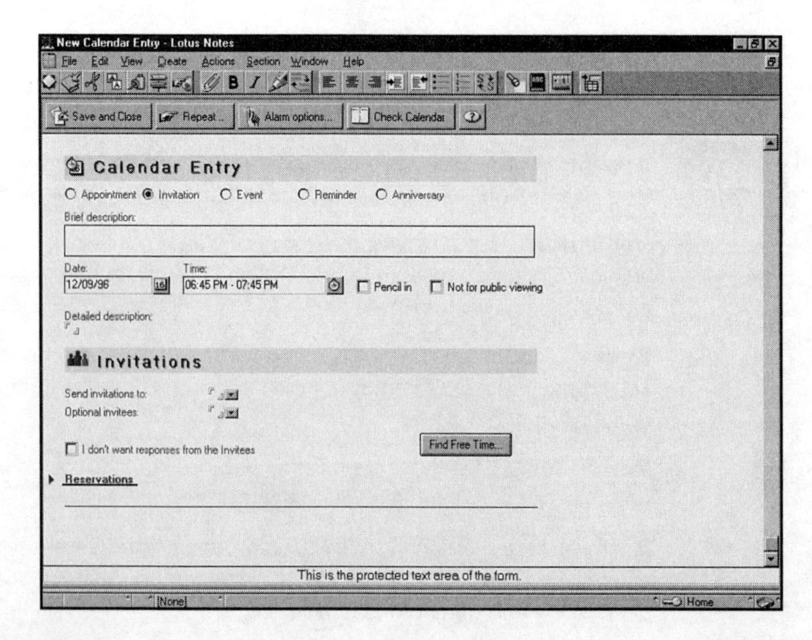

Figure 22.1 Create an invitation to a meeting using Notes Calendar feature.

You can create a calendar entry by following these steps:

1. To create a calendar entry, open your mail database and choose the **Calendar** view. Do one of the following:
    - Click the **New Entry** button on the Action Bar.
    - Choose **Create**, **Calendar Entry**.
    - Double-click the day you want to create an entry for in the calendar.
2. Choose the entry type you want to create: **Appointment**, **Invitation**, **Event**, **Reminder**, or **Anniversary**.
3. Enter a description, the date, time, and any other details or options you want.
4. To create a repeated entry, click the **Repeat** button on the Action Bar. The Repeat Rules dialog box appears. Select the days, dates, and any other repeating options and choose **OK** to return to the Calendar Entry document.
5. To set an alarm, click the **Alarm Options** button on the Action Bar. If you haven't enabled alarms in your Calendar Profile, a dialog box appears and asks if you want to do that now; choose **Yes**.
6. In the Set Alarm dialog box, choose whether to sound the alarm before, after, or on the specified time; if you choose before or after, enter the number of minutes the alarm will ring before or after the entry time. Choose **OK**.
7. Choose the **Save** and **Close** button to close the entry and enter it into your calendar.

Inviting Others to Meetings

You can create an appointment or meeting in your calendar, called an Invitation, and invite others to attend. Notes creates the invitations and e-mails them to all invitees, listing the date, time, and duration of the meeting as well as a description. You also can check the free time of the invitees if you want to choose a meeting time that's convenient for all.

To invite others to a meeting, follow these steps:

1. Create a new entry that is an Invitation. Enter the date, time, description, and other details (refer to the previous section).

2. Click the **Send Invitations To** down arrow in the Invitations area of the document and choose the names from the address book; alternatively, enter the names in the provided field. You can choose from the following:

    Send Invitations to—Enter the names of those you require to attend.

    Optional Invitees—Enter the names of those who may attend the meeting if they want to.

3. To view the free time of the invitees, click the **Click here to find free time for all invitees**. The Free Time dialog box appears, as shown in Figure 22.2.

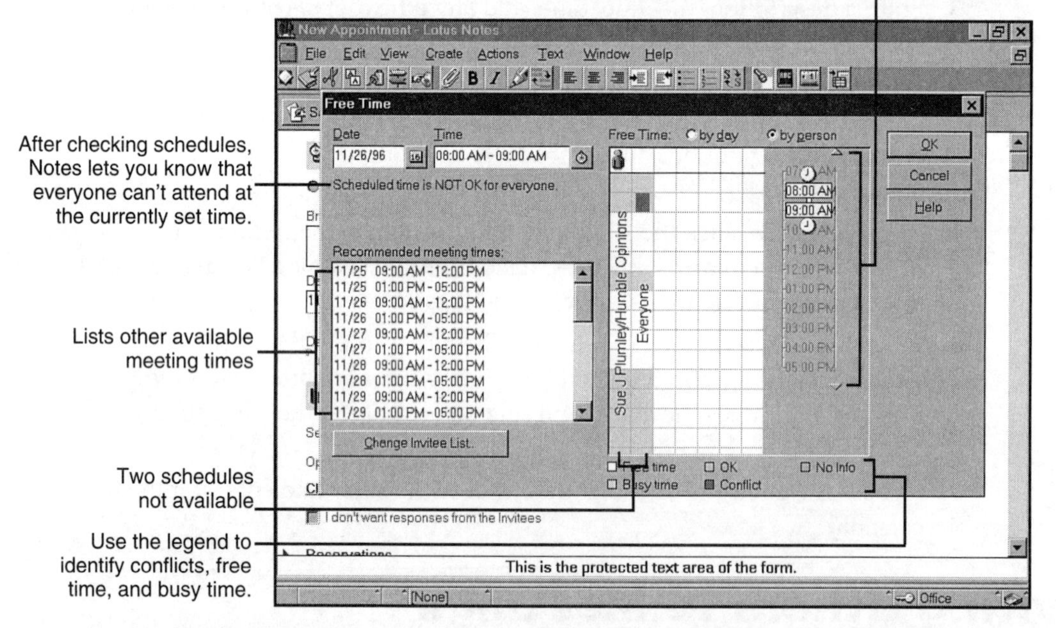

Figure 22.2 Check to see if your invitees can attend your meeting.

What If Schedules Aren't Available? If an invitee's schedule isn't available to you (the free time is kept in a separate database on the server), that person has not enabled you to see his schedule or you are working remotely. The best thing to do in this case is to send the invitation and ask for a response.

4. Check the individual schedules in the Free Time window to the right of the dialog box. You can check either by day or by person.

5. You can change the date and time, and even the people you've invited to the meeting, in the Free Time dialog box.
6. Choose **OK** when you're finished with scheduling around the free time.
7. Click the **Save** and **Close** button to save the appointment. Notes displays a dialog box asking if you want to send invitations; choose **Yes**.

After you send the invitations, your appointment appears on your calendar. You can view or edit the appointment at any time by double-clicking the appointment.

CAUTION

No Response from an Invitee? Invitees do not have to respond to your messages; however, if an invitee is not using Notes, cc:Mail, or Office Vision, he cannot respond. You can only send invitations to others on the Notes network.

Responding to Invitations

When you receive an invitation from someone, it appears as a mail message in your Inbox. The subject begins with Invitation, so it's easy to find. You can open the message and respond to it through Notes e-mail.

To respond to an invitation, follow these steps:

1. In your Inbox, open the Invitation. Notes displays the Invitation document (as shown in Figure 22.3).

TIP

Who Else Is Invited? Click the **Invitees** option at the bottom of the Meeting Invitation document to see who else has been invited to the meeting.

2. Choose one of the following options from the Action Bar:

    Close—Closes the invitation without further action.

    Accept—Sends a message saying you will attend the meeting.

    Decline—Sends a message saying you cannot attend the meeting.

    Other—Displays the Options dialog box from which you can choose the following options: **Accept**, **Decline**, **Delegate**, or **Propose Alternative Time/Location**. Select one and choose **OK**.

   If you choose to Delegate the meeting, the Delegate To dialog box appears; enter the person's name to whom you want to delegate the meeting and choose **OK**.

If you choose the Propose Alternate Time/Location option, Notes adds a section to the message called "Proposed Change." Enter the reason for the change, proposed date and time, or proposed time. Click the **Send Counter Proposal** button on the Action Bar and Notes sends the message for you.

If you choose Check Calendar, Notes displays your calendar so you can check your schedule before you reply. Press **Esc** to return to the Invitation and respond.

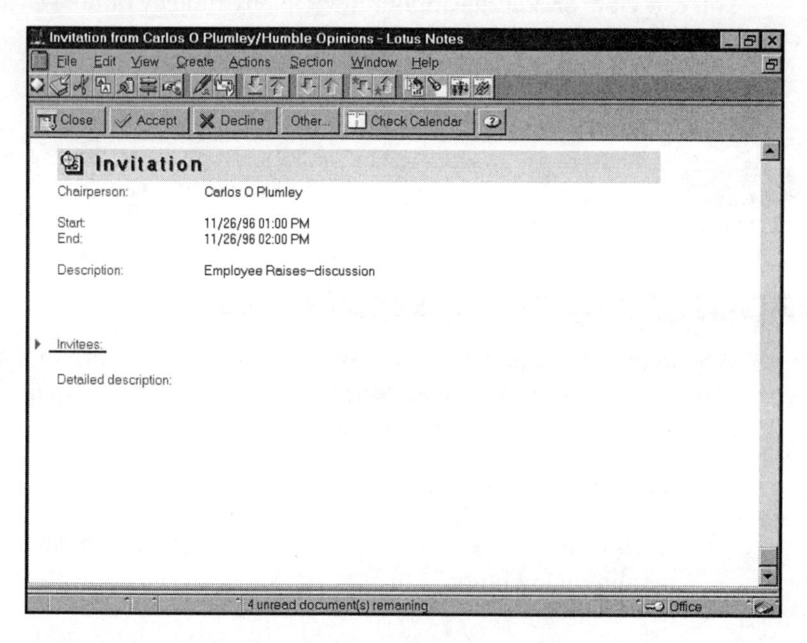

Figure 22.3 View the meeting invitation and then respond.

3. After you select an option, Notes displays the appropriate Status dialog box informing you of its next action, such as sending your acceptance of the invitation. Notes then closes the Invitation and returns to your mail database.

In this lesson, you learn to make calendar entries, invite people to meetings, and to respond to invitations. In the next lesson, you will learn to customize Notes.

Customizing Notes

In this lesson, you learn to customize Notes by changing SmartIcons, arranging workspace pages, changing mail setup, and setting user location.

Changing SmartIcons

In Notes, you can use SmartIcons as shortcuts for common tasks and commands. However, you might find that you don't often use the SmartIcons that Notes displays by default. You can modify the SmartIcon bar to include whichever SmartIcons you prefer. To change the displayed SmartIcons, follow these steps:

1. In your workspace, choose **File**, **Tools**, **SmartIcons**. The SmartIcons dialog box appears (see Figure 23.1). The list on the left shows all available icons; the list on the right shows the icons in the bar that's currently displayed.

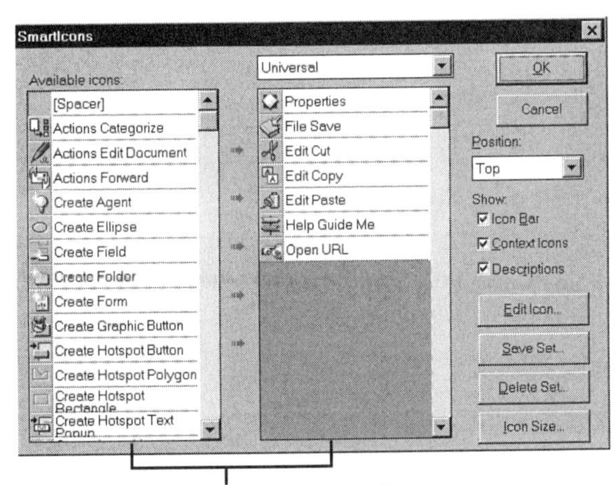

Figure 23.1 Modify the current SmartIcon bar or create your own bar.

2. To add an icon to the selected icon bar, drag it from the list of Available icons to the list on the right. To remove an icon from the list on the right, drag it to the list on the left.

TIP **Don't Like the Order?** You can move icons around in the icon list on the right. Simply drag each icon to the desired location.

3. When you finish adding and rearranging icons, click **Save Set** to save the changes you made to the icon bar. The Save Set of SmartIcons dialog box appears (see Figure 23.2).

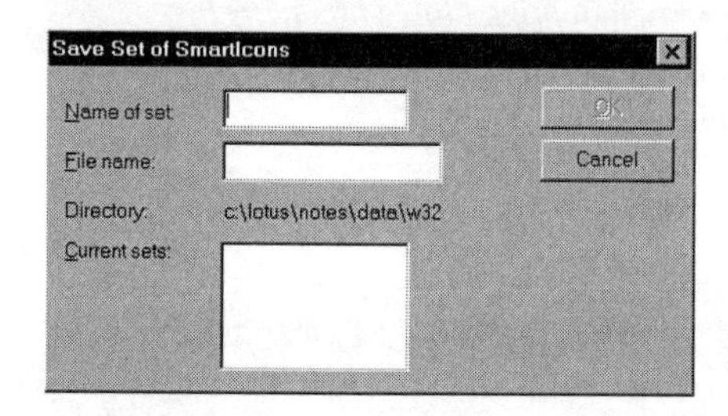

Figure 23.2 Save the set of SmartIcons so you can use it anytime.

4. In the Name of set text box, enter a brief descriptive name.
5. In the File name text box, enter a name for the icon file. Use eight characters or fewer, and add the .SMI extension for ease in file management.
6. Click **OK** to close the Save Set of SmartIcons dialog box. The new SmartIcon bar appears in the drop-down list of SmartIcon bars above the list on the right. You can choose to display this icon bar or any other.
7. In that top drop-down list, choose the icon bar you want to display and click **OK**. Notes displays the selected icon bar in the workspace.

TIP **Change Positions** You can change the position of the SmartIcon bar, moving it to the left, right, or bottom of the Notes workspace. To do so, open the **Position** drop-down list in the SmartIcons dialog box and select a new location for the bar.

Changing User Preferences

Notes enables you to change a number of settings that affect your workspace and how you work in Notes. You can control such things as when Notes scans for unread documents, when it should prompt you to empty the trash, and whether it saves a copy of the mail you send. You'll find these options in the User Preferences dialog box (shown in Figure 23.3). To open the User Preferences dialog box, choose **File**, **Tools**, **User Preferences**.

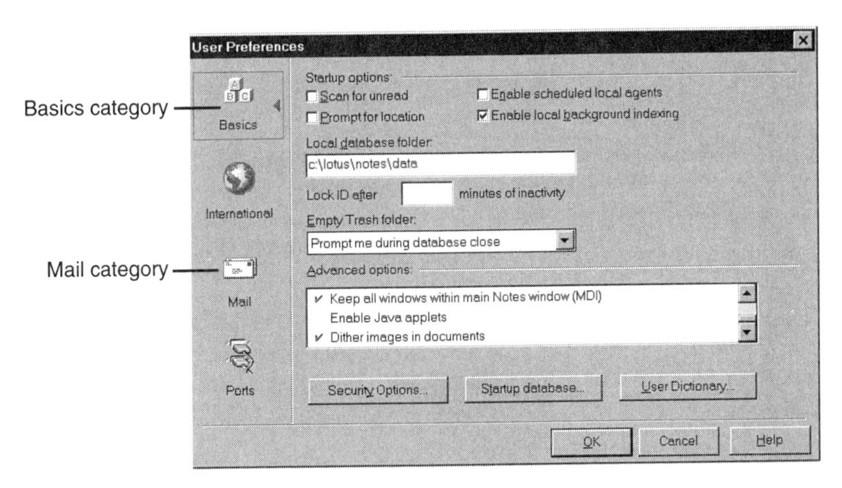

Figure 23.3 You might change the options in the Basics or the Mail category.

TIP **More Information** This lesson covers only the common, most basic options you can customize in User Preferences. If you need more information about customizing User Preferences, see Que's *Special Edition Using Lotus Notes*.

Changing Basics Options

Click the Basics icon to access the Basics category in the User Preferences dialog box (refer to Figure 23.3). There you can work with the following options: Startup options, Local database folder, Empty Trash folder, User Dictionary, and Advanced options. Table 23.1 describes the common settings for each of these areas.

Table 23.1 Basics Options

Option	*Description*
Startup options	Contains check boxes for commands you can have Notes perform automatically at startup. Choose the Scan for unread check box to indicate Notes should scan for unread mail and documents in selected databases on your workspace when you first start Notes. (For more information on scanning databases, see Lesson 12.)
Local database folder	Displays the path to the folder on your hard drive that holds your database files. You can change the path if you want to store your databases in another folder.
Empty Trash folder	Governs how Notes empties your trash folder. Choose whether you want to be prompted when you close the database, whether you always want it emptied when you close the database, or whether you want to empty it manually. (To learn more about using the trash folder, see Lesson 5.)
User Dictionary	Enables you to view words you've added to your User Dictionary during spell checking. You can add, update, and delete any of these words. (For more information about spell checking, see Lesson 20.)
Advanced options	Contains a list of options that control how you use Notes. A check mark appears beside active options. Click an option to select or deselect it.

CAUTION

Scared of the Advanced Options? If you're unsure of an option's meaning, read about the option in Notes' Help system before you activate it. If you do check an option and you don't like the results, open the User Preferences dialog box and deselect it.

Changing Mail Options

You can change Mail options by clicking the **Mail** category icon in the User Preferences dialog box. Figure 23.4 shows the Mail options, and Table 23.2 describes them.

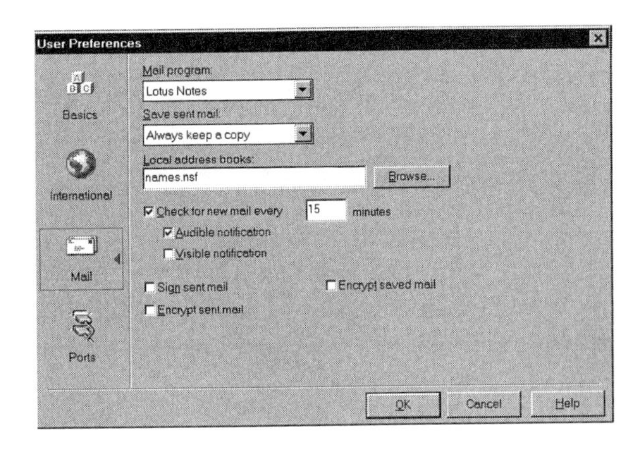

Figure 23.4 The options in the Mail category.

Table 23.2 Mail Options

Option	*Description*
Mail program	Displays the name of the mail program you're using, such as Lotus Notes or cc:Mail.
Save sent mail	Controls whether Notes keeps a copy of the mail messages you send or prompts so you can decide which messages to keep a copy of.
Local address books	Lists the path and file name of your local address book. You can enter a new path and file name, or you can click the Browse button to search for another path.
Check for new mail every ___ minutes	Tells Notes how often to automatically check for new mail addressed to you.
Audible notification	Controls whether Notes sounds a beep or any other sound upon receipt of new mail.
Visible notification	Controls whether Notes displays a message in the Status bar upon receipt of new mail.
Sign sent mail	Tells Notes to always add your name, date, and time signature to your mail (see Lesson 7).
Encrypt sent mail	Tells Notes to always protect the mail you send so it can be opened only by the person to whom it's addressed (see Lesson 7).
Encrypt saved mail	Tells Notes to always protect the mail you save so others cannot view it.

When you finish changing settings in the User Preferences dialog box, click **OK** to close it.

Changing Your Password

Depending on how your Notes network is set up, you may be required to enter your password when you first log on to Notes, or you may have to enter a password only when you want to modify documents and databases. You can change your Notes password at any time to ensure that your mail and databases are safe from others in your company.

Follow these steps to change your password:

1. Choose **File**, **Tools**, **User ID**. Enter your password if prompted. The User ID dialog box appears (see Figure 23.5).
2. Click the **Set Password** button, and the Enter Password dialog box appears.
3. Enter your password. (A series of Xs appears in the text box to ensure your privacy.) Click **OK**, and the Set Password dialog box appears.

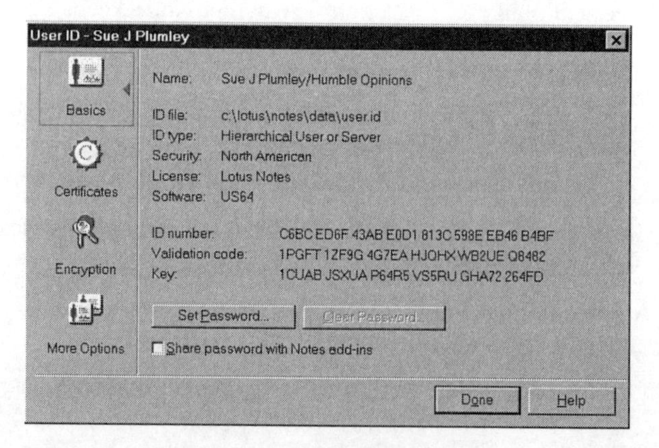

Figure 23.5 Change your password periodically to secure your system.

4. Enter your new password and click **OK**, and the Set Password confirmation dialog box appears.

TIP **Case-Sensitive** In Notes, passwords are case-sensitive. If you enter any uppercase letters when you set your password, you must use uppercase each time you enter your password or you won't be able to access your Notes workspace.

5. Enter your new password again and click **OK** to confirm it.
6. Click **Done** to close the dialog box.

In this lesson, you learned to change SmartIcon bars, user preferences, and your password. In the next lesson, you will learn to link and embed data in Notes.

Linking Information

In this lesson, you learn about linking and embedding data to your database documents.

Understanding Linking and Embedding

Most Windows applications enable object linking and embedding (OLE) between applications and between documents; Notes is no exception. You use linking and embedding as a method of sharing data between documents so you can save time in your work. You also use these features so that your data can quickly and easily be updated.

For example, suppose you create a document about the first quarter sales within a Notes database. Suppose also that you have all of your sales figures in an Excel spreadsheet. You can link a copy of the spreadsheet to the Notes document so that your readers can open the spreadsheet file and view your data. And as a bonus, if you choose to link the document, any changes you make in the Excel spreadsheet automatically update the link in your Notes document.

When you *link* data, you copy the data from one document or application (called the source), and you paste the data in a special way to another document or application (called the destination). A connection, or link, exists between the two documents so that any changes in the source are automatically updated in the destination.

When you *embed* data, you actually create one document within another. For example, you might want to place a picture in a Notes database document. In the Notes document, you open the graphics application (the source), create the picture, and then save the picture within the Notes document (the destination). Anytime you want to edit the picture, you double-click it, and the source application opens so you can edit the picture.

CAUTION

I Can't Edit! In order to edit data you've linked or embedded from another application to a Notes document, you must have the source application installed on your computer.

You can link and embed text, pictures, spreadsheets, tables, or sound and video clips, all of which are called *objects*. There are many advantages to linking and embedding objects. Linking saves disk space and makes use of objects you've already created and want to use again. In addition, linking enables you to use one source and many different destinations; and all destinations are automatically updated when you make changes to the source. Embedding, on the other hand, uses more disk space, but it makes editing the object within the document a quick and easy task. Embedding also enables you to change the object in the destination document without changing the source document.

Linking Data

In Lesson 20, you learned how to create a link (doclink) between documents within Notes. Now you learn to link data between Notes and another application.

To link data from another application to Notes, follow these steps:

1. In the source application, select the data you want to link and choose **Edit, Copy** (as shown in Figure 24.1). Windows copies the data to the Clipboard.
2. Using the Windows 95 taskbar or the Task List, switch to the Notes application and open the database and document to which you want to link the data.
3. Position the insertion point where you want the link and choose **Edit, Paste Special**. The Paste Special dialog box appears (see Figure 24.2).
4. Choose the **Paste link to source** option.
5. In the **As** list, select the type of data you're pasting (if it's not already selected).
6. Click **OK** to paste the data to the Notes document. Figure 24.3 shows an Excel table in a Notes document.

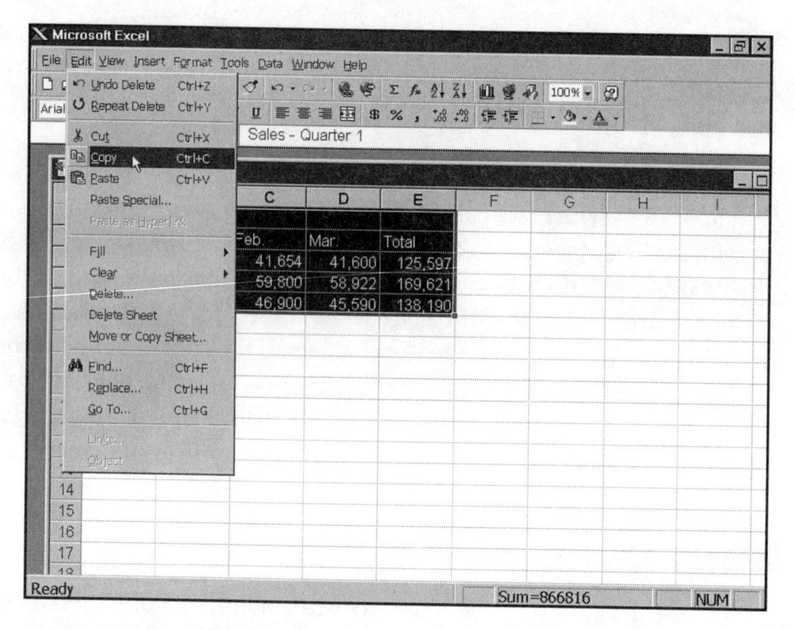

Figure 24.1 You can link data from Excel to a Notes document, for example.

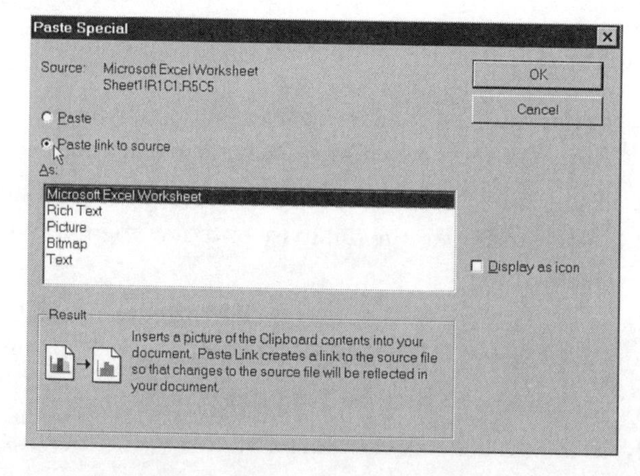

Figure 24.2 Paste the data on the Clipboard as a link in the Notes document.

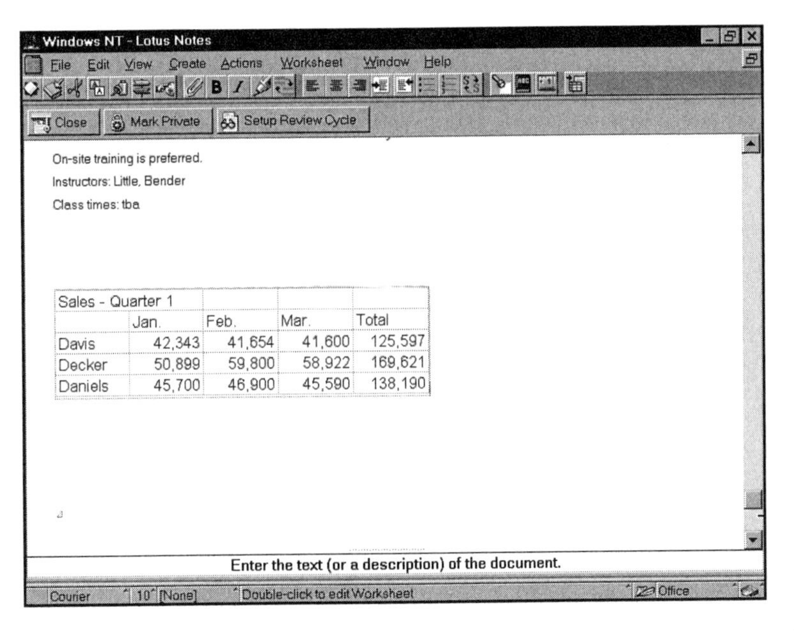

Figure 24.3 An Excel spreadsheet that's linked to a Notes document is automatically updated.

TIP **Quick Edit** To edit a linked item, double-click it, and the source application opens with the data ready to edit. When you change data in the source application, the data automatically changes in the destination.

Embedding Data

When you embed data, you create an object—text, table, picture, or sound file—within the destination document. Embedding uses more disk space and more memory because when you create or change an embedded object in the destination document, you must actually open and use two programs at one time.

Follow these steps to embed data:

1. In edit mode, position the insertion point in the Notes document where you want to create the embedded object.
2. Choose **Create**, **Object**. The Create Object dialog box appears (see Figure 24.4).

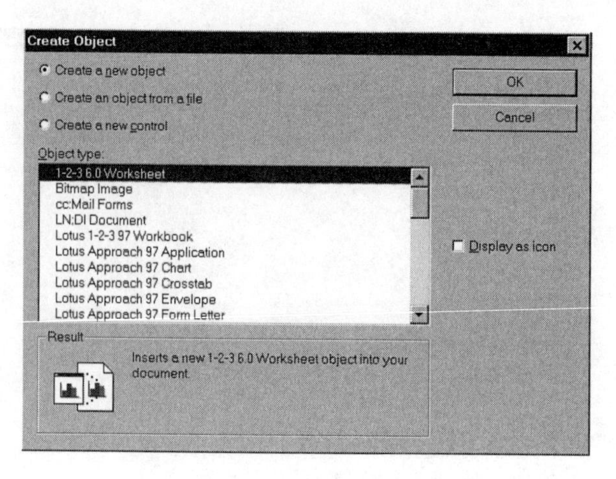

Figure 24.4 Choose the type of object you want to create.

3. Choose **Create a new object** if you want to create an object using one of the applications listed. Choose **Create an object from a file** if you want to embed an existing object.
4. In the Object type list, select the kind of object you want to add to the Notes document. (What types of objects you can create depends on the programs installed to your computer.)
5. Click **OK**, and the application opens within the Notes document with all the tools and menus you need to create the object. Figure 24.5 shows a Notes document with the Windows Paint program open, ready for the user to create an embedded object.
6. When you finish creating the object, click anywhere in the Notes document outside of the object's frame. The source application closes, and the object appears in the Notes document (see Figure 24.6).

Frame The box that appears around many embedded or linked objects in a Notes document. You can usually click and drag the bottom-right corner of the frame to resize the object within the document.

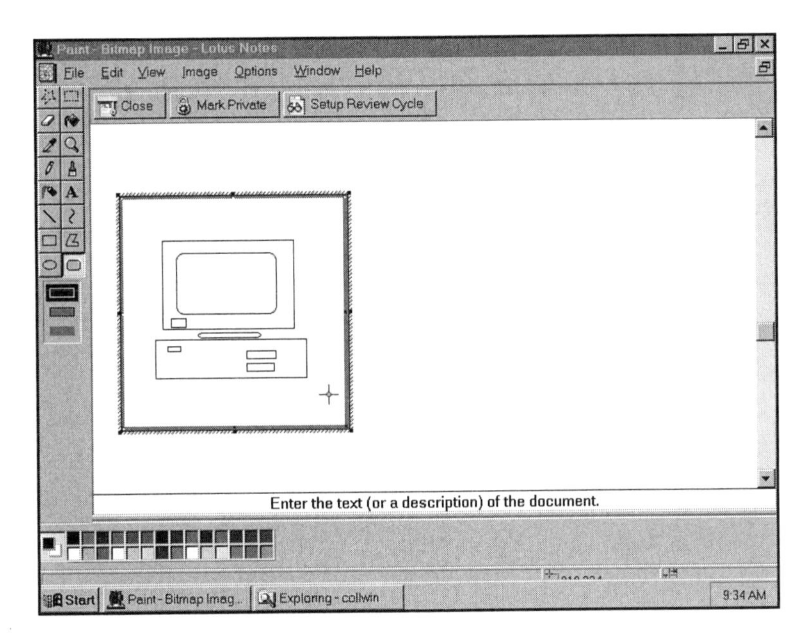

Figure 24.5 The Paint program is open within Notes.

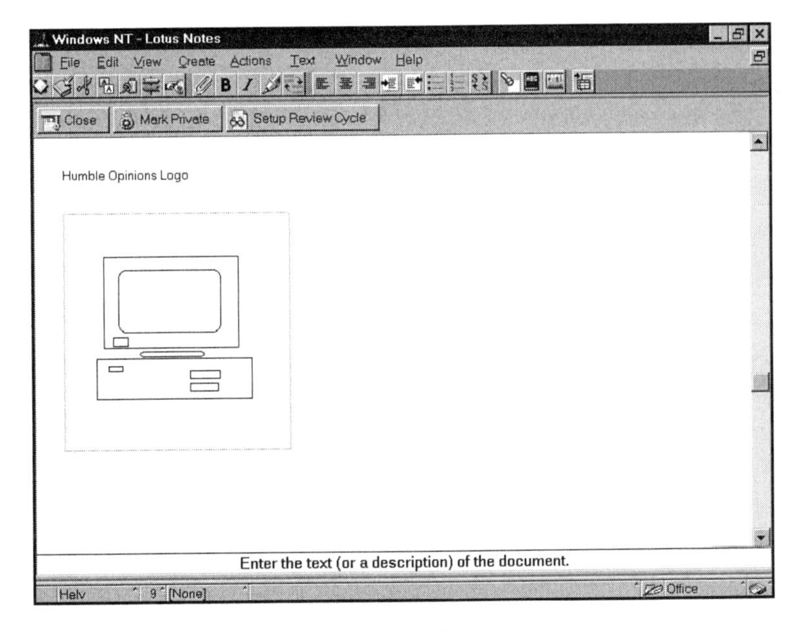

Figure 24.6 An embedded Paint object in a Notes document.

To edit any embedded object, double-click the object, and the source application opens. Edit the object as you want. When you finish, click outside the frame of the object to close the source application.

Updating Links

When you open a document that contains linked data, Notes displays a message asking if you want to refresh the links in that document. Click **Yes** to update the links and to update all data in the object. To update the changes in the Notes document at any other time, change to Edit mode and choose **View, Refresh**.

If you click No when you're asked to update a link, the links are broken. Once the links are broken, any changes made to the source are not updated in the destination document. You can still double-click the object and open the source application, but the changes you make there will not be updated in the destination.

Shortcut To refresh the view at any time—and thus update the links—press **F9**.

In this lesson, you learned to link data and embed data and to update links. In the next lesson, you learn to work remotely with Notes.

Working Remotely with Notes

In this lesson, you learn how to set up a modem, how to connect to and disconnect from a network, and how to replicate mail and databases.

Understanding Remote Connections

Domino includes many features that help you connect remotely to your network by way of a modem instead of a direct cable. You use remote connections with Domino when you're working away from the office, at home, or on the road with a notebook computer. You can complete your work—mail, document creation, task lists, and so on—on your computer without being attached to the network. Then when you're ready, you call up the server and transfer the data from your Notes program to the network.

Before you plan to connect to the server remotely, check with your Domino administrator to make sure you have a certified Domino User ID and appropriate access to the Domino server. You also need to make sure that the server is set up to receive incoming calls through a modem. Finally, you should know the exact name of your server.

Remote Connection A network connection that uses a modem and phone lines instead of a direct cable. For a remote connection to work, both the server and the remote computer must have Domino installed. In addition, each one must have a modem and must be attached to a phone line.

When you work on a computer that's attached to the network with cables, the mail you send and the documents you create and update are immediately transferred and updated on the server. However, when you work remotely, you must first create copies (or replicas) of the databases you want to use on your remote computer and save them to your local hard disk.

When you first copy (or *replicate*) the databases, they match the databases on the server exactly. As you work on the copied databases though, they begin to differ from the databases on the server. Not only are you making changes to your copy of the database, but other users are making changes to the original database back at the office. That's why remote connections are necessary.

When you connect remotely to the server, Domino locates the changed databases and updates them with your changes (your new mail, newly created documents, and edited or deleted documents, for example). And of course, Domino also updates your databases to reflect the changes other people have made to the original databases.

Configuring for the Modem

Before you can connect to the network, you must modify some settings in your computer. The changes you need to make include enabling the communications port, setting up your modem, entering the server in your address book, and setting up Domino for Remote Mail.

TIP **Disconnect Call Waiting?** When working with a modem, you use a phone line that's normally used for verbal (voice) communication. Therefore, you should disconnect such phone services as call waiting so that your connection will not be interrupted and terminated.

Setting the Port

You use communications ports to connect to the network. When working at the office, as you have throughout this book, you use the LAN port. When working remotely, you use a communications port such as COM1 or COM2. To set the port (let Domino know which port you're using), follow these steps:

1. Choose **File, Tools, User Preferences**. The User Preferences dialog box appears.

2. Choose the **Ports** category (bottom left of the dialog box), and the Ports options shown in Figure 25.1 appear.

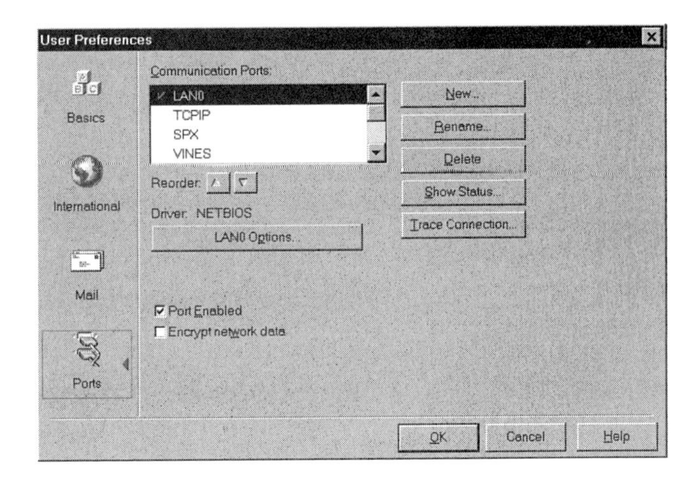

Figure 25.1 You must set the port before you can use a remote connection.

3. In the **Communication Ports** list, select the COM port to which your phone line is attached.
4. Select the **Port Enabled** check box.
5. Click **OK** to implement these settings and close the User Preferences dialog box. Alternatively, you can set additional options for your modem, as explained in the next section.

TIP **Encrypt?** Click the **Encrypt network data** check box if you're transferring highly sensitive data and you do not want anyone to tap into it. Note, however, that using this option slows down the speed of the transmission and increases the chances of transmission errors and terminations.

You can—and should—also set your modem speed, dialing mode, and modem type, as well as a few other options from the User Preferences dialog box. To configure additional options, perform these steps:

1. In the User Preferences dialog box, click the **XXX Options** button (where *XXX* is the name of the selected port, as in COM2 Options). The Additional Setup dialog box appears (see Figure 25.2).

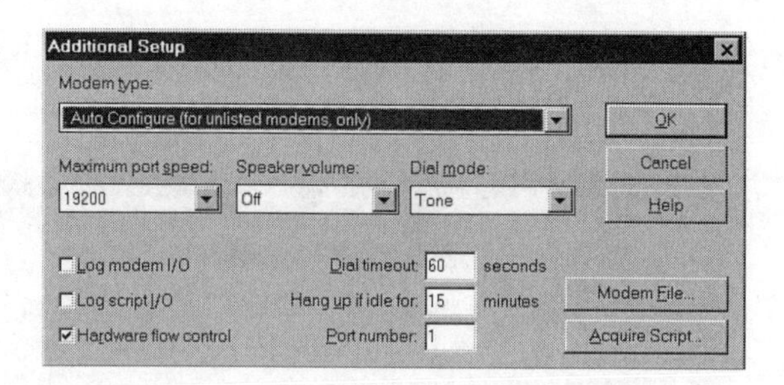

Figure 25.2 Configure specific settings for your modem.

2. In the Modem type list box, select the type of modem you're using.
3. Set the rest of the options. Several are explained in Table 25.1.
4. Click **OK** to close the Additional Setup dialog box, and then click **OK** again to close the User Preferences dialog box.

Table 25.1 Modem Settings

Setting	*Description*
Maximum port speed	Set the maximum bps (baud per second) speed your modem can use, such as 14.4, 19.2, or 38.4. (The setting 38.4 represents the port speed; use it if your modem is 28.8 bps.)
Speaker volume	Set the volume to off, low, medium, or high. The sounds you'll hear are the dial tone, the dialing, and the two modems communicating. It's a good idea to at least keep the setting on low so you can tell whether your modem is connecting and when in the sequence there's a problem (for example, if there's no dial tone or no communication between modems).
Dial mode	Indicate whether your phone uses Tone or Pulse dialing.
Dial timeout	Enter a number of seconds for Domino to continue to try dialing before hanging up.
Hang up if idle for	Enter the number of minutes of no activity that Domino should wait before hanging up.

Setting a Location

You must set up a location when using a remote connection. For example, you can use *Travel* or *Home* instead of the Office location that you've used throughout this book. The only difference between Travel and Home is in the way you set them up. You can, for example, set up the Travel location so that you can use your calling card number when you're in a hotel or remote office location. Additionally, you can set up the Home location with permanent settings for dial out numbers, area codes, and so on (but Travel location settings will change).

To set a location, click the location button in the Status bar (the second box from the right end) and choose either **Home** or **Travel**. Alternatively, you can choose **File**, **Mobile**, **Choose Current Location**, select the location from a list, and click **OK**.

CAUTION

Location Settings You should ask your Domino administrator for help setting up the location options if they are not already set. Creating locations is beyond the scope of this book.

Creating a Server Connection

Another setting you must complete includes the connection to the server. You'll need to know the exact name of the server, as well as the phone number you need to connect to the modem on the server. You can get both from your Domino Administrator. Follow these steps to create the server connection.

1. Choose **File**, **Mobile**, **Server Phone Numbers**. Your Address Book database appears in the Server/Connections view.
2. Choose **Create**, **Server Connection**. The Server Connection sheet appears (see Figure 25.3).
3. In the Connection type area, confirm or select **Dialup Modem**.
4. In the brackets next to Server name, enter the exact name of your server.
5. In the Area code brackets, enter the server's area code.
6. In the Phone number brackets, enter the server's phone number.
7. Choose **File**, **Save** to save the information, and then choose **File**, **Close** to close this sheet.
8. Close the Address Book database.

CAUTION

Trouble? If you are unsure of any setting in the Server Connection sheet, ask your Domino Administrator for assistance.

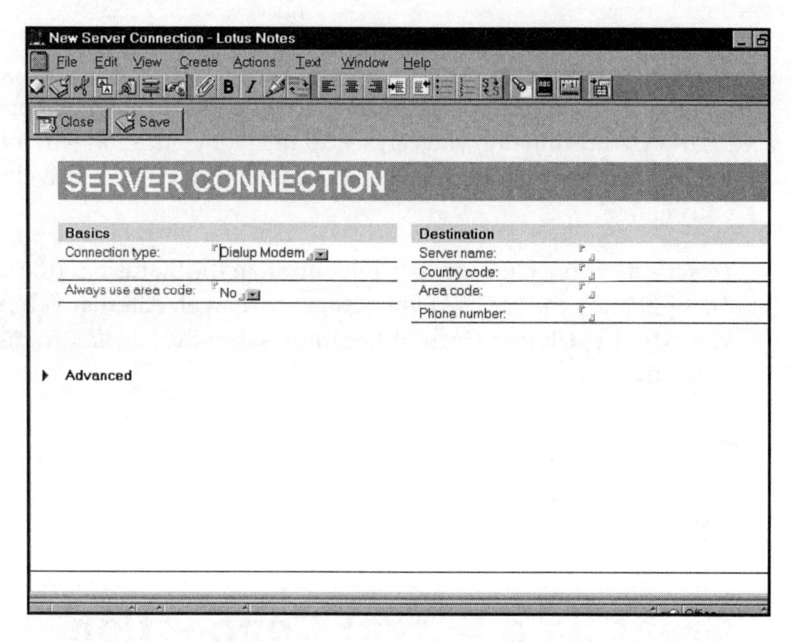

Figure 25.3 Set up your server connection.

Connecting to the Network

Connecting to the network from a remote computer is simply a matter of calling the server. Domino takes care of the connection details so you can continue with your work. Disconnecting is also easy; however, make sure you save and close all databases before you disconnect from the network.

To call the network server, follow these steps:

1. Choose **File**, **Mobile**, **Call Server**. The Call Server dialog box appears.
2. In the list of servers, select the server.
3. (Optional) Make any last-minute or temporary changes to the port, timeout, or call setup settings described in Table 25.1.
4. Click **Auto Dial**. Domino dials the server and connects your remote computer to the network, from which you can replicate mail and databases.

To disconnect from the server, choose **File**, **Mobile**, **Hang Up**.

Replicating Databases

You can *replicate*, or copy, your databases to and from the server for use when you're working remotely. Doing so ensures that you'll always have up-to-date material with which to work and that your coworkers will have access to changes you make to the databases as well.

Follow the steps below to replicate a Domino database:

1. After connecting to the server, select the database on your workspace by clicking it.
2. Choose **File**, **Replication**, **Replicate**, and the Replicate database dialog box appears (see Figure 25.4).

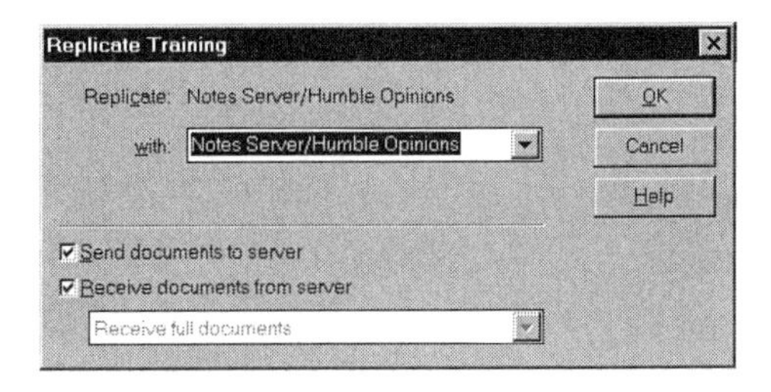

Figure 25.4 The Replicate database dialog box.

3. In the **with** text box, select a different server from the list if you don't want to replicate to the currently selected server.
4. Select the **Send documents to server** check box if you want to replicate to the server; select **Receive documents from server** if you want to replicate to your workstation. If you choose to receive documents, use the drop-down list to indicate whether you want to receive full documents or document summaries (document summaries contain only basic document information such as the title and author).
5. Click **OK**.

Sending and Receiving Mail

Domino's replicate feature also works in the mailbox. When you replicate mail, you send mail to and receive mail from the network using a remote connection, and Domino updates your mailbox accordingly.

To replicate mail, follow these steps:

1. After connecting to the network, choose the **Replicator** tab.
2. Choose the **Send & Receive Mail** tool button. Domino sends your mail to the server and receives any new mail.

TIP **Send Only** If you want to send outgoing mail without receiving incoming mail, select the check box to the left of the **Send outgoing mail** icon and click the **Start** tool button. Domino sends your mail to the network.

Lotus Notes 4.5 Web Navigator

Understanding the Internet and the Web

In this lesson, you'll learn about the Internet and the Web. You'll also learn about protocols and Internet tools.

What Are the Internet and the Web?

Welcome to the world of the Internet and the Web!

Before we get down to the details of the Internet and the Web, let's clear up a common misunderstanding. The Web is part of the Internet and is a thing, not a place. For some reason, many newcomers to the Internet and Web think that they are two different places. Hopefully, a little background on each will clear this up.

- **The Internet** is a worldwide conglomeration of computer networks. The Internet is not owned and operated by any one company. (This is one of the defining characteristics of the Internet.) It is one network of computers who can talk to one another, that in turn, talk to another network of computers, and so on and so forth.
- **The Web** is a collection of documents accessible through the Internet. These documents contain a special technology called *hypertext*. When you click your mouse on hypertext, you'll be taken to a new document, maybe even to a different computer. This works much like the green words you see in help files that you use in Windows and many other Windows products.

Grasping Protocols

In order for computers to communicate over the Internet they follow sets of agreed-upon rules that are called *protocols*. The people who came up with these rules were not only clever, they came up with cute names for their protocols, such as "gopher" and "World Wide Web." Other long, descriptive names that nobody really wanted to pronounce or write out, were shortened to acronyms, such as HyperText Markup Language (HTML) and Transmission Control Protocol/Internet Protocol (TCP/IP).

It's a good idea to understand some of these protocols as you "surf the Web." You really don't need to memorize or even fully understand all of these terms, but you'll find that as you use the Web, this list will be a good reference for you.

Surfing the Web We're not sure exactly who said it first, or when this term caught on, but it means to look around the Internet, just like we use the term "channel surfing" with our TV remote control.

Internet Protocol (IP) This is one of the most basic protocols. All computers that communicate with one another on the Internet do so using IP. This determines how data will be transferred from one computer to another, the route the data takes, and the order of the data when it arrives at the second computer.

Transmission Control Protocol (TCP) Another basic protocol. It enhances IP and gives you a way of correcting transmission errors, setting up and breaking down a communications session between the computers, and lots of other things. Because TCP and IP generally work hand-in-hand, people generally refer to them together as TCP/IP.

File Transfer Protocol (FTP) Defines how to transfer a generic file from one computer to another. The file could be a text file, a program, a picture–anything. FTP will transfer it.

HyperText Markup Language and HyperText Transport Protocol (HTML and HTTP) Together they drive the World Wide Web. HTML defines a method of adding formatting to text files, so that when you view them with an HTML viewer, you see things like headlines, emphasized words, centered paragraphs, and embedded pictures. HTTP defines how computers will send HTML files back and forth.

Clients and Servers

One of the things that might help clarify what's going on when your computer talks to another computer is the concept of clients and servers. On a network, computers will often assume either the role of client or server. That is, one computer—the server—will offer some service to the world. The other computer—the client—will make use of that service.

When you use the Internet, your computer is almost always acting as a client and communicating with a server of some kind. If you're transferring a file, you are using FTP client software to transfer the file to or from a computer running FTP server software. If you're surfing the Web, you use your Web browser as a client. A Web browser communicates with a Web server, which serves up Web pages to your browser. Even the copy of Notes you work with is a client. It requests that the Domino server serve up views and documents from the Notes databases that it maintains.

Understanding Tools

From its outset, the purpose of the Internet was to help communication and research. It is to those ends that the various Internet programs are aimed, such as Internet mail programs, Internet News Groups and Mailing Lists. Other tools, such as Gopher, Archie, Veronica, WAIS, and Web servers, are intended to help locate published material—that is, to further your research activities.

Here is a brief description of the most common Internet tools:

Telnet A protocol that defines how one computer can act like a terminal on another computer. Using a telnet program, you can log onto another computer and run programs on it, just as though you were sitting at its own console.

Mailing Lists Mailing lists are a way of participating in group discussions on the Internet. Mailing list server computers maintain mailing lists. Using your e-mail program, you can send a request to be added to a mailing list (or removed from it). Then, anyone can send messages addressed to the mailing list itself. The mail server will forward the message to everyone on the mailing list.

UseNet News Another way of participating in group discussions. News servers store messages and forward them to one another using a protocol called NNTP (Net News

Transfer Protocol). You can read and post messages on the servers using a News Reader program.

Archie Archie servers maintain lists of the names of programs and documents and their locations on other computers on the Internet. If you need to locate a program, you can request its location from an Archie server either with an Archie client program or using Telnet or e-mail.

WAIS Wide Area Information Servers maintain searchable, full-text indexes of documents. If you need to find information about a particular subject, you can search for more than titles, as with Archie and other data-locating engines. WAIS allows you to search through the contents of the files in the database. By doing this, you may find information that the author or indexer of a document might never have realized you would want.

Gopher Gopher servers present content in the form of cascading menus. You pick items from menus. Each menu item can be another menu, a program, or a file of some kind. The strength of Gopher remains that any menu item may actually be on gopher server that is different from the one that presented the menu to you in the first place. So by picking items from gopher menus, you actually jump from gopher server to gopher server.

Veronica Veronica servers maintain searchable databases of gopher server contents. If you get tired of searching menus for what you want, you can compose a search request of a Veronica server, which will present the search results in the form of a Gopher menu.

Java Java is a programming language you can use to build small applications (called "applets") that you can embed in Web pages. When a surfer downloads the Web page, his/her browser (if it is Java-aware) executes the Java applet. To the Web surfer, the executing applet may appear as a scrolling text display, an animated picture, a clock keeping real time, a stock ticker reeling off stock quotes, a graph that changes as the surfer enters numbers into a form, or any number of other whimsical or useful things, limited only by the programmer's imagination and the Web surfer's browser and patience. Big Java applets might take a long time to download.

Hypertext: The Heart of the Web

The World Wide Web, or simply the Web, is just another Internet tool. The other tools are useful to get work done, but the World Wide Web is positively exciting. There are two reasons for this: hypertext searching and the HyperText Markup Language (HTML).

Hypertext is like computerized footnotes. If you look at the bottom of the page in a book with footnotes, or maybe at the end of a footnoted article, you'll find that little number or asterisk followed by a reference. That reference might be another book or magazine article that provides additional information about the topic being discussed. Well, not only can the Web provide you with that reference, it can also take you directly to that reference, even if it's located on another computer entirely. You leap instantly through *hypertext* from one Web page located on this computer to another page located on that computer (another *Web site*) halfway around the world.

HyperText Markup Language (HTML) is a set of standard notations that can be embedded in a string of text. When you view the text with an HTML reader, it interprets the HTML notations as formatting commands. Plain text becomes *formatted* text, complete with headlines, italics, centered paragraphs and, best of all, pictures. Recently HTML has been enhanced even further so that a Web page can include audio clips, video clips, and embedded programs.

Embedded Programs Programs that are incorporated in a document. When a browser encounters it, the browser actually runs the program or calls another application to run the program.

The Web Navigator: Your Ticket to the Web

The Web Navigator is a Web browser, allowing you to send requests to Web servers and display pages sent by the Web server in your Notes database. What differentiates the Web Navigator from other browsers (for example, Netscape Navigator or Microsoft Internet Explorer) is that it translates HTML pages into Notes documents while you are surfing the Web. What you see on your screen (while on the Web) is an actual Notes document. Depending on your version of Notes, the pages you view on the Web are stored as Notes documents in Notes databases.

In this lesson, you learned about the Internet and the World Wide Web. You also learned some new terminology. In the next lesson, you'll learn how Lotus Notes and the Web Navigator work.

Understanding How the Web Navigator Works

In this lesson, you'll learn how Lotus Notes works to help you access the Internet. You'll also learn how the Web Navigator is customizable by your company.

The Two Versions of Web Navigator

The Web Navigator is a Web browser built into Notes. It works in conjunction with a Notes database that converts Web pages retrieved by the browser into Notes documents, then stores them in the database. That's a big distinction from your other Notes databases, which give you access to Notes documents.

There are two versions of Web Navigator:

The Server Web Navigator, which is a shared browser and database and resides on your Notes server.

The Personal Web Navigator, which is built into your Notes client along with a local database residing on your workstation.

With Web Navigator you can:

- Browse the Web and save Web pages in the Personal Web Navigator or the Public Web Navigator database.
- Send Web pages to other Notes users via Notes mail.
- Retrieve previously viewed Web pages without reconnecting to the Internet.

- Save Web pages in any Notes database to which you have access rights.
- Rate and categorize Web pages.
- Use built-in agents to locate and return Web pages to you, or create your own agents.
- Access Web pages that contain Java applets.
- Create "Web tours" that can be rerun at a later time.

The Public Web Navigator

The Server Web Navigator runs on your Notes server. It creates and uses a shared database called Web Navigator. Your Notes server must have access to the Internet or your company's intranet for the Server Web Navigator to function properly. When you browse the Web, each Web page that you retrieve is converted into a Notes document and stored in the Server Web Navigator database.

Shared Database A database that is located on the server and can be accessed by more than one person at a time. A local database, on the other hand, is stored on your hard drive and accessible only by you.

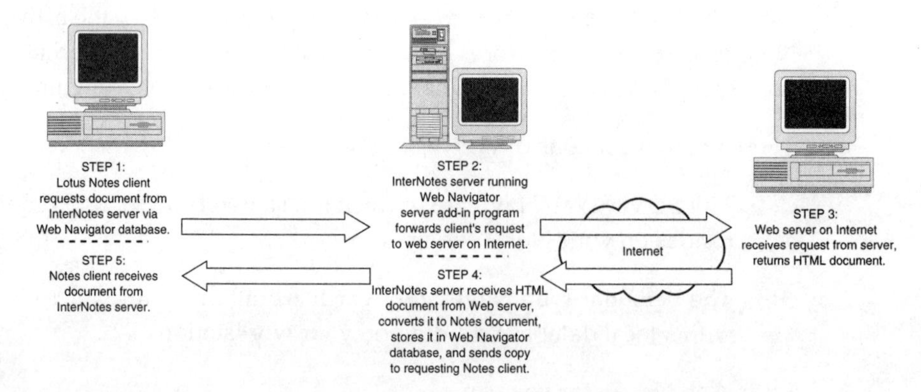

Figure 2.1 How the Server Web Navigator accesses the Internet.

If you are using the Server Web Navigator, you should be aware that:

- Your Notes Systems Administrator can set the size limit on this database. He can also set limitations on the "age" of documents stored in the database.

- Your Notes System Administrator can customize the Navigator, so icons and screens might look and act differently than you see in this guide. Our "look" is based on the default. If your icons look different, have fun and explore.
- Your Notes Administrator can restrict the Web sites you can visit and the time of day you can visit them. If you cannot reach an Internet address using the Public Web Navigator, check with your Notes Administrator.

The Personal Web Navigator

The Personal Web Navigator runs on your own computer and creates and uses a local database (called Personal Web Navigator) on your computer's hard drive. It enables you to access the Web directly if you have an Internet connection, such as a dial-up connection through an Internet Service Provider. When you browse the Web, each Web page that you retrieve is converted into a Notes document and stored in the Personal Web Navigator database.

The Personal Web Navigator does not require Internet access through a Domino server. You can use your Personal Web Navigator from home, if you have a modem and an Internet Service Provider.

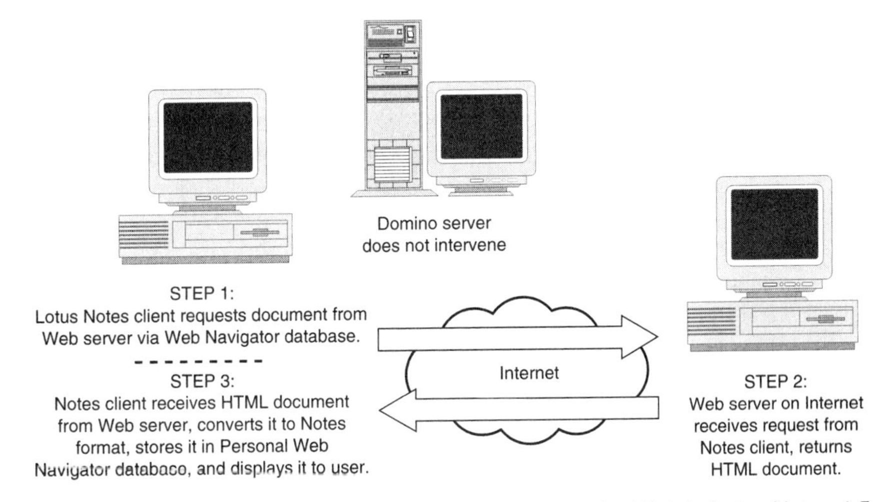

Figure 2.2 How the Personal Web Navigator accesses the Web in Lotus Notes 4.5.

Recognizing Clients and Servers

When you access the Internet, your computer is acting as a client. By either passing through the Notes server, (or connecting directly to a computer on the Internet that is acting as a server) you, the client, are requesting service from another computer, the server.

It is similar to the connection you have at work with your file server. The file server on your office network is where you often store work that you create in other software programs (other than Notes). The place you store your files on that server is often called your F: drive. When you retrieve a file, you're asking the server to send it to you.

So, it's very likely that you can be a Notes client, a file server client, *and* an Internet client.

Internet or Intranet?

In some companies, the Web Navigator is used on an *intra*net, which is a closed or internal network.

Why use an intranet? In some organizations, it's cost effective to share company information this way. The protocols and rules are the same as the Internet—the difference is that it's a closed network, available only to employees connected to the network inside of the company. The information available on the intranet is *company* information, usually proprietary in nature, and not accessible to outsiders.

A company can establish an intranet by installing the TCP/IP protocol, a Web server, and Web browsers. A Web server will publish documents and information in HTML format so that people with Web browsers can access this information. This Web server acts the same as the Web servers you connect with when you go out to the Internet. Except on an intranet, you never have to go out to the Internet to get this information; you simply type in the address of your company Web server, and you have access to the information you need. (We'll cover addresses more thoroughly in Lesson 4.)

You might be saying to yourself, "If my company has Lotus Notes, why would we need a Web server? Can't I get everything I need in Notes?" The answer is maybe yes and maybe no. The power and design of Lotus Notes makes it every bit as effective for sharing information within a company as does a Web server on an intranet. But what if your Web server and your Web applications were installed before the company purchased Lotus Notes? What if there are already applications built for an existing intranet and those applications are not Notes applications? Well, if that information is published to the *intra*net, you can access it with your Web Navigator.

If you are on an intranet, how does this affect you and the way you can use this guide? Well, being on an intranet does not necessarily preclude having access to the Internet. You may have both. Check with your Notes or Network Administrators to see whether you have permission to access both the intranet and the Internet. If you have only intranet access, your only restriction will be the inability to reach an Internet address.

In this lesson, you learned how the Web Navigator works and some of the potential limitations of the product. In the next lesson, you'll access the Web Navigator and configure it for your use.

Setting Up the Web Navigator

In this lesson, you'll learn how to set up and open the Web Navigator. You'll also learn how to configure the databases so that you can access the Internet.

The Web Navigator requires information regarding Internet access in order to perform properly. This information must be provided by you in a location document.

CAUTION

If You Use Both Web Navigators, Be Careful Setting Up! If you intend to use *both* the Personal and the Server Web Navigator, make certain that you use two different location documents (one for home and one for the office) when you are following the instructions for setting up the Navigators. If, after setting up the Personal Web Navigator, you do not change location documents before setting up the Server Web Navigator, the two Navigators will not operate properly. If you experience problems, you can delete the Personal Web Navigator database from your hard drive (PerWeb45.nsf) and start again at the installation instructions contained in this lesson. Be certain to delete the *database*, not just the icon. You might want to have multiple Web Navigator databases for the purpose of segregating and manipulating various types of Web data. To handle this, you will want to create multiple location documents to specify the use of multiple Web Navigator databases.

Setting Up the Personal Web Navigator

The Personal Web Navigator allows Internet access from your workstation (your own computer). You will need one of the following types of Internet connection:

- **Direct Connection** A direct connection is a leased telephone line, such as a T1 line, that connects your PC or network with an Internet Service

Provider. Through that connection, you can connect with any other computer on the Internet. It is unlikely that you have a leased line at home, but your Local Area Network (LAN) at work might be connected by router and leased line directly to the Internet. Your computer, connected to such a LAN, is effectively always on the Internet.

- **Proxy Connection** A proxy connection places another computer (a proxy server) between you and the Internet. The proxy server acts as a *firewall* with your LAN on the inside and the Internet on the outside. The proxy server filters, caches, and passes incoming and outgoing requests between you (inside the firewall) and the Internet (outside the firewall).
- **Dial-Up Connection** A dial-up connection (also considered a direct connection) enables you to connect your computer to the Internet through a dial-up modem that connects to an Internet Service Provider (ISP). This is the most common connection used by personal PC users while at home and on the road. Your ISP might be a local company with only local phone numbers for you to call; or it might be a large company such as CompuServe or America Online, which provide local phone numbers all over the U.S. and foreign countries.

It is most likely that you will use a dial-up connection for your Personal Web Navigator. If you are using a proxy or a direct connection at work, consult your Notes or Network Administrator for configuring the Personal Web Navigator. Odds are, if your workplace allows the Personal Web Navigator for your use, they will also configure it for you. The possibility exists that some corporations will disallow the use of the Personal Web Navigator, and give you access only to the Server Web Navigator.

The instructions given here assume that you are configuring the Personal Web Navigator for use on your laptop or your PC at home, and that you have a location document for home. It also assumes that you have a dial-up connection to an ISP. Before you begin these steps, you'll need to have established:

- A dial-up connecton to the Internet.
- TCP/IP installed on your system. If you have *winsock* or *PPP*, you do have TCP/IP.

Winsock and PPP Point to Point Protocol (PPP) is a dial-up protocol that extends TCP/IP across telephone connections. Winsock is the Windows version of PPP.

If you're already using an ISP and a Web browser other than Notes, you probably have a dial-up connection configured in your operating system. After you've taken the following steps to configure the Personal Web Navigator, you'll initiate that dial-up connection. Once connected, you can simply open an URL as described herein. To begin opening Web pages through your Web Navigator, you'll need to edit or create a new Location document in your Personal Address Book. We recommend that you edit your current location document (i.e., your "home" location).

URL Uniform Resource Locator, the address that you will use to locate a Web site. See Lesson 6 for more detailed information on URLs.

To provide Notes with the information needed to run the Personal Web Navigator:

1. Click once on the location indicator on your status bar and select **Edit Current** from the list of choices.
2. The location document appears (see Figure 3.1). In the Internet browser field located in the Internet Browser section, choose **Notes** as your browser.

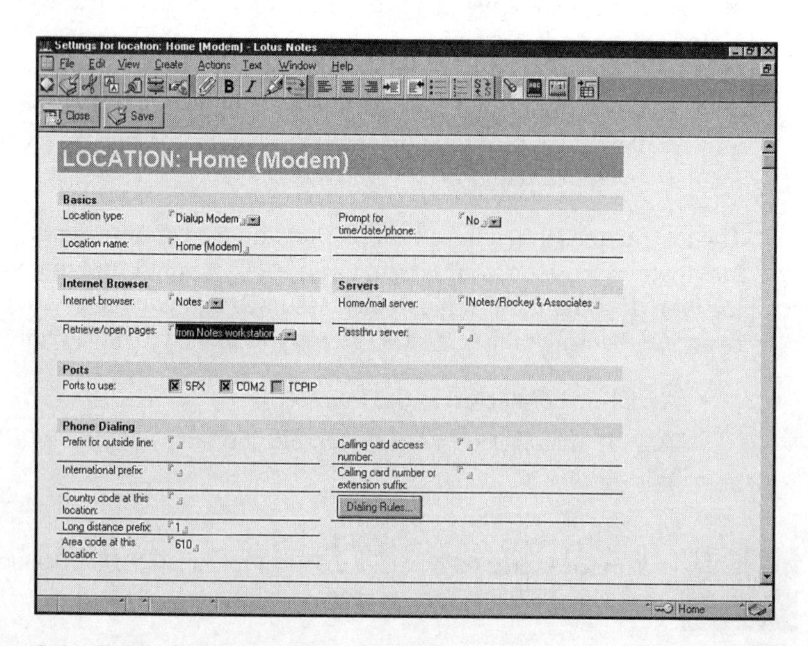

Figure 3.1 The location document.

3. In the Retrieve/open pages field select **From Notes workstation**. This selection is important. It is the trigger that notifies Notes *which* database you will be using, the Personal or the Server Web Navigator. Selecting From Notes workstation will result in the creation of the Personal Web Navigator database.
4. Make certain that you have a COM port in use for your modem. This will already be selected if you are using Notes remotely and replicating to your server.
5. **Save** and **Close** this document.
6. Choose **File**, **Open URL** from the menu. (You'll learn more about URLs in Lesson 6.)
7. Enter the URL of the Web site you want to visit. For testing purposes, enter **www.Lotus.com** to visit the Lotus Web site. Since you haven't dialed into your ISP yet, you won't reach this Web site. The purpose for this step isn't to actually reach the Web site, but to force Notes to create the database and place the icon on your desktop. After a few seconds, your browser will be activated. Press the **Esc** key when you receive an error message (the error message will tell you that the URL can't be located) to close the browser and return to your Notes workspace.
8. You will see the new icon for the Personal Web Navigator on your workspace.
9. At the Notes workspace, select **File**, **Tools**, **User Preferences**. The User Preferences window appears as shown in Figure 3.2.

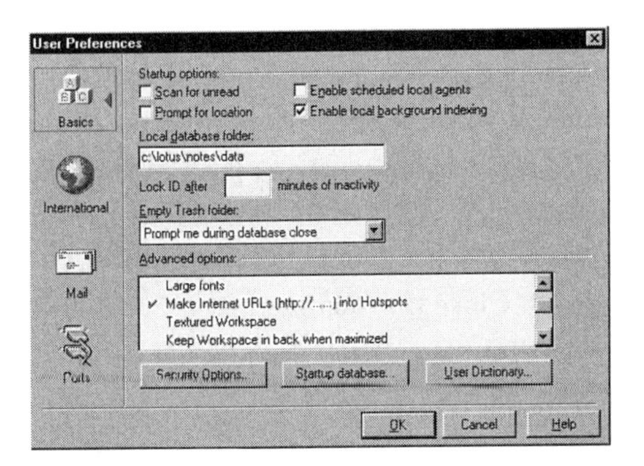

Figure 3.2 The User Preferences window.

10. Click the **Basics** icon to display the Advanced Options window.
11. In the Advanced Options window, place a check mark next to the **Make Internet URLs (http://.....) into Hotspots** selection.
12. Click the **OK** button to close this window.

Setting Up the Server Web Navigator

The Server Web Navigator enables you to access the Internet through your Domino server. If your company has not set up the Server Web Navigator for you, you can set it up yourself. Verify with your Notes or Network Administrator that your PC and your Domino server meet the system requirements to use the Server Web Navigator. If you have the Web Navigator icon on your workspace, you may skip this section.

If you have not installed the Personal Web Navigator, follow these steps to set up the Server Web Navigator. If you have installed the Personal Web Navigator, create a new location document, select that location document, and follow along:

1. Make certain that your current location is correct. If you are at the office, it will probably say "office." Click once on the location indicator on your status bar. Select **Edit Current**. Your currently selected Location document appears (see Figure 3.3).
2. In the Internet browser field located in the Internet Browser section, choose **Notes** as your browser.
3. In the Retrieve/open pages field, select **From server**.
4. Enter the hierarchical name of your Web server in the server field. If you are unsure of the name, ask your Notes Administrator.
5. If you connect to the Internet through a proxy, enter the name or IP address of the proxy in the Web Proxy field found in the Basics Section. If you are unsure of your connection, consult your Notes Administrator.
6. **Save** and **Close** the document.
7. Choose **File**, **Open URL** from the menu.
8. Enter the URL of the Web site you want to visit. For testing purposes, enter **www.Lotus.com** to visit the Lotus Web site.

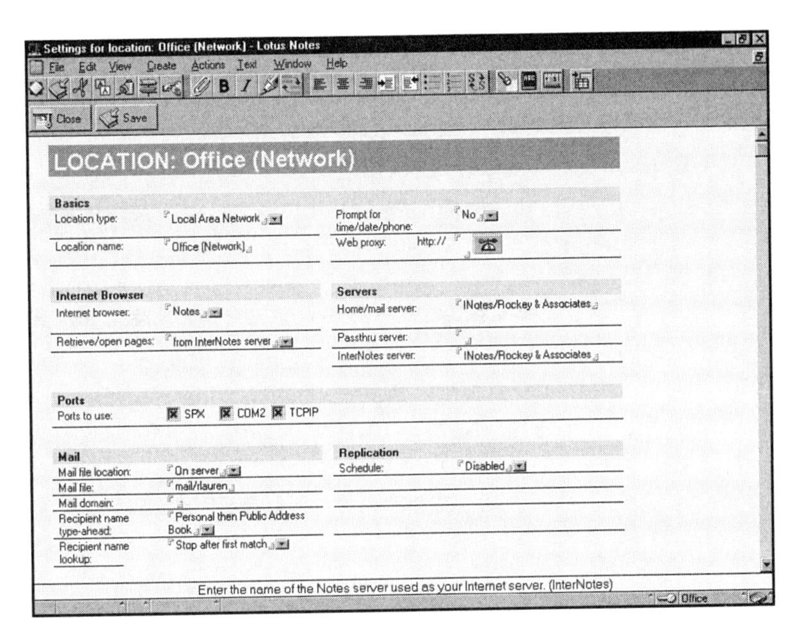

Figure 3.3 Location Document for Office.

9. Once the Lotus Web site is visible on your screen, you can be assured that you have successfully reached the Internet. To continue with your setup, press the **Esc** key once. Your Notes workspace will be visible and you will see the new Web Navigator icon on your workspace.
10. When you return to your workspace, the icon for the Web Navigator will be visible on your workspace. Double-click the **Web Navigator** icon to open the database. You will see a message welcoming you to the Web Navigator and asking whether you want to edit the settings of your Internet Options document.
11. Choose **Yes** to set up your Internet Options document.
12. You do not need to fill out this entire document in detail. For installation purposes, you should fill out the section called **Collaboration options**. This will enable you to share Web pages with other Notes users.

Where's the Message? If you do not see the message to edit your Internet Options document, simply click once on your Personal Web Navigator icon and select **Actions**, **Internet Options** then continue with the next step.

13. In the Server field, type the name of your Server. In the Database field type **PUBWEB45.nsf** to indicate that pages you rate and share will be shared and rated on the Server Web Navigator.
14. **Save** and **Close** this document.
15. At the Notes workspace, select **File, Tools, User Preferences**. The User Preferences window appears as shown in Figure 3.4.

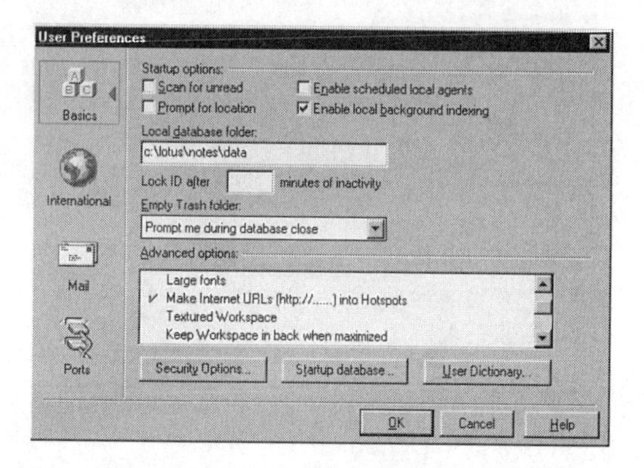

Figure 3.4 The User Preferences window.

16. Click the **Basics** icon.
17. In the Advanced Options window, be certain that a check mark appears next to the **Make Internet URLs (http://.....) into Hotspots** selection. If it does not, click once to place a check mark there.
18. Click the **OK** button to close this window.

Opening the Web Navigator Database

To open the Server or Personal Web Navigator, double-click the database icon. If this is the very first time you've opened the database, you will be looking at a document called the About Database document. This document describes the purpose of the database. If you have opened the Web Navigator before, you won't see this document because by default it is displayed only the first time the database is opened. To see the About Database document again, simply click the Web Navigator icon to select it, then open the **Help** menu and click **About this Database** (see Figure 3.5).

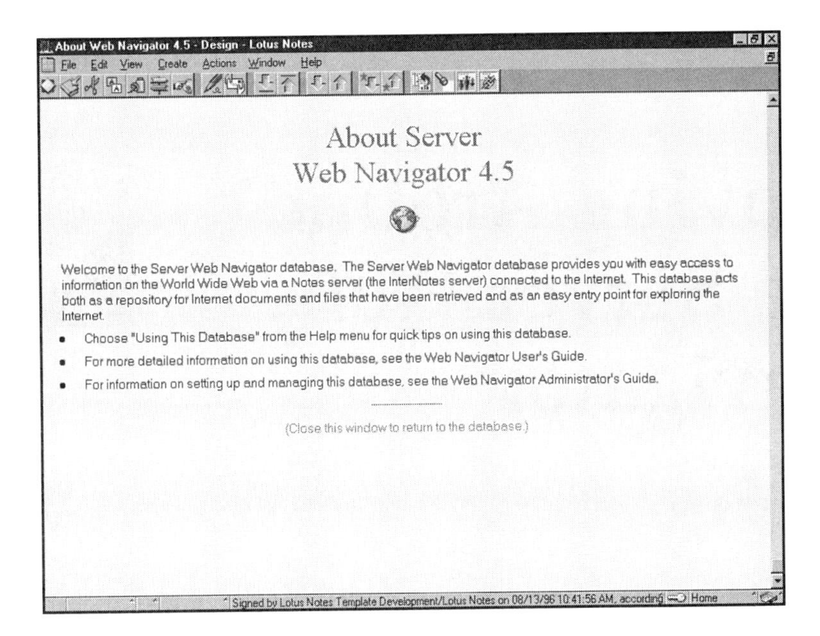

Figure 3.5 The Personal Web Navigator About Document.

A **Using this Database** document is also available for most of your Notes databases, including the Web Navigator. This document provides highlights on how to use the database. To access the Using this Database document, open the **Help** menu and click **Using this Database**. When you've finished reading the document, press the **Esc** key until you return to your Notes workspace. You'll learn more about moving around the Web Navigator in Lessons 4 and 5.

TIP **About this Database** You will find an About Database and Using this Database document for most of your Notes databases. To view these documents for a different Notes database, simply click the **database** icon in your workspace, open the **Help** menu, and click **About this Database** or **Using this Database**.

In this lesson, you learned how to access and configure the Personal and Server Web Navigator(s). In the next lesson, you'll learn how to move around in the Server Web Navigator.

Moving Around the Server Web Navigator

In this lesson, you'll explore the Server Web Navigator and take a look at its different views and documents.

Understanding Documents

Like other Lotus Notes databases, the Server Web Navigator contains views, folders, and documents. Moving around, searching, finding, and saving documents is similar to the methods you use in other Lotus Notes databases.

There are three types of documents available in the Server Web Navigator. They are:

- **Web pages** These pages are converted to Notes documents when you retrieve them from the Web. They look and act just as they did on the Web, complete with hypertext and links. Web page documents make up the bulk of the database. Which Web page documents you see in your database is strictly dependent upon which Web pages have been retrieved by you and others in your company. Figure 4.1 shows a sample Web page.
- **Web tour documents** Web tour documents contain the history of a visit to Web sites. They are also Notes documents and from these Web tour documents, you can retrace a Web site visit. Creating Web tour documents is explained further in Lesson 13. Figure 4.2 shows a Web tour document.

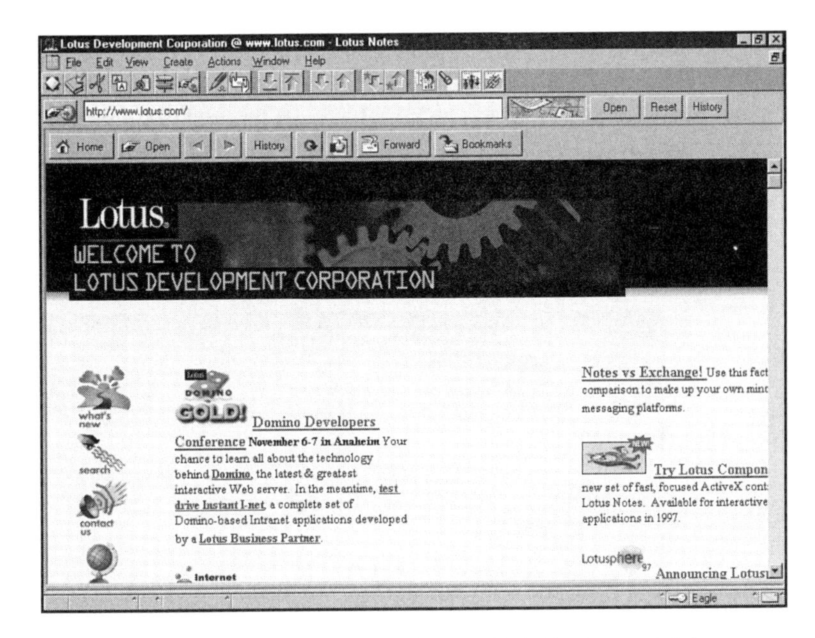

Figure 4.1 An Example Web page in the Server Web Navigator database.

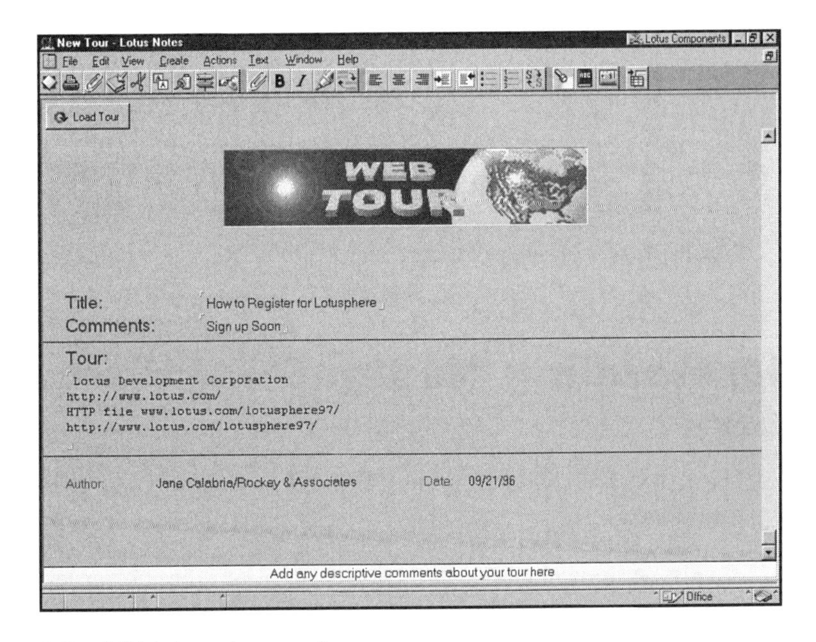

Figure 4.2 A Web tour document.

- **Rating documents** Rating documents are created to rate and recommend Web sites to other users of the Web Navigator. You might be researching a project and find a Web site that could be valuable to others on the project. When you create a rating document for this site, it will be listed in one of the Recommended Views. How to fill out Rating documents is explained in Lesson 14. Figure 4.3 shows a Rating view in which you can see Web page titles, scores, and comments by the people who rated those pages.

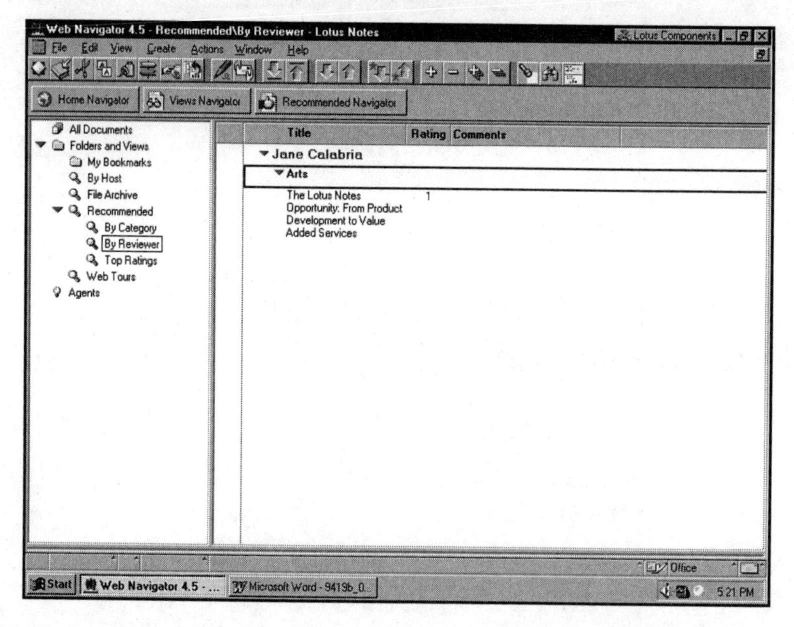

Figure 4.3 A Rating document view.

Understanding Navigators, Views, and Folders

The Server Web Navigator has graphical navigators to help you move around the database.

The first graphical navigators you see are found on the Server Web Navigator home page. The Sampler icons (see Figure 4.4) are navigators that can be customized by your Notes Administrator. If no customizing has been done, then these icons will take you to a search page where you can fill in a specific topic that falls within each category. (We'll cover more about searches in Lesson 10.) Figure 4.4 shows the default icons and the categories they represent for finding Web pages, but icons and the categories might be different.

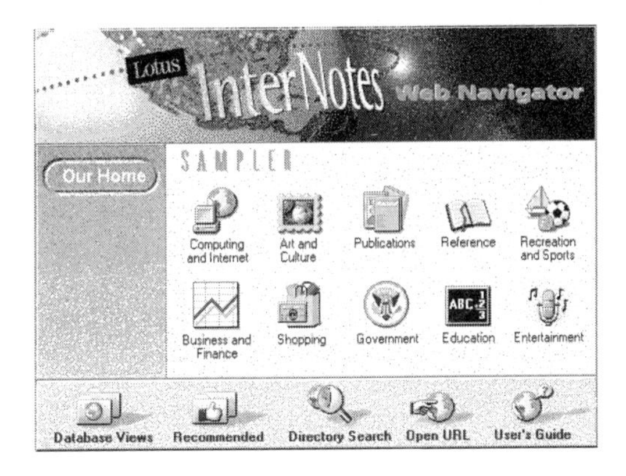

Figure 4.4 Sample icons on the Home Page.

Home Page Different? If the Sample icons in your database look or act differently than the ones displayed here, don't panic—explore! The Server Web Navigator Home Page is completely customizable by your Notes Administrator and Developers, and they may have changed its look as well as its navigators.

If you have the default sampler and you click one of the Sampler icons, you'll see a navigator that takes you to various Web sites listed in the navigator. As shown in Figure 4.5, you can click the Entertainment sampler icon, which gives you a choice of three Web sites where you can find information on entertainment.

To return to the home navigator page, click the **Back to Home** button or press **Esc**. The icons along the bottom of the home page will open to different views, searches, URLs, and even to the Web Navigator User's Guide, as shown in Figure 4.6.

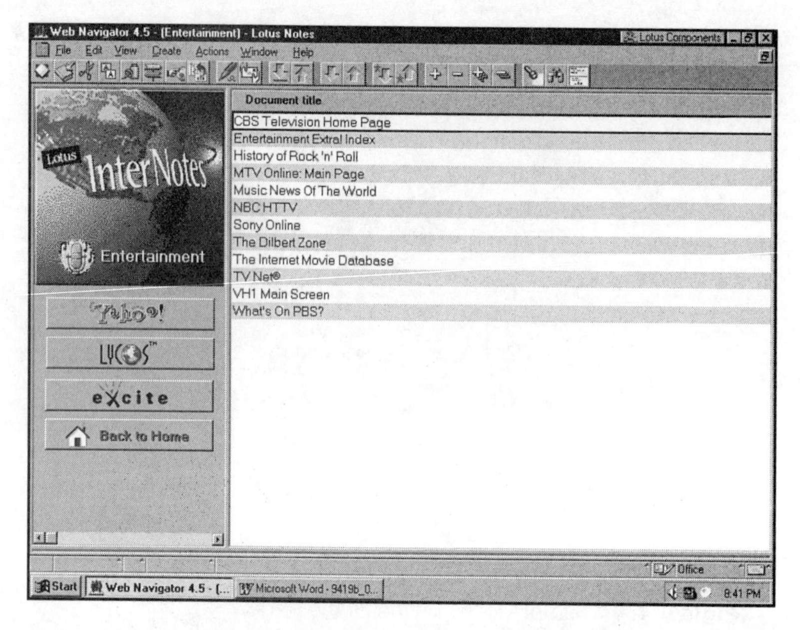

Figure 4.5 The Entertainment navigator.

Figure 4.6 More views, searches, and user's guides.

Table 4.1 The Default Icons

Icon	*Description*
Database Views	Takes you to the View Navigator where you can see a list of the Web pages already stored in the database
Recommended	Opens the Recommended Navigator where you can see the Rated documents

Icon	*Description*
Directory Search	Displays a search form that lets you perform searches with Internet search engines. Lesson 11 discusses search engines in more detail.
Open URL	Displays a dialog box in which you enter the URL of a Web page in order to open it
User's Guide	Accesses the online Web Navigator user's information

When you or another user retrieves a page off the Web, the Server Web Navigator turns it into a Notes document. That document gets stored in the Server Web Navigator database. To see the Notes version of these documents, open the Database View.

1. Click the Database Views icon at the bottom of the home page.
2. The View Navigator appears (see Figure 4.7).
3. Click the **All Documents** button, if you're not already seeing a list of all the documents in the database.
4. Double-click a document to read it.

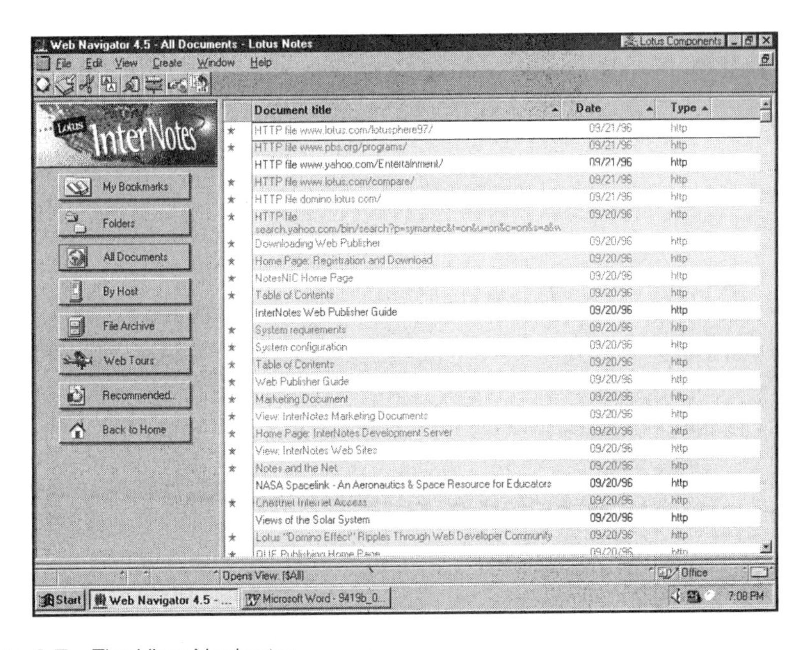

Figure 4.7 The View Navigator.

Table 4.2 The View Navigator Buttons

Button	*Click this Button to*
My Bookmarks	Open pages you saved in your Bookmarks folder. To add a page to the Bookmarks folder, drag and drop the page onto this button. You add pages to the Bookmarks folder from the Web by clicking Bookmarks, selecting My Bookmarks in the Move to Folder dialog box, and clicking Add.
Folders	See traditional folders instead of the View Navigator.
All Documents	See all the Web pages stored in this database.
By Host	Show all the Web pages stored in the database by their host site.
File Archive	See all the Web pages with file attachments.
Web Tours	Display all the saved Web Tours.
Recommended	See the Recommended Navigator.
Back to Home	Return to the Home Navigator.

Click the **Back to Home** button to return to the Home Navigator or press **Esc**.

The home page has one more button we haven't explored, Our Home. This button takes you to your company home page, if your company has one, or to a sample home page for the Notes Network Information Center. However, given the customization available to Notes administrators and application developers, your Home Navigator might not have this button or might have a button with a different label. If Our Home is there, give it a try!

The Action Bar

To access the Server Web Navigator window, double-click any document contained in the database. The action bar buttons at the top of the Server Web Navigator window (see Figure 4.8) help you browse the Web.

Figure 4.8 The Action Bar of the Server Web Navigator.

Table 4.3 Action Buttons

Button		*Click to*
Home	Home	Go back to the Home Page Navigator.
Open	Open	Open the Open URL dialog box.
Previous		Go to the previous page in the History file.
Next		Go to the next page in the History file.
History	History	Open the History dialog box to save pages to the history or go to other pages listed in the history.
Reload		Reload the current Web page from the Internet server.
Recommend		Open the dialog box to enter your rating of the current Web page.
Forward	Forward	Forward the Web page through e-mail.
Bookmarks	Bookmarks	Store the current Web page in the Bookmarks folder.

You'll learn more about using the action toolbar in Lesson 9.

The Search Bar

You can use the search bar to enter an URL and then open a Web page, or you can search Web pages for text you enter in the search bar.

If you don't see the search bar, select View, Search Bar.

There are two versions of the search bar:

 Open URL icon

 Search icon

Make sure the proper icon is showing at the left of the search bar for the type of search you want to perform (see Figure 4.9). When you click the Open URL button, the icon toggles to the Search icon as shown in Figure 4.10.

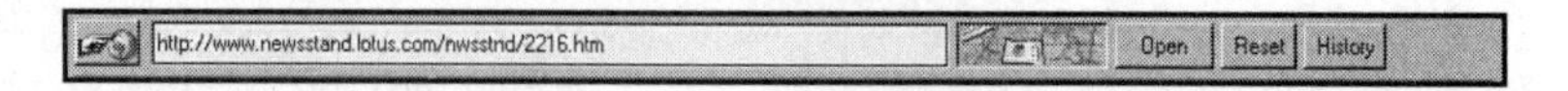

Figure 4.9 The search bar with the Open URL icon showing.

Table 4.4 The Buttons on the Open URL Search Bar

Button		*Description*
Open URL		Sets which type of search bar you're using.
URL Name		Enter the URL you want here.
Progress	Add Condition	Movement indicates activity Indicator on the Web. You can click on this indicator to stop a Web search.
Open	Open	Press to open the specified URL.
Reset	Reset	Press to clear the URL name.
History	History	Go to a particular page if you've saved it in the History.

You'll learn more about opening URLs and accessing Web pages in Lesson 6.

When you want to search for text within the pages of the database, you need to click the Open URL icon to switch it to the Search icon (see Figure 4.10). To search for text, your database must be full-text indexed. For more on full-text indexing, see Lesson 10.

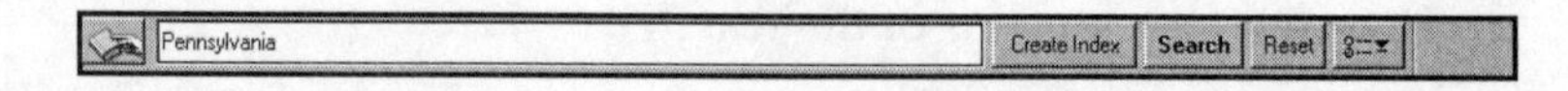

Figure 4.10 The search bar with the Search icon showing.

Table 4.5 The Buttons on the Text Search Bar

Button		*Description*
Search		Sets the search bar to search for text in the database.
Text		Enter the word or phrase you're looking for.
Create Index	Create Index	Use this button if your database is not already full-text indexed.
Add	Add Condition	Replaces the Create Index Condition button after you create a full-text index. When clicked, opens the Search Builder dialog box.
Search	Search	Click this to activate the search.
Reset	Reset	Click this to clear the search string.
Search Menu		Shows a drop-down menu of search options.

In this lesson, you looked at the views, navigators, and documents of the Server Web Navigator. In the next lesson, you'll be doing the same thing for the Personal Web Navigator.

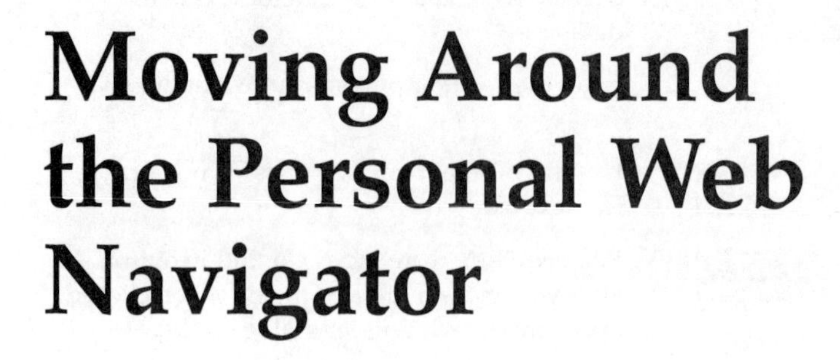

Moving Around the Personal Web Navigator

In this lesson, you'll take a look at the Personal Web Navigator and learn how to move around in it.

Understanding Documents

The Personal Web Navigator is a Notes database that contains views, folders, and documents. Changing views, opening, saving, searching, and finding documents works very much like other Notes databases.

In the Personal Web Navigator, there are two types of documents:

- **Web page** The Web pages are converted to Notes documents when you retrieve them from the Web, but they look and act just as they did on the Web, including the hypertext and links. Web pages make up the bulk of the Personal Web Navigator database. Which Web documents you see are dependent on which Web pages you retrieved. Figure 5.1 shows a typical Web page document.
- **Web Tour** Web Tour documents contain the history of a visit to Web sites so you can retrace a visit later. Web Tour documents are also Notes documents. Creating Web Tour documents is explained further in Lesson 13, "Sharing Web Pages." Figure 5.2 shows a Web Tour document.

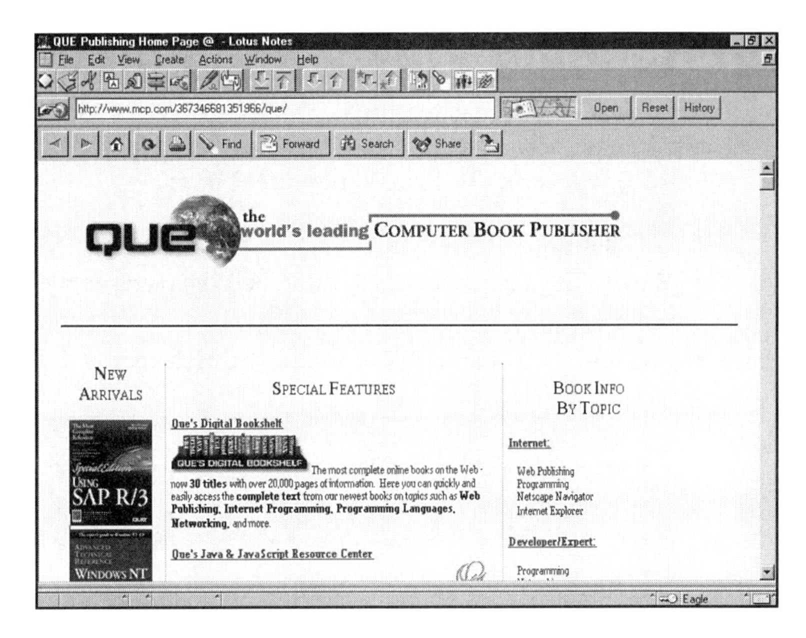

Figure 5.1 An example Web page document in the Personal Web Navigator.

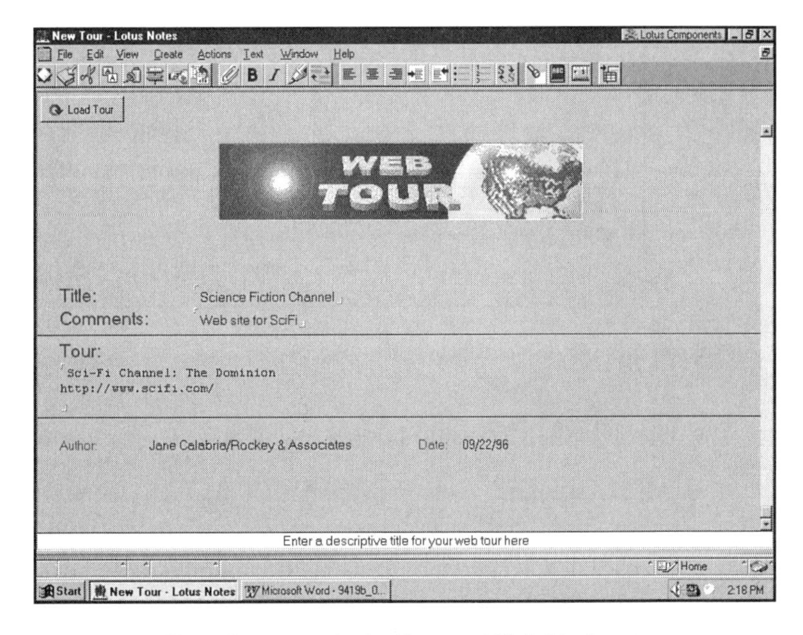

Figure 5.2 A Web Tour document in the Personal Web Navigator.

Understanding Views and Folders

The Personal Web Navigator, unlike the Server Web Navigator, does not have graphical navigators. Its interface resembles that of most Notes databases (see Figure 5.3). The screen is divided into three panes:

- **Navigation** This shows all the views and folders.
- **View** This pane displays a list of the Web pages in the current folder or view.
- **Preview** This particular pane shows the current Web page.

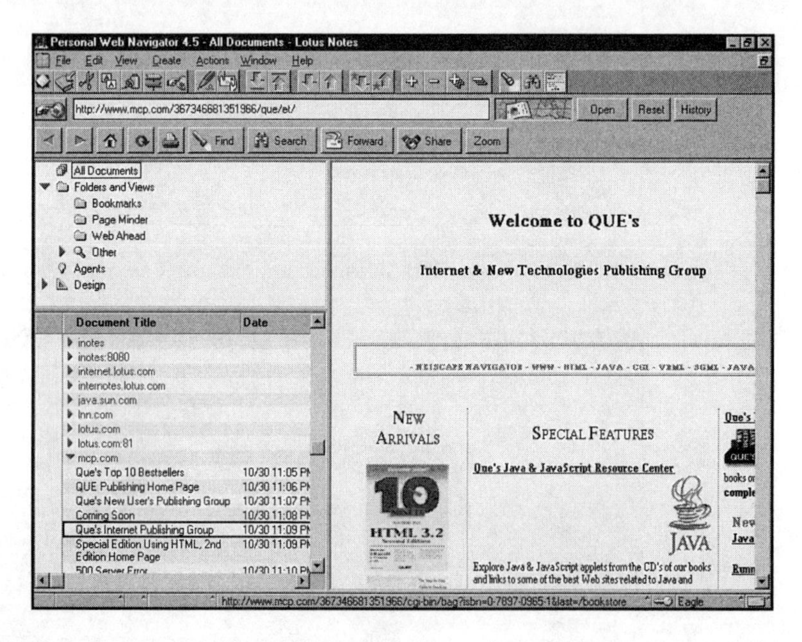

Figure 5.3 The Personal Web Navigator.

The default list of views and folders includes:

- **All Documents** This view shows all the Web pages you retrieved.
- **Bookmarks** Use this folder to save your favorite Web pages for quick access later. To add a page to the Bookmarks folder, drag and drop the page onto this folder. When you're on the Web, add pages to the Bookmarks folder by clicking the **Move to Folder** action button (visible when you are on the Web), selecting **Bookmarks** as the folder, and choosing **Add**.

- **Page Minder** To start an agent that reminds you when a particular Web page changes, drag that Web page onto the Page Minder folder.
- **Web Ahead** To start an agent that retrieves all the URLs on a Web page, drag that Web page onto the Web Ahead folder. The agent will run as scheduled. (More on Web Ahead in Lesson 13.)

The following views are listed under Other, an expandable category. You might have to click on the triangle located next to the word "Other" to expand and see the following views:

- **File Archive** Select this view to see all the Web pages with file attachments.
- **House Cleaning** Select this view to see Web pages listed by size so you know which ones to reduce to a link. Reducing a page to a link will save disk space.
- **Web Tours** Select this view to see all the Web Tour documents you've made.

The Action Bar

The action bar buttons (described in Table 5.1) at the top of the Personal Web Navigator window (refer to Figure 5.3) help you browse the Web.

Table 5.1 Action Buttons

Button	*Click to*
Previous	Go to the previous page in the History list.
Next	Go to the next page in the History list.
Home	Go to the page you defined in Internet Options as your home Web page.
Reload	Reload the current Web page from the Internet server.
Print	Print the current page.
Find	Find pages from any of the views or find text on a Web page.
Search	Use the Internet search engine you specified in Internet Options.
Forward	Forward the Web page through e-mail.

continues

Table 5.1 Continued

Button	*Click to*
Share	Share the Web page according to the specifications you made in Internet Options.
Zoom	Go to a full-page view of the Web page.

You'll learn more about using the action toolbar in Lesson 9.

The Search Bar

You can use the search bar to enter an URL and then open a Web page, or you can search Web pages for text you enter in the search bar (see Table 5.2). If you don't see the search bar, select **View**, **Search Bar**. There are two versions of the search bar—one for opening the URL and the other for searching text:

The Open URL icon

The Search icon

Make sure the proper icon is showing at the left of the search bar for the type of search you want to perform. When you click the Open URL button (see Figure 5.4), the icon toggles to the Search icon and vice versa.

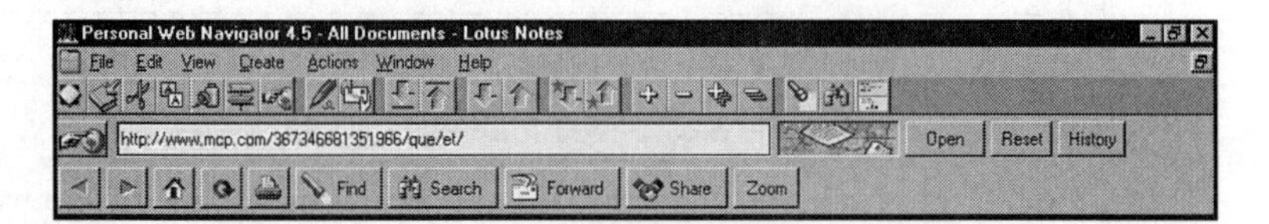

Figure 5.4 The search bar with the Open URL button showing.

Table 5.2 The Buttons on the Open URL Search Bar

Button	*Description*
Open URL	Sets which type of search bar you're using.
URL Name	Enter the URL you want here.
Progress Indicator	Displays a graphic which is animated when Notes is retrieving a Web page.

Button	*Description*
Open	Press to open the specified URL.
Reset	Press to clear the URL name.
History	Go to a particular page if you've saved it in the History.

You'll learn more about opening URLs and accessing Web pages in Lesson 6.

When you want to search for text within the pages of the database, you need to click the Open URL icon to switch it to the Search icon (see Figure 5.5). To search for text, your database must be full-text indexed (see Table 5.3). You'll learn more about full-text indexing in Lesson 11.

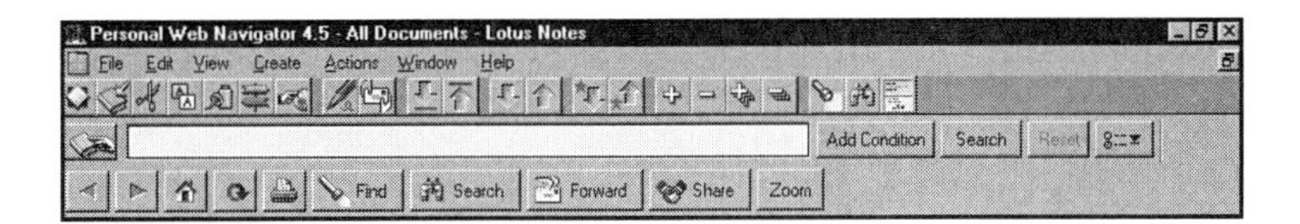

Figure 5.5 The search bar with the Search icon showing.

Table 5.3 The Buttons on the Text Search Bar

Button	*Description*
Search	Sets the search bar to search for text in the database.
Text	Enter the word or phrase you're looking for.
Create Index	Use this button if your database is not already full-text indexed.
Add Condition	If your database is full-text indexed, use the Add Condition button to further refine your search criteria.
Search	Click this to activate the search.
Reset	Click this to clear the search string.
Search Menu	Shows a drop-down menu of search options.

You'll learn more about searching the database and Web pages in Lesson 11.

In this lesson, we introduced you to the Personal Web Navigator screen and how to see its views, folders, and documents. In the next lesson, you'll visit a Web site.

Visiting a Web Site

In this lesson, you will visit some Web sites. You'll also learn about reading URLs, and you'll view your Web pages in both the Personal and Public Web Navigator databases.

Reading URLs

Every file on every computer on the Internet has an address at which it can be located. All Internet computers use something called Uniform Resource Locators, or URLs, to specify the locations of files. An URL looks something like this:

http://www.mcp.com/que/file name

and is broken down into four basic parts, each with its own unique name and function:

Protocol//name of computer and Internet domain/directory/file name

- The protocol indicates the type of resource being described. In the preceding example, the resource type, **http**, tells us the document is a Web page and tells the computers to use the Hypertext Transport Protocol to transfer the file to your computer.
- The name of the computer and Internet domain follows the protocol, and is preceded by a double slash. The computer name consists of three parts:

  Its host name, in this case **www**.

  The domain it is in, in this case **mcp**.

  Its super domain, in this case **com**, meaning that mcp is a commercial enterprise.

- The directories precede the file name and are separated from each other (if there is more than one directory) and the file name by single forward slashes.

- The file name comes immediately after the directory. It is separated from the directory by a single slash. The file may be located in the root directory or a subdirectory.

When you want to tell your computer to locate a file, you can enter the file's URL by typing it in manually. Or, the URL may be embedded in the image on your screen, so that, for example, if you click a highlighted word, your browser reads "behind" that word an URL for another file or page, and goes and retrieves that resource.

Deciphering URLs

URLs seem a little backwards because you read them from right to left. The rightmost location is the file name, next is the directory, followed by the zone, then the name of the computer, and finally the protocol. Now, you won't always know the file name (which is the name of the page) you are looking for, so it's not unusual to visit a site by typing the protocol and the name and domain of the computer:

http://www.mcp.com

The last (or, first if you read from right to left) piece of information, the domain, can be interpreted by you. There are three-letter domains and two-letter domains. Two-letter domains indicate a country and are used widely outside of the United States. Three-letter domains indicate a domain *type* such as "com" for commercial and are used mostly within the United States. Tables 6.1 and 6.2 list some two-letter and three-letter domains.

Table 6.1 Partial Listing of Three-Letter Domains

Domain	*What It Represents*
com	Commercial establishments
edu	Educational institutions (schools, colleges)
gov	Government agencies and departments
int	International organizations
mil	Military sites
net	Networking organizations
org	Professional organizations

Table 6.2 Partial Listing of Two-Letter Domains

Domain	*What It Represents*
AU	Australia
CA	Canada
FR	France
IE	Ireland
IL	Israel
JP	Japan
NL	Netherlands
TW	Taiwan
UK	United Kingdom
US	United States

Visiting a Web Site

Are you ready to visit a Web site? There are several ways to accomplish this. For this lesson, you'll learn the quickest and easiest technique.

TIP **Wrong Address?** When typing addresses, it's important to use the exact space, periods, symbols, and capitalization you see in the examples. Typing the address incorrectly could result in failing to locate the Web site you are seeking.

1. Select **File, Open URL** from the menu.
2. The Open URL dialog box will appear (see Figure 6.1). Type **www.mcp.com/que** (you don't need to type the protocol, HTTP; Notes will fill that in for you). This is the URL for the Que Books division of the Macmillan Computer Publishing Company.
3. Click the OK button.
4. After a few moments, you should now see the home page for Que Books (a good resource for purchasing books for all of that new software you keep getting at work). It's a big home page, and doesn't fit within your screen, so use the scroll bars or Page Up or Page Down to examine this page.

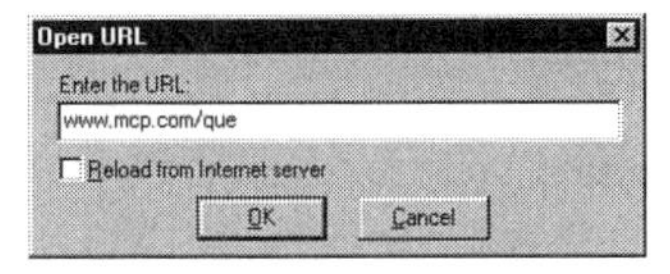

Figure 6.1 The Open URL dialog box.

5. Notice the blue text on the screen? This is an example of *hypertext* that we discussed in Lesson 1. If you place your mouse on hypertext, you'll see your cursor change from a pointer to a hand. Try it! Hold your mouse over the words `Que's Software Library`.

   You'll also notice that if you hold your mouse pointer over the graphics on this page, your cursor will change from a pointer to a hand. It's very likely that the page you are seeing will differ slightly from the one you see in Figure 6.2.

Figure 6.2 The Que Books home page showing hypertext.

Also, Web pages change all the time. New information is added; designs might be updated so it would be fruitless for us to walk you through too many pages on this site, because the links, text, and information will be different. But you can continue this little "surf" on your own. Click text and navigators to move around the site.

CAUTION

Can't Get There? Earlier, we mentioned that access to the Internet can be and is often controlled by your company. If you're using the Public Web Navigator and can't reach any of these Web sites, call your Help Desk or your Notes Administrator and ask for site addresses that you *can* access. Write down a few and simply replace those addresses with the three we have given you here.

After you've moved around a few pages, leave this Web site and go check out the solar system. Click the Open icon on the action bar as shown in Figure 6.2. In the Open URL dialog box, type **http://bang.lanl.gov/solarsys/**. After a few moments, you should see something similar to Figure 6.3.

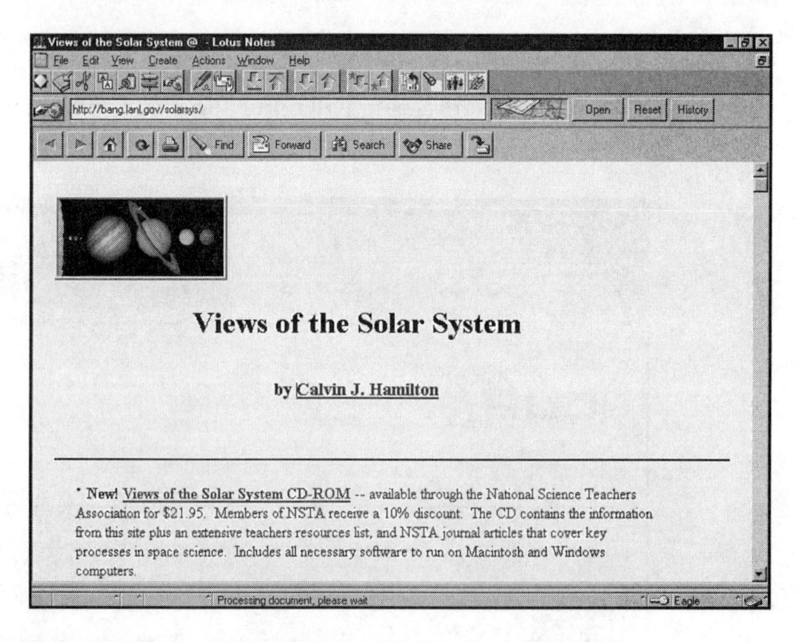

Figure 6.3 http://bang.lanl.gov/solarsys/.

After you've roamed around a litte on this page, go look at one more space site: NASA's site, which includes the shuttle launch schedule (see Figure 6.4). Click the **Open** icon on the action bar and in the Open URL dialog box, type **http://spacelink.msfc.nasa.gov**.

Let's leave the Web and learn more about Web sites while you are disconnected. It's easy to disconnect—just click the **Home** icon on the action bar.

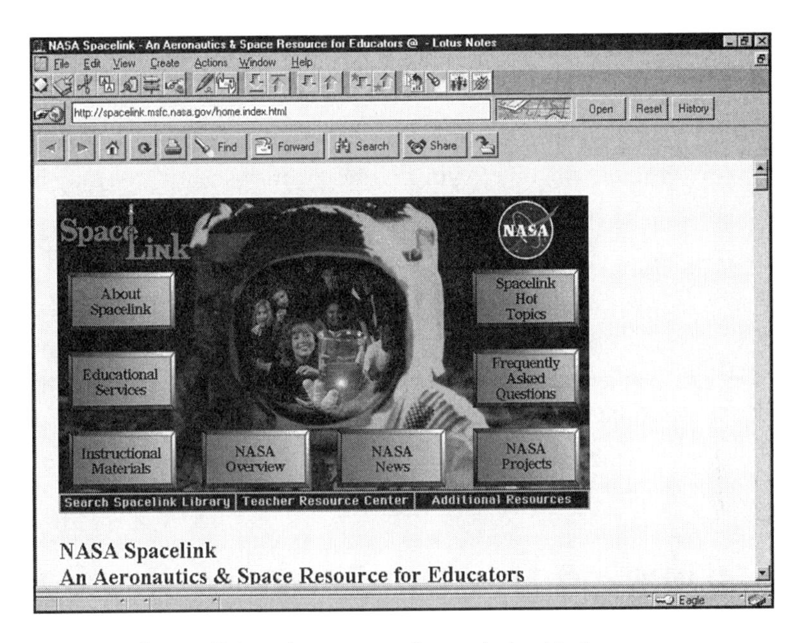

Figure 6.4 http://spacelink.msfc.nasa.gov/home.index.html

Understanding Caching

A cache is a storage bin (or directory). *Caching* is to send files to the storage bin. When you use the Public Web Navigator, each page that you visit on the Internet is converted to a Notes document and cached into the Web Navigator database on your Notes server. (Yes, each and every one!) If you are using your Personal Web Navigator, the pages are stored in your Personal Web Navigator database.

If you need to see a page again, you can retrieve the document from the Notes database copy, instead of going back to the Internet. (It's much faster that way.) Of course, the cached document you're retrieving from the Notes database is *static* (or is unchanging information), and is no longer an HTML page. It is a Notes document.

We've already said that Internet pages change frequently. You might need to see the current page instead of the cached Notes document. To do that, you would simply click the **Reload** button on the action bar. That would force the Notes server to pull the *current* copy of that Web page from the Web, replacing the one you're viewing. If you're using the Personal Web Navigator, you'll need to dial into your ISP to reload from the Internet.

All of this caching can make for a lot of stored pages on the Notes server! There are options available to your Notes Administrator that may be used to solve this problem, such as:

- Purge the documents stored on the InterNotes server.
- Instruct the InterNotes server to delete duplicate copies of pages (what if you visit the same site that someone else in the company visited yesterday? You'd have two copies). By purging duplicate copies, the most current one would be stored as an InterNotes document, the other deleted.
- Instruct the Notes server to delete documents after a specified period of time.

Viewing the Contents of the Server Web Navigator

Accessing stored Notes documents from the Navigator databases is much faster than retrieving the original pages on the Web. In this section, you will learn how to access Notes documents from the Server Web Navigator.

1. Start at the home page of the Public Web Navigator (see Figure 6.5).
2. Click the Database Views icon. The Database Views screen appears (see Figure 6.6).
3. You are now seeing a view that contains the entire contents of the Server Web Navigator Database located on the InterNotes server, as shown in the previous figure. Scroll through the list to find the documents you created by visiting Web sites. Notice the stars on some documents. Just like other Notes databases, those marks represent documents that you have not yet read in this database. The text of those documents is shown in red. The documents from the sites you just visited will undoubtedly display with unread marks.
4. You can find your page by sorting the titles of the documents, or the date column. To change the sort order of each, click the triangle located in the column header of this view.

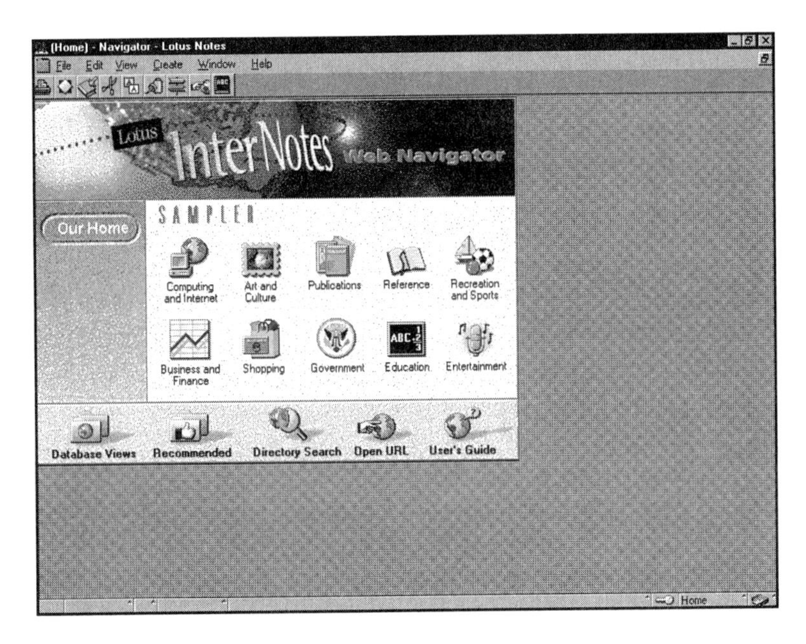

Figure 6.5 The Server Web Navigator Home Page.

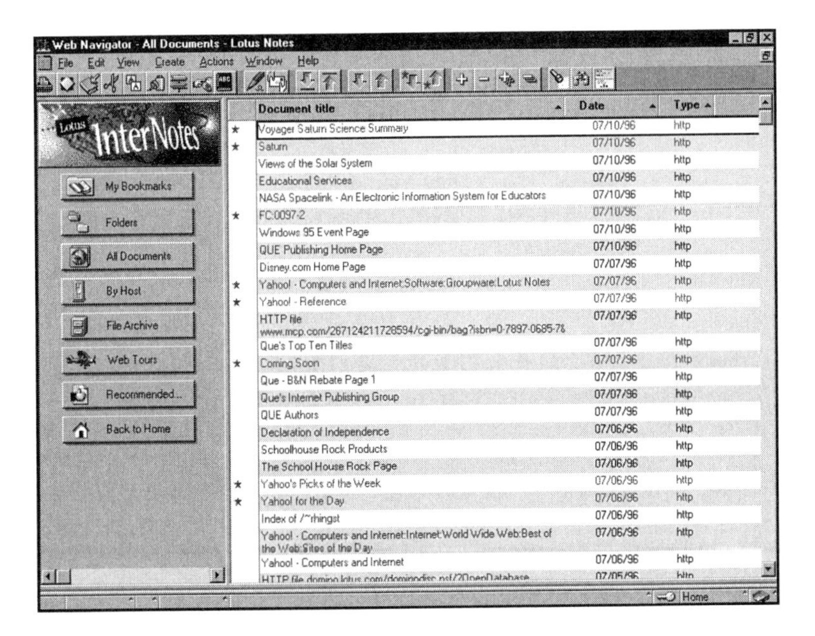

Figure 6.6 The Database View.

5. Find one of your documents (a Web page you just visited in the previous sections of this chapter) and double-click the document name.
6. This is a page you viewed on the Web, cached to the InterNotes server, and converted into a Notes document. If this document were several days old, you could click the Reload button in the action bar, and your InterNotes server would take you back to the Internet and refresh this page with the most current one.
7. What's really impressive about this document is that the hypertext is still "active." If you now click hypertext that you had not clicked while you were on the Web, the InterNotes server will take you back out to the Web to this new page you've never even seen! You can test this by holding your mouse pointer over a piece of hypertext or graphics. See the cursor change to a hand? Double-click, and you'll be surfing once again.
8. After you've completed your latest adventure, return to the home page of the Navigator by clicking the **Home** button.

Viewing the Contents of the Personal Web Navigator

The Personal Web Navigator doesn't have a home navigator like the Server Web Navigator has. Upon opening the database, it looks much like other Notes databases, with a list of available views in the navigator pane on the left of the screen. To open the Personal Web Navigator:

1. Double-click the Personal Web Navigator icon to open the database.
2. Double-click a document to open it.
3. Press **Esc** to exit the page.

Surfing is fun, but there's lots more to it than a few mouse clicks. You'll learn more advanced features in the following chapters.

In this lesson, you visited a few Web sites, used hypertext to move from page to page, and opened a cached Web page converted into a Notes document. In the next lesson, you'll learn some more Web terms and learn more about how hypertext works.

Understanding Links

In this lesson, you'll learn about the different types of Internet links and how they function.

Types of Links

Links are embedded pointers to other Web pages. They appear as colored text, pictures, or buttons. When you use your mouse to point to a link, your cursor might turn into the image of a hand, as you saw in Lesson 6. If you hold down the mouse button while pointing to a link, the Web Navigator status bar will display the URL of the link. When you double-click a link, the Web Navigator will send a request for the page that link points to. Web Navigator knows which page to get, since the URL is embedded in the link.

Host Site is simply a computer that runs a server program and stores files accessible through that server. You can identify a host site by reading the computer name in an URL (see Lesson 6 for help on reading URLs).

Several kinds of links are used on the Web, and they act as pointers to help you reach your destination. It would be impossible for you to know the URL, or address, of every Web page you want to visit. So, Web page designers create links that contain URLs. Point and click, point and click—that's all you really need to do when you're moving around a Web site.

Link? How Can I Tell If It's a Link? It may not be as important to know what *kind* of link you're using, as long as you know it's a link. If you point your cursor to something, and the cursor changes from a pointer to a hand, it's a link!

Graphics Links

A *graphics link* is simply a picture with an embedded pointer (see Figure 7.1). When you double-click the picture, your computer sends out a request for the page or object named in the pointer.

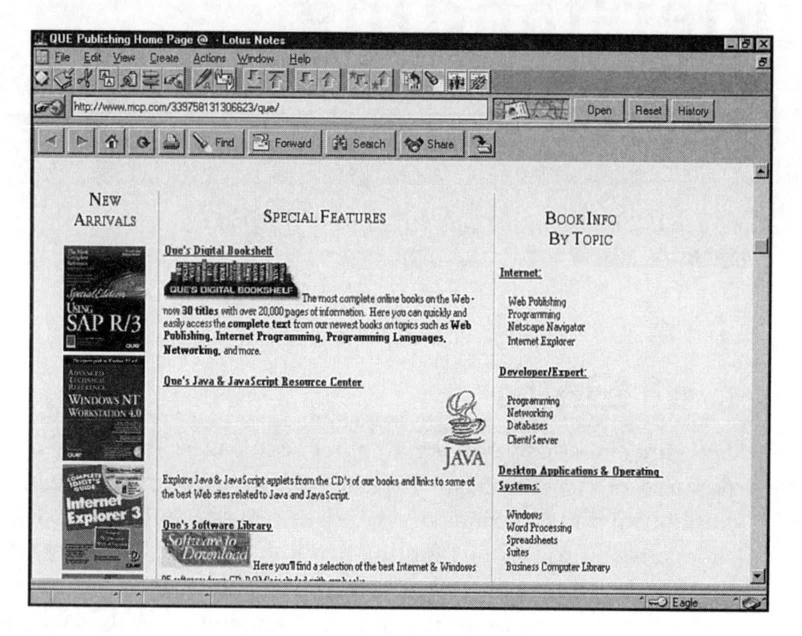

Figure 7.1 Graphics Link.

An *image map* works much the same as a graphics link, except that you can't hold down the mouse button and see URLs. It is a single, usually large and colorful picture that has different portions of it mapped to different pointers. That is, one part of the picture will hold a pointer to Web page x, another part will hold a pointer to Web page y, and a third will hold a pointer to Web page z. You retrieve different pages depending on what part of the picture you click. Click an image map and you're at a new page (see Figure 7.2).

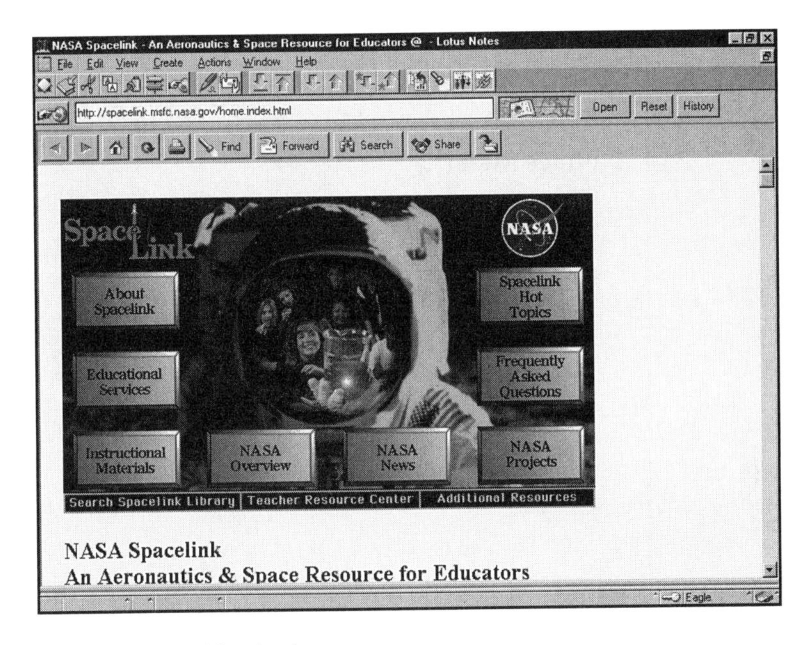

Figure 7.2 An Image Map is shown.

Gopher Links

A *Gopher link* is a link to a Gopher menu. (See Lesson 1 for more information on gophers.) You can recognize a Gopher link because its URL begins with "gopher:". To see the URL embedded in any link, point at it with your mouse and hold down the mouse button (see Figure 7.3). The Web Navigator status bar will display the URL.

TIP **Gopher** Don't forget to include Gopher in your URL or you won't be able to find the Gopher server you're looking for. To address a Gopher site: type **Gopher://name of computer and zone/file name**.

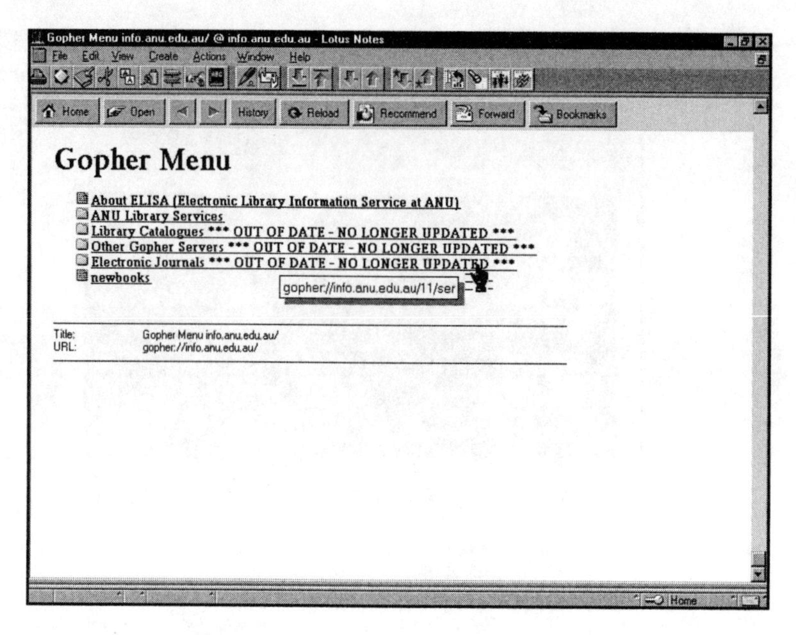

Figure 7.3 Gopher Links.

FTP Links

A File Transfer Protocol (FTP) link is a link to an FTP server (see Figure 7.4). You can recognize an FTP link because its URL begins with "ftp:".

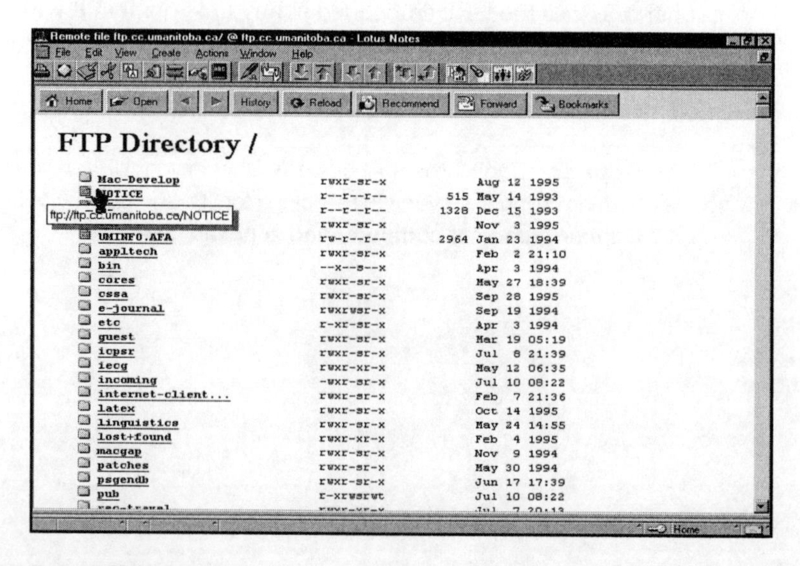

Figure 7.4 FTP Link.

TIP **Remember Your URLs** To reach an FTP server, the URL should read: **FTP://name of computer and zone/file name**.

Mailto Links

A *mailto link* (which begins with "mailto:") pops up a pre-addressed mail memo form when you double-click it. Then, you write the memo and send it. *If* your Notes server is configured for Internet mail and *if* you are using Notes mail, then double-clicking a mailto link would bring up a Notes Mail Memo, with the address line filled out with an Internet address that was contained in the mailto link. (This assures that you won't make any typing errors when typing the address.) Lesson 12 discusses Internet e-mail in more detail.

Hypertext Links

Some links are created by using hypertext. You saw in Lesson 6 what happened when we double-clicked hypertext, but if you hold down your mouse key on hypertext (don't click), the Web Navigator status bar will display the URL.

You've also seen that hypertext is usually underlined, and often in a different color so that it stands out and makes it clear to you that clicking that text will take you to a different page or site. If you return or go back a page after you have visited a linked page, the hypertext will appear in a different color on your screen. This allows you to easily see where you've been. So, if on a home page, you have hypertext displayed in purple that points you to another page, you can visit that page, click to go back home, and the hypertext might now appear in red, distinguishing it from the links you have not visited.

Hypertext originally involved just text. Now it can involve pictures, programs, and video or sound clips. To put it simply, hypertext is something that includes an embedded link to something else (see Figure 7.5).

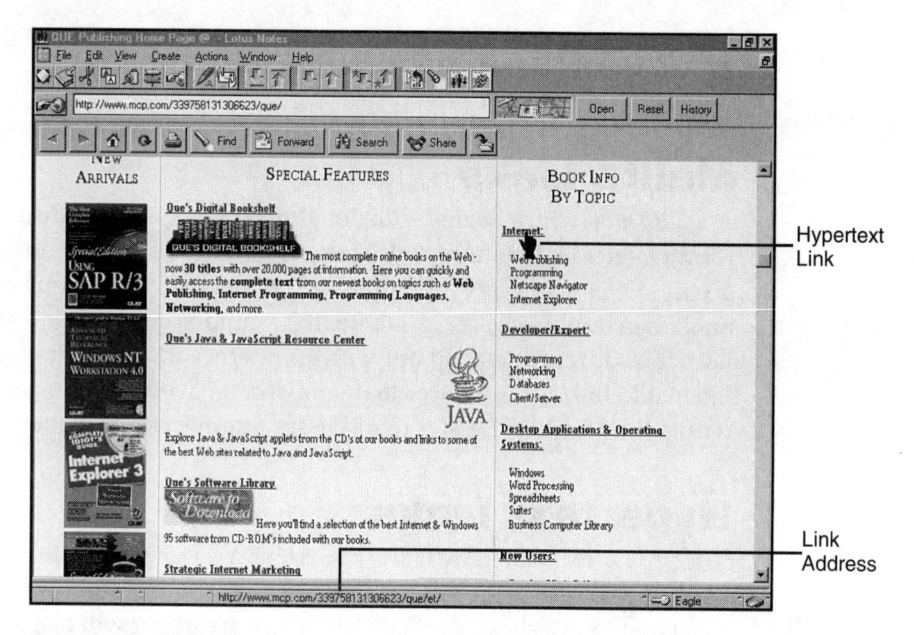

Figure 7.5 Hypertext Link

In this lesson, you learned about links. In the next lesson, you'll learn more about navigating around the Web Navigators.

Interactive Forms on the Internet

In this lesson, you'll learn about filling out forms on the Internet and authenticating with Internet servers.

Filling Out Forms

When you visit a Web site, you might want to provide information to an Internet Server by filling out a form at its site. Some sites will ask general information about you or about your interests in their sites.

Many sites will use HTML forms to gather information. The Web Navigator creates a Notes form from the HTML form so you can fill out the information and submit it back to the Internet. If you receive a response from the Internet server, that response will be saved for you by Lotus Notes. Figure 8.1 shows a typical Web form for supplying information to an Internet Server.

Figure 8.2 shows a typical response sent by the Internet Server after you have submitted a form.

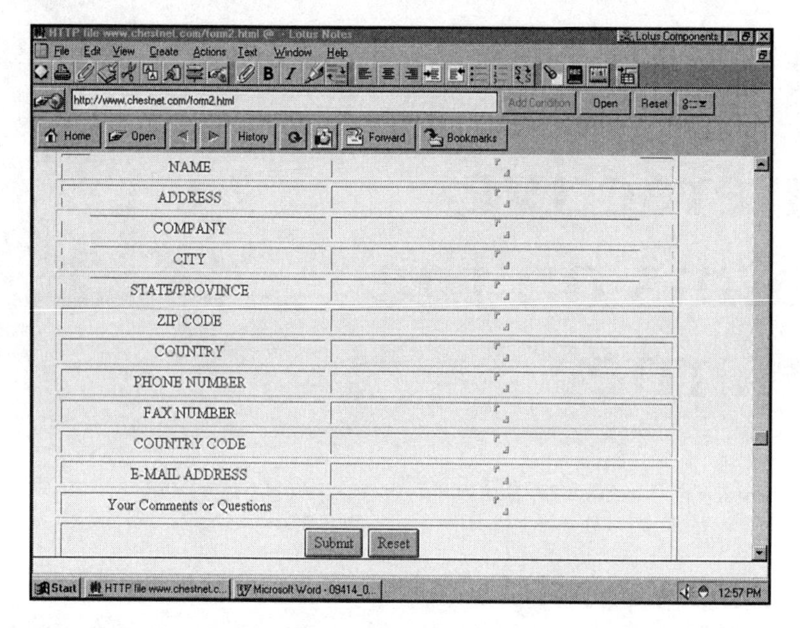

Figure 8.1 Filling out a Web form.

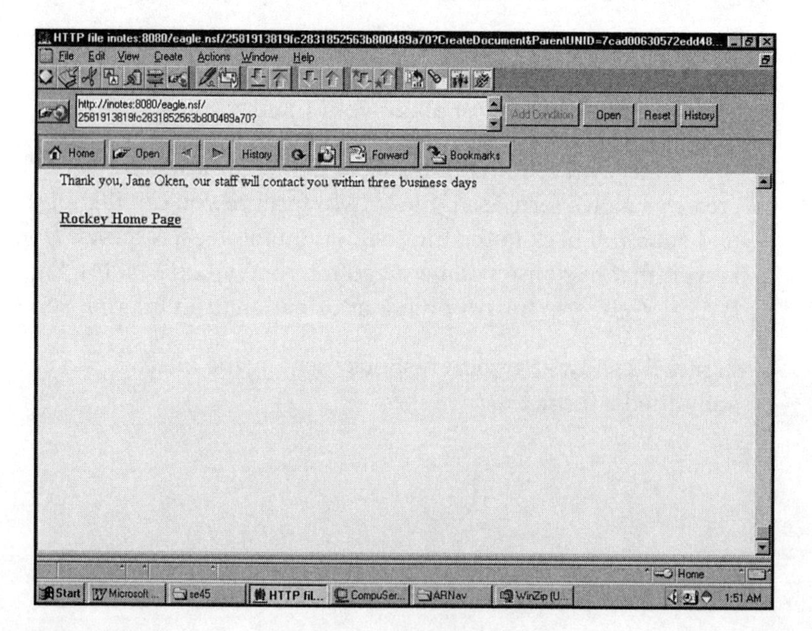

Figure 8.2 Receiving a submit response from an Internet Server.

Authenticating with Internet Servers

Some Internet sites will require that you verify who you are before you can access certain pages or information. You'll be required to supply a name and a password. That name and password might be provided to you via e-mail by the host site, or in some cases, you can register online. Once you fill out a form, you will either be assigned a password by the company whose site you are visiting, or you will be able to create your own password. The next time you visit the site, you will see a request to authenticate as shown in Figure 8.3. Fill in your name and password, and access will be granted to you.

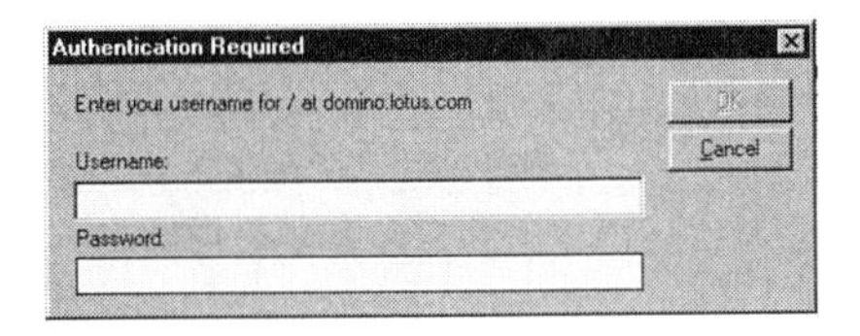

Figure 8.3 Request to authenticate.

If you are registering for, or visiting an authenticated site while using the Server Web Navigator, Notes will encrypt and save these response documents in a private folder. When Lotus Notes creates this private folder, you'll see the message as shown in Figure 8.4.

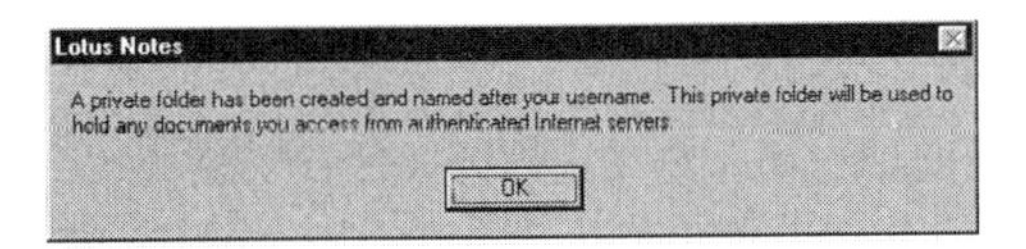

Figure 8.4 Private folder creation dialog box.

The folder is created only when you are authenticating the Internet. The purpose behind this folder is security. If you are a member of some exclusive group on another Internet Server, then the information you see and retrieve while at that Web site should not be accessible to other Notes users in the shared Public Web Navigator. Therefore, Notes creates a private folder to which only you have access. The name of the folder is your name, and the folder is located on the server. Only you will be able to see it. To access the folder:

1. Open the **Public Web Navigator Database**.
2. In the Home Page Navigator, select **Database Views**.
3. In the View Navigator, select **Folders**.

4. Double-click your folder to see its contents.
5. Double-click any document in the folder to view it.

Figure 8.5 shows the folder view of the Public Web Navigator with a private folder.

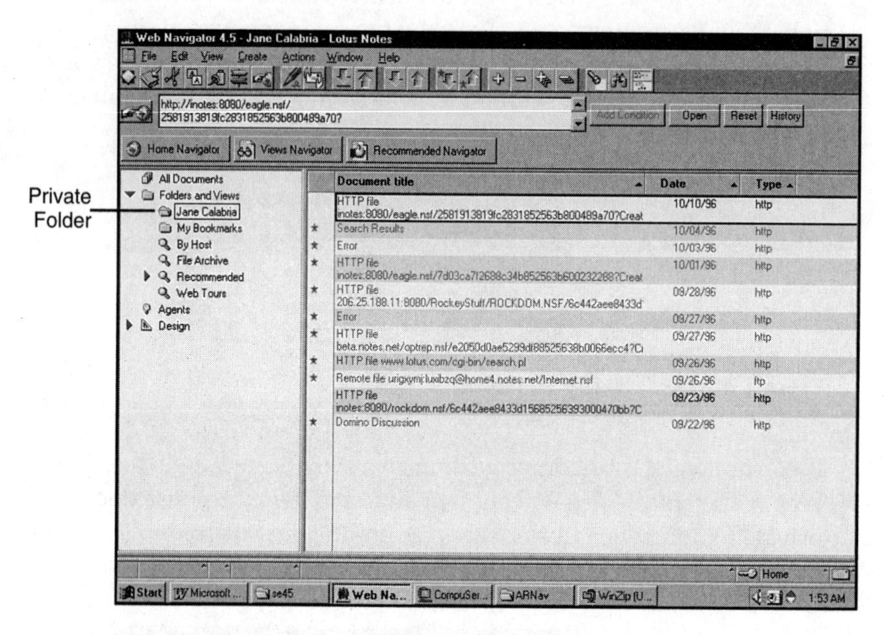

Figure 8.5 Private folder on the Public Web Navigator database.

In this lesson, you learned about filling out forms on the Internet, authenticating with Internet servers, and about private folders on the Public Web Navigator. In the next lesson, you'll learn about SmartIcons and how to manipulate them.

Using SmartIcons

In this lesson, you learn about SmartIcons and how to manipulate them to your liking.

Using SmartIcons

SmartIcons (a Lotus term) are the icons located on the toolbar. Most of your Windows products contain a toolbar with icons that act as shortcuts or alternatives to using the menu. Some people find it faster to click a SmartIcon than it is to look through the menus to find choices such as opening a database or bolding text. Figure 9.1 shows the SmartIcons in the Personal Web Navigator.

SmartIcons in Notes are *context-sensitive*, which means they change depending on what window you have open or what task you're working on. In the Web Navigator, you'll see a slightly different set of SmartIcons when you are looking at document listings than when you're in a Web page. The same is true of the Server Web Navigator.

Figure 9.1 The SmartIcons.

Understanding SmartIcons with the SmartIcons Description

You can have Lotus Notes help you understand the function of each SmartIcon by turning on the feature to show the SmartIcons description. After you elect to show descriptions, a brief description of the icon will appear in a bubble when you hold down your mouse pointer over the icon (see Figure 9.2).

Figure 9.2 The bubble description of the icon.

To have the descriptions appear:

1. Choose **File**, **Tools**, **SmartIcons** from the menu. The SmartIcons dialog box appears.
2. Under **Show**, select **Descriptions**.
3. Click **OK**.

Figure 9.3 Shows the File, Tools, SmartIcons dialog box.

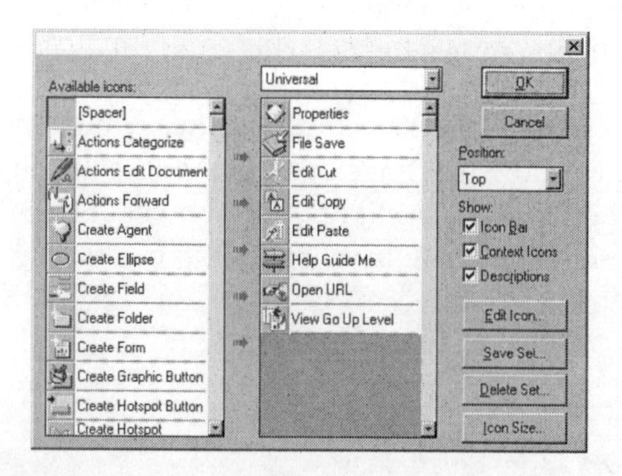

Figure 9.3 The SmartIcons dialog box.

Customizing SmartIcons

You might want to customize your SmartIcon set, adding an icon for a menu choice that you use often. To customize the SmartIcons on your toolbar:

1. Choose **File, Tools, SmartIcons** from the menu.

2. The SmartIcons dialog box will appear (see Figure 9.3). The left panel shows available icons; the right panel shows icons that are currently selected for your Universal Set (the set in use). Scroll through the left panel of available icons until you locate the printer icon that is labeled File Print.
3. Use your mouse to drag the icon you want from the left panel to the right panel. Position it on the right panel in the exact position you want it to appear on your toolbar. The icons after it will move down.
4. Click **OK** to save your changes and close the window. You now see your new icon on the toolbar.

Changing the Size of Your SmartIcons

You can also change the size of your SmartIcons. To do so:

1. Choose **File**, **Tools**, **SmartIcons** from the menu.
2. The SmartIcons dialog box will display. Click the **Icon Size** button. The Icon Size dialog box will appear (see Figure 9.4).

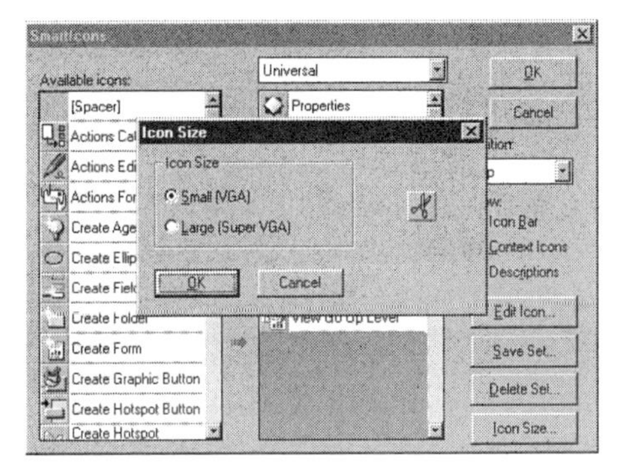

Figure 9.4 The Icon Size dialog box.

3. The default size for icons is small. Select **Large** to change the icon size.
4. Click **OK** to close the Icon Size dialog box.
5. Click **OK** in the SmartIcons dialog box to save your changes and close the window.

Changing the Position of the SmartIcon Palette

You might want to change the position of your SmartIcon palette. The default position for your SmartIcon palette is at the top of the screen. You can select Left, Right, Top, Bottom, or Floating. Figure 9.5 shows a floating palette.

Floating Palette A floating palette is one that is in its own window rather than being anchored on the edge of the screen (as in right, left, top, or bottom). You can move the floating window around the screen by dragging its title bar and you can resize the window by dragging its borders.

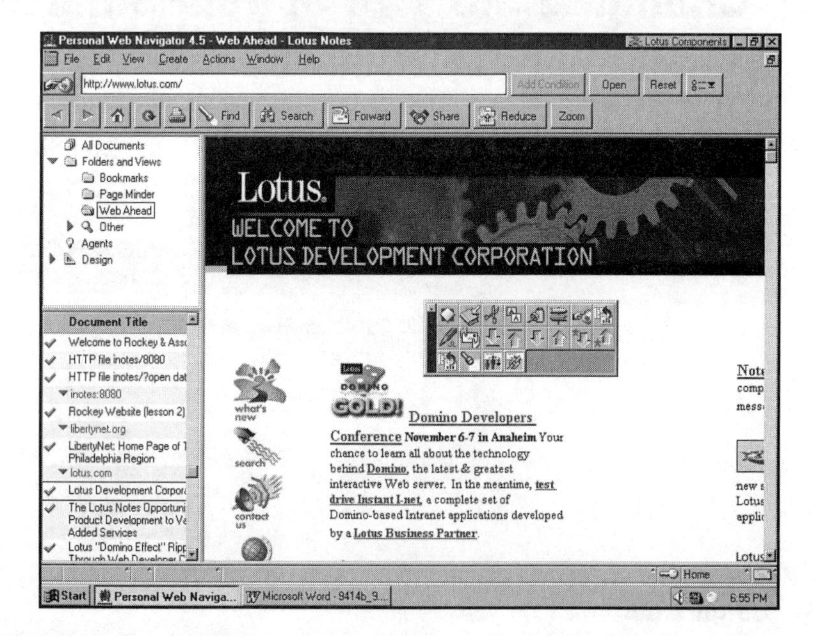

Figure 9.5 The SmartIcons as a floating palette.

To change the position of your SmartIcon palette:

1. Choose **File, Tools, SmartIcons** from the menu.
2. The SmartIcons dialog box will display. Click the **Position** drop-down menu. Select the position you would like for your SmartIcon set. Figure 9.6 shows the SmartIcons dialog box with the position choices displayed.

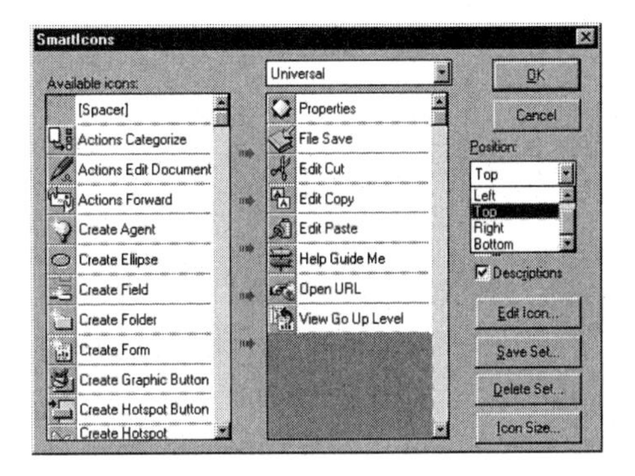

Figure 9.6 Changing the SmartIcons position.

3. Click **OK** in the SmartIcons dialog box to save your changes and close the window.
4. The SmartIcon set will now appear in its new position.

Modifying the Open URL SmartIcon

The Open URL SmartIcon is not unique to the Navigator. You can open a Web page directly from your Notes workspace by clicking Open URL. You don't even have to open the Navigator. However, you can modify the icon to have it open a specific Web page:

1. Choose **File**, **Tools**, **SmartIcons**. Figure 9.7 shows the File, Tools, SmartIcons dialog box.
2. From the list box at the top right of the SmartIcons dialog box, select the SmartIcons set you want to modify (unless you added a set, the only choice is Universal).
3. Click the Open URL icon from the list of available icons.
4. Click **Edit Icon**. Figure 9.8 shows the Edit SmartIcons dialog box.
5. Click **Formula**. Figure 9.9 shows the SmartIcons Formula dialog box.
6. Enter the following formula: **@URLOpen ("URLName")** where *URLName* is the name of the page you want to open.
7. Click **OK**.

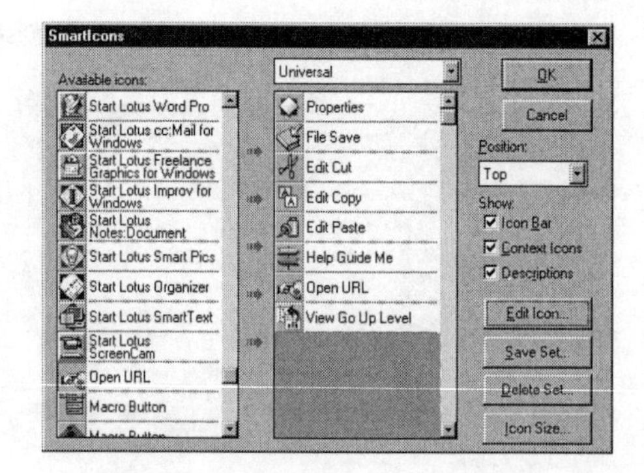

Figure 9.7 The SmartIcons dialog box.

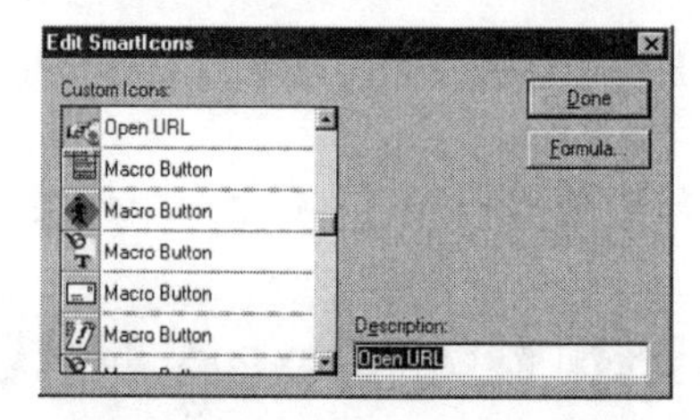

Figure 9.8 The Edit SmartIcons dialog box.

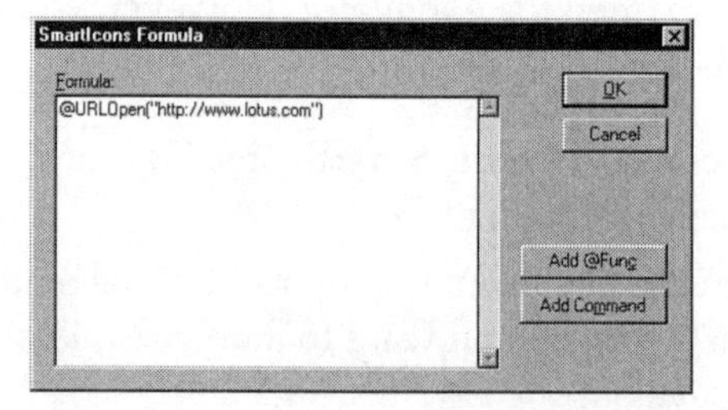

Figure 9.9 The SmartIcons Formula dialog box.

8. Click **Done** in the Edit SmartIcons dialog box.
9. Click **OK**.

For more information on writing Notes formulas, see Part III "Application Development."

Creating a SmartIcon

You might want to make one to search a specific Internet server for information you enter in a dialog box.

1. Choose **File, Tools, SmartIcons**.
2. From the list box at the top right of the SmartIcons dialog box, select the SmartIcons set you want to modify (unless you added a set, the only choice is Universal).
3. Select one of the custom icons from the list of available icons on the left of your screen (you might have to scroll down to see all the available choices).
4. Click **Edit Icon**.
5. Enter a brief description for the icon. Figure 9.10 shows the Edit SmartIcons dialog box.

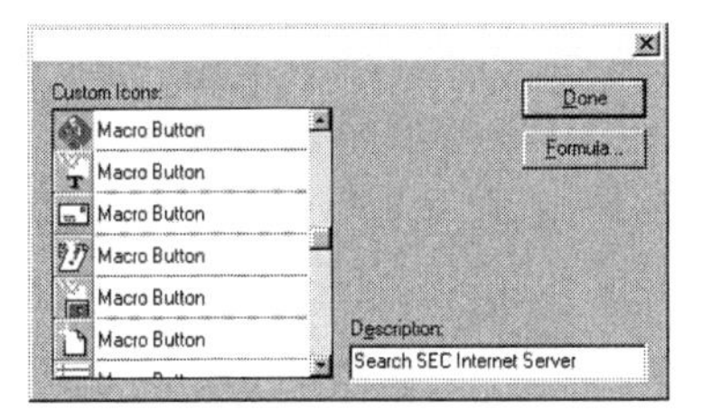

Figure 9.10 The Edit SmartIcons dialog box.

6. Click **Formula**.
7. Enter the following formula substituting a Web address for *URLName* (be certain to use the exact characters and spacing):

   search_string := @Prompt([OkCancelEdit]; "Search Criteria"; "Please enter a search string: "; " "); @URLOpen("URLName" + search_string)
8. Click **OK**.
9. Click **Done** in the Edit SmartIcons dialog box.
10. Click **OK**.

In this lesson, you learned about SmartIcons and how they particularly apply to the Navigators. In the next lesson, you'll learn how to search for information on the Web.

Understanding Notes Searches

In this lesson, you will learn how to index your Personal Web Navigator and how to search both the Personal and Server Web Navigators for information contained in stored documents.

Searching a Database

With Lotus Notes and the Web Navigator(s), there are two kinds of searches you can perform: searching the documents stored in the Web Navigator database(s), and searching for information on the Internet. This lesson deals with searching the database. Lesson 11 covers searching the Internet.

Creating a Full Text Index

Whether you want to search the Personal Web Navigator or the Server Web Navigator, the method is the same with the exception of one initial step. You will need to create a full text index for your Personal Web Navigator in order for Notes to search its contents. You cannot create a full text index on the Server Web Navigator, as you must have designer or manager access to do so. Odds are, your Server Web Navigator has been full text indexed by your Notes database manager. If you are not using the Personal Web Navigator, you can skip this section.

Index The method used by Notes to store the catalogued contents of a database so that Notes can search and locate words or phrases you request. If you search for the word "mail," Notes will return a list of all documents that contain the word "mail."

To index the Personal Web Navigator:

1. At the Notes workspace, right-click the Personal Web Navigator icon to bring up the properties box.
2. Select **Database Properties**.
3. In the Database Properties box, click the tab labeled **Full Text** as shown in Figure 10.1.

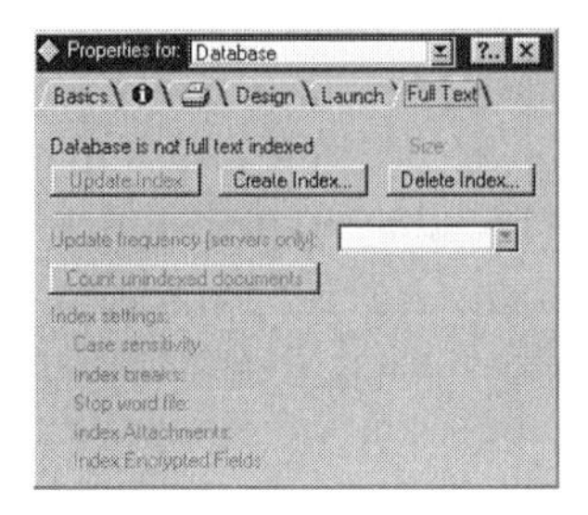

Figure 10.1 The Properties box with the Full Text tab selected.

4. Click the button labeled **Create Index**. The Full Text Create Index dialog box will appear as shown in Figure 10.2.

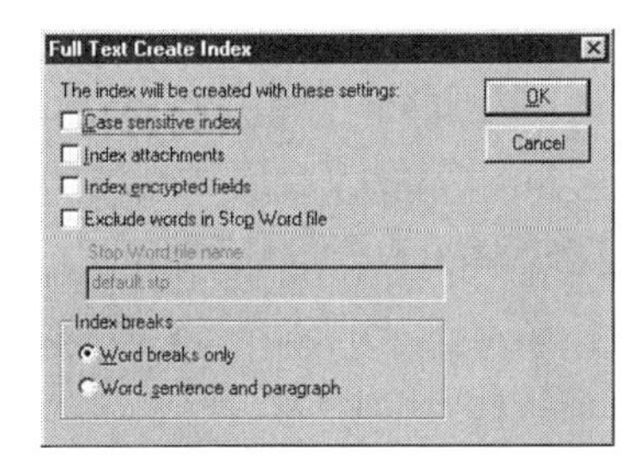

Figure 10.2 The Full Text Create Index dialog box.

5. Select the indexing options you want. Options for indexing are explained in the following list:
   - **Case-Sensitive Index** Checking this makes case-sensitive searches possible. To do a case-sensitive search, you would type "exactcase Apple" to find only Apple and not apple or APPLE. Leaving it blank means that you can't do a case-sensitive search.

- **Index attachments** Indexes attachments that you have stored in the document (such as WordPro documents). If you index attachments, your index file will be much larger than if you elect not to index attachments.
- **Index encrypted fields** This option indexes encrypted text.
- **Exclude words in Stop Word File** Will not include words such as "and," "the," or "is."
- **Word Breaks only** This will ignore the placement of the word in the document. If you search for apple and orange, it will return all occurrences of apple and orange in the same document, even if they are not together on the same page.
- **Word sentence and paragraph** This option searches by proximity. Searching for apple and orange would only return documents in which apple and orange are found in the same sentence or paragraph.

6. Click **OK** to start the indexing. Close the Database Properties box by clicking the "X" in the upper-right corner. The indexing should only take a moment, and you'll know it's finished when you open the database and the search bar appears.

Updating Your Index

Notes will not update your index, so it's up to you to do so manually. To update the index on your Personal Web Navigator:

1. At the Notes workspace, right-click the **Personal Web Navigator** icon to bring up the properties box.
2. Select **Database Properties**.
3. In the properties box, click the tab labeled **Full Text**.
4. Click the **Update Index** button. When the update is finished, close the properties box.

Searching the Web Navigator Databases

The search bar needs to be displayed to search either the Personal or the Server Web Navigators.

To view the search bar in the Web Navigators:

1. In the Server Web Navigator, open the database and select the **Database Views** icon. In the Personal Web Navigator, open the database and from the menu select **View, Search Bar**.
2. Be certain the Search icon is to the left of the Search bar as shown in Figure 10.3. If the Open URL icon is showing, click the **Open URL** icon to toggle to the search icon.

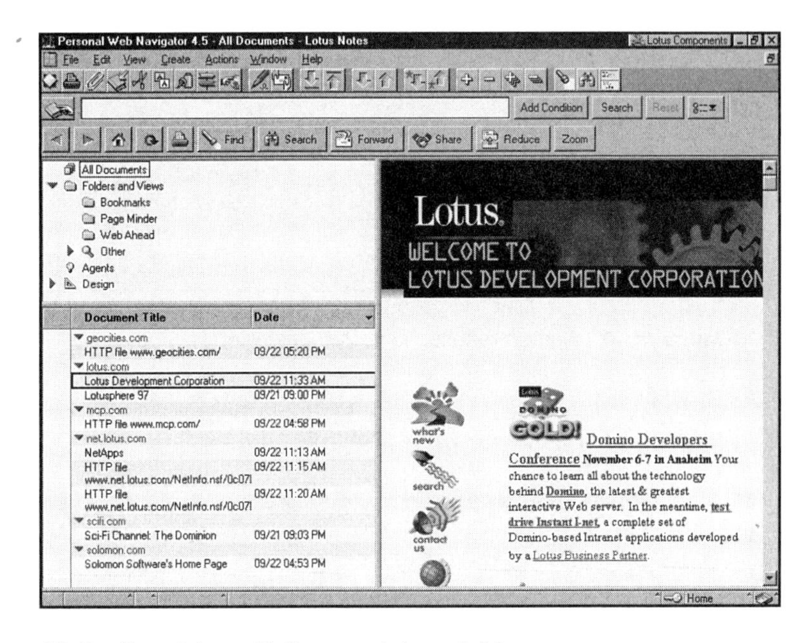

Figure 10.3 Search bar with the search icon visible.

3. Enter the text to search for.
4. Click **Search**.

The results of your search are displayed and weighted according to their occurrence. Figure 10.4 shows the results of a search for the Phrase "Notes 4.5" in the Personal Web Navigator. The documents are listed according to the amount of times the word Lotus was found in the documents, with the highest occurrence first on the list. The dark gray bar indicates that "Notes 4.5" was found more times than in the documents with lighter gray bars. The status bar shows the number of documents containing the phrase "Notes 4.5."

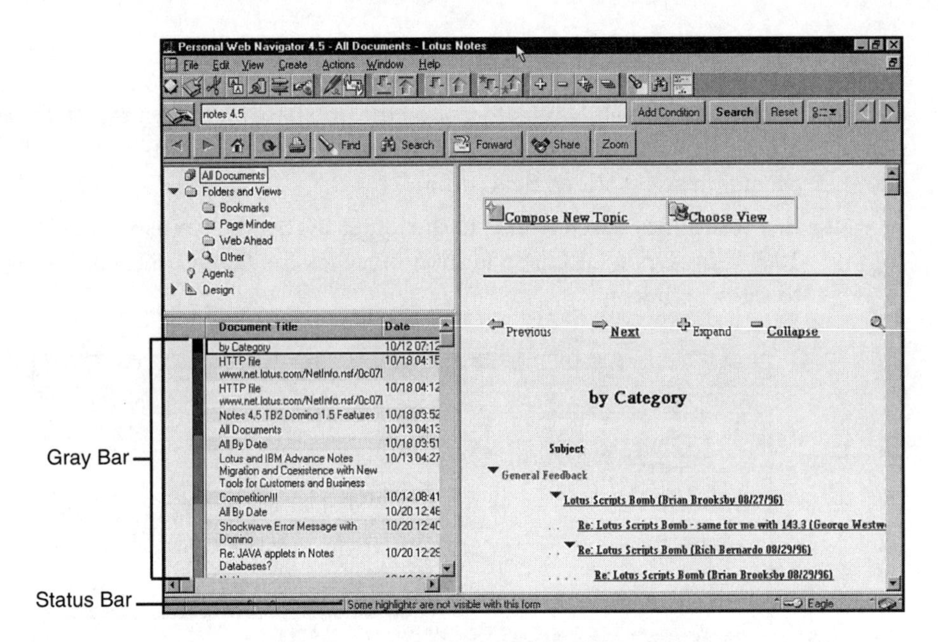

Figure 10.4 Search results in the Personal Web Navigator.

Figure 10.5 shows the results of the search for "Notes 4.5" in the Server Web Navigator. The same gray bar principle applies.

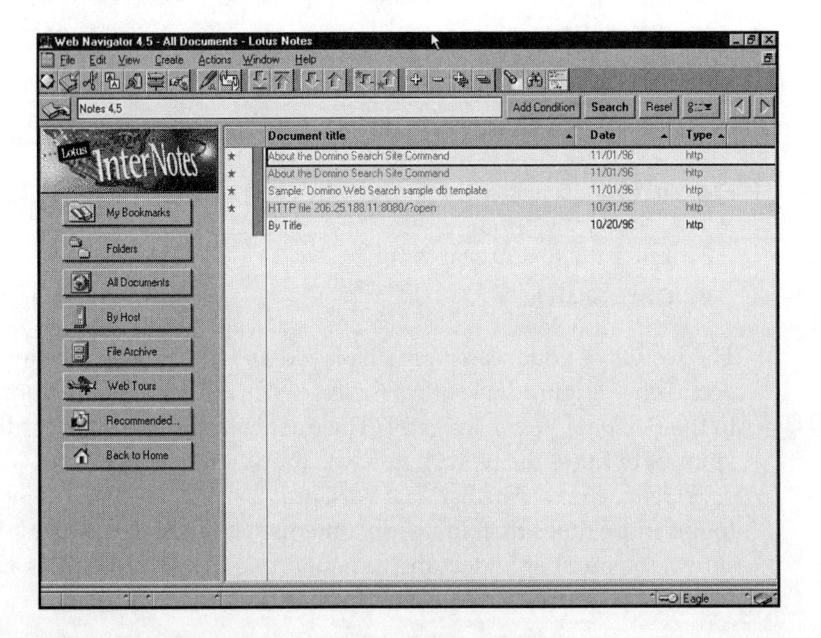

Figure 10.5 Search results in the Server Web Navigator.

When Notes performed the search for "Notes 4.5," it placed a box around each word that matched your search criteria. To view the occurrences of the phrase "Notes 4.5" in documents, double-click a document in either the Personal or Server Web Navigator. Figure 10.6 shows "Notes 4.5" outlined each time it is found in the document.

For example, to find "Lotus" or "Internet":

1. Click the **Reset** button to delete your previous search text from the search bar.
2. Click the **Add Condition** button. The Search Builder dialog box appears as shown in Figure 10.7.
3. Select **Any** in the Search for field.
4. Select **Words and Phrases** in the condition field. Type **Lotus** in the first field and **Internet** in the second field.
5. Click **OK** to add the condition to the search bar.
6. Now click **Search**.

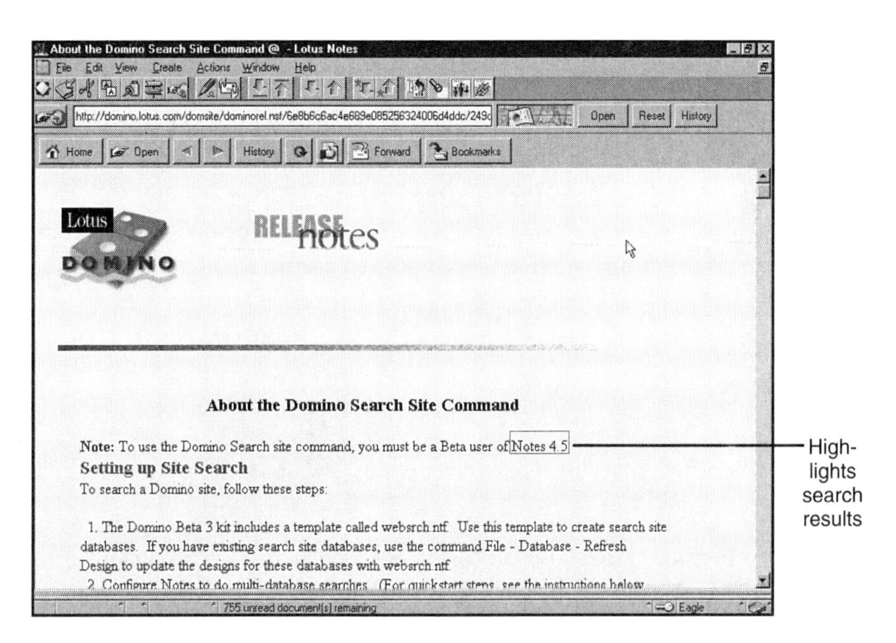

Figure 10.6 Highlighted search results.

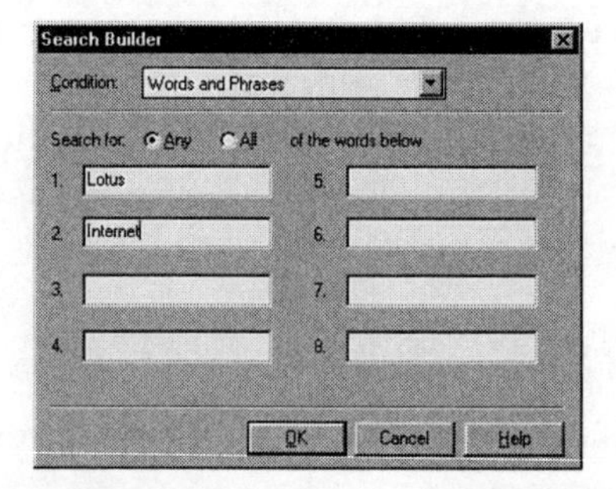

Figure 10.7 Search Builder dialog box.

To find "Lotus" and "Internet":

1. Double-click in the search bar on the search criteria **Lotus Internet**.
2. In the Search Builder dialog box, select **All** in the Search for field.
3. Click **OK** to add the condition to the search bar.
4. Click **Search**.

To save a search, follow these steps:

1. Fill in your search criteria in the search bar.

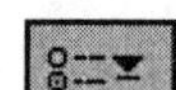

2. Click the **Options** button in the search bar.
3. Select **Save Search As** and give the search a name. Click **OK**.
4. To reuse your saved search, click the **Options** button on the search bar. Select your saved search as shown in Figure 10.8.

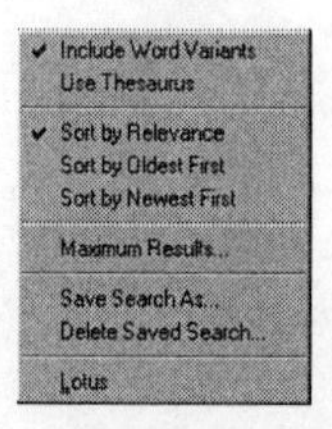

Figure 10.8 Saved search as found in the Options button.

Using Quick Search

Quick Search is available in both the Personal and Server Web Navigators. Quick Search searches categories and document titles only in a view. To perform a Quick Search, simply start typing the word you want to search while in any view in the Navigator(s). Be certain that your cursor is *not* in the search bar. The Quick Search dialog box will appear. Finish typing your word or letter and click **OK**. If you type the letter **P**, Notes will take you to the first document whose title begins with P. Figure 10.9 shows the Quick Search dialog box.

Figure 10.9 Quick Search dialog box.

In this lesson, you learned how to search the Web Navigator databases using a simple Quick Search and a full text search. In the next lesson, you will learn how to search the Internet.

Searching, Saving, and Downloading

In this lesson, you will learn how to use search tools and how to download files from the Web.

Understanding Search Tools

Up until now, you worked your way around the Web by typing in an URL to go to a specific site. But what if you want to search for information on Elvis? You could try typing www.Elvis.com (is this a real Web site?). Or a more efficient way to search the Web is to use a *search tool* (also referred to as a *search engine*). With a search tool you can type "Elvis" and it will search the Web for sites that contain "Elvis" and return to you a list of links pointing to those sites with the most *hits* at the top of the list.

Hit This a match between your search parameters and information found on a home page on the Internet. The more specific your search parameters, the smaller number of hits you will find.

Searching for "Elvis" might return a lot of hits—perhaps thousands, certainly hundreds, and probably more than you need. So, to narrow your search and find a better match, you can supply additional information to the search tool. For example, Elvis AND Sands AND LasVegas AND October 1996 is bound to return fewer hits.

Different search tools maintain different lists of Web pages and after working with a few, you'll find the one you like best. When you select a search tool to use, the Navigators will take you to the home page of that search tool where you can type your search criteria. Although you can use any search tool, the Navigators make it easy for you to choose Yahoo!, Lycos, Excite, or AltaVista (which are some of the more popular search tools available).

Searching with the Server Web Navigator

To access the search tools in the Server Web Navigator:

1. Open the Server Web Navigator database.
2. Click the **Directory Search** icon.
3. Enter your topic to search in the text box as shown in Figure 11.1.

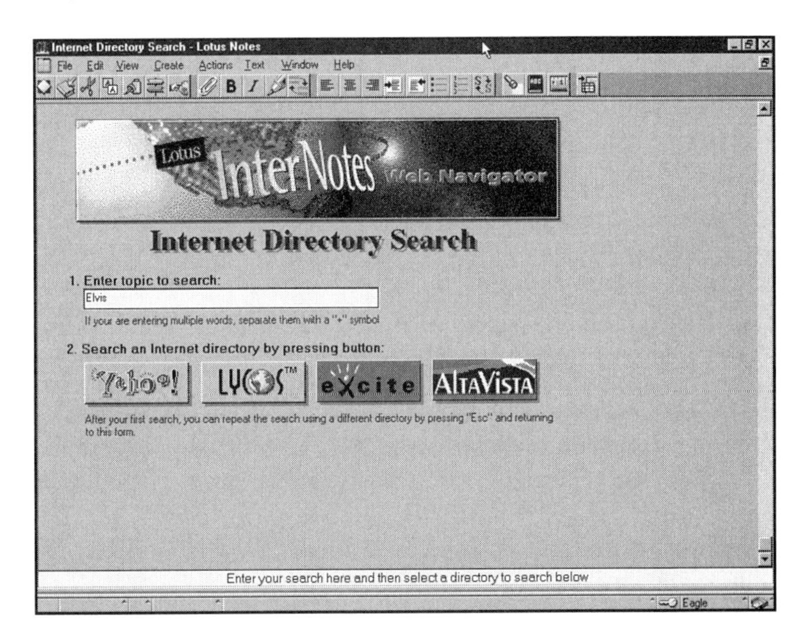

Figure 11.1 Searching for Elvis.

4. Click the search tool you want to use (**Yahoo!**, **Lycos**, **Excite**, or **AltaVista**).
5. Web Navigator takes you to the site you requested (Yahoo!, Lycos, Excite, or AltaVista), and the results of your search are displayed on your screen. Figure 11.2 shows the results of searching Yahoo! for "Elvis."

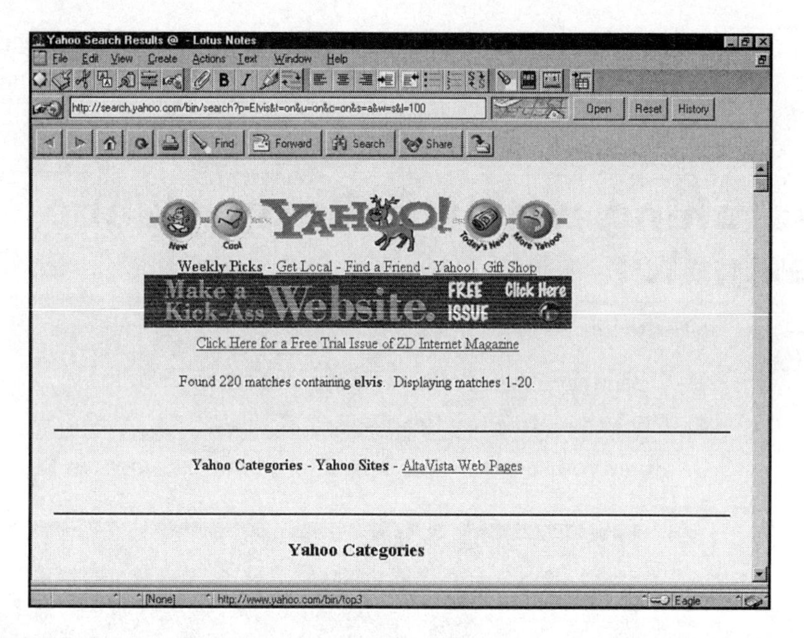

Figure 11.2 Yahoo! finds Elvis.

6. By scrolling down the Yahoo! page, you see some of the links to Elvis sightings as shown in Figure 11.3.
7. You can now scroll through the Elvis list. When you find a page you want to read, click the underlined text.

TIP **Search for Yourself!** If you prefer to use a search tool that is not listed on the home page of the Server Web Navigator, simply use the Open URL command or icon and type the URL of the search tool. You can find some search tool URLs in this lesson under "Understanding Search Tools."

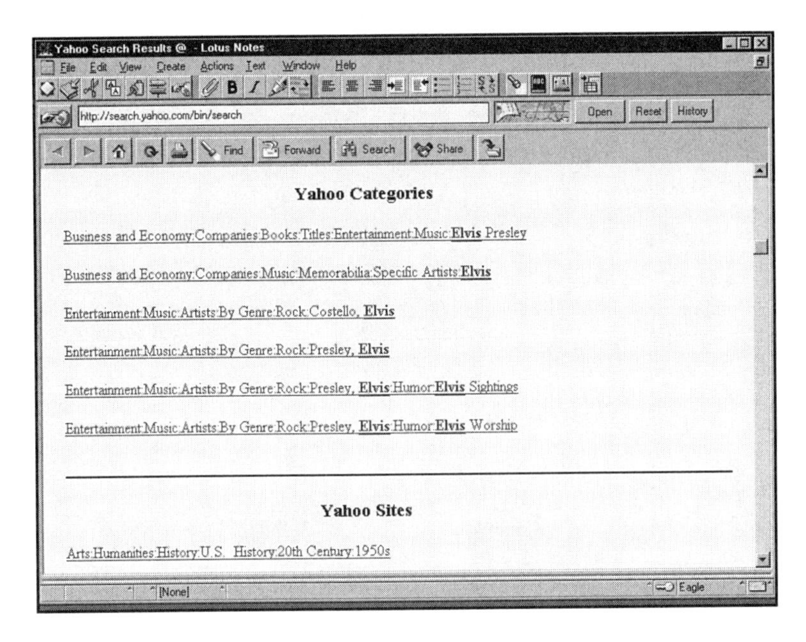

Figure 11.3 Links to Elvis sightings.

Searching with the Personal Web Navigator

The Personal Web Navigator enables you to select your preferred search tool (although it's not quite as intuitive as in the Server Web Navigator). To access a search tool, you can either type in the URL, or you can set a preferred search tool in your Internet Options document. To set a preferred search tool (engine):

1. From the workspace, select the **Personal Web Navigator** and choose **Actions, Internet Options** from the menu.
2. In the **Search Options** section, select the search engine you prefer in the **Preferred Search Engine** field. If you select AltaVista, Excite, Lycos, or Yahoo!, **Save** and **Close** this document. If you choose **Other**, a new field will appear in this section and you must provide an URL in the new text field as shown in Figure 11.4. Then save and close this document.

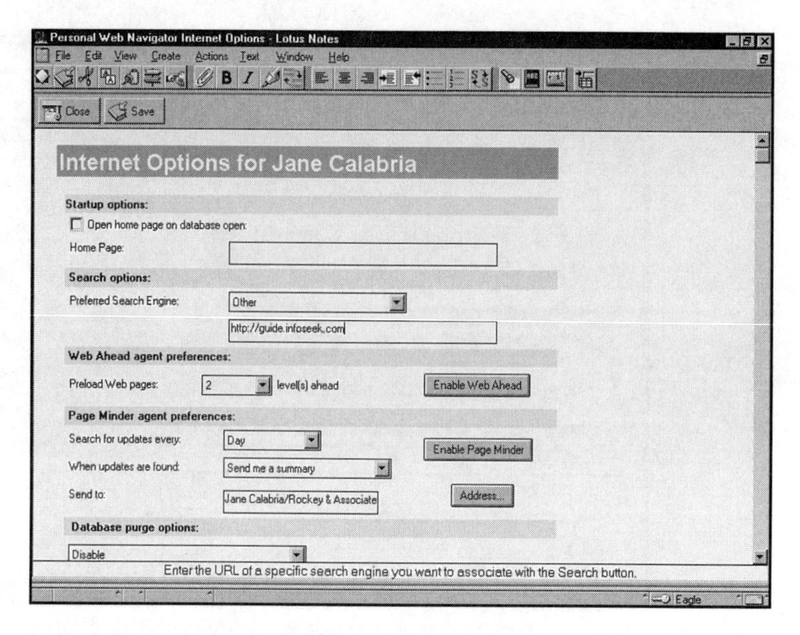

Figure 11.4 Choosing a Preferred Search Engine.

Choosing a Preferred Search Engine

To use the search engine you just selected:

1. Open the **Personal Web Navigator**.
2. Open a page in the database by double-clicking it. It doesn't matter which page you open, but you must have a page open to use the search engine. You can't be in preview mode.

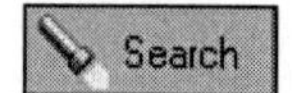

3. Click the **Search** icon on the action bar.
4. The Web Navigator will take you to the Search Engine Web page to start your search.

TIP **Title** You can perform searches on some Web pages. If a Web page is indexed, the Web Navigators will display a search button on the action bar. Often a Web page that is indexed will indicate that it is indexed. Visit **http://www.sec.gov/cgi-bin/srch-edgar** to see an example of an indexed Web page.

Using Bookmarks

Now that you have mastered the science of searching for information on the Internet, let's go over one of the most frustrating experiences that occur with new and experienced users. You initiate a search and drill deeper and deeper down through one layer of information after another. The address of the home page or site you have reached is:

http:\\www.bongo\technotes\dir_423\idea\ohno\iamlost\littlefeat.

The phone rings, the system goes down, you get distracted and did not make note of the address of this very important home page. How do you ever find it again?

You can save the page, with its hotspot links in the Bookmarks folder. When using the Server Web Navigator, the Bookmarks folder is a private folder, stored on the Notes server and its contents are accessible by you only. If your Notes Administrator has elected to periodically purge the Server Web Navigator database, the contents of the Bookmarks folder and any subfolders you create under it will not be deleted during the purge. When using the Personal Web Navigator, the folder is also private but is stored on your hard drive.

Saving in Bookmarks in the Server Web Navigator

To add a page to your My Bookmarks folder while using the Server Web Navigator while surfing the Web:

1. Open the page on the Web.

2. Click the **My Bookmarks** button in the action bar.
3. The Move to Folder dialog box will appear (see Figure 11.5). Select the **My Bookmarks** folder and choose **Add**.

TIP **Drag It!** You can also add a page to the My Bookmarks folder from the Server Web Navigator view pane. Just drag and drop the page into the My Bookmarks Navigator button or folder icon.

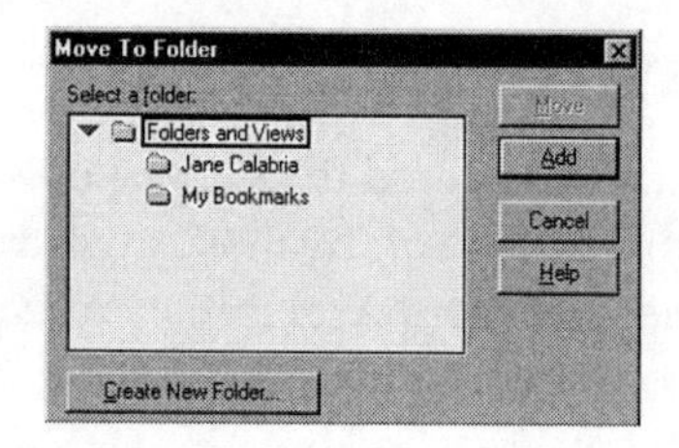

Figure 11.5 Move to Folder dialog box.

Saving Bookmarks in the Personal Web Navigator

To add a page to the Bookmarks folder using the Personal Web Navigator while surfing the Web (these icons will not appear on the action bar when in preview mode, only when you have a document open, or when you are surfing the Web):

1. Click the **Folder** button of the action bar. The Move to Folder dialog box appears.
2. Select the **Bookmarks** folder and choose **Add**.

TIP **Drag It!** To add a page to the Bookmarks folder from the view pane of the Personal Web Navigator, simply drag and drop the page into the Bookmarks folder icon in the navigation pane.

Downloading Files from the Web

When you need to retrieve a file from a Web page, double-click the file name listed in the Web page, click the download option or the Web page, or follow the instructions for downloading. Just prior to the download, a Properties box will appear as shown in Figure 11.6.

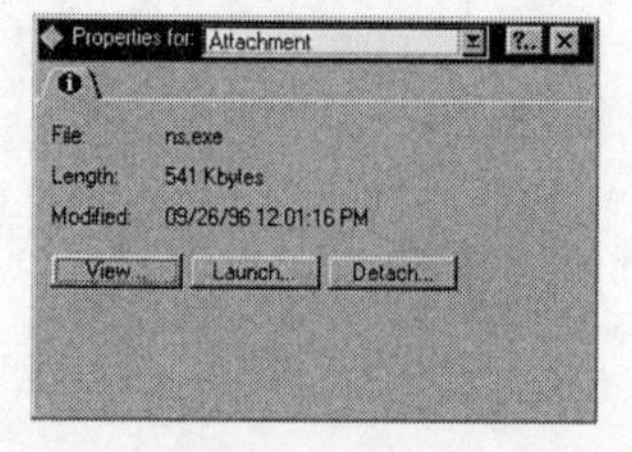

Figure 11.6 Properties box for attachment (download).

Select **Detach**. Select a drive and directory to download the file. Click **Detach**. Now you will see the Save Attachment dialog box, as shown in Figure 11.7.

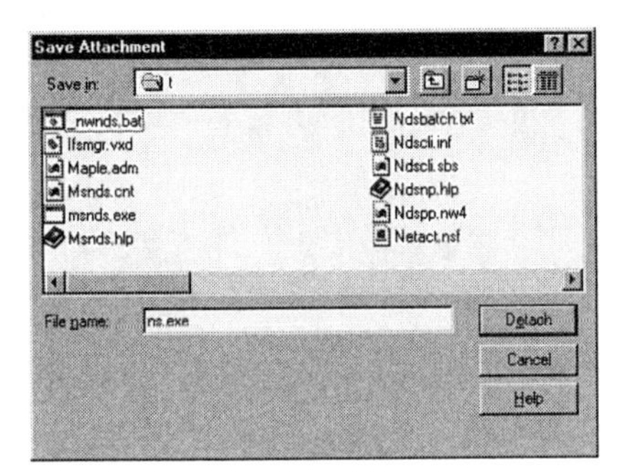

Figure 11.7 Save Attachment dialog box.

In this lesson, you learned about various search tools and how to use them. You also learned how to select a preferred search tool and how to download files from the Web. In the next lesson, you will learn about using history and creating Web Tours.

Using History, Web Tours, Web Ahead, and Page Minder

In this lesson, you will learn how to return to specific pages you've visited, how to save a listing of what you've visited, how to retrieve Web pages that appear as URLs on another Web page, and how to get an alert each time a specific Web page updates.

Using History

While surfing the Web, you might want to go "back" a few pages. Maybe the link you clicked was the wrong link. You can go back or forward a page by clicking the Previous and Next buttons in the action bar of the Web Navigators.

The Previous Button

The Next Button

You can see a list of Web pages you've browsed through in the current session, which is referred to as checking your History.

To check your History in the Personal Web Navigator:

- Choose **Actions, History** or click the History Button on the Action Bar or the Search Bar.

To check your History in the Public Web Navigator:

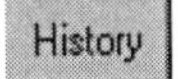

- Click the **History** button on the Action Bar or on the Search Bar to open the History dialog box (see Figure 12.1).

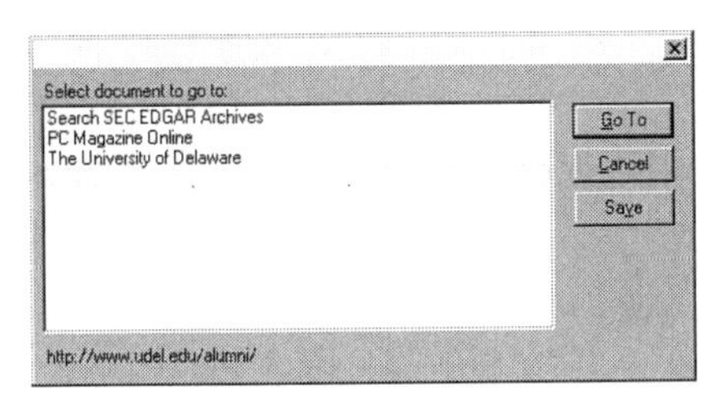

Figure 12.1 The History Dialog Box.

- To go to a specific Web page, select the name of the page and then click the **Go To** button.

Creating a Web Tour

History maintains a list of Web pages that you viewed in your current session, but the history disappears at the end of the session. If you want to keep a particular list of pages to refer to later, create a Web Tour. A Web Tour is a Notes document that is the saved history.

To create a Web Tour:

1. After you've been browsing the Web and you decide you'd like to save the list of pages you looked at, select **Actions**, **History** from the menu. If you're in the Public Web Navigator, click the **History** button on the action bar.
2. Click the **Save** button in the History dialog box (see Figure 12.1).
3. A Web Tour document (see Figure 12.2) opens showing a list of the URLs from this session (the first line of each entry is the title of the URL and the second line is the actual URL).

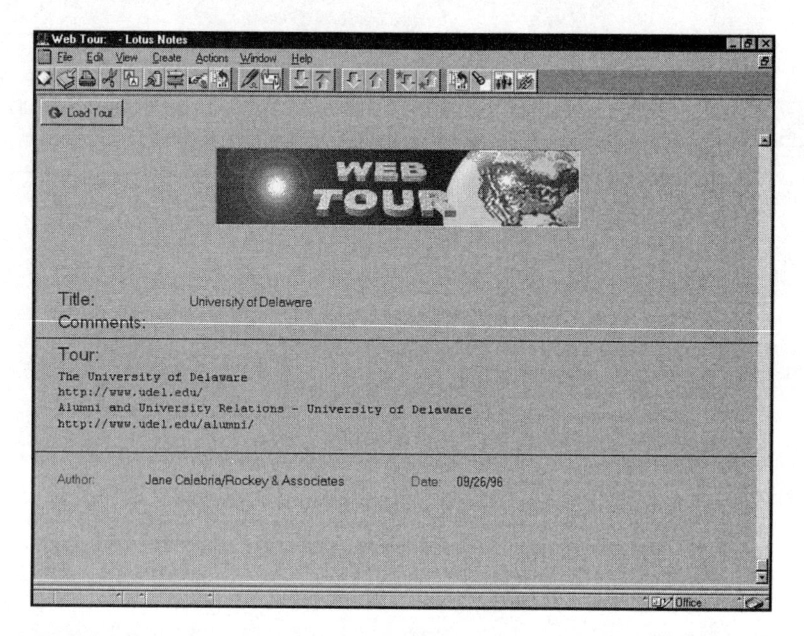

Figure 12.2 A Web Tour document.

4. Enter the title of the tour in the Tour field.
5. If you want to change the order of the URLs, edit the contents of the document.
6. Enter a description of the Tour in the Comments field.
7. Press **Esc**.
8. Click **Yes** to save the document.

Loading a Web Tour

When you want to revisit the pages you saved in your Web Tour document, reload it into your history list.

In the Public Web Navigator:

1. Click the **Database Views** icon on your Home Navigator Page.
2. Click **Web Tours**.
3. Select the Web Tour you want to use and open the document.
4. Click the **Load Tour** button.

If you're using the Personal Web Navigator, follow these steps:

1. Go to the **Other**, **Web Tours** view.
2. Select the Web Tour you want to use and open the document.
3. Click **Load Tour**.

Once you've loaded the Web Tour, use the previous, next, and history buttons to move through the Web pages.

Using Web Ahead

On most Web pages, you find links that point to the URLs of other Web pages. You could spend a lot of time browsing through all these Web pages, but the Personal Web Navigator has an agent that makes this easier for you.

The Web Ahead agent retrieves all the Web pages specified as URLs on a particular Web page and saves them in your database. Then you can view them later at your leisure. You can determine how many levels (up to 4) down from the original URL you want the agent to retrieve. This agent runs in the background, so you can work on other pages and databases while it's running. However, Web Ahead runs only while your Notes workstation is on.

Before you use it the first time, you must enable the Web Ahead agent (but you have to do this only once):

1. Choose **File**, **Tools**, **User Preferences**. You will see a dialog box much like the one shown in Figure 12.3.

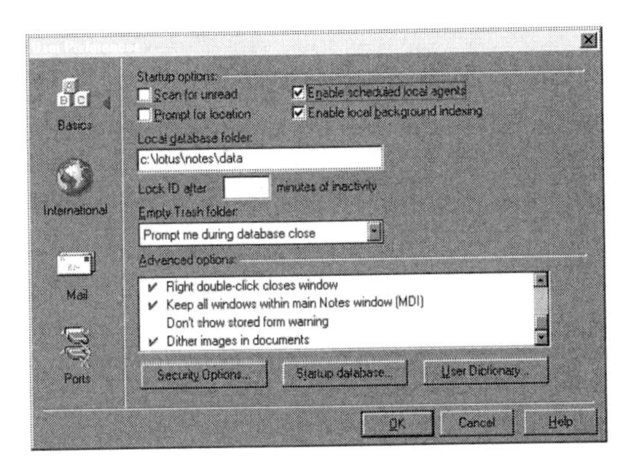

Figure 12.3 The User Preference dialog box.

2. Select **Enable scheduled local agents** and then click **OK**.
3. Open the Internet Options document by choosing **Actions, Internet Options** from the menu.
4. Click the **Enable Web Ahead** button.
5. When the Choose Server to Run On dialog box appears, select **Local**.
6. Click **OK**.

To run the Web Ahead agent:

1. Choose **Actions, Internet Options** to open the Internet Options document (see Figure 12.4).

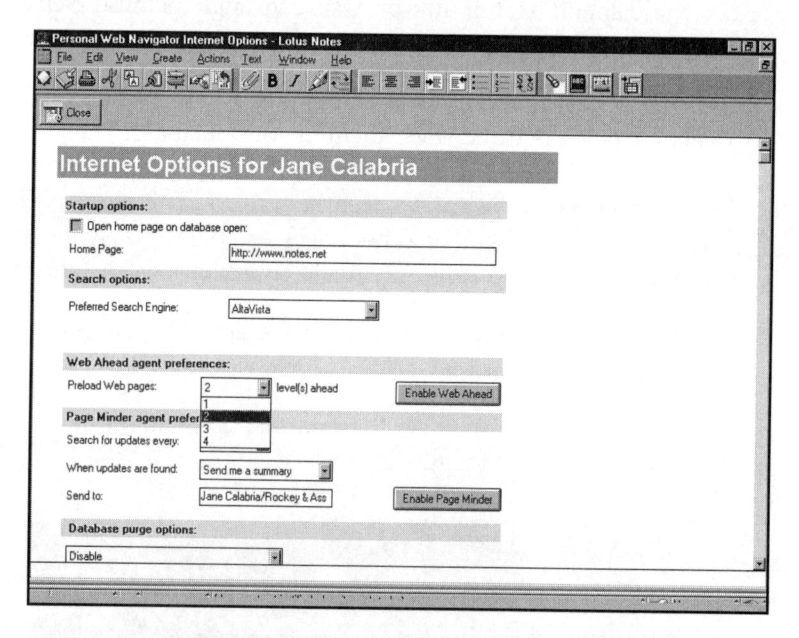

Figure 12.4 The Internet Options Document.

2. Under Web Ahead preferences, enter the number of levels of pages you want to retrieve from 1 to 4.
3. Exit and save the document.
4. Select the Web page on which you want to run the agent.
5. Drag the Web page onto the Web Ahead folder and the agent begins to run (see Figure 12.5).

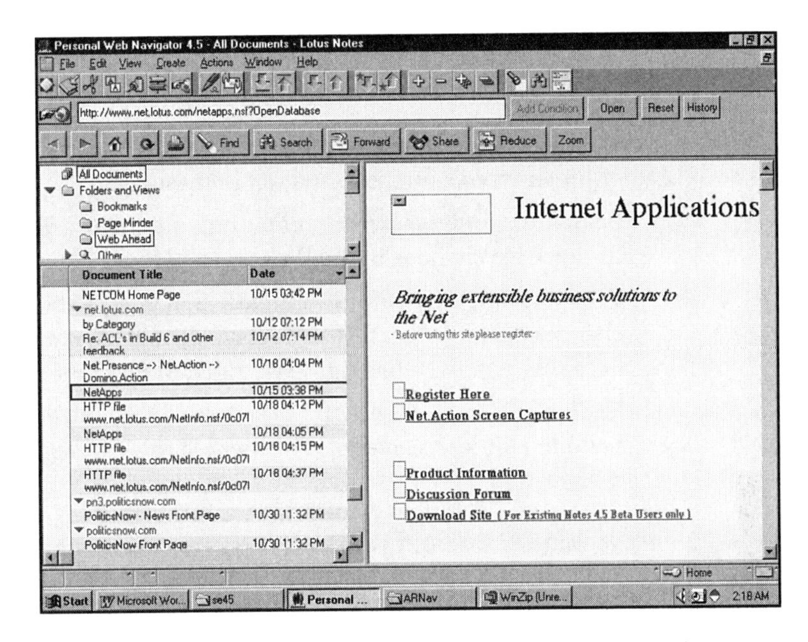

Figure 12.5 Drag the Web page onto the Web Ahead folder to run the agent.

Running Page Minder

The Personal Web Navigator has another agent you should try. It's the Page Minder. This agent keeps tabs on a designated Web page and lets you know when the contents of the page change.

The first time you want to run this agent you must enable it, but you have to do that only once. To enable the Page Minder agent:

1. Choose **File, Tools, User Preferences**.
2. Select **Enable scheduled local agents**.
3. Open the Internet Options document by choosing **Actions, Internet Options** from the menu. The Internet Options document appears (refer to Figure 12.4).
4. Click the **Enable Page Minder** button.
5. From the Choose Server to Run On dialog box, select **Local**.
6. Click **OK**.

To run the Page Minder agent:

1. Choose **Actions**.
2. The Internet Options document appears (refer to Figure 12.4). For the Page Minder preferences, enter information in these fields:

 Search for updates every Enter how frequently you want the agent to check for changes in the Web page—Hour, 4 Hours, Day, or Week.

 When updates are found Set how you want to be alerted when changes occur. Select **SMAS** to have the agent send you a message notifying you that the page is changed or Send me the actual page to have the agent send you the newly updated Web page.

 Send to Enter the name of the person to alert when the page content changes.

CAUTION

Page Minder Doesn't Run? The Page Minder runs at the schedule you set, but only if your Notes workstation is running.

3. Exit and save the document.
4. Select the Web page you want to track.
5. Drag the document onto the Page Minder folder to activate the agent.

TIP **Agents and Authentication** You can run agents on authenticated Internet servers if you have successfully retrieved that page during the *current* session. After you close a session, you have essentially logged off of an authenticated session. But during the session, Notes saves your username and password in a field on the Web page so that even if you leave the site of the authenticated server, you can return without signing in again. Refer to Lesson 8 for more on authenticating with Internet servers.

In this lesson, you learned how to save a list of the Web pages you visited, how to retrieve pages linked to other Web pages, and how to keep track of changes to specific Web pages. In the next lesson, you will learn to save and share documents and folders.

Sharing Web Pages

In this lesson, you learn how to share your Web pages with other Notes users by making recommendations in the Server Web Navigator, or by mailing Web pages to other Notes users.

Recommending Web Pages from the Server Web Navigator

The Server Web Navigator enables you to make recommendations about useful or interesting Web pages to others within your company who are also Notes users. Since the Server Web Navigator is a shared database, when you make a recommendation, anyone who can access the Server Web Navigator database can see your recommendations, and you can see theirs.

To recommend a Web page while using the Server Web Navigator:

1. Open the Web page you want to recommend.
2. Click the **Recommend** button in the Action Bar.
3. A dialog box appears as shown in Figure 13.1.

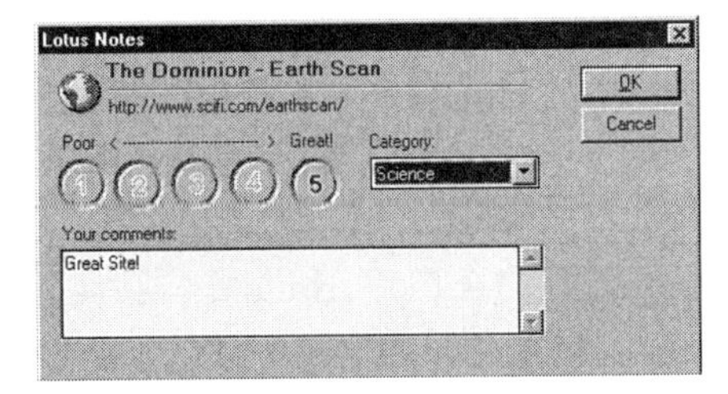

Figure 13.1 The Recommend dialog box.

4. Select a rating from 1 to 5 for this page. Number 1 is a low, or poor, rating and 5 is the highest rating.
5. Add your comments about this page in the comments text field.
6. Select a category for your recommendation. The categories are:

Arts	Business
Computers	Culture
Education	Entertainment
Finance	Government
Internet	Publications
Recreation	Reference
Science	Shopping
Sports	

7. Click **OK** to save this recommendation.

Recommending or Sharing a Document from the Personal Web Navigator

To recommend a Web page using the Personal Web Navigator, you first need to supply the name of your InterNotes server in your Internet Options document as explained in Lesson 3. You must also be connected to your InterNotes server for most of these sharing and recommending options. Only the forwarding of an URL will work remotely.

1. Open the **Personal Web Navigator**.
2. Click a document in the Navigator pane, or open a document.

3. Click the **Share** button in the Action Bar. The Share Options dialog box appears (see Figure 13.2).

   This dialog box is different than the one you see in the Server Web Navigator, and gives you three options:

   - **Forward only the URL** This option forwards the URL to others via e-mail. When you select this option, you are prompted for a name. You can fill in the name or click the address icon to select a name from your Personal Address Book. No mail message is created, so you won't have the opportunity to comment with the URL you are sending. Since you are only mailing the URL, you can use this feature while remote. The recipient will receive a mail memo, and the body of the memo will contain the URL only.

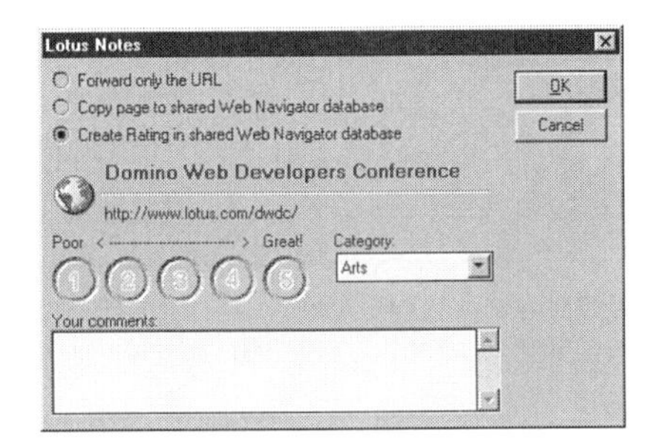

Figure 13.2 The Share Options dialog box.

- **Copy page to shared Web Navigator Database** This will send a copy of the page to the All Documents view of the Server Web Navigator.
- **Create Rating in shared Web Navigator Database** This will prompt you to create a rating as you would in the Server Web Navigator database and sends the page with its rating to the Recommend view of the Server Web Navigator.

4. Click **OK** to send this document and close the dialog box.

Viewing Recommended Web Pages

To view the Web pages you and others have recommended in the Server Web Navigator:

1. Open the Server Web Navigator.
2. Click the **Recommended** button in the Navigator home page.
3. The Navigator pane on the left of the screen allows you to view the contents of the recommended Web pages in three ways:
   - **By Category** A list of classifications chosen when Web page ratings were created. A good view for finding pages by topics.
   - **By Reviewer** Sorted by the person who rated the Web page.
   - **Top Ten** Shows the top ten pages with the highest cumulative ratings.

The other two buttons on the Navigator pane will take you to the Navigator Home Page (Back to home) or to the Database Views page (Database Views).

Forwarding Web Pages

You can forward (mail) a Web page to other Notes users from any view in your Personal Web Navigator or from an open document in the Server Web Navigator. Click the Forward icon, and Notes will open a mail memo. The Web page is the body of the mail memo, and the subject line is automatically filled in with the title of the Web page. Figure 13.3 shows a Web page ready to be forwarded.

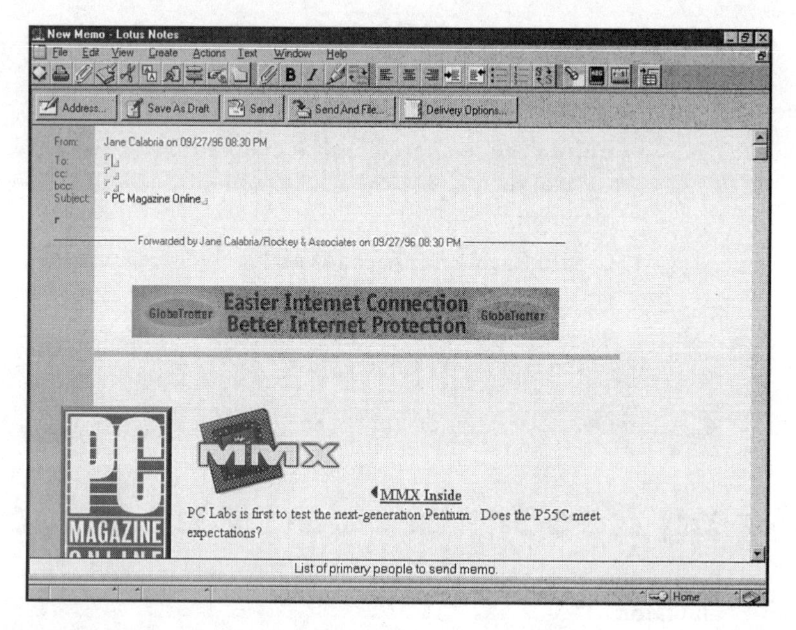

Figure 13.3 Forwarding a Web page.

In this lesson, you learned how to recommend, rate, and share Web pages with other Notes users. You also learned how to forward Web pages and URLs. In the next lesson, you will learn about viewing Java applets and HTML code.

Viewing Java Applets and HTML Code

In this lesson, you learn about Java Applets and how to view them. You also learn about viewing HTML code.

Viewing Java Applets

As we mentioned in Lesson 1, Java is a programming language that enables you to build small applications called applets. Applets can be embedded within a Web page by including them in an HTML code with the <APPLET> tag; they are then run from a browser. Notes temporarily copies the <APPLET> tag into the RAM of your PC and the Java applet is then run by the Java interpreter that comes with Notes. Java applets are very popular and can run animated pictures and voice clips. Lotus Notes supports running Java applets on your Windows 95 and Windows NT machines.

Is It Secure? Allowing Java applets to play on your PC brings up questions of security. Since these applets are actual programs, what if the program harms your PC? Whether intentional or not, there is a risk. With Java applets, the program is embedded in the page and after you open the page, you have opened the program. Lotus Notes enables you to decide *whether* you want to enable Java applets and *from whom* (which host) you will allow Java applets to be received. Additionally, Notes does not permit any outside host access to any of your system resources (files, environment variables, password files, and so on).

TIP **It Can Take Longer to See Pages with Java Applets!** If you don't enable applets, you will still see the Web pages you are visiting, minus the applets. If you are using the Public Web Navigator, check with your Notes Administrator to see whether Java applets are enabled.

Configuring the Personal Web Navigator for Java Applets

For Java applets to run on your computer, you must enable the Java applet function in Notes and check your location document to see that the access level for Java applets is set correctly. To configure your Personal Web Navigator:

1. From the Notes workspace, choose **File**, **Tools**, **User Preferences** from the menu.
2. In the Advanced Options section of the User Preferences box, verify that the Enable Java applets preference is checked. If it is not, click it once to place a check mark beside it (see Figure 14.1).

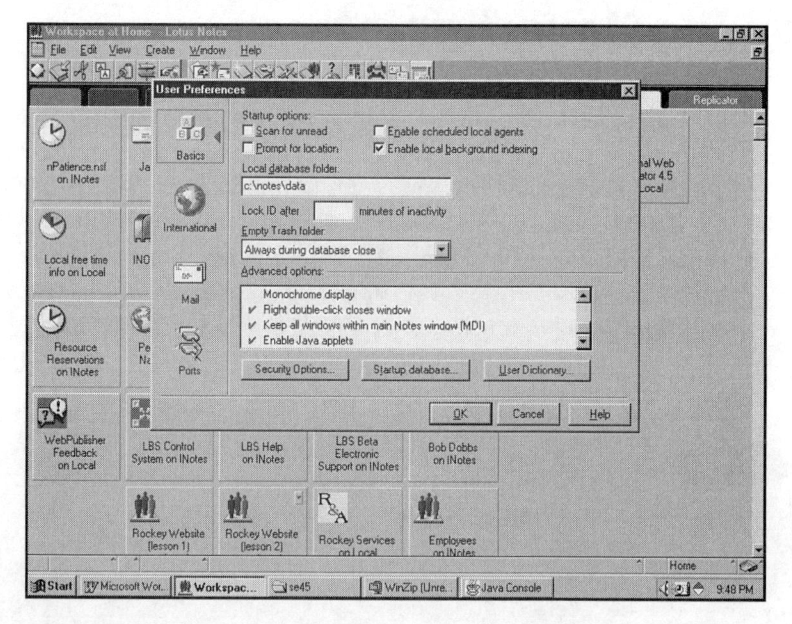

Figure 14.1 Advanced Options section of User Preferences.

3. Click **OK** to save your changes and close the window.
4. Open your Location document by clicking the location in the status bar and selecting **Edit Current**.

5. Click to open the collapsed **Advanced Section**. Go to the Java Applet Security section. The default for Network access for any trusted hosts is to allow access to any trusted host. Set your Java options in the following fields:

Trusted Hosts: Computers from which you can comfortably assume all Java applets received will be benign. Enter the host's domain name or IP address. If you leave this field blank, the information you provide in Network access for untrusted hosts will apply for all hosts.

Network access for trusted hosts: The degree of access to system and network resources on your computer that you will permit to a Java applet received from a trusted host.

Disable Java: Notes does not run Java applets received from trusted hosts.

No access allowed: Notes does not permit a Java applet to expose your computer's system or network resources to any computer.

Allow access only to originating host: Notes permits the Java applet to expose your computer's resources only to the computer from which it obtained the Java applet.

Allow access to any trusted host: Notes permits the Java applet to expose your computer's resources to any computer in your list of trusted hosts. This is the default setting.

Allow access to any host: Notes permits the Java applet to expose your computer's resources to any other computer.

Network access for untrusted hosts: Untrusted hosts are computers from which you cannot comfortably assume all Java applets received will be benign. Untrusted hosts include all computers not listed in the Trusted Hosts field unless that field is empty, in which case all hosts are treated as trusted hosts. The choices for this field are **Disable Java**, **No access allowed**, and **Allow access only to originating host**, each of which is defined as for trusted hosts. See those definitions listed previously.

Trust HTTP Proxy: This field is relevant only if you access the Internet through an HTTP proxy server. The default is No, meaning that your computer makes its own determination of whether the host from which a Java applet is received is a trusted host. If you cannot run a Java applet, it might be because your computer cannot resolve the Web server's host name to its IP address. Changing this field to **Yes** tells your computer to assume that your HTTP proxy server successfully resolved the host name to its IP address, and to run the applet according to the Trusted host/Untrusted host settings of the other fields in this section.

6. Save and exit the Location Document.

Viewing HTML Code

Sometimes you visit a Web page and say to yourself, "How did they do that?" Really impressive colors, formatting, and graphics help entice people to your site. (In Parts III, IV, and V of this book, you learn about building Notes applications and optimizing those applications for publication to the Web, as well as learning more about HTML code.) Here, you can learn how to view the HTML code behind Web pages.

If you are using the Public Web Navigator, check with your Notes Administrator to see whether the option has been set for HTML code. If you are using the Personal Web Navigator, edit your Internet Options page by checking off the **Save HTML in Note?** field under the Presentation preferences section (see Figure 14.2).

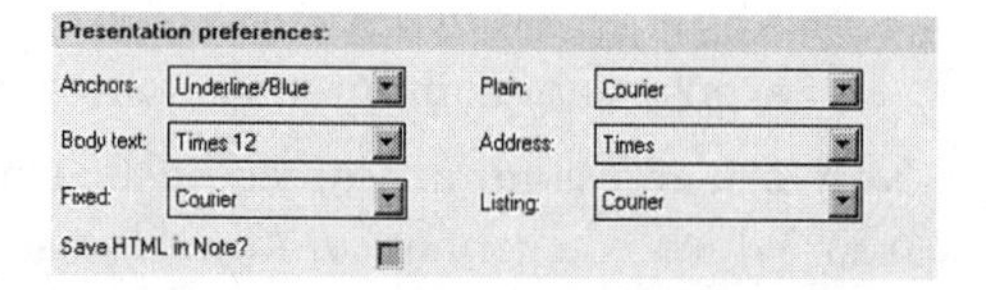

Figure 14.2 Save HTML field.

To view HTML code:

1. Select the Web page in either the Public or Personal Web Navigator.
2. Choose **File, Document Properties** from the menu.
3. Go to the **Fields** tab.
4. Check the HTML Source field in the left column to see the HTML code in the right column as shown in Figure 14.3.

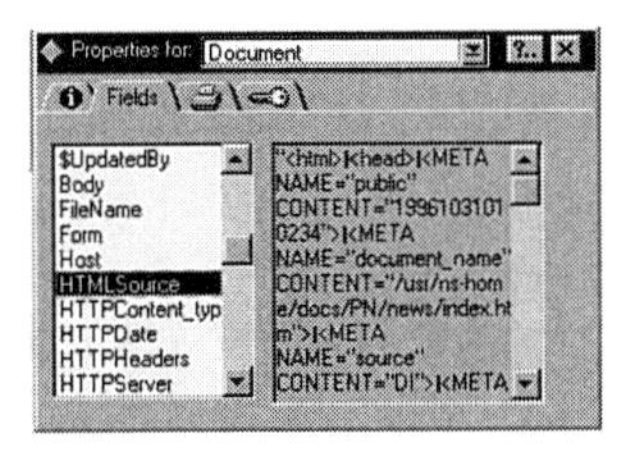

Figure 14.3 Choose HTML Source to see HTML code in right field.

TIP **To Better View the HTML Source** Notes displays the HTML code in a very small window in the field properties box. You can select and copy the contents of that field to the clipboard for better viewing.

In this lesson, you learned what Java applets are, and how to run them on your Personal Web Navigator. You also learned how to configure both Navigators to enable you to view HTML code. In the next lesson, you will learn how to fine-tune the Personal Web Navigator.

Fine-Tuning the Personal Web Navigator

In this lesson, you learn how to fine-tune your Personal Web Navigator to make surfing and saving an efficient process.

Multiple Web Retrievals

If you have a fast PC and a fast Internet connection, you can retrieve several Web pages at the same time. The Personal Web Navigator enables you to retrieve up to six pages simultaneously. To allow multiple Web retrievals:

1. Edit your Location Document (see Figure 15.1) by clicking the Location on the status bar and selecting **Edit Current**.
2. In the Concurrent Retrievals field (found under the Web Retrieval Configuration section), select the number of pages you want to be able to retrieve simultaneously. This field will be available only if the *Retrieve/ Open pages* file is set to "From Notes Workstation."
3. Save your changes and close the document.

Once you have edited your Location Document, you can retrieve several Web pages at one time. For each Web page you want to open, choose **File**, **Open URL** from the menu. As the pages are retrieved, Personal Web Navigator will open a new Window. To see the pages, select **Window** from the menu and move from page to page from the Window menu, or click **Cascade** to see all of your Web pages.

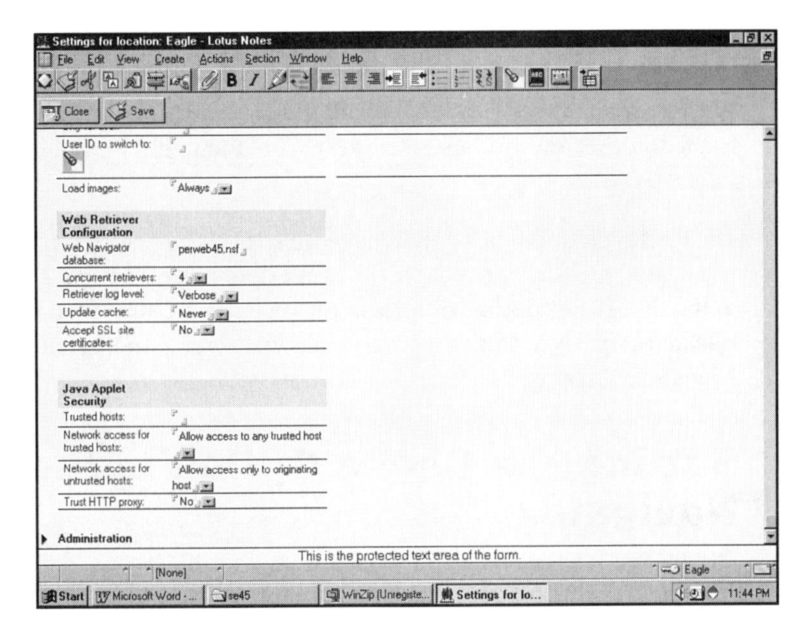

Figure 15.1 The Location Document.

Viewing the Most Current Version of a Web Page

Web pages are updated constantly. When you visit a Web site, you want current information, not last week's news. So, there is a chance that a Web page stored in your database could be out of date a day later. On the other hand, opening a Web page from the Notes database is a lot faster than opening a Web page on the Web. So, how can you balance between opening pages from the Web or the database?

Consider the Web page contents. It's highly unlikely that the Web pages you retrieved on the History of Chocolate in America are going to change. On the other hand, the Chocolate Lovers home page, which leads you to the history of chocolate, might change daily...and you wouldn't want to miss the daily chocolate chuckles!

Understanding the Cache Option

With a constant Internet connection, the Navigators can be instructed to go out to the Internet and update, or refresh Web documents. This is called setting the Cache Options.

The Cache Option will apply when you *open* a page stored in the database. If pages are stored in the database and not opened by anyone, Notes does not go to the Internet to update or refresh the page. The Cache Options can be set to reload a Web page from the Internet server when you open it from either Navigator database.

Setting the Cache Option in the Server Navigator

To find out what Caching Options are set for your Server Web Navigator, check with your Notes Administrator as only he can set caching options for the Server Web Navigator. Your Notes Administrator might have the caching options set to never. If that's the case, when you open a document from the Web Navigator database, be certain to open it by reloading it if you need to know that you will see the most current version of the page.

Setting the Cache Option in the Personal Web Navigator

You set the Caching Options for your Personal Web Navigator. If you're dialing into an ISP, the Caching Options you set will apply only while you are connected to the ISP. Obviously, when you're working offline, Notes can't access the Internet to update the pages. Remember, updating will occur only when you *open* a page in the database, so don't assume that because you've dialed into an ISP, every page in your database is current as of the last time you dialed in.

To set the Cache Options for your Personal Web Navigator:

1. Edit your Location Document by clicking the Location on the status bar and selecting **Edit Current**.
2. In the Update Cache (see Figure 15.2) field, found under the Web Retriever Configuration section (available only if the *Retrieve/Open pages* field is set to "From Notes Workstation"), choose one of the following:
    - **Never** Select this option if you do not want your Web pages refreshed. This is the default setting. With **Never** as your choice, you

would have to click the reload button on the action bar to refresh your Web page, or select **Reload from Internet Server** when you type an URL in the Open URL dialog box.

- **Once per session** Select this option to refresh your Web page at the time you open it from the database, and not again during your session.
- **Every time** Select this option to refresh a Web page every time you open it from the database during a session.

3. Save your changes and close the document.

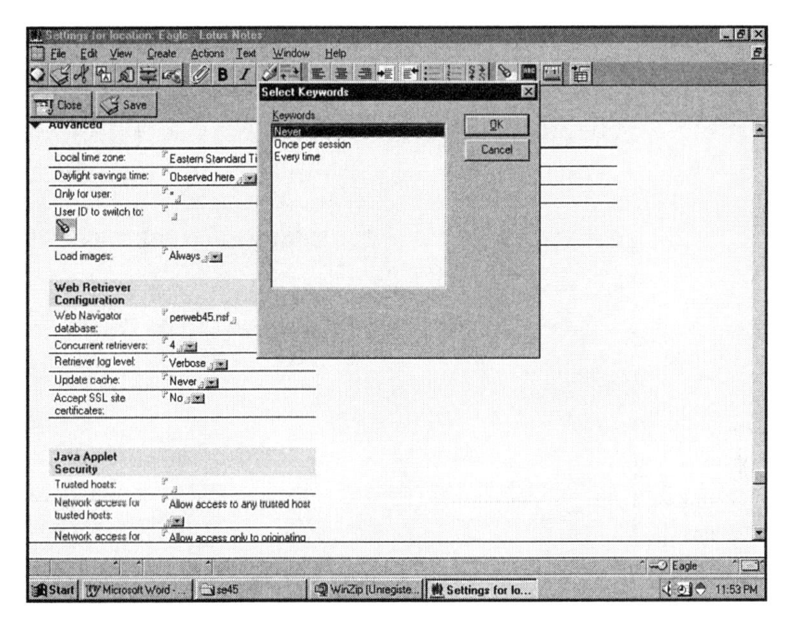

Figure 15.2 Update Cache Options.

Managing the Size of Your Database

With the Personal Web Navigator, Web surfing can result in disk space drowning. Remember that each page is Cached into your database. To control the size of your database, you should set purge (deletion) options for your database in the Internet Options document. Once you set the purge options, Notes will execute the purge each time you open the database.

To control the size of your database:

1. Select the **Personal Web Navigator** and choose **Actions, Internet Options** from the menu.
2. In the Database purge options section, select one of these options (see Figure 15.3):

   - **Reduce full pages to links if not read within ___ days** Indicate the number of days that a Web page should be stored as a full doc. If you choose 10 days, on the 11th day, the document will be reduced to an URL.
   - **Remove pages from database if not read within ___ days** Indicate the number of days that you would like to store a Web page that you haven't viewed. If you choose 10 days, on the 11th day the page will be purged, or deleted.
   - **Disable** Nothing will ever be purged from the database.

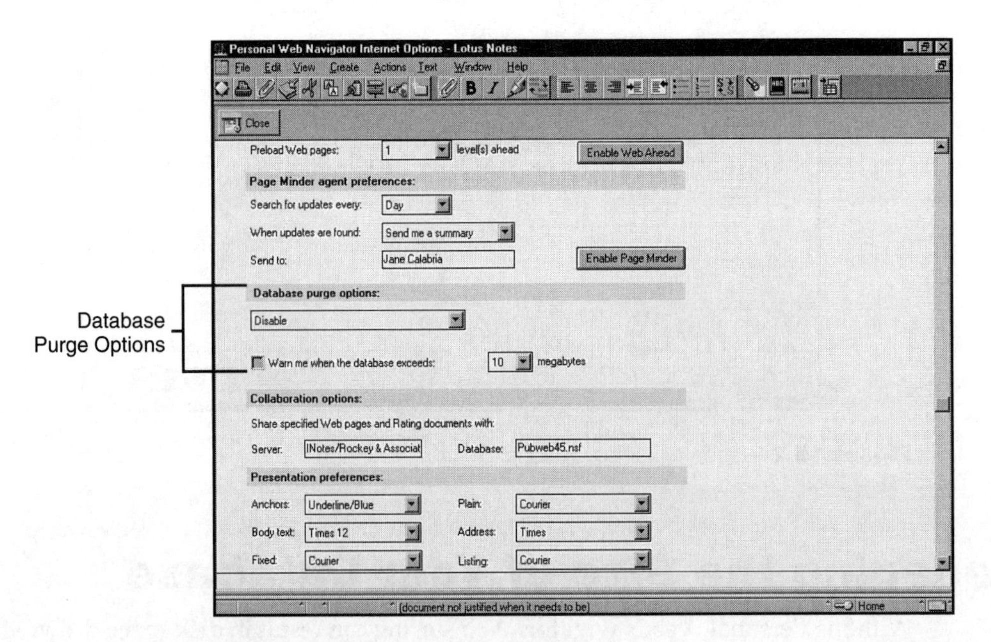

Figure 15.3 The Database Purge Options.

Keeping Track of Database Size

You can also keep track of the overall size of the database by asking Notes to notify you if the database exceeds a certain size. If you tell Notes that you want to be notified if the database exceeds 100 megabytes, when the database exceeds 100 megabytes, you will see a message box indicating that it has. To specify the size limit, open your Internet Options document and in the Database purge options section, check the **Warn me when the database exceeds** box and then type a size (in megabytes).

In this lesson, you learned how to activate multiple Web retrievals and how to manage the size of your database. In the next lesson, you'll learn how to use Notes Help databases.

Using Lotus Notes Help

In this lesson, you'll learn how to access and use Lotus Notes Help.

Understanding Lotus Notes Help

Lotus Notes has two versions of Help and, like all information stored in Lotus Notes, Help is a database. That fact might not be obvious to you, because you can access Help in so many ways. In other Notes databases, the only way to access the information contained in the database is to open the database itself. With Help, you don't have to double-click the database icon because you also can access it from the Help menu.

There are two versions of Help available, and each has its own unique icon on your workspace:

- The full version of Help (file name: Help4.nsf) is a larger database complete with navigators and is usually stored on the Notes server. It is accessible to users who are constantly connected to the Notes server.

- Notes Help Lite is the database used for desktops or laptops that have minimal disk space available and whose operator might need to access help when not connected to the Notes server. In Notes Help Lite, you'll find the most frequently used help topics (although you'll have less information and fewer views available).

If you aren't sure of which version you have, Help or Help Lite, look for the help database icon on your workspace. If don't have the database icon on your workspace, you can add it by opening the **File** menu and selecting **Database**, **Open**. Select **Notes Help** or **Notes Help Lite** from the database list on the server.

Getting Around in Help

Moving around and finding information in the Help database is done in the same way you move around and find information in other Notes databases, through views and searches. But as we said, you can get to the information in the database in one of several ways:

- You can use the menu (**Help**, **Help Topics**) and you'll see the Help database table of contents.
- You can press the **F1** key and you'll see a list of hypertext options that help you answer the question, **"What do you want to do?"**
- You can use the **Guide Me** option for accessing context-sensitive help.

Context-Sensitive Screen elements (menus and SmartIcons) change according to the task you are performing. For example, when you are in Edit mode, you'll see icons for text attributes, such as bold and italic. When you're in Read mode, those icons will not be visible.

Getting Help by Using the Menu

Let's take a look at using the menu to access Help. From your workspace, open the **Help** menu and select **Help Topics**. You'll see the main view of the Help database, called the Index view. The Index view is the default view. This view displays the contents of the entire database as seen in Figure 16.1.

This view takes advantage of expanded and collapsed views. Notice the little triangles that appear in front of some of the view topics? If the triangle is pointing to the right, this means that the line of text you see is a *category*. A category is not an actual document; it is a group description for the documents listed underneath it. To see those documents, click the triangle. The triangle will now point down and the documents will show beneath the category.

To select a help topic, select the topic you want to see on the right panel of your screen, and double-click the topic.

When the triangle points to the right, this is called a *collapsed* view.

When the triangle points down, this is called an *expanded* view. One way to expand and collapse views is to click the triangle. If the category is collapsed, clicking once will expand it. If the category is expanded, clicking once will collapse it. You can also use the SmartIcons located on the toolbar to expand and collapse views. You can also use the Expand All and Collapse All buttons on the Action bar.

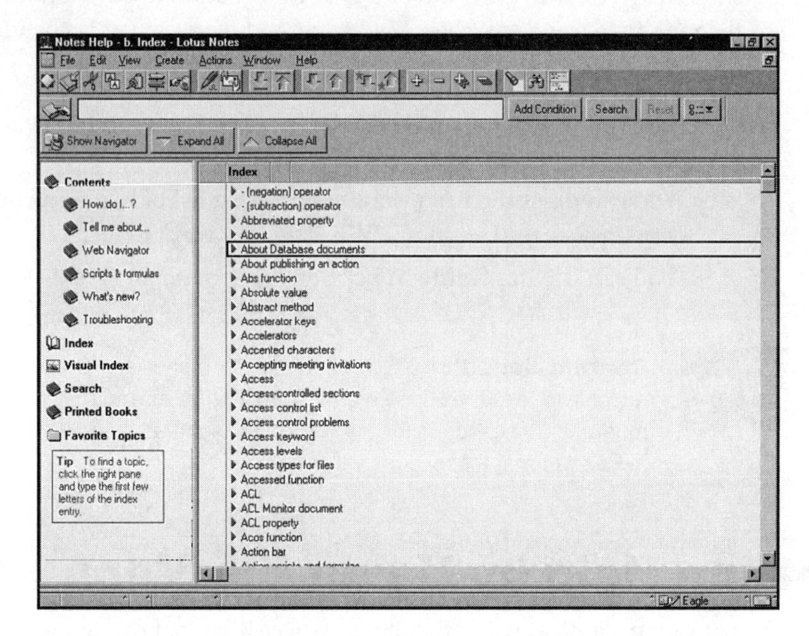

Figure 16.1 The Help Database Index View.

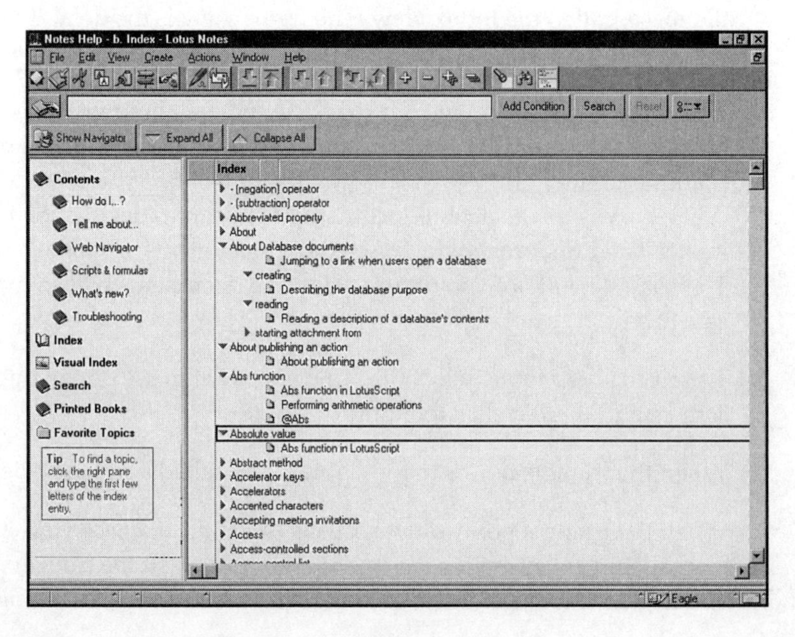

Figure 16.2 Help Topic Category (expanded view).

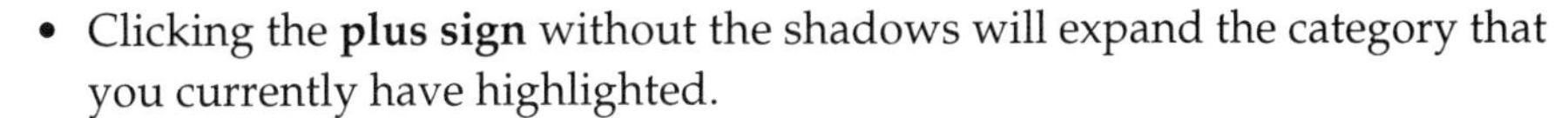

- Clicking the **plus sign** without the shadows will expand the category that you currently have highlighted.

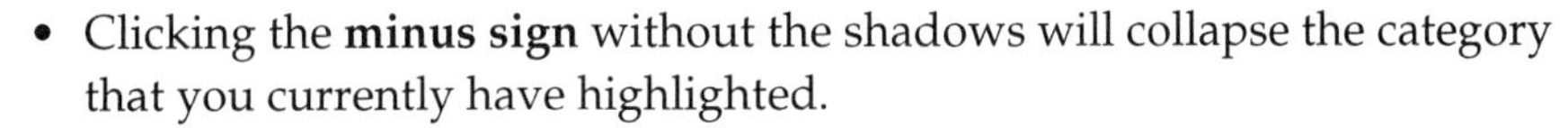

- Clicking the **minus sign** without the shadows will collapse the category that you currently have highlighted.

- Clicking the **plus sign** with the shadows will expand all categories in the database.

- Clicking the **minus sign** with the shadows will collapse all categories in the database.

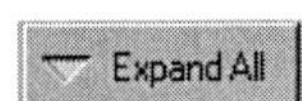

- Clicking the **Expand All** button on the Action bar will expand all categories in the database.

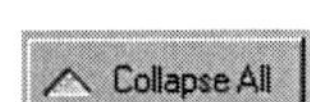

- Clicking the **Collapse All** button on the Action bar will collapse all the categories in the database.

To read a help topic, simply double-click the document you want to read. Press **Esc** to return to the Index view. In the left panel of the Index view are navigators to other available views (see Figure 16.3).

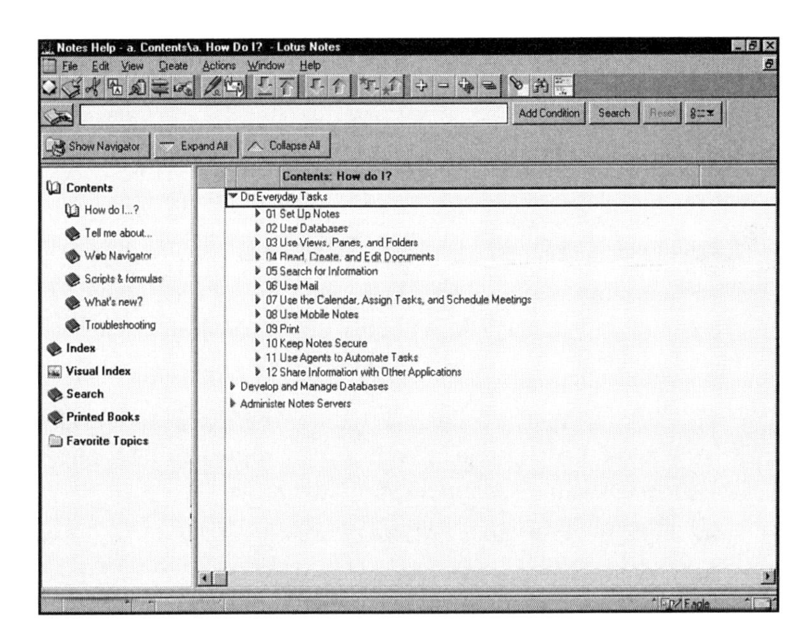

Figure 16.3 The Help Database Index View Navigators.

- **How do I..?** contains a list of task-oriented functions such as "Ways to address mail."

- **Tell me about...** provides shortcuts, notes, database design, and management concepts.
- **Web Navigator** contains Help information on the Navigators.
- **Scripts and Formulas** contains information on Lotus Script and Formulas.
- **What's new?** contains information about Notes Release 4 for users of previous versions.
- **Troubleshooting** lists and answers common questions and meanings of error messages.
- **Index** displays a list of categorized help topics. This is the default view for the database.
- **Visual Index** is available if using Help4.nsf. Topics are graphically represented.
- **Search** lists topics alphabetically, without categories.
- **Printed Books** contains Notes documentation in book form, such as Programmers Guide and User Guide.

As you select a view navigator on the *left* of your screen, the contents will change on the *right* of your screen. Each time you change views, you can navigate to another view, or press the **Esc** key to return to your workspace. You can disable the navigator by clicking the Navigator button on the action bar. This will take you to the Folders view.

Using the Visual Index

The Visual Index view displays the contents of the database with navigators as shown in Figure 16.4. You will only have this view available if you are using Help (not Help Lite). To see the Visual Index View:

1. Click the **Visual Index** Navigator. The Visual Index View displays navigators on the left pane of your screen, representing topics. Let's investigate the Workspace Management Navigator.
2. Click the **Workspace Management** Navigator.
3. A picture of the workspace is shown. Tiny yellow bubbles act as hotspots to lead you to help on a given topic as shown in Figure 16.5.

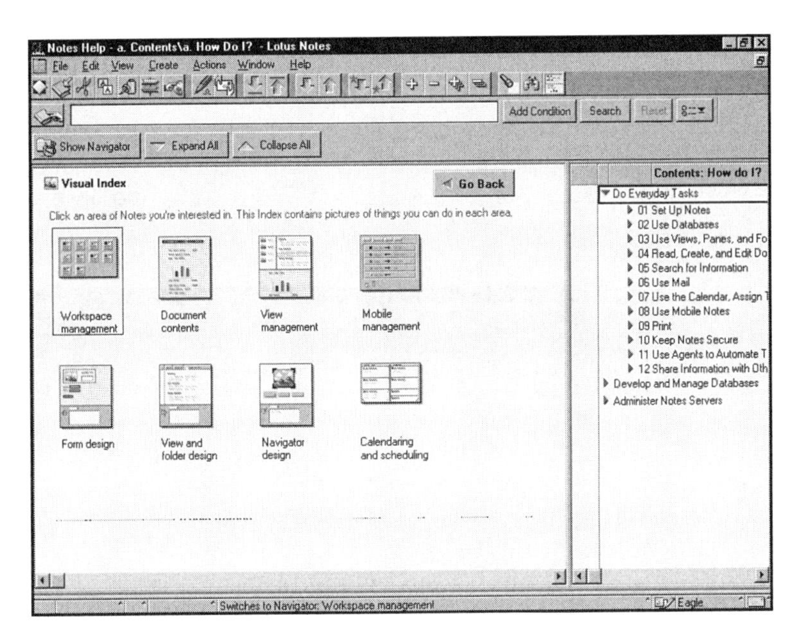

Figure 16.4 The Notes Help Database Visual Index View.

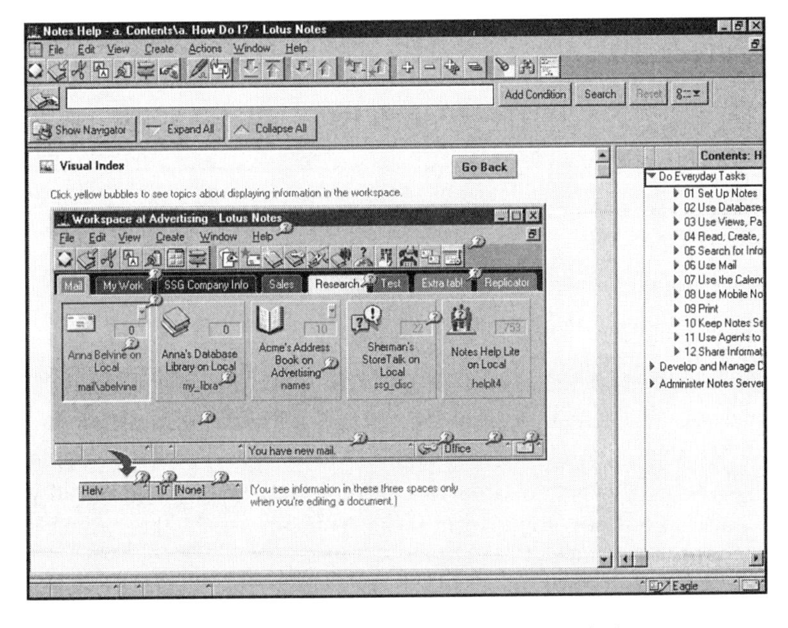

Figure 16.5 Tiny yellow bubbles act as hotspots for getting help.

4. Click the tiny yellow bubble that points to the "My Work" tab in the picture of the workspace. The help topic `Entering a name on a workspace tab`: will display Figure 16.6.
5. Click the **Go Back** button in the form to return to the workspace navigator, then again to return to the Visual Index view, and once again to return to the Index view.

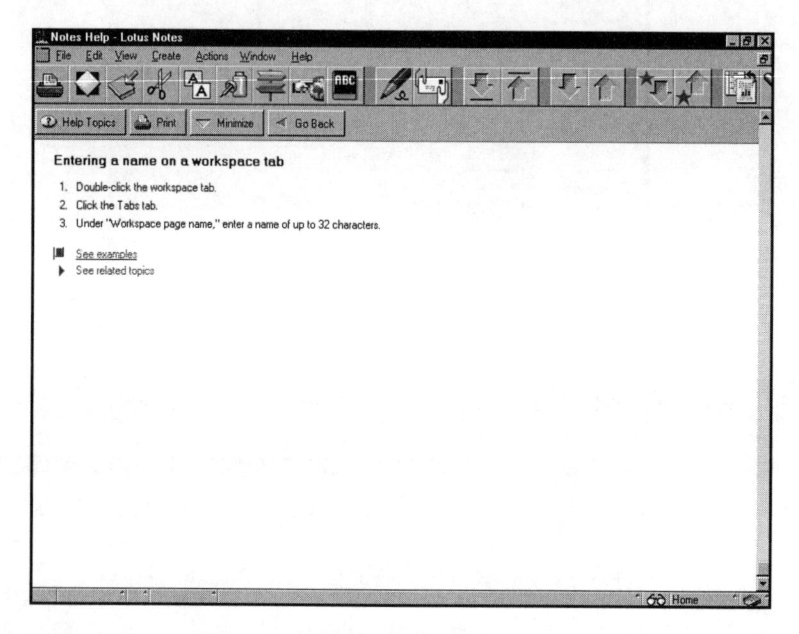

Figure 16.6 Click a bubble for help on that topic.

Using the "Guide Me" Feature of Help

Another way to access Help is to use the context-sensitive Guide Me feature of Notes. To activate Guide Me, press the **F1** key. When you use this key, instead of showing you the views we just discussed, Notes will display a list of topics asking you `What do you want to do?` followed by topics that you double-click to search out how to perform tasks. You can use **F1** at any time, from any place while working in Lotus Notes.

Let's open the Web Navigator database and experiment with the **F1** key. From your Lotus Notes workspace, double-click the **Web Navigator** icon, then perform the following steps:

1. Click the **Database Views** icon located on the Web Navigator home page.
2. The All Documents view will appear with the Views Navigator. Press the **F1** key for help.
3. A screen will display asking `What do you want to do?`. (See Figure 16.7.) Double-click **Print**.

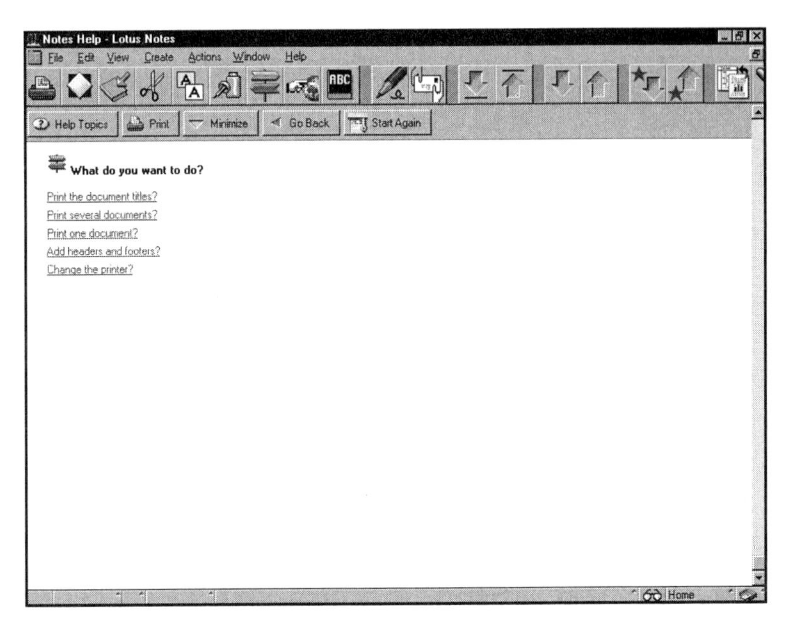

Figure 16.7 Using Context-Senstive Help.

4. A list of print topics appears. Double-click **Print one document?**
5. Now you can read the instructions for printing a document. To exit this screen, press the **Esc** key four times to return to the Web Navigator home page.

In this lesson, you learned to access Lotus Notes Help.

Application Development

Beginning an Application

In this lesson, you learn about Lotus Notes application types, what steps you should follow in creating an application, and how to create a database file.

What Is a Lotus Notes Application?

Lotus Notes applications typically support or automate business functions by helping you create, collect, share, and manage almost any kind of information. Notes can distribute the information widely, as you can access the information across a network or by dial-up telephone connections. Notes applications can incorporate information from external sources and can export data to external databases. Notes developers can define who has access to applications and the degree of access.

There are five general categories of Notes applications:

- **Broadcast** For keeping an organization informed about current events or the latest facts on subjects of mutual interest. Typical broadcast applications are newsletters, industry news bulletin boards, or postings of meeting agendas and minutes.
- **Reference** Online libraries of reference information that can be periodically updated. Company policies and procedures manuals, software and hardware documentation, employee benefits information, market research information, and technical support information all work well as reference applications.
- **Discussion** Discussion applications are just that—online discussions, where participants read one another's contributions and reply to them if they want. The views are laid out so one can easily see who is replying to whom. You might use a discussion application for brainstorming ideas, as a suggestion box, or for polling opinions.

- **Tracking** Perfect for following the status of a project that changes rapidly, and where multiple people contribute frequent updates to the database. Typical tracking applications include sales call tracking, project tracking, customer service tracking, service call tracking, event planning, and collections management.
- **Workflow** Automation of routine tasks. Use a workflow type application to process purchase requests, handle insurance claims, submit and approve expense reports, work on a marketing plan, or route loan approvals.

As functional as Notes applications are, in some circumstances other application tools might work better than Lotus Notes. You should probably use a relational database manager, a spreadsheet program, or a financial modeling application if your application:

- Requires continual access to real-time data (Notes users should be able to tolerate a 30- to 60-minute delay).
- Requires databases which are four gigabytes or more in size.
- Involves complex, processing-intensive calculations (Notes doesn't have the range of financial and mathematical functions you get in a spreadsheet or financial modeling programs).
- Requires file or record locking (Notes users in different locations can edit the same document simultaneously).

What Is a Notes Database?

A Notes application consists of one or more databases designed to perform a specific function. A Notes *database* is a collection of documents used to manage large amounts of related information. As long as you have access rights to a database, you can read or add information to the database. The database also contains the design elements that make the database functional for Notes users, the access levels for database users, and settings that define how the database captures and stores information.

There are several elements involved in the database structure:

- **Forms** Forms provide the structure for entering and displaying data. They are the windows through which users see the fields of a document in order to view the data in the database. They are also the document templates, which determine how documents will look when viewed; they also determine what fields will appear.

- **Documents** Documents *store* the information entered into the fields on a form in the database. How the document is displayed to the user depends on the form used to create the document, or the form used to display the document (each piece of information in the document is stored with a field name tag that provides the key for knowing which piece of information to display with what field tag on the form). When users compose a document, they choose a form that defines the type of document they will create, they enter data in the appropriate fields, then they save the document.
- **Fields** You enter data into fields. Designers add specific areas on forms to collect different types of data or to compute data from other information. These areas are fields, and each field contains one kind of information. Together, the fields on a form define what data each document contains.
- **Views** Views are tabular lists of documents. Views function as tables of contents for the database. Each row represents information from a single document. Each column displays information from a single field, a group of fields, or a the result of a formula that uses field information.

The Steps to Creating an Application

When you're ready to build an application, you should follow these steps to get the best results:

1. Establish the needs of the users through interviews and by analyzing their current systems.
2. Sketch out a design for the database on paper.
3. Gather user feedback on your design, make note of any modifications to the plan, and obtain approval to proceed.
4. Create the database file.
5. Design the forms and define the fields on the forms.
6. Create the views.
7. Set up the Access Control List to specify the user access levels for the database.
8. Make the About Database and Using Database documents.
9. Create the database icon.
10. Set up a pilot program to test the application with a small group of users.
11. Make the necessary modifications to the database based on the user feedback.

12. Give access rights to the remainder of the user community.
13. Provide training for the new application.
14. Document your work.

TIP **Planning Is So Important!** The most important part of application development is planning. You want to avoid any midstream and last-minute changes that make it necessary to redesign whole sections of your application. If you plan well and have your client sign off on your plans, you might save surprises down the road. Reworking is always harder than doing it right initially. However, even the best-laid plans will be subject to some changes, so be flexible.

If you follow along closely with the figures in this part of the book, you will see an application developing that will eventually be published on the World Wide Web (see Parts IV and V of this book). In this application, Rockey & Associates, a company that provides computer training and consulting services, will advertise its services. The application will include schedules and descriptions of courses, free seminars, and satellite broadcasts the company offers. It will also include information about Rockey's instructors and directions to the training locations.

Creating a Database File

After you have your application design worked out on paper, you're ready to implement it in Notes by creating the database file.

You have three choices about how you want to create the database:

- Create a database using a template.
- Copy an existing database.
- Create a new database from scratch.

Notes provides some design assistance in setting up the database file. Lotus Notes includes several database design templates. You can choose one that is similar to the design you want to create. Templates will save you time, because you only have to modify the design to fit your needs.

The application templates include what is listed in Table 1.1.

Table 1.1 Notes Templates

Template	*Type*	*Description*
Approval Cycle	Workflow	Builds a standard approval cycle into a database. Has pre-made approval subform and approval logic that you can add to any form. Includes agent to manage overdue approvals.
Discussion	Discussion	An electronic conference room for groups sharing ideas. Includes archiving capabilities, interest profile (users can automatically mail themselves document links to topics of interest).
Document Library	Reference	An electronic library to store reference documents. Includes author-initiated review cycle, archiving capabilities.
Lotus® SmartSuite	Reference	Document library for 96 Library SmartSuite 96. Automatically launches, stores, and supports review cycles of documents created with SmartSuite products.
Microsoft® Office	Reference	Document library for Microsoft Library Office. Automatically launches, stores, and supports review cycles of documents created with Office products.
Personal Journal	Discussion	An electronic diary for creating and organizing private ideas and documents. Includes graphic navigators.
Room Reservations	Tracking	Schedules and tracks the use of conference rooms. Can customize to track other shared resources.

TIP **Review/Approval Cycles** Very little activity takes place in any company that is not subject to review and approval. If you submit an expense report, your boss has to review and approve it before you get paid. If you ask a bank to lend you money, the loan officer will carefully review and possibly approve your application, an appraiser will review and approve the collateral, a credit analyst will review and approve your credit history and finally, the Board of Directors will reject—er—approve the actual loan. This is the Review/Approval Cycle. Notes can automate and track the whole thing.

Create a New Database File Using a Template

The easiest way to create a new database is to base it on an existing design. That way you don't have to reinvent the wheel. You just have to customize it. Here are the steps:

1. Choose **File**, **Database**, **New** from the menu.
2. The New Database dialog box appears (see Figure 1.1). `Local` should appear in the Server list box. Accept this selection.

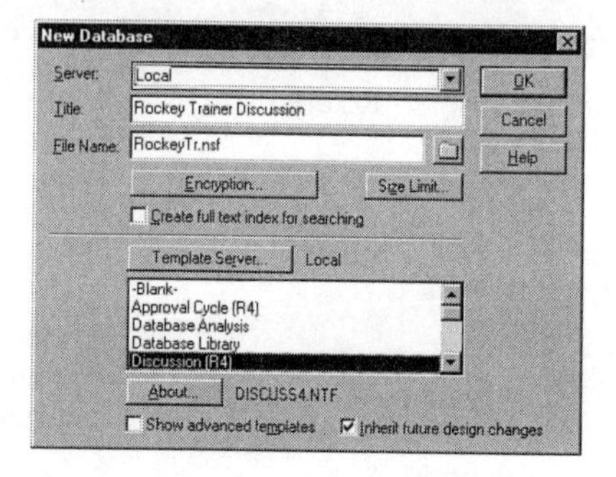

Figure 1.1 The New Database dialog box with a template selected.

TIP **Make It Local!** You should always create a new database on your own workstation hard disk or in a personal directory or folder on your network to prevent users from accessing the application before you're finished designing it.

3. In the Title box, type the name of the database as you want it to appear on the database icon and in the list of databases for the server. The maximum length is 32 characters. Try to keep it short and simple so it's easy to see and to remember.
4. For the File Name, enter the filename or use the one that Notes has entered. Depending on the operating system your computer uses, you may be limited to eight characters for the filename. Notes will automatically add a period and the file extension NSF.

5. Ignore the Encryption button. It is for use by *users* who take individual copies of sensitive databases out of the office with them on their laptops. Depending on how concerned the user is that the database might get into the wrong hands, he could choose "strong," "medium," or "simple." Strong is unbreakable but slows access to the database. Medium is easier but still difficult to break. Simple is very easy to break.

Encryption Encodes the database so that only the person who chose the Encryption option can read the database.

6. Ignore the Size Limit button for now. When you are ready to distribute (roll out) your database to the user community, you will have to choose the maximum possible size of the database: 1, 2, 3, or 4 gigabytes.
7. Ignore the Create full text index for searching box for now. Full text indexing enables users to search the database for words or phrases. You will make a decision about full text indexing at the time you roll out the database (see Lesson 15 for more information).
8. Template files are stored locally and on the server. You might have different templates on your server than those on your workstation. Click the **Template Server** button only if you need to change this.
9. From the list of available templates, choose the one on which you are basing your application.
10. Click the **About** button to see the About Database document, if it exists.
11. If you don't see the template you want, check **Show advanced templates**. You'll see more templates on this list.
12. Do not check the Inherit future design changes box.

Inherit Future Design Changes When you base a new database on a template, you effectively make a copy of the template, its forms, views and so on. If you choose to inherit future design changes, changes to the original template will overwrite changes you made to your database.

13. Click **OK**.

Copying an Existing Database

Just as basing your design on a template saves time, copying an existing database can also save design time. After you make a copy of a database, you can modify the copy to meet your needs, adding forms, fields, views, and so on.

1. Select the icon for the database you want to copy.
2. Choose **File**, **Database**, **New Copy** from the menu (see Figure 1.2).

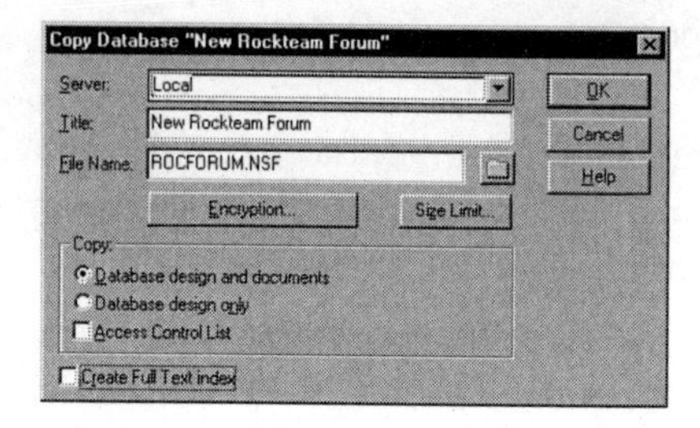

Figure 1.2 The Copy Database dialog box.

3. Leave `Local` as the selection for the Server. This tells Notes to create the new copy on your computer.
4. In the Title box, enter the title for your database. The maximum length is 32 characters. It's a good idea to change the title, so no one will be confused as to what copy to choose from the File Database Open dialog box or from the workspace.
5. In the File Name box, change the filename of the database extension.
6. Ignore the Encryption button.
7. Ignore the Size Limit. This is important at the time of roll-out.
8. Select **Database design only**. Choose **Database design and documents** only if you want to copy *all* the documents into your new database.
9. Disable **Access Control List**, as you'll want to create your own ACL for the database. Another reason to disable ACL is that you might not have designer access to the database you're copying, and you'd be denied access to your new one if you copied the ACL.
10. Ignore the Create Full Text index box.
11. Click once on **OK**.
12. Do not check Inherit future design changes for the reasons discussed in the previous list.

Creating a New Database from Scratch

If you must, you can create a database from scratch. This is not recommended for a novice database designer.

1. Choose **File**, **Database**, **New** from the menu.
2. The New Database dialog box appears as in Figure 1.1. `Local` should appear in the Server list box. Accept this selection.

TIP **Keep It Local!** You should always create a new database on your own workstation hard disk or in a personal directory or folder on your network to prevent users from accessing the application before you're finished designing it.

3. In the Title box, type the name of the database as you want it to appear on the database icon.
4. For the File Name, enter the filename or use the one that Notes has entered. You might be limited to eight characters.
5. Ignore the Encryption button.
6. Ignore the Size Limit button.
7. Do not check Inherit future design changes.
8. From the list of available templates, choose the one on which you are basing your application or select **Blank** to start the application from scratch.
9. Click once on **OK**.

In this lesson, you learned what a Notes application is, what types of applications you can create, what a Notes database is, and how to create your own database. In the next lesson, you'll learn about making forms.

Making Forms

In this lesson, you learn about starting a new form, giving it a name, setting the form properties, and saving the form.

Plan Your Form

Before you sit down to create a form in Lotus Notes, you should sketch out the form on paper. You should pay attention to the layout of the form in relation to how it will be used. Also, don't forget these tips (which you'll learn how to do in this chapter):

- Consider placing the most important field information at the top, so people who quickly read through documents will not have to page down to find what they want.
- Group related information together.
- Space the text and fields on the form so people can readily see the fields and won't have to jump all over the page to enter data.
- Use colors to differentiate text that will not be changed from fields that have to be filled in.
- Add graphics and colored backgrounds for variety or to differentiate each form.
- Plan which fields you need to include on the form, what types of information need to be entered in those fields, and which fields need to be computed. Think about the names you want to assign the fields. Remember that fields are computed from the top down and from left to right, and place fields that are dependent on information to the right of or below the fields from which the information will be drawn.

Computed Fields Fields whose values Notes calculates automatically.

Once you have the design mapped out, your application will be much easier to create in Notes.

Form Types

When you create a form, one of your first decisions is what *type* of form it will be—Document a Response or Response to Response.

- A **document** is a type of form independent of all other forms. It stands alone. It does not *respond* to other forms. It is sometimes referred to as a *main* document.
- A **response** form is subordinate to and dependent on the form type Document. A Response form typically appears in views indented beneath its parent—the Document form.
- A **response to response** form is always subordinate to and dependent on its parent: the Document, Response, or Response to Response form. A Response to Response form also appears in views indented beneath its parent.

Think of a typical customer-tracking database that stores information about each customer. You need to store information about each person that you have contact with at each customer. You need to store information about your activities with respect to each customer or contact. Start by creating a form called Customer Profile that includes basic information about a customer. This form would be the form type *document*.

Since there could be more than one contact per customer, create a second form, Contact Profile, that contains information about a contact. Since each contact is associated with a particular company, this form would naturally be a form type *response*. Each Contact Profile created would then automatically be associated with some Customer Profile.

Finally, you would create forms for different types of actions, such as a meeting or phone conversation record. Since these might be associated with either a Customer *or* a Contact, they would be form type *response to response*.

Figure 2.1 Shows a view containing a main document, response document, and response to response document.

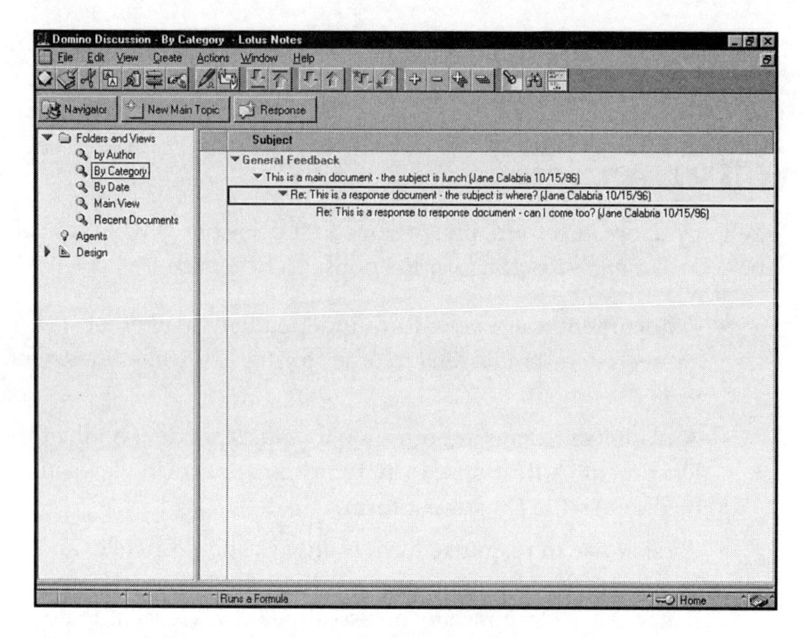

Figure 2.1 A document with a response and a response to a response.

Understanding the Design Window

Now that you have a database, you need to create forms in that database that will be used to enter data. To start a form:

1. Open the database.
2. Choose **Create**, **Design**, **Form** from the menu. The Design window appears.

You are now in the Design window (see Figure 2.2). The top part of the window, called the form builder, is a blank page that will become the form.

The bottom part of the screen is the Design pane. In the Design pane is the Define list box, which tells you what object of the form you're working on. The Define list box says `Untitled (Form)`, meaning that you're working on the form itself. The Event box says `Window Title`. If you enter a formula in the large white box below the event (the formula box), the formula will define the title of the window for documents created with this form.

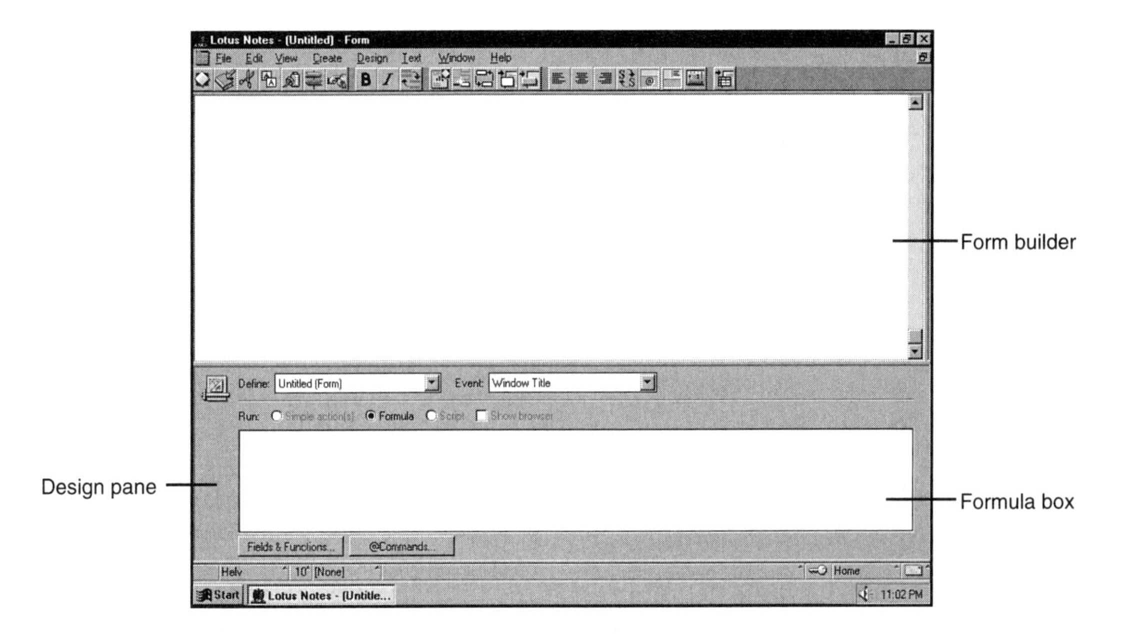

Figure 2.2 The Design window.

There are three Run options above the formula box:

- **Simple actions** Select this to choose from a list of Notes functions. The selected action will be performed.
- **Formula** Choose this to enter a Notes formula in the formula box. Two buttons will appear to help you create these formulas: Fields & Functions and @Commands. When you click these buttons, lists of available Fields & Functions and @Commands will appear. You learn more about formulas in Lesson 5, "Formulas and @Functions."
- **Script** Pick this to add LotusScript, Notes' programming language. If you select this, you can enable the browser by checking the box next to **Show browser**. LotusScript programming is beyond the scope of this book and is used for advanced programming.

Customize Your Work Area You can size the Design pane by dragging on its top border. To make it disappear from the screen, double-click the border or choose **View**, **Design pane** from the menu. Do the same thing to make it reappear (the border is right above the status bar).

Creating the Form

Now that you have the form builder window open, you should name the form and set its basic properties. To do this, you need to open the Form Properties box by choosing **Design, Form Properties** from the menu (see Figure 2.3).

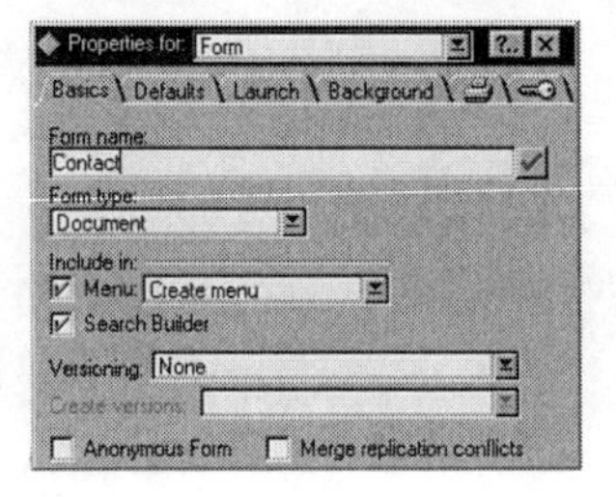

Figure 2.3 The Form Properties box.

Click the Background tab to select a color for the form background from the Color list box (see Figure 2.4). Because they may be hard on the eyes, stay away from vibrant, dark colors. You might think a dark background with white text looks good, but you'll get a shock when you try to create a view showing documents created with this form. You won't see the text; it's white on white. You'll have to change the view background color or the color of the text in the view.

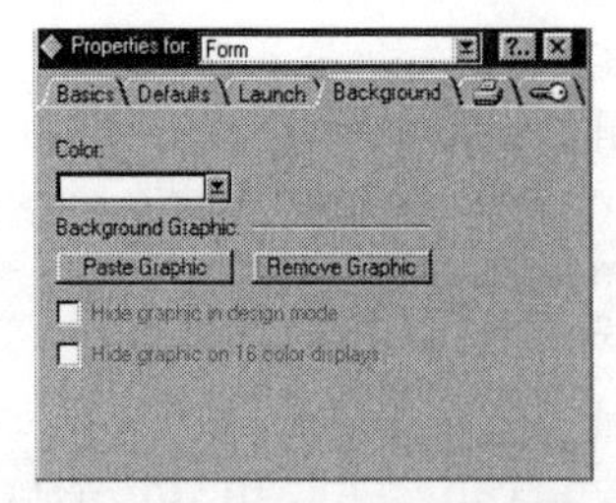

Figure 2.4 The Form Properties box with the Background tab selected.

If you want to use a picture to make a background for your form, open the picture in the graphics application where you created it, copy it to the Clipboard using the **Edit**, **Copy** command, and then switch back to Notes. Click the **Paste Graphic** button on the Background page of the Form Properties box. If your graphic is small, Notes will repeat it several times to fill the entire screen; this is called "tiling." You want to be careful in choosing a graphic for your background because a busy graphic will make the text difficult to read.

We'll be working more with Form properties in the section entitled "Selecting Form Properties" later in this lesson.

Naming the Form

Enter the name of the form in the Form name box. Also, click once on the green check button at the end of the box. By clicking that button, you activate a check of your syntax.

The form name can be up to 256 characters long but Notes only displays the first 64 characters on the menu, so keep the name simple and descriptive. You can use any combination of letters, numbers, spaces, and punctuation. Be aware that Notes form names are case-sensitive, so "RESPONSE" will be treated as a different form than "Response."

The form name affects those who will be using the form to create documents. As a Notes user, you are accustomed to creating documents by accessing forms listed under **Create** on the Notes menu bar. As a Notes designer, you determine whether and how your Notes forms will appear on that menu for others to access (see Selecting Form Properties in this lesson). In naming your form, consider how the form name will appear on the Create menu:

- **Keyboard Shortcuts** Because users can type the underlined letter of a menu entry as a keyboard shortcut, you may want to be sure all your form names begin with a different letter. The first letter is normally underlined in the menu because that is the default keyboard shortcut. However, if two forms begin with the same letter, the form's default keyboard shortcut is the next letter not used by a preceding form. This can be awkward for your users. If you can't assign form names with different first letters, type an underscore (_) before the letter you want to use as the shortcut. Make sure you don't use the same letter more than once in the same menu list.
- **Order** The names on the Create menu are normally listed in alphabetical order. If you want the forms in different order, you'll have to put numbers or letters in front of the names. Numbers work well for less than nine forms, but once you add more than 9, the form named 10 will appear in a list before the form named 2 because the sort order is alphabetical.
- **Cascading** If you have several forms with the same words at the beginning or that are response levels to a parent document, you may want to create a cascading menu to group them together. In the form name of each form, enter the main name followed by a backslash (\) and then enter the name that should appear on the cascading menu. For example, if you have

both a course description form and a course inquiry form, you might name them Course\Description and Course\Inquiry. Course appears on the Create menu and when you click Course, a cascading menu displays Description and Inquiry.

- **Synonyms** Synonyms are internal form names; they don't appear on the menu for users and are a tool for the designer when form names are used in formulas. For example, a form named Registrations for Night Classes might work well for users, but not for the designer who has to type out that name in a formula. You should make a practice of using synonyms. To create a form name synonym, enter a vertical bar (|) after the form name and then enter the synonym (Registrations for Night Classes | Night).

  A short form name is no excuse for omitting synonyms. For example, a form called Orders is part of a database you completed and rolled out six months ago. Today, the order department expands its services and now wants to call the existing Orders form Domestic Orders. A design request has been made for you to create an International Orders form, which needs new fields added to support international commerce. Renaming the Orders form Domestic Orders could have an unpredictable effect on your documents created with the form Orders, particularly if you used the form name in any formulas. Creating a synonym, Orders | Orders allows you to continue to use Orders in your formulas and renaming the form Domestic Orders | Orders has no negative effect.

- **Consistency** When you have multiple databases with similar forms containing the same information, standardize the names so users can recognize them easily (for example, Client Contact, Client Call Report, and so forth).

Selecting Form Properties

Now that the form is named, you need to select the other properties associated with the form.

1. In the Form type box, choose **document**, **response**, or **response to response**. The default setting is Document.
2. From the Background list box, select a color for the form background. Because they might be hard on the eyes, stay away from vibrant, dark colors. You might think a dark background with white text looks good, but when you try to create a view showing documents created with this form, you won't see the text—it's white on white. You'll have to change the view background color or the color of the text in the view. Pastel shades make a good background and dark colors are good for text.

3. By default, the Include in options Menu and Search Builder are enabled. If you don't want this form to appear on the Create menu, disable the Menu option. If you want it to appear under Other on the Create menu, select Create - Other dialog from the drop-down list box next to Menu. Having Search Builder enabled makes it possible to search documents created with this form using the full text index.
4. To track revisions of documents, choose an option other than None from the Versioning box to display the updates differently in a view.
   - **New versions become responses** Shows the original document first with all successive versions below. Use this when the original document is the point of reference. This option also prevents replication and saves conflicts when updates become responses.
   - **Prior versions become responses** Lists the latest revision first in the view. Make this selection when the latest update is where you want to focus, and older versions become backup or reference documentation. You can't prevent replication or save conflicts with this choice.
   - **New versions become siblings** Lists the original document first, but all successive versions are listed below it as main documents. Use this when you don't expect every main document to be revised because it will be hard to find updates in the view. This prevents replication or saves conflicts of the main document.

Save Conflict A Save conflict occurs when two users on the same network edit and save the same document at the same time. A *replication conflict* occurs when two users using different replica copies of the database edit and save the same document and then the database is replicated. One version of the document becomes the main document, and the other becomes the "Replication or Save Conflict" document. Someone, usually the Notes administrator, has to resolve the conflict by editing one of the documents to include the changes made in the other. Then one of the documents gets deleted.

5. When you choose one of the versioning options, the Create versions box gives you two choices. When you select **Automatic - File, Save**, Notes creates new versions as new documents automatically whenever users save a document. If you choose **Manual - File, New Version**, a new document is created only when users select **File, Save as New Version** from the menu. (With this option, users have more control over when they create new versions.)

6. Enable **Anonymous Forms** when you want to create a form that doesn't record the names of the people who create or edit documents. This would be useful for a voting ballot form, an instructor evaluation form, or an anonymous complaint form.
7. If you want to avoid replication conflicts , you can enable **Merge replication conflicts**. With this enabled, replication conflicts will only occur if the same field in the same document is modified by more than one person at the same time.

Replication Conflict If two users edit the same document on different servers between replications, a replication conflict might occur when the servers replicate. For more information on replication, refer to Part I, "Lotus Notes 4.5."

8. Sometimes forms get renamed or deleted from the database, but there are still documents in existence that were created with those forms. In order to display those documents, Notes uses the default form. The information might appear differently than in the original, but at least some of it can be seen. There can be only one default form in a database. To make a form the default form, click the **Default** tab on the Properties box. Check **Default database form**.

Saving the Form

There are several methods of saving the form.

- Choose **File**, **Save** from the menu or press **Ctrl+S** . This saves the form but enables you to continue working on it.
- Press **Esc**. Notes will then prompt you `Do you want to save this new form?` Answer **Yes** to save it, **No** to close it without saving it, or **Cancel** to go back to the form without saving or closing it.
- Choose **File**, **Close** from the menu. Notes will then prompt you `Do you want to save this new form?` Answer **Yes** to save it, **No** to close it without saving it, or **Cancel** to go back to the form without saving or closing it.

After you save your form, you can see the form listed in the forms design view. Expand Design in the Navigator pane. Choose **Forms**. You see your form in the View pane. Double-click to open it in Design mode.

In this lesson, you learned how to start a new form, give it a name, set the form properties, and save the form. In the next lesson, you learn about adding static text to the form.

Adding Static Text to a Form

In this lesson, you learn about adding text to your form and how to format that text.

What Is Static Text?

Static text is the text that appears on the form but isn't part of a field. It defines what the user should enter in a field and provides instructions on how to complete the form. To enter static text, position your cursor where you want to place the static text on the form and simply type the text. Use word processing fundamentals such as arrow keys to move left, right, up, down, and around the form. The Delete and Backspace keys will remove unneeded characters.

Character Formatting

When you format text, you change the appearance of the text. Size, font, color, and style are formatting attributes you can use to differentiate areas of your form.

You can format text in one of two ways:

- You can turn on the formatting feature when you come to the point in your text where you want the formatting to start, and then turn it off once you have completed the formatting. For example, if you are typing a sentence and you come to a word that you want to be bold, you can turn on the bold format, type the word, turn off the bold format, and then continue typing.

- You select the text to which you want to apply the format, then you turn on the formatting. Notes applies the format only to the selected text.

The best way to apply formats is to use the Text Properties box. To open the Text Properties box, choose **Text, Text Properties**. Then click the first tab of the Properties box (see Figure 3.1).

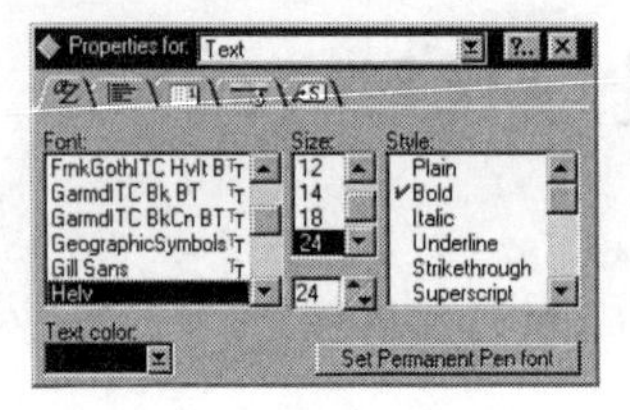

Figure 3.1 The Text Properties box.

The formatting options are all listed in the Properties box. Just click one to select it. Notes immediately applies the format to text you have selected. If you haven't selected text, Notes applies the format to the next text you type.

Fonts

Text in Notes normally appears in a font called Helv (Helvetica). Lotus recommends a sans serif font like Helv because it's easier to read on-screen. But if the documents created from the form are more likely to be printed, you might want to use a serif font such as Times New Roman because serif fonts are considered easier to read than sans serif fonts.

Serif/Sans Serif Serifs are the short, horizontal bars at the tops and bottoms of text characters. If a typeface has serifs, it's known as a serif typeface or serif font. If it does not have serifs, it's known as a sans serif font.

- To change the font, click the Font button on the status bar and then pick the font you want from the pop-up list. Or, you can make a font choice from the Properties box by clicking the name of the font you want to use.

Use Just a Few Fonts Just because you have a large number of fonts, you should still be judicious in your font use. A great number of fonts available for computers are decorative; they're fine to use for a couple of words, but they're difficult to read in large blocks of text. Simple is best. Save fun fonts for special occasions or emphasis. Also, not everyone shares the fonts you have on your computer. When you don't know what font set your users have, you should use Helv, Arial, or Times New Roman for Windows users.

Size

Size of type is measured in points—the larger the number of points, the larger the text. The default size of text in Notes is 10 points, which is easy to read on screen. As with fonts, you should be consistent in your use of sizes for form titles, section titles, and field headings, not to mention text.

- To change the font size, click the Size button on the status bar and pick one of the sizes from the pop-up menu. Or, you can choose the size you want from the Properties box by clicking one of the listed choices. If you want a size other than the ones listed, use the text size box below the list. Either type the size in the box, or use the small up and down arrows to select the size.

Font Style

You can change the type styles to bold, italic, underline, strikethrough, superscript, and subscript.

Use **bold**, *italic*, and underline for emphasis. You can also use these type styles in combination, such as ***bold and ivAlic***.

~~Strikethrough~~ is used only to show when text that has been struck from a document, so you probably won't use it when you design a form.

You only use superscript when text must appear above the line, as with the notation of a trademark™. Finally, use subscript when you need to write chemical formulas, such as H_2O.

- To change the style, choose **Text**, and then **Bold** or **Italic** or **Underline**. These choices also have keyboard shortcuts that are noted on the menu next to the formatting choice. However, when you are applying many attributes to text, it's best to work from the Properties box.

TIP **Neatness Counts!** Don't be careless in applying font styles. Save bold, underlined, and italic for emphasis and be consistent to avoid confusing the users.

Color

One of the best ways to add emphasis and emotion to your text is to add color.

- To add color to text, choose **Text, Color** and then select a color name from the list. Not all of the 16 available colors are listed on the menu. When you click Other to see more colors, the Properties box opens. You can also select a color from the Text Color list on the Properties box. Instead of color names, this list shows samples. Just click the color swatch you want to apply it to the text.

TIP **Neatness Counts Here, Too** Don't abuse colors. Just because you can change them doesn't mean you should. Stick to one or two on a form. The easiest-to-read combination is still black text on a white or light-colored background.

Paragraph Formatting

When you have longer sections of text, when you need to control the spacing of the text, or when you want to emphasize headings, you'll want to use paragraph formatting.

Aligning Paragraphs

You can change the alignment of a paragraph, so it is flush left, flush right, centered, or justified.

1. With the document in the edit mode, select the paragraph or paragraphs you want to change.
2. Choose **Text, Text Properties**.
3. Click the **Alignment** tab (see Figure 3.2).

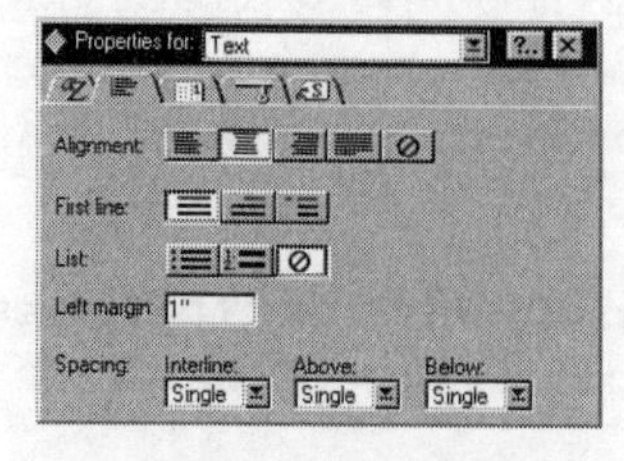

Figure 3.2 The Text Properties box with the Alignment page showing.

4. Click one of the alignment icons: Left, Center, Right, Full, No Wrap.

Left align Aligns text flush to the left margin, but leaves text uneven on the right margin.

Center align Centers the text between the left and right margins.

Right align Aligns text flush to the right margin but leaves it ragged on the left margin.

Full align Aligns text flush with both the left and right margins.

No wrap Turns off word wrapping and displays text as one continuous string.

You can also align paragraphs with the Text Align Paragraph Left, Text Align Paragraph Center, and Text Align Paragraph Right SmartIcons. Or, you can choose **Text**, **Align Paragraph** and then select **Left**, **Center**, **Right**, **Full**, or **No Wrap**.

Indenting Paragraphs

Lotus Notes gives you a number of ways to indent paragraphs. Indenting moves the beginning of the first line of the paragraph to the right by a specified amount. Outdenting moves the beginning of the first line of the paragraph to the left by a specified amount.

To set indents using the Text Properties box:

1. With the document in the edit mode, select the paragraph or paragraphs you want to indent.
2. Choose **Text**, **Text Properties**.
3. Click the **Alignment** tab.
4. Click one of the First line icons: Normal, Indent, or Outdent.

   Normal Returns the first line of the paragraph to flush with the rest of the paragraph.

   Indent Indents the first line of the paragraph(s).

   Outdent Outdents the first line of the paragraph(s).
5. For indented or outdented paragraphs, enter the amount you want to indent or outdent the paragraph.

To set indents using the Ruler:

1. With the document in the edit mode, select the paragraph or paragraphs to indent.
2. Choose **View, Ruler** (see Figure 3.3).

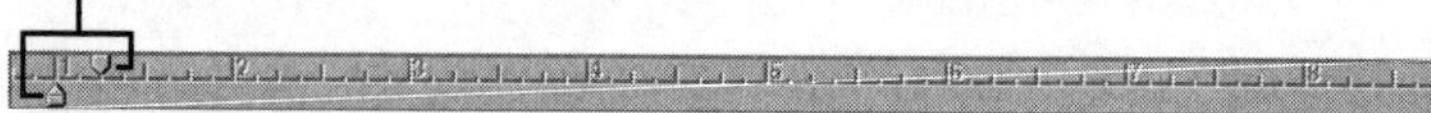

Figure 3.3 Ruler showing indent pentagons.

3. Drag the upper pentagon pointer to where you want the first line of the paragraph(s) to start, or drag the lower pentagon pointer to where you want the remaining lines of the selected paragraph(s) to start.

   Drag the lower pentagon to where you want it and then double-click it to move both pointers at the same time.

TIP **So, You Don't Like Mice?** Lotus Notes also has keyboard shortcuts for indenting paragraphs:

- Press **F7** to indent the first line of the selected paragraph(s).
- Press **Shift+F7** to outdent the first line of the selected paragraph(s).
- Press **F8** to indent the entire selected paragraph(s).
- Press **Shift + F8** to outdent the entire selected paragraph(s).

Bullets and Numbers

You can add bullets or numbers to selected paragraphs.

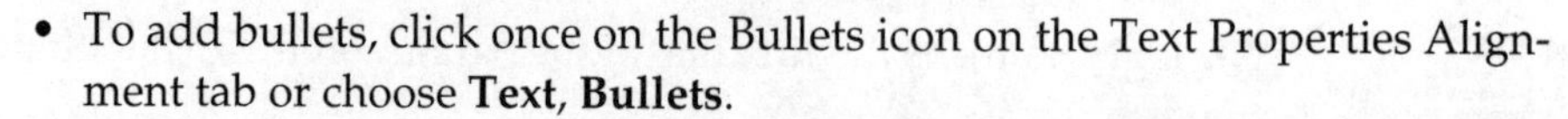

- To add bullets, click once on the Bullets icon on the Text Properties Alignment tab or choose **Text, Bullets**.

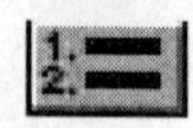

- To add numbers, click once on the Numbers icon on the Text Properties Alignment tab or choose **Text, Numbers**.

Line and Paragraph Spacing

You can set the spacing between lines in a paragraph, as well as the amount of space before and after paragraphs.

1. With the document in the edit mode, select the paragraph(s) you want to change.
2. Choose **Text**, **Text Properties**.
3. Click the **Alignment** tab.
4. To set the spacing between lines within a paragraph, select **Single**, **Double**, or **1 1/2** from the Interline list box.

   To set the amount of space you want between paragraphs, select **Single**, **Double**, or **1 1/2** from either the Above or Below list box.

If you choose **Text**, **Spacing**, you can also set the Interline spacing.

Setting Tabs

By default, tabs are set every one-half inch in Lotus Notes, but sometimes you need to set your own tabs. Using tabs, for instance, can help line up your fields and make it easier to enter data. You can set tabs from the Properties box or from the Ruler.

To set tabs from the Properties box:

1. With your document in the edit mode, select the paragraph(s) for which you want to set tabs.
2. Choose **Text**, **Text Properties**.
3. Click the **Page** tab (see Figure 3.4).

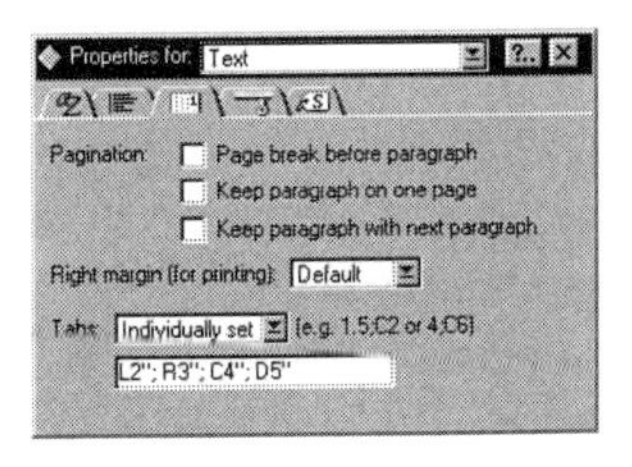

Figure 3.4 The Text Properties box with the Page tab showing.

4. In the Tabs box, choose **Individually set** and enter the tab stops you want (if you enter more than one, separate them with semicolons), or select **Evenly spaced** and enter the interval between tab stops. Always enter the numbers followed by the inch mark (").
5. If you want to enter left, right, center, or decimal tabs, type an **L**, **R**, **C**, or **D** before the number (L1" would result in a left aligned tab at 1"). A decimal tab would cause a column of numbers to align on the decimal point.

To set tabs using the Ruler:

1. With the document in the edit mode, select the paragraph(s) to which you want to add tabs.
2. Choose **View, Ruler** (see Figure 3.5).

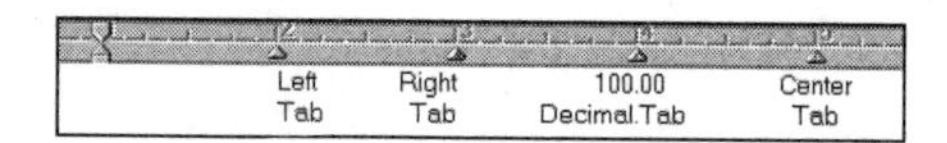

Figure 3.5 The Ruler with tab settings.

3. On the Ruler, click where you want a left tab, right-click where you want a right tab, press **Shift** and click where you want a decimal tab, and press **Shift** and right-click where you want a centered tab.

To remove a tab from the Ruler, click it. To change the type of tab, right-click the tab and select a new tab type.

Keeping Paragraphs on One Page or Together

You may want to keep a paragraph from breaking in the middle at the automatic page break. You can enter a manual page break to control where your page breaks by choosing **Create, Page Break** where you want the new page to start. Alternatively, you can format the paragraph(s) to keep the lines all on one page. You may also want to be sure that two paragraphs are kept together and not split by the page break, which is especially true if one paragraph is a headline.

1. With the document in edit mode, click in the paragraph you want to keep on one page or click in the first of two consecutive paragraphs you want to keep on that page.
2. Choose **Text, Text Properties**.

3. Click the **Page** tab.
4. Under Pagination, select **Keep paragraph on one page** or **Keep paragraph with next paragraph**.

Where's the Page Break? To see where the page breaks, choose **View**, **Show**, **Page Breaks**. Page breaks appear as solid lines across the screen.

Using Named Styles

If you find yourself frequently using the same set of formatting commands, it's time for you to try named styles. Named styles keep a group of formatting commands together, so you can apply them all at once.

1. With your document in edit mode, format a paragraph with the properties you want to save as a named style.
2. Click the paragraph.
3. Choose **Text**, **Text Properties**.
4. Click the **Named Styles** tab.
5. Click **Create Style** and enter a name for the paragraph style. The Create Named Style dialog box appears (see Figure 3.6).

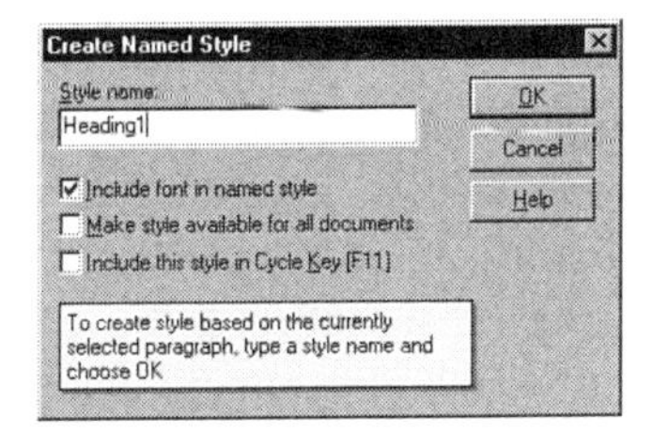

Figure 3.6 The Create Named Style dialog box.

6. Check **Include font in named style** if you want to save the font as part of the named style.
7. Check **Make style available for all documents** if you want to use the named style outside of this one document.
8. Check **Include this style in Cycle Key [F11]** so it becomes one of the styles available when you press F11 to cycle through the named styles.
9. Click **OK**.

Once you have created the named style, you can apply it to other paragraphs.

1. With your document in the edit mode, select the paragraph(s) to which you want to apply the named style.
2. Choose **Text, Named Styles** and select a style from the menu.

   Or, click the **Named Styles** indicator on the status bar and select a style for the pop-up list.

   Or, press **F11** to cycle through the named styles.

Changing and Deleting a Named Style

If you need to change a named style:

1. Format a paragraph with the new properties you want for the named style.
2. Choose **Text, Text Properties** and then click the **Named Styles** tab.
3. Click **Redefine Style** and select the named style whose properties you want to replace with those of the selected paragraph. Then click **OK** once.

To delete a named style:

1. Choose **Text, Text Properties** and click the **Named Styles** tab.
2. Click the **Delete Styles** button.
3. Choose the name of the style you want to delete, and then click **OK**.

Figure 3.7 shows the beginning of a form. Although you can't see it here, a cyan background has been chosen, and the text has been kept black (and bold) for easy reading. The font is 10 point Helv, and each field label is followed by a colon. Finally, the line that separates the address from the directions is simply an underline set in a dark blue effect. To keep the underline from wrapping around on smaller screens, the alignment of that paragraph is "No Wrap."

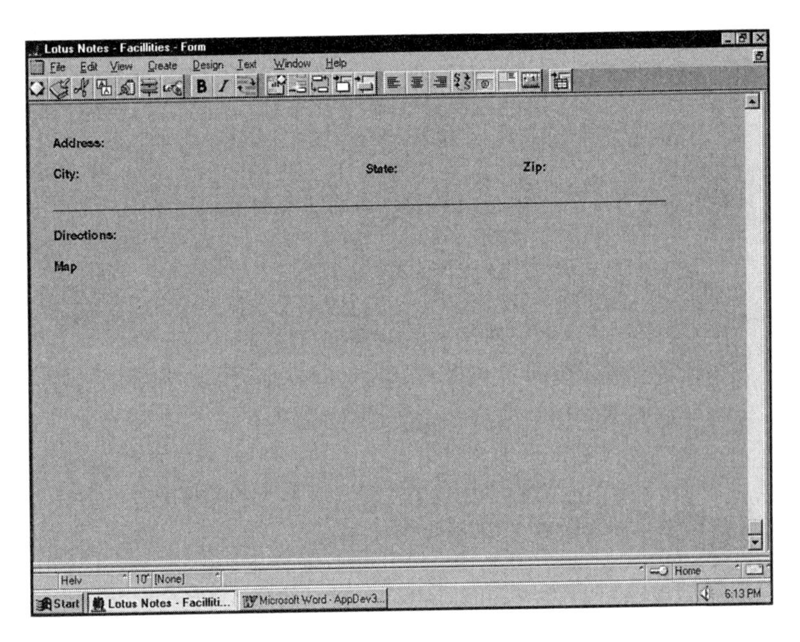

Figure 3.7 Static text on a new form.

In this lesson, you learned how to enter static text on a form and how to format text for the best appearance. In the next lesson, you learn about adding fields to the form.

Adding Fields

In this lesson, you learn about using fields in a form and what types of fields you can create.

Understanding Notes Fields

Fields are the method by which you enter and sort data in Notes. Forms cannot accept any kind of data, except data entered through the use of fields. For example, to enter information to track clients, you need to create fields for the client name, address, phone number, and so on.

The elements of a field are:

1. Field name
2. Data type
3. A computed or editable attribute
4. Display options
5. Formulas or scripts

Naming Fields

Consistency is important in creating names for your fields. In naming fields, keep these rules in mind:

- Each field name within a form must be unique. For example, a client form might have several address fields, one for the street address, one for the P.O. Box, one for the city, and so on. Name those fields Address1, Address2, and City so each is unique.
- The maximum length for a field name is 32 characters They are, by convention, words run together with the first letter of each word capitalized (for example, CourseDescription).

- Field names cannot begin with a number, and should not begin with $ or @. These symbols are reserved for special use by Notes.
- Field names should not contain spaces. Use an underline character (_) to mark a space if you have to.

You will use field names in formulas, so try to keep your field names short. Notes has some reserved field names that have predefined uses. Refer to Table 1.1 on your tear-out card for a list of those names.

Editable versus Computed Fields

All field types must have either an editable or computed attribute.

- **Editable Fields** are fields where you can change the values. In these fields, you can enter text, time, dates, and numbers or select from a list of keyword choices.
- **Computed Fields** are fields where you can't change the values. Values in these fields appear automatically—they are based on formula calculations or they are pulled from other systems or database information.

  There are three types of computed fields:

  > **Computed** fields are recalculated every time a document is created, saved, or refreshed.
  >
  > **Computed when composed** fields are calculated when the document is created and are never recalculated.
  >
  > **Computed for display fields** are recalculated when a document is opened for reading or editing. The results of these fields are not stored in the document.

Field Data Types

Lotus Notes has eight field data types. A data type sets the kind of data that a field can hold. It's important to define the proper data type. For example, you cannot calculate numbers that you enter into a field whose data type is defined as *text*. Notes field data types are defined in Table 4.1.

Table 4.1 Field Data Types

Data Type	*Contains*
Authors	List of names of people who can edit a document created with that form (it excludes unlisted people from editing those documents)

Table 4.1 Continued

Data Type	*Contains*
Keyword	List of text choices shown as dialog lists, radio buttons, or check boxes
Names	User or server names as they appear in the Notes ID
Number	Numerals 0 to 9 (used for mathematical calculations), +, -, decimal point, scientific notation (E), and constant (e)
Readers	List of names of people or servers who can read a document created with that form (it excludes unlisted people from readership)
Rich Text	Formatted text, text, graphics, pop-ups, buttons, attachments, tables, and embedded objects. Rich text fields can't be displayed in a view and their values can't be returned in most formulas. See Lesson 9 for more on views.
Text	Letters, punctuation, spaces, and non-mathematical numbers (such as phone numbers and ZIP codes)
Time	Numbers separated by punctuation, as MM/DD/YY HH:MM:SS, to define date and time information

Field Display Options

The Number and Time field data types have display options that appear on the Basics tab of the Field Properties box. You can select the **General**, **Fixed**, **Scientific**, or **Currency** format for the values. You can choose the number of decimal places for display. You can also determine how percentages and negative numbers will appear or add a thousands separator (a comma). Figure 4.1 shows the options for display for numbers.

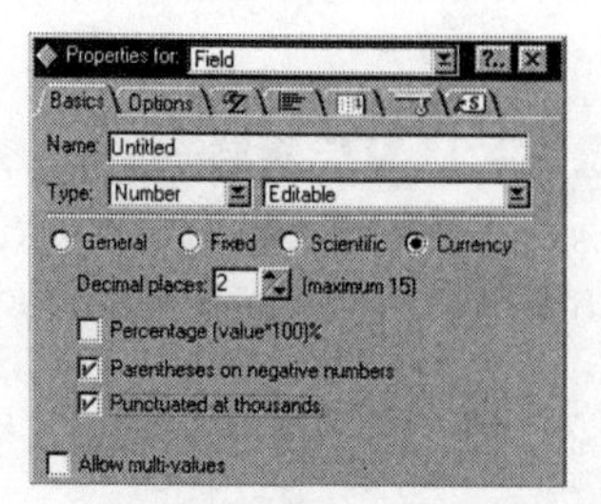

Figure 4.1 Field Properties box with Number type selected.

In a Time field, you can select the date format and the time format (mm/dd/yy, and so on). Figure 4.2 shows the options for display for time.

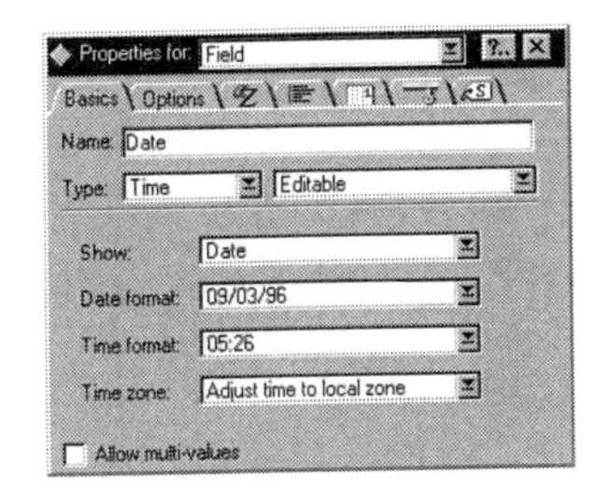

Figure 4.2 Field Properties box with Time field chosen.

In all fields, you can also select fonts and other text attributes found on the AZ tab of the Field Properties box.

Field Formulas and Scripts

Field formulas determine the value of a field. Not all fields have formulas. You use formulas to calculate a field value, set a default value, and to translate or validate the user's input. For more on formulas, see Lesson 5.

Creating Fields

When you are ready to add a field to your form, follow these steps:

1. With the form opened in design mode, position your cursor where you want the field to appear. Place your field following or underneath your static text. For example, if you have static text that says "Customer name," place your cursor a few spaces after the static text.
2. Choose **Create**, **Field** from the menu.
3. On the Basics page of the Field Properties box, enter the name of the field in the Name box (e.g., a field for entering a first name might be called Fname). Figure 4.3 shows the Field Properties box.

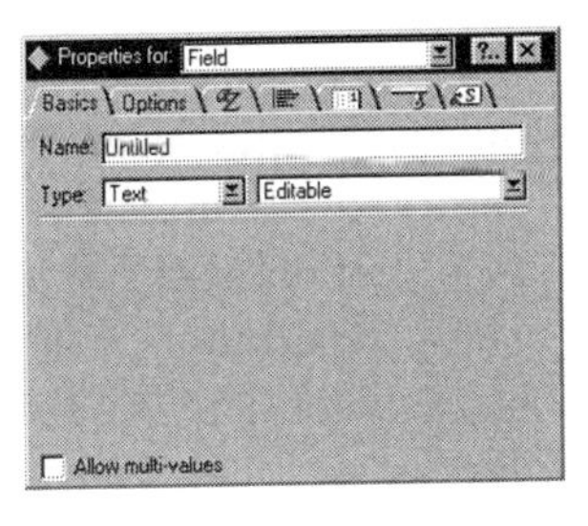

Figure 4.3 The Field Properties box.

4. Select the Type of field (refer to the list in Table 4.1).
5. Choose whether the field will be **Editable**, **Computed, Computer for display**, or **Computed when composed.**

   If you pick the Keyword type of field, you can list the keywords you want to appear (see Figure 4.4). Check **Allow values not in list** if you want users to have the ability to use words not included in your list. If you allow values not included in your list, those new values will not be added to your original list. **Check Allow multi-values** if you want the users to be able to pick more than one keyword (not available for radio buttons).

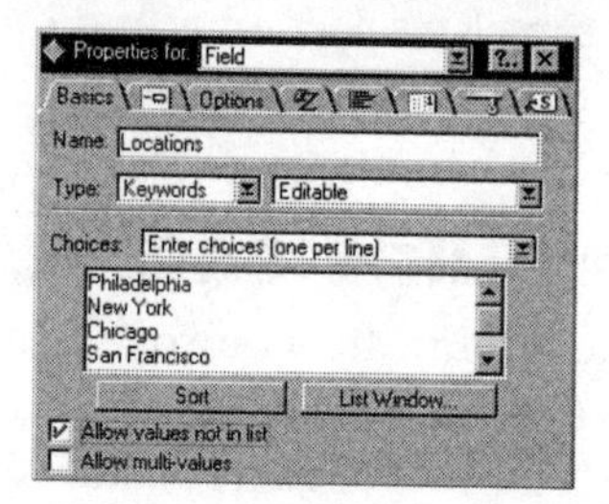

Figure 4.4 Field Properties box with Keywords selected.

On the second tab of the Field Properties box (the field tab), you can choose how you want to show the keywords: as a dialog list box, as radio buttons, or as check boxes (see Figure 4.5).

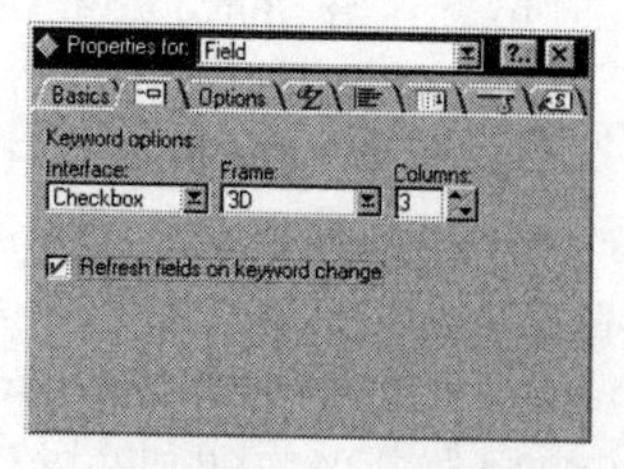

Figure 4.5 Keyword options page of Field Properties box.

6. Click the **Options** tab of the Properties box and enter any helpful text in the Help description box (for instance, `Select the location nearest your home`; see Figure 4.6). If the user has selected **View**, **Show**, **Field help** from the menu, this help description will appear at the bottom of the screen when the cursor is in the field (this text is small so it's often overlooked by users—you might want to put your help information directly on the form).

7. Beginning again at step one, continue to add fields to your form.

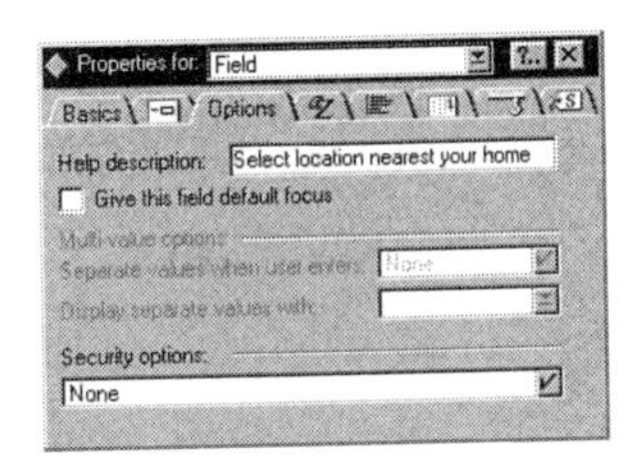

Figure 4.6 The Options page of the Field Properties box.

In the example shown in Figure 4.7, a keyword field is inserted at the top of the form to enter the name of the facility. The text attributes for that field are set at 18-point bold Helvetica. The rest of the fields are editable text fields except for the FacilityMap field, which is a rich text field so a picture of a map can be stored there. Each field on this form starts with Facility to avoid confusion when other forms are used to inherit information from this form. By using the form name in the field name, you'll know which fields came from which forms. Note that Facility is a long word to be included in a field name (remember field names should be as short as possible). It would be easier to use F for facility, or Fac. Facility was spelled out for the sake of this example. You also see static text on this form, such as Address and City.

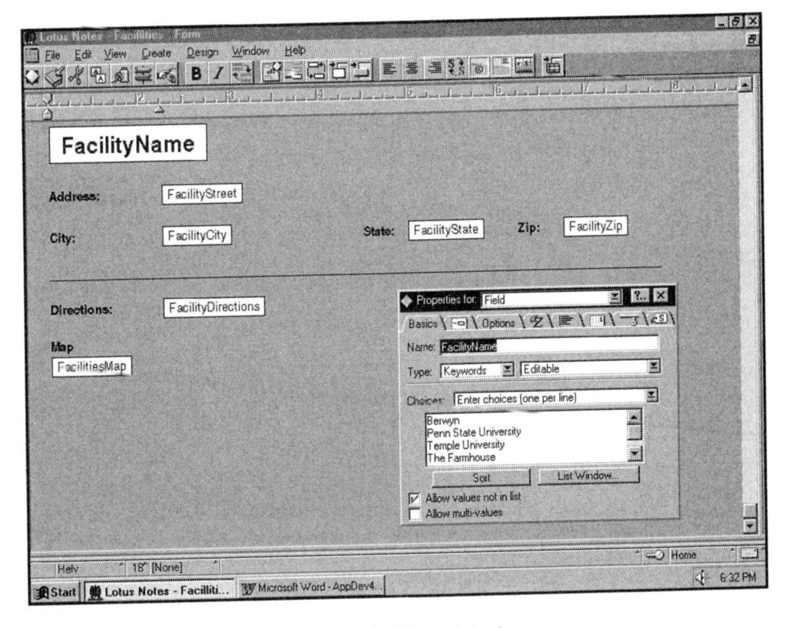

Figure 4.7 The Facilities form with the fields added.

Shared Fields

Each of the fields you have added to the form have been single-use fields. Single-use fields are designed for use within one form and their definitions (elements) are stored in that form. Notes also permits you to create shared fields. All shared field definitions are stored together in a shared field design document. A shared field can be used in multiple forms. If the definition of a shared field changes, the change automatically appears in all forms that contain the shared field. The value of a shared field, however, is not part of its definition and is therefore not necessarily the same from form to form. If you need to include a single field in many forms, using a shared field is a good way to do it. If you need to include multiple fields in many forms, you should use subforms. See Lesson 7 for more information on subforms.

To define a shared field, choose **Create**, **Design**, **Shared Field**. Then define the field as you would any field. To include a shared field in a form, choose **Create**, **Insert Shared Field**.

In this lesson, you learned about the different types of Notes fields and how to add fields to a form. In the next lesson, you learn about formulas and @functions.

Formulas and @Functions

In this lesson, you learn about formulas and @functions, when to use them, why you need them, and how to use them.

Understanding Formulas and @Functions

Formulas are central to Lotus Notes. @Functions are central to formulas. Formulas and @Functions calculate field and column values, automate difficult or tedious tasks, and generally make your databases more useful and usable in a score of ways.

Before you read any further, look at the Tear-Out Card in this book. The Tear-Out Card contains useful information about formulas and @functions and you may want to have it handy while reading this lesson and while designing your databases.

What Is a Formula?

A *formula* is an expression that performs a function. It can determine field values, define what documents will appear in a view, or calculate values for a column. A formula can be as simple as a field name or concatenation of field names, or as complex as a multiple statement with combined functions. It can call up @Functions (which you'll learn about later in this lesson) and @Commands (which you'll learn about in Lesson 12) to perform specialized functions.

Concatenation The stringing together of field names and text constants. For example, if your form has City, State, and Zip fields but you want a column in a view to show a combination such as Philadelphia, PA 19101, you need a concatenation formula:

City + ", " + State + " " + Zip

Do not confuse concatenation with addition. They both use plus signs (+), but addition is a *mathematical* function.

The algebraic expression $x + y$ is a formula, where x and y are variables or *operands*. The plus (+) is the *operator*. Formulas are therefore combinations of operands and operators. Operands in Notes can include field names, constants, or @Functions.

When Do You Use a Formula?

You can use formulas to perform a variety of tasks in Notes as described in Table 5.1.

Table 5.1 Where to Use Formulas

Use Formulas in:	*In Order to:*
Forms	Compute fields
	Determine actions
	Display data differently
	Hide fields under specified conditions
	Set the window title
	Provide a default value
	Translate input
	Verify input
Views	Select documents for the view
	Determine column values
	Perform actions

Formula Components

There are a number of building blocks that make up formulas. These are the formula components.

Variables

Variables have different values at different times. They can stand by themselves as formulas. For example, if you want to show the value of the field *FacilityName* in a view column, the formula for the view column would simply be this: FacilityName.

Variables can be used in arithmetic formulas. For example, if the field *NetPrice* has *$100* in it, and the field *GrossPrice* has the formula *NetPrice * 1.06* in it, the user would see *$106* in the *GrossPrice* field.

Variables can be strung together with operators and text in a concatenation as in the following formula:

```
FacilityCity + ", " + FacilityState + " " + FacilityZip
```

FacilityCity, FacilityState, and FacilityZip are field names. The quotation marks (") enclose static text (the comma and spaces). The plus signs (+) concatenate everything to produce something like "Philadelphia, PA 19103." You can also use field names as arguments for @functions:

```
@If(FacilityCity = "Philadelphia"; "Home game"; "Away game")
```

This formula says that if the contents of the FacilityCity field are equal to Philadelphia, then this is a home game; otherwise, it's an away game.

Notes formulas also make use of *temporary variables*. A temporary variable is one that you set at the beginning of a formula for use later on in the formula, and only in the formula. Use temporary variables to make long, complex formulas easier to read. Here is an example:

```
Price := Cost * 1.28;
Tax := Price * .06;
Price + Tax
```

The preceding formula includes three expressions, separated from one another by semicolons. The first expression creates a temporary variable (Price) and assigns to it the value of Cost multiplied by 1.28. The second expression creates a temporary variable (Tax) and assigns to it the value of Price multiplied by .06. The third expression adds the values of the temporary variables (Price and Tax) and inserts the result into the field that contains this formula.

Constants

Constants are values that don't change. There are three types of constants:

- **Number** Number constants include numerals from 0 to 9, + (plus), - (minus), exponent (E), or constant (e).
- **Text** Text constants are any set of characters that appear in a formula in quotation marks (" "), such as "Philadelphia." If you want to use quotation marks in a text string, you must precede the quotation mark with a backslash (\).
- **Time** Time constants are any set of characters in Notes date or time format that appear in a formula in square brackets ([ ]) such as [09/05/96].

Operators

You assign, modify, or combine values into new values by using operators. There are five types of operators:

- Arithmetic operators (+, -, *, /) add, subtract, multiply, and divide numbers with each other. They produce a numeric result.

TIP **Order of Precedence** Arithmetic operators evaluate in the following order: Parentheses, Exponents, Multiplication and Division, and then Addition and Subtraction. For example:

6 + 4/2 = 8

(6 + 4)/2 = 5

- The Assignment operator (:=) assigns values to variables. The following example assigns the value "Philadelphia" to the variable name City:

  City := "Philadelphia"

- Comparison operators (=, <>, !=, ><, <, >, ,=, >=) compare one value to another, determining whether one is equal to, greater than, or less than the other. Comparison operations always produce a result of *true* or *false*. The following examples all produce a result of *true*:

  2 + 2 > 3
  "Philadelphia != "Superbowl contender"

- The Text Concatenation operator (+) connects blocks of text to each other to create a single block of text. The following example results in "Philadelphia, PA 19131":

  City + ", " + State + " " + Zip

- Logical operators (AND or &, OR or |, NOT or !) permit you to combine logical values in a single expression. The following example states that, on 4th down and less than one yard to go, the play will be "Quarterback Sneak"; otherwise "Punt":

  @If(Down = 4 AND YardsToGo < 1; "Quarterback Sneak"; "Punt")

Keywords

Keywords in Notes formulas perform special functions. They always appear in uppercase.

DEFAULT Associates a value with a field. If the field already exists in a document, the current value is used. Otherwise, Notes creates the field in the document and the default value defined in the statement. In this example, the value in the Topic field is used if Topic exists. Otherwise, the value of MainSubject is placed in the Topic field.

DEFAULT Topic := MainSubject

ENVIRONMENT Assigns a value to an environment variable from the user's NOTES.INI file or Notes Preferences file. The formula below converts the counter number to text and saves it as an environmental variable called Order.

ENVIRONMENT Order := @Text(Counter)

FIELD Assigns a value to a field in the current document. If the field doesn't exist, Notes creates it. If it does exist, Notes replaces the contents of the field. This example formula creates a new field called Name that adds

"Dr. " to the beginning of the name. It is not a visible field, unless you add it to the form, but it exists in the document and you can use it in formulas.

FIELD Name := "Dr. " + LName

REM Inserts remarks (documentation) into a formula that are ignored in evaluating the formula. REM lines are always ended by a semicolon. Remarks must be in quotes and cannot include semicolons or other separators used in formulas.

REM "This formula assigns variables to calculate the correct date";

Formula Syntax Rules

All programming languages have syntax rules, and Notes formulas do, too. You have to know where to put spaces, when to use quotation marks, when to capitalize letters, and where to use parentheses. Refer to Table 1.3 on your Tear-Out Card for more on syntax rules.

One of the most common syntax errors is the failure to include the proper number of open "(" and closed ")" parentheses. There must be an equal number of open and closed parentheses, and Notes will not allow you to complete the entry of your formula if parentheses are not in balance.

Semicolons are used to separate multiple statements or arguments and colons are used to separate lists. In the following example, the semicolon separates the first and second arguments of the @IsMember function. The colon separates the members of the list in the second argument. The @IsMember function asks if the item in the first argument is a member of the list in the second argument. This would be true if the field *Country* has either *United States* or *France* entered as its value.

@IsMember(Country ; "United States" : "France")

@Functions

The @functions perform specialized tasks in Notes formulas. You can use them to format text strings, generate dates and times, format dates and times, evaluate conditional statements, calculate numeric values, calculate values in a list, convert text to numbers or numbers to text, or activate agents, actions, buttons, hotspots, or SmartIcons.

There are about 200 @functions in Lotus Notes, and they're all listed in the *Programmer's Guide, Part 2*. Also refer to the Tear-Out Card for tables of @functions.

An @function calculates a return value and replaces itself with that value; the return value can be text, a number, time, or a logical value (true = 1, false = 0).

One of the most frequently used @functions is the @If statement, which evaluates a condition to true or false. The syntax for @If is: @If(condition1; action1; condition2; action2; else-action). If the condition is true, it performs the first action; if it is false, it evaluates the next condition, and so on. If none of the conditions are true, it evaluates the else-action. The following formula says we eat peanut butter and jelly if we have the ingredients; otherwise, we call out for pizza.

> @If(@IsMember("peanut butter"; Cupboard) & @IsMember("Jelly"; Refrigerator); "Peanut butter and jelly"; "Domino's")

TIP **@If Guidelines** @If statements are useful for testing conditions and making decisions. They must always have an odd number of arguments. They can handle up to 99 conditions.

Syntax and @Functions

Although some @functions take no arguments (such as @Created), most do take arguments. Arguments are the values the formula uses to perform the operation specified by the @function. For example, in the formula @Min(Retainer; Earnings), the function @Min specifies that the operation select the smaller of the two arguments. @Sum(3; 5; 2; 9; 15; -3) specifies that all the numbers be totalled.

When an @function uses arguments, the syntax rules are as follows:

1. Separate multiple arguments with semicolons.
2. Enclose arguments in parentheses.
3. Enclose keyword arguments in square brackets, such as @Name([CN]; @UserName). These @functions require keyword arguments: @Abstract, @Command, @PostedCommand, @DocMark, @GetPortsList, @PickList, @MailSend, @Name, and @Prompt.

Types of @Functions

You can categorize an @function as one of seven types: arithmetic operations, data conversion, date/time operations, list operations, logical operations, string manipulation, or special.

Arithmetic Operations

Use arithmetic @functions to make calculations using numeric values. See Table 2.1 on your Tear-Out Card. The following is an example:

@Sum(3;5;7) produces the total of all the arguments
@Average(3; 5; 7) produces the average of all the arguments

Data Conversion

Because you must use data of the same type in formulas, you'll need to convert text to numbers, numbers to text, or dates to text. See Table 2.2 of the Tear-Out Card. Here are some examples:

@Text(12) converts the number 12 to a text string "12"
@TextToNumber("12") converts the text string "12" to the number 12

When you use @Text(*value;format-string*), the format string you choose significantly affects the appearance of the returned value. For example, if you just use @Text(*value*) with a time/date value you will get all the date and time information, down to the second. If you only want the date, you need to include a format string that limits the output to Date only. Likewise, if you want @Text(price) to return a dollar sign and two digits (such as $25.00), you need to include a format string to that effect.

There are four categories of date/time format strings. Although you can include up to four components in your format string, you can only choose one from each category. For example, @Text(Date; "D0S0") returns 8/19/96, but @Text(Date; "T1S1") returns 10:15.

There are also format strings for numbers. You can combine any of these into a string, but separate the components with commas. For example, @Text(Price; "C") will return $25.00 when the value in the Price field is 25. "C" designates "currency" format with two decimal places.

Date/Time Operations

Use date and time @functions to generate or manipulate time and date values. Here are some examples:

@Created results in the creation date of a document
@Month(Date) extracts the number of the month (1-12) from the variable Date

List Operations

Notes is particularly strong in its ability to manipulate lists of elements. Use list @functions to evaluate, manipulate, and calculate from lists. Here are some examples:

@Elements(*list*) returns the number of elements in a *list*
@IsMember(*string*; *list*) returns true if *string* is a member of *list*
@Member(*value*; *list*) returns the position of *value* in *list*
@Unique(*list*) removes duplicate values from *list*

Logical Operations

Use the @If function to evaluate conditions and produce true or false results. The basic @If function is written as:

@If(condition; action; else-action)

If you want to evaluate more than one condition, you must have an odd number of arguments and you can't exceed 99 arguments:

@If(condition1; action1; condition2; action2; else-action)

In the preceding statement, the first condition that is true causes its action to process and no further evaluation takes place. Only if none of the conditions is true does the else-action process.

String Manipulation

When you're working with text, you might need to select part of a text string or format the text string in order to get the results you want. That's what string manipulation @functions are for. They work only on text fields. They can take variables or constants as arguments, including case-sensitive arguments, but they require quotation marks around arguments that are constants. Some examples include the following:

@Left(*string*; *n*) returns the *n* leftmost characters of *string*
@Middle(*string*; *substring*; *n*) returns *n* characters of string, beginning immediately after *substring*
@Trim(*string*) strips extra spaces from *string*
@ProperCase(*string*) capitalizes the first letter of every word in *string*

Special Functions

There are a number of @functions that perform useful tasks such as: accessing information about the user environment, about the document hierarchy, or about the database and views.

@UserName returns the name of the current user
@DbName returns the location and name of the current database
@Responses returns the number of responses to the currently selected document that appear in the current view

In this lesson, you learned about formulas, the components of formulas, and when and how to use formulas. You also learned about @functions. In the next lesson, you learn about Computed and Editable fields.

Computed versus Editable Fields

In this lesson, you learn the differences between computed and editable fields, the types of computed and editable fields, and what types of formulas to use in those fields.

The Differences Between Computed and Editable Fields

All field types are either editable or computed. Editable fields are ones in which users can change the values. Computed fields are ones in which users can't change the values because values are based upon formulas and the users see only the result of the formula.

There are three types of computed fields:

- **Computed** fields are recalculated every time a document is created, saved, or refreshed.
- **Computed for Display** fields are calculated when the document is created and are never recalculated.
- **Computed when Composed** fields are recalculated when a document is opened for reading or editing. The results of these fields are not stored in the document.

Computed

When the information you need in a particular field depends on data from other fields, select a computed field type. Computed fields recalculate every time a document is created, saved, or refreshed. Notes saves the value in the computed field with the document.

If you were preparing a form for computing employee hours, a typical formula for a computed field might be:

Hours * Rate

To enter a formula for a field:

1. Open the form in the Design mode.
2. Click the particular field to select it, or create a new field.
3. Click the drop-down in the Field Properties box to set the field properties. Choose **Computed**, **Computed for display**, or **Computed when composed**.
4. In the Design pane, select **Value** from the Event list box (see Figure 6.1).

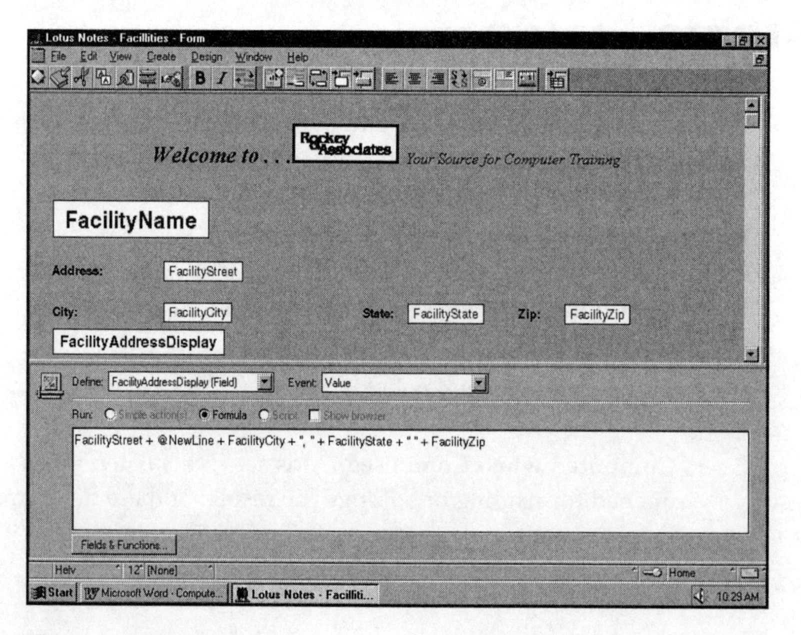

Figure 6.1 The Design pane.

5. If it hasn't already been selected, click the **Formula** radio button (located right above the Formula box) as the Run option.
6. In the formula box, enter a field name, a text string in quotation marks, or an @function formula. @functions are found in Lesson 5, and on Table 2.2 of your Tear-Out Card.
7. Complete the formula and then click the green check mark.
8. Save the form.

You can click the **Fields & Functions** button to get help in selecting the proper field names and proper @function syntax (see Figure 6.2).

1. From the dialog box, choose **Fields** or **Functions** depending on which you need to see. If you select **Fields**, a list of fields displays. If you select **Functions**, a list of @functions displays. If you are uncertain of the definition of an @function in the list, click once the @function and press the F1 key. A Help screen will appear defining that @function as shown in Figure 6.3.

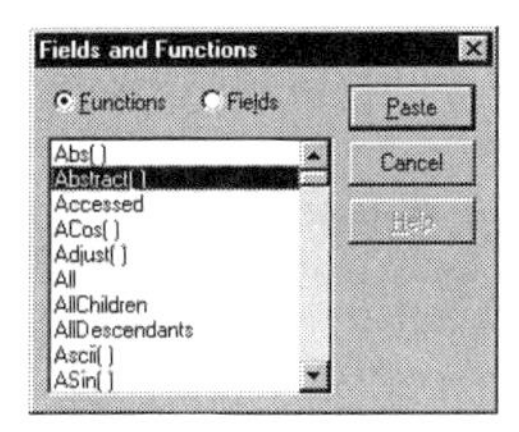

Figure 6.2 The Fields and Functions dialog box.

2. Select the field or function you need, and then click **Paste**.

Normally, computed fields recalculate when a document is created or saved or when the user manually refreshes the document by pressing **F9** or making the menu selection **View, Refresh**.

- If you want the computed fields in your document to recalculate as the user enters or edits information, open the Form Properties box, choose the **Default** tab, and select **Automatically refresh fields**.

Although this may slow down the display time for your document, at least your users will see the results of their input and it's especially useful when fields at the end of the document are dependent on values at the beginning.

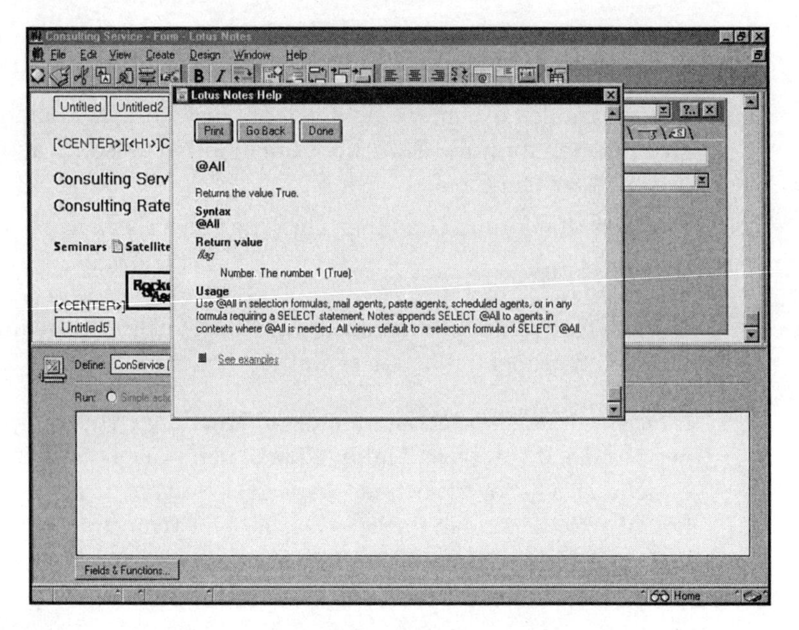

Figure 6.3 Press F1 to access the @function Help Screen.

Computed for Display

Computed for Display fields recalculate when a document is opened for reading or editing, but the results are not stored in the document. You might create a field to display the current time or date, but because that information changes second to second it is not useful to save it, so make it a Computed for Display field.

Here's another use for a Computed for Display field. In a form called Facilities, in which users enter information on the facility name, street address, city, state, and Zip Code, you want the fields spread apart for easy data entry. But when another person opens a document on a facility and reads this information, you might not want the information to be so spread out. Create a Computed for Display field that combines the address in a more readable form. It pulls the information from other fields on the form, so it doesn't need to be saved with the form. This field formula (see Figure 6.4) might read:

```
FacilityStreet + @NewLine + FacilityCity + ", " + FacilityState + " " +
FacilityZip
```

where FacilityStreet, FacilityCity, FacilityState and FacilityZip are field names and will return the value of those fields. @NewLine is an @function which tells Notes to start a new line.

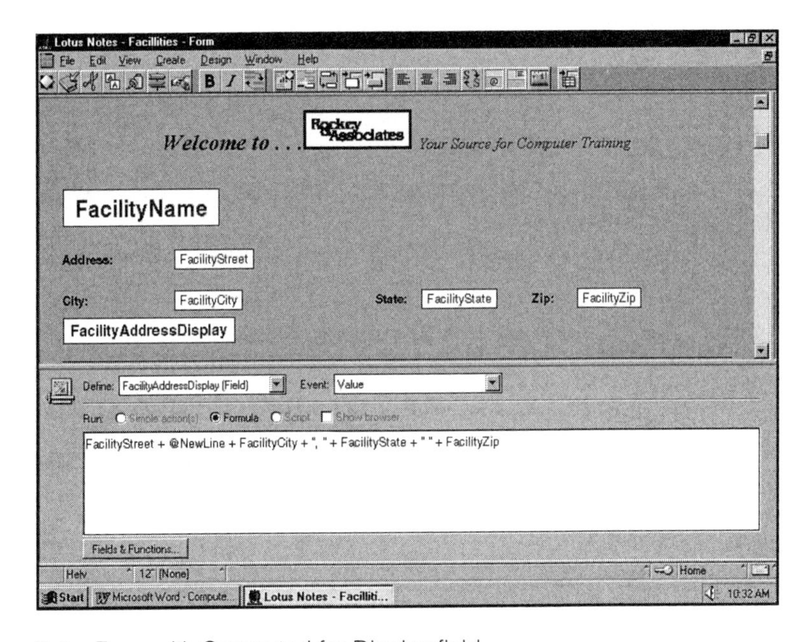

Figure 6.4 Form with Computed for Display field.

Figure 6.5 shows the form as it would be seen by those responsible for entering the data. The fields are spread apart, making it clear to the user what information is expected in which field.

Figure 6.6 shows the Computed for Display field showing the address flush left on the form and displayed as one might expect to see an address on a letterhead or form.

In this example of a computed field, you would want to hide the Computed for Display field when the document is being edited, showing it only when the document is being read. You would also want to hide the original address fields (notice they do not show in Figure 6.6) when the document is being read, or the reader will see the Computed for Display fields as well as the original fields spread out over the document. Lesson 7 discusses hiding fields in this manner.

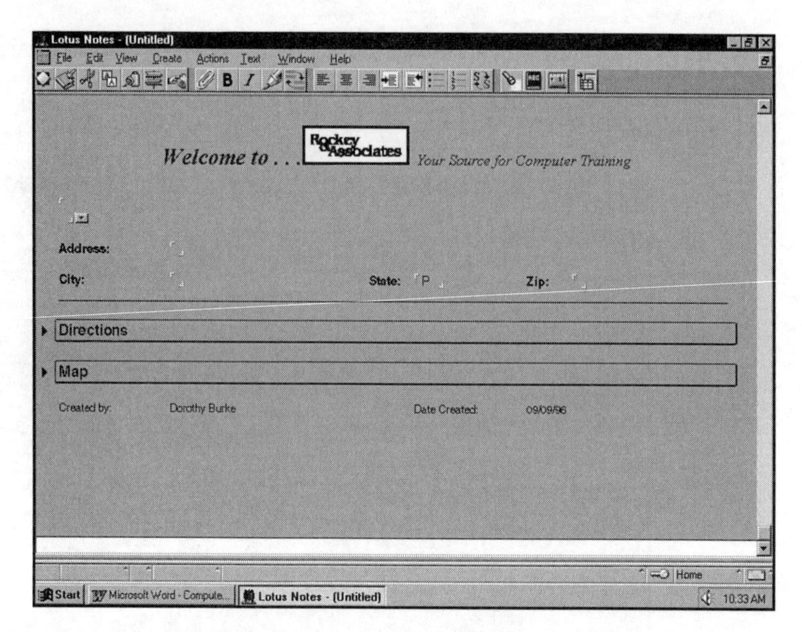

Figure 6.5 Form as seen by person entering information.

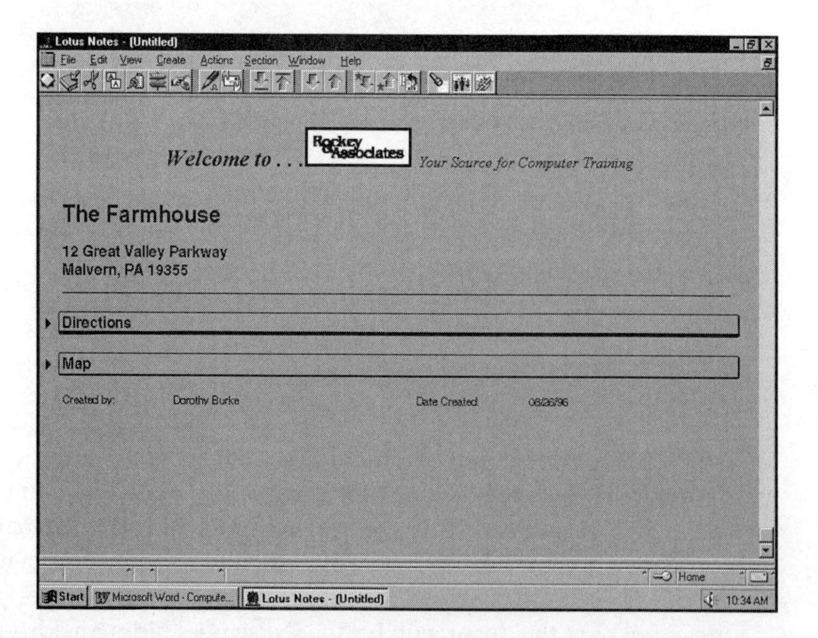

Figure 6.6 Document as seen by reader, with information neatly organized.

Computed When Composed

When a document is created, Notes automatically calculates all the Computed when Composed fields. They are never recalculated, although the values in these fields are saved with the document. You use these fields to gather information about the creation date or author's name, or to inherit information from another document.

An example of a Computed when Composed field might be one that returns the common name of the author of the document. The formula for this field is:

```
@Name([CN]; @UserName)
```

If you want to capture the date a document was created, the formula for this field is:

```
@Created
```

Editable Field Formulas

Users can change the information in editable fields, but you can still use formulas for them. Unlike computed fields that only contain one formula, each editable field can involve up to three formulas: a default value formula, an input validation formula, and an input translation formula. Choose the type of formula you're entering from the Event drop-down list on the Design pane.

Default Value

Use default value formulas to make it easier for your users to enter information in documents. The default value is the data that would appear in the field most often. By providing this value, you give the users the freedom to accept the default value and skip the field or edit the field if the information is different than what they need. For example, if you have a field where the user is asked to enter his or her state, but most of the users are located in the same state, you would want to make the default value formula for the state field a two-letter abbreviation (PA for Pennsylvania). The users can change it if they need to, but most will bypass this field because the information entered is correct.

TIP **Default Values** You can use a text string (in quotes), a field name, or a formula (such as @Now to put in the current date) as a default value formula. Notes evaluates a default value formula when the document is created.

To enter a default value formula:

1. Select the field on your form for which you want to enter a default value formula.
2. In the Field Properties box, make sure you're on the Basics tab.
3. Choose **Editable.**
4. From the Event drop-down list box on the Design pane, choose **Default Value**.
5. In the formula window, enter the formula, field, or text string.
6. Click the green check mark.
7. Save the form.

Input Translation

To standardize the input from your users to a desired format use an input translation formula. Input translation formulas convert user entries based on the formula you put in the field. This gives your documents consistency while letting the users have the freedom to enter the text as they choose.

For example, the following input translation formula makes sure that the state abbreviation entered into the field FacilityState is always capitalized:

```
@UpperCase(FacilityState)
```

To enter an input translation formula:

1. Select the field on your form for which you want to enter the input translation formula.
2. In the Field Properties box, make sure you're on the Basics page.
3. Choose **Editable**.
4. From the Event drop-down list box on the Design pane, choose **Input Translation**.
5. In the formula window, enter the formula, field, or text string.
6. Click the green check mark.
7. Save the form.

Input Validation

On some forms, there is information you must have, and you don't want the users to skip those fields when creating the document. You can make an error message appear when the user tries to save the document if they don't complete the field or complete it incorrectly.

For example, if you want to force users to enter the same state value in the field FacilityState, the input validation formula would be:

> @If(FacilityState = ""; @Failure("Please enter the state where the facility is located"); @Success)

Where FacilityState is a field name and if it is left blank ("": @Failure), the user will see the message `Please enter the state where the facility is located;` otherwise, the input is accepted (@Success). To enter an input validation formula:

1. Select the field on your form for which you want to enter an input validation formula.
2. In the Field Properties box, make sure you're on the Basics page.
3. Choose **Editable**.
4. From the Event drop-down list box on the Design pane, choose **Input Validation**.
5. In the formula window, enter the formula, field, or text string.
6. Click the green check mark.
7. Save the form.

Notes evaluates input validation formulas when the document is saved or recalculated but after any input translation formulas.

In this lesson, you learned about computed and editable fields and how to use them in your forms. In the next lesson, you'll learn to enhance your forms and make developing them easier.

Enhancing Forms

In this lesson, you learn how to make your forms look and work better by adding tables, collapsible sections, and graphics. You learn how to inherit information from other documents and how to hide fields you don't want certain users to see. Finally, you also learn how to use subforms to add consistency to your forms and save you some development time.

Creating Tables

Use tables to organize the information on your form. They're especially useful for creating side-by-side paragraphs or evenly spaced fields.

To add a table to your form:

1. Have the form open in the Design mode.
2. Position your cursor where you want the table to start.
3. Choose **Create, Table** from the menu (see Figure 7.1).

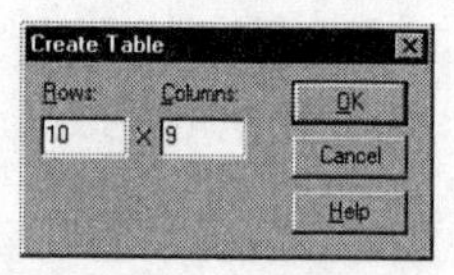

Figure 7.1 Create Table dialog box.

4. Enter the number of Rows and Columns you want in the table (you can always insert and delete rows and columns later if needed).
5. Click once on **OK**.

If you didn't specify the correct number of columns or rows when you created the table, you can insert or delete columns or rows (see Table 7.1).

Table 7.1 Adding or Removing Columns or Rows

To	*Do this*
Add a column	Click in the column where you want to insert a new one (new columns appear to the left of this column). Choose **Table**, **Insert Column**.
Add column at the right of the table	Choose **Table**, **Append Column**.
Add a row	Click in the row where you want to insert a new one (new rows appear above this row). Choose **Table**, **Insert Row**.
Add a row at the bottom of the table	Choose **Table**, **Append Row**.
To add more than one column or row	Position your cursor where you want to insert the columns or rows. Choose **Table**, **Insert Special**. Specify the number of columns or rows, and then select **Column(s)** or **Row(s)**. Click **Insert**.
Delete a column or columns	Click in the column or select the columns you want to remove. Choose Table, **Delete Selected Column(s)**. Click **Yes** to confirm the deletion.
Delete a row or rows	Click in the row or select the rows you want to remove. Choose **Table**, **Delete Selected Row(s).** Click **Yes** to confirm the deletion.
Delete a specified number of columns or rows	Place your cursor in the first column or row of the ones you want to delete. Choose **Table**, **Delete Special**. Specify the number of columns or rows you want to delete, select **Column(s)** or **Row(s)**, and click **Delete**. Choose **Yes** to confirm the deletion.

You can use **Edit**, **Copy** to copy rows or columns of data in a table. **Edit**, **Cut** will remove selected columns or rows and store them in the Clipboard. You can then use **Edit**, **Paste** to put them in a new position (where you have your cursor).

Setting Borders for Your Table

You can also control how your table looks. To set borders on the table:

1. Select the cells of the table to which you want to add borders.
2. Choose **Table, Table Properties** (see Figure 7.2).
3. Click the **Cell Borders** tab.

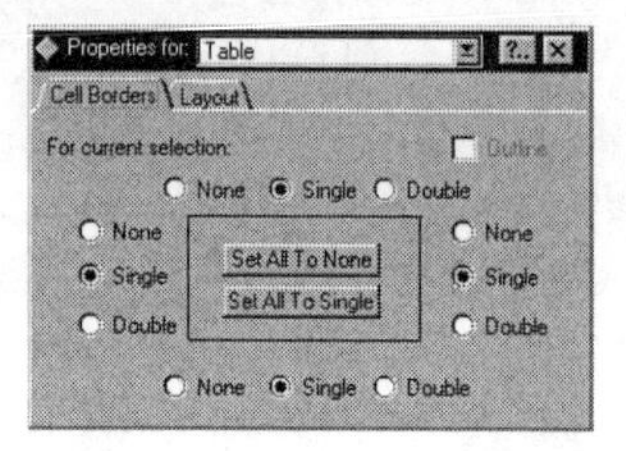

Figure 7.2 Table Properties box with Cell Borders tab selected.

4. Check **Outline** to set the borders for *only* the outside lines of the current selection.
5. Select a border style. The choices are Standard, Extruded, and Embossed. Try each one to see which you prefer.
6. To set the borders on all sides to single, click the **Set All to Single** button. To not have any borders, click the **Set All to None** button. You can select a border thickness for each side of the selected cells by choosing a thickness from zero to 10 for each side. The sides of the cell correspond to the measurements in the property box (left, top, right, bottom).

Setting the Width of Your Table and Columns

To set the overall width of the table so the column widths will adjust to fit the table in the window, perform the following:

1. Click anywhere in the table.
2. Choose **Table, Table Properties**.
3. Click the **Layout** tab (see Figure 7.3).

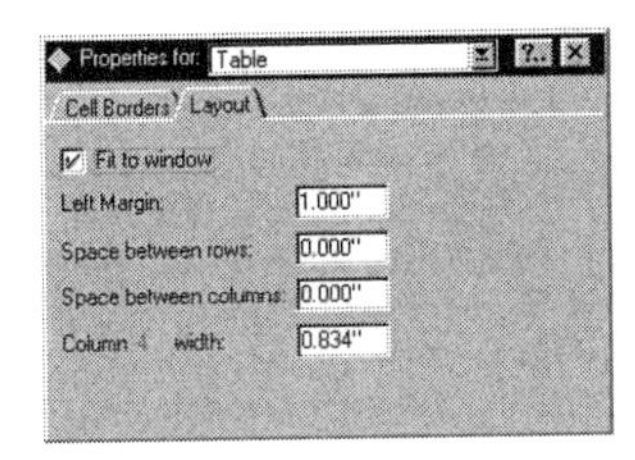

Figure 7.3 Table Properties box with Layout tab selected.

4. Select **Fit to window** to automatically size the table to fit the window.

To change a cell width, space between columns, left margin for the cells, or space between rows, perform the following:

1. Click the column you want to change.
2. Choose **Table**, **Table Properties**.
3. Click the **Layout** tab.
4. Enter the cell width, space between columns, left margin, or space between rows (refer to Figure 7.3).

To change the background color of a cell or cells:

1. Select the cells you want to change.
2. Choose **Table**, **Table Properties**.
3. Click the **Colors** tab.
4. Select a background color for the cells. If you want to apply the color to the entire table, click **Apply to Entire Table**. If you want to make the color transparent, click **Make Transparent**.

Making Collapsible Sections

Make longer forms more manageable for your users by incorporating collapsible sections. By gathering all the information for one topic into a section, the user sees only the line of text that makes up the section title (unless the section is expanded). Where there are many sections, the users ignore those sections that don't apply to them or interest them.

To create a section on your form:

1. Open the form in the design mode.
2. Select the fields and text you want to be part of the section by holding down the mouse key and dragging over the area to select it.
3. Choose **Create**, **Section**, **Standard** from the menu.
4. Place your cursor in the section you just created and right-click your mouse to bring up the Section Properties box as shown in Figure 7.4.

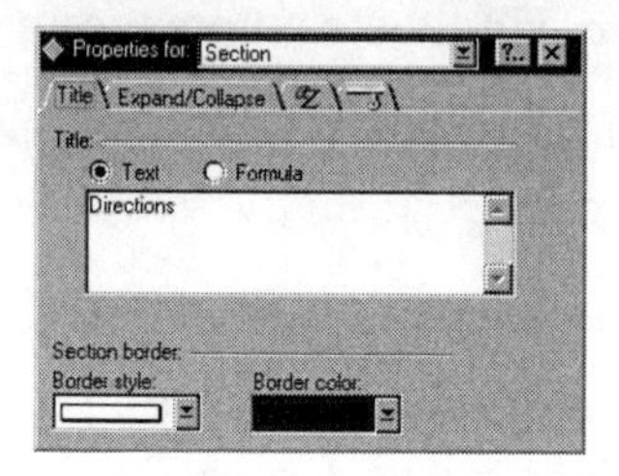

Figure 7.4 The Section Properties box.

5. In the Section Properties box, enter the title for the section if the text that automatically appears in the box is not what you want to use. Don't use carriage returns, hotspots, or buttons in the section.
6. Set the appearance of the section border by choosing a Border style and Border color from the appropriate list boxes.
7. Click the **Expand/Collapse** tab on the Section Properties box. Choose whether you want to Expand or Collapse the section in the preview pane, when opened for reading, when opened for editing, or when printed. Select **Hide title when expanded** if you don't want your users to see the section title when all the fields and text in the section are displayed (see Figure 7.5).

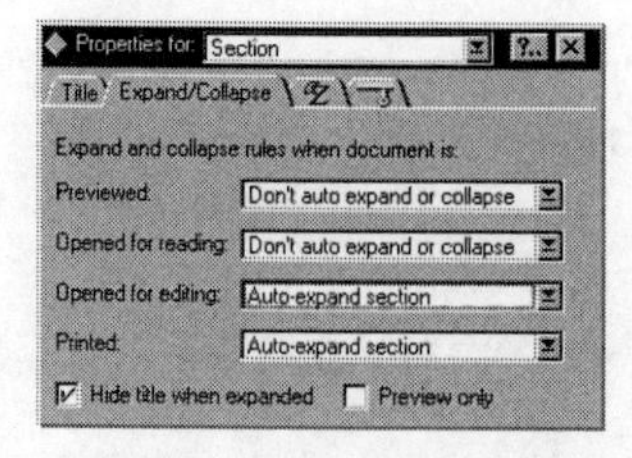

Figure 7.5 The Section Properties box with the Expand/Collapse tab selected.

8. Click the **Font** tab to select a font, font size, font style, and color for the title.
9. Click the **Hide-When** tab if you want to hide the section when the user is editing or reading this document (see Figure 7.6).

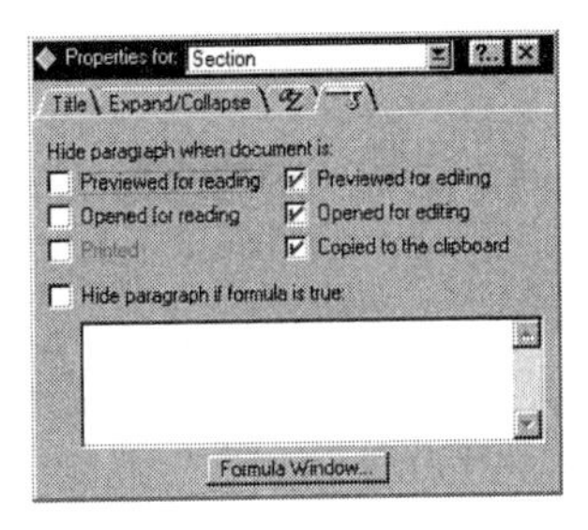

Figure 7.6 The Section Properties box with the Hide-When tab selected.

You can also create sections that can only be read or edited by those who have a certain access level. To do this:

1. Follow steps 1 and 2 of creating a section on a form.
2. Choose **Create**, **Section**, **Controlled-Access**.
3. In the Section Properties box, enter the title for the section if the text that automatically appears in the box is not what you want to use. Don't use carriage returns, hotspots, or buttons in section titles.
4. Type in a Section Field Name if you don't want to use the name that automatically appeared. Use regular field naming rules to give this a name.
5. Click the **Editors** tab and set the options for expanding or collapsing the section. Choose whether you want to expand or collapse the section in the preview pane, when the section is opened for reading, opened for editing, when it is printed, or if you want it set the same as the last time the user viewed it (see Figure 7.7).

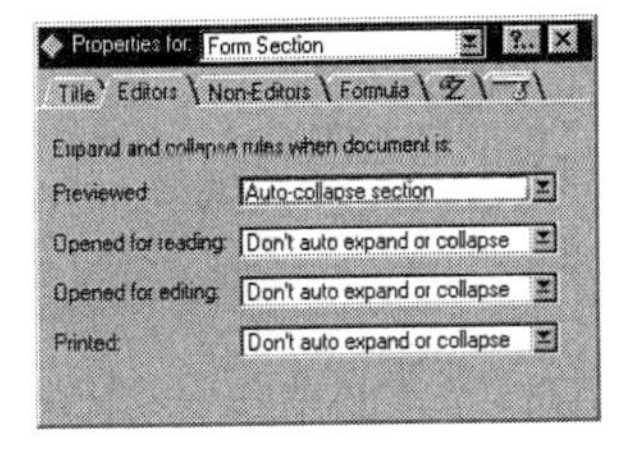

Figure 7.7 The Section Properties box with the Editors tab selected.

6. Click the **Non-Editors** tab. The selections are the same as the Editors tab. Choose how you want this section to appear for those who do not have Editor privileges (see Lesson 8 for more on security). You can also select **Hide title when expanded** if you don't want your users to see the section title when all the fields and text in the section are displayed (see Figure 7.8).

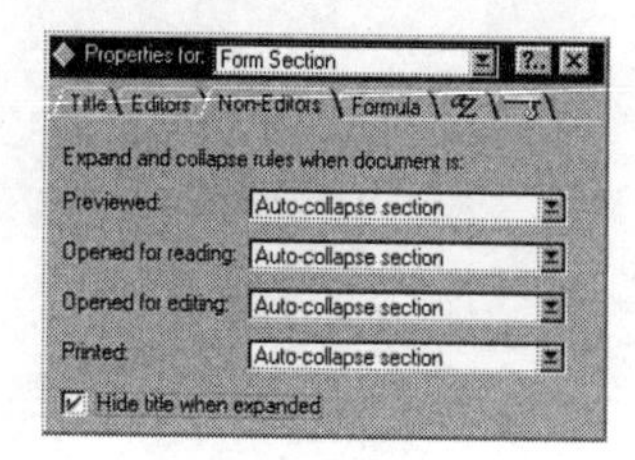

Figure 7.8 Section Properties box with the Non-Editors tab selected.

7. To restrict who can edit the section, click the **Formula** tab. If you want the document's author to specify the section editors, choose **Editable** as the section Type. Otherwise, select **Computed** to define this group with a formula. Enter the formula and then click the green check mark.

Section access formulas must result in a text list containing one or more names. Use group names or roles from the access control list for more flexibility. Enclose the names in quotation marks and concatenate them with colons:

"Supervisors" : "Henry Taurus" : "Mary Ann Whiting"

If you have documents that require approval, such as expense accounts or employee evaluations, you can place the fields for that approval information in a collapsible section with restricted access. That way, the average reader or the employee can't see the approval fields, but the supervisor or human resources department can.

Creating Subforms

If you find yourself repeating the same fields and text on different forms, you can save yourself a lot of time (and enforce consistency) by creating a subform that holds that information. Then you can insert that subform into any form you're creating. Use a subform for document author and creation date, logos, letterhead, or for signature or approval areas. A subform is designed in the same way that you create a form: You can add fields, static text, graphics, and so on.

Forms that contain subforms inherit any changes to the original subform. If you change your logo on the letterhead subform, for instance, your logo will change on every form that uses that subform.

To create a subform:

1. From the menu, choose **Create**, **Design**, **Subform**. The Subform Properties box appears (see Figure 7.9).

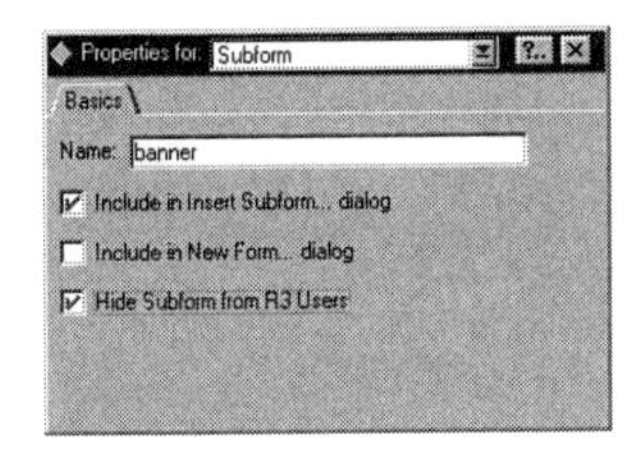

Figure 7.9 The Subform Properties box.

2. In the Subform Properties box, give the subform a name.
3. Select the appropriate subform options.
4. Add the elements (fields, text, tables, sections, and so on) to your subform as you would to a form.
5. Save and close the subform.

To put the subform in a form:

1. Open the form that you want the subform to be part of in design mode and position your cursor where you want the subform to appear.
2. From the menu, choose **Create**, **Insert Subform**.
3. Pick the subform you want to use from the list in the dialog box.
4. Click once on **OK**.

In Figure 7.10, you can see how a subform contains information that is consistent throughout an application and which can then be placed at the top of most of your forms.

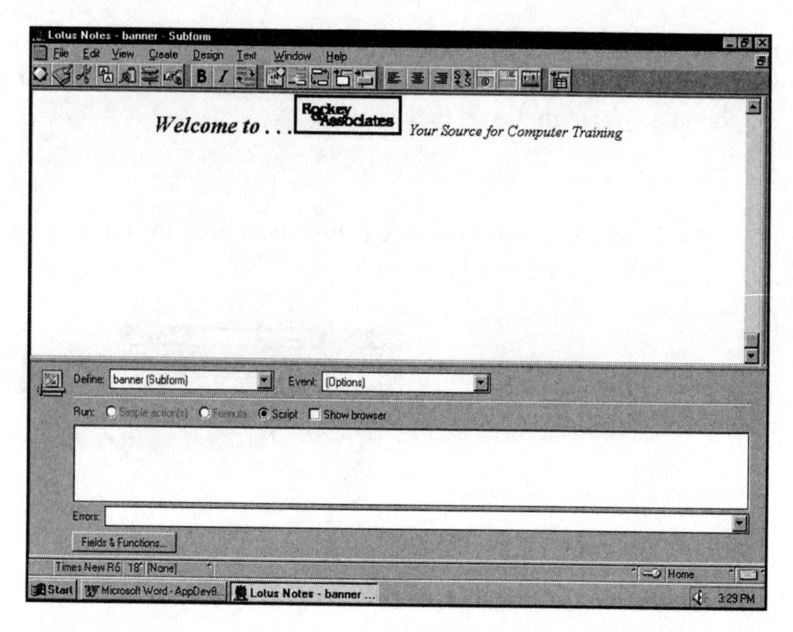

Figure 7.10 A subform.

Inheriting Information from Other Documents

You can arrange for some of your field information to be filled in automatically by pulling information from another document, or *inheriting* information. This works really well for a discussion database, where you have response and response to response documents. Users normally select the parent document when they formulate their response. Inheritance relies on the parent document being selected at the time the new document is created. However, you do not need response documents to inherit information from other documents.

To make inheritance work in your form:

- Open the Form Properties box and choose the **Default** tab (see Figure 7.11).

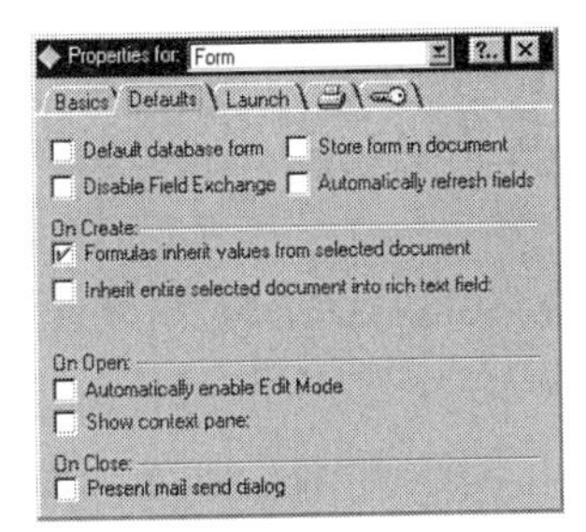

Figure 7.11 Form Properties box with the Defaults tab selected.

- Under On Create, select **Formulas inherit values from selected document**.
- Create the fields that will inherit the information, and then write a formula for each field that uses the name of a field in the parent document. The fields can be editable with a default value formula but they are more often Computed when Composed fields.

You can also create a form that inherits the full contents of the document the user selects:

- Create a rich text field on the form to store the inherited document.
- In the Form Properties box, choose the **Default** tab.
- Under On Create, select **Inherit entire selected document into rich text field**. Select the rich text field and assign it one of the full document display options, **Collapsible rich text** or **Rich text**. Choosing Collapsible rich text displays the inherited document as a collapsed section, so the user has the option of viewing that document or not.

Hiding Text and Fields

There are times when you don't want your users to see certain fields in a document. These may be fields that you put in the form for your own purposes; they're involved in calculations but the users don't need to see them. Most designers put fields like this at the bottom of a form. You want these fields available to you so you can diagnose problems, but you'll need to hide them from the users before you roll out your application.

When you have computed for display fields, you may want to hide them when the document is being created or edited and display them when the document is being read.

To hide fields:

1. Open the form in design mode.
2. Select the field(s) and any related text or buttons you want to hide.
3. Open the Field Properties box and click the **Hide-When** tab (see Figure 7.12).

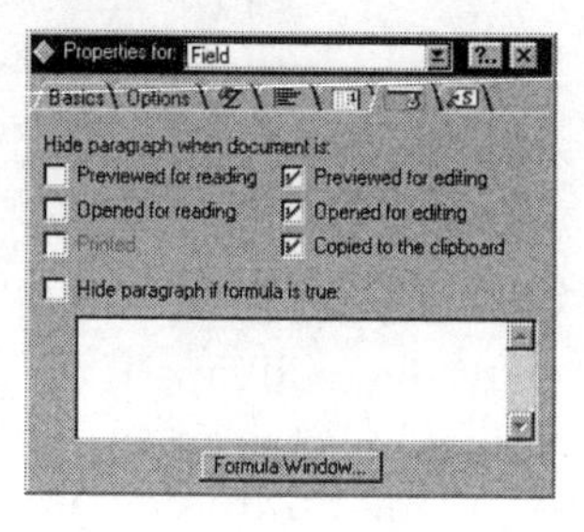

Figure 7.12 The Field Properties box with the Hide-When tab selected.

4. Under `Hide paragraph when document is`, select the appropriate options:

   Previewed for reading When this is selected, users won't be able to see the information when they read documents in the preview pane.

   Previewed for editing Check this and users won't be able to see the information when they edit documents in the preview pane.

   Opened for reading When this is selected, users who open documents to read them won't be able to see the information.

   Opened for editing Check this and users who create or edit documents won't be able to see the information.

   Printed When this is selected, the information doesn't appear on printed documents. This option is only available if you have selected Previewed for Reading or Opened for Reading.

   Copied to the Clipboard Check this and the information won't appear when documents are copied to and pasted from the Clipboard.

5. (Optional) Choose **Hide paragraph if formula is true** to enter a formula that sets the conditions under which the information is invisible.
6. Save the form.

Adding Graphics

The graphics on your forms should not be overwhelming. Keep the size, position, and colors of the graphics within reason. Remember, the purpose of the form is to gather and disseminate information.

Figure 7.13 illustrates a diploma graphic that was placed on a course description form. This makes it obvious to the user which form is open. Also, it brightens and lightens up the application to have graphics in it.

Documents Are Slow to Open! Be aware that graphics take more time to display than text, so they might slow down your application.

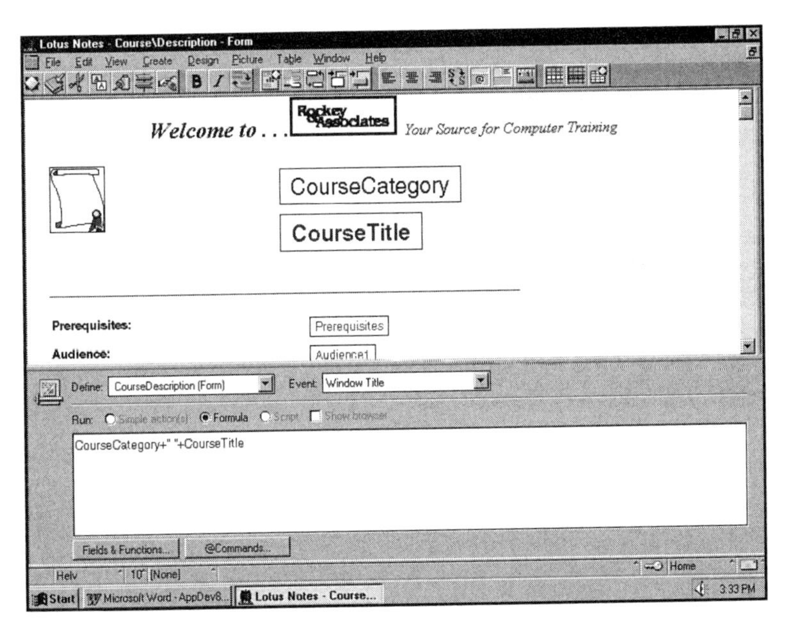

Figure 7.13 A Diploma graphic on a course description form.

Lotus Notes accepts graphics in these formats: Lotus PIC files (.PIC), ANSI metafiles (.CGM, .GMF), JPEG files (.JPG), TIFF 5.0 files (.TIF), as well as .BMP, .GIF, and .PCX files. You can import your graphics files or copy and paste them into your forms.

To add graphics to a form using the Clipboard:

1. Open the picture in its source application.
2. Select the picture.
3. From the menu, choose **Edit**, **Copy**.
4. Switch to Lotus Notes.
5. Open the form in design mode.
6. Position your cursor where you want the picture to appear.
7. Select **Edit**, **Paste** from the menu.

To import a graphic file:

1. Open the form in design mode.
2. Position your cursor where you want the picture to appear.
3. Choose **File**, **Import** from the menu.
4. Select the name of the picture file.
5. Click once on **OK**.

Once you have the graphic in your form, you can change its size:

1. Click the picture to select it. You can tell it's selected because a small black box appears in the lower-right corner. This small black box is a *handle*.
2. Drag the handle away from the center of the graphic to enlarge the picture and toward the center to reduce its size. You can see the picture's current width and height (displayed as a percentage of its original width and height) above the status bar.

If you incorrectly sized the graphic and you want to return it to its original proportions, don't use Undo. Instead, select the picture by clicking it, open the Picture Properties box, and select **Reset width and height to 100%**.

Making Layout Regions

Layout regions are design elements that give you flexibility in designing your forms. In a layout region, you can arrange static text, fields, graphics, buttons, and graphic buttons by clicking and dragging them. The size of a field in a layout region is adjustable, and you can place fields on top of graphics or static text.

Creating a Layout Region

To make a layout region on a form:

1. Open the form in the design mode.
2. Position the cursor where you want the layout region to appear on the form.
3. From the menu choose **Create**, **Layout Region**, **New Layout Region**.
4. In the Layout Properties box (see Figure 7.14), set the position and size of the layout region by entering values in the Left box (to specify the left margin), the Width box, and the Height box. Optionally, you can drag the handles on the outer edge of the layout region to size it.

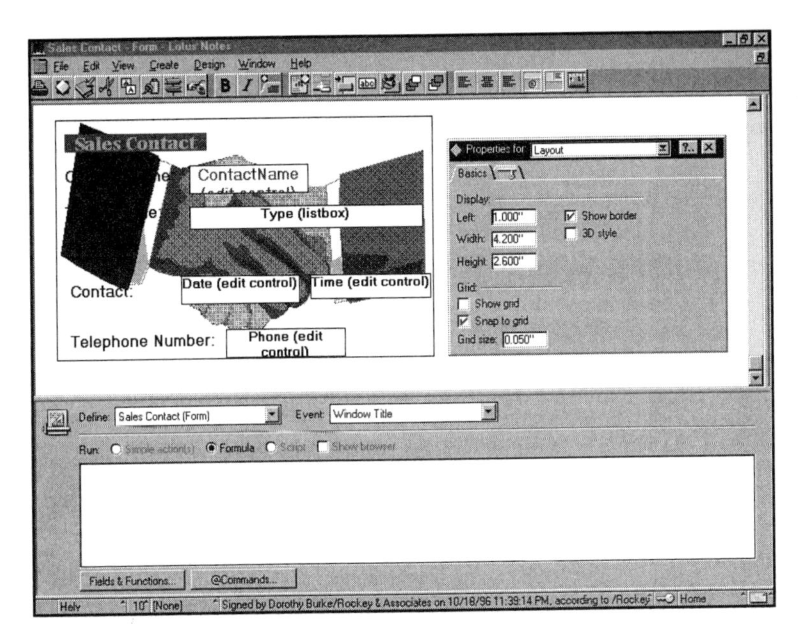

Figure 7.14 The Layout Properties box.

5. Specify how you want the layout region to look by checking **Show border** to add a line around the layout region or **3D** style to color the region gray and give it a three-dimensional appearance.
6. If you plan to add elements to the region, check **Show grid** to display a non-printing dot overlay that will help you line up the elements as you place them in the region. Check **Snap to grid** to have the elements align to the grid as if it were a magnet. The value in Grid size sets how far apart the dots are in the grid.

7. Add whatever elements you like to the layout region.
8. Close and save the form.

CAUTION

Not For the Web In Parts IV and V, you learn about publishing applications to the Web. InterNotes Web Publisher and Domino did not support layout regions at the time of this printing, so you might not see that part of your form when you view your application with a Web browser. However, Lotus has stated its intention to make it possible for Domino to publish layout regions in a future release.

Adding Elements to a Layout Region

You can add static text, graphics (both as a background and as graphic buttons), fields, and buttons to a layout region. You can't add attachments, hotspots, links, objects, pop-ups, sections, tables, or rich text fields.

To add static text to a layout region:

1. Click the layout region to select it. Small black squares called handles will appear in each corner and in the middle of each side of the region to indicate that it is selected.
2. From the menu, choose **Create**, **Layout Region**, **Text**. The text `(Untitled)` appears in the middle of the layout region, surrounded by handles. This is the static text *block*.
3. In the Control Properties box (see Figure 7.15), delete `(Untitled)` from the Text box and enter your static text there. Click green check to accept your text entry.
4. Under Layout options, set the position of the static text block in the layout region by entering values in the Left and Top boxes, or by using the mouse point in the middle of the static text block on the layout region and dragging it to its new position.
5. Specify the dimensions of the text box by entering values in the Width and Height boxes, or point to one of the handles on the text block and drag away from or toward the center of the text block to size it.
6. To specify the horizontal position of the text within the text block, choose an option from the Alignment list box (**Left**, **Center**, **Right**). Center the text vertically within the text block by checking **Center vertically**.

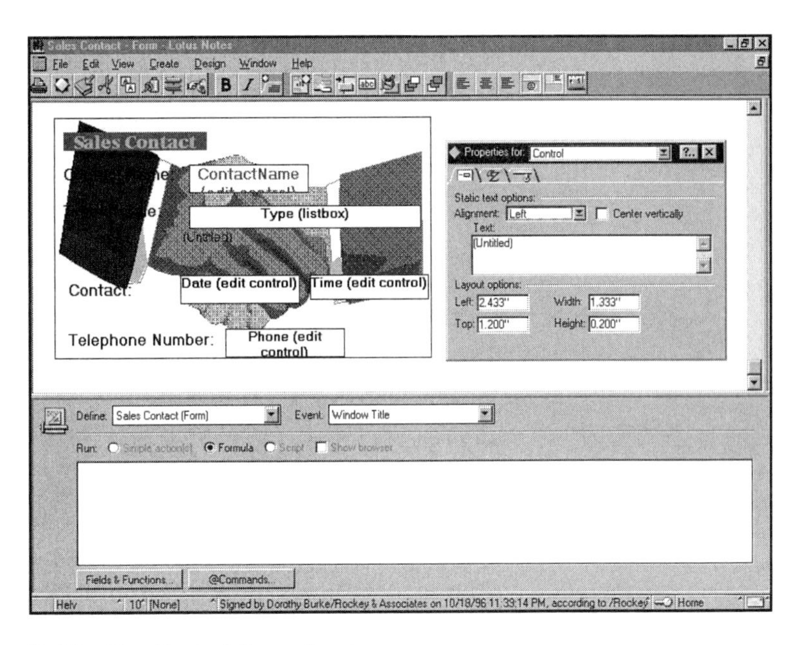

Figure 7.15 The Control Properties box.

7. Click the **Style** tab of the Control Properties box to select the Font, Size, Style, and Text color of the text in the block (see Figure 7.16).

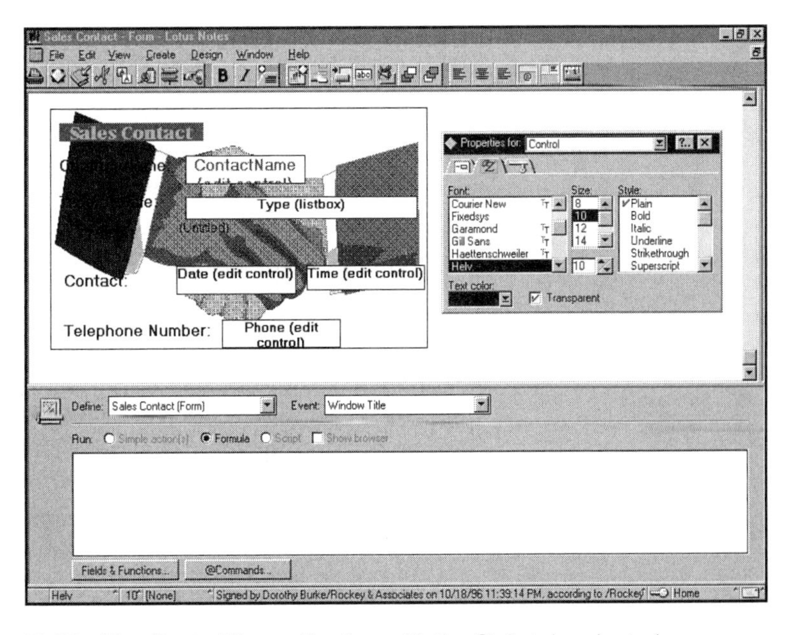

Figure 7.16 The Control Properties box with the Style tab selected.

8. If you want to be able to see the layout region background through the text block, check **Transparent**. If not, remove the check mark from the Transparent option and select a background color for the text block.
9. Repeat the preceding steps to add each piece of static text. Then save the form to save the text.

To add fields to the layout region:

1. Click the layout region to select it.
2. Choose **Create, Field** from the menu. A box appears on the layout region with the text `Untitled (edit control)` inside and handles on the outside border.
3. Assign a name to the field in the Field Properties box.
4. Select the Type of field (Rich Text is not available).

   If you choose a Keyword type, you now have different options for displaying keywords in a form: **Checkbox**, **Radio button**, **Listbox**, or **Combobox**. The Listbox has a small up and down arrow at the end of the field so the user can scroll up or down the list of keyword options. The Combobox has a single down arrow, so the list drops down for the user to see all the choices.

   If you choose a Time type and decide to display the time as a date, users will see a pop-up button that displays a calendar when they click it (see Figure 7.17). If you select a Time type and display it as time, allowing multiple values, your users will see a pop-up that allows them to set the time (see Figure 7.18). These features are available as part of Calendaring and Scheduling.
5. Choose **Editable** or a **Computed** option for the field.
6. Click the second tab of the Field Properties box to select Edit control options (see Figure 7.19). Check **Multiline** to allow users to press **Enter** and make multiple lines of text in a field, **Scroll Bar** (lets the user scroll through the text in a field with lots of data), or **Border** to add an outline around the field box.
7. Point in the middle of the box and drag it to the desired position (you can also specify the position by entering values in the Left and Top boxes under Layout options in the Properties box). Drag one of the handles to size the field box (or enter the Width value on the Properties box).

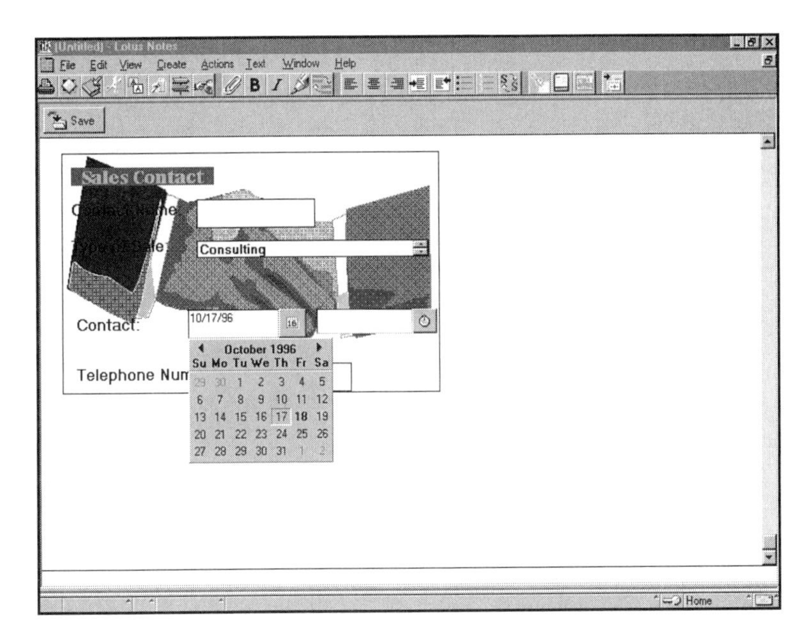

Figure 7.17 The Calendar pop-up.

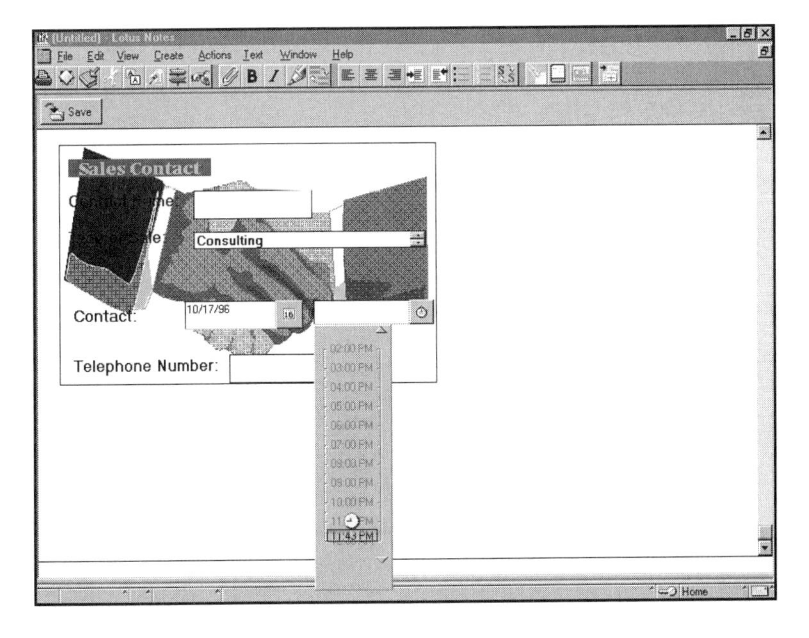

Figure 7.18 Time pop-up.

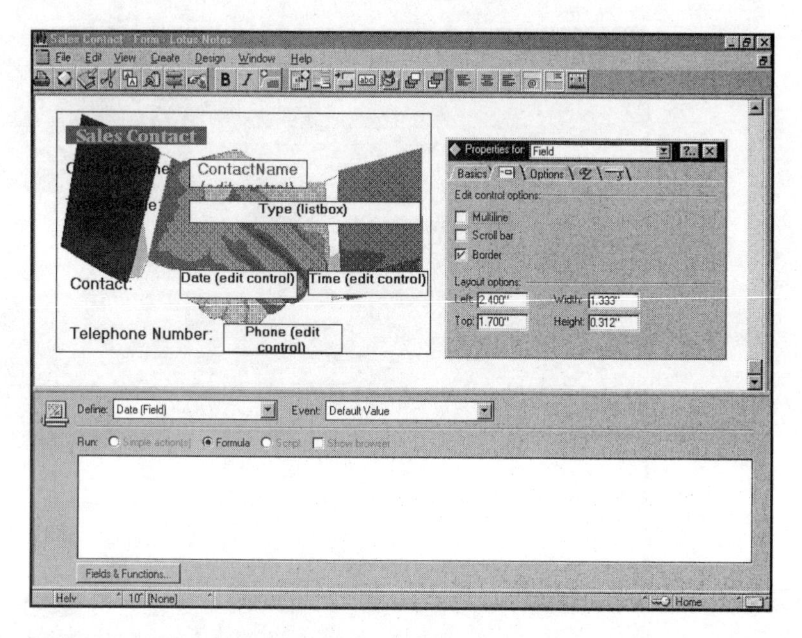

Figure 7.19 Control options of Field Properties box.

To add graphics to a layout region:

1. In a graphics application program, open a graphic file or create a new graphic object.
2. Select the graphic object and copy it to the Clipboard by choosing **Edit**, **Copy** from the menu.
3. Close the graphic application and switch to Lotus Notes.
4. Open your form in the design mode and select the layout region by clicking it.
5. If you want to create a graphic button to which you can assign actions, choose **Create**, **Layout Region**, **Graphic Button** from the menu. If you want a graphic background for the layout region, choose **Create**, **Layout Region**, **Graphic** from the menu (see Figure 7.20).
6. In the Control Properties box, set the position of the graphic by entering values in the Left and Top boxes.
7. If you have other elements in the layout region and want to place them on top of the graphic, choose **Design**, **Sent to Back** to move the graphic behind the other elements.
8. Save the form to save the graphic.

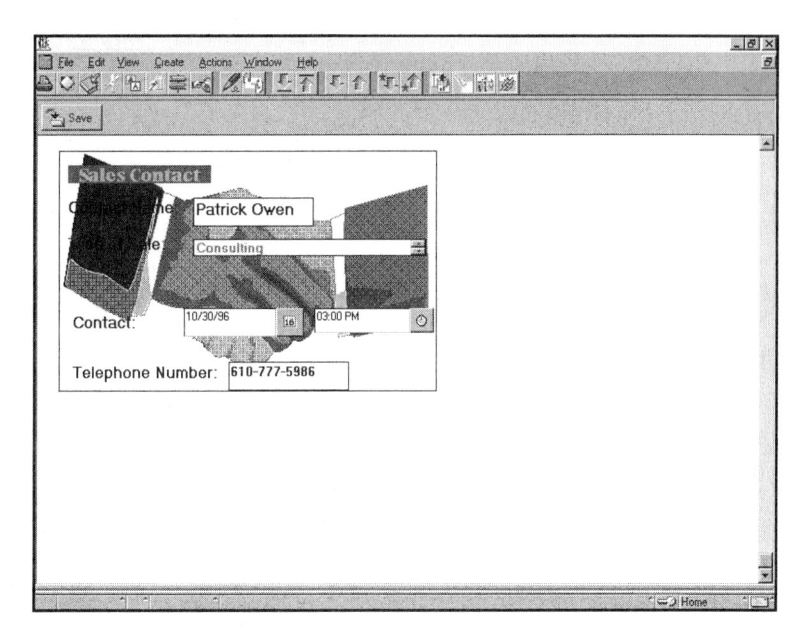

Figure 7.20 A layout region with a graphic background.

Hiding Layout Regions

As with sections and paragraphs, you can hide layout regions under certain conditions.

1. Click the layout region to select it.
2. On the Layout Properties box, click the **Hide** tab.
3. Under Hide paragraph when document is, select the conditions when you don't want users to see the layout region: **Previewed for reading, Opened for reading**, **Printed**, **Previewed for editing**, **Opened for editing**, or **Copied to the clipboard.**

   To program options, check **Hide paragraph if formula is true** and enter the appropriate formula.

In this lesson, you learned about adding tables, collapsible sections, and graphics to your forms to enhance their appearance. You also saw how subforms are used as a way of handling repetitive design, how inheritance brings information from other documents, and how hiding can make fields invisible to certain users. In the next lesson, you'll learn about creating views.

Implementing Security

In this lesson, you learn what the access control levels are and how you can use them to limit user access to databases.

The Database Access Control List

Every database has an Access Control List (ACL) that defines who has entry to the database and what each entrant can do in the database: Notes defines seven levels of access to a database:

- **No Access** This denies access to the database altogether. If you have No Access, you cannot even add the database icon to your workspace.
- **Depositor** Depositors can create new documents, but they can't read or edit any of the documents in the database—including the ones they created themselves. You might be granted this access level to cast a ballot in a voting database, for example.
- **Reader** A reader can read the documents in the database, but can't create or edit documents. You might have this level of access to a company policy database, so you can read policies but can't create or change them.
- **Author** As an author, you can create and read documents. You cannot normally edit any document, including those you create. However, if any document, whether you created it or not, has a field of data type *Authors* in which your name appears, then you will be able to edit that document.
- **Editor** If you have editor access, you can do everything an author does, plus you can edit any documents in the database. For example, a manager who approves the expense reports submitted by others needs editor access to those documents.

- **Designer** A designer can do everything an editor does, but can also create or change any design elements of the database. In order to create a new call report form in a database, for instance, you would need designer access.
- **Manager** Someone with manager access can do everything a designer can, and can also modify the access control list—can add new users to it, delete users from it, and can modify the degree of access enjoyed by other users. The Manager can also modify the database's replication settings and delete a database from the server.

A newly created database inherits its ACL settings from its Design Template, if it has one. Otherwise, a new database's default ACL entries are as follows:

Entry	Access Level
Default	Designer
Local Domain Servers group	Manager
Other Domain Servers group	Manager
(person who created the database)	Manager

While you are designing the database, it doesn't really matter what the ACL settings are. But before you roll out the database to the users, you should decide who gets what level of access and set the ACL accordingly. Otherwise, the default ACL will let any user change the design of your database.

To see or change ACL settings (you can only change settings, of course, if you have Manager access), choose **File**, **Database, Access Control**. The Access Control List dialog box appears. It has four different panels, accessible by clicking the four icons on the left side of the dialog box. We care only about the first panel at this time. See Figure 8.1.

The People, Servers, Groups window lists all users by default, but you can limit the display by changing the setting of the People, Servers, Groups field from `Show All` to one of the access levels. The types of users listed include people, servers, and groups that might themselves include people, servers, or other groups. The very first listing is for -Default-. This listing covers any user not otherwise listed either individually or as a member of a listed group.

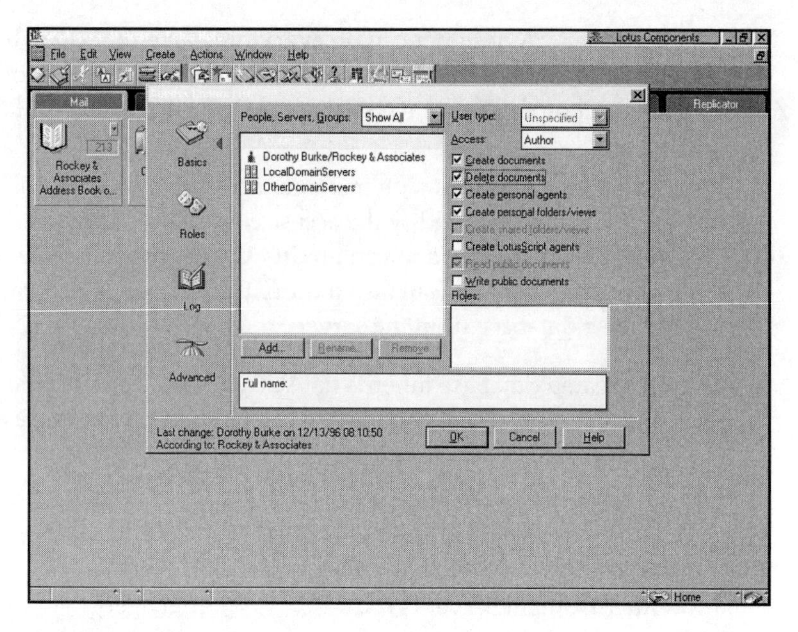

Figure 8.1 The Access Control List dialog box.

To see the level of access granted to a listed user, select the user in the list. That user's access level appears in the Access field in the upper-right corner of the dialog box. Also, if a User type has been specified, that also appears in the upper-right corner.

In addition to giving a general level of access to a user, you may refine that access by checking the boxes on the right side of the dialog box. Depending on the general level of access, you might be able to take away the right to create or delete documents, to create personal agents, views, or folders, to create shared views or folders, to create LotusScript agents, or to read or write public documents.

To add a user to the ACL, click the **Add** button. The Add User dialog box appears (see Figure 8.2). Either type in the name of a person, server, or group, or click the "user" icon to choose people or groups (but not servers) from a list. If you type in the names of users, be sure to enter their *fully distinguished name* (Jane Calabria/Rockey & Associates) not just their common name (Jane Calabria). This assures that if there are two Jane Calabrias in the organization, they each get only their own level of access to the database.

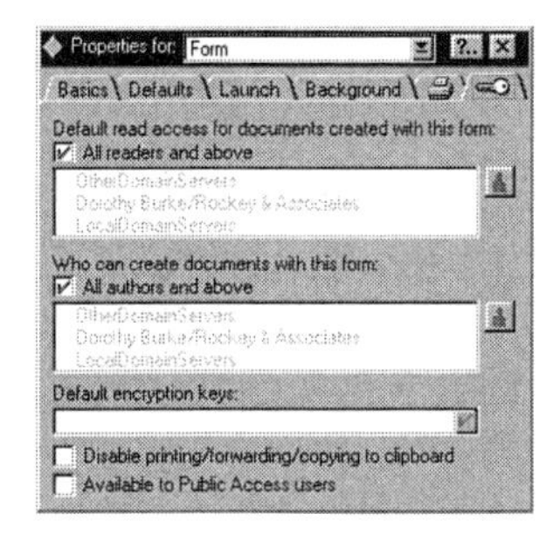

Figure 8.2 The Add User dialog box.

If you click the user icon to choose from a list, you will see the Names dialog box, which displays a list of people and groups from any address book you have access to (see Figure 8.3). You can select people or groups in the left-hand window, then click the **Add** button to copy the names to the right-hand window. After you have added the names that you want to the right-hand window, click **OK**. The dialog box will close and the selected names will appear in the Access Control List dialog box.

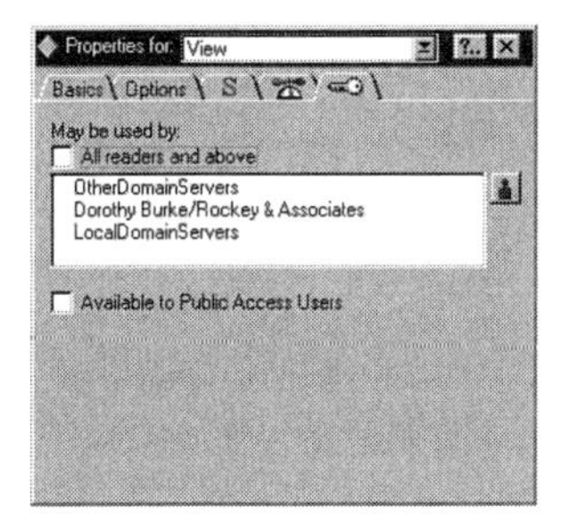

Figure 8.3 The Names dialog box.

Select each newly added user and specify a User type and an Access level. Refine the access level by checking or removing check marks from the check boxes. Add a person to a Role, if any appear in the Roles box, by clicking the Role to make a check mark appear.

You can also rename someone. Select the user to be renamed, then click the **rename** button. The Rename User dialog box appears. Type the user's correct name or pick it from a list.

Finally, you can remove a user from the Access Control List. Select the person you want to remove, then click the **Remove** button.

Using Groups

Naming individuals in access control lists is a lot more work than you may have to do and it can backfire on you. If one individual leaves or is replaced, you will have to change that person's name in every ACL the name is in. However, if you use group names in the ACL, then you have to update only the group in the address book when the membership changes.

To create a group:

1. Open the public address book for your company.
2. Select **Groups** under Folders and Views in the navigator pane. See Figure 8.4.

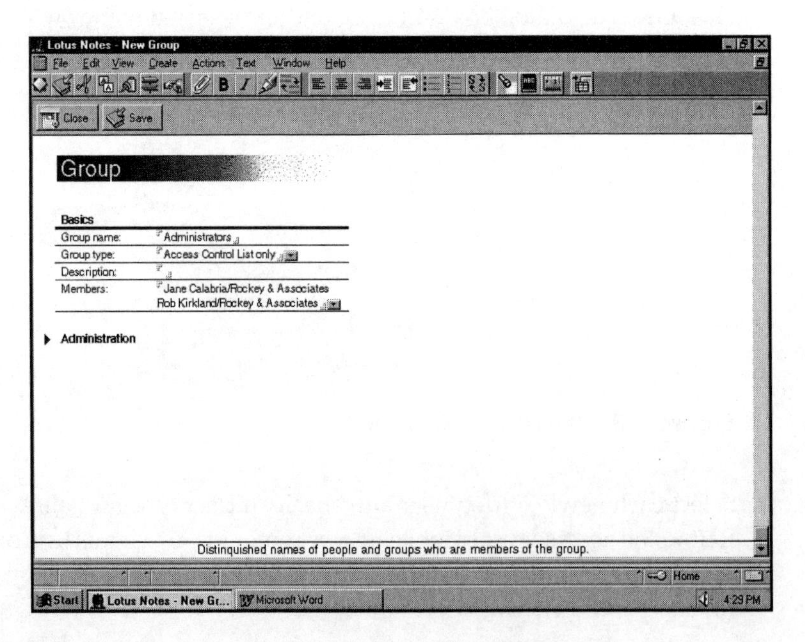

Figure 8.4 The Group document from the public address book.

3. Click the **Add Group** action button or choose **Create, Group** from the menu.

4. Under Group Name, add the name you'll be using in the ACL.
5. For Group Type, select **Multi-purpose** or **Access Control List only**. Multi-purpose means you can later use the group either in an Access Control List or as a mailing list. If you choose Access Control List only, you will not be able to add this group to the To: or cc: or bcc: fields of a mail message.
6. In Description, enter any descriptive text you want. What you type here should help anyone who looks at this document understand the purpose of this group.
7. In Members, select the names you want to include in this group.
8. Close and save the Group document.

In this lesson, you learned what the access control levels are and how to implement them. In the next lesson, you'll learn about creating views in your applications.

Creating Views

In this lesson, you learn about the types of views, how to create views, and how to create column formulas in views.

Types of Views

A view shows a list of documents, like a table of contents for your database. You can have more than one view in a database, each one showing a different group of documents or the same documents in a different way.

There are three types of views:

- **Private** Any user with reader access to a database can create a view for his own use. A private view is not shared by other users in the database. Instead of being stored on the server, it's kept in a file called DESKTOP.DSK on the user's own hard disk.
- **Shared** A shared view is stored on the server and is available to all users with sufficient access rights. Only users with designer or manager access to the database can create shared views. (See Lesson 8, "Implementing Security," for more about security.)
- **Shared, personal on first use** These views are initially stored on the server and are created by someone with designer or manager access to the database. Once the view is used by a person, the view automatically becomes a private view for that person and is stored on that person's desktop. For example, you design a sales tracking system so each salesperson can keep track of his own clients. You make the view shared, personal on first use. As each salesperson calls up that view, it becomes a private view for that person and shows only that person's information. Every salesperson has the same view structure but doesn't see anyone else's sales contacts.

Pick Your View Type Carefully! Once you create a view, you can't change your mind about the type of view it is. You must delete it and re-create it.

Creating a View

Before you start creating the view in Notes, spend a little time planning how you want the view to look, what documents and fields you want to see, how you want to see response documents, and if you want any special features like categories and icons. Sketch the view out on paper.

To create a view:

1. Choose **Create, View** from the menu. The Create View dialog box appears (see Figure 9.1).

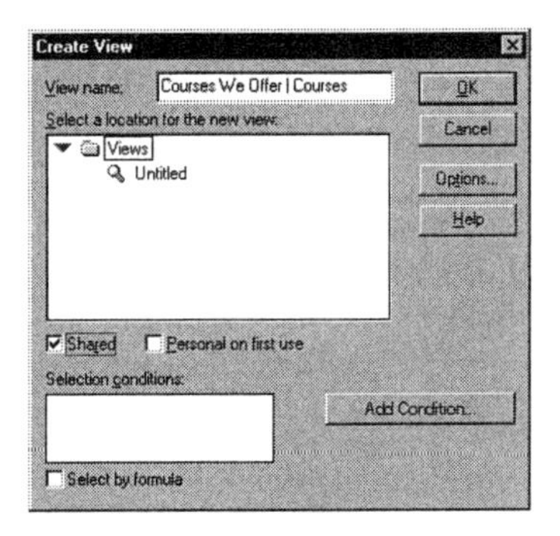

Figure 9.1 The Create View dialog box.

2. In the Create View dialog box, enter the name of the view in the View name box. Like forms, you can use synonyms in your view names (see Lesson 2, "Making Forms," for more on synonyms). View names can be up to 256 characters long, but only the first 32 appear in dialog boxes and on menus.
3. Check a view type. Notes assumes you want to create a private view until you check **Shared**. If you want to create a Shared, Personal on first use view, you must check **Shared** first to see the **Personal on first use** option.
4. Under Selection conditions, check **Select by formula** if you want to enter a selection formula for the documents you want to include in this view.

When you check this option, the **Fields & Functions** button appears. Use this to find @functions and field names you need to put in the formula. If the window is too small to enter your formula, click the **Formula Window** button to get a bigger screen.

If you don't check Select by formula, you can still limit what documents appear in the view. Click the **Add Condition** button and use the Search Builder dialog box to build a condition for what appears in the view. Click **OK** when you're done.

5. Click the **Options** button if you want to inherit the view design from an existing view or folder. Choose the view or folder whose design you want and then click **OK**.
6. Click once on **OK**.

Selecting the Documents to Show

There are two ways to select what documents you're going to display in your view: the Search Builder and the Selection formula. If you set no selection conditions or formulas, Notes assumes you want to include all the documents in the view.

To use the Search Builder window:

1. Click the **Add Condition** button in the Create View dialog box (see Figure 9.2).

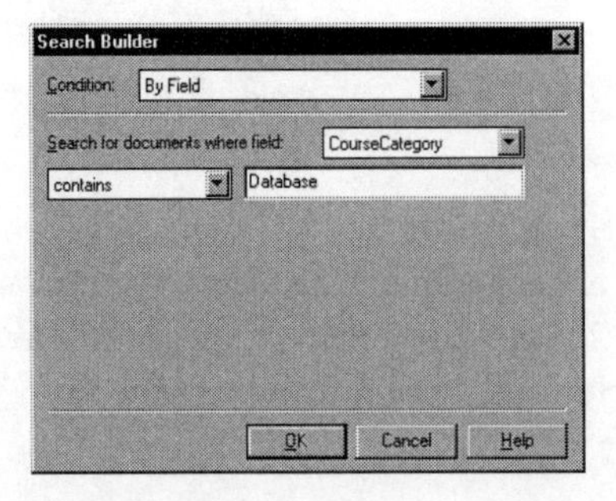

Figure 9.2 The Search Builder dialog box.

2. From the Condition list box, choose how you want to select documents for the view: **By Author, By Date, By Field, By Form,** or **By Form Used**.

3. Depending on your choice of condition, the remainder of the dialog box changes. For instance, if you selected **By Author** the conditions you set up are for the author of the document to contain or not contain the names you specify. If you selected **By Field**, you can specify what field and what text string it does or does not contain.
4. Click **OK**.

Selection formulas always begin with the keyword SELECT. To select all the documents, enter:

SELECT @All

To specify a particular form, you might enter a formula like this:

SELECT Form = "CourseDescription"

To enter a Selection formula for a view:

1. Check **Select by formula** at the bottom of the Create View dialog box.
2. Enter the formula in the Selection conditions window.
3. If you need help with the formula syntax or the field names, click the **Fields & Functions** button. Select **Field** or **Function**. Choose the field or function you want from the list and then click **OK**.
4. If you need more room to write your formula, click the **Formula Window** button to get a bigger screen. Click **Done** when you want to return to the Create View dialog box.
5. Click **OK**.

Creating Columns

When you first start a view, it has only one column, and that contains the number of the document (see Figure 9.3).

To create a new column, do one of the following:

- Double-click the column heading to the right of any existing columns.
- Choose **Create**, **Insert new column** from the menu. This makes a new column to the left of the current column.
- Choose **Create**, **Append new column**. This makes a new column to the far right of any existing columns.

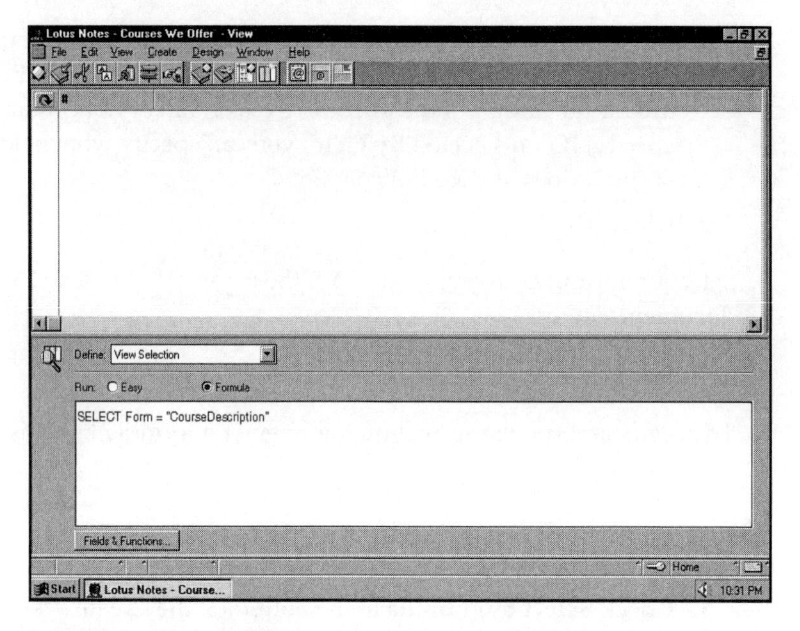

Figure 9.3 New view in Design mode.

When you make changes to your view design, you'll need to refresh the screen to see how your documents are affected. Press **F9** or click the refresh icon in the left corner.

In the Column Properties box, enter a name for the new column in the Title box. Set the width of the column by entering a value in the Width box or by dragging the column heading boundary (see Figure 9.4).

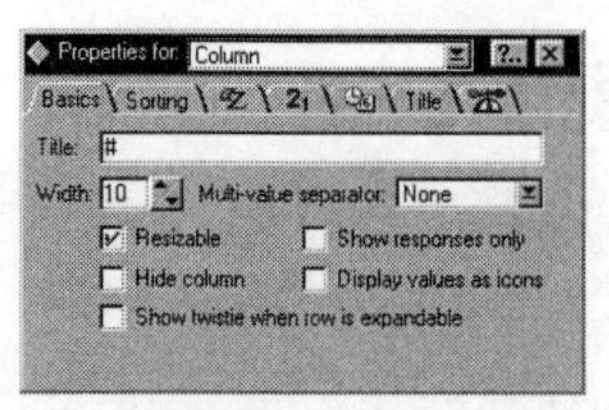

Figure 9.4 The Column Properties box.

- To remove a column, click the heading to select the column and press the **Delete** key.

- To move a column, click the heading to select the column and then choose **Edit**, **Cut** from the menu. Click where you want the column to appear and choose **Edit**, **Paste** from the menu.

Assigning Values

To tell Notes what to put in the column, you must enter a simple function (pick one from a list), a field name, or a formula in the design pane. The formula can be as simple as a field name or a concatenation, it can calculate a value, or it can be an @function.

For example, if you want to add a column that shows the date the document was created, choose the **Simple Function** option for Display and select the created date from the list.

If you want your column to display information from document fields, you must enter a formula. Select the **Formula** option and then enter your formula. The formula can be as simple as a field name or a concatenation of fields, or it can be a complicated set of conditional statements depending on what you need to appear in the column (see Lesson 5, "Formulas and @Functions"). For example, to display the city and state information in one column, you might use a formula like this:

```
City + ", " + State
```

In this lesson, you learned about the types of views, how to create views, how to choose what documents show in the view, and how to add columns. In the next lesson, you'll learn about creating folders.

Creating Folders

10

In this lesson, you learn how folders and views differ and how they're alike. You'll learn what types of folders you can create and the steps to take to make a folder.

Differences Between Folders and Views

Folders and views are similar, but the contents of a view are determined by a selection formula while the user decides the contents of a folder. Users determine the contents of folders by dragging documents from a view into folders.

Folders display documents in rows, just like views. Like views, the columns each show one type of information about the listed documents based on a formula, a simple function, or a field name. In fact, you can base the design of a folder on a view.

Types of Folders

Just like views, there are three types of folders:

- **Private** Any user with reader access to a database can create a folder for his or her own use. A private folder isn't shared by other users in the database. It's a good idea for users to create their own folders to store documents they refer to frequently.
- **Shared** A shared folder is stored on the server and is available to all users with sufficient access rights. Only users with designer or manager access to the database can create shared folders.
- **Shared, personal on first use** These folders are initially stored on the server and are created by someone with designer or manager access to the database. Once the folder is used by a person, the folder automatically becomes a private folder for that person and is stored on that person's desktop.

Creating a Folder

To create a folder:

1. From the menu, choose **Create, Folder**. The Create Folder dialog box appears (see Figure 10.1).

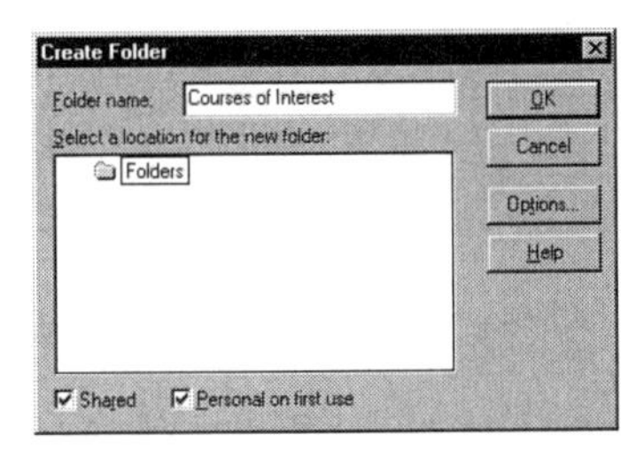

Figure 10.1 The Create Folder dialog box.

2. Enter a Folder name.
3. Check **Shared**. Otherwise, Notes assumes that this is a private folder.
4. Once you check Shared, the **Personal on first use option** becomes available. Check this option if you're creating a folder that will be distributed to users to open as a private folder.
5. Select the folder under which you want your new folder to show in the navigator pane or click **Folders** (or **Private Folders** if you're making a private folder) to store your folder at the top level.
6. Click **Options** and select the name of the view or folder on which you're basing the design of this folder or choose **Blank**. Click **OK** (see Figure 10.2).

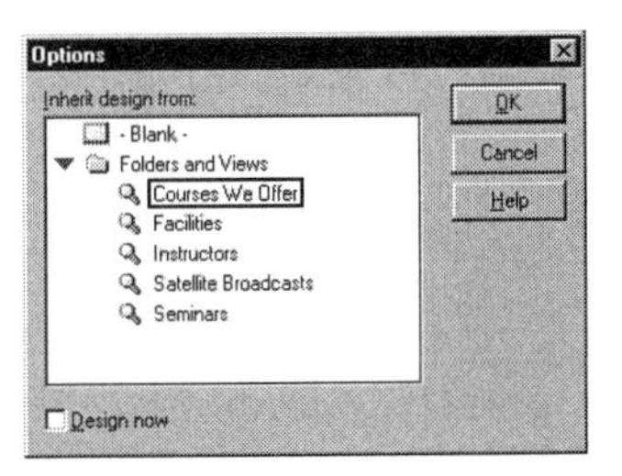

Figure 10.2 The Options dialog box.

7. Click **OK**.

For example, Figure 10.3 shows a shared, personal on first use folder named `Courses of Interest`. This is created for users to store course descriptions they refer to often. The design of the folder is based on the `Courses We Offer` view that displays all the course description documents.

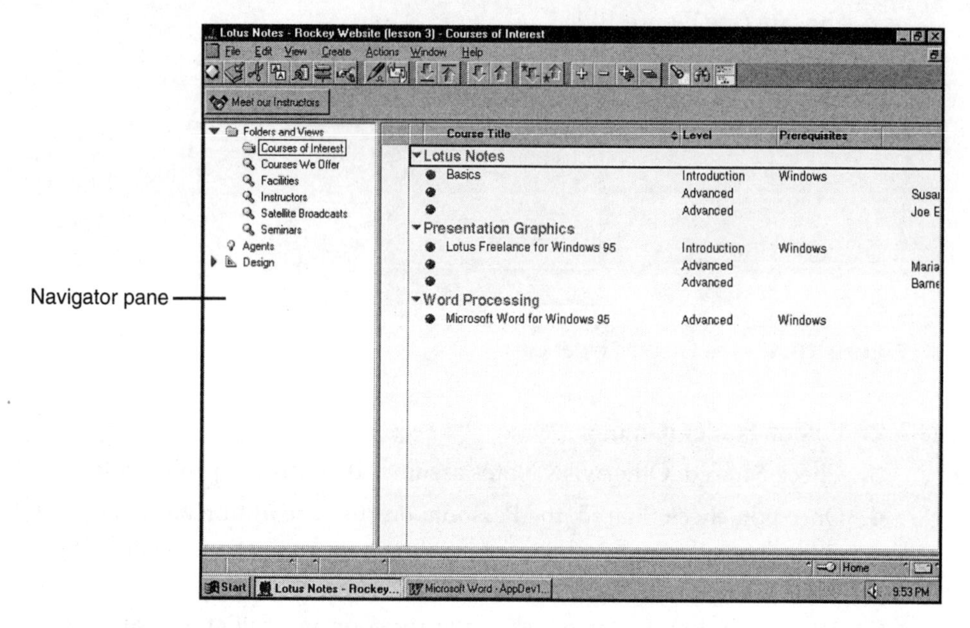

Figure 10.3 The Navigator Pane of a sample application.

In this lesson, you learned how a folder is like a view and how it is not and what steps you need to take to create a folder. In the next lesson, you'll learn about enhancing views.

Enhancing Views

In this lesson, you learn about making your views more user-friendly by sorting the documents or enabling users to sort them, by showing categories (like topic headings), by displaying icons to give visual signals about documents, or by alternating row colors to separate the document rows.

Sorting and Categorizing

You can set up your Notes view to sort the documents in ascending (A to Z, 1 to 10) or descending (Z to A, 10 to 1) fashion, using the contents of one or more columns as the sorting criteria. Notes can sort the documents automatically, or you can make it possible for the user to sort the individual columns.

Categorizing groups sorted the columns and creates headings for the documents in each category. It's possible to collapse category headings, and users can expand the categories when they need to see the documents in a particular category. This is very useful for views that might contain thousands of documents.

Keep in mind these properties of sorting:

- Sorting in Notes occurs in this order: numbers, letters, accented letters, punctuation, and special characters
- Sorting is case-sensitive ("name" will appear before "Name," which comes before "NAME")
- If there are two or more sort columns, the order of the sort is determined in column order from left to right, so place your most important sort column at the left of the other sort columns
- Place categorized columns to the left of any other sort columns

To sort a view:

1. Open the view in Design mode.
2. Double-click the header of the column you want to sort.
3. In the Column Properties box, select the **Sorting** tab (see Figure 11.1).

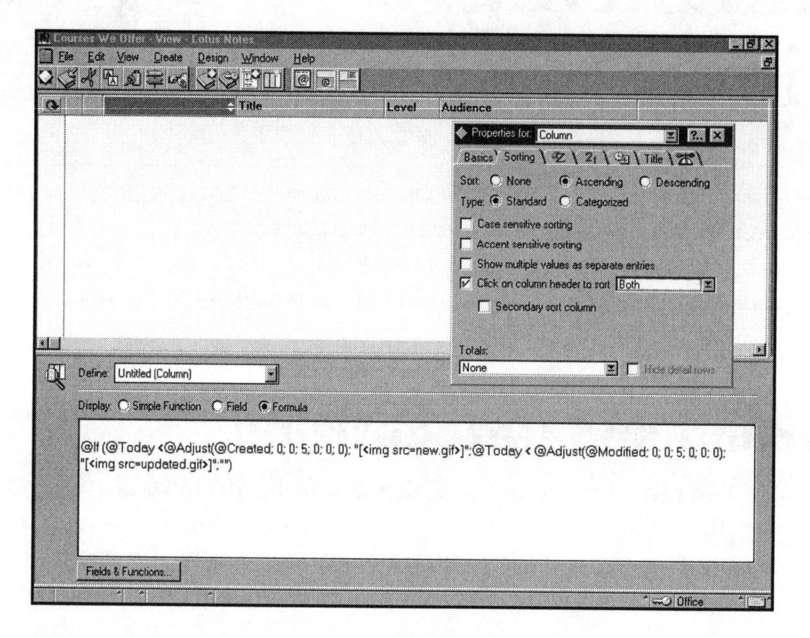

Figure 11.1 The Column Properties box with the Sorting tab selected.

4. From the Sort options, choose **Ascending** or **Descending**.
5. Select a Type: **Standard** or **Categorized**.
6. Enable **Case sensitive sorting** or **Accent sensitive sorting** by checking either or both of those options.
7. If you want your users to sort documents as they want, check **Click on column header to sort**. Then select **Ascending**, **Descending**, or **Both** from the list box (see Figure 11.2).
8. Save the view.

If you chose to sort by categories, go to the **Basics** page of the properties box and check **Show twistie when row is expandable**. This provides users with a visual aid on expandable rows in the form of a small triangle called a "twistie." Users click the twistie to expand a collapsed row or collapse an expanded row.

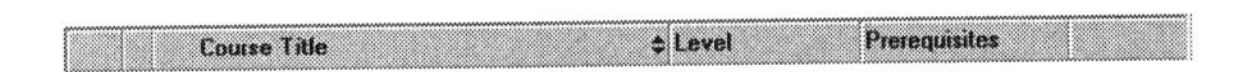

Figure 11.2 Column header with up and down arrows to enable users to sort the column in ascending or descending order.

The sample application shown in Figure 11.3 has a Courses We Offer view. The first column of the view is only one character wide, and the value assigned to the column is the field CourseCategory. The twistie shows that the row is expandable. This column is sorted in ascending order and is categorized. This column is placed first so the view is sorted by the type of courses offered.

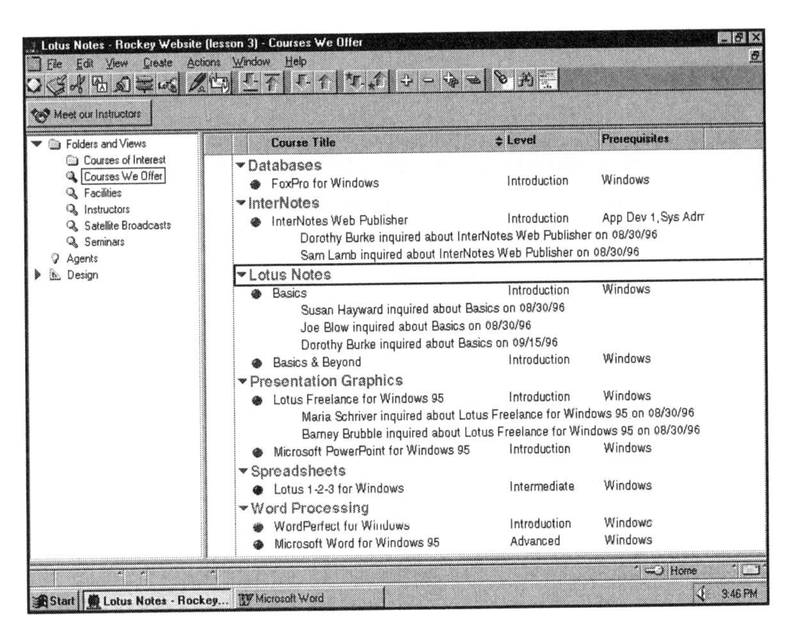

Figure 11.3 The Courses We Offer View from a sample application.

Hidden Columns

Use a hidden column when you want to sort your view based on a particular field but you don't want to show the field values in your view. To hide a column, select it by clicking the column header and then choose **Hide column** from the Column Properties box.

In order to illustrate how this works, let's look again at the example, Courses We Offer View (shown in Figure 11.3). Once the courses are categorized, the courses are shown in order by course level (Introduction, Intermediate, and Advanced). To do this, a column was created after the category and then hidden. The content of that hidden column is the Level field (see Figure 11.4).

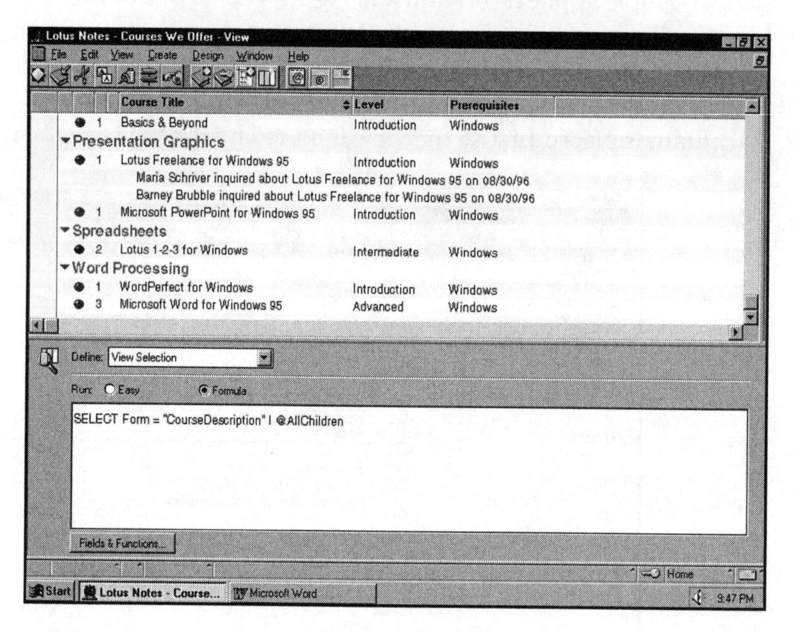

Figure 11.4 The Courses We Offer view in Design mode.

The Level field in the example Course Description form is a keyword field, and the keyword choices are `Introduction`, `Intermediate`, and `Advanced`. Keyword selections automatically appear in alphabetical order. To display the keyword text in level order in the Course Description form, a synonym was created for each keyword entry (see Figure 11.5).

Keyword Synonym Synonyms are internal names that Notes stores as the value of the field (instead of the keyword itself). Like form name synonyms, this enables you to use shorter names and to change the keywords without affecting formulas referencing the synonyms.

TIP **Trouble Sorting High, Medium, and Low?** A very popular use of a keyword field is to enable users to select a priority of High, Medium, or Low from a keyword field. Categorizing in ascending order on that field in a view would produce High, Low, and Medium. To produce a sort of High, Medium, and Low, assign synonyms to each keyword as follows: High|1, Medium|2, Low|1, and sort and categorize the column in ascending order.

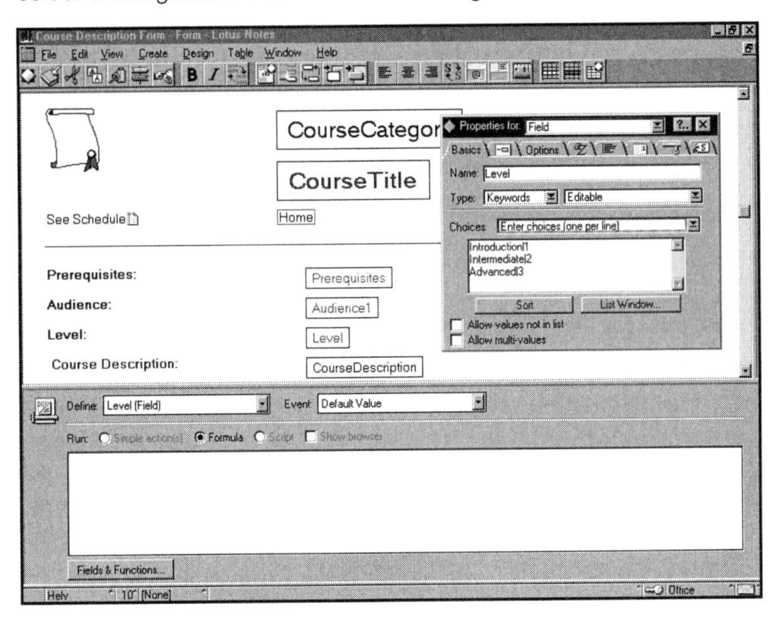

Figure 11.5 The Field Properties box showing the keywords for the Level field of the Course Description form.

Keyword synonyms do not appear on forms but they do appear in views. The contents of the new column shows numbers (refer to Figure 11.4). The column is hidden so users can't see these numbers. The column is also set in ascending order with a standard sort so the course descriptions will appear in order by level.

You'll notice a Level category was included that shows the words for the level. In that column the formula reads:

```
@If(Level = "1"; "Introduction"; Level = "2"; "Intermediate"; "Advanced")
```

Displaying Values as Icons

Visual signals like icons in columns make your view look "cool" and quickly let your users know what type of document is in that row.

In the Courses We Offer view, icons were used to distinguish the course levels. Green bullets were used for Introduction courses, blue bullets for Intermediate courses, and red bullets for Advanced courses. These icons appear in a column placed before the hidden column. This new column is not sorted.

To put the icons in the columns, check **Display values as icons** in the Column Properties box. Then enter a formula to show the icons. For the icons shown in the Courses We Offer view, the formula was:

```
@If(Level = "1"; 114; Level = "2"; 117; 115)
```

Where did these values come from and what do they mean? In the Lotus Notes *Application Developer's Guide* section on displaying icons in a column, there is a table of available icons. You pick the icon you want and find the number of that icon. Enter the number in your formula. You can also find this table in Notes Help under "Displaying an Icon in a Column."

Responses Only Columns

In applications that have response and response to response documents, you want to show those documents in the view in such a way that your users will be able to immediately identify them as being responses instead of main documents.

Because columns to the right of the **responses only** column will display only data referring to the main document, you need to be careful where you put this column (cut and paste the column elsewhere if you don't place it correctly the first time).

There can be only one **responses only** column per view.

To display response documents as grouped under the main document and indented:

1. In the View Properties box, select the **Options** tab, and check **Show response documents in a hierarchy**.
2. If your view selection formula is not SELECT = @All, rewrite the formula to include the response documents.

3. Create a new column. In the Column Properties box, select **Show responses only**.

In the Courses We Offer example view, a **responses only** column is just before the Course Title column. In order to make the response documents appear correctly, each of the steps previously outlined was followed. The selection formula was changed in the Design mode for the view, where the following formula was entered in the design pane:

```
SELECT Form = "CourseDescription" | @AllChildren
```

See Table 2.8 on the Tear Out Card for @functions relating to response documents.

Because the designer wanted to display specific information from the response document (based on an Inquiry form), the following formula for this column was entered:

```
InqName + " inquired about " + InqCourseTitle + " on " +
@Text(@Created;"D0S0")
```

Adding the **responses only** column affected the column in which the icons are displayed. All the icons for the response documents showed up as red bullets, which indicated that the courses were from the advanced level. That happened because the formula for that column said that if the levels were not introductory or intermediate then use the advanced icon. The formula for that column was changed to read:

```
@If(@IsResponseDoc; ""; @If(Level = "1"; 114; Level = "2"; 117; 115))
```

View Properties

You can make your view easier to read by changing the background color and adding alternating rows.

With the view in Design mode, select the **Style** tab (see Figure 11.6) from the View Properties box and make the appropriate selections:

Here is a summary of the options on the Style tab:

- **Background** Select a color for the background of the view.
- **Column total** Choose a color to accent column totals when you've specified that the column should be totaled.

- **Unread rows** Pick a color to highlight documents that the user hasn't read.
- **Alternate rows** Select a color to alternate with the background color, to give the view a striped appearance.
- **Show selection margin** Select this to provide a margin in the view, enabling users to select documents with a check mark in that margin.
- **Extend last column to window width** Check this to stretch the last column out to take up the rest of the window.
- **Show column headings** Select this to display your column headings. If you don't select this, your column headings won't show in your view. After you select it, choose whether you want **Beveled headings** or **Simple headings**.
- **Lines per heading** Use this to allow more than one line per column heading.
- **Lines per row** Increase the number of lines per row to accommodate large amounts of text (as in a product description). The text will wrap in that column.
- **Shrink row to content** If you increased the number of lines in a row, choose this option to shrink the row if the text is not long enough to completely fill the number of lines you specified.
- **Row spacing** Set the spacing between rows to **Single**, 1/4, 1/2, 3/4, or **Double** spacing.

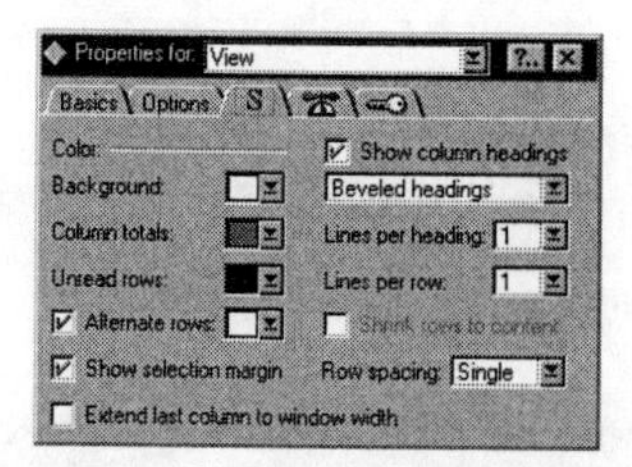

Figure 11.6 The View Properties box with the Style tab selected.

In this lesson, you learned how to sort documents in a view, to use hidden sort columns, to add category headings that expand or collapse, to add icons to columns, to change the background color of views, and to add alternating rows. In the next lesson, you'll automate some tasks by creating actions and action buttons.

Actions

In this lesson, you learn about Actions and how they add automation to forms, views, and folders.

What Are Actions?

Actions automate functions that can be performed on documents based on their forms, views, and folders they are displayed in. They can appear as commands on the Actions menu or as buttons on the Action Bar. Figure 12.1 shows Actions as buttons on the Action Bar.

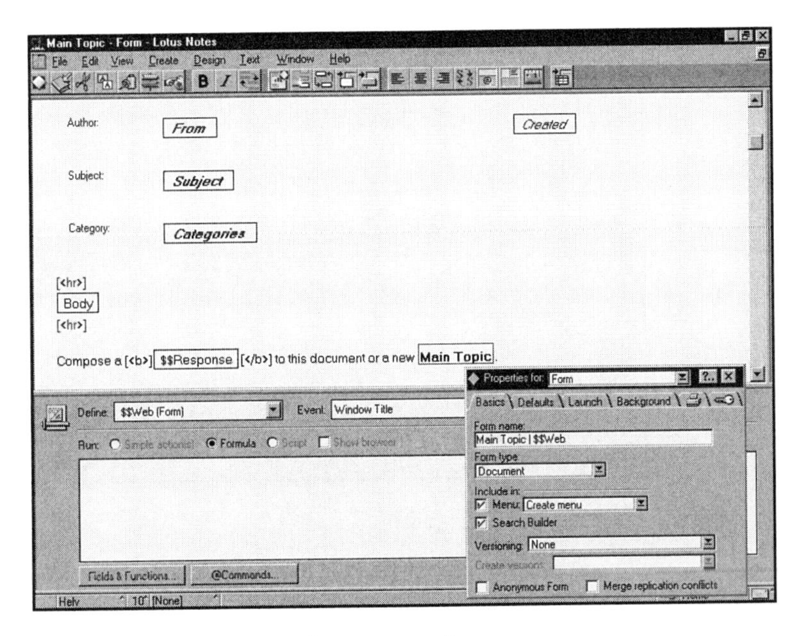

Figure 12.1 The Action buttons for a new mail memo.

These are the categories of Actions:

- **System supplied actions** Forms, folders, and views have default Actions that automatically appear on the Actions menu. They include Categorize, Edit Document, Send Document, Forward, Move to Folder, and Remove from Folder. You can change the properties of these Actions to create buttons on the Action Bar.
- **Custom Actions** You can create custom Actions that can be simple functions you select from the Add Actions list, they can be based on @function or @command formulas, or they can be programmed using LotusScript.

To see the list of Actions associated with a form, folder, or view, you must be in the Design mode. Then select **View**, **Action Pane** from the menu. There are asterisks in front of the default Actions in the list. Figure 12.2 shows the Action Pane.

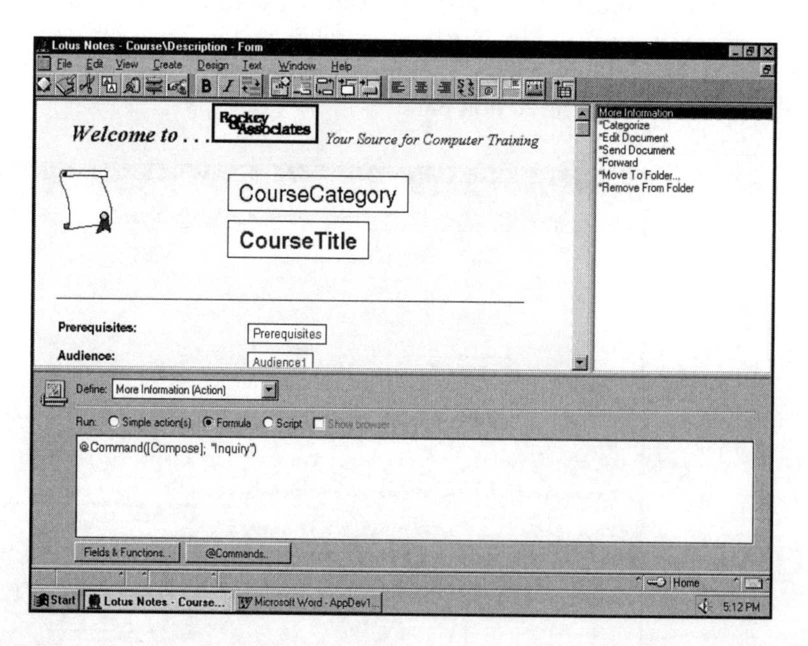

Figure 12.2 The Action Pane.

Using @Commands

The @commands are a special branch of the @function formulas. You generally use @commands to automate menu commands in a formula for Actions, buttons, hotspots, and SmartIcons.

@Commands are split into two categories:

- **@Commands** Notes evaluates all formulas (including @commands) from top to bottom and left to right. Most @commands are evaluated in the sequence they appear. There are some exceptions that are noted in Notes Help in the document "Order of evaluation for formula statements."
- **@PostedCommands** @PostedCommands are processed last in a formula, that is, they will run after all other @functions and @commands in the formula.

The syntax for an @command formula is:

@Command([Command]; Parameter)

where *Command* is the name of the Notes command you're activating and *Parameter* defines what the command acts on. @Commands can include several parameters, and parameters are not required for all @commands. Table 12.1 lists some frequently used @commands:

Table 12.1 Frequently Used @Commands

@Command	*Does this*
@Command([Compose]; server; database; form)	Creates a new blank document. Only use server and database parameters if the form is not in the current database. For example, use:([Compose]; "Inquiry") when the Inquiry form is in the current database.
@Command([CreateFolder])	Opens the Create Folder dialog box.
@Command([EditDocument])	Places the document you're currently reading in edit mode.
@Command([EditFind])	Displays the Find dialog box.

continues

Table 12.1 Continued

@Command	*Does this*
@Command([FileCloseWindow])	Closes the current window (doesn't apply to Notes workspace window), but prompts user to save before closing if the document hasn't already been saved.
@Command([FileExit])	Closes Notes and all its active windows, but doesn't prompt user to save files.
@Command([FilePrint]) or @Command([FilePrint]; *"NumberCopies"*; *"FromPage"*; *"ToPage"*; "Draft"; "printview"; *"FormName"*; *"PageBreak"*; *"ResetPages"*)	Prints currently selected or open documents. Parameters are optional but can help specify what you want printed and how. Specify an empty string ("") if you don't use a parameter. Specify "draft" for draft quality printing. Specify "printview" to print a view.
@Command([FileSave])	Saves the current document or a form, subform, view, folder, agent, or navigator in design view.
@Command([Help])	Opens online Help in the index view.
@Command([OpenNavigator])	Displays the navigator defined for that database.
@Command([OpenView])	Opens the specified view *"viewname."*
@Command([ToolsSpellCheck])	Activates the spelling checker.
@Command([ViewNavigatorsFolders])	Displays Folders and Views navigator.

A complete list of all the @commands appears in the *Programmer's Guide Part 2.*

Creating Actions

To create an Action, open the form, folder, or view in Design mode.

1. Choose **Create**, **Action** from the menu.
2. In the Action Properties Box (see Figure 12.3), enter a title for the Action. Keep it short because it must fit on a button or in the menu.

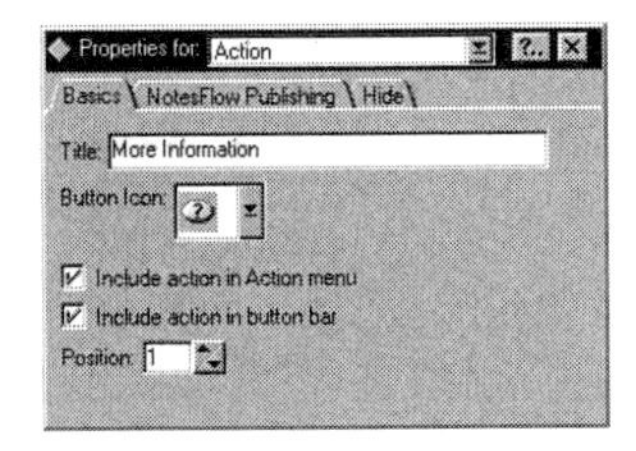

Figure 12.3 The Action Properties Box.

3. Check **Include action in Action menu** if you want your Action to be on that menu.
4. Check **Include action in button bar** if you want to add a button to the Action Bar.
5. If you want to place an icon on the Action button, select a button icon from the drop-down list of available icons.
6. Choose a Run option in the design pane: Simple action(s), Formula, or Script.

   If you choose Simple action(s), click the Add Action button to see the Add Action dialog box (see Figure 12.4) and select an action from the list.

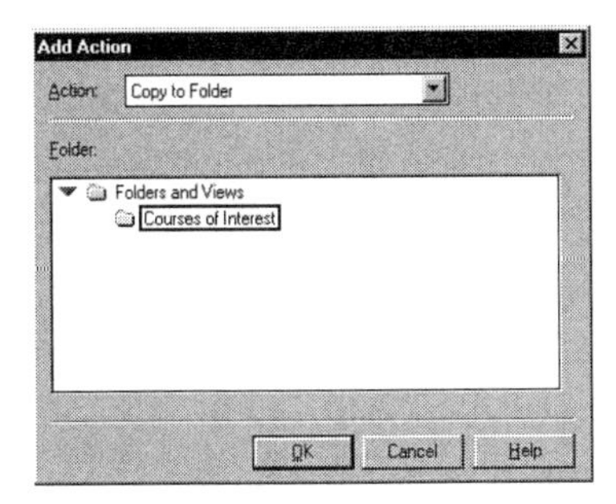

Figure 12.4 The Add Action dialog box.

If you select Formula, enter a formula using the Fields and Functions and @commands button to help you. Figure 12.5 shows the dialog box when you select **Paste, @command**.

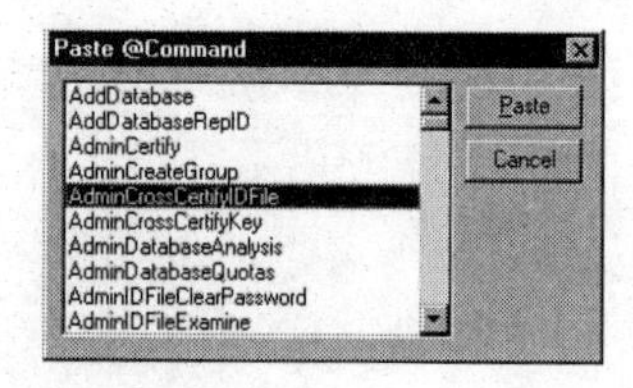

Figure 12.5 The Paste @Command dialog box.

7. Close and save the form, folder, or view. Test it.

Figure 12.6 shows two buttons with icons on the Action Bar. The `Meet Our Instructors` Action button takes users to a different view called the Instructors view. This Action button uses an @command formula:

@Command([ViewChange]; "Instructors")

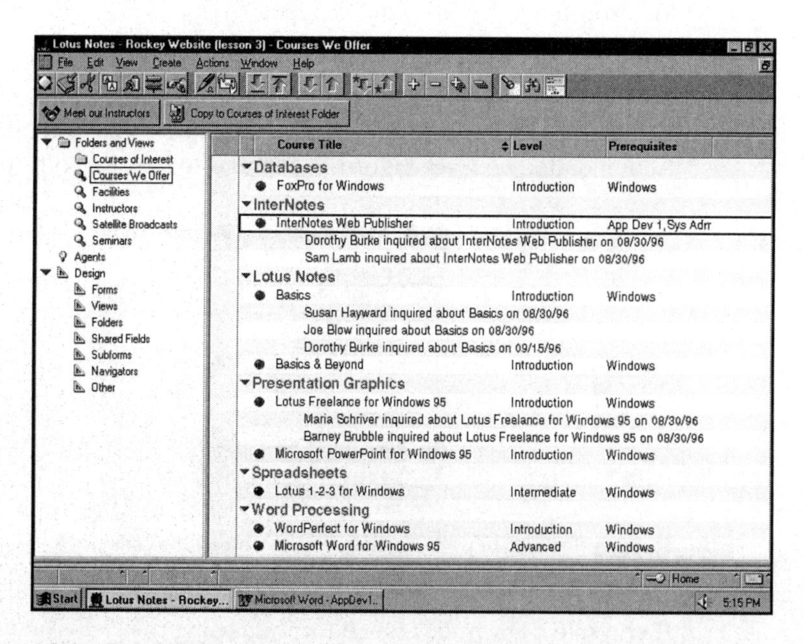

Figure 12.6 The Courses We Offer view has two Action buttons.

The `Copy to Courses of Interest Folder` Action button allows users to store course descriptions in a folder called Courses of Interest. A simple Action called Copy to Folder was used (refer to Figure 12.4).

In this lesson, you learned how to automate functions in your views, folders, and forms. In the next lesson, you'll learn about navigators.

Navigators

In this lesson, you learn what navigators are, how to create them, how to add graphics and hotspots, and how to make an image map.

Creating Navigators

You can use graphical navigators to give your users a way to find documents or take actions that is easier than selecting folders, views, or menu commands (see Figure 13.1). Users can point and click buttons or objects, instead of searching through a list of folders or views. The hotspots you add to the navigator can open a view, open a folder, open a link, open another navigator, or run a formula.

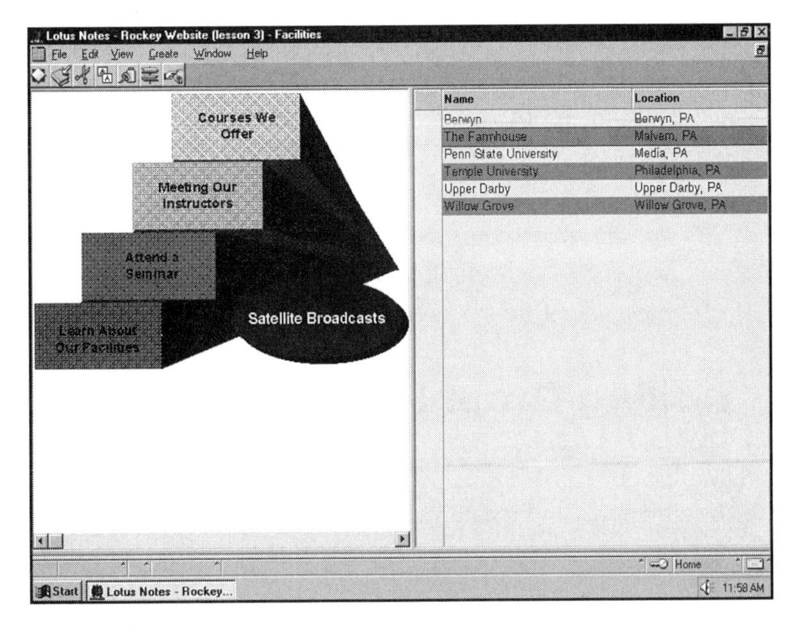

Figure 13.1 A Sample Navigator.

You can create graphics in other programs and paste them into the navigator you're designing, or you can draw some of the elements using the navigator drawing tools.

To create a navigator from scratch:

1. Select the database for which you want to design a navigator.
2. Choose **Create, Design, Navigator**.
3. Open the Navigator Properties box (see Figure 13.2).

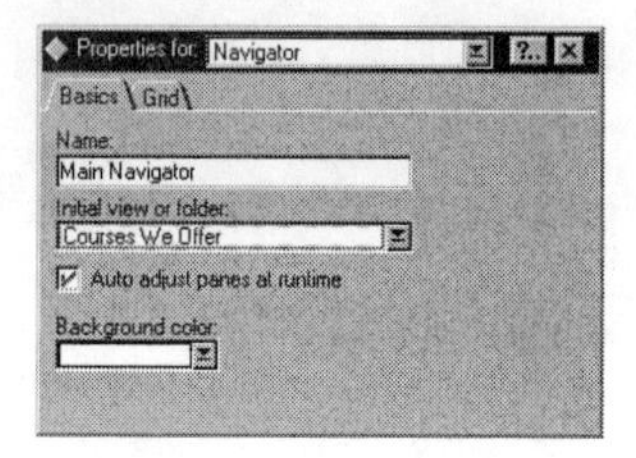

Figure 13.2 The Navigator Properties box.

4. In the Name box, enter a name for the navigator. Keep it short and descriptive; only the first 32 characters appear on the menu.
5. From the Initial view or folder list box, select the view or folder you want to appear when the navigator first opens.
6. Check **Adjust panes at runtime** to have the view pane automatically adjust to allow room for the navigator.
7. If you want to set a background for the navigator, choose a Background color from the list box.
8. Add objects to the navigator (graphic elements, text, drawings, and so on as described throughout this lesson).
9. Save and close the navigator.

Adding Graphic Elements

There are two ways you can add graphic elements to a navigator: Create a graphic object in another program and paste it into the navigator, or use the drawing tools and create your own objects.

To create graphic buttons by pasting graphics from other programs:

1. Create the graphic element in the other program (clip art from a graphics presentation program was used to make the one shown in Figure 13.1). Lotus Notes accepts bitmap files or metafiles. Make it the right size, because you won't be able to size it once you put it into Notes. For more information on graphics, see Part IV, "InterNotes Web Publisher."

CAUTION

Bitmaps and Metafiles If you have trouble pasting a graphic element from your source program into your navigator, Notes might not accept it because the graphic is not a bitmap or metafile. A solution for this problem is to first paste the graphic into Windows Paintbrush or Windows 95 Paint. Then cut and paste it from one of those applications. Their native graphic format is BMP (bitmap), and Notes accepts graphics from those applications readily.

2. Select the graphic element and choose **Edit, Copy**.
3. Switch to Notes (you can close the graphics program if you choose).
4. Open the database and go to the design mode by selecting **View, Design** from the menu.
5. Double-click the navigator.
6. Position the cursor where you want to place the graphic.
7. Select **Create, Graphic Button** (see Figure 13.3).

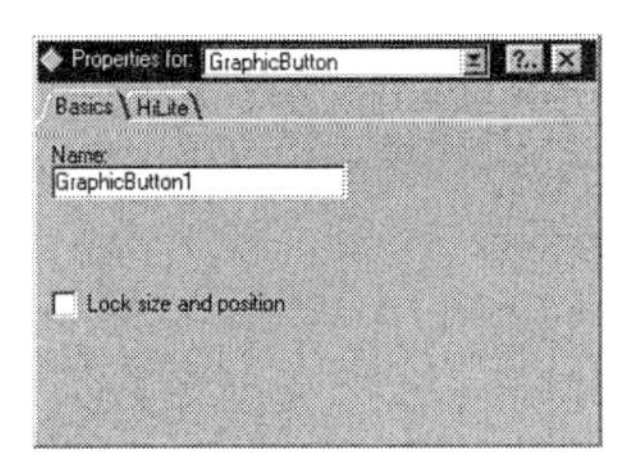

Figure 13.3 The Design pane for a graphic button.

8. In the Design pane, select a Run option: **Simple action(s)**, **Formula**, or **Script**.

If you select Simple action(s), choose an action from the Action list: **Open another Navigator**, **Open a View**, **Alias a Folder** (the current folder is replaced by the folder activated by the navigator), or **Open a Link** (users can open an existing database, view, or document link that was created by selecting the database, view, or document and choosing **Edit**, **Copy as Link**). Select the view, folder, navigator, or link this action will open (you must **Paste** the link in).

If you select Formula, enter a formula using the **Fields & Functions** button and the **@Command** button to help you construct it. You would need a formula if the choices for simple actions are insufficient—for example, if you want to put an @Command associated with your navigator, to create a new document.

9. Save the navigator.

You can make the drawing objects from scratch:

1. With the navigator in design mode, select the item you want to draw from the Create menu: **Button**, **Text, Rectangle**, **Rounded Rectangle**, **Ellipse**, **Polygon**, **or Polyline** (see Figure 13.4).

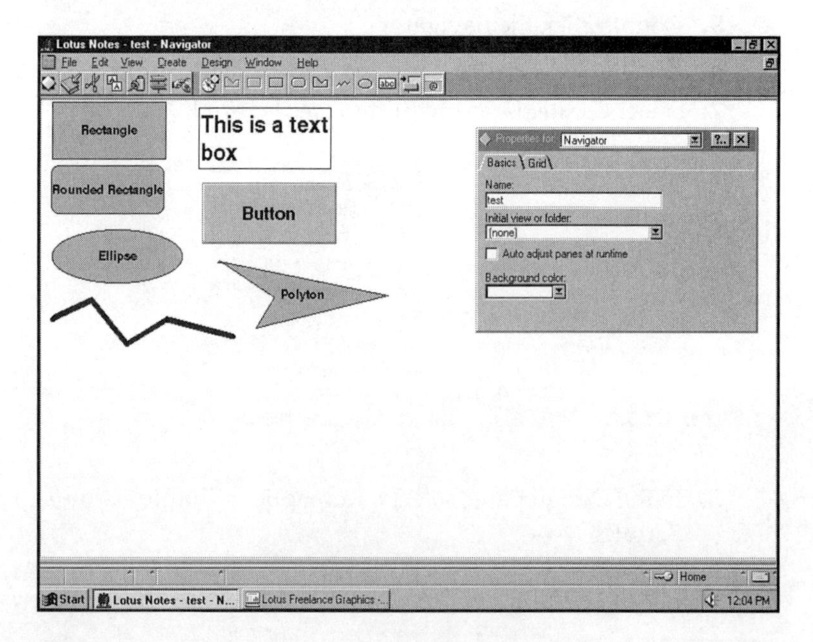

Figure 13.4 The objects you can draw in a navigator.

2. Draw the object. The Properties box will appear for that object after you have completed drawing.

   Buttons, text boxes, rectangles, rounded rectangles, and ellipses are all drawn in the same fashion. Position your cursor where you want the top-left corner of the object to start, hold down the mouse button, drag to the diagonally opposite corner, and then release the mouse button. Holding down **Shift** as you drag makes the rectangular objects square and the ellipse a circle.

   Polygons and polylines (these are connected lines, not shapes) are drawn in much the same way. Click once where you want the object to begin and then click at each bend or corner. To complete the polygon, you must make the last point the same as the first. Double-click when you are finished drawing the object.

3. Define the properties for the object.

4. In the Design pane, select a Run option: **Simple action(s)**, **Formula**, or **Script**.

   If you select Simple action(s), choose an action from the Action list: **Open another Navigator**, **Open a View**, **Alias a Folder**, or **Open a Link**. Select the view, folder, navigator, or link this action will open.

   If you select Formula, enter a formula using the **Fields & Functions** button and the **@Command** button to help you construct it.

5. Save the navigator.

TIP **Drawing Tips** If you want to draw more than one of a particular type of object, hold down the **Shift** key as you choose **Create** and the shape. When you're finished, select **Create** and the name of the shape to discontinue the creation mode.

For precision drawing (and this is helpful if you aren't as familiar with drawing programs as you are with Notes), open the Navigator Properties box to the **Grid** page. Select **Snap to grid**. It will help you line objects up on the screen.

Buttons, rectangles, rounded rectangles, text boxes, and ellipses have similar properties. For each of these objects, you need to add a caption. This is the text that appears on the object. Text wraps in the text box and you can size it if your text is larger than the box you have drawn (see Figure 13.5).

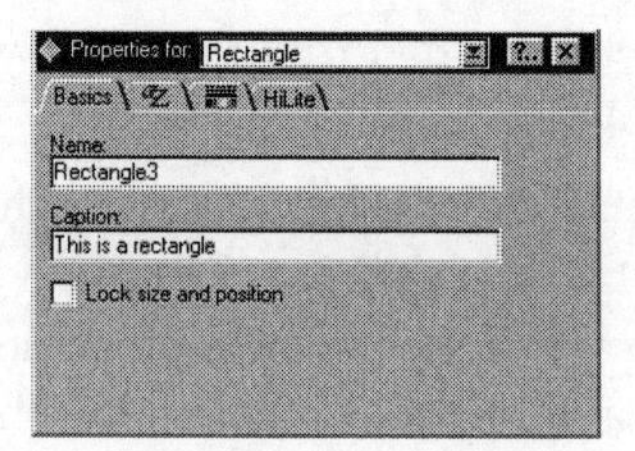

Figure 13.5 Basics page of the Rectangle Properties box.

You can set the font characteristics of the object's text, the fill color of the object, and the outline color of the object (see Figure 13.6).

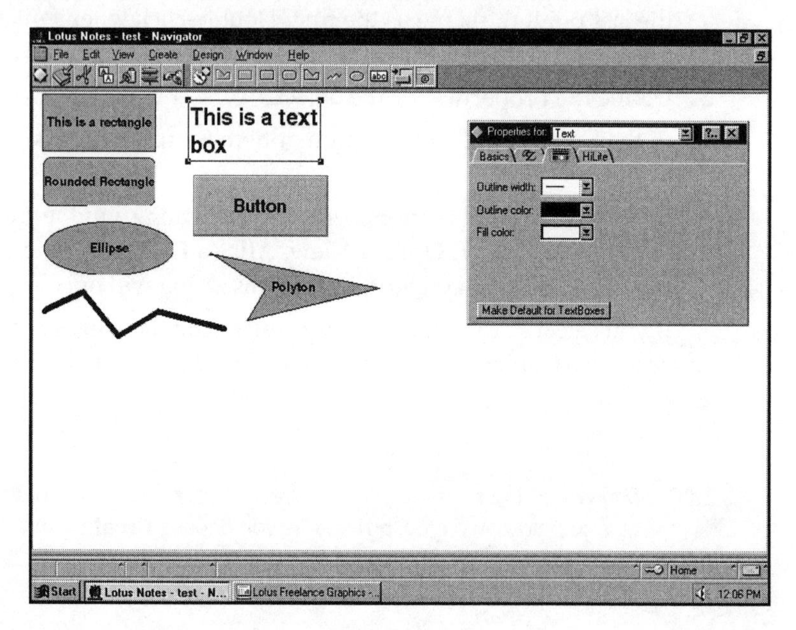

Figure 13.6 The Colors page of the Text Properties box.

The button attributes are slightly different. Here you choose the face color, the depth of the bevel, and the color of the outline. Setting the polyline attributes includes choosing the width of the line and its color.

All these graphic objects have HiLite settings. You can choose whether you want highlighting to show when the user's mouse pointer touches the object, when the user clicks the object, or both. Then select the color of the highlighting outline, the width of the line, and the highlighting fill color (see Figure 13.7).

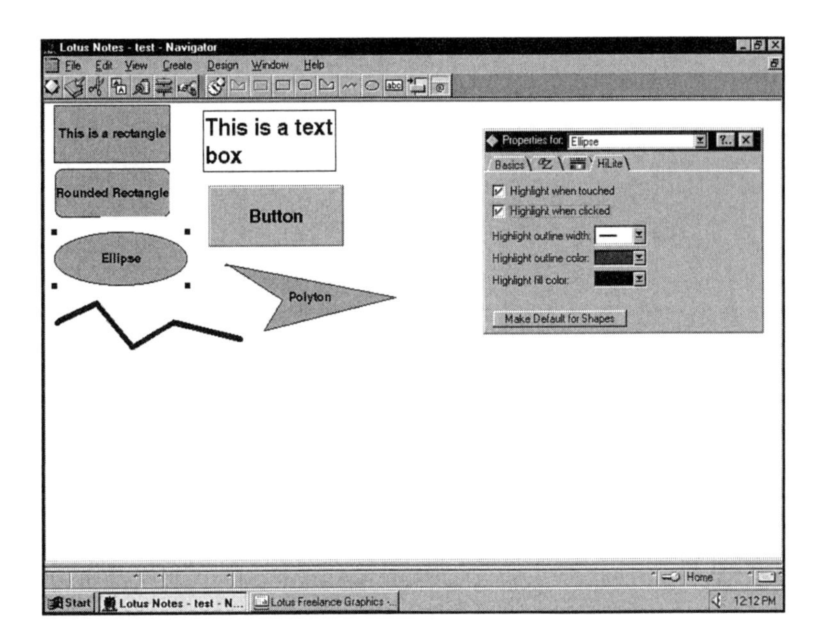

Figure 13.7 The Ellipse Properties box with the HiLite tab selected.

Except for graphic buttons, you can change the size, shape, or position for these graphic objects.

To size an object:

1. Select the object by clicking it once.
2. Position your cursor on one of the four sizing corners.
3. Drag the mouse pointer away from or toward the center of the object to resize it proportionally. Drag in any direction if you don't care about keeping the size uniform.

As you add objects, you might want to move, delete them, and so on. The following list describes how to work with objects:

- To keep an object at its current size and position, select **Lock size and position** from the Properties box for that object.
- To move an object, point in the middle of the object and drag it to its new position.
- To delete an object, select the object and choose **Edit**, **Clear** or simply press the **Delete** key.

- If one object is overlapping another that you need to reach but can't, select the top object and choose **Design, Send to Back**. This puts the selected object on the bottom of the stack, and the object you want to work with is now on top of the stack. If you can select the object in the back by clicking a piece of the object that is showing, choose **Design, Bring to Front** to put that object on top of the stack.

Adding Hotspots

If you don't assign actions to graphic objects, they become simple graphic elements (part of the picture), as is the ellipse and its shadow in the navigator in Figure 13.1. You'll need to add hotspots to initiate actions where you didn't assign actions to the objects.

To add a hotspot:

1. With the navigator in the design mode, choose **Create, Hotspot Rectangle** or **Create, Hotspot Polygon**.
2. Draw the hotspot on the navigator using the same skills you've now mastered for drawing graphic objects.
3. Set properties for the hotspot. You can choose if you want highlighting to show when the user's mouse pointer touches the object, when the user clicks the object, or both. Then select the color of the highlighting outline and the width of the line.
4. Select a Run option in the design pane, to either run a **Simple action** or to use a **Formula**.
5. Save the navigator.

Using Image Maps

An image map is a large graphic that acts like a background for your navigator. You can add hotspots so users can click specific areas on the image and activate an action. In the navigator shown in Figure 13.1, an image map was used. The image was copied from a graphics program and then hotspots were added. However, the ellipse was added using the drawing tools in Notes.

To create an image map, you must start with a graphic background. You may have only one graphic background per navigator. The graphic background is always positioned in the top-left corner, and you can't move it.

1. Create the graphic background in another program. Notes only allows you to import bitmap files or metafiles.
2. Select the graphic element and then choose **Edit, Copy**.
3. Close the program and switch to Notes.
4. Open the navigator in design mode.
5. Choose **Create, Graphic Background** from the menu.
6. Add hotspots as needed.
7. Save the navigator.

TIP **Use Text Boxes for Text!** The text on the navigator shown in Figure 13.1 was added in the graphics program, but you should consider adding the text to your image map in Notes by using text boxes. That way, it's easier to change the text later.

Once you've completed your navigator, test your design by selecting **Design, Test Navigator** from the menu.

In this lesson, you learned how to create a navigator, how to add graphic elements, how to create hotspots, and how to make image maps. In the next lesson, you'll learn about agents.

Agents

In this lesson, you learn what agents are, how to create them, and how to trigger them.

Understanding Agents

Agents are like macros. They enable you to automate repetitive tasks or build powerful tools that you can use to execute complex programs. An *agent* is similar to an action in that they both automate tasks, but unlike actions, agents are not attached to a form or a view. Anytime the database that the agent was created for is open, the agent is available. Because an agent isn't tied to a form or a view, it can perform other useful tasks such as managing documents, manipulating fields, sending messages, and bringing in information from other applications.

Users can create their own agents to automate their own tasks. This type of agent is a *personal* agent and can be used only by the person who designed it. As an application designer you're more likely to create *shared* agents that can be used by many people. After you've created an agent, you can't change the personal or shared settings.

Creating Agents

Before you create an agent, be sure you've considered what you want the agent to do, how you want to trigger the agent, and what the consequences of triggering the agent will be.

To create an agent:

1. Select the database for which you are creating the agent.
2. Choose **Create**, **Agent**. The Agent window opens (see Figure 14.1).

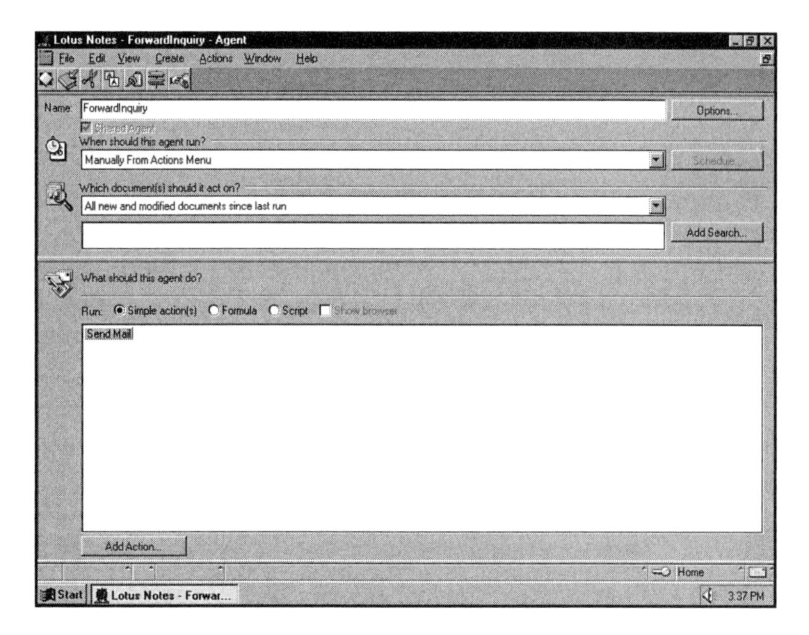

Figure 14.1 The Agent window.

3. In the Agent window, enter a Name for the agent.

   The full agent name, including cascading names, can't be more than 127 bytes (which is not necessarily the same as 127 characters).

Cascading Names on a Menu You can group together several agents that perform similar functions. Decide on a descriptive name for the top-level agent. When that agent is selected from the menu, a submenu will appear with the additional agents. This is called cascading.

Consider how the agents will be listed in the menu. Try to start each agent with a different letter to make keyboard shortcuts easier, or use the underscore (_) before the letter you want to use as the keyboard shortcut (C_reate, for example).

Agents normally appear in alphabetical order on the menu. If you want your agents in a different order, use a number or letter designation before each agent name.

Keep your agent names consistent where you are using the same type of agent in more than one database. Consistency helps the users recognize the agent and what it does.

4. Check **Shared Agent** unless you're creating a personal agent.
5. Select one of the options under `When should this agent run?`: **Manually from Actions Menu**, **Manually from Agent List**, **If New Mail Has Arrived**, **If Documents Have Been Created or Modified**, **If Documents Have Been Pasted**, **On Schedule Hourly**, **On Schedule Daily**, **On Schedule Weekly**, **On Schedule Monthly**, and **On Schedule Never**.

   Users can manually run an agent when a database is selected or open by choosing **Actions** and then the name of the agent from the menu (see Figure 14.2).

   A *hidden* agent (one that isn't on the menu) can be run from the Agents List. The user selects **Agent** from the navigator pane, clicks the appropriate agent name in the list to select it, and then chooses **Actions**, **Run** from the menu.

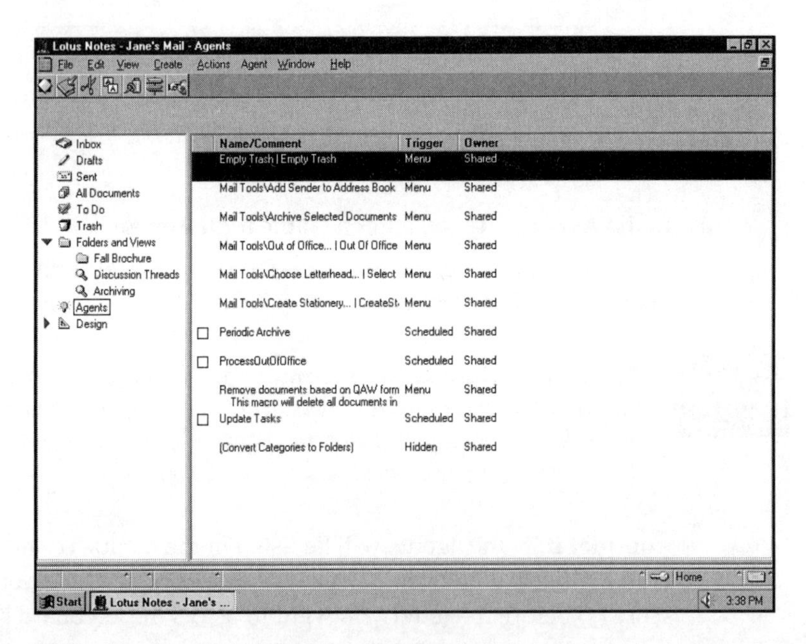

Figure 14.2 The Agents List from the Mail Database.

A condition-triggered agent, such as "If New Mail Has Arrived," occurs when the condition criteria have been met.

Scheduled agents run on a time schedule that you must set. When you select this type of trigger, click the **Schedule** button and set up the schedule you want to use (see Figure 14.3).

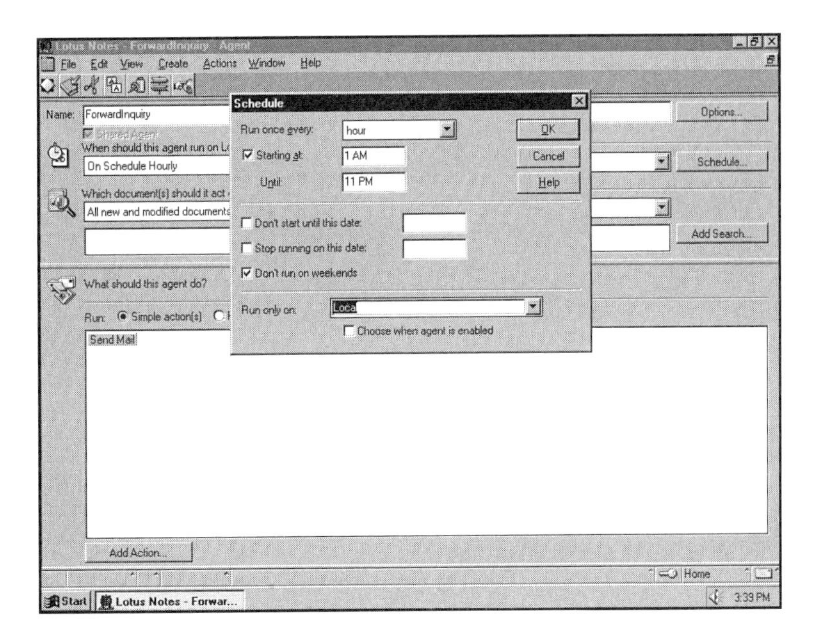

Figure 14.3 The Schedule dialog box.

6. Select an option for `Which document(s) should it act on?`: **All documents in database**, **All new and modified documents since last run**, **All unread documents in view, All documents in view**, **Selected documents**, or **Run once** [@Commands may be used].
7. If you want the agent to search for something, click the **Search** button to open the Search Builder dialog box. You can specify that the agent search **By Author**, **By Date, By Field**, **By Form**, **By Form Used**, **In Folder**, or **By Words and Phrases**. Then fill in the information for which you want to search and click **OK**. If you choose By Words and phrases, the Search Builder dialog box will appear so that you can fill in your conditions.
8. Select a Run option under `What should the agent do?`: **Simple action(s)** (click the **Add Action** button to select the simple action you want to run; see Figure 14.4), **Formula** (enter in the formula pane using the help of the **Fields & Functions** and **@Commands** buttons), or **Script**.
9. Close and save the agent.

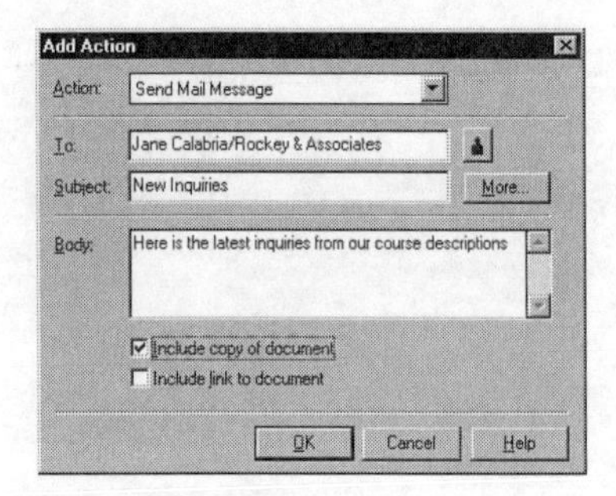

Figure 14.4 The Add Action dialog box.

In this lesson, you learned what agents are and how to make them. In the next lesson, you'll learn how to put some finishing touches on your application design.

Final Touches

In this lesson, you learn how to add the finishing touches to your application by creating the About Database and Using Database documents, making the database icon, and then documenting your work.

Creating About Database and Using Database Documents

The About Database document appears by default the first time a user opens a database. It also appears when a user looks up the database in the Database Catalog. Your About Database document should include a statement about the database's purpose, who should use the database, some basic guidelines for using the database, the date the database was implemented, and the name and address of the database manager.

To create the About Database document for a database:

1. Choose **View**, **Design** from the menu.
2. Under Design in the navigator, select **Other** (see Figure 15.1).
3. Double-click **"About Database"** document.
4. When the document opens, you see a blank screen, which is really a huge rich text field. You may place text, buttons, hotspots, links, and graphics there (see a sample About Database document in Figure 15.2).
5. Save the document.

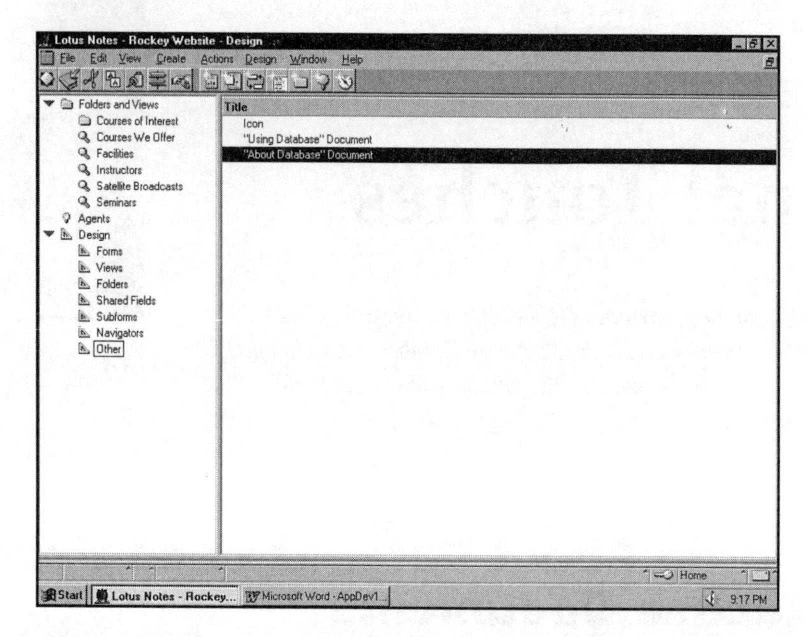

Figure 15.1 The Design view with Other selected.

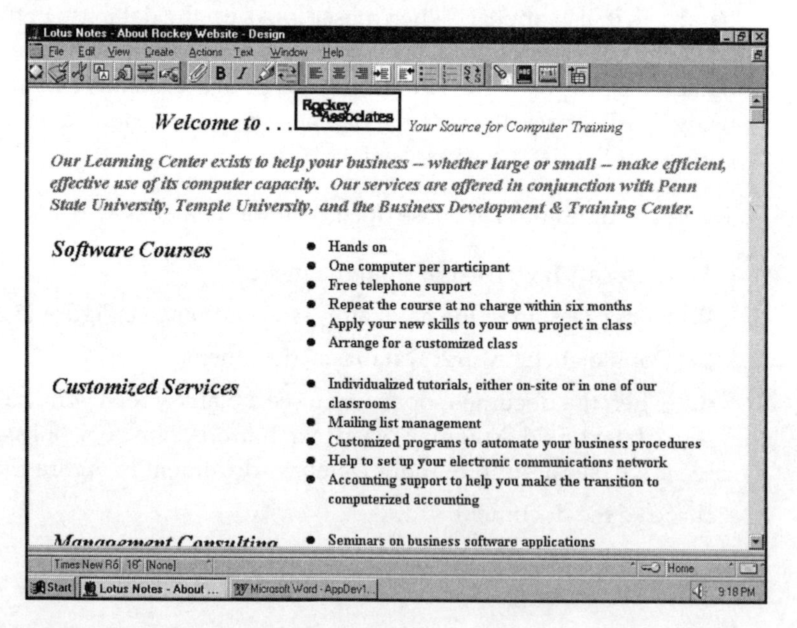

Figure 15.2 The About Database document from a sample application.

The Using Database document is meant to supply help information to the user (users access this document by choosing **Help**, **Using This Database**). You should include a brief description of the database, how it works, and what it is intended to do. Explain what each form is and how it is to be used, and do the same for the views. If this application follows a work process, make it clear what the process is and what steps the user is to follow. Any agents you have made should be described, along with instructions on when to run those agents.

To create the Using Database document:

1. Choose **View**, **Design** from the menu.
2. Under Design in the navigator, select **Other**.
3. Double-click **"Using Database" document**.
4. When the document opens, you see a blank screen, which is really a huge rich text field. You may place text, buttons, hotspots, links, and graphics there (see a sample Using Database document in Figure 15.3).
5. Save the document.

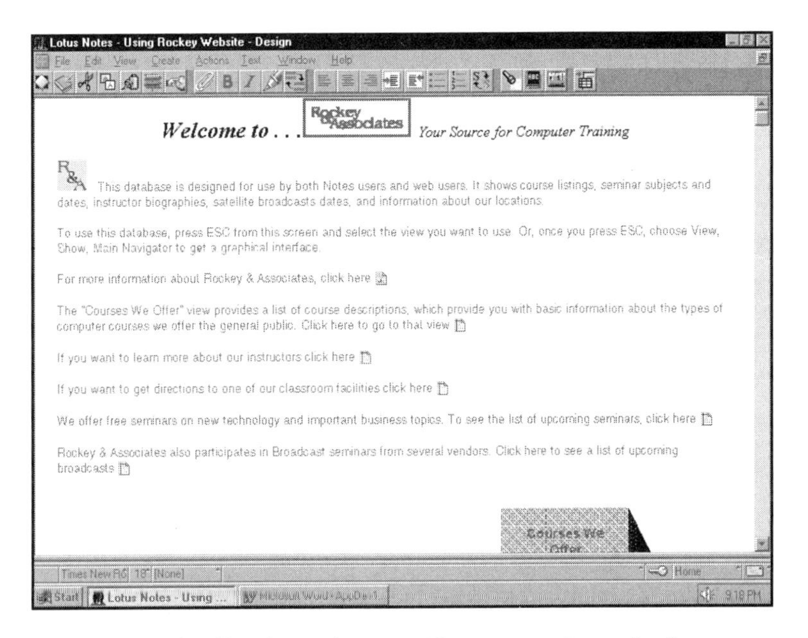

Figure 15.3 The Using Database document from a sample application.

Making a Database Icon

The database icon quickly shows the user which database this is. To make the icon, you can copy an existing one in another database, create one from scratch, or import a bitmap. For the example application shown in Figure 15.4, a drawing was made in Windows 95 Paint and then cut and pasted into the application.

Figure 15.4 The database icon from a sample application.

To create a database icon:

1. Open the database.
2. In the navigator pane, select **Design**, **Other**.
3. Double-click **Icon**. The Design Icon dialog box appears (see Figure 15.5).

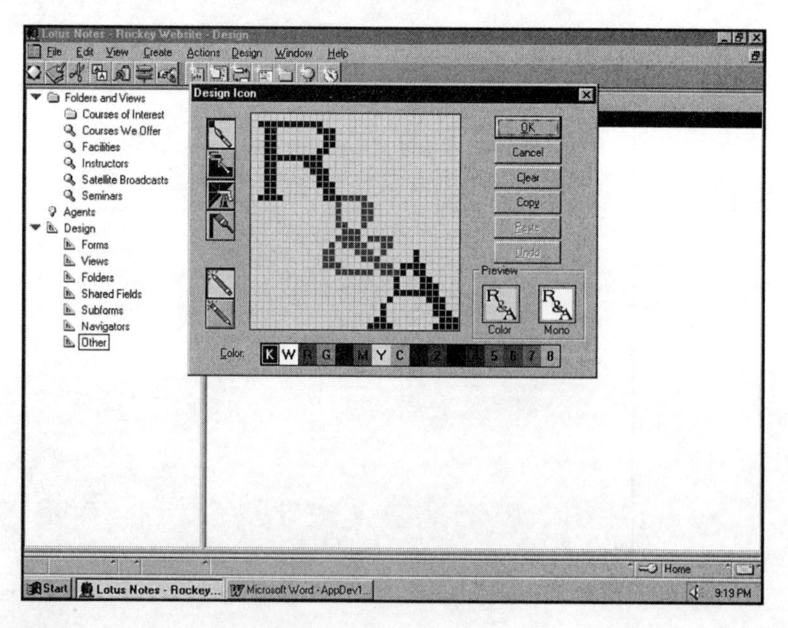

Figure 15.5 The Design Icon dialog box.

4. Click **Clear** to remove the default icon picture.
5. Click **Paste** if you have copied a bitmap from another application into the Clipboard. Or, use the drawing tools to make your own icon (see Table 15.1).
6. When your drawing is complete, click **OK**.

Table 15.1 The Icon Drawing Tools

Drawing Tool	*What It Does*
	Fills one pixel at a time with the selected color
	Fills with the selected color any pixels that are connected and of the same color
	Fills an area of connected pixels in all directions with the selected color
	Fills with the selected color any pixels that are connected in a straight line horizontally or vertically and have the same color
	When on, painting tools fill pixels using the currently selected color
	When on, it resets to the background color when you use one of the painting tools
Color	Click one of the color swatches to make that the current color selection

Documenting the Application

After you have completed all the other steps in preparing the application, you'll be ready to test it. Before you do, you should document the application on paper. You can make a design synopsis for each database you create that will provide documentation on just about everything, including all the formulas you put in each field on each form.

To document the application:

1. Select the database icon on your workspace.
2. Choose **File, Database, Design Synopsis** (see Figure 15.6).

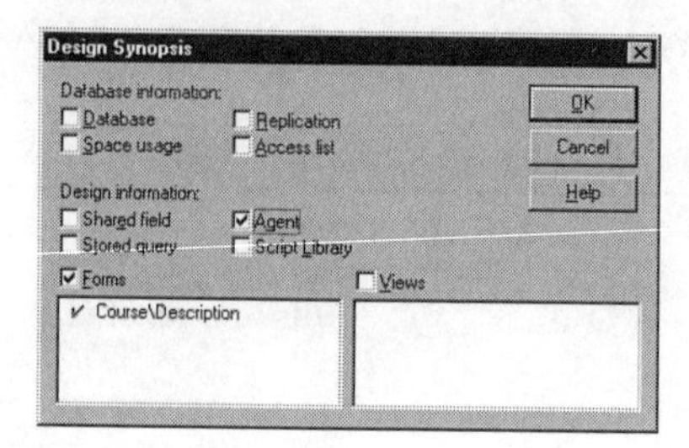

Figure 15.6 The Design Synopsis dialog box.

3. Check the database, form, and view information that you want printed out.
4. Click **OK**.

Don't Use Your Original Database File When Testing Keep a copy of the database in case there are changes to be made, or in case the server copy gets damaged for some reason.

Rolling Out the Application

Now that you're satisfied that your application is ready for user testing, you need to select a group of users who can do your initial testing. It's best to get a cross section of users so you get feedback from different perspectives. A test for a sales contact database should include managers, supervisors, salespeople, and support personnel in the test group.

Remove any working documents and views from your databases before you open them up to your test group. Working documents refers to those documents and views you have created just for your testing purposes. You don't want your test group to see the fictitious customer you created named "Fred Flintstone."

Up to now, you've been working on your own desktop and storing your application database(s) there or in a private directory on your server. You need to replicate a copy of the database file(s) to the server. Set the access control list of the replica or copy so only you and your test group can use it.

Because you want feedback from your test group, you might want to make a form just for this purpose so you get information on bugs, complaints about awkward parts of the application, and praise about things that work well. You'll also want suggestions for improvements or enhancements. If you don't want to make a form, at least set up a procedure to have your test group mail you feedback regularly.

Make fixes and enhancements on a regular basis (don't wait until the end of the test period), and announce them to your test group before you add them to the server copy.

Once you have a workable application (one that most of your test group agrees on), you're ready to open up the application for general use. Make sure you change the Access Control List to include all the users of the application.

Decide on an unveiling date. You might want to have a trial period where everyone can use the application but the old procedure is being used simultaneously. This is a "comfort" period to allow users to see that the new system works as well or better than whatever was in place before Notes. This gives users the opportunity to use the old system still in place (for a while). Schedule your training during the comfort period. Announce when the comfort period will end, so users know when the system is "up for real."

At the end of the comfort period, remove any unnecessary documents that might have been created as users were learning the system.

In this lesson, you learned how to finish the database by creating About Database and Using Database documents, the database icon, design documentation, and how to roll out your application.

InterNotes Web Publisher

Understanding InterNotes Web Publisher

In this lesson, you learn about the InterNotes Web Publisher and its capabilities. You also learn how to prepare for the publication of your Notes databases to the Web.

What Is InterNotes Web Publisher?

As you learned in Part II, "Lotus Notes 4.5 Web Navigator," the Internet is a worldwide network of computers, some of which are servers and some of which are clients. Servers store information of various kinds for the benefit of client computers. There are many kinds of servers including Lotus Notes servers and Web Hypertext Transport Protocol (HTTP) servers. HTTP servers are Web servers that provide information to Web users.

InterNotes Web Publisher is a server program that converts Notes databases into Hypertext Markup Language (HTML) files and copies the files to the HTTP server so that people browsing the Web can retrieve them.

Some of the InterNotes Web Publisher features include:

- *Document conversion* Converts Notes documents and views into HTML pages, and data entered into HTML forms into Notes documents.
- *HTML publishing* Publishes Notes databases as HTML pages on HTTP servers.
- *HTML maintenance* Maintains the Notes-originated HTML pages and their links by updating them whenever the underlying Notes database is updated.

- *Search engine* Extends Notes' full-text search capability to Web users. They enter a query into a field in a search form. InterNotes Web Publisher conveys the query to Notes, which conducts the search. InterNotes Web Publisher then conveys the results of the search to the user as a list of links to the HTML pages that meet the search criteria.
- *Information retrieval* Publishes Notes forms as HTML forms that Web browser users can fill in. When a Web user submits a form, InterNotes Web Publisher conveys it back to the underlying Notes database as a standard Notes document. That document can then become a part of a standard Notes workflow application, or InterNotes Web Publisher can republish it as an HTML document.
- *Discussion site* Because InterNotes Web Publisher permits the republishing of forms completed by Web users as HTML documents, your Web site can be used as a discussion database. You can effectively extend the utility of Notes' discussion databases to your Web users.

How Publishing Works

Lotus Notes servers maintain databases of information stored in a proprietary format that was not, until recently, compatible with any of the standard Internet protocols. Therefore, you could only retrieve information from Notes servers using a Notes client. However, recently Lotus developed two different tools to make Notes databases available to the Internet: the InterNotes Web Publisher and the Domino Web Server (discussed in Part V, "Domino").

Following are important aspects of how InterNotes Web Publisher functions:

- It converts Notes databases residing on a Notes server into HTML files and copies those files to a Web server. Web Publisher also uses CGI programming to permit users who receive Notes documents via a Web server to send information back through the Web server to the Notes server. But this works only if the Notes server software and the Web server software are running on the same physical computer. If the two server programs run on separate computers, then InterNotes Web Publisher cannot receive information back from the Web user.
- The Web Publisher publishes static information on a scheduled basis. Documents you create in Notes won't be published to the Web until a scheduled time, unless you force their publication. Conversely, forms filled out by Web users, as in a discussion database, will not appear on the Web until the database is republished.

CGI: Common Gateway Interface Defines a way of transferring information between two programs that were not designed to share information with each other. Web browsers were designed to receive information from Web servers, but your average Web server cannot receive and process information from a browser without the help of extra programming. CGI provides that missing programming.

Two Ways to Publish

You can publish Notes databases in two ways:

- If you are in a hurry, you can take any Notes database and publish it as is. The About [this database] document will become the home page for the database, which will include a list of all the views in the Notes database. Clicking one of the listed views retrieves the view, which will list the documents in the view; clicking a document retrieves that document.
- Alternately, you can redesign the database to make it more attractive or more functional when published to the Web. This takes more effort, but the resulting set of Web pages will appear (presumably) more attractive and more useful to the Web user.

Make It a Two-Way Street! If you want to permit the Web user to send information back to the Notes server, you must add special fields and programming to your Notes database. Again, this takes more effort, but the result will be a more functional Notes database.

What Happens When You Publish

When you publish a Notes database to the Web server, a program called *webpub*, running on the Notes server, converts the About [this database] document, the views, and the data documents in the database to HTML files, and copies those files into the Web server's data directories. If you have enhanced the Notes database with search queries or forms to be completed and returned by Web users, then a CGI script called *inotes*, residing on the Web server, sends the completed queries or forms back to the Notes server. A counterpart program, also called *inotes*, converts the returning data into Notes format, which the Notes server can then process.

Filling Out a Database Publishing Record

For each database you want to publish, a Database Publishing Record must be completed (usually by the Web Master—the person who maintains your Web site). Become familiar with the information contained in the Database Publishing Record so that you can inform the Web Master of your publishing needs such as which views to publish and so on.

If the Web Publisher Configuration database icon does not appear on your workspace, follow these steps (if you do have this icon, skip to the next section, "Publishing Your Database."

1. Choose **File**, **Database**, **Open** from the menu.
2. In the Server field, enter the name of the server on which the database resides; or click the arrow to the right of the field, and pick the server's name from the drop-down list that appears. Then, if no databases appear in the Database field, choose **Open**.
3. In the Database field, choose the **Web Publisher Configuration** database; then choose **Add Icon.**

You are now ready to publish your Database. Proceed to the next section.

Publishing Your Database

Open the Web Publisher Configuration Database. You see the All Documents by Form Name view. Included in this view is the WebMaster Options document, in which the Web Master sets the default settings for InterNotes Web Publisher, and the Database Publishing Records of any databases that have previously been published.

CAUTION

My Screen Is Different If this is the first time you've opened the database, the About the Web Publisher document will appear first. After reading it, press **Esc** to clear it from the screen. It will not appear again unless you want to see it (select **Help**, **About This Database** from the menu).

To create a new Database Publishing Record:

1. Choose **Create**, **Database Publishing Record**. You will see the top portion of a new Database Publishing Record, as shown in Figure 1.1 with default values in some of the fields. Scroll down to view all the fields.

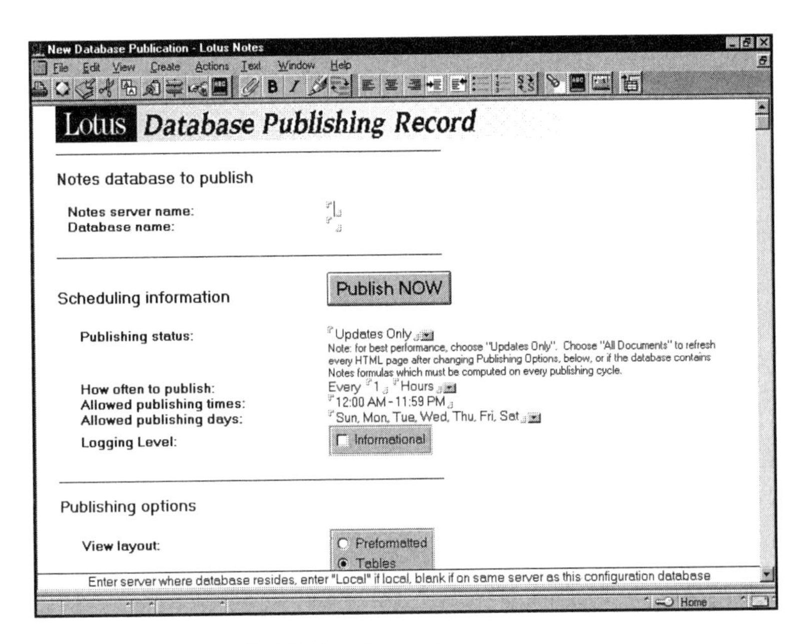

Figure 1.1 The Database Publishing Record.

2. To publish the database with as little fuss as possible, you must complete the following fields:

 Notes server name: You may leave this field blank if the database resides on the InterNotes server. If the database only resides on other servers, fill in the name of one of the resident servers.

 Database name: Enter the relative path name of the database here.

Relative Path Name: The path name of a file is its full name and indicates not only the file name but also the location of the file in the file system. A *relative* path name is a partial path name, which indicates a file's location relative to another location within the file system. In the case of Notes database names, all names are relative to the root data directory.

 Is This the Home Page database? The answer to this question should be **Yes** for *only one* Notes database. It should be **No** for all others. The Home Page database is the one Web users see when they first arrive at your site. They get to all the other databases via links you set up in the Home Page database.

3. You can publish your database now, safely ignoring the rest of the fields. However, some of the following fields may interest you, especially if you want to stop publishing a database. The remaining fields are also helpful if you want to affect which parts of the database get published or how the database looks when published. If you're not interested, proceed to step 4:

   Publishing status: The choices are **Updates Only**, **All Documents**, **Disable**, and **Remove from Web site**. If you are publishing a database for the first time, choose **Updates Only**. If the database has been publishing and you have made changes to the design of the database or in the options in this document, choose **All Documents** to republish every document. If you want to stop publishing temporarily, choose **Disable**. If you want to discontinue all publication of a database, choose **Remove from Web site**.

   How often to publish: You can publish as often as every minute or as seldom as once every few weeks. Publish dynamic, updated databases frequently, and publish static databases less frequently.

   Font mappings: You probably want to leave this set at its default, which is enabled. If you don't like the way Notes fonts appear when the Notes doc-uments are converted to HTML documents, you can change the numbers in the Font size fields. If you have the luxury of designing a Notes database from scratch for publication to the Web, you can define and apply Notes paragraph styles called Heading 1, Heading 2, and so on. These style names will map directly to the corresponding HTML styles. In this case, you can disable Font mapping altogether in the Database Publishing Record.

   Views to publish: If you don't want to publish every view in a Notes database, you can list here the views you do want to publish. Enter the view names precisely as they are entered in the Notes database (including case and spacing) with one exception. If a view name includes underscores, you must omit the underscores when entering the view name in the Database Publishing Record.

TIP **More Extensive Help Is Available** For more information on filling out the Database Publishing Record, how to install InterNotes Web Publisher, and system administration for the Notes server, see the *InterNotes Web Publisher Guide* available from Lotus Development Corporation, Cambridge, Massachusetts.

4. Click the **Publish NOW** button (refer to Figure 1.1).

Viewing a Database Through a Web Browser

After you publish your database, you can access it by entering the name of your HTTP server followed by the database directory. The name of the database directory is the name of the database itself, without the .nsf extension. To access a database called RealRock.nsf, type

http://*hostname*/realrock

where *hostname* is the name of the HTTP server.

In this lesson, you learned about InterNotes Web Publisher and how it publishes Notes databases to the Web. You also learned how to fill out a Database Publishing Record. In the next lesson, you'll learn about planning your Notes applications for Web publication with InterNotes Web Publisher.

Application Design Considerations

In this lesson, you learn how to plan for publishing your Notes databases to the Web. You also learn which features of Notes 4.5 will not convert through the InterNotes Web Publisher.

The Importance of Planning

To plan and execute your application design for Notes databases on the Web, you need to have some Notes application development knowledge. In Part III, you learned most of the basics of application development. With the new skills you learn in Part IV, you can plan and deliver a Notes Web application.

To begin the planning of your Web site, decide if you want to create:

- Separate databases: one for the Web, one for Notes users.
- One database with two sets of forms and views: one set for Web users and one set for Notes users.
- One database: If you're working with multiple databases, do you want multiple databases to publish, or do you want to build one Web database that extracts and sends information to other Notes databases?

Base your decision upon the complexity of your existing or planned databases, using the knowledge you obtain from reading this section.

When designing your application, you also need to consider what you want Web users to *see* and *do* at your Web site. InterNotes Web Publisher and your HTTP server give Web users the ability to:

- Open databases, views, and documents
- Fill out and submit interactive forms
- Search the site

You determine which databases and views to publish. You can create interactive forms for Web users to send information to you. And you can provide search capabilities for your databases on the Web.

TIP **Practice Makes Perfect** If you have an existing database that you want to publish to the Web, you might want to copy the database and work with the copy until you're happy with the results. If the database contains a large number of documents, copy it without the documents, and then cut and paste some documents into it so you have documents to work with during your development stage.

Notes Features and Functions Not Supported in Web Applications

Not everything that you can do in Notes can be done on the Web. Following are some of the Notes Features and Functions that won't translate well to the Web. Keep this in mind when designing your applications.

- **Text** Except for bold and italic, Notes rich text attributes are not converted to HTML by the InterNotes Web Publisher. You can include HTML code for text attributes in Notes documents. See Lesson 3, "Using HTML," for more information on text and text formatting.
- **@commands** Since most @commands are really targeted for workstations, they won't apply to Web users (to learn more about @functions, refer to Part III, "Application Development"). There are a few @commands that will be converted to URLs on the Web by InterNotes Web Publisher. Support @commands are:

  @Command([Compose]) Works, but the server argument does not apply.

  @Command([EditClear]) Works in forms, not supported in view actions, deletes the current document.

  @Command([EditDocument]) Works in forms, not supported in view actions, edits the current document.

  @Command([FileOpenDatabase]) Only accepts database, view, and navigator name arguments. Only accepts for *published* databases.

  @Command([OpenNavigator]) Only accepts the navigator argument.

  @Command([OpenView]) Only accepts the view name argument.

- These @Commands relate only to Notes views, not Web views:

  @Command([NavigateNext])

  @Command([NavigatePrev])

  @Command([NavigateNextMain]

  @Command([NavigatePrevMain])

- **Graphics** Graphics won't appear on the Web in forms using $$Response while they are being filled out by Web users. Once the document is saved, the graphics will appear. See Lesson 9, "Using Graphics," for more information on graphics.
- **Buttons** Only *submit* buttons are supported. Any other buttons will be viewed as submit buttons by InterNotes Web Publisher during conversion.
- **Collapsible Views** Not supported.
- **Layout Regions** Not supported.
- **OLE objects** Not supported, but see Lesson 14 for more details.
- **On Open Options and On Refresh Options** Not supported.
- **@Functions** Lotus Notes has over 100 @functions and many would not apply to applications built for the Web. Included in Table 2.1 are those that are not supported.

Table 2.1 @Functions Not Supported by InterNotes Web Publisher

@DBLookup	@DBColumn	@DBCommand
@DocMark	@DeleteDocument	@GetPortsList
@MailSend	@IsNewDoc	@IsDocBeingEdited
@IsDocBeingMailed	@IsDocBeingRecalculated	@IsDocBeingSaved
@URLGetHeader	@URLHistory	@UserAccess
@UserPrivileges		

Web Field Names

Naming fields with certain field names will send instructions to InterNotes Web Publisher regarding the performance of these fields on the Web. The lessons on InterNotes Web Publisher describe these fields and their use:

- **$$Web** Tells InterNotes Web Publisher to publish a form. See Lesson 7, "Creating Notes Forms," for more information.

- **$$Home** Identifies a form alias for the home page if you are not using the *default* home page, which is the About Database document. See Lesson 7 for more information.
- **$$AboutDatabase** Places the About Database document within the home page if you use $$Home to identify a home page. See Lesson 7 for more information.
- $$**ImageMapBody** Tells InterNotes Web Publisher to publish an image map. Include this field in the forms that you want your image map to appear. Put the actual name of the Image Map in the Help Description box of the Field Properties. See Lesson 10, "Understanding Image Maps," for more information.
- **$$ViewList** Instructs InterNotes Web Publisher to include a list of all views in the database on the page in which you create this field. See Lesson 8, "Working with Views," for more information.
- **$$ViewTemplate** A form alias that instructs InterNotes Web Publisher to use the form as a template for each view published. See Lesson 8 for more details.
- **$$ViewBody** Instructs InterNotes Web Publisher to include the *contents* of a specific view on a page. Put the actual name of the view in the Help Description box of the Field Properties. See Lesson 8 for more information.
- **$$ViewName** An alias for forms that allows unique templates for each view published, where ViewName is the actual name of the view to include on the form. See Lesson 8 for more information.
- **$$Return** Tells InterNotes Web Publisher to create a customized response Web page that will display for Web users when they submit a form. See Lesson 13, "Creating Response Forms and Searches," for more information.
- **$$Response** References a response form. Placed on a main document form, this tells InterNotes Web Publisher which form to use as a response form. Place the response form name in the Help Description box of the Field Properties. See Lesson 13 for more information.
- **$$ViewSearchBar** Places a search bar on the home page or view page for Web users. See Lesson 13 for more information.

In this lesson, you learned some considerations for planning your Web applications. You also learned which features of Notes will not publish well to the Web, and some new fields that are specifically for Web publishing. In the next lesson, you'll learn about HTML and how to use HTML in Notes forms and documents.

Using HTML

In this lesson, you learn what HTML is, how it affects page formatting on the Web, which Lotus Notes formatting features it doesn't support, and how to add HTML code to your Notes documents.

Understanding HTML

Hypertext Markup Language (HTML) lets you save a document with formatted text, graphics, rules, sound, and video (if you have the necessary hardware) in a text-only ASCII file that any computer can read. HTML works with *tags*, which are keywords that indicate what type of content will follow. These tags appear between angle brackets (<) and (>). A Web browser interprets the HTML tags and then shows the properly formatted document on the screen.

InterNotes Web Publisher will convert your Notes documents to HTML for you. But some Notes attributes don't translate into HTML code, so you might need to include HTML code in your Notes forms and Home Page design, which you'll learn in this lesson.

Notes Formatting Features Not Supported in HTML

Documents in a Lotus Notes database will not look the same when they appear on a Web browser. HTML does not support all Lotus Notes formatting features, so InterNotes Web Publisher has to make compromises during conversion.

Listed as follows are some of the features that may be lost. Knowing this may help you in designing your database:

- **Alignment** All text is automatically left aligned, so you will lose any alignment settings you made unless the text is in a table, or you have inserted HTML alignment codes.
- **Borders** HTML does not support different cell borders within a table. Whatever border is assigned to the top-left cell of the table becomes the border applied to all the cells in the table.
- **Buttons** InterNotes Web Publisher does not translate buttons.
- **Column Widths in Tables** HTML sizes each column in the table to the width of the widest entry, regardless of the column settings in the Notes table.
- **Font and Style Attributes** Except for bold and italic, HTML does not support rich text attributes. Underline, strikethrough, and color attributes will not carry over.
- **Text Size** Font sizes do not map directly from Notes documents to HTML documents. How they map depends on the way you mapped fonts to HTML heading tags—by using paragraph styles in Lotus Notes or through fields in the database publishing record.

Adding HTML to Notes Forms and Documents

If you want to preserve some of the Lotus Notes formatting that doesn't convert to HTML, you can incorporate HTML code into your Notes forms or store *existing* HTML files in your Lotus Notes database.

The easiest and quickest way to apply HTML formatting is to enter the code directly on a Lotus Notes form or document using HTML *passthrough*. Type a bracket ()[followed by a less than sign (<) to indicate that HTML passthrough follows. Enter the raw HTML code. Then type a greater than sign (>) followed by a closed bracket (]). The passthrough appears on the form in this format:

[<html code>]

where html code is the keyword instruction you want to include.

TIP **HTML Passthrough** Notes doesn't use your HTML code, but enables it to be passed on through InterNotes Web Publisher to the HTTP server. So, we call it "HTML passthrough."

Some of the most-used codes are:

[<B>] your text **[</B>]** Makes your text bold.

[<I>] your text **[</I>]** Makes your text italic.

[<STRIKE>] your text **[</STRIKE>]** Applies strikethrough to your text.

[<U>] your text **[</U>]** Underlines your text.

[<CENTER>] your text **[</CENTER>]** Centers your text.

[<BASEFONT SIZE =*n*>] Sets the relative font size for the entire page, where ***n*** equals a number between 1 and 7 (3 is normal). Use only one BASEFONT setting per document.

[<FONT SIZE = *n*] your text [</FONT>] Sets the relative font size for *your text*, where ***n*** equals a number between 1 and 7.

[<H*n*>] and [</H*n*>] Begins and ends a header section where ***n*** is the header number (1,2,3, and so on). Use like chapter headers; the lower the header number you supply, the larger the font will appear.

[<BODY>] Contains the bulk of your Web page, including formatting that applies to the entire page. This code is necessary only if you want to apply a color (see [<Text=rrggbb>]) to your text, and that color will apply to all text on the page.

[<TEXT=#*rrggbb*>] Sets the font color. You must replace the ***rr***, ***gg***, and ***bb*** letters with the hexadecimal equivalent. Many desktop publishing programs provide color tables of common colors and their hexadecimal values. Each color has a value for its red, green, and blue components (***rr***,***gg***,***bb***). Not all Web browsers will accept your color changes.

A few of the color codes are listed here:

Red	#C91F16
Orange	#F1A60A
Apple Green	#CED500
Green	#80B812
Avocado	#CECDB4
Blue Green	#088D6C
Ocean Blue	#0994A6

Blue	#0D84C4
Dark Blue	#06438A
Dark Purple	#5B0B5A
Light Purple	#940B63
Dark Gray	#A7A7A7

[<HR SIZE=*n*>] Sets the height of the horizontal rule in pixels where ***n*** is the number of pixels (such as 1,5,6, and so on) and shows the rule on the Web page.

[<HR WIDTH=*n*>] Sets the width of the horizontal rule in pixels where ***n*** is the number of pixels (such as 100, 200, 350, 500, and so on) and shows the rule on the Web page.

[<HR WIDTH=*n*>] Sets the width of the horizontal rule as a percentage of the screen's width where ***n*** is the percentage—for example, 25%, 75%, 100%, and shows the rule on the Web page.

[<HR SIZE=n WIDTH=n>] Sets both the height and width of the horizontal rule where ***n*** is the number of pixels and shows the rule on the Web page.

Specifying a Title for the HTML Page

As you learned in Part III, "Application Development", Notes enables you to determine the information that appears in the title bar of a window. By default, InterNotes Web Publisher handles window titles in this way:

Window Title for the Home Page: database name

Window Title for a document: view name from which the document was selected

You can specify the title you want the users to see on a specific form by defining a title in the design mode of a form. Since the home page is a *document* (the About Database document) and not a *form,* you cannot specify a title for the home page.

TIP **Placing a Title on the Home Page** In Lesson 7, "Creating Notes Forms," you'll create a form that will contain the About Database document within it, enabling you to place a title on the home page.

To create a title for a Notes form:

1. In design mode, open the form you want to design by choosing **Design**, **Form**, **Form Name**.
2. Choose **Window Title** from the **Event** box.
3. In the Formula pane, enter a formula for the window title, or simply enter the title surrounded by quotation marks. The InterNotes Web Publisher will use this information to generate the title for the HTML page on the Web. Figure 3.1 shows a formula for the title in the Formula pane. Figure 3.2 shows the title as it appears through a Web browser.

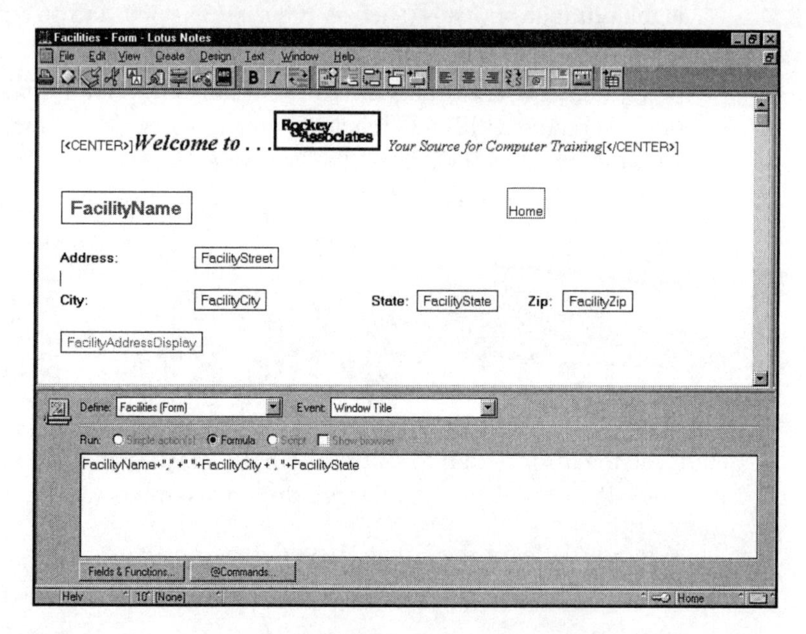

Figure 3.1 The Formula pane showing a window title formula.

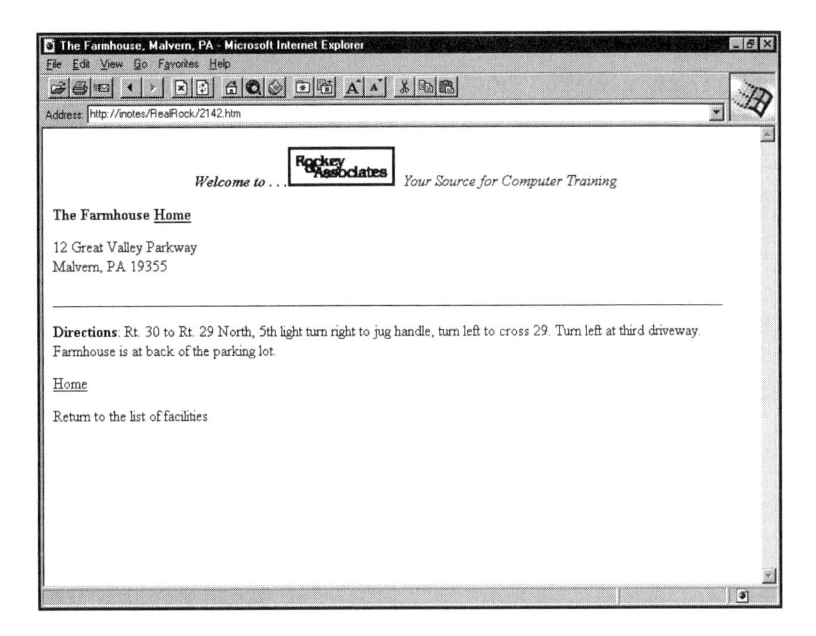

Figure 3.2 A Window Title as it appears in a Web browser.

If you want to include existing HTML pages, you can create a Notes form with a special field named HTML. Create a document using this form to paste the pages into the HTML field. The InterNotes Web Publisher will create a separate HTML file containing the output, which will display as a separate page on the Web.

To create the separate HTML file:

1. Choose **Create**, **Design**, **Form** from the menu to open a new, blank form.
2. Choose **Design**, **Form Properties** from the menu, or click the **Properties** SmartIcon. The Form Properties dialog box appears (see Figure 3.3).

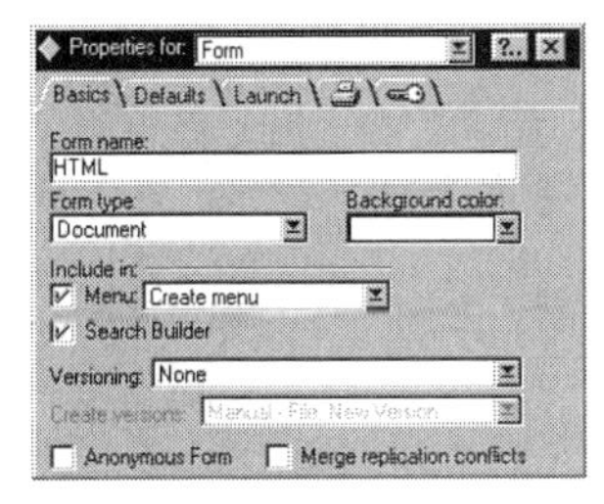

Figure 3.3 The Form Properties box.

3. In the **Form name** field, enter the name of the form. (For simplicity, you can name the form **HTML**.)
4. Under **Include in**, check **Menu**; select **Create Menu** from the list box.
5. Choose **Create**, **Field** from the menu, or click the **Create Field** SmartIcon. The Field Properties dialog box appears, as shown in Figure 3.4.

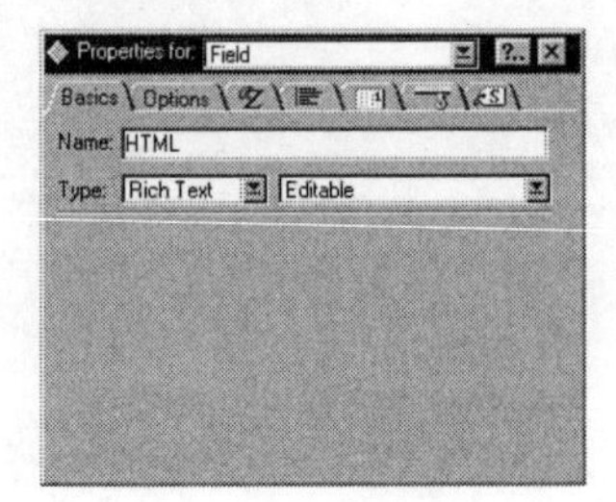

Figure 3.4 The Field Properties box.

6. In the Field Properties box, type **HTML** in the **Name** field. This field *must* be named **HTML**.
7. In the **Type** box, select **Rich Text**. Make the field Editable. This is the field where you enter or paste HTML code. Although you may enter additional fields or text, InterNotes Web Publisher will convert only the contents of the HTML field.
8. Save the form and close it.

To use this form, do the following:

1. Choose **Create** from the menu, and select the name of the form you just created (see Figure 3.5).
2. Click in the HTML field you created.
3. Paste the HTML code you copied from another document or enter the HTML code. If the code refers to other files (such as graphic images), insert those files as attachments in the HTML fields.
4. Save and close the document.

Give GIFs Unique File Names Be sure all GIF files associated with HTML code in a single database have unique names. The Web Publisher detaches any attached files in an HTML document to the output HTML directory of the database. Therefore, if you have two documents using the HTML form in the same database and you use the same file names for the GIF files attached to each document, one of the GIF files will overwrite the other.

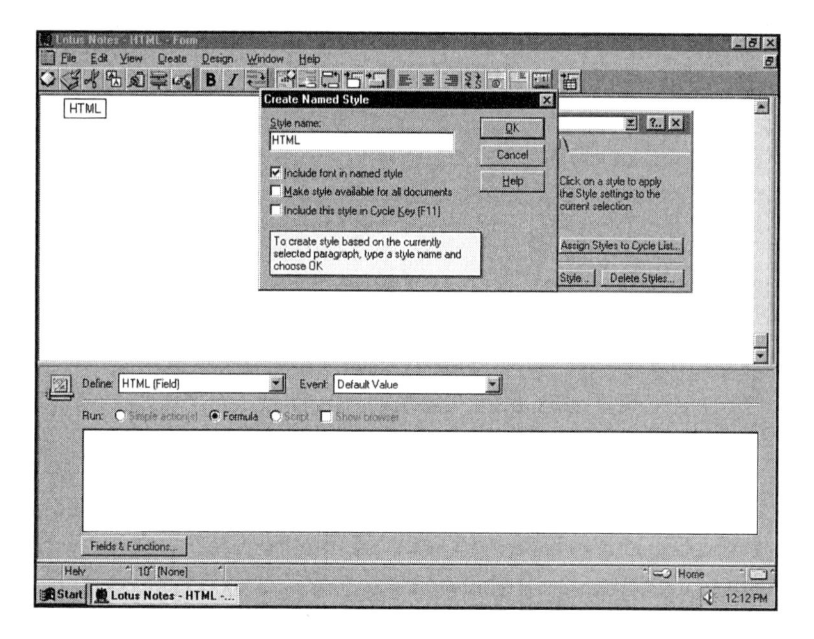

Figure 3.5 The Create Named Style dialog box.

In this lesson, you learned about HTML and how to use it in Lotus Notes to format pages for the Web. You also learned to add HTML titles to Notes forms. In the next lesson, you'll learn how to create a home page.

Creating a Home Page

In this lesson, you learn how to create a home page using the About Database document. You also learn how to add HTML code to your home page.

Understanding Home Pages

For every database that you publish, you need a home page. By default, that home page is the database's About Database document. The home page lists all views for the database as hypertext. This is a function of InterNotes Web Publisher and happens automatically.

Your site home page name, once converted to HTML, depends upon the HTTP server you use. This book refers to the home page as default.htm, the name given by the HTTP server. Check with your Notes Administrator or Web Administrator to find the name given to your home pages.

Although each database has a home page, you can have only one *site* home page. Lesson 1, "Understanding InterNotes Web Publisher," contains instructions for filling out the Database Publishing Record in which you can indicate which database contains your site home page.

When you're designing a site home page, be sure to place links to your other databases as described here and in Lesson 5, "Working with Links."

Using the About Database Document

To create a database home page, you'll start your design at the About Database document. You determine whether this home page becomes the *site* home page or the *database* home page on the Web as described in Lesson 3, "Using HTML."

If you want to customize your home page and have it contain only one view, or you want to customize the display of your views, you can create special Notes forms in the database prior to publication. You'll learn about custom home pages and custom views in Lessons 6 and 8.

In this example, we have decided that the home page will be a *site* home page; in subsequent work, you will make that determination yourself before designing a page. Later in Lesson 6, you will create a custom home page *form* that includes the contents of the About Database document and additional graphics, navigators, and links to views.

TIP **Design and Test Immediately** This application was developed working on an intranet; it was designed and then published immediately to the Web. If possible, set up a small intranet between you and your Web server for the purpose of design. Alternately, you can set up a second set of output directories on your Web server just for test databases. Because this set of output directories is not included in your published set of database links, Web users cannot see it. For more details, see the "Creating More than One Web Publisher Configuration Database" in Chapter 4 of the *Lotus InterNotes Web Publisher Guide* or consult with your Lotus Notes Administrator.

To design a home page:

1. Open an existing database, or create a new database and open it. (This example uses an existing database, with a blank home page.)
2. Click **Design** in the Navigator pane and select **Other**.

TIP **Databases and Templates** If you create a new database based upon a template, deselect **Inherit Design from template** in the Properties box or all of the forms you create in this database will be lost whenever the master design template updates. Better yet, do your design *in* the template. If you don't want to alter the template, make a copy of it by using **File**, **Database**, **New Copy**.

3. Double-click the **About Database** document. If this is a new database, your screen appears blank. If this is an existing database, you need to edit your About Database document so it appears exactly as you want it to appear on the Web.
4. Add and format your *static* text on your home page. Keep in mind that alignment will be lost on the Web, as everything left aligns when converted. If you want to center align, you can use HTML script as described

later in this lesson, or you can use tables on your home page to align blocks of text side by side. Figure 4.1 shows a two-column, one-row table to place our text and graphics side by side. Refer to Lesson 3 for more on HTML code.

Figure 4.1 A table on the About Database document, the home page.

TIP **Don't Cross the Border** If you use tables to align graphics and text, be sure to turn off all borders of your table before publishing. You won't want Web users to see the tables you used as placeholders. On the other hand, you may find it helpful to leave on the borders while you're in design mode.

5. (Optional) If you are publishing and testing on the Web or your intranet as you design, save and publish your database now and view it on the Web. Periodically republish so you can see the results of your work.

Figure 4.2 shows the home page published to the Web, with the borders removed from the table. (Microsoft Internet Explorer was used to browse the intranet.) Views that existed in the database automatically publish to the Web as hypertext links on the home page.

Untitled Views If you're working with a brand new database, don't forget that Lotus Notes will automatically generate a default view (named **untitled**) for your database, even before you design anything. If you publish your database during testing before you design any views in your database, your untitled view will show as a bullet on your home page without any text. Don't panic; continue to design your database views as you normally would, and remember to delete or rename the untitled default view from Notes.

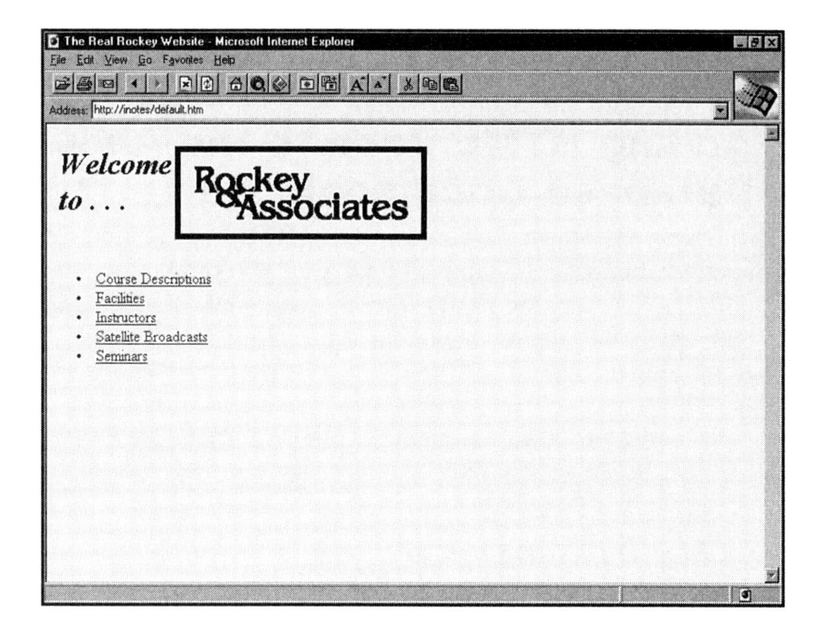

Figure 4.2 The home page published to the Web.

Notice that the views in the database show as hypertext links with bullets in front of them. This is part of the InterNotes Web Publisher conversion.

If you compare Figures 4.1 and 4.2, you can see that the table is full screen width in Lotus Notes, and left-aligned on the Web. The blank spaces in the Notes application did to translate to the Web. HTML does not recognize Notes' blank spaces in the tables. We will add code later in this lesson to correct this.

You may want to add a link from this page to other published Notes databases. You can create links by using Notes Links, link hotspots, underlined text with a Notes link, or graphics with a Notes Links. Links are covered extensively in Lesson 5, "Working with Links," but here is a foretaste. To create the Database Link:

1. From your workspace, select the Database to which you want to link.
2. Choose **Edit**, **Copy as Link**, **Database Link**.
3. Switch back to the design mode of your About Database document.
4. Type some static text that tells the Web user where the link is going. If you are linking to a discussion database, you might type **Join our discussion database** on your home page and then choose **Edit**, **Paste** to paste the database link into your page.
5. Save your home page; publish your database.

Adding HTML Code to the About Database Document

In Lesson 3, you learned about adding HTML code to Notes documents and forms. In building the sample home page, you can remove the table that contains the company logo and center the logo on the page. Figure 4.3 shows the edited About Database document as viewed in Lotus Notes, with the HTML code applied.

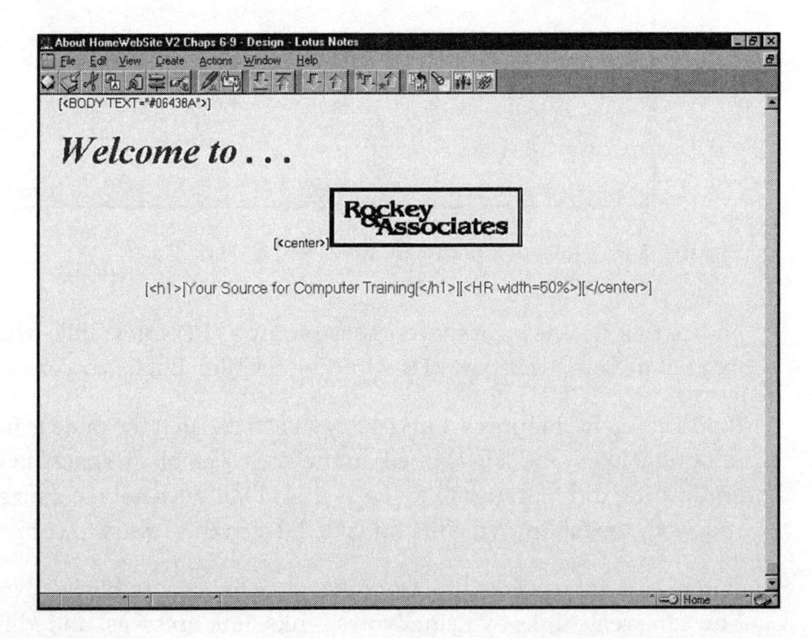

Figure 4.3 HTML code on Lotus Notes About Database document.

The following is an explanation of the HTML code:

- center our logo and header [<center>] [</center>]
- identify a header line [<h1>] [</h1>]
- apply color to the header [<BODY TEXT="#06438A">]

In Figure 4.4, you can see the results of the HTML code as viewed on the Web. As you progress through the InterNotes Web Publisher sections, you'll see the example home page built on, later adding links, graphics, and navigators.

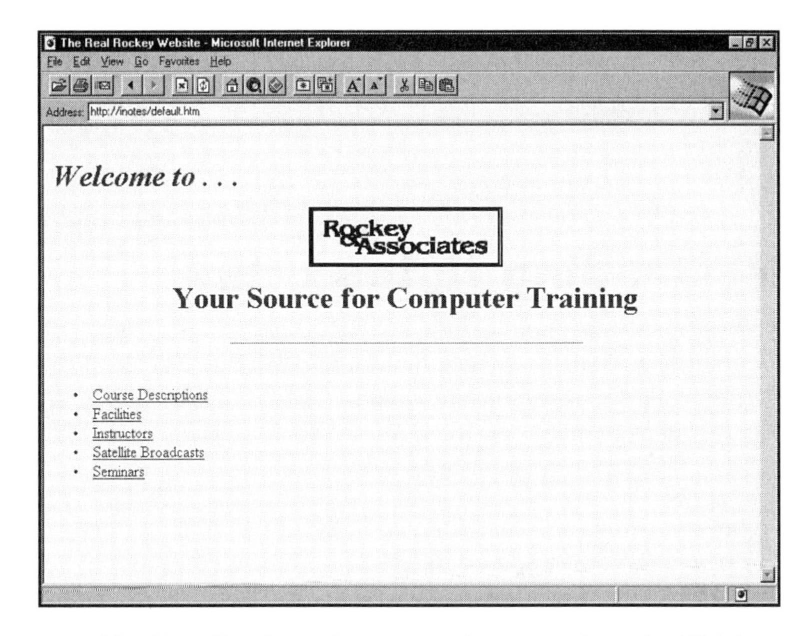

Figure 4.4 The About Database document as it appears through a Web browser.

CAUTION

This Looks *Terrible* in Notes! You may want to consider hiding any HTML code so Notes users see only the good-looking forms you designed for them.

In this lesson, you learned how to create a home page using the About Database document. You also learned how to apply HTML code to the page and how to link to another published database. In the next lesson, you learn more about using Notes links.

Working with Links

In this lesson, you learn how to use Lotus Notes document links, view links, and create database links in your Notes documents.

Understanding Notes Links

Notes Links that you include in your database design work effectively in your published database. In fact, InterNotes Web Publisher will *generate* most of your view links for you (much of what is covered in this chapter are links that are exceptions to that rule). InterNotes Web Publisher *converts* your document links, view links, and database links to hypertext.

Beyond using the Notes Copy as Link command, you can also make link hotspots by creating bordered text immediately followed by a Notes link, or by pasting a graphic followed by a Notes link. When you create link hotspots or paste graphics followed by a Notes link, the icon for the Notes link doesn't show, and the text or graphic becomes the hotspot. Since the Notes database, view, and document icons all look the same on the Web, some people prefer to use graphics or text.

There are times when only an URL link or an Action Hotspot with an @URLOpen formula will work for you. Table 5.1 summarizes types of links and when to use them. Some of these links are discussed in this Lesson, others are discussed in Lesson 6 "Using URLS in Links."

Table 5.1 Lotus Notes and URL Links

To Link to this	*Use this*
A Notes Document	Notes Document Link or Notes Link Hotspot
A Notes View	Notes View Link or Notes Link Hotspot
A Notes Database	Notes Database Link or Notes Link Hotspot
Another Database Home page	URL Link Hotspot containing the path to the HTML page
Another Web Site	URL Link

Document Links

Document Links will link to other published Notes documents within any published database. When Notes database managers change or update the source link or document in Notes, the InterNotes Web Publisher will change or update the hypertext the next time the database is published.

To create a Document Link:

1. Open the document to which you want to link.
2. Choose **Edit**, **Copy as Link**, **Document Link**.
3. Close the document.
4. In design mode, open the form where you want to place the document link. Place your cursor where you want the link icon to appear.
5. Choose **Edit**, **Paste,** or click the **Edit Paste** SmartIcon.
6. The document link icon appears. Add any static text you need to define the link—perhaps a description of what the link is pointing to.
7. Save the form.
8. To test the link in Lotus Notes, open a document created with the form, and click the Document Link icon.
9. Publish the database to test your link on the Web. Open the document in the Web browser, and click your Document Link to see the results.

View Links

View links will link to published views within the same published Notes database. If you want, your users can return to a view once they select a document from that view. Of course, their Web browser has a way of tracking back but it's a nice touch to have a link to do so. To establish links to views, you should put the View Link in the form related to the view.

To create a view link:

1. Open the view to which you want to link.
2. Choose **Edit**, **Copy as Link**, **View Link**.
3. Open the form where you want to place the link.
4. Position your cursor where you want the link to appear.
5. Choose **Edit**, **Paste,** or click the **Edit Paste** SmartIcon. The link appears, as shown in Figure 5.1.

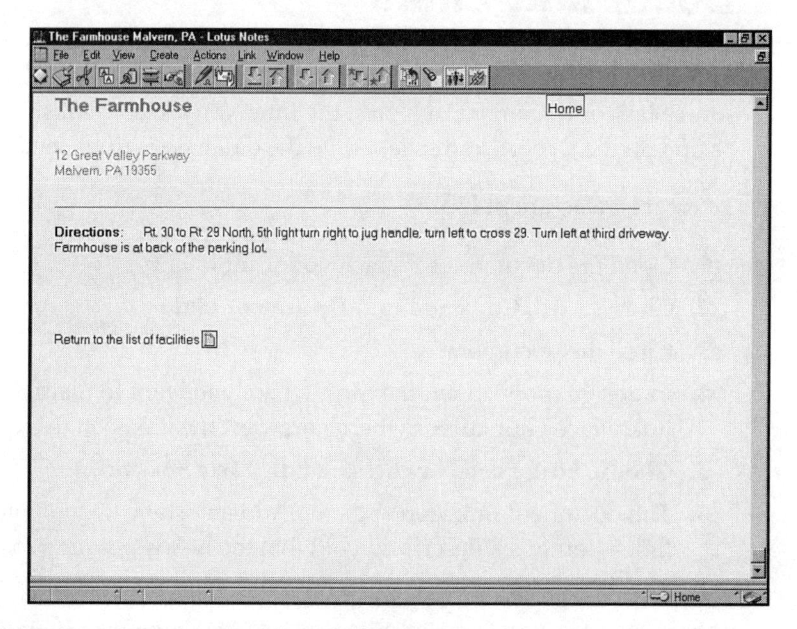

Figure 5.1 The View Link icon in Lotus Notes.

6. Add any static text you need to direct your users in using the link.
7. Save and close the form.
8. To test the link in Lotus Notes, open a document created with the form, and click the View Link icon to see if it returns you to the appropriate view.
9. You also need to test your view link on the Web. Publish the database; then open the form in your Web browser. Click your link (see Figure 5.2).

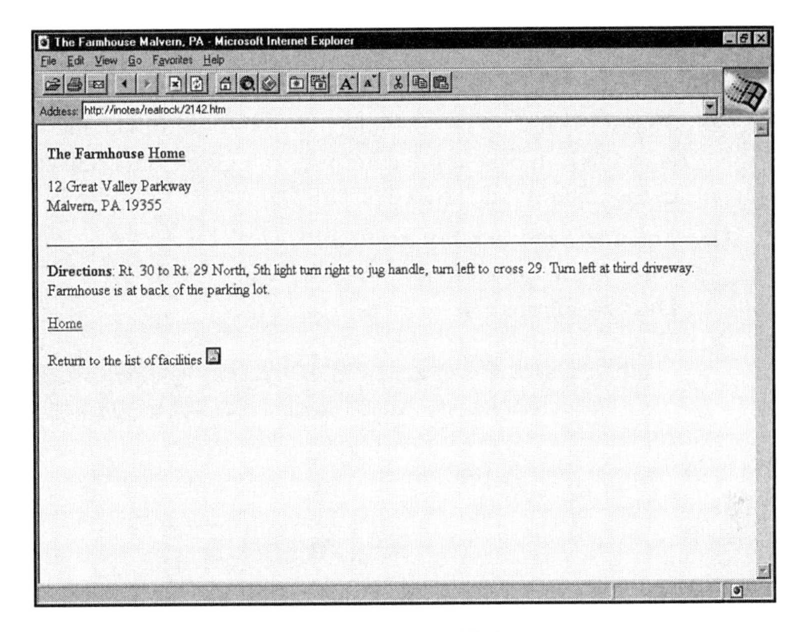

Figure 5.2 The View Link as it appears on the Web.

Database Links

Database links will link to the default view of other published Notes databases. You may want to include database links on your home page. (You can place database links in forms other than the About Document.) This example uses a home page.

To create a database link:

1. From your Lotus Notes workspace, select the database icon for the database you want to link to.
2. Choose **Edit, Copy as Link, Database Link**.
3. Switch to your database you want to link *from*. Open the Design view and then click **Design Other** in the navigator.
4. Open the About Database document (your home page).
5. Position your cursor where you want the link to appear.
6. Choose **Edit, Paste** from the menu, or click the **Edit Paste** SmartIcon.

7. Add any static text you need to give directions to the users.
8. Save the form and close it.
9. To test the link in Lotus Notes, open the About Database document, and click the Database Link icon to see if it gives you access to the default view of the other database (see Figure 5.3).
10. You also need to test your database link on the Web. Publish both databases; then open the home page in your Web browser. Click your database link (see Figure 5.4).

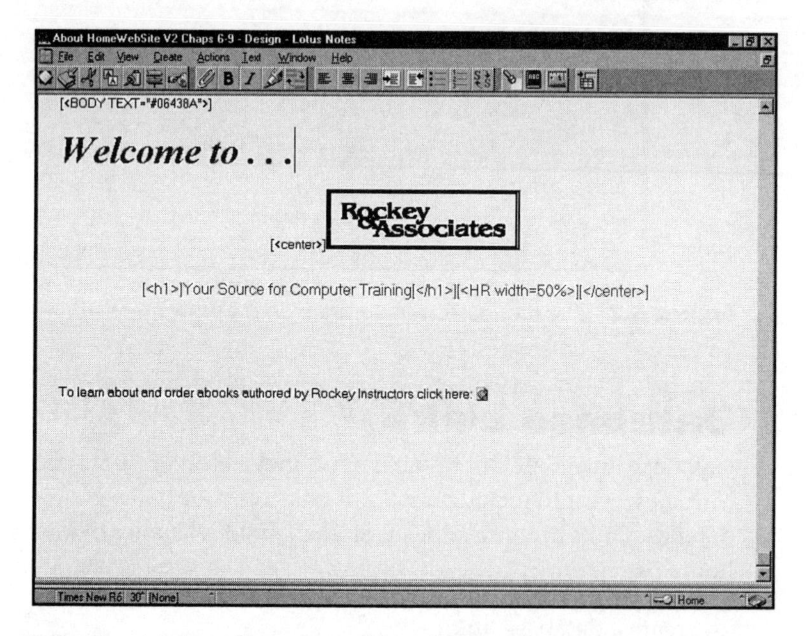

Figure 5.3 The database link on your About Database document.

My Links Don't Link! Links *must* point to *published* databases, forms, and views. If you link to a database that you are *planning* to publish, the link will not be converted to HTML and will not show in your Web browser, even though it is functional in Notes.

If you want to link to the home page of another published Notes database, see Lesson 6.

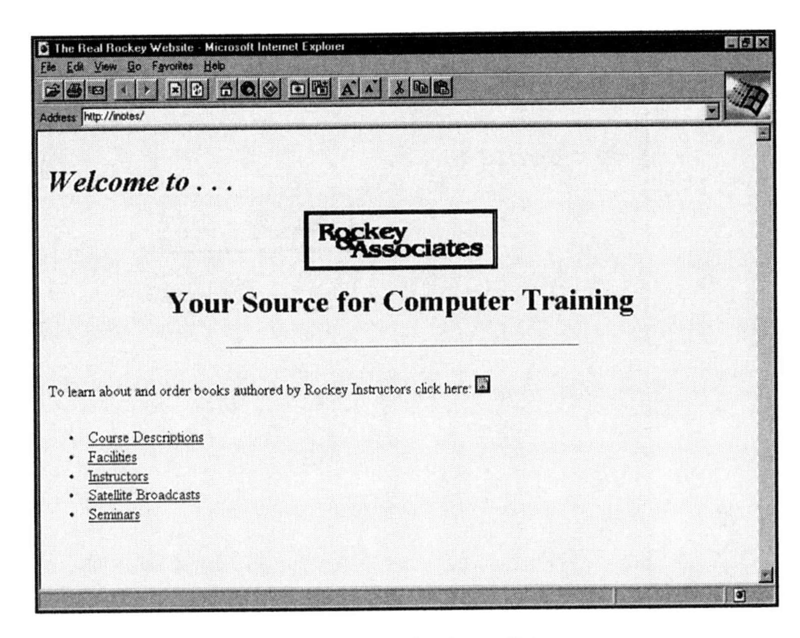

Figure 5.4 The home page containing a database link.

Link Hotspots

Link Hotspots use text or graphics as the link instead of a database or document icon. With these, you can link to a document, view, or database. When the user clicks the text or graphics, he will link to the target form or view. You can only place Link Hotspots in a form or rich text field in a document.

1. Open the view or document, or select the database on your workspace to which you want to link.
2. Choose **Edit**, **Copy as Link**. Then choose **Document**, **View** or **Database Link**.
3. Open the form or document where you want to place the link. In Edit mode, highlight the text or graphic that will become the hotspot.
4. Choose **Create**, **Hotspot**, **Link Hotspot** from the menu (see Figure 5.5).
5. Test your link.

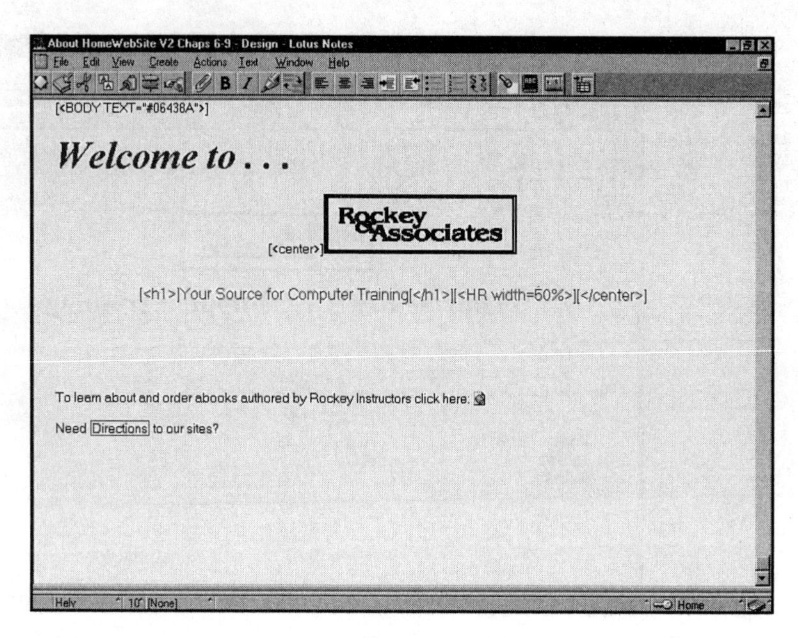

Figure 5.5 The Link Hotspot as it will appear on the Web.

In this lesson, you learned how to create Notes links and saw the results of those links on the Web. In the next lesson, you'll learn how and when to use URL links.

Using URLs in Links

In this lesson, you learn how to create, and when to use, URL links. You also learn how to use action hotspots.

Understanding URLs and Links

In Lesson 5, you learned how to use Lotus Notes links to link Web users to other published Notes documents, views, and databases. But what if you want to link to another Web site, or to a page on your own site that did not originate as a document in a Notes database? You can't use Notes links in that case. Instead, you need to use URLs in your links so that Notes can find the site or page you're pointing to. This lesson explains ways that you can use URLs.

Also, if you want to link to Notes home pages in other published Notes databases (within your site), you need to provide the exact location of those pages in the Web server's output directories. Without that location, Notes can't find the page you're linking to. In order to provide the location, you need to understand how InterNotes Web Publisher and the HTTP server that it publishes work together to store the HTML files.

CAUTION

Broken Links? If you use an *URL* instead of a *Notes* link (and you can do this at any time, on any document or form), there may be cases where the links are lost because the source database changed. Replication can have a negative effect on URL links. By using Notes links when possible, the InterNotes Web Publisher will update those links when changes are made to documents.

URLs and Links to Other Web Sites

There are two kinds of URLs, *explicit* and *relative*. An explicit URL is a complete address: **http://www.lotus.com/dirname/filename**, for example. Use explicit URLs to link to external Web sites.

A relative URL is not a complete address, and need not be, since you use relative URLs to link to pages within the same site. A relative URL requires only the HTML directory and page names.

You can use URLs in:

URL links	Action Hotspots
An HTML	Passthrough URL Anchors
URL Graphics	URL Graphic Pop-Ups

URL Links

You can create an URL link on a Notes form or document by providing the full URL in square brackets, preceded by some underlined text. When your Web users click the underlined text, they will link to the HTML page with that URL. It's important to note that this kind of URL link will not work for your Notes users viewing this database in Notes. Underlined text followed by an URL within Notes will have no connection whatsoever to the Web or other Web sites. If both Notes and Web users access your database, you should use an Action Hotspot for your URL links.

To create an URL link:

1. Open the document/form in **Edit, Design** mode where you want to place the link.
2. Underline the text that will work as your hypertext.
3. Immediately after the text, type the URL in square brackets. Be certain not to place any spaces between the last letter of the text and the left bracket containing the URL, as shown in this example:

   To visit the Lotus Site[http: / / www.lotus.com]

4. Save your document and publish the database.
5. Test the link from within a browser.

URLs Appear as Underlined Text in Web Pages Underline only the text preceding an URL, not the URL itself. If you don't, the entire line of text and URL will appear on the Web site as normal underlined text. No link will be created.

Action Hotspots

Action Hotspots work in the same manner as URL links, but Action Hotspots will work both within Notes and on the Web.

To create an Action Hotspot:

1. Open the view or document; or select the database on your workspace to which you want to link.
2. Choose **Edit**, **Copy as Link**. Then choose **View**, **Document or Database Link**.
3. Open the form where you want to place the link. In Edit mode, highlight the text or graphic that will become the hotspot.
4. Choose **Create**, **Hotspot**, **Action Hotspot** from the menu.
5. In the design pane, use the **@URLOpen** command and enter the URL for the site. Remember to place quotes around the URL, as shown in Figure 6.1.
6. Save your document, publish your database, and test the link.

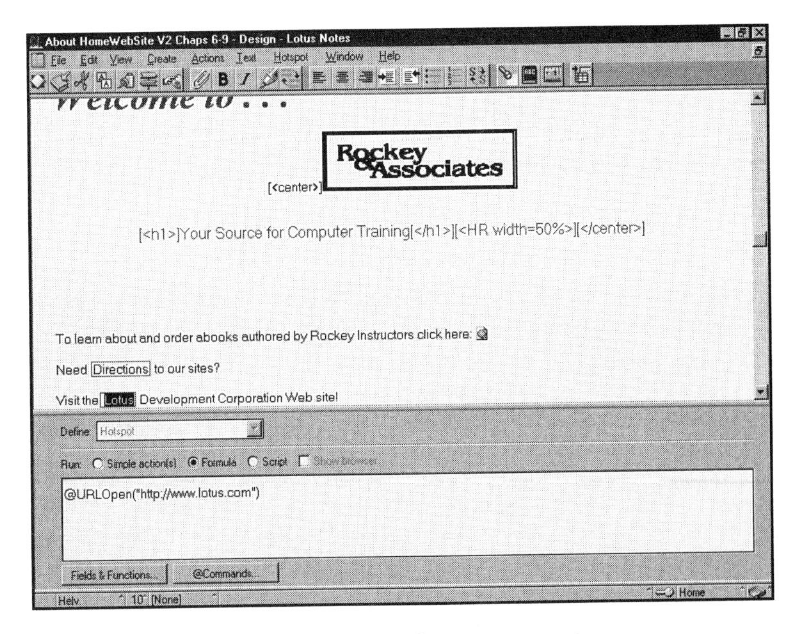

Figure 6.1 Action Hotspot with the @URLOpen command.

To edit an Action Hotspot:

1. Open your document in Edit mode.
2. Click inside the hotspot.
3. Choose **Hotspot, Edit Hotspot** from the menu. The Design pane appears.
4. Make your changes in the Design pane. Save your document and publish your database.

URL graphics and URL graphic pop-ups are described in Lesson 9, "Using Graphics." Also, Lesson 7, "Creating Notes Forms," and Lesson 8, "Working with Views," define how to use URLs in forms and views.

Links to Home Pages

You have to use URLs to link to home pages. If you use Notes database links, they will link you to the default view of a database. You can use document links within the About Database document (the home page) and in the Using document, but you can't create a document link that links you from another document to either of those pages. Since you know that one of your About Database documents is your site home page, and the About Database document for every database you publish is that database's home page, you also need to know how to link users to those home pages; you do this with *relative* URLs.

A relative URL does not include the entire address. Since you are accessing HTML pages on the same HTTP server, you need only include the relative path and the document name. For example:

Home[default.htm]

This link takes you to the home page (where the home page is "default.htm") of your current database. Since that page is in the same directory as the page you are linking from, it is only necessary to specify the file name. Since you leave the rest of the path out, the computer assumes the target file is in the same directory as the source file.

Figure 6.2 shows the output HTML directory as structured by InterNotes Web Publisher. In this example, you can see that the site home page resides in the root output directory for Notes-derived files. All other documents reside in subdirectories of the root output directory. Each published Notes database has a corresponding subdirectory of the same name as the database's file name. All published documents from the Notes database are published to that database's subdirectory.

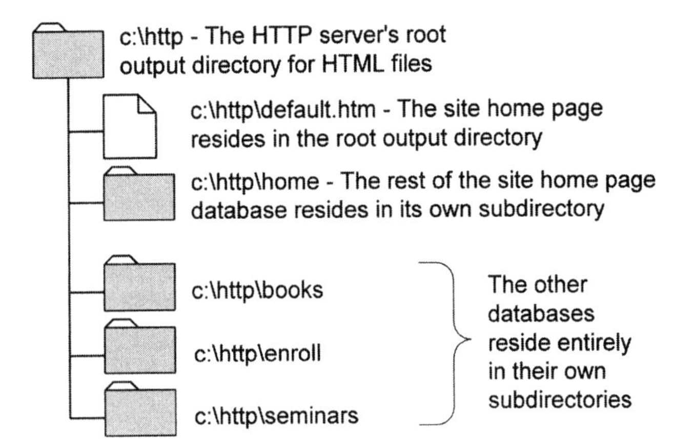

Figure 6.2 Data directory structure of HTTP server in which all HTML pages are derived from Lotus Notes databases.

Figure 6.3 shows the same directory structure as Figure 6.2 but with several example HTML files added. Using the example files in Figure 6.3, you can see that Table 6.1 demonstrates the syntax for URL links to the site and database home pages.

In all examples, you may omit the target file name if it is the home page.

Table 6.1 Examples of Relative Links

To link	*Use this Syntax*	*Comment*
From C to B	[default.htm] or [.]	When source and target are in the same directory, use the file name alone. Or use [.], which means "current directory."
From C to D	[../enroll/]	Source and target are in sibling directories. [..] means "parent directory."
From C to A	[/]	Target is in the root [/] directory.
From A to B	[books/]	Target is in a child directory of the source directory.

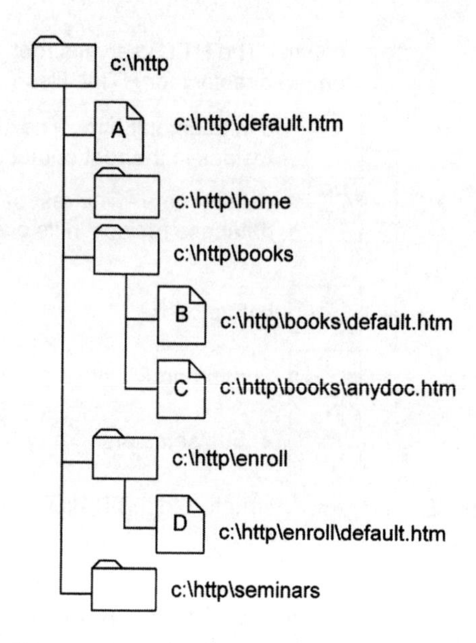

Figure 6.3 Use this diagram in the examples in Table 6.1.

In this lesson, you learned how to create and use URL links. You also learned about the HTML directory and how to point URLs to the proper directory. In the next lesson, you learn how to create custom home page forms.

Creating Notes Forms

In this lesson, you learn how to create Notes forms for use on the Web. You also learn how to create custom home page forms, whose content will include the About Database document.

Creating Custom Home Page Forms

TIP **Notes to HTML** The InterNotes Web Publisher can convert Notes forms that you create in Notes to HTML. See Part III, "Application Development," for more information on creating standard Notes forms.

Although the About Database document will publish as the default home page, there are certain disadvantages to using a document instead of a form as the home page. You might want to include search capabilities, fields, or form attributes in your home page. These are not things that you can place on a Notes document.

Alternatively, you can create a home page form and incorporate your About Database document into such a form. Your home page form can have any name, but must have the alias of $$Home. This alias tells the InterNotes Web Publisher to make the contents of this form the home page for the database. You can have customized home pages for each database.

TIP **Forget Now, Pay Later** Except for special fields that begin with **$$**, fields you add must have the field type **Computed for Display**.

To include the contents of your About Database document into a form (if you followed Lesson 4, you can use the About Database home page you created), insert a field at the position that you want the About database contents to appear. Name that field **$$AboutDatabase**. You don't need to define the $$AboutDatabase fields except for this name. Data types, fields formulas, and so on won't have any effect in this type of field.

To create a custom home page form:

1. Open the database and select **Create**, **Design**, **Form** from the menu.
2. Name the form something descriptive such as **Home page**.
3. In the Form Properties box, enter the form's name followed by the alias ($$Home). For example:

   Rockey on the Web | $$Home

4. Create a field called **$$AboutDatabase**. Place this field on the form where you want the contents of the About Database document to appear as shown in Figure 7.1.
5. Be sure to deselect **Inherit Design from Template** in the Database Properties box. Failure to do this will mean that your form will be lost whenever the master design template is updated.

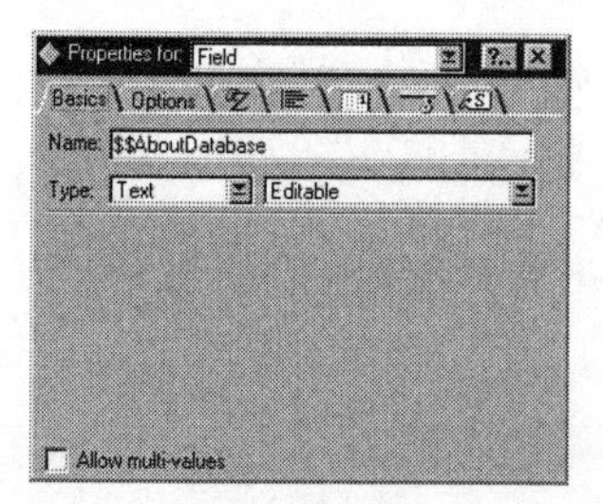

Figure 7.1 The Home page form in Design mode, showing the $$AboutDatabase field.

6. Unlike the About Database document, a list of available views will not automatically be placed on this document by the InterNotes Web Publisher. You must add the database view list to this new form. To add the database view list, create a field named **$$ViewList**. This will tell InterNotes Web Publisher to place a linked list of all published views in the About Database form in place of this field as shown in Figure 7.2.

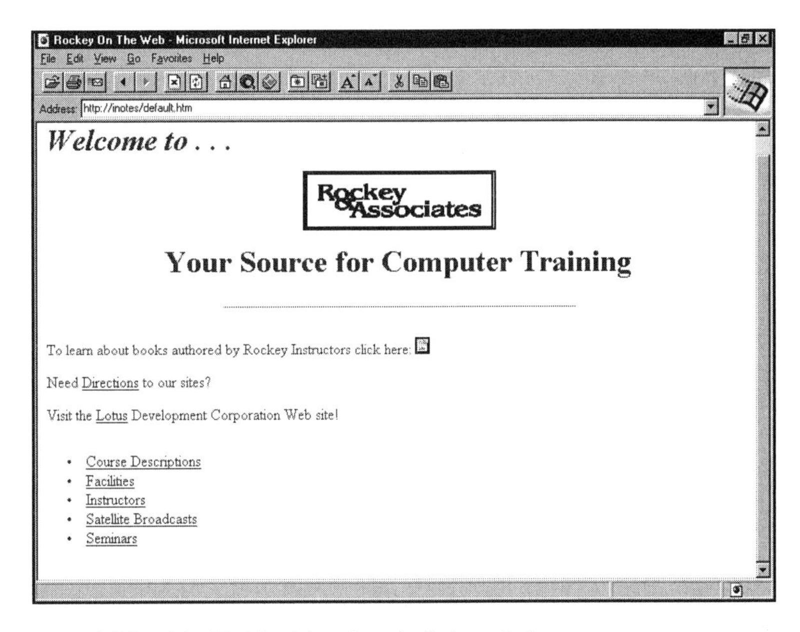

Figure 7.2 $$ViewList Field adds a list of all views to home page.

Other fields that you can use on this form are:

- **$$ViewBody** Adds the contents of a specific database view to the home page or to any document resulting from a form in which you put this field. When you use this field, you must enter the name of the view you want to include in the Help Description box of the Field Properties box.
- **$$ImageMapBody** Includes a specific image map on the form. When you use this field, you must enter the name of the navigator you want to include in the Help Description box of the Field Properties box. Lesson 11, "Creating Interactive Forms," demonstrates the use of this field.

At any time, changes you make to the About Database document will be reflected in the Home page form. The $$ViewList field from Figure 7.2 was cut from the bottom of the About Database form and pasted in at the top. Figure 7.3 shows the results—the views now appear before the links.

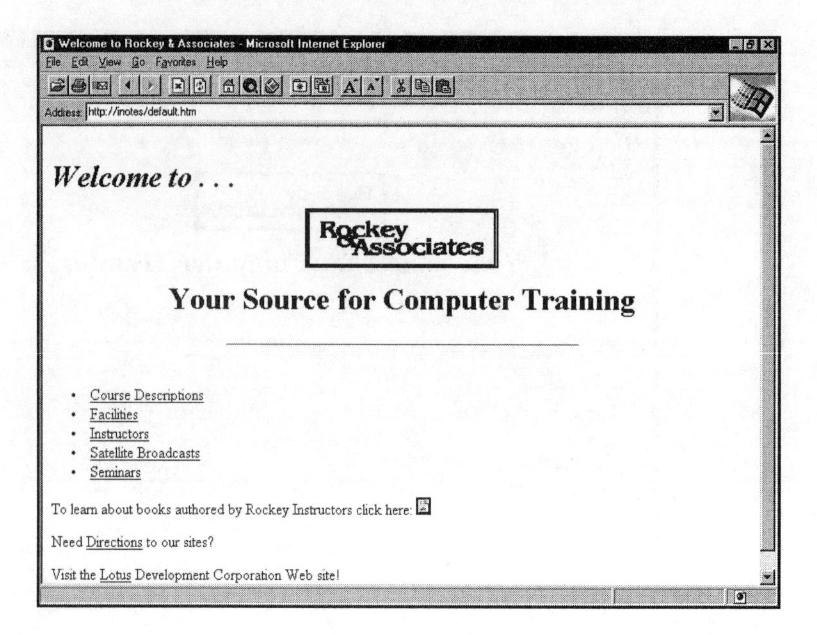

Figure 7.3 Redesigned home page.

Creating Banners

Banner is not a term or function used within Lotus Notes. But you can create a subform that appears as a banner at the top of every Web page.

To create a banner subform follow these steps:

1. Open the database and select **Create**, **Design**, **Subform** from the menu.
2. Design your subform that you want to use as the banner.
3. Like a form, the entire subform is a rich text field. You can include fields, graphics, and anything that you can place in a rich text field, within your subform. Figure 7.4 shows a subform with graphics, static text, and HTML code to center the information.
4. Add the subform to each of your Notes forms by opening the form in Design mode and selecting **Create**, **Insert Subform** from the menu. The Insert Subform dialog box appears listing all of your subforms, as shown in Figure 7.5. Select the subform and click **OK** to close the dialog box.
5. Publish your database and look at it in a Web browser. Figure 7.6 shows a form on the Web with the banner subform.

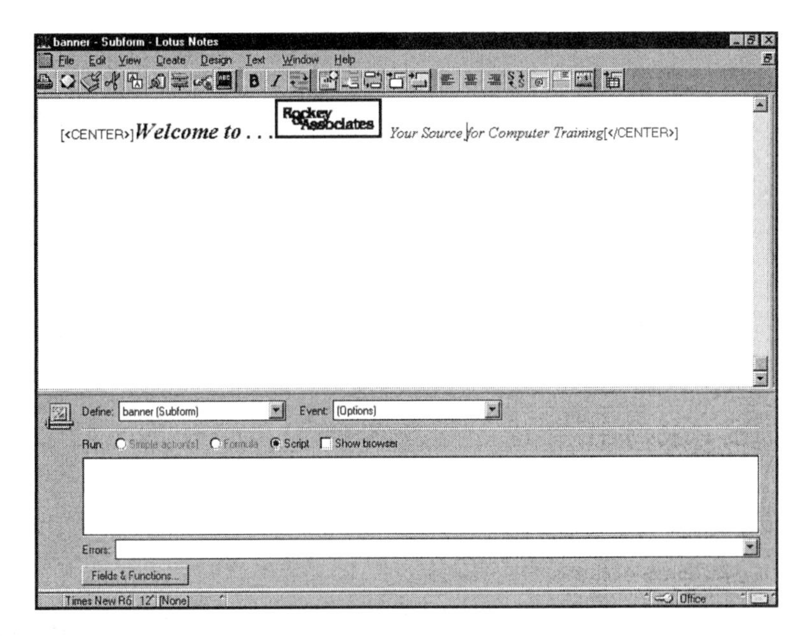

Figure 7.4 The subform designed to become a banner.

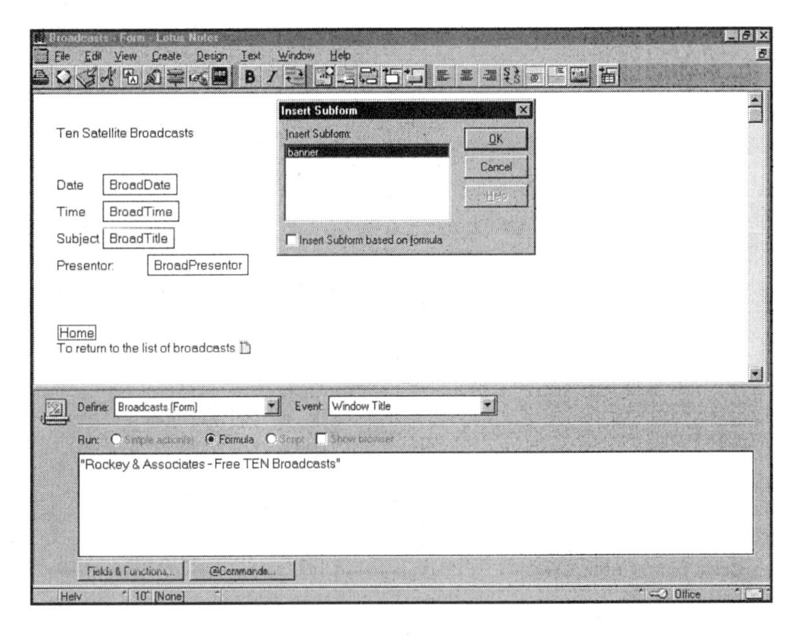

Figure 7.5 The Insert Subform dialog box.

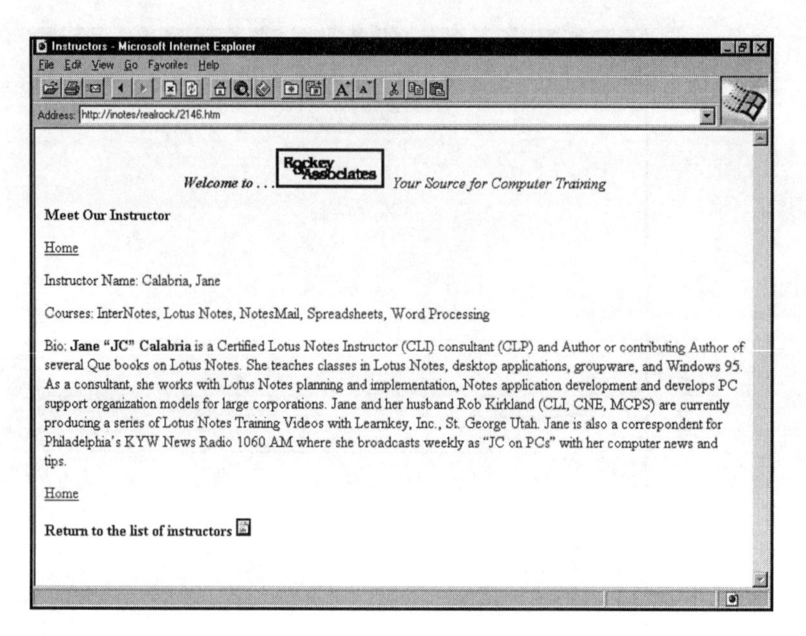

Figure 7.6 A Notes form with a banner subform as viewed on the Web.

Of course, you might not want to include this subform in each of your Notes forms (you can create as many subforms as you want). Depending upon the structure of your database, you might want to create a set of subforms to use within your Notes forms.

Specifying a Title for the Home Page

As you read in Lesson 3, "Using HTML," you can add titles to forms so that the title will publish to the Web and will appear as a window title in your browser. If you don't create a window title, the default for your window title is your database name as seen in Figure 7.5. Now that the home page has become a form, you can add a window title.

To add a title to your home page:

1. Open the Home page form (the one with the alias $$Home) in Design mode.

2. In the Design pane, select **Window Title** as the **Event,** and type your window title in the formula box. Place quotes around your window title (see Figure 7.7).

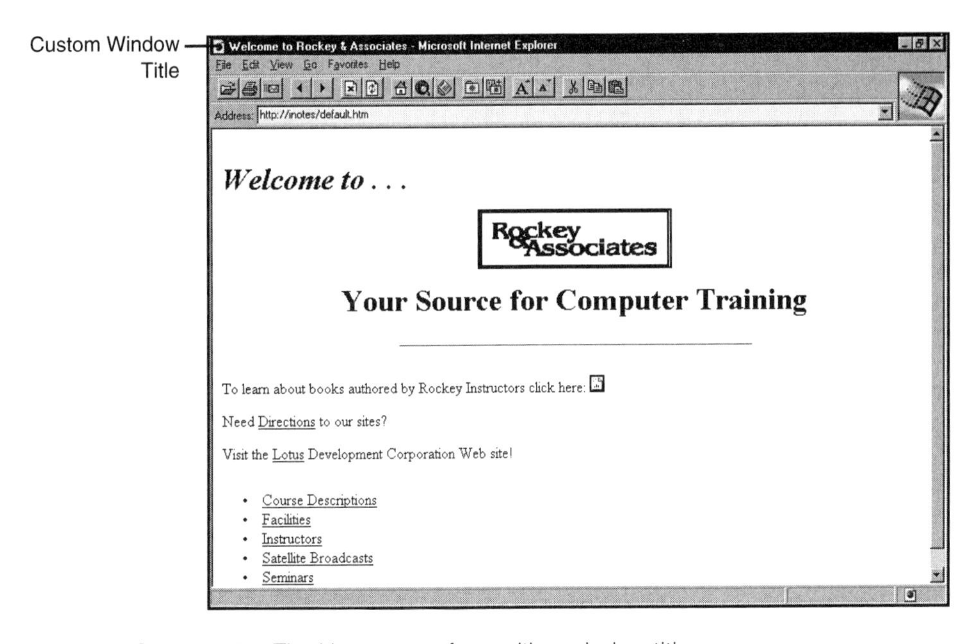

Figure 7.7 The Home page form with a window title.

3. Save and publish your database.

In this lesson, you learned how to create custom home page forms and banners, as well as how to specify a title for the home page. In the next lesson, you learn about creating custom view forms.

Working with Views

In this lesson, you learn how to create custom view pages and how to display icons in views.

Working with Views

Just as you created a form for your home page in Lesson 7, you can create a form for your views. Without custom view forms, your views will appear somewhat drab on the Web. Figure 8.1 shows a view as it appears on the Web without a custom form.

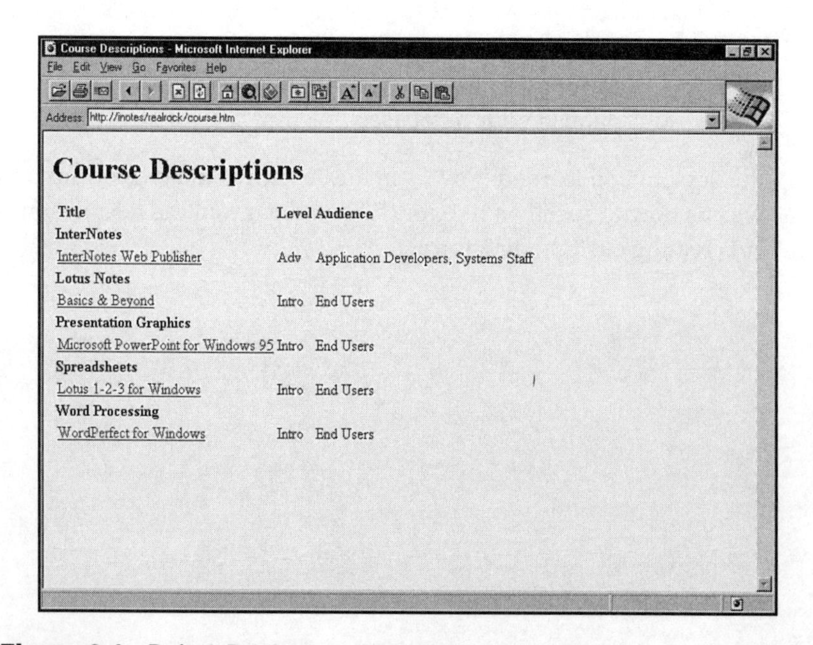

Figure 8.1 Default Publication of a view—without a form.

Although the view in Figure 8.1 *works* and looks fine, you might want to add graphics, banners, a different title (by default, the window title is the view name), icons, or bullets to the view page. To do this, start by creating a new form.

Generating Custom View Pages

As you learned in Lesson 7, "Creating Notes Forms," the form's *alias* is the key that tells InterNotes Web Publisher to publish the contents of this form. Unlike the $$Home alias you encountered in Lesson 7, which publishes only one form, and only the contents of that one form, the $$ViewTemplate alias creates a form that acts like a template for *all views* in the database.

TIP **Develop a Consistent Look for Your Site** If you want a custom page for each of your different views, you can create a form for each view and use the alias $$*viewname*, where *viewname* is the actual name of the view.

You can use standard Notes fields, graphics, and text in your view form. All fields must be Computed for Display field types except for the following fields that are special Notes fields used for Web publication:

- **$$ViewList** Provides a list of *all* the database views on the page.
- **$$ViewBody** Includes the contents of a specific database view on the page.
- **$$ImageMapBody** Includes a specific image map on the page.

As a convenience to Web users, you can include links to the home page or other databases on this view form template.

To create a custom view form (template):

1. Open the database and select **Create, Design, Form** from the menu.

CAUTION **The View Form Template Appears on Page One Only!** When you use a view form template, the InterNotes Web Publisher will use the template for the first page of the view. If the view contains multiple pages, later pages will not have the template on them.

2. Open the Form Properties box and name the form. Give it an alias of **$$ViewTemplate** if you want to use only one template for all views. If you want to use a different template for each (as was used in Figure 8.2), give

the form a name and use an alias of **$$*viewname*,** where *viewname* is the actual name of the view. Keep in mind that the name you give this form is the name that will appear in the browser title bar on the Web. Figure 8.2 shows the Form Properties box with the name and alias filled in.

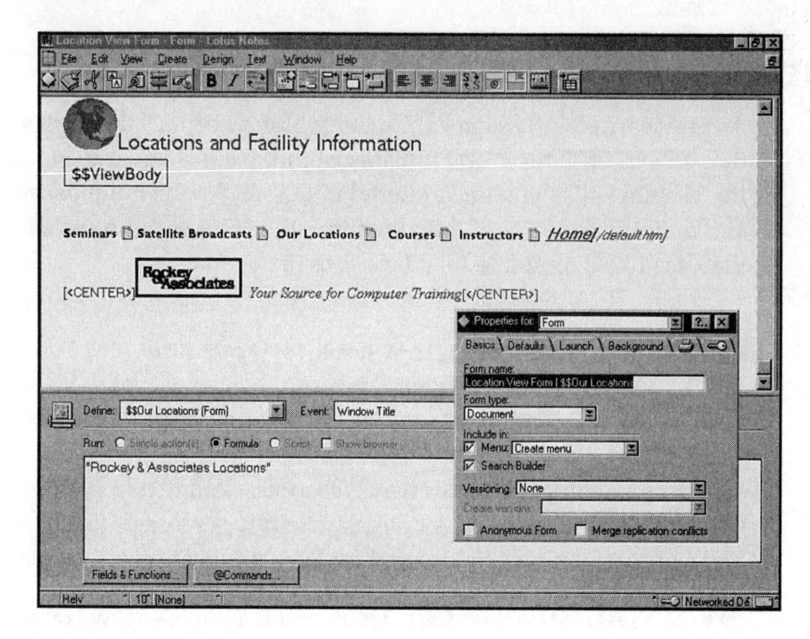

Figure 8.2 $$ViewBody field with view name in Help description.

3. Enter the other fields, graphics, subforms, and so on, you want to include in this form.
4. To include the contents of a view in this template, add a `$$ViewBody` field. Enter the name of the view you want to appear on this page in the `Help description` field of the Field Properties box, and select the **Options** tab (see Figure 8.3).
5. In the Design pane, select **Window Title** as the Event and type your window title in the formula box. Place quotes around your window title.
6. To create a hypertext link to the home page, type and underline the word **Home** followed by the URL. The URL link for this home page is simply a forward slash / surrounded by square brackets. Be certain not to place a space between the word and the URL. This is called placing an *URL passthrough* on your view (URL passthroughs are discussed in Lesson 3). Your home page link might look like this:

   Home[/default.htm]

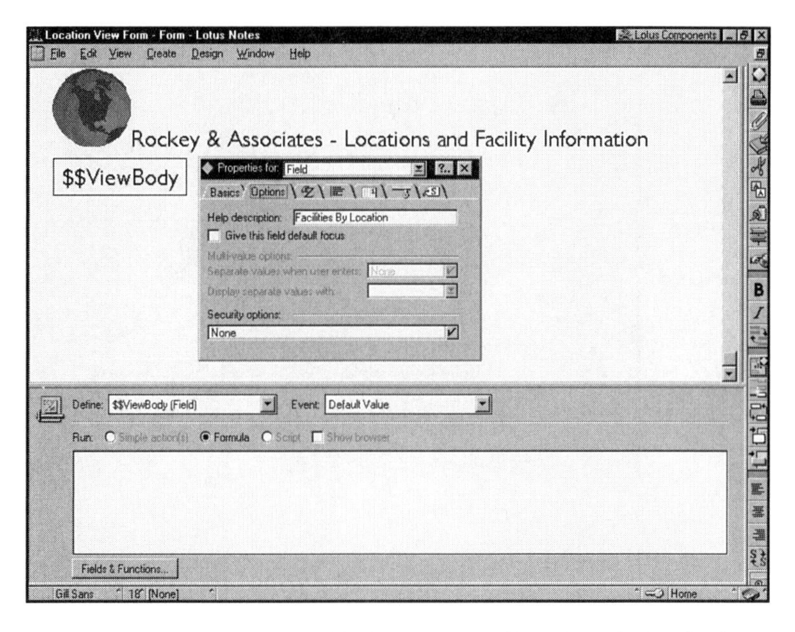

Figure 8.3 Form Properties box with view name in Help description field.

7. You can use a subform on this form. By using a subform, we'll only have to make these changes in one subform—Notes will update other forms that include the subform. (See Lesson 7 for information on creating subforms.)
8. When you finish creating your form, save the form and publish the database.

TIP **One Form, Multiple Views** You can have more than one $$ViewBody field on your form, enabling you to list more than one view. Name the fields **$$ViewBody_1**, **$$ViewBody_2**, and so on, and put their corresponding view names in the Help description field of the Field Properties box or InfoBox.

Displaying Bullets in Views

Displaying bullets in views involves using graphics or .gif files. Lesson 9, "Using Graphics," covers graphics more extensively but this is a good time to get a head start because bullets are easy to add to your views.

To create bullets, you first need a .gif file of a bullet. Store the bullet.gif file as an attachment in your Using Database document. Figure 8.4 shows some .gif files stored for use on our Web site.

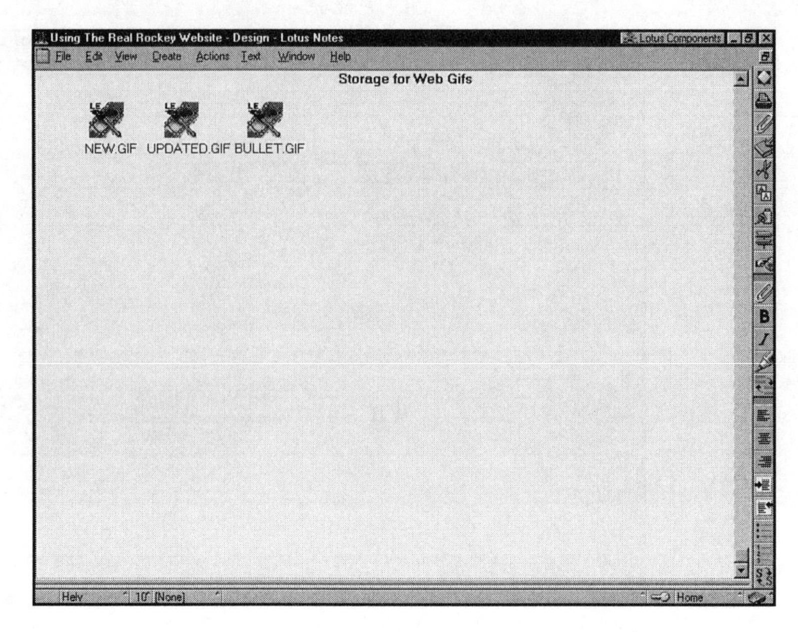

Figure 8.4 The Using Database document as a storage place for .gif files.

Where's the .gifs? You can store your .gif files within your Notes database to make it easy to locate and use them. If you store them in one of these documents, you need not tell InterNotes Web Publisher where to find them. When it publishes these documents, it automatically creates pointers to the .gif files, which are invisible to you. You need only name the .gif file in the document where you want to use it (in the Help Using Database document, the About Database document, or a Notes document containing the HTML field).

To display a bullet in each row of a view:

1. Open in Design mode the view in which you want to place the bullets.
2. Insert a column with no title and a width of one character. The placement of the column is important. Place the column to the right of any category columns in your view. Figure 8.5 shows a view, Course Descriptions, in Design mode. In column one, we sort by course category. Column two contains the course title. We placed the new column for bullets to the right of our category column and before our title column.
3. Edit the column formula to read:

   ```
   temp := @NoteID;"[img src=bullet.gif>]"
   ```

4. Save the form and publish the database.

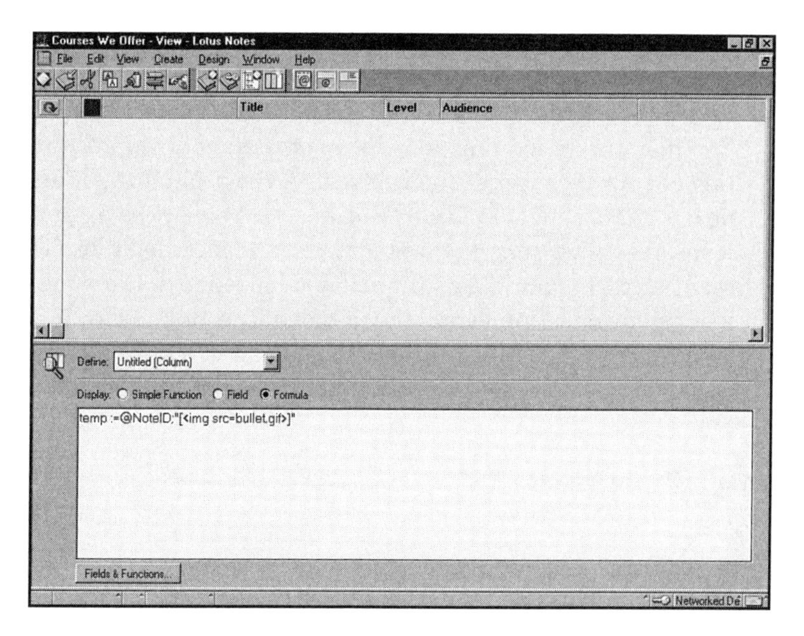

Figure 8.5 Formula to add bullets to a column.

Bullets will now appear on each line of your view on the Web, as shown in Figure 8.6

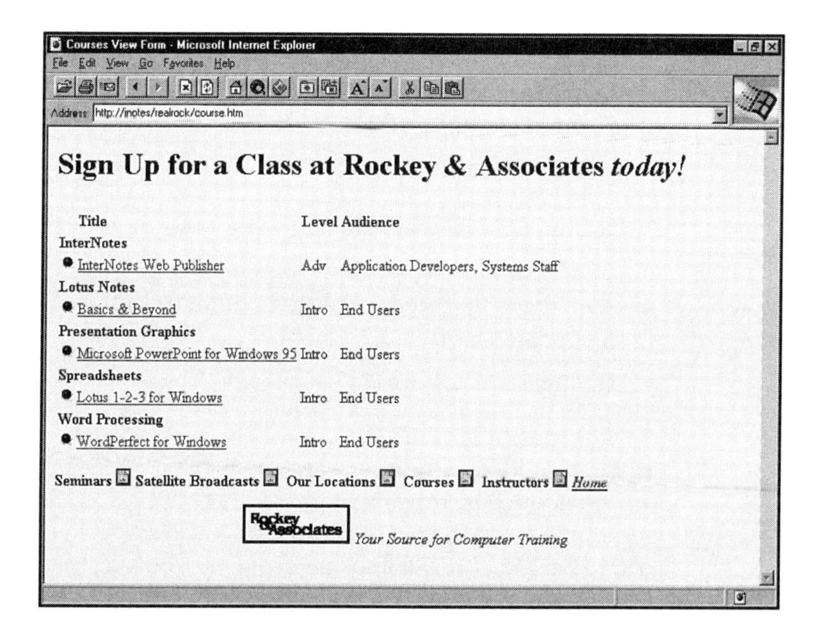

Figure 8.6 Bullets in view as seen on the Web.

Showing Icons Next to New and Updated Documents

You might want to bring new documents or modified documents to the attention of your Web users. You can write a view column formula that will put icons next to those new or modified documents. You'll need a .gif file for each of the icons. We called ours new and updated and included those words on the icons themselves. In your view formula, you'll need to indicate the parameters for placing the new icon versus the updated icon, and the formula needs to contain instructions for all other documents. If documents are neither new nor updated, then no icon will be placed next to the document in the view.

Formulas Part III, "Application Development," covers formulas more extensively.

After you have the .gif files stored in your Using document, About document, or in a document containing an HTML field, you can edit your view to use these .gifs. To show these icons next to new and updated documents:

1. In Design mode, open the view in which you want to use the icons.
2. Insert a new column; then enter a formula for the use of the icons. You might try this formula:

    @If (@Today < @Adjust(@Created; 0; 0; 5; 0; 0; 0); "[<img src=new.gif>]"; @Today < @Adjust(@Modified; 0; 0; 5; 0; 0; 0); "[<img src=updated.gif>]";"")

    The results of this formula are:

    - Documents that were created within five days of today will display the new icon.
    - Documents that were modified within five days of today will display the updated icon.
    - All other documents will display no icon.

It Worked Yesterday! In order for this type of formula to work correctly, the Publishing Record (described in Lesson 1, "Understanding InterNotes Web Publisher") for this database should be set to publish the database at least once a day. Also, the Publishing Record must be publishing *all documents*, or the InterNotes Web Publisher will not publish the view unless there are changes in the database that affect the view.

Figure 8.7 shows the results of our view column formula on the Web.

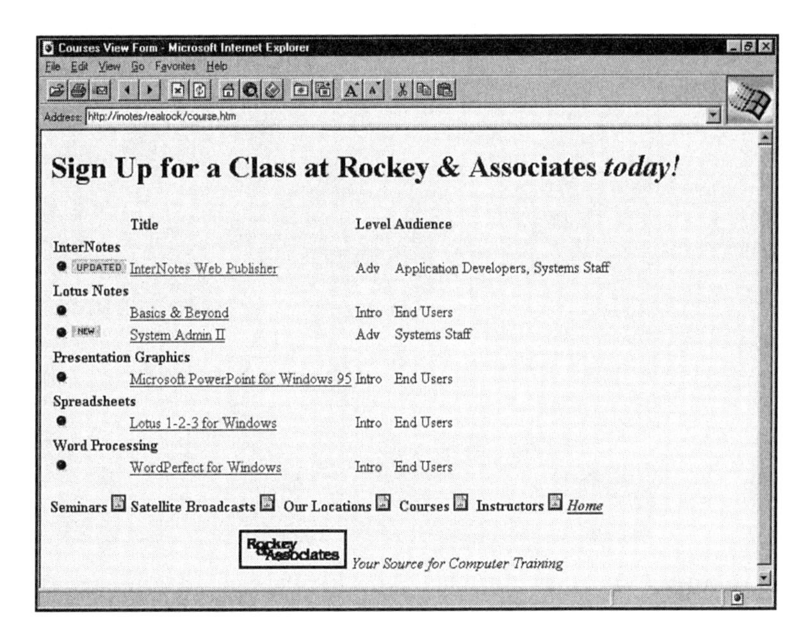

Figure 8.7 Icons next to new and updated documents.

Selecting Views to Publish

You can specify which views to publish by listing them in the Publishing Record of the database. In the Views to Publish field, list the names of the views you want to publish. If you leave this field blank, all the views in the database will be published.

Don't Use Parentheses in View Name! Be certain to list these views *exactly* as they are named, including spaces and case. If you put the view name in parentheses to hide it from the menu, the view won't publish.

Figure 8.8 shows a selection of views filled in the Views to Publish field of a Publishing Record.

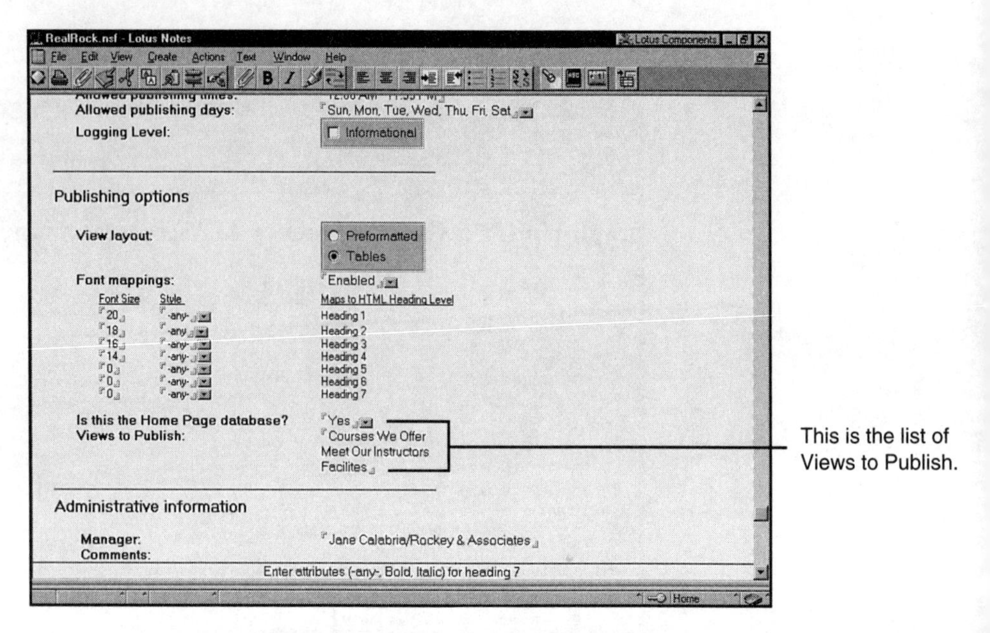

Figure 8.8 Specifying which views to publish in the Publishing Record.

In this lesson, you learned how to select views to be published, and how to create custom view pages. You also learned how to display bullets in views. In the next lesson, you'll learn about using graphics.

Using Graphics

In this lesson, you learn how to use graphics as hotspots and how to create bitmap backgrounds for your Web pages.

Understanding Graphics Files

There are two kinds of computer graphics: vector graphics and bitmap graphics. Vector graphics are pictures made up of mathematically described objects, such as lines, arcs, ellipses, and rectangles. Bitmap graphics are pictures made up of an array of dots of different colors and shades. Notes documents can include both kinds of graphics. Web browsers can display only bitmap graphics, and only two types of bitmap graphics: GIF and JPEG.

GIF: Graphics Interchange Format A compressed bitmap file format first made popular by CompuServe. GIF files use "lossless" compression—the compressed version of a file is identical to the pre-compressed version.

JPEG A compressed bitmap file format developed by the Joint Photographic Experts Group. JPEG uses "lossy" compression, which permits you to compress a file more if you are willing to give up fidelity to the original version. The more fidelity you are willing to lose, the more you can compress the file. This type of compression is good for photographs.

Unlike other Web site limitations, where graphics must always be .jpg or .gif files, the InterNotes Web Publisher allows you to paste a graphic (.bmp, .pcx) or scanned image into a Notes document. It will convert that image for use on the Web.

The InterNotes Web Publisher will automatically take your graphic and convert it to .gif. Also, Web Publisher will store it in the appropriate directory on the Web site with a link in the document so the graphic displays in the right spot on your document. This allows you great flexibility in the use of various graphic formats in your Notes documents.

Lesson 8 describes how to create formulas for graphics (bullets and symbols) in views. Lesson 4 shows how to paste graphics into home pages. In Lesson 7, you learned to paste graphics into forms and subforms. In this lesson, you use graphics as Notes links and as document backgrounds.

Graphics as Hotspot Pop-Ups

You can use graphics as hotspots with defined URLs, for linking to external or internal sites, documents, views, or databases. Here are some things to consider:

- Bitmaps must be 16-color image type to publish properly. You may have difficulty with black and white, since black and white is considered two colors.

Bitmap A bitmap is an array of dots. Some dots are darker than others or they are a different color. When you hold the array far enough away and look at it, instead of seeing dots, you see an image. For example, a photograph in a newspaper is a bitmap. Hold a newspaper photograph up close and you can see the light and dark dots that make it up.

- Graphics that you use for your Web site need not be high resolution, because most monitors see only 72 dots per inch. Most high-resolution monitors see only 96dpi so there isn't any point in having a high-resolution (300dpi) image.

dpi Dots per inch is a measure of resolution. A high-resolution display or printer uses more dots per inch to render an object. The higher the resolution, the smoother the edges of objects look. The lower the resolution, the more jagged the edges of objects look.

Resolution Refers to the amount of detail you can see in an object. The higher the resolution, the more detail you can *resolve.* To obtain higher resolution, a display or printer must either magnify the object or display it using more dots per inch.

- Size your graphics before you paste them into Notes. Although you can size them on a Notes document or form, when published to the Web, the image reverts to its original size, before you sized it in Notes.

To create a graphic pop-up:

1. Open your document or form in Design mode.

2. Paste your graphic into the document or form.
3. Highlight your graphic and choose **Create**, **Hotspot**, **Text Pop-up** from the menu. (You really do create a graphic pop-up by choosing Text pop-up from the menu.)
4. The Properties box for the HotSpot Pop-up will appear. Type the URL to which you want to link in the Popup text box. Be certain to place square brackets around the URL. If this URL points to an external Web site, you must enter the entire address. If this URL points to a site on your server, you can use a relative address as explained in Lesson 6. Figure 9.1 shows the Properties box containing an explicit URL for this pop-up.
5. Save your form, publish your database, and test it with a browser.

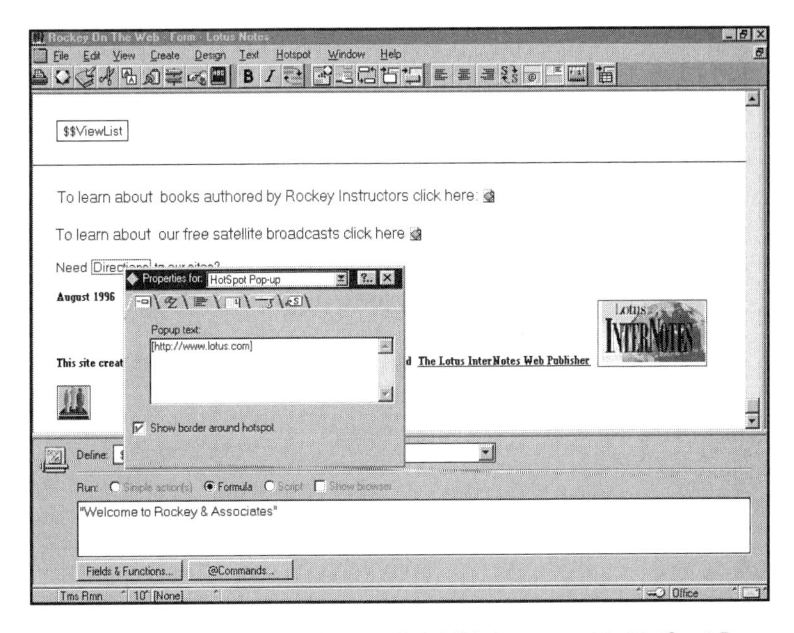

Figure 9.1 Properties box containing explicit URL for a graphic HotSpot Pop-up.

Graphics as Anchors

You can use graphics as *anchors* for your Web site. Anchors are links in which the user clicks a graphic instead of underlined text or icons, but you'll need to use bitmap graphics. Graphic anchors can link to relative or explicit URLs. You can also use Notes document links, database links, or view links.

You might want to use anchors if your view has many documents and pages. Suppose you have published your entire catalog of products to the Web. You may have categories in your view, but a Web user will still have to browse through pages and pages until they find the category for widgets. Furthermore, your potential customer may not even know that you call these things widgets.

You might consider placing graphic anchors on your category view form representing each of your categories. This would give your Web users a choice—to scroll through the list of items by category, or to click a graphic anchor that can then take them to the widgets view. You can build a view for each of your categories with a selection formula to display only those documents within that category.

To create graphics as anchors:

1. In Design mode, open the form or document in which you want to place your anchor graphics.
2. Paste your bitmap graphic where you want it to appear on the form.
3. Immediately following your bitmap, establish your link by either using a Notes Link (as described in Lesson 5) or typing an URL after the graphic. Don't leave any spaces between the bitmap and the Notes Link or URL. Figure 9.2 shows a view form in Design mode.

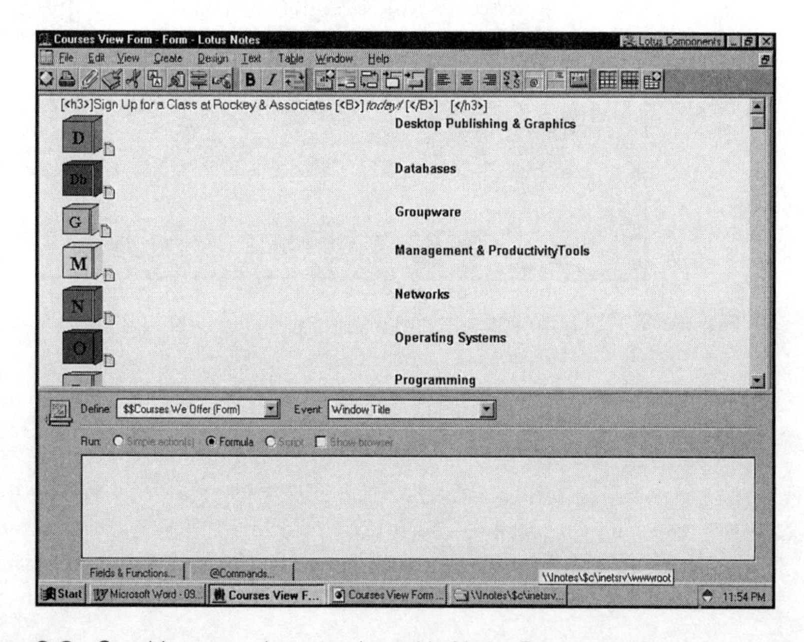

Figure 9.2 Graphics as anchors as viewed in Notes Design mode.

4. Save your document or form, publish the database, and test it with a browser.

When your form is published, Web users will not see the link that immediately follows the graphic anchor but will see the anchor as a hotspot. Figure 9.3 shows a published view form through a Web browser.

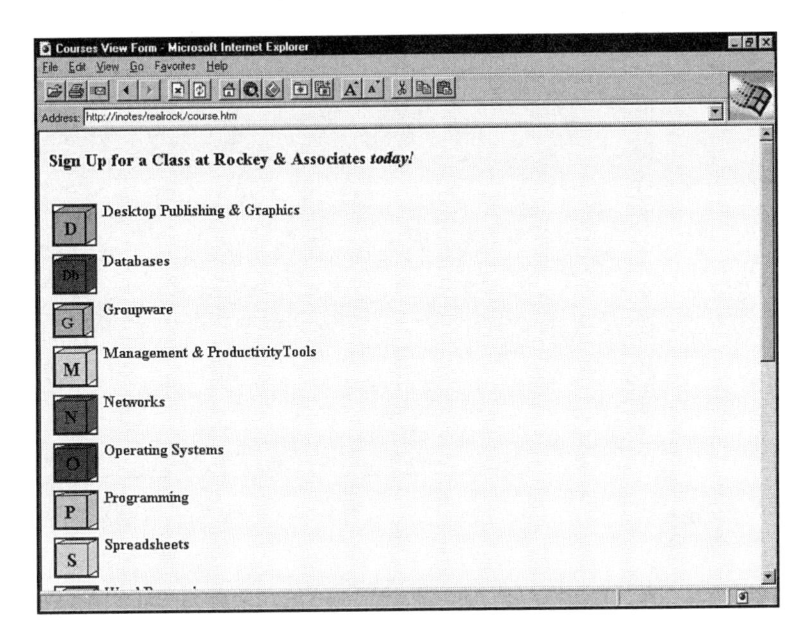

Figure 9.3 Graphics as anchors as viewed through a Web browser.

Using Graphics as Background Bitmaps

You can use .gif files to create background images for your forms. To create a background image:

1. Attach your .gif file to your Using Database document, About Database document, or a document with an HTML field.
2. Open in Design mode the form that you want to place the background on in Design mode.
3. At the top of the form, before anything else on the form, type the following HTML code where *filename* is the name of your file:

   <BODY BACKGROUND="*FILENAME*.GIF">]

4. Save the document and publish the database. Figure 9.4 shows a background bitmap as seen through a Web browser.

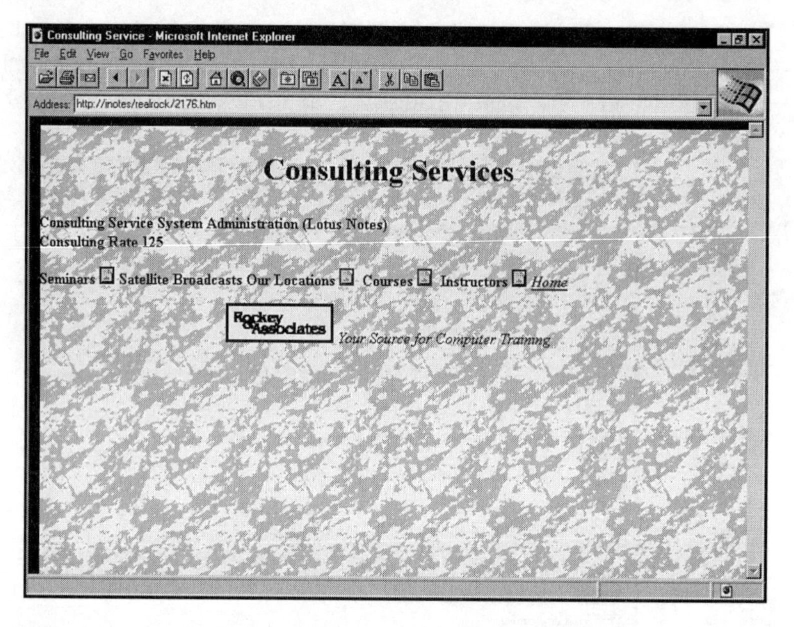

Figure 9.4 Background bitmap on Notes document as seen through a Web browser.

TIP **Tools You Can Use** The InterNotes Web Publisher comes with a Web Publisher Toolkit database. This toolkit contains graphics, tips, and tools that you can use in the design of your Web application. One of those tools is a series of colored lines that you can paste into your forms as separators. See the Graphics-separator bars document in the Toolkit, and refer to Lesson 14 for more information on how to use the Toolkit.

In this lesson, you learned how to use graphics as hotspots, background bitmaps, and anchors. In the next lesson, you learn how to create and use image maps.

Understanding Image Maps

In this lesson, you learn what an image map is and how to create an image map from a Notes navigator. You also learn how you can open views and other navigators from an image map.

Using Image Maps

An *image map* is a picture, regions of which are linked to a series of URLs, Notes documents, views, databases, or are used to run actions. To create an image map, start by creating a navigator and paste your picture as a graphic background in the navigator. Here are some tips to keep in mind when using navigators in this way:

- You can define action hotspots for the regions of the navigator.
- The image you use for your navigator in Notes must be a bitmap (.bmp file).
- Only bitmaps will work as Navigators.

Table 10.1 describes ways you can use navigators, as well as the steps you need to take to complete each task.

Table 10.1 Using Navigators

To	*Select*
Open another navigator	Run simple action.
	Open another navigator.
	Select the navigator.

continues

Table 10.1 Continued

To	*Select*
Open a view	Run simple action. Open a view. Select the view.
Alias a folder	(Folders don't publish to the Web properly. You should not use this option for your Web database.)
Open a link	Run simple action. Open a link. Paste your link (if copied as link).
Use an @function	Run formula. Enter your formula in the formula box.
Use LotusScript	Run script. Enter your script in the script box (this allows you to perform sophisticated processing that is not covered in this book).

Creating Image Maps

Start your image map by creating a graphic in a program that supports bitmap graphic formats. Save the graphic and follow these steps:

1. Copy the bitmap to the Clipboard.
2. Open the database in which you are going to use this image map. From the menu, select **Create, Design, Navigator**.
3. To paste your bitmap into the navigator screen, select **Create, Graphic Background**.

CAUTION

Don't Use Edit, Paste to Paste Your Graphic! When you paste your graphic into the navigator, you must use the **Create**, **Graphic background** menu commands.

4. Right-click to open the Properties box and name your navigator.
5. Determine which areas of your navigator will act as hotspots. To make an area an active hotspot, select **Create, Hotspot Rectangle** (or **Hotspot Polygon** if the area on your image is odd shaped). Your pointer will become a crosshair.
6. Click and drag over the area you want to become the hotspot. Release the mouse button after you have identified the area. If you release the mouse button too soon or your hotspot is not the right size, you can resize it by pulling on the handles.
7. Define what action this hotspot will perform by providing the information in the formula pane. Table 10.1 lists the options available.
8. Repeat steps 5, 6, and 7 until you have completed all hotspots for your navigator. Save your navigator.
9. Open the form in which you want to place your navigator. Follow the directions in this lesson for opening another navigator, opening a view, opening a link, or using an @function.

To Open Another Navigator

You can use navigators to open other navigators. For an example, see the Server Web Navigator database. To create a navigator that opens another navigator:

1. Follow steps 1 through 6 of "Creating Image Maps."
2. Select **Simple Action(s)** as the **Run** option.
3. Select **Open another Navigator** in the **Action** list box.
4. A new list box appears to the right of the Action list box. This new box contains a list of all of your available navigators. Select the navigator you want to open (see Figure 10.1).
5. Continue at step 8 in the previous section,"Creating Image Maps."

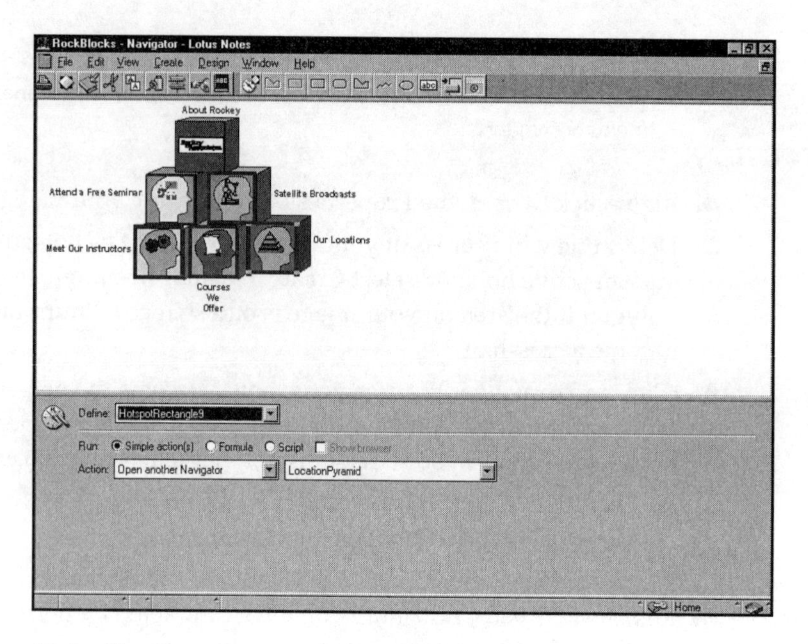

Figure 10.1 The Open another Navigator Design pane.

To Open a View

The most common use of navigators is to open views. If you use a simple action, you can open a view within the same database. To create a navigator to open a view:

1. Follow steps 1 through 6 of the "Creating Image Maps" section.
2. Select **Simple Action(s)** as the **Run** option.
3. Select **Open a View** in the Action list box.
4. A new list box appears to the right of the Action list box. This new box contains a list of all of your available views. Select the view you want to open.
5. Continue at step 8 of the "Creating Image Maps" section.

To Open a Link

Another use of navigators is to link to other databases, views, or documents. Use a Notes link in your simple action. To create a navigator to open a link:

1. Follow steps 1 through 6 of the "Creating Image Maps" section.
2. Select **Simple Action(s)** as the **Run** option.
3. Select **Open a Link** in the Action list box.
4. Open the Window menu, switch to your workspace, and open the database, document, or view to which you want to link. Select **Edit, Copy as Link;** then choose **Document Link, View Link,** or **Database Link**.
5. Switch back to your navigator. A new button appears to the right of the Action list box (see Figure 10.2). Click this **Paste Link** button to paste your Notes link.
6. Continue at step 8 of the "Creating Image Maps" section.

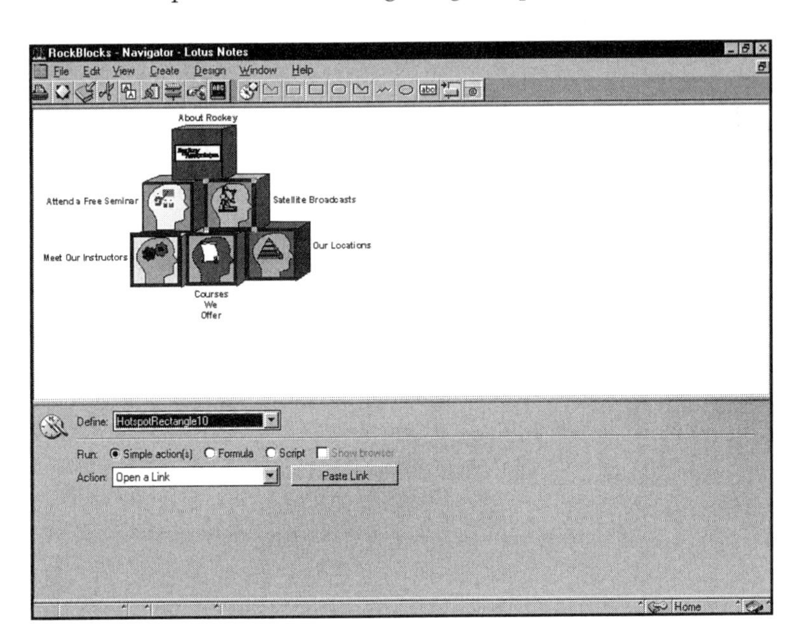

Figure 10.2 The Open a Link Design pane.

To Use an @function

You can use an @function to create a navigator that opens an URL. An example of this would be a navigator that links to a Web site. To use an @function in your navigator formula:

1. Follow steps 1 through 6 of the "Creating Image Maps" section.
2. Select **Formula** as the **Run** option.
3. Enter your formula in the formula box (see Figure 10.3). You can use a new @function that may not be listed in your @function list, as it is available only with the Lotus Notes Web products. This new @function is:

   @*URL*Open("URL")

   where *URL* is the full address, or explicit URL.
4. Continue at step 8 of the "Creating Image Maps" section.

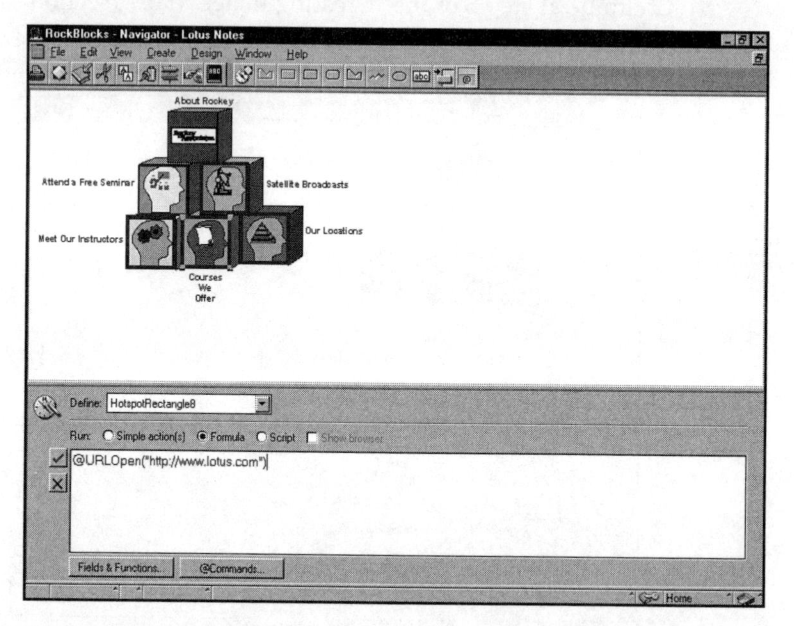

Figure 10.3 Formula Design pane.

In this lesson, you learned about image maps and how to use them in your Notes documents for publication on the Web. In the next lesson, you'll learn how to create interactive Web forms.

Creating Interactive Forms

In this lesson, you learn how to create interactive forms so Web users can enter information that will be converted back to Notes documents.

Understanding Interactive Forms

Interactive forms are powerful. They extend the functionality of publishing Notes databases on the Web by enabling the user to submit information back to the Notes database; this information can subsequently be manipulated and acted on by agents in Notes.

For the sake of this book, and in Notes' terms, interactive forms are:

- Designed in Notes as forms and are form *type* documents (not response documents)
- Converted to HTML by InterNotes Web Publisher and published to a Web server
- Filled out by Web users
- Delivered to a Notes server by Notes CGI script
- Converted to Notes documents by InterNotes Web Publisher

Not a Response Form? An interactive form may also be referred to as a *response*. In this lesson, the term *response form* is used exclusively for a type of Notes document, not a type of Web form. Lesson 12, "More Interactive Forms," covers Notes response forms used on the Web.

With interactive forms, Web users can inquire about products and services, ask to be added to your mailing list, or request additional information about your company. Interactive forms act like other Notes forms—just as Notes users create documents by filling in forms, Web users can create Notes documents by filling in interactive forms.

Other Notes functions and features you can use in interactive forms include:

- HTML code to override Notes field defaults such as restricting the size and maximum length of Notes text fields
- @functions, including default formulas, input translation formulas, and input validation formulas
- Keyword fields, including check boxes and radio buttons
- Subforms, both computed and named

A Quick Tour of Interactive Form Design

To understand the combined use of forms, subforms, main documents, response documents, and interactive forms, follow this example of an online registration process for Web users to register themselves for free seminars.

- **The home page in Notes Design mode** The home page is a form of type document (Rockey on the Web*)*. It has the alias $$Home to identify it as the home page for the database. It contains the $$ImageMap field, and the $$AboutDatabase field. This form also has a Notes link to a different database, and an URL link to a different Web site (see Figure 11.1).
- **The home page as viewed on the Web** Web users click the Image Map to learn about free seminars (see Figure 11.2).
- **The list of seminars in Notes Design mode** The list of seminars is a form of type document (Seminar View Form*)*. It contains two subforms (the Banner subform used repeatedly throughout the application for a consistent look and the Home Navigator subform used throughout the application for navigational purposes). The view of available seminars is a result of the $$ViewBody field as discussed in Lesson 8, "Working with Views," which displays a named view *(*Attend a Free Seminar*)* (see Figure 11.3*)*.

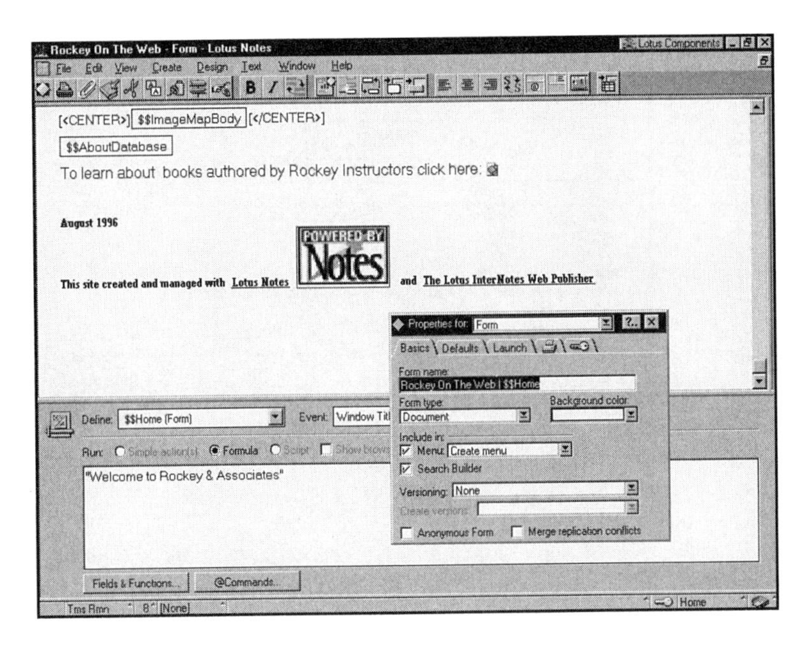

Figure 11.1 The home page in Notes Design mode.

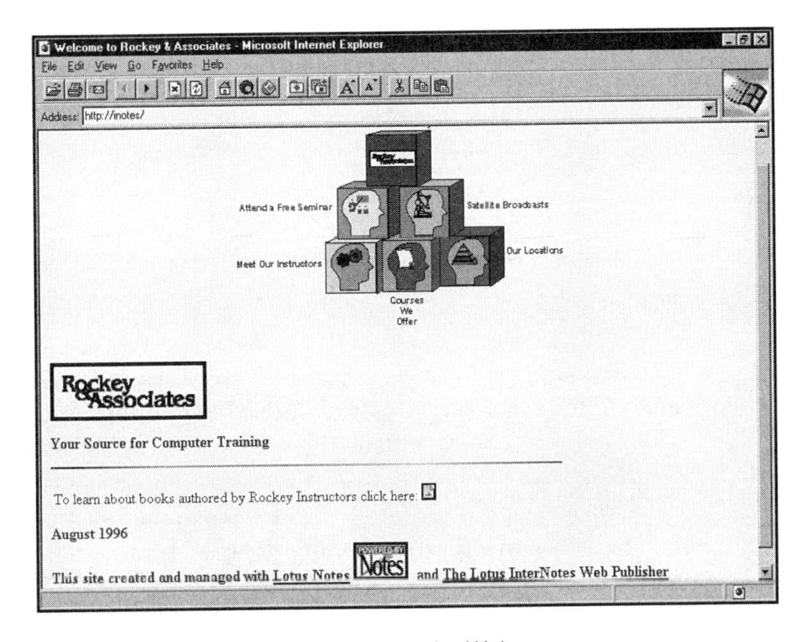

Figure 11.2 The home page as viewed on the Web.

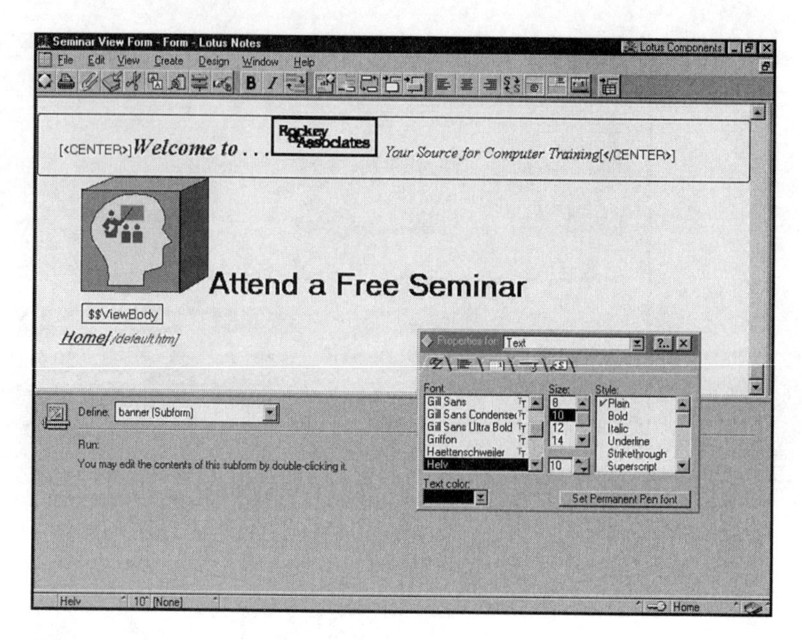

Figure 11.3 The list of seminars in Design mode.

- **The list of seminars on the Web** (Seminar View Form) The Web user selects a seminar of interest by clicking its hypertext link (see Figure 11.4).
- **The Seminar form in Notes Design mode** (Seminars) This is a form type document and contains information about a specific seminar. This form contains the Banner subform and an URL link called Register that links to the registration form (SemReg.htm) (see Figure 11.5).
- **The Seminar form as viewed on the Web** Web users read about the seminar and can click the hypertext **Register** to register for this seminar (see Figure 11.6).
- **The Registration form** (SemReg) **in Notes Design mode with the $$Web alias** This tells InterNotes Web Publisher to publish this form to the Web. This is a form type document and contains a graphic and a special InterNotes Web Publisher field, $$Return. This field formula creates a customized response to the Web users when they submit the form, thanking them by name for their inquiry. Figure 11.7 shows the formula for the $$Return field.

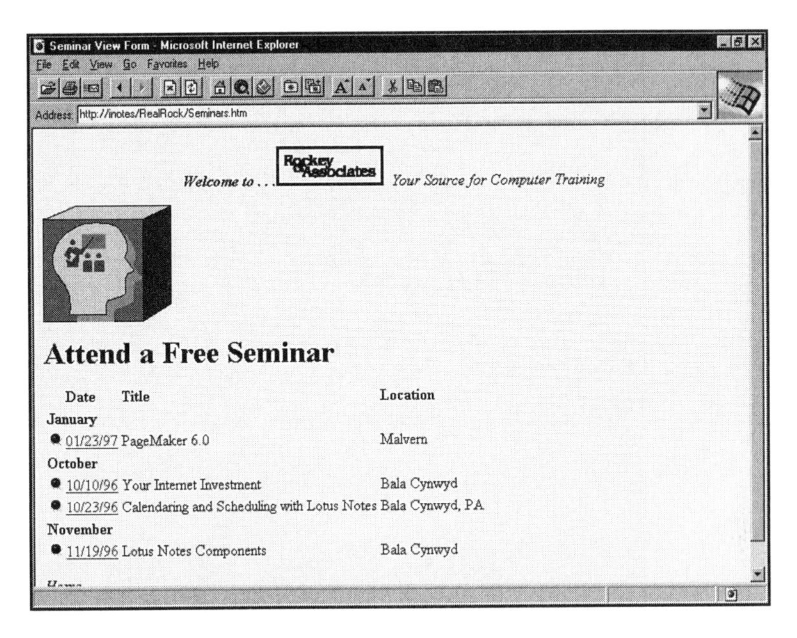

Figure 11.4 The list of seminars as viewed on the Web.

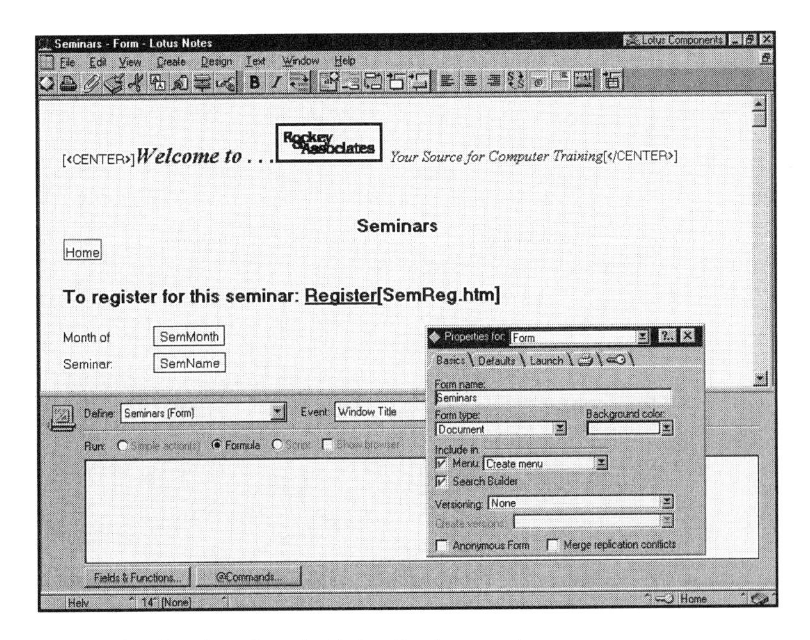

Figure 11.5 The Seminar form in Notes Design mode.

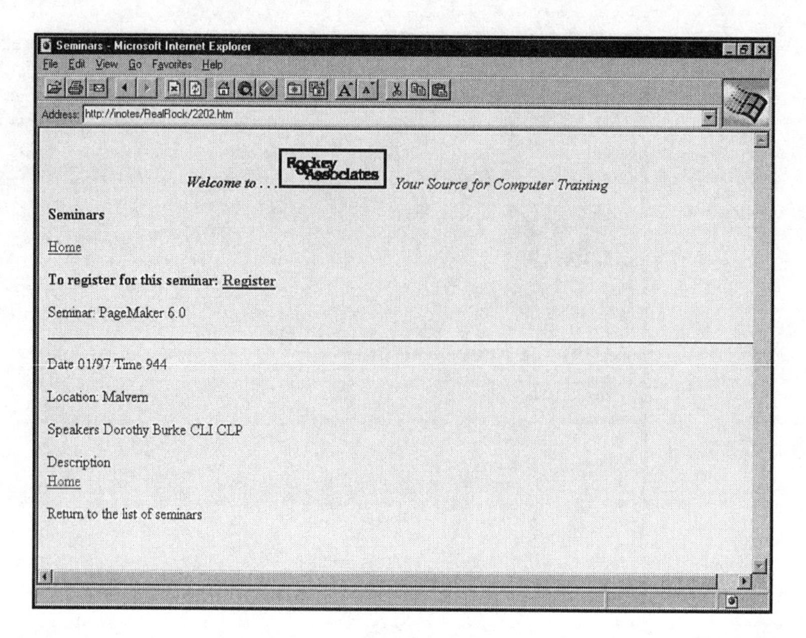

Figure 11.6 The Seminar form on the Web.

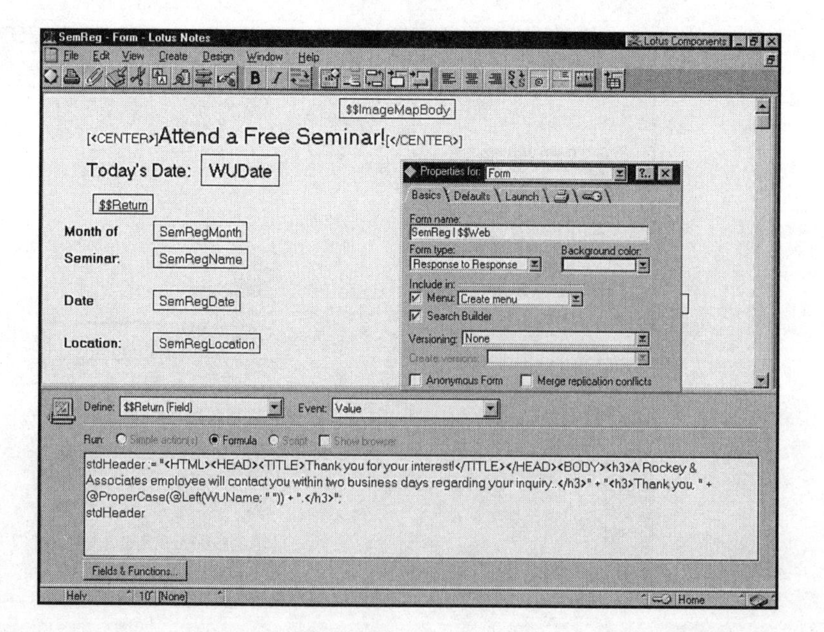

Figure 11.7 The Registration form.

- **The Registration form as viewed on the Web** (SemReg)**as seen by Web users** When Web users complete the form, they click the **Submit** button (see Figure 11.8).

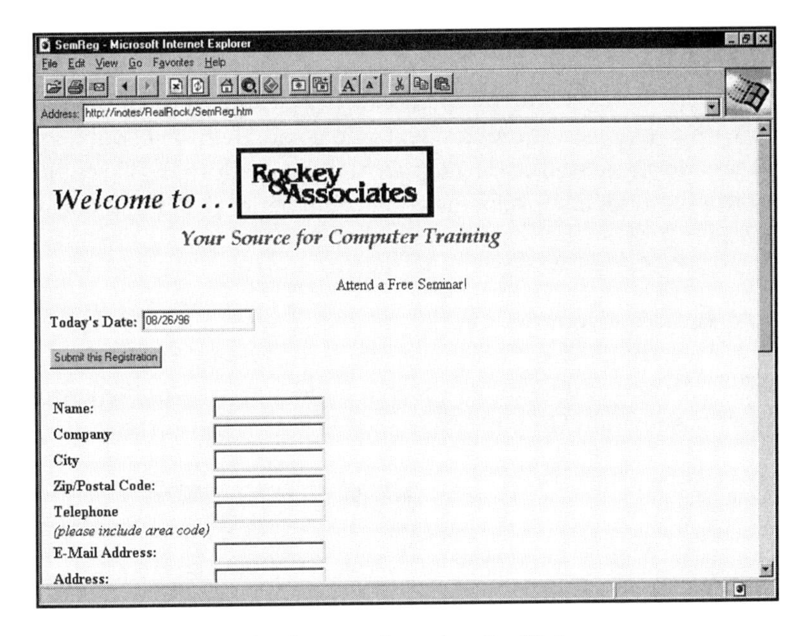

Figure 11.8 The Registration form as viewed on the Web.

There are four processes involved in the creation of interactive forms. They are:

- Create the Notes form that will be the interactive form.
- Give the form an alias of $$Web. This special alias tells Notes to convert the form to HTML for publication on the Web.
- Create a link from the form to the HTML file associated with the form.
- Publish the database.

CAUTION

I Don't See the Documents! The Notes server, InterNotes Web Publisher, and the HTTP server must *all* be installed on the same computer for interactive forms to be received back into Notes databases. In addition, the database that contains the form must be on that same computer. Check with your Notes systems administrator for assistance.

For more information on creating Notes forms, see Part III, "Application Development."

Creating Interactive Forms

Use good development practices when designing your interactive forms. Start with a few fields, graphics, text, and so on; then save, publish, and test. These are the steps used to develop any Notes application. This will help you to troubleshoot any problems you may experience along the way.

To create an interactive form:

1. Create your form in Lotus Notes. Give it an alias of $$Web. If you don't want this form to appear for your Notes users, deselect the Include in Menu and Include in Search Builder options of the Form Property box as shown in Figure 11.9.

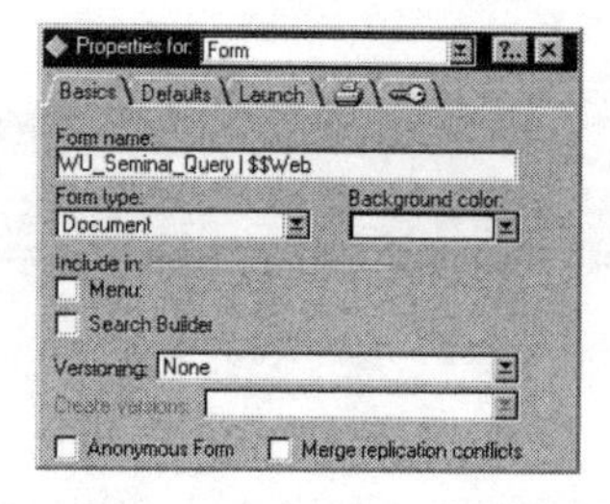

Figure 11.9 The Form Properties box.

2. Put all of the fields and information you need on the form, including graphics and formulas. You can even include subforms, as shown in Figure 11.10. You might consider putting all or parts of your form in a table to help with alignment on the Web.

TIP **Using Subforms** Subforms can be extremely helpful; for example, you can use subforms for banners, footers, and the section of your interactive forms that asks basic Web user information (name, e-mail address, company, phone number, and so on). Note that computed subforms might not work as expected when published. It is a good idea to avoid them on forms that will be published.

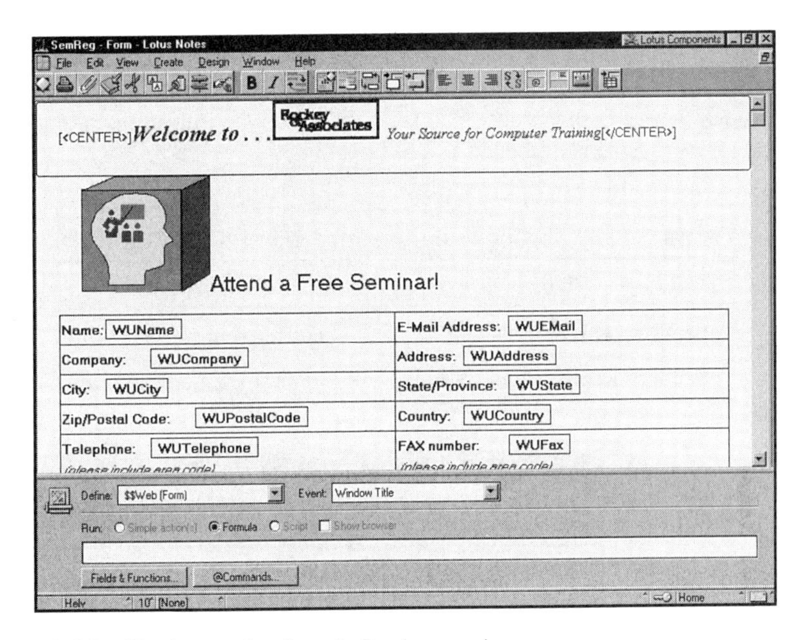

Figure 11.10 The interactive form in Design mode.

3. Create a link *to* the form. For example, if you allow Web users to register for a seminar, you'll create a link on the page that lists the seminar to the interactive registration form. In order to link to the new form (the one with the $$Web alias), you need to know the name of the HTML file created by Notes for that form. Table 11.1 shows how HTML file names will be associated with your Notes form names. The first name of the form will be the HTML file name, followed by an .htm extension. If your form name contains spaces, they are replaced by a plus sign (+) in the HTML file name.
4. After you create your link, you can save your interactive form and test it on the Web. If you are building the form in steps, as suggested, you can save and test at any time. Just be certain to have your link created *to* your form so you can access it easily (see Figure 11.11).
5. Create a view so that you can view the interactive forms in Notes, or include the form name in a selection formula for an existing view.

TIP **Submit Button** Because you have identified your form as an interactive form for publication to InterNotes Web Publisher, a Submit button will be placed on your form automatically. When a Web user fills out the form, he will click the **Submit** button, and the form will be converted into a Notes document, stored in the database, and found in the appropriate view.

Action Buttons Don't Publish Notes buttons won't publish, so it's not even a good idea to create them for Web users. All buttons will be translated as Submit buttons by the InterNotes Web Publisher. You cannot change the action or function of a Submit button.

Table 11.1 Linking to the Interactive Form—HTML File Names

Name of Form in Notes	*HTML File Name*
SemReg | $$Web	SemReg.htm
Seminar Registration | $$Web	Seminar+Registration.htm

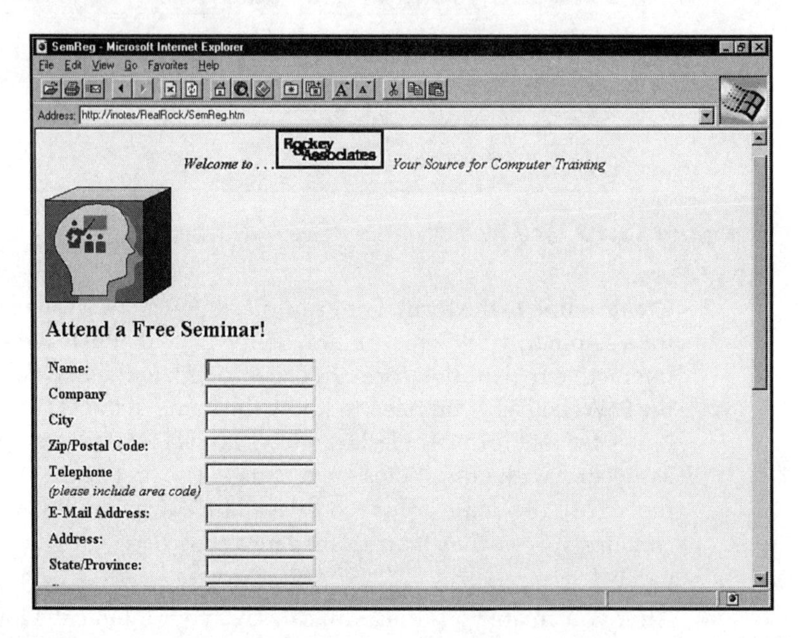

Figure 11.11 The interactive form as seen through a Web browser.

In this lesson, you learned how to create interactive forms. In the next lesson, you will learn formulas and tricks to creating forms.

More Interactive Forms

In this lesson, you learn more formulas and tricks for creating interactive forms for Web users. You learn how to use input validation formulas, create customized responses to your Web users, and how to change the face of the submit button.

Interactive Form Tips, Tricks, and Formulas

You're now ready to start fine-tuning your Web applications. One of your Web application design objectives should be to make Web users feel like they are a part of your site. You want them interacting with your information and even participating in your databases. To help you along in your design, here are some tips and tricks for using interactive forms:

Requiring a Web user to provide a name in your interactive form You can use many types of Notes formulas and functions in your Notes field, including default value, input validation, and input translation formulas. For example, if you *require* a Web user to put their name in your form, you might enter the following formula where *WUName* is the name field for the Web User:

```
@If(WUName = ""; @Failure("<HTML><HEAD><TITLE>Name
Required</TITLE></HEAD><BODY><h3>You must enter a name.
</h3><hr><a href=\"/RealRock/SemReg.htm\">Back</a></BODY>
</HTML>"); @Success)
```

If the Web user tried to submit the form without entering his name, InterNotes Web Publisher would display a Web page with the message `You must enter a name` followed by the word `back` that will link back to the form so the Web user can fill in the required information. Notice that HTML code for the text formatting **<h3>** is included in the formula. You have a lot of flexibility in your form and field design.

Creating a customized response to your Web user If you want to create a customized Web page response to your Web user when he submits this form, add a **$$Return field** to the form. The formula for this *computed* field should contain the message (including the HTML code) you want to return to your Web user and can also contain URLs to other sites. This field is not required. If you don't include this field, then InterNotes Web Publisher will display a Web page with the message `Your form has been processed` when users submit the form. The following example thanks the Web users for their inquiry by displaying a Web page that says `A Rockey & Associates Employee will contact you within two business days. Thank you, (firstname)` where (*firstname*) is the name the Web user provided when filling in the form:

```
stdHeader := "<HTML><HEAD><TITLE>Thank you for your interest!
</TITLE></HEAD><BODY><h3>A Rockey & Associates employee will
contact you within two business days regarding your inquiry..</h3>" +
"<h3>Thank you, " + @ProperCase(@Left(WUName; " ")) + ".</
h3>";stdHeader
```

Setting a Maximum for the length of a text field In the Help Description field of the Field Properties box, enter the HTML code for the display size and maximum characters accepted:

```
[<SIZE=40 MAXLENGTH=60>]
```

This help description will display 40 characters in the field and accept a total of 60.

Linking to another page based on user input In the formula for the $$Return field, include a link to an URL. For example, if a user signs up for a free seminar and answers **yes** to the question `Would you be interested in receiving our mailing list of courses?`, the `See a list of our courses` message with a link to the courses view will display. The formula reads:

```
Example:@If(MailList="yes";"<H2>See a list of our <a href=/realrock/
courses.htm\">courses</a></H2>"
```

Customizing the Submit Button You can create a customized Submit button. Remember that it is the *only* Notes button that will work because InterNotes Web Publisher ignores all button formulas. To create the button, select **Create, Hotspot, Button** from the menu. If you don't create a Submit button, InterNotes Web Publisher will create one for you when your interactive form is published. If you want to create your own, you can:

- Create multiple Submit buttons for the form (all will have the same function).
- Customize the Button Text (the default button will say `Submit`).
- Position the button wherever you want on your form (by default, InterNotes Web Publisher will place it at the bottom of the form).

Don't forget default values and input translation formulas. These may not be considered "interactive" with your Web user, but could be very important in your Notes applications. For example, a default value formula might be `@Today` in a date field. An Input Translation Formula might read `@Trim(@ProperCase(`*`fieldname`*`))` for example. For more information on default values, input validation formulas and other kinds of formulas, refer to Part III, "Application Development."

In this lesson, you learned field formulas that can help you create a response to Web users. You also learned how to set the maximum length of a field and how to use input validation and translation formulas. In the next lesson, you'll learn how to create response forms.

Creating Response Forms and Searches

In this lesson, you learn how to create response forms, as used in discussion databases. You also learn how to create a searchable Web site.

More Interactivity

Discussion databases are one of the most popular types of databases in Lotus Notes. The ability to follow a threaded discussion is extremely useful for Notes users, and InterNotes Web Publisher gives you the opportunity to extend that capability to your Web users. You can also enable Web users to search your databases from the Web by building *search bars*, and you can gather information about your Web users through CGI variables.

Including the following four features in your Notes-driven Web site, along with interactive forms (Lessons 11 and 12), can put your Web site up with the best of them! The keys to a successful Web site include:

- Good management
- Interesting and frequently updated graphics
- Timely information
- Interactivity

You're at the last part of interactivity. If you've been building your Web site as you read through the previous lessons, adding these last features brings your basic design phase near a close.

Creating Response Forms

Using Notes application development skills, you create Notes response forms that InterNotes Web Publisher will publish to the Web. Response forms allow documents to appear indented beneath their main document. For more information on response documents, see Part III, "Application Development."

Applying response capabilities to your Web site involves only two steps:

- Create the response form.
- Add a $$Response field to the main form and place the name of the Response form in the Help Description of the Field Properties box. This field forms the link to the response form.

The standard use of response forms is in discussion databases. Figure 13.1 shows the response form of a discussion database in Design mode. This form is given an alias $$Web that tells InterNotes Web Publisher to publish the form to the Web.

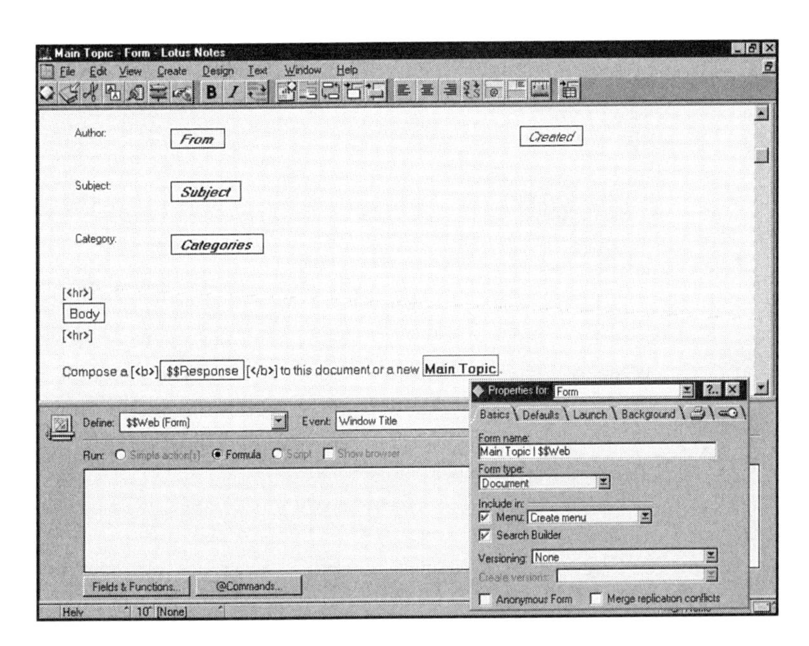

Figure 13.1 Response form in Design mode.

The main document for this database has a $$Response field. The name of the response form is listed in the Properties Help description box.

Figure 13.2 shows a discussion database view on the Web. As a result of creating response type documents, you can see that the response forms are indented under the main topic.

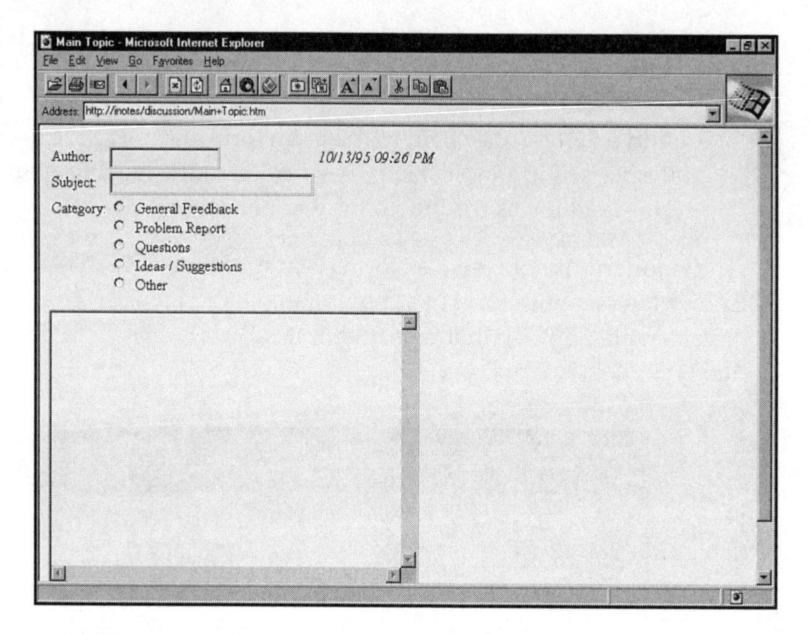

Figure 13.2 Response form on the Web.

CAUTION

Where's the Graphics? If you include graphics in a response form, you may not see those graphics on the Web while the response document is being created by the Web user. Once the form is saved and becomes a document, the graphics will appear.

Using CGI Scripts in Forms

CGI (Common Gateway Interface) Script provides a way of transferring information between two programs that were not designed to share information with each other.

InterNotes Web Publisher includes a CGI script called *inotes.exe* that resides in the companion Web server's script directory. The inotes.exe CGI script is the component part of InterNotes Web Publisher that delivers Web user input (search queries and submitted forms) back to the Notes server for processing.

Here is some information on CGI variables, for both interactive forms and response forms:

- You can add fields to any interactive form where the field name of a given field is one of the listed CGI variables. If you do so, the inotes CGI script will automatically gather the information from the user and deliver it to the Notes server for further processing.
- You can add fields to a response form that will allow you to capture information from Web users. The field name is actually the CGI environment variable to your forms that allows you to capture information from Web users. You should apply Hide when editing attributes to these fields so Web users don't see the fields.

Here are some common CGI variables (and their Notes field names) recognized by inotes.exe:

Auth_Type	Protocol-specific authentication method used to validate the user.
Content_Length	Length of content.
Content_Type	Content type for attached information.
Gateway_Interface	The CGI specification revision for the server.
HTTP_Accept	From the HTTP headers, the MIME type that the client will accept.
HTTP_User_Agent	The browser that the client is using.
Path_Info	The extra information attached at the end of the pathname untranslated.
Path_Translated	The PATH_Info translated.
Query_String	The information after the ? in the URL that is referencing the script.
Remote_Addr	The IP address of the remote host.
Remote_Host	The name of the remote host.

Remote_Ident	The remote user name retrieved from the server.
Remote_User	The username used for authentication.
Request_Method	Method used to make the request.
Script_Name	The virtual path of the script being executed.
Server_Name	The name of the server as hostname, DNS, or IP address as it appears in self-referenced URLs.
Server_Port	The port number that the request was sent to.
Server_Protocol	The information protocol for the request, shown by name and revision.
Server_Software	The information server software answering the request, by name and version.

Understanding Searches

You'll want to make it easy for Web users to search for information in your databases. The InterNotes Web Publisher gives you the tools you need:

- The Web user enters search criteria in an HTML form and submits it.
- Web Publisher then searches the Notes database and gives the Web user a list of links to documents that match the search criteria. This search includes only those documents in the Notes database that have not changed since the last publication date. Newer documents will not be included in the search results.

CAUTION

Remember In order to make searches work for your Web site, the InterNotes Web Publisher, the Notes server, the HTTP server, and the databases you want to search must all be installed on the same computer. Each database must have a full-text index (refer to Part III, "Application Development," for more information on creating a full-text index for a database).

To make searches work for your database, you must place *search bars* on your forms into which users will enter the search query (see Figure 13.3). Full-text search works much the same way on the Web as it does in Notes. The user can search for words, phrases, numbers, or dates. Queries can include wildcards or logical operators (AND, OR).

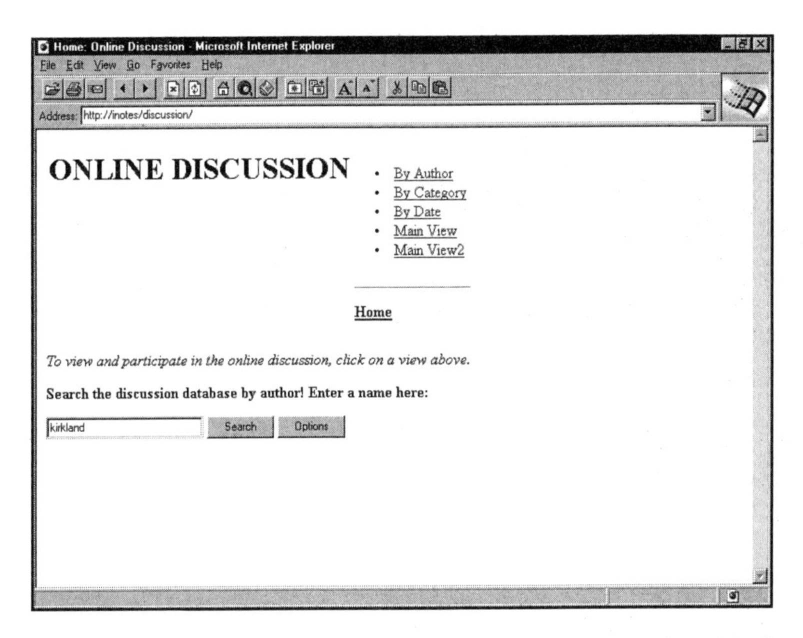

Figure 13.3 The search bar as it appears in the Web browser version of the home page.

When the Web Publisher displays the search results, it uses an existing view to present them to the Web user. A search bar appears at the top of the view, so the user can initiate additional searches from there without returning to the page where the original search bar was located. Additional searches work only on the results of the previous search.

Creating Search Bars

Search bars can appear on the home page or view pages of any database you publish. Before you can create the search bar, however, you must create a form to customize the display of the page. See Lesson 4 for more information on creating custom home pages and Lesson 8 about creating custom view forms.

The search bar appears on your form where you place a $$ViewSearchBar field. If the field appears on the home page form, you must specify a view where InterNotes Web Publisher can display the search results.

To include a search bar on your home page or view page:

1. Open your home page form.
2. Position your cursor where you want the search bar to appear.
3. Choose **Create, Field** from the menu.
4. Name the field **$$ViewSearchBar** (see Figure 13.4).

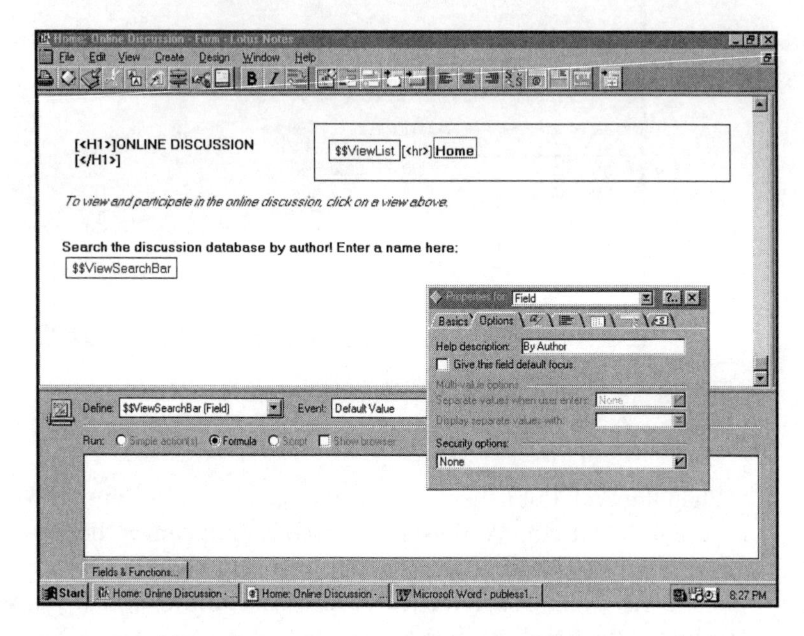

Figure 13.4 The $$ViewSearchBar field on the home page form.

5. On the Options page of the Properties box, enter the name of the view you want to use to display your search results in the `Help Description` box (see Figure 13.5).
6. Save and close the form.

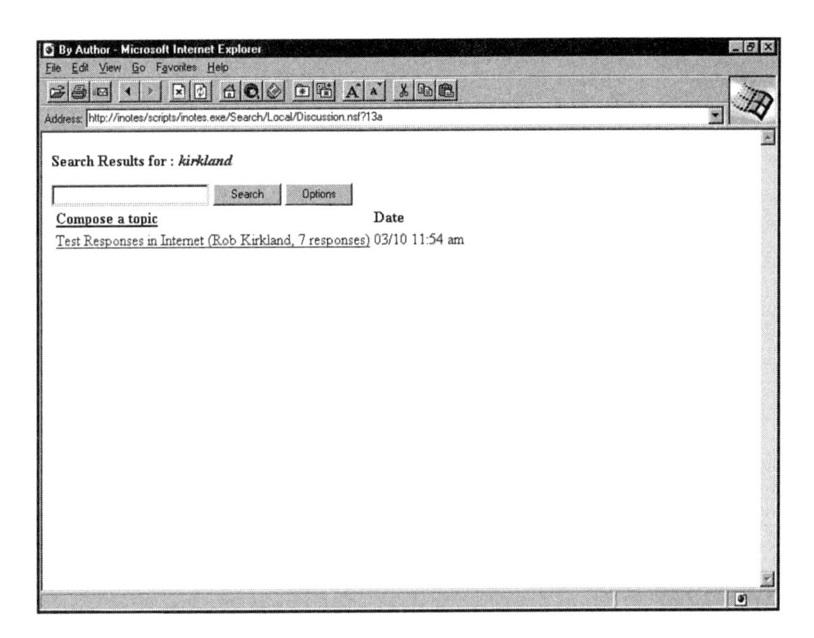

Figure 13.5 The search results on a view page.

Avoiding Graphic Placeholders

Any graphics you used on your view form or in a subform attached to your view form won't appear when you see the search results. Instead, all you see are little graphic placeholders where your graphics should be. That's because this result form is CGI generated. You may not be happy with this result.

To create a workaround, look at the history of how you built this view:

- Let's suppose you had a view called **courses**. You then created a form for this view that contains your company logo. You called this form **courses on the Web** and you added the $$ViewBody field. And in the $$ViewBody Help Description field of the Properties box, you placed the view name **courses**.
- Now, you create a search bar on your home page to search **courses**, and you name the *view* **courses** (not the form name **courses on the Web**) as the view to search. Because you have created the form **courses on the Web**, InterNotes Web Publisher will print the resulting *form*, not the view, and you'll have graphic placeholders on your view.

The workaround to this is to create a second view, **courses2**. This view should not be included in any forms with graphics. Use courses2 as the view for the $$ViewBody field on your home page, and your search results will not have graphic placeholders.

Searching from the Web

When you insert a $$ViewSearchBar field on a form, InterNotes Web Publisher publishes the search bar with two buttons on it: a Search button and an Options button as seen in Figure 13.6. These buttons are created by InterNotes Web Publisher when you include the $$ViewSearchBar field. Remember that InterNotes Web Publisher will not publish any buttons that you design in your form except for the submit button.

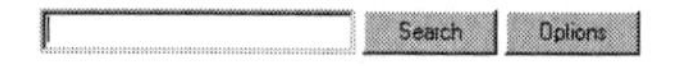

Figure 13.6 The search bar.

The Options button opens a dialog box that lets Web users specify how they want to see the search results. They can limit the number of documents that appear as a result of the search and have the results sorted.

The sort options include:

- **Sorted by Relevance** Selecting this Show Results option sorts the documents that meet the search criteria by the number of occurrences of the search string that appear in each document. Therefore, a document where the search string appears four times would probably be higher ranked in the sort than a document with only one reference. However, the ranking also depends on the length of the document, so a shorter document with fewer references may be ranked higher than a long document with the same number of references (see Figure 13.7).
- **Sorted by Date (Ascending)** Use this option when you want to see the resulting documents in date order, with the oldest document appearing last.
- **Sorted by Date (Descending)** Use this option when you want to see the resulting documents in date order, with the most recent document appearing first.

- **Include Word Variants** Check this Query Option to search for words that have the same root as the word in your search string. Thus, if your search string is **embed**, the search will include **embedded**, **embedding**, **embeds**, and **embed**.

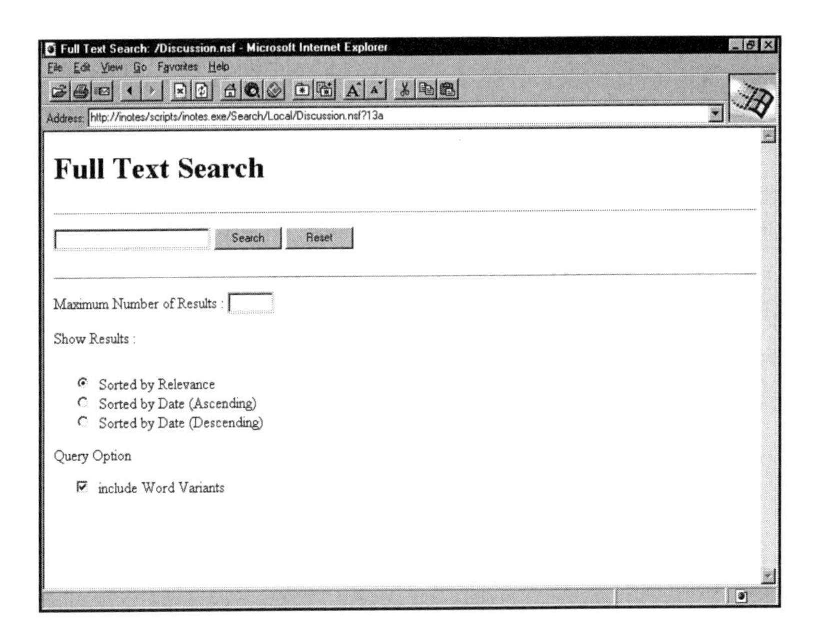

Figure 13.7 The Full Text Search dialog box.

In this lesson, you learned how to add search bars to your home and view pages. In the next lesson, you'll learn about using attachments and how to write formulas that differentiate between Web users and Notes users.

Publisher Pointers

In this lesson, you learn some pointers for fine-tuning your application for the Web.

Using Attachments

The attachments you place in your Notes documents will appear on the Web (see Figure 14.1).

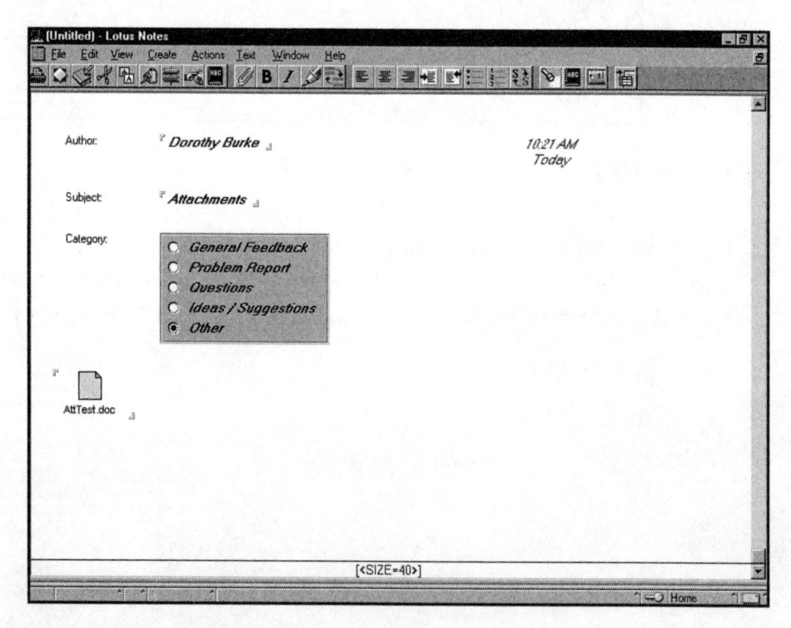

Figure 14.1 The attachment as it appears on the Web page.

Web users can **Shift-Click** an attachment to save it to a file. From that point, the method of saving the file differs depending on the Web browser you're using.

OLE and the Web

Lotus Notes supports object linking and embedding (OLE), but if you place an OLE object in a document that publishes to the Web, the link will be lost. The object acts the same as any pasted object. Double-clicking it does not activate the link because the link is nonexistent on the Web.

This also affects Lotus Components. If you are using Components, for example, you can embed a spreadsheet in your Notes document in which you can put values and formulas. A Notes user who has components installed can open and edit that Component object. Components rely on OLE; therefore, publishing a component to the Web has only one result: The Web user can see the component but cannot edit it. The spreadsheet will appear on the Web as if you took a picture of it—with columns, rows, titles, and data.

Using Different Forms for Web versus Notes Users

When you want to use the same database for both Notes users and Web users, Notes users are going to see the HTML code you've placed on your forms when they work with those documents. For example, if you've used a link to another view or document, the Web users will see the hypertext but the Notes users will see code.

The solution to this is to use separate forms for the different user groups:

- The forms should contain the same fields, but the document for the Notes users will have the button while the Web form will have the HTML code.
- The Notes response form and the Web response form will also be similar. Add a hidden Form field on the Notes documents naming the corresponding Web form.
- If you name the Notes document **Suggestion** and its response document **Comments**, you might call your Web documents **WebSuggestion** and **WebComments**. Then on the Suggestion document, the hidden field would contain WebSuggestion; the Comments document hidden field would contain WebComments.

The second part of this solution is to also create separate but similar views:

- In the view for Notes, users enter the following formula: **@If(@IsNewDoc; @Success; Form = "WebSuggestion"; "Suggestion"; Form = "WebComments"; "Comments"; @Success)**.
- As a result, all your documents will have a form value of **WebSuggestion** or **WebComments**, Web documents because you used these names when you created them and Notes documents because you defined a form variable with these values. When Notes users create new documents, the formula has no effect.

The benefit here is that all of the documents will open in Notes, and Notes users will see them using the Suggestion or Comments forms. But when you publish the database to the Web, use the view you prepared for Web use. You do not need to specify a formula for this view because all the documents have a form value of either WebSuggestion or WebComments.

Using Formulas that Detect Web versus Notes

Another solution to some of the problems that occur when you use the same database for both Web and Notes users is to use formulas that evaluate differently for the Notes client than they do for the Web user.

The success of this solution hangs on a new R4 @ function: @UserRoles. When you use the @UserRoles function, you get a list of the roles assigned to the current user. The InterNotes Web Publisher sees $$WebPublisher as one of the values returned by @UserRoles. Because of this, you can use a formula that evaluates as TRUE if the page is on the Web and FALSE if it isn't.

Consider these examples:

- The following formula tests *x* for a text string beginning with **$$Web** and accepts it anywhere in the list returned by the @UserRoles function. **@Contains(@Implode("*x*" : @UserRoles; "<>"); "<>$$Web")**
- This formula will hide a paragraph for Notes users but will show it on the Web if you choose the **Hide-When attribute, Hide paragraph if formula is true**

  @If(@Contains(@Implode("*x*" : @UserRoles; "<>");"<>$$Web") @False; @True).
- If you'd like to display documents using their Notes forms in Notes but want to use a form on the Web that is specific to the Web, try using this form formula:

```
@If(@Contains(@Implode("x" : @UserRoles; "<>"); "<>$$Web"); "Web"
+ Form; "").
```

The @UserRoles feature will work in some situations but not in others. The following list describes where this feature is effective and where it is not.

@UserRoles Will Work for:	*@UserRoles Will Not Work for:*
Computed fields in documents	Agent formulas (they aren't supported by the Web Publisher in any case)
Computed subform formulas	Button formulas (they aren't supported by the Web Publisher in any case)
Default value formulas	Selective replication formulas (which wouldn't involve the Web Publisher anyway)
Form formulas in views	View column formulas
Hide-paragraph formulas	View selection formulas
Input translation formulas	
Input validation formulas	
Keyword formulas (used to compute the list of keywords on a form)	
Window title formulas on documents	

Interesting Effects with Tables and Horizontal Lines

Tables created in Notes will appear on the Web, but Notes doesn't support merging cells. You can simulate the merging of cells by adding HTML code to give the table that appearance on the Web.

Figure 14.2 shows a table in a Notes document that has one row and two columns. We then entered our text and HTML code for horizontal rules to create the appearance of a merged cell in the first column, as shown in Figure 14.3.

In this lesson, you learned some advanced features and pointers for Web publication. In the next lesson, you'll learn how to get help concerning Web Publisher.

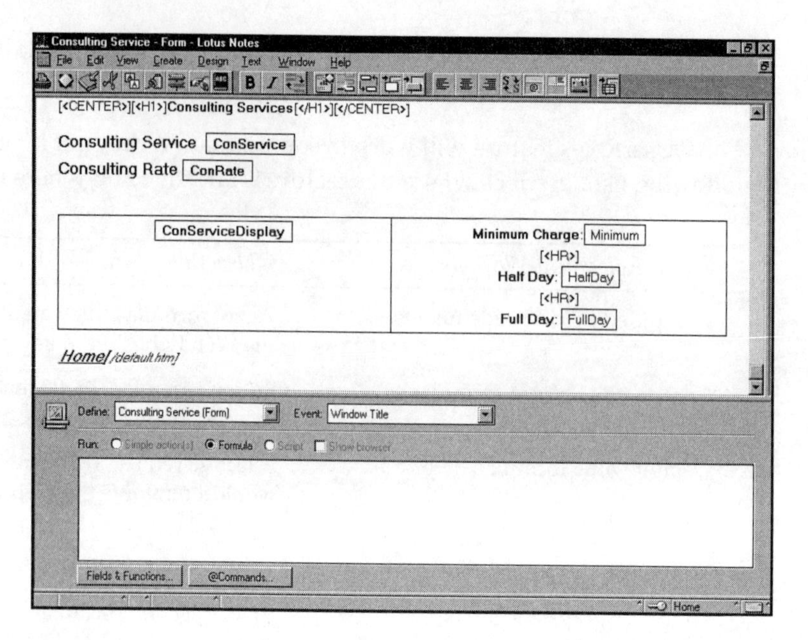

Figure 14.2 The Notes table with the HTML codes.

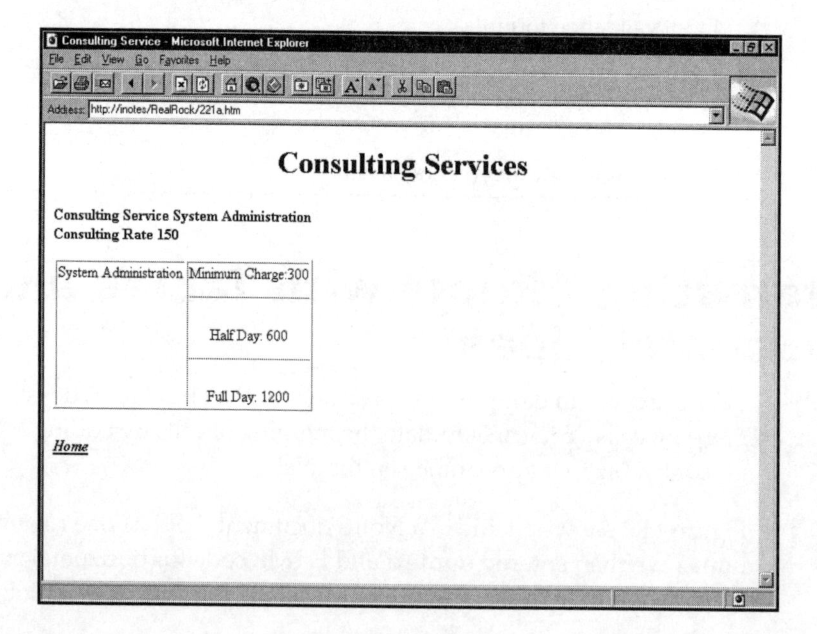

Figure 14.3 The table as it appears on the Web.

Getting Help

15

In this lesson, you learn where to go for help when you're working with Lotus Notes and the InterNotes Web Publisher.

Several databases come with InterNotes Web Publisher. Two are help type databases: the Web Publisher Guide and the Web Publisher Toolkit (see Figure 15.1).

Figure 15.1 The Web Publisher Guide and the Web Publisher Toolkit database icons.

A third database, Mercury Sports, is a sample Web site. When you enable publication, Web Publisher begins publishing Mercury Sports automatically. Use this database to see how a Web site and Web pages work.

The Web Publisher Guide

The *Web Publisher Guide* is a Lotus Notes database that acts as an online manual on how to install, configure, and use the InterNotes Web Publisher. This book assumes a knowledge of network systems or Lotus Notes application development.

There are Index and Table of Contents views to help you find the topics in which you're interested (see Figure 15.2). Double-click the document you want to read. The documents contain step-by-step instructions, as well as brief explanations of concepts. Stars appear in the left margin to indicate unread pages, so you'll know if you already checked a particular document. Use the `My Favorite Documents` folder to store pages you refer to often.

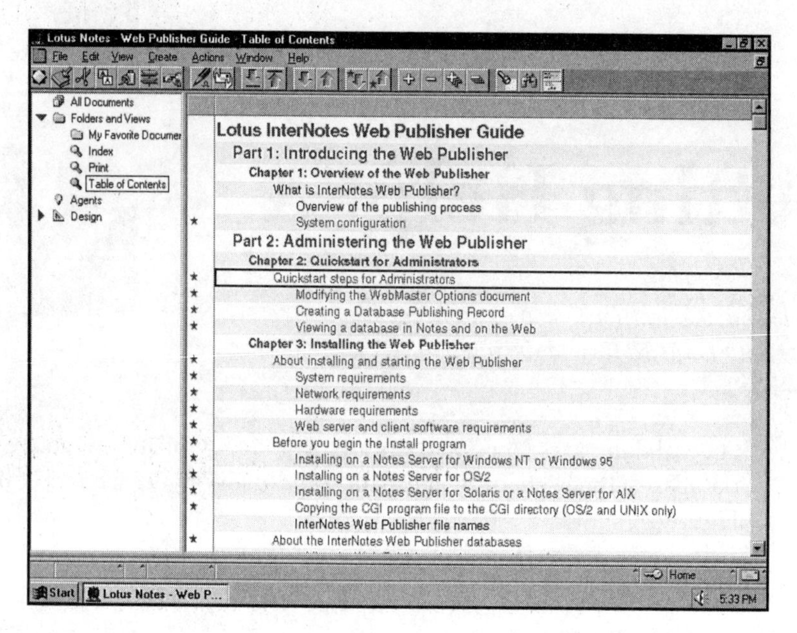

Figure 15.2 The Table of Contents view of the Web Publisher Guide.

You may also print documents from the Web Publisher Guide.

1. Open the Web Publisher Guide database and switch to the **Print** view.
2. Select the documents you want to print.
3. Choose **File, Page Setup** from the menu.
4. Set the starting page number and the page margins.
5. Click **OK**.
6. Choose **File, Print** from the menu.
7. Set the number of **Copies** you want to print.
8. From the **Document separation** drop-down list, choose **Extra Line**.
9. Click **OK**.

To print the entire book, click the **Print it all** button on the action bar.

The Web Publisher Toolkit

The Web Publisher Toolkit provides examples, tips, tricks, and techniques on how to publish your Notes database on the Web. You can view the documents by category or by title.

This database is particularly useful for incorporating HTML code because it shows examples of where it needs to be used and how it works. For example, if you need to add a horizontal rule, there is a document called "HTML - Horizontal Rules" that gives you specific code for the width of the rule and the length of the rule, either in pixels or percentage of screen width. There is also specific help on using URLs in your documents (see Figure 15.3).

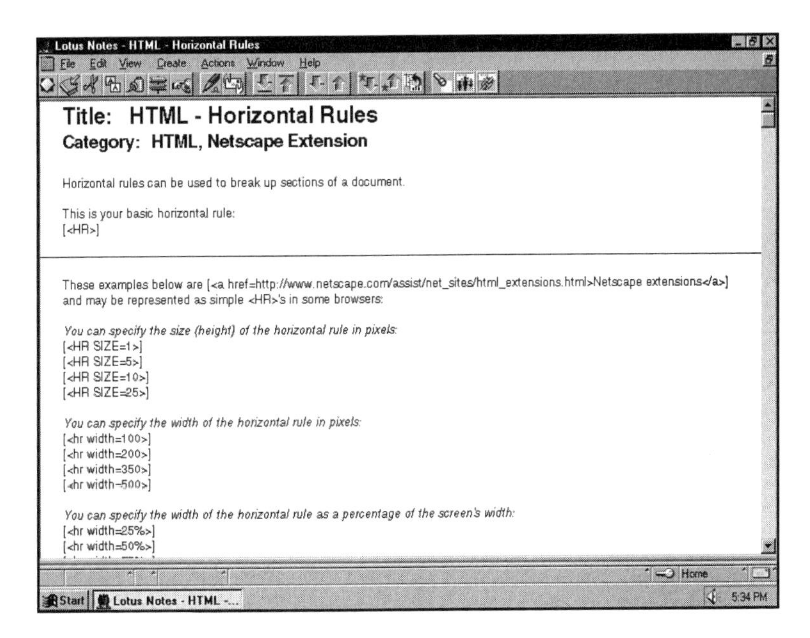

Figure 15.3 HTML - Horizontal Rules document from the Web Publisher Kit.

Select either the **Normal** or the **By Category** view to see a list of the documents in this database. Then double-click the document you want to read.

In this lesson, you learned where to get help when you're working with Lotus Notes 4.5 and the InterNotes Web Publisher.

Domino

Understanding Domino

In this lesson, you learn about Domino's HTTP Service and its capabilities. You also learn about Notes features supported by the HTTP Service and how it compares to InterNotes Web Publisher.

What Is Domino?

Domino is Lotus's new name for its Notes server. Lotus renamed it to emphasize its new connectivity to the World Wide Web. Domino includes, along with the services that it always provided to Notes users, an HTTP server that dynamically serves Lotus Notes applications to the Web. Domino "speaks" HTTP and translates Notes views, documents, navigators, and links into HTML for Web users to see. With Domino, there is no "publishing" intervention as there is with InterNotes Web Publisher. When you make a change to a Notes database or document in Notes, as soon as you save your change, you can see the change on the translated Web page.

With Domino, any Web browser can access the Notes server through Domino and:

- Access Notes databases and views
- Perform full-text searches of Notes databases
- Create, edit, and delete Notes documents (if authorized)
- Read and respond to Notes mail.

Understanding How Domino Works

A Domino server has many *server tasks* running on it simultaneously. Among the server tasks are the database server, which serves up Notes databases, and the HTTP service, which serves up HTML documents. When Notes clients request access to Notes databases, the database server provides the access. When a Web client requests an HTML document, the HTTP server task provides it. When a Web client requests access to a Notes database, the HTTP server task passes the request through to the database server and, if access is granted, converts the Notes views, documents, and forms from Notes format to HTML format, then delivers the resulting HTML pages to the Web client. If a Web client submits a form or query, the HTTP server task converts it to Notes format and submits it to the Notes database server, which processes it appropriately (see Figure 1.1).

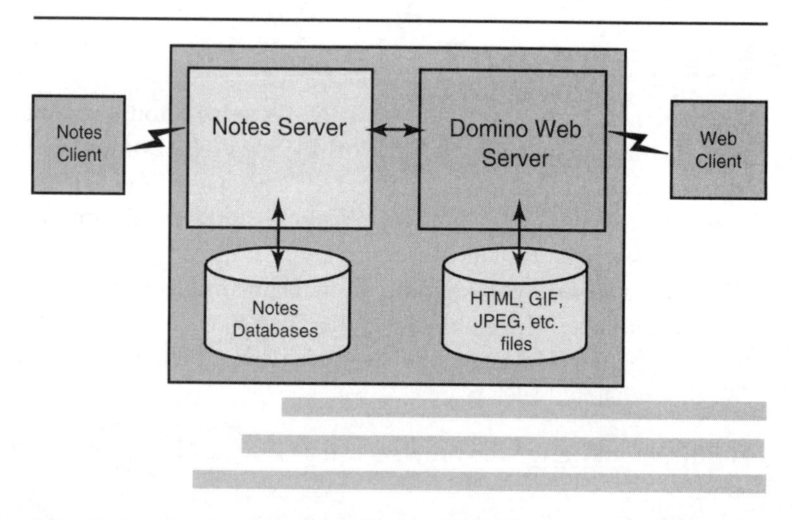

Figure 1.1 Architecture of a Domino server.

In essence, Domino is a combination Notes/Web server. Unlike InterNotes Web Publisher, it isn't necessary to tell Domino which databases to publish and to fill out forms containing information on those databases. Once the Domino software is installed on your Notes server (and your Notes Administrator runs the HTTP server task on the Notes server), Web users can retrieve your Notes databases. This is not to say that anyone with a Web browser can access every database. There is Notes database security through database, view, form, and document access lists, and field security. These are all valid forms of security with Domino.

Viewing a Domino Web Site with a Web Browser

Domino automatically links related elements in a database to one another. That is, a Notes view consists of a list of links to the Notes documents that appear in the view. Notes database designers can also link databases to one another or to other sites by adding links manually. Database designers can add links in the form of standard Notes links or special URL links. Domino extends the URL interface to include some of the Notes naming structures to the Web client. A Domino link can contain a path to a Notes object (database, document, view, and so on) and the action you want to perform. A URL link includes the URL of an external document or site. Here is a sample of some Domino URLs (where *domino* is the server name, *lotus.com* the domain name, *dominodisc.nsf* the database name, and *main topic* the view name):

- Open a site home page: **http://domino.lotus.com**
- Open a Domino server: **http://domino.lotus.com/?Open**. This displays a list of databases on the server.
- Open a database on a Domino server: **http://domino.lotus.com/dominodisc.nsf/?Open**
- Open a view: **http://domino.lotus.com/dominodisc.nsf/main+topic**

In this lesson, you learned about Domino's HTTP service and which Notes functions and design features it will support. You also learned about some Notes features not supported by Domino's HTTP service. In the next lesson, you'll learn how to prepare your Web site.

Designing a Web Site

In this lesson, you learn about planning a Web site and about the components of a Domino Web site. You also see the default view at a Domino site.

Domino Web Site Components

The database designer (you) and the Notes Administrator determine *which* databases, documents, forms, and views are accessible to Web users. The components of a Domino Web site are:

- **Databases** Every Domino Web site exposes at least one Notes database to the HTTP server for Web viewing. However, you are not limited to one database; your site can contain many databases. A combination of the database ACL, the database properties settings, and the Server document control access to a database. You and the Notes Administrator work together to set access rights.
- **Forms** A Web user can access forms on the Web only if the database designer provides an Action Bar action, an Action hotspot, or an URL link to the form. When the Web user fills out a form, Domino converts and saves it as a Notes document.
- **Documents** You control which documents the Web user can see by using selection formulas in your views.
- **Fields** You control which fields are accessible to Web users through form design and Hide-when formulas.
- **Views** You control which views are accessible to Web users through View access lists. Collapsible views will publish as such to the Web.

- **Navigators** Will appear as image maps on a Web page.
- **Home Pages** Every site needs a home page. With Domino, you can also have a home page for every database.
- **Links** Notes databases, documents, and view links, as well as URL links, are supported by Domino. Use your Notes application development skills to create links. See Part III, "Application Development," for more information.
- **Formulas** Most of your Notes formulas and @functions will work. Exceptions are noted throughout this part of the book.
- **Agents and Actions** Actions can trigger agents or agents can be triggered by the submission of a form by Web users. Actions will appear as buttons on the Action bar above the view or document.

Notes Design Features & Functions Not Supported in Domino

Not all Notes design features and functions perform well on the Web. Those that don't fall into three categories:

1. Those not applicable to Web users.
2. Those not applicable to workstations.
3. Those that Domino cannot translate or convert to HTML.

Some of the Notes design features and functions that Domino cannot translate to HTML (#3 in the previous list) are listed next. This list is subject to change, because Lotus continually improves this product and periodically makes updates available on the World Wide Web. For an up-to-date list, visit the Lotus Web site at **www.lotus.com**. There you can find discussion databases, Lotus Release Notes (last-minute information on Domino and its performance), and files to download, such as database templates and supplemental help databases.

We've condensed this list by selecting items that are most likely to affect you. This list includes the Notes features and functions you learned in Part III, "Application Development."

Domino does not support the following form properties for Web users:

- Automatically Refresh fields
- On Create: Formulas inherit values from selected document
- On Open: Automatically enable edit mode
- On Open: Show context pane

Domino does not support the following form design elements for Web users:

- Buttons (other than one submit button per form)
- Layout Regions
- OLE objects

Domino does not support the following field properties for Web users:

- Compute after validation
- Field help
- Give this field default focus

Domino does not support the following view properties for Web users:

- On Refresh Options
- Style Options for row colors, beveled column headings, unread rows, and show selection margin
- Click column header to sort
- Resizable column
- "Show twisties" when a row is expandable

Planning Your Web Site

In planning your Domino Web site, you have three steps to take before you get to design mode. You need to decide whether to publish one or many databases to the Web. Then decide which of the databases will contain your site home page. Finally, you should talk with your Notes Administrator and develop a strategy for security on the Web. By default, all of the databases that reside on the Domino server appear in a list to Web users who know how to use the /?Open command at your Domino site. You might want to control what can be seen on that list.

Decision 1 One Database or Many?

Your Web site can contain one multipurpose database or several single-purpose databases. This depends on the purpose of your site. If you're designing the databases for the sole purpose of having a Web presence, you might be tempted to design just one multipurpose database. But there are advantages to having several single-purpose databases:

- Single-function databases are easier to create, manage, and understand.
- You can easily distribute design and content responsibilities to different departments or people.
- Smaller databases are easier to manage and replicate.

Figure 2.1 shows a diagram of a planned Web site.

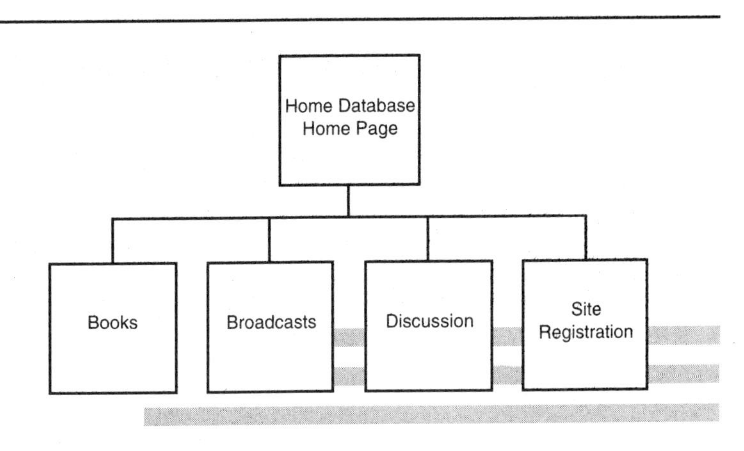

Figure 2.1 Diagram of planning our Web site.

Decision 2 Who's on First?

A Site home page is defined in the Server document. (Consult with your Notes Administrator concerning this document.) To identify the database that contains your site home page, the Notes Administrator will need to change the Home URL field in the Server document to include the name of the database. Once the database is identified in the Home URL field, Web users will see either the About Database document or the navigator you elected to launch on open. You will learn more about home pages in Lessons 3 and 4.

Figure 2.2 shows the Server document and the Home URL containing a default database. The database in this field contains the site home page.

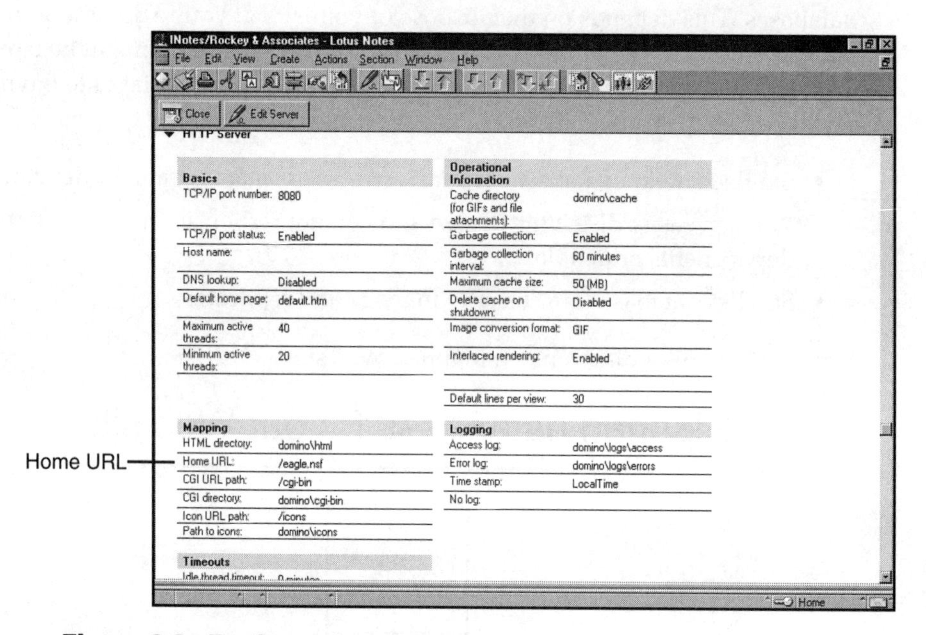

Figure 2.2 The Server document.

Decision 3 Controlling Databases on the Default View

If you don't identify a home URL, visitors to your site will see a list of databases on your server in the form of a view. (See the example in Figure 2.3.) You can have a Web site up and running in minutes if this view is acceptable to you as your site home page.

The potential dangers with this view are that Web users can see the list of databases on your Domino server. Even though they can't access all databases (you can control this through the ACL), you might not want them to even see the list. You can control which databases appear on this list in the Properties box of your database. Disable the List in Database Catalog option on the Design page of the Properties box and the database will not appear in this list.

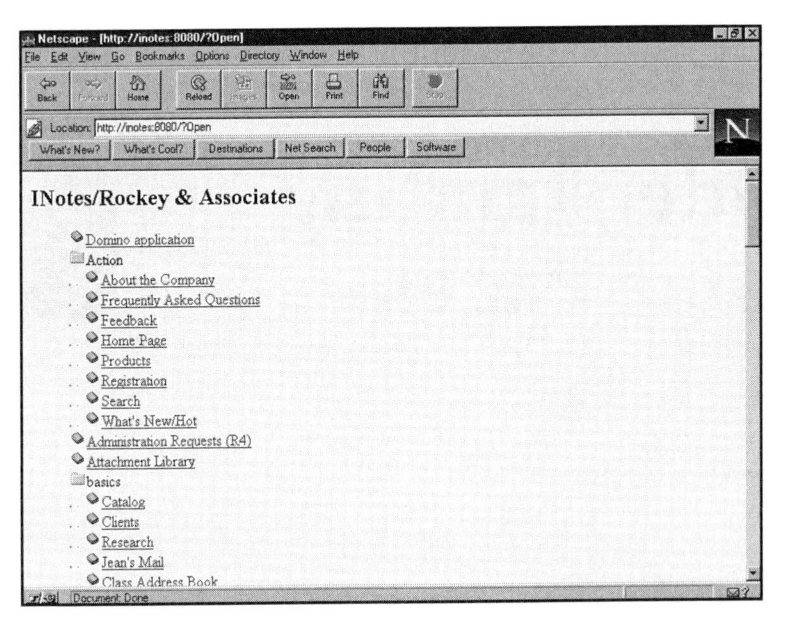

Figure 2.3 The default view of a Domino site for which no home page has been designated.

I Can't Find the Database! When you disable the List in Database Catalog option on the design page of the Properties box, your database will not appear in the list of available databases when you choose File, Database, Open from the menu. Type the database's file name in the Open dialog box and you will be able to open the database.

In Lesson 1, "Understanding Domino," you learned about Domino URLs and syntax. Disabling a database from the database view does not restrict access to it. If a Web user knows the name of your database (for example, all Notes address books are names.nsf), he can access the database with a Domino URL. Of course, he must have rights to open the database.

In this lesson, you learned the first steps to designing a Web site. You also learned which Domino features and functions will not work properly for Web users. In the next lesson, you'll learn about home pages.

Understanding Home Pages

In this lesson, you learn what a home page is and how to create a site home page using the About Database document. You also learn how to decide between using the About Database document or a Navigator for your home page.

Home Page Basics

A home page is the first screen you see when you visit a site on the Internet. Because it introduces the site, a home page should be attractive and useful. It should contain links to other documents, views, databases, or sites. The home page should also tell Web users how to get more information about your site or your company. With Domino, you can use either a Navigator as your home page or the About Database document of a database.

In addition to a site home page, you can create a home page for each database, using either the About Database document or a Navigator. If you don't create a home page for each database, the default view of the database is the view the Web user will see. (For more information on default views, see Part III, "Application Development.")

TIP **Don't Forget to Ask!** Once you've decided upon and designed your home page, you'll need to remember to ask your Notes Administrator to identify the site home page by entering the URL in the server document (see Lesson 2, "Designing a Web Site").

Creating the Site Home Page Using the About Database Document

The About Database document is essentially one big rich text field. You can add graphics and text, but not fields or subforms. The advantage of the About Database document is the ability to change it easily. If you use a navigator, you have to make changes to the original graphics in order to change any text, so it's not as flexible as the About Database document. To create the About Database document:

1. Open the database. Under Design in the Navigator pane, select **Other**. Double-click the **About Database** document.
2. Type any text that you want to appear on your home page. You can include tables or you can paste graphics (like logos), text, or links in the About Database document.
3. If you want to align graphics next to each other on the page, insert them into a table. Figure 3.1 shows a table with two graphics inserted.

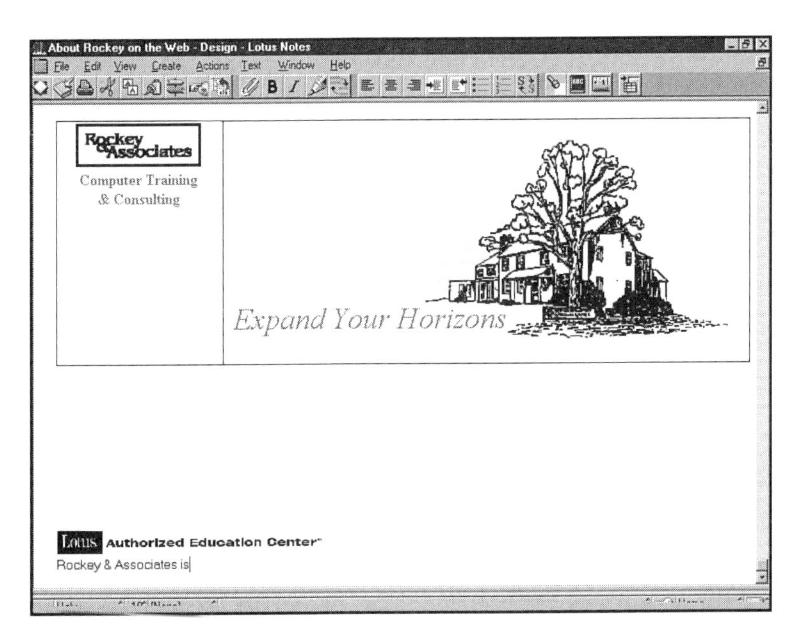

Figure 3.1 Using tables to align graphics.

4. If you use a table, remove the table borders so they don't publish to the Web. To remove the borders, select the whole table, click the Properties icon on the toolbar to bring up the Properties box, select **Table** in the

Properties for field, and then click the **Borders** tab in the Properties box. Click the button labeled **Set all to 0**. Figure 3.2 shows the Table Properties box with the Borders tab selected.

5. Exit and save the finished About Database document.

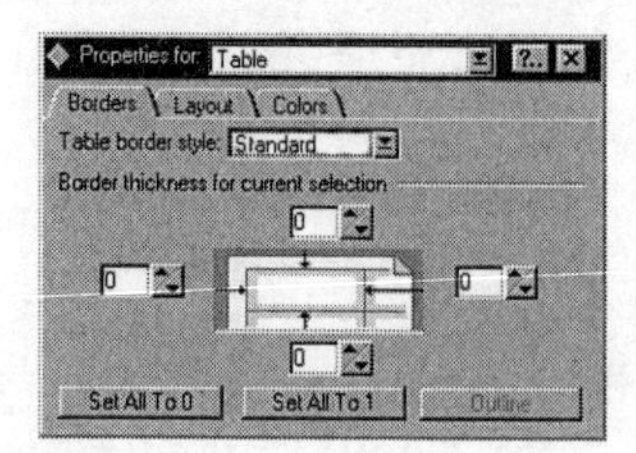

Figure 3.2 Properties box for table.

Putting Links on the Home Page

Without links to your database views and links to other databases you are publishing, your home page would be essentially useless. The next step is to add links. Part III, "Application Development," and Lessons 5 and 6 in this part also cover links, but we want links on our home page in order to test it, so we're going to do a few links here. To create the links:

1. From a view or the workspace, select the document, view, or database to which you want to link.
2. Choose **Edit, Copy as Link** and then select **Document Link**, **View Link**, or **Database Link**.
3. Return to the About Database document.
4. Enter the text you want to use as the hypertext and then select it.
5. Underline the text by choosing **Underline** from the Text Properties box.
6. With the text still selected, choose **Create, Hotspot, Link Hotspot**.
7. Save the About Database document.

Figure 3.3 shows links in design mode. Note the table and the extra cells that set the spacing for the link text.

Figure 3.4 shows a home page as seen on a Web browser. We'll show you how to create the bullets and the "New" icon in Lesson 5, "Using and Customizing Forms and Subforms."

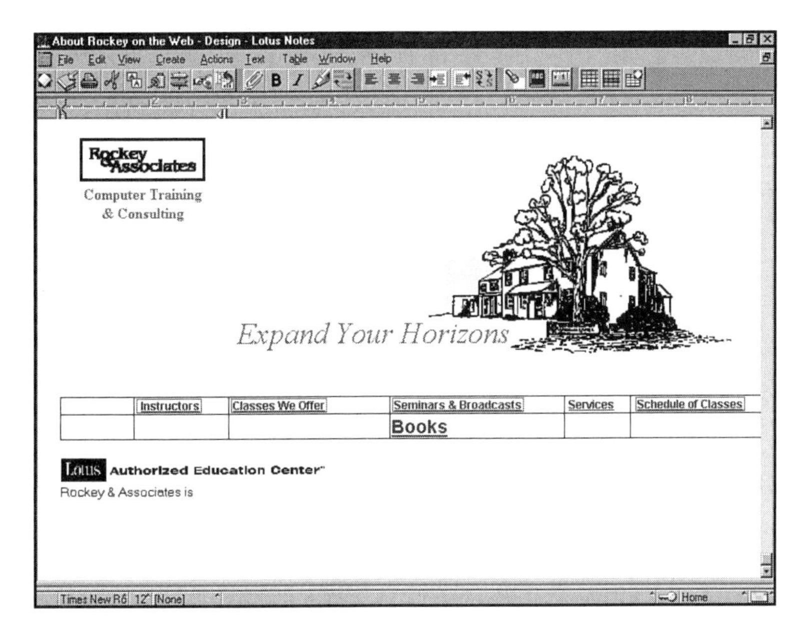

Figure 3.3 Links on the About Database document.

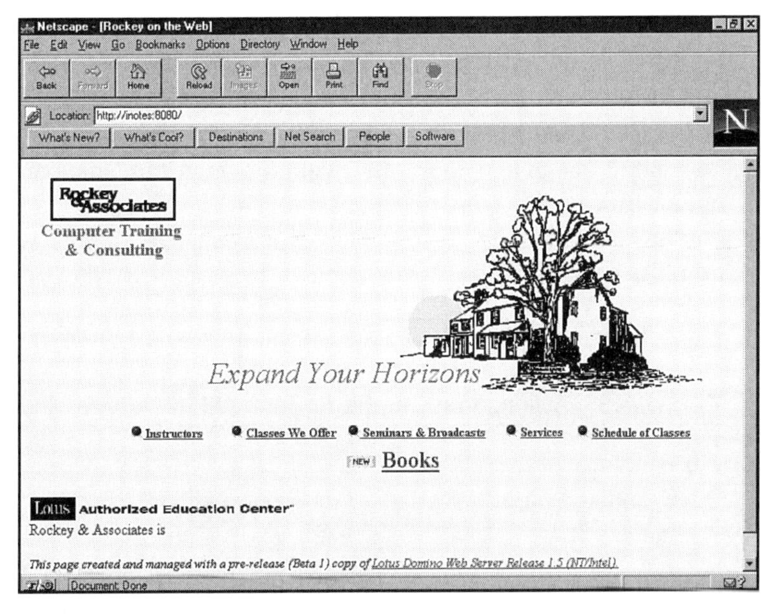

Figure 3.4 The site home page as it appears on the Web.

In this lesson, you learned how to design a site home page using the About Database document. In the next lesson, you learn how to design a graphic Navigator.

Navigators

In this lesson, you learn about Navigators and Image Maps. You also learn how to create graphic hotspots for Navigators.

Understanding Navigators and Image Maps

A Navigator will appear as an image map on the Web. An image map is a graphic in which regions of the graphic are linked to a series of URLs. Navigators enable an image map to link to URLs, Notes documents, views, or databases, or they are used to run actions.

If you want an image map on your site or database home page, you paste a graphic into a Notes Navigator. The graphic must be pasted into the Navigator as a *graphic background.* You then define action hotspots for the regions of the Navigator. The image you use for your Navigator in Notes must be a bitmap, not a vector graphic. Only bitmaps will work as Navigator/Image maps. When you need to change the text on your home page, you'll have to do so in the graphics package in which you created the graphic used in your Navigator.

You can use Navigators to perform the actions listed in Table 4.1.

Table 4.1 Actions that Can Be Performed from Image Map Hotspots

To	*Select*
Open another Navigator	Run Simple Action Open another Navigator Select the Navigator
Open a View	Run Simple Action Open a View Select the View

continues

Table 4.1 Continued

To	*Select*
Open a Link	Run Simple Action Open a Link Paste your link (Must be copied as link)
Use an @Function	Run Formula Enter your formula in the formula box.
Use LotusScript	Run Script Enter your script in the script box. (This allows you to perform sophisticated processing that is not covered in this book.)

Creating Image Maps

To create an image map:

1. Create a bitmap graphic in a graphics program.
2. Copy the bitmap to the clipboard.
3. Open the database in which you are going to use this image map. From the menu, select **Create**, **Design**, **Navigator**.
4. To paste your bitmap into the navigator screen, select **Create**, **Graphic Background**. Figure 4.1 shows the graphic background pasted into a Navigator. The text that surrounds the Navigator was part of the original graphic.

CAUTION

Don't Use Edit, Paste to Paste Your Graphic! Domino does not convert a pasted image. When you paste your graphic into the Navigator, it's critical that you use the menu commands: **Create**, **Graphic background**.

5. Right-click the mouse to bring up the Properties box and name your Navigator.
6. Determine which areas of your Navigator will act as "hotspots." To make an area an active hotspot, select **Create**, **Hotspot Rectangle** (or hotspot polygon if the area on your image is odd shaped). Your pointer will become a crosshair.

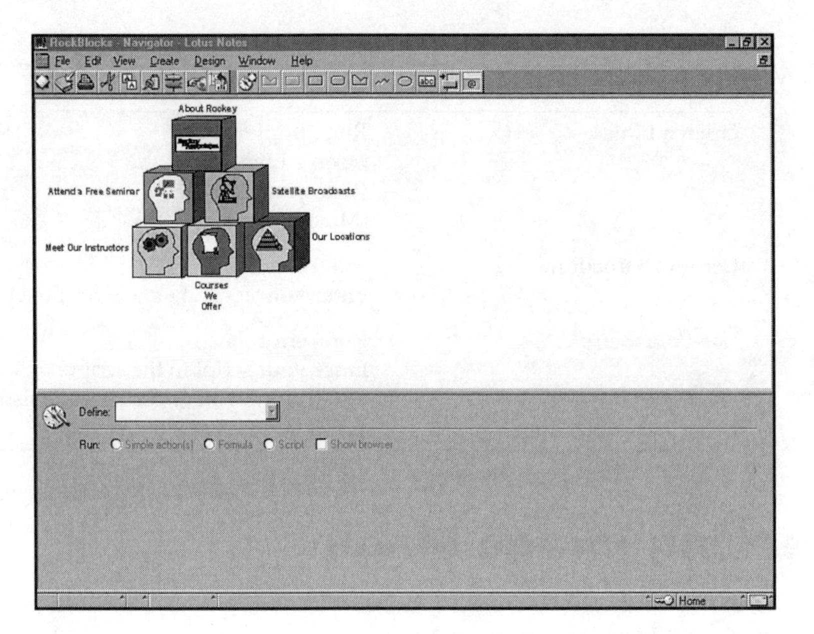

Figure 4.1 Graphic background in Navigator.

7. Click and drag over the area you want to become the hotspot. Release the mouse button after you have identified the area. If you release the mouse button too soon or your hotspot is not the right size, you can resize it by pulling on the handles.
8. Define what action this hotspot will perform by providing the information in the formula pane. Table 4.1 lists the options available. Step-by-step instructions for each of these actions appear next.
9. Repeat steps 6, 7, and 8 until you have completed all the hotspots for your Navigator. Save your Navigator and close this window.

Now that you have created the Navigator, you need to make it the default initial view for the database.

1. Return to your Notes Workspace. For the Navigator to become the home page of the Database, you need to select the Navigator as the initial view of the database. Right-click the database icon. When the pop-up menu appears, choose **Database Properties**.

2. Click the launch tab of the Properties Box. In the **On Database Open** field, select **Open designated Navigator**. In the drop-down list under **Navigator**, select the name of your Navigator. Close the properties box. See Figure 4.2.

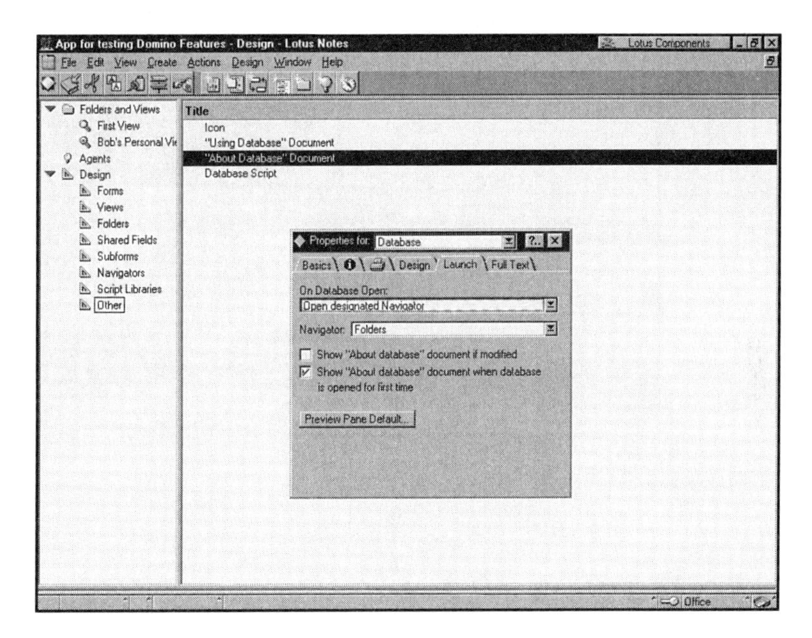

Figure 4.2 The Launch panel of the Database Properties box.

Test your Navigator by opening the database on the Web or through a Web browser on your intranet.

To Open Another Navigator

1. Follow steps 1 through 7 of "Creating Image Maps."
2. Select **Simple Action(s)** as the **Run** option.
3. Select **Open another Navigator** in the Action list box.
4. A new list box will appear to the right of the Action list box. This new box will contain a list of all of your available Navigators. Select the Navigator you want to open (see Figure 4.3).
5. Continue at step 9 of "Creating Image Maps."

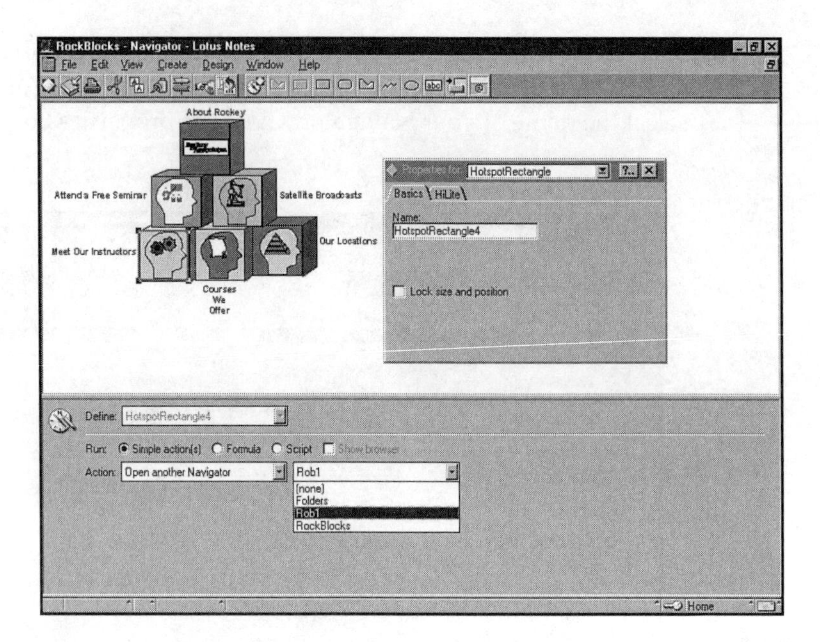

Figure 4.3 Open another Navigator.

To Open a View

1. Follow steps 1 through 7 of "Creating Image Maps."
2. Select **Simple Action(s)** as the **Run** option.
3. Select **Open a View** in the Action list box.
4. A new list box appears to the right of the Action list box. This new box contains a list of all of your available views. Select the view you want to open.
5. Continue at step 9 of "Creating Image Maps."

To Open a Link

1. Follow steps 1 through 7 of "Creating Image Maps."
2. Select **Simple Action(s)** as the **Run** option.
3. Select **Open a Link** in the Action list box.
4. Using the Window command from the menu, switch to your workspace and open the database, view, or document to which you want to link. Select **Edit**, **Copy as Link**, then choose **Document Link**, **View Link,** or **Database Link**.

5. Switch back to your Navigator. A new button labeled **Paste Link** appears to the right of the Action list box (see Figure 4.4). Click this button to paste your Notes link.
6. Continue at step 9 of "Creating Image Maps."

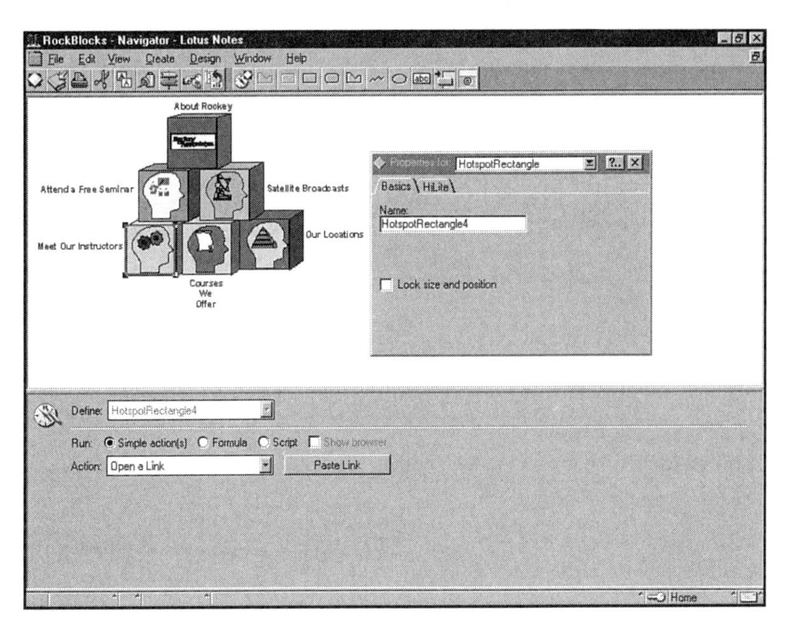

Figure 4.4 Open a Link design pane.

To Use an @Function

1. Follow steps 1 through 7 of "Creating Image Maps."
2. Select **Formula** as the Run option.
3. Enter your formula in the formula box (see Figure 4.5). Use the @function @URLOpen("*URL*") where ("URL") is the full address, or explicit URL.
4. Continue at step 9 of "Creating Image Maps."

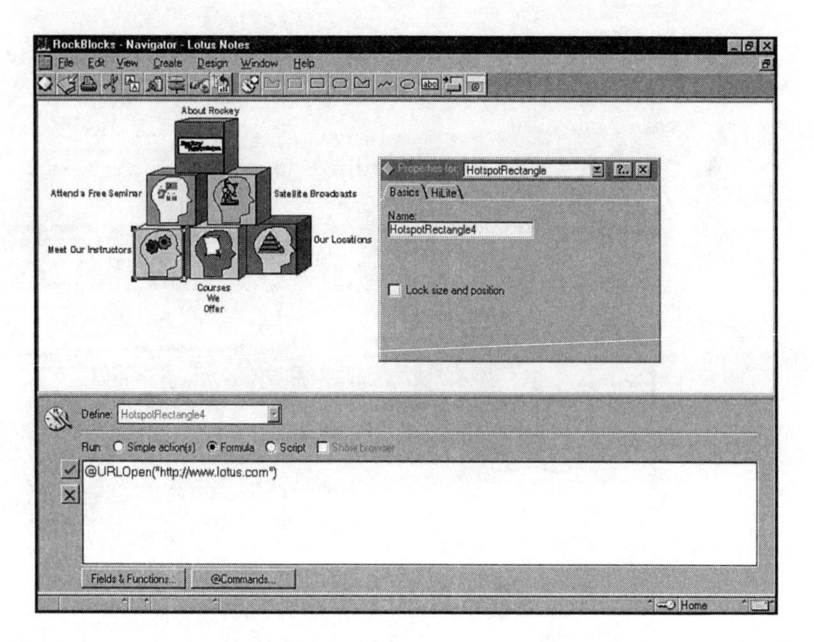

Figure 4.5 Formula design pane.

In this lesson, you learned what Navigators are used for and how to create them. You also learned how to create action hotspots for Navigators. In the next lesson, you'll learn how to use forms and subforms.

Using and Customizing Forms and Subforms

In this lesson, you learn how to prepare forms and subforms for the Web. You also learn how to make input forms for Web users with customized responses to their input.

Forms for Web Users: Some Considerations

You learned about creating forms and subforms in Part III, "Application Development." The forms and subforms you created in Notes will be converted to HTML by Domino. When creating forms for Web users, consider the following:

- Text formatting: Domino will convert Notes text formatting features to HTML tags. Not all Notes text formatting will appear to Web users and not all browsers support all of the HTML tags used by Domino.
- HTML, URLs, and CGI variables: You can include HTML code, URLs, and CGI variables in your forms and documents. For more information, refer to Part IV, "InterNotes Web Publisher."
- Form access: Web users will not be able to create documents by choosing them from a menu, as Notes users can. To make forms accessible to Web users, you must create an Action Bar action, an Action hotspot, or an HTML link to the form.
- Buttons: Except for items on the Action bar of a form or view, all Notes buttons become Submit buttons when Domino converts them. It's not necessary to create any Submit buttons at all, because Domino will

automatically generate a Submit button for Web user forms. This lesson provides the steps to customize the label of the Submit button.

Submit Button When you fill in a form on the World Wide Web, you return the completed form to the Web server by clicking a button. This button is called a Submit button because the word Submit usually appears on it.

Formatting Text

Domino supports the following Notes text formatting features:

- Font colors
- Typeface styles (monospace versus proportional). To preserve spaces, use Courier.
- Font Sizes (mapped by Domino to HTML sizes shown in Table 5.1)
- Bullets
- Named Styles

Domino does not map font sizes to HTML headers. Table 5.1 lists the Notes font size as it is mapped by Domino to HTML sizes.

Table 5.1 Font Size Mapping—Domino to HTML

Notes Font Size	*HTML Font Size*
<=8	1
<=10	2
<=12	3
<=14	4
<=18	5
<=24	6
>24	7

The actual size of HTML font sizes 1 through 7 depends on what browser you use. Different browsers map the HTML font sizes to different type sizes. HTML size 3 is usually the default for body text, so you should define the font size of body text in your Notes forms to be greater than 10 points and less than or equal to 12 points.

Domino supports the following paragraph formatting:

- Center and right align.
- Inter-paragraph spacing, such as double.

HTML does not support inter*line* spacing, Notes indentation, or tabs, so any such formatting in Notes is ignored.

Accessing Forms

Domino can gather information provided by Web users and make that information available in Notes by translating your Notes forms to HTML forms, and translating the completed HTML form back to a Notes document. But you need to point the way for the Web user so that he can access your form.

Figure 5.1 displays a Notes form as viewed through a Web browser. This form contains information about a Notes class. Web users can register for this class by clicking the Action **Register for this Course**. When creating Actions, you can refer to Lesson 12 of Part III, "Application Development."

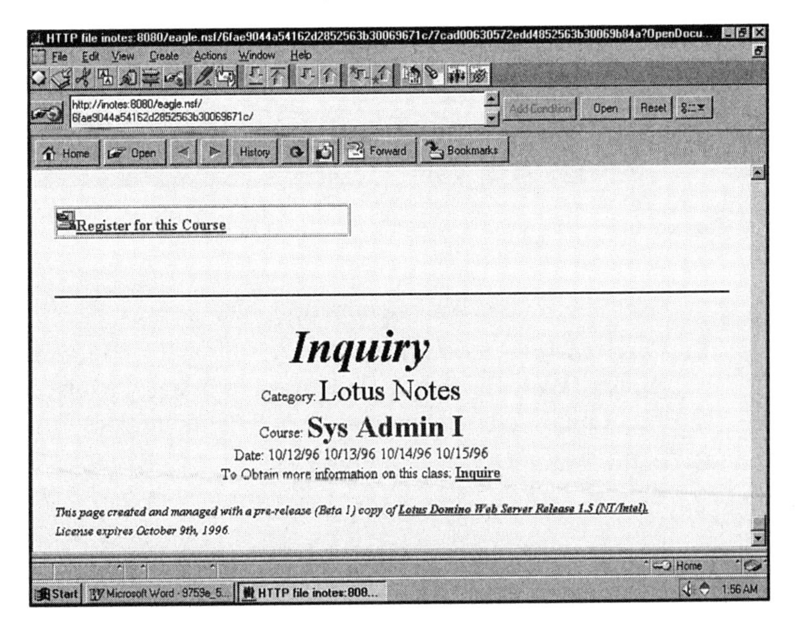

Figure 5.1 A Notes Action on the Web.

Using Actions

To create an Action to access a form:

1. Open the form that will contain the Action in Design mode.
2. Choose **Create, Action** from the menu. Click the Action pane icon in the toolbar.
3. The Action Properties Box appears as shown in Figure 5.2. Type a title for your action. Remember that the title will appear as a button label. Don't make it too long.

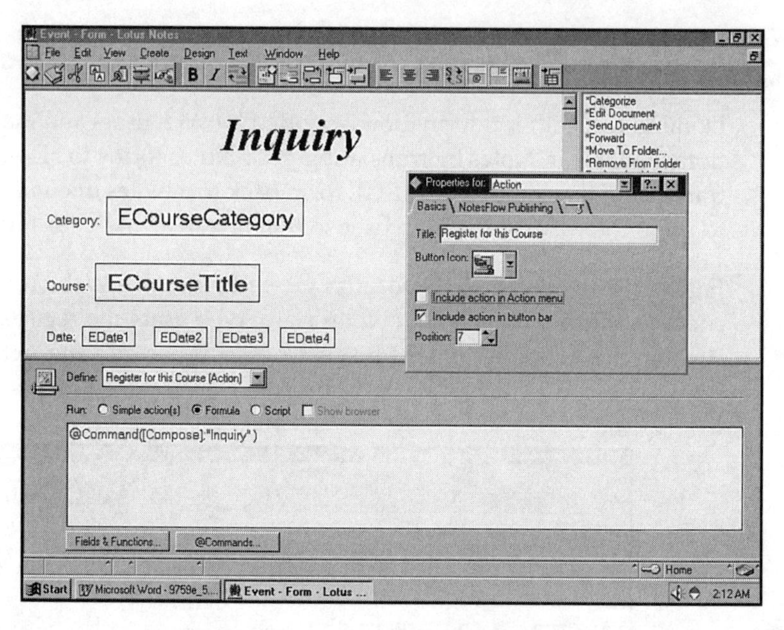

Figure 5.2 The Action Properties Box and Action Formula.

4. Select an icon for your Action (optional).
5. Check **Include action in button bar** (the action menu option does not apply to Web users). You don't need to change or select the position of the icon, unless you have more than one Action for this form.
6. In the formula pane, select **Formula**.
7. Enter the following formula.

   @Command([Compose];"*formname*")

   where "*formname*" is the form name you want filled in by the Web user (refer to Figure 5.2).

8. Save and close the form.

After the Web user fills in the form, he simply clicks the Submit button created by Domino on the form. Domino then creates a new document in the Notes database. When Web users click the Submit button, Domino responds with a confirmation message that reads `Form processed`.

TIP **Actions** You can create Actions in views. See Lesson 6, "Working with Views", for more information.

Using Action Hotspots

To create an Action Hotspot to access a form:

1. Open the form that will contain the Action hotspot in Design mode.
2. Type the text or paste the graphic into the form that will become the hotspot. Select the text or graphic and choose **Create, Hotspot, Action Hotspot** from the menu as shown in Figure 5.3.

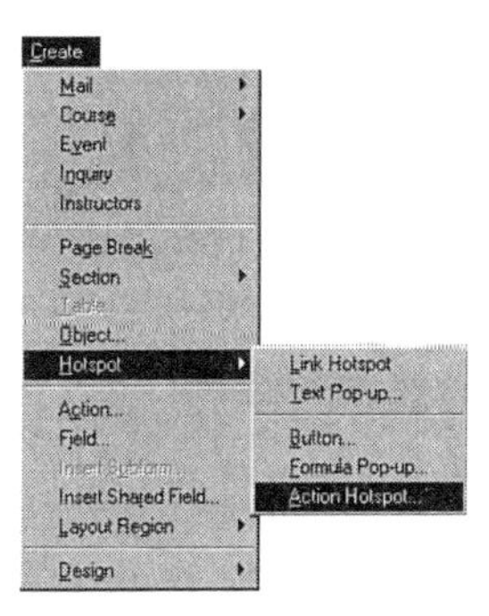

Figure 5.3 Creating an Action Hotspot.

3. In the formula pane, enter the formula for composing the form:

   @Command([compose]; "formname")

   where *formname* is the name of your form.
4. Save and close this form.

Using HTML Links

You can use HTML code and Domino URL syntax to access a form. Include the HTML code directly on the page. The syntax to link to a form is:

> [<a href="/databasename/formname?Openform">Text you wish to appear on form</a>]

Figure 5.4 shows an example of an HTML link.

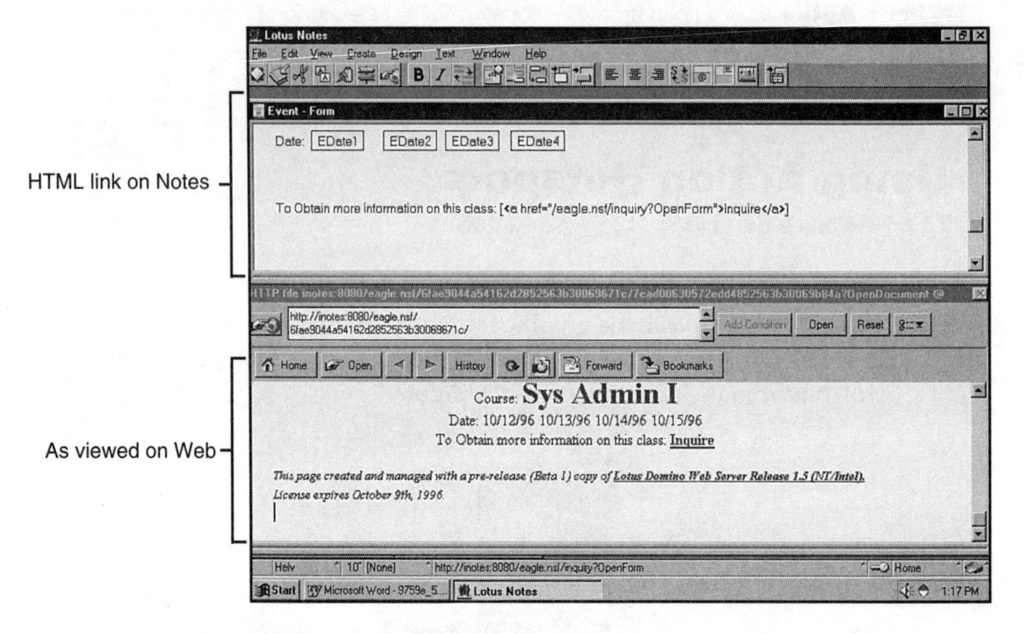

Figure 5.4 Form link syntax.

Customizing the Submit Button

When the Web user clicks your Action, the form you selected in your action formula will appear for him, ready to be completed. Figure 5.5 shows a Notes form on the Web that contains a Submit button generated by Domino. Remember, you don't need to create this button. Domino places its Submit button at the bottom of the form. You can, however, customize this button by changing its label or its position.

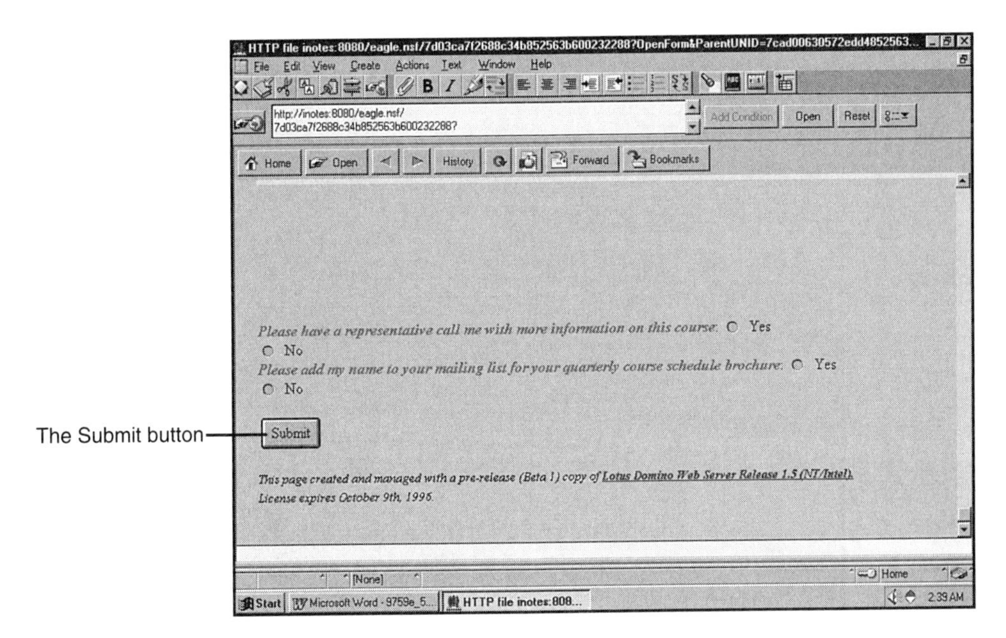

Figure 5.5 The Submit button generated by Domino.

To customize the Submit button:

1. Position your cursor in the form where you want the button to appear.
2. Select **Create**, **Hotspot**, **Button** from the menu.
3. Type a title for your button in the Button Properties Box. If you want to change the *position* of the button that Domino creates, but not the label, type **Submit** as your button title. Don't do anything else. Domino will ignore all other settings.
4. Save and close this form. Figure 5.6 shows a customized Submit button as viewed through a Web browser.

TIP **Where Have All the Buttons Gone?** Unlike InterNotes Web Publisher, Domino will only use the *first* button you create. All buttons are treated as Submit buttons. If you create multiple buttons or write any formula for a button, Domino will ignore your hard work!

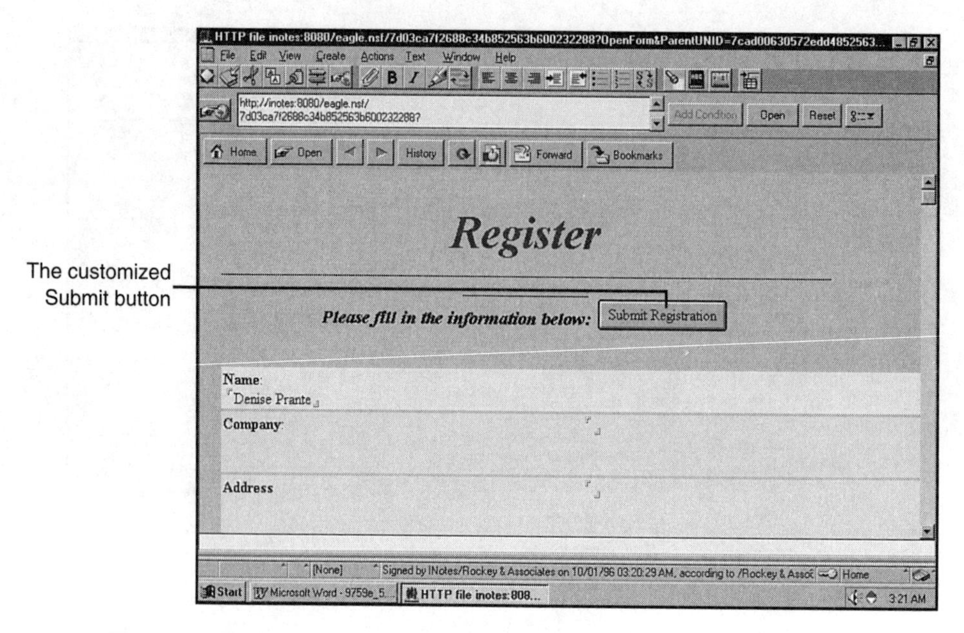

Figure 5.6 You can customize the Submit button.

Customizing Response Messages

Each time a Web user submits an input form, Domino responds by generating an HTML page with a message: "Form processed." You can customize this message to send a more personal and friendly message to your visitor.

To create a customized response:

1. Add a field to your form with the field name of $$Return. Make this field a Computed field.
2. Type the following formula in the formula pane. "InqName" in the formula is a field in the form where the user's name appears. This formula includes HTML code. In addition to personalizing a response message, it provides the Web user with a link to return to the site home page. The code <p> means "Paragraph" and moves the following text down one line:

    "Thank you, " + InqName + ", our staff will contact you within three business days." + "<p><a href=\"http://inotes:8080\">Rockey Home Page</a>"

3. Save and close the form. Figure 5.7 shows the message as it appears on a Web browser after a visitor has submitted his input form.

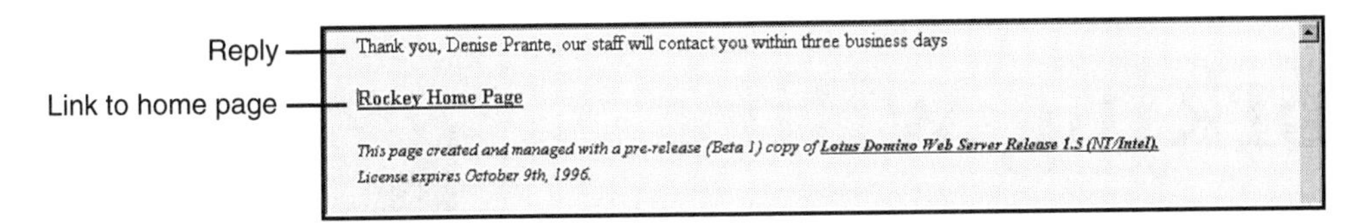

Figure 5.7 A customized response message.

Viewing Web-Generated Forms

Domino now translates the HTML input form into a Notes document. Figure 5.8 shows the Notes view, listing Web users who have registered for courses. Open the document to see the entire form.

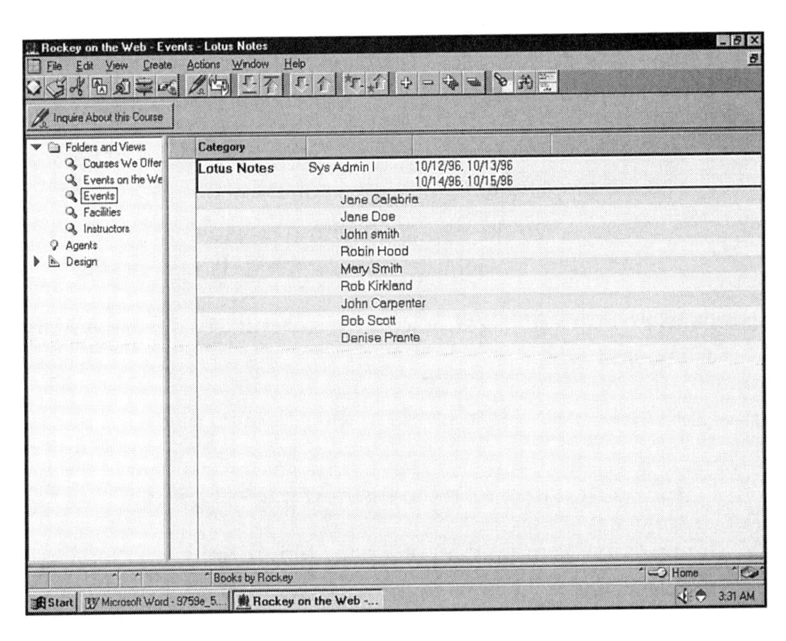

Figure 5.8 Web input forms become Notes documents.

In this lesson, you learned how to make interactive Web forms and how to view Web input forms in Notes. You also learned how to customize buttons and responses to Web users. In the next lesson, you learn about views.

Working with Views

In this lesson, you learn how Domino handles views and searches. You also learn how to create Actions for views.

Understanding Views

Domino supports most of the view functions, although you should keep these considerations in mind:

- Alternate row colors are not supported. Refer to Lesson 1, "Understanding Domino," for a list of view properties not supported by Domino.
- Notes views are expandable and collapsible by Web users and twisties are converted. By default, views open fully expanded.

Domino also adds a set of icons to expand, collapse, navigate, and search views as shown here:

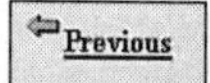

- The *Previous* icon refers to the previous page of a view.

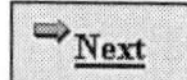

- The *Next* icon refers to the next page of a view.

If your view is more than one page of information, Web users can click the previous and next icons to move forward or back.

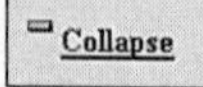

- The *Collapse* icon will collapse the entire view.

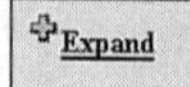

- The *Expand* icon will expand the entire view.

To collapse or expand a category of the view, Web users click the triangle (that is, the "twistie") located to the left of the category.

- The *Search* icon brings up a screen in which the user can enter search criteria, and is described more fully later in this lesson.

Using Actions in Views

You can create Actions in views. Such Actions can assist Web users and Notes users (who are using a Web browser) to navigate your site and work with documents. Depending on your database and its purpose, you might want to provide an Action to create a document, as described in Lesson 4, "Navigators," or you might want to create an Action to help users navigate through other available views.

For example, your views for a document database might include: By author, By Date, or By title. When the Web user is looking at the "By Author" view, Actions on the action bar can point him to the other views or to the site home page as shown in Figure 6.1.

Creating an @URLOpen Action

To create a view Action for the Web user to navigate to the home page:

1. In Design mode open the view that will contain the Action.
2. Choose **Create**, **Action** from the menu. Click the Action Pane icon in the toolbar.
3. The Action Properties Box appears. Type a title for your Action such as "Home Page." Remember that the title will appear as a button label. Don't make it too long.
4. Select an icon for your Action (optional).
5. Check the box labeled **Include action in button bar**. You don't need to change or select the position of the icon, unless you have more than one Action for this form.
6. In the formula pane, select **Formula**.

7. Enter the formula:

   @URLOpen("http://*URL*/*databasename.nsf*/?Open")

   where *URL* is the URL for your site and *databasename*.nsf is the file name of the database.

8. Save and close the view.

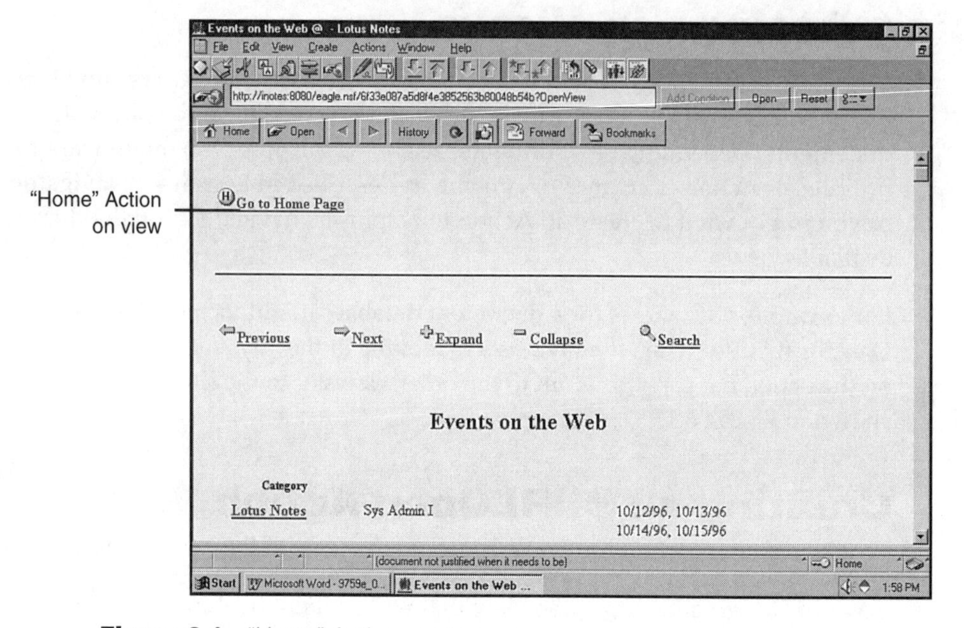

Figure 6.1 "Home" Action on view.

Because the Home Page Action is such a useful Action for each of your views in the database, you might want to include it in every view. You don't need to redesign it. You can copy it from view to view as follows:

1. Open the view that contains the Action.
2. Click the Action Pane icon in the toolbar.
3. Select the Action you want to copy.
4. Select **Edit, Copy** from the menu.
5. Open the view you want to copy the Action to.
6. Select **Edit, Paste** from the menu.

Creating an Action to Open a View

To create a view Action for a Web user to navigate to another view:

1. Open the view that will contain the Action in Design mode.
2. Choose **Create, Action** from the menu. Click the Action Pane icon in the toolbar.
3. The Action Properties Box appears. Type a title for your Action such as "View By Category." Remember that the title will appear as a button label. Don't make it too long.
4. Select an icon for your Action (optional).
5. Check **Include action in button bar**. You don't need to change or select the position of the icon, unless you have more than one Action for this form.
6. In the formula pane, select **Formula**.
7. Enter the formula:

   ```
   @Command([OpenView];"By Category")
   ```

   where "By Category" is the name of your view.
8. Save and close the view. Figure 6.2 shows three view Actions.

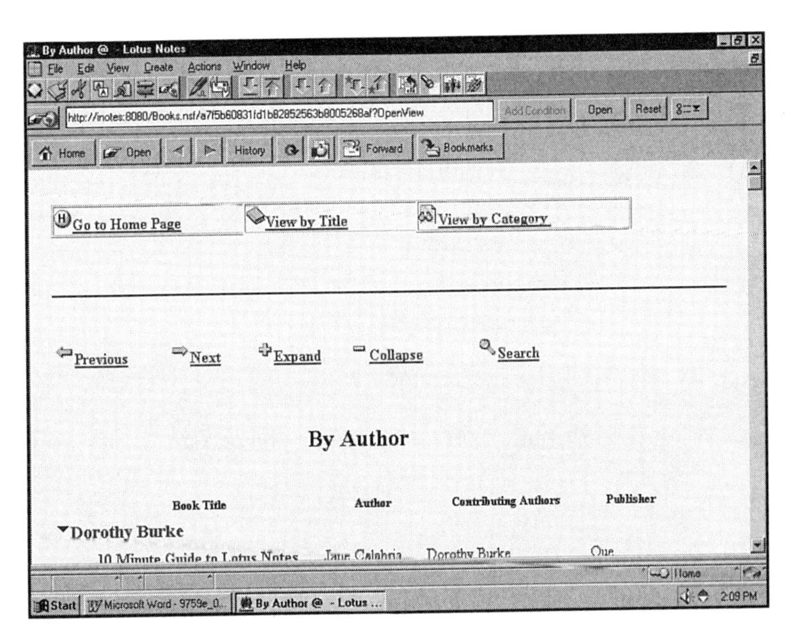

Figure 6.2 View Actions on View.

Using Icons in View Columns

As you learned in Part III, "Application Development," you can use icons in view columns to alert users to new information. In your Notes mail database, icons are used when you send attachments (with the paper clip) or send mail as a high priority (with a red exclamation mark). Although icons in view columns will not translate to the Web, you can use .gif files. (GIF is a standard HTML graphics file format). To use .gif files with Domino, a copy of the .gif file must be located on the Domino server, in the icons directory. Ask your Notes administrator for assistance in copying those files to the proper directory.

Once you have the .gif files you would like to use, you can create a formula to define its use in your view. For example, you might have a .gif file that is a picture of the word "new." You can have this .gif file appear in a column if a document is new to your Web site and you want to bring this to the attention of Web visitors. Figure 6.3 shows a .gif file in a view on the Web.

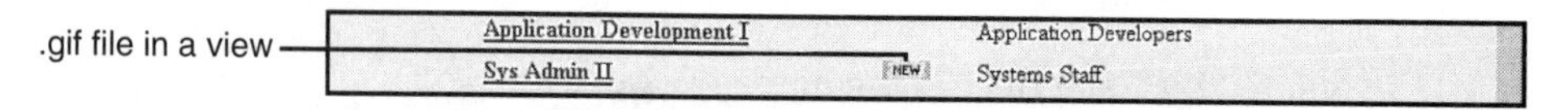

Figure 6.3 Using .gif files in views.

To create a formula that uses .gif files in view columns:

1. Create or edit the view in which you want to use the .gif file.
2. Enter a formula in the column where you want the .gif to appear. In the following example, the .gif file is called "new" and will appear if the document is less than five days old.

   ```
   @If(@Now < @Adjust(@Created; 0; 0; 5; 0; 0; 0); "[<img src=/icons/
   new.gif\ border=0>]";"")
   ```

3. Save and close your view.

For more information on formulas for view columns, see Part III, "Application Development."

No GIFs? If your icons are refusing to show on the Web, first test your formula in Notes to see if your syntax for the formula is correct. Then, check the path (/icons) for your .gif file to be certain that you have correctly typed the path. Check with your Notes administrator to see if the .gif file is in the proper directory on your Domino server. If your Notes administrator is storing the .gif files in a different directory, you need to change your formula to include the proper path.

Understanding Searches

A database must be full-text indexed so that Web searches can find information in it. Domino places the search bar and creates the search results page for Web users. For more information on creating indexes, see Lesson 10 of Part IV, "InterNotes Web Publisher."

Figure 6.4 shows the search page generated by Domino as a result of the Web user clicking the search icon on a view.

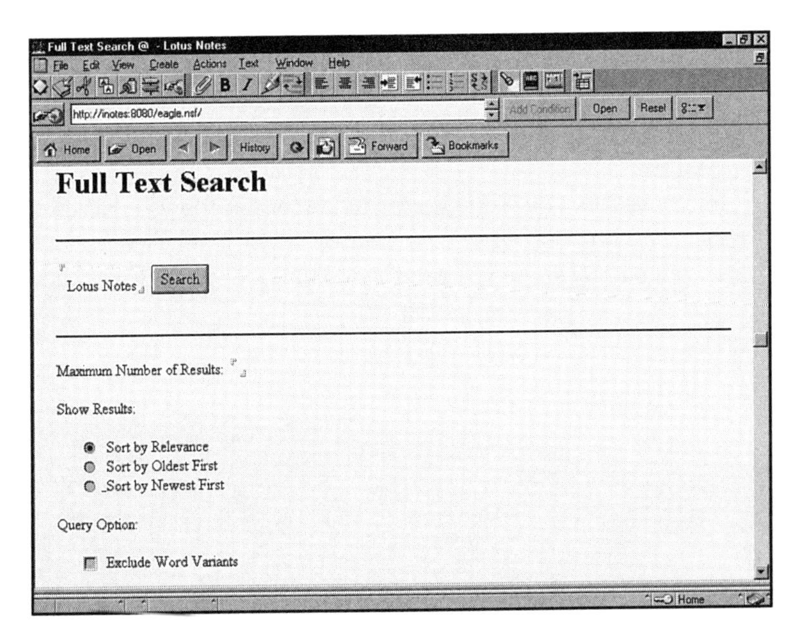

Figure 6.4 Domino search page.

The results of the "Lotus Notes" search are shown in Figure 6.5. This page was generated by Domino.

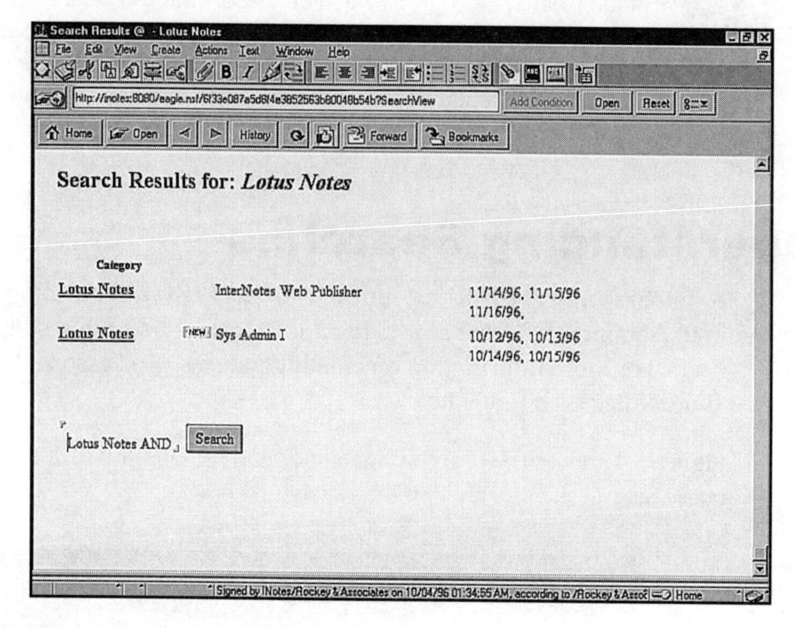

Figure 6.5 Domino search results.

In this lesson, you learned how to customize views for Web users and how to include icons in your view columns. You also learned how Domino creates search pages for the Web. In the next lesson, you'll learn about security.

Understanding Security

In this lesson, you learn about Notes and Domino security. You also learn how to hide portions of your database from Web users.

Levels of Security

Although it is the responsibility of the Notes Administrator and not the database designer to control access to your site, you need to be familiar with the processes the Notes Administrator has invoked to protect your site.

With Domino running and the Notes server connected to the Internet or intranet, any Web user can access your databases. Since you don't want just any Net surfer browsing around in your Notes databases—and perhaps making changes in them—you should invoke Notes security features to protect them.

Notes has very strong security features. To gain access to databases on a standard (non-HTTP) Notes server, a Notes user has to first authenticate with the server, then the user must qualify on the server's access list, then get past a series of access lists in each database. In the authentication process, both the user and the server have to prove to each other that they are members of trusted organizations and they have to prove their identities. This involves a series of encryptions and decryptions of information using public and private keys. After the server has authenticated the user, the server may still refuse the user access to the server if the user is in a Not Access Server field. The server may also bar the user if the user is not in an Access Server field in the Server's access list.

If the user gets past this checkpoint, the server will consider any user request to access a database. The server will consult the database's Access Control List, where the user may be listed, either individually or as a member of a group, as having Manager access, Designer access, Editor access, Author access, Reader access, Depositor access, or No access. Or the user may not be listed at all, in which case the user will be granted the Default level of access, which is set by the Database Manager.

Notes Release 4 permits the relaxing of Notes security by allowing unauthenticated users to access the server and its databases. An unauthenticated user is one whose identity the server has not ascertained and who, therefore, is essentially anonymous to the server. You can control the degree of access such users have by adding Anonymous to any access list and specifying the degree of access that an Anonymous user shall have. If you don't add Anonymous to a database Access Control List, then anonymous users receive Default access.

Domino also permits "authentication" of Web users. Authenticated Web users are no longer anonymous but are identified by the server. Once this is the case, you can add Web user names to database ACLs to assign access levels to them individually or, better yet, you can add their names to groups defined in the Public Address Book, then add the groups to database ACLs. In this way, you assign access levels to Web users collectively.

Domino supports two kinds of authentication of Web users: Web Authentication and SSL (Secure Sockets Layer) Authentication. With Web Authentication, you create a Person document for a Web user. The Person document has at least two fields completed: The Full Name field and the HTTP Password field. When a Web user tries to enter a restricted database (one for which Anonymous or Default access is No Access) or when a Web user tries to perform a restricted activity (such as creating, editing, or deleting a document), Domino will ask the user for his name and password. If the user enters a name and password that match those in a Person document, then the user is authenticated (but not nearly so thoroughly as Notes users are).

The easiest way to set up Web Authentication is to download the User Registration database from the Lotus Web site (http://www.lotus.com). This database allows anonymous users to fill in a registration form, then uses the information in the form to create a Person document for the user in your Public Address Book and to add the user to a Public Address Book group called Web Users.

SSL Authentication involves issuing certificates to Web users in a way similar to that used for Notes users. The certificates are signed by the issuer and include public and private keys. This method of authentication is as thorough and secure as Notes' own authentication method. For more information about SSL Authentication, see the *Domino Documentation* database that comes with Domino and the *Notes and the Internet* database that can be downloaded from the Lotus Web site (http://www.lotus.com).

The database designer's responsibility for access control lies in the following:

- View access lists, which restrict who can use a view to see documents.
- Form access lists, which restrict who can use a form to see documents.
- Readers fields and $Readers fields, which may forbid the viewing of a particular document.
- Authors fields, which may forbid the editing of a particular document.
- Section access lists, which may forbid the reading or editing of a section of a document.
- Encrypted fields, which may forbid the reading of those fields in a document. These are not supported by Domino.

For more information on access control, see Part III, "Application Development."

Hiding Information

If you want to hide forms, sections, paragraphs, or fields from Web users (a good example would be CGI variables) you can use the skills you learned in Part III, "Application Development," and use the following hide-when formula:

```
@IsMember ("$$WebClient";@UserRoles)
```

Here's how the formula works:

- @UserRoles returns any Roles that the current user fulfills. These are the Roles that appear in the database ACL, mostly. However, if a user is coming in from the Web, @UserRoles returns "$$WebClient."
- @IsMember asks if $$WebClient is a member of the list of Roles returned by @UserRoles. If it *is* a member, as it would be if the user is coming from the Web, then @IsMember returns "1," true. If it is *not* a member, as it

would not be if the user is coming in from a Notes client, then @IsMember returns "0," false. The whole thing taken together is true if the user is a member of $$WebClient, in which case the Action will be hidden from that user.

If you want to hide information from Notes users, preface the formula with an exclamation point which means NOT:

```
!@IsMember ("$$WebClient";@UserRoles)
```

In this case, the whole thing taken together is true if the user is *not* a member of $$WebClient, in which case the Action will be hidden from that user.

In this lesson, you learned about Domino and Notes security and how to hide parts of your database from Web users. In the next lesson, you'll learn how to make your Web site distinct.

Combining Forms with Views and Navigators

In this lesson, you learn about dressing up documents, views, and Navigators so your Web site doesn't look like every other Domino Web site.

Embedding View Lists, Views, and Navigators in Forms

One way to make your Domino Web site look unique is to embed a list of Notes views, a single Notes view, or a Notes graphical Navigator into a Notes form. Any document created with the Notes form automatically appears with a view, view list, or one or more Navigators embedded in it.

To embed a list of views, a view, or a Navigator into a form, you insert a special Web-only field in the form. The fields you can insert are displayed in Table 8.1.

Table 8.1 View and Navigator Fields

Field Name	*Field Value*	*Other Information*
$$ViewList	None	Displays a list of views and folders.
$$ViewBody	View name in quotation marks or a formula that computes to a view name	Displays the specified view. You may use only one $$ViewBody field per form.

continues

Table 8.1 Continued

Field Name	*Field Value*	*Other Information*
$$NavigatorBody $$NavigatorBody_n	Navigator name in quotation marks or a formula that computes to a Navigator	Displays the specified Navigator. You may insert more than one Navigator in a name form by inserting multiple fields named $$NavigatorBody_1, $$NavigatorBody_2, and so on.

Enter these fields in a form by following these steps:

1. In Design mode, open the form or subform in which you want the view list, view body, or Navigator to appear.
2. Move the text cursor to the position in the form (or subform) where you want the view list, view body, or Navigator to appear. This can be anywhere in the form, including in a table, in a collapsed section, or in a left-aligned, centered, or right-aligned paragraph.
3. Insert a field at the cursor position by choosing **Create**, **Field** in the menu.
4. In the Field Properties Box, name the field **$$ViewList**, **$$ViewBody**, **$$NavigatorBody**, or **$$NavigatorBody_n**.
5. Set the field Type as **Text**. The field may be **Editable** or **Computed**. If you named the field $$ViewList, this is all you have to do; you can now save and close the form, then test it by viewing it in a Web browser. If you named the field one of the other names, proceed to step 6.
6. For $$ViewBody, $$NavigatorBody, or $$NavigatorBody_n fields, enter the alias (or name if there is no alias) of the view or navigator, surrounded by quotation marks, in the formula box, or enter a formula that resolves to the alias or name of a view or navigator (see Figure 8.1). Save and close the form.
7. Test the form by viewing it in a Web browser (see Figure 8.2).

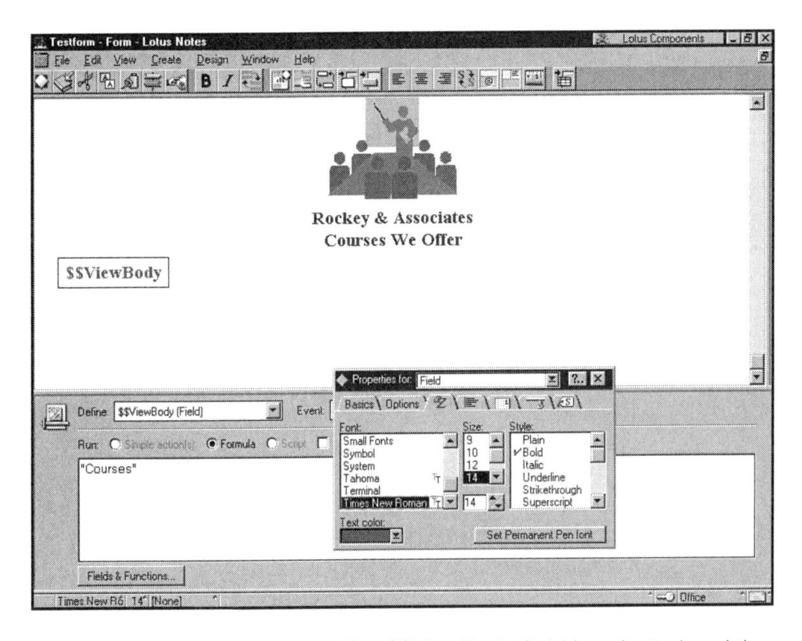

Figure 8.1 A form in Design mode. The $$ViewBody field is selected and the name of a view appears in the formula box.

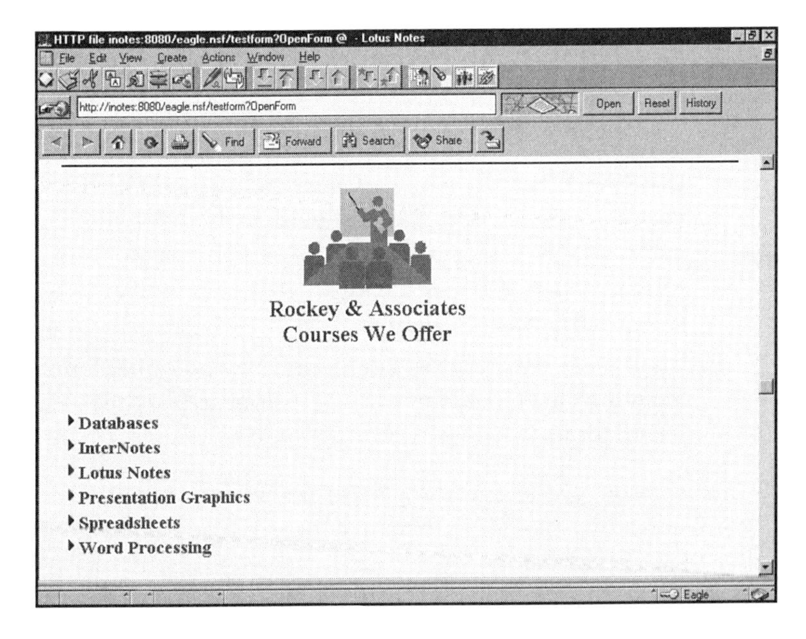

Figure 8.2 The same form as viewed in a Web browser.

Framing Views and Navigators with Forms

Another way to make your Web site look different from other Domino Web sites is to define a Notes form as a frame for a Notes view or Navigator. In this case, whenever a Web user retrieves the view or Navigator, it will appear within the defined form. When you retrieve a view or Navigator, it appears framed in a form; that is, it has custom text and graphics above and below it. Does this sound very close to embedding a view, view list, or Navigator in a form? The difference is that, with embedding, when you retrieve a document, it appears with a view, view list, or one or more Navigators embedded in it.

To create a special form that Domino will use to frame a view or Navigator when a Web user retrieves that view or Navigator, you take the two following special steps when creating the form:

1. Name the form with one of the following special names:

    $$ViewTemplate for *viewname*, where *viewname* is the name or alias of a view

    $$ViewTemplateDefault

    $$NavigatorTemplate for *navigatorname*, where *navigatorname* is the name or alias of a Navigator

    $$NavigatorTemplateDefault

    Use $$ViewTemplate for *viewname* and $$NavigatorTemplate for *navigatorname* for a form that should be used only with one view or Navigator. Use $$ViewTemplateDefault or $$NavigatorTemplateDefault for a form that should be used with all views or Navigators that are not otherwise associated with another view or Navigator template form.

2. Insert a $$ViewBody field or $$ViewNavigator field in the form where you want the view(s) or Navigator(s) to appear. See the previous section of this lesson for instructions regarding these two fields.

In this lesson, you learned how to display views, view lists, and Navigators in a form either by embedding them in a form or by defining a form as a frame for the view or Navigator.

Domino.Action

What Is Domino.Action?

In this lesson, you are introduced to Domino.Action. You learn what it does and how to install it. You also learn what the SiteCreator is and how it works.

Understanding Domino.Action

Domino.Action is a Lotus Notes application that creates and maintains a whole, Domino-based World Wide Web site with Lotus Notes databases. It simplifies the creation of a Web site by working from preset designs into which you plug site- or company-specific information and graphics. Domino.Action leads you through the design process in a step-by-step manner in which you:

- Enter your company information and choose the content areas to be included in your site
- Decide how you want your site to look by specifying the page layout and the images that will be included
- Decide how you want your users to work with the site

Domino.Action then generates your Web site as a set of databases that can be used by both Web browsers and Notes clients.

Domino.Action lets you take advantage of Notes' workflow, security, and document-management features for your Web site. When you use Domino.Action, you can control who can author, edit, and approve Web pages for your site, and you can distribute the authoring, editing, and approval tasks to other Notes users. For example, if an employee in your sales department normally populates your Notes database containing your product line, you can continue to have that individual author product documents. Domino.Action and the Domino 4.5 server together will convert the Notes database to the Web.

Setting Up Domino.Action

The Domino.Action application consists of two database templates: SiteCreator (SiteAct.ntf) for configuring and generating the databases that make up your site, and Library (LibAct.ntf), which stores the design elements that SiteCreator uses to build the site.

You need to create two databases from the templates provided. The templates will install to your Domino server data directory automatically during the installation/upgrade of the Domino server to version 4.5. You'll use these templates to generate the Domino.Action Site Creator database and the Domino.Action Library database. These, in turn, you will use to generate a set of databases that will constitute your Web site.

You can set up the Site Creator and Library databases on a Domino server or on your workstation. The Web site databases must, however, reside on a domino server running Domino's HTTP service and connected to the Internet or an intranet. The HTTP service is a server task; if you're not certain it's running, consult with your Notes Administrator.

The SiteCreator database lets you select and configure the elements of your site. You can decide where you want your site to be, how you want it to appear, and how you want visitors to interact with your site. When you set it up the way you want, SiteCreator generates your Web site as a set of Notes databases that you can use either in Notes or in a Web browser.

To create the SiteCreator database for your Web site:

1. Choose **File**, **Database**, **New**. The New Database dialog box appears (see Figure 1.1).

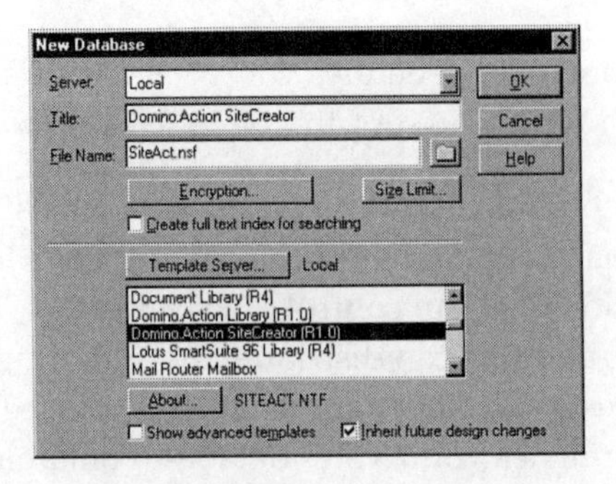

Figure 1.1 The New Database dialog box.

2. Specify the server (Local or the Domino server) in the Server box.
3. Enter a title for the database in the Title box. This is the title that appears on the database icon. You can choose SiteCreator if this is the only site you're going to make using the SiteCreator template, or you can make up a title that is specific to your Web site.
4. In the File Name box, enter the name of the database (with an .NSF file extension) or accept the name that Notes generated.
5. From the list of templates, find and highlight the **Domino.Action SiteCreator** template (SiteAct.ntf).
6. Leave a check mark in the check box entitled Inherit future design changes.
7. Click **OK**.

The second database you need is the Library, which includes forms, subforms, views, and other design elements that may be used to build your site. During the site generation process, the SiteCreator looks through the Library for the design elements you selected during your setup. When SiteCreator generates the site, several databases are created by marrying the information you supply in the Site Configuration document to the resources of the Domino.Action Library. When the database first starts up, the Domino logo and copyright notice appear. Click **OK** or press **Esc** to make this screen disappear.

To create the Library database:

1. Choose **File**, **Database**, **New**. The New Database dialog box appears (refer to Figure 1.1).
2. Specify the server (Local or the Domino server) in the Server box.
3. Enter a title for the database in the Title box. This is the title that appears on the database icon. You can choose "Library" if you're only making one Web site, or you can make up a title that is specific to your Web site.
4. In the File Name box, enter the name of the database (with an .NSF file extension) or accept the name Notes generated.
5. From the list of templates, find and highlight the **Domino.Action Library template (LibAct.ntf)**.
6. Leave a check mark in the check box entitled Inherit future design changes.
7. Click **OK**.

The About Database document will appear. Press **Esc** to close it. Now you can begin building your Web site.

How the SiteCreator Works

You configure your Web site in the SiteCreator database by making a series of choices in a profile document. Then you make a series of design decisions about how your site should look and act. The design elements that will make up the Web site are stored in the Library database.

Profile Document A Notes document that contains the basic outline of how to configure a process, procedure, database, or document.

As part of the Web site creation process, you install the AppAssembler module, which pulls together the design elements and your configuration choices to generate the databases that will make up your Web site. Finally, you set the access controls and the approval process.

AppAssembler Module The "program" portion of the Domino.Action application that pulls together the design components and your specifications to create the databases that make up your Web site.

When you double-click the SiteCreator database icon and open the database, you'll see a screen that is split into three panes (see Figure 1.2). The lower-left pane displays the contents of the Action view. There are four categories in the view. Under the Quickstart: SiteCreator category there are five documents: The SiteCreator Overview document, one document for each of the three steps necessary to create a site, and one document entitled Finish Your Site. The documents under the User's Guide category provide valuable information on putting your site together; and you should refer to Before You Begin for pointers on what you should know prior to starting step 1. Administration Tasks provide instructions or suggestions you may need after you have set up the Web site. The Release Notes - Release 1.0 document contains information on how this particular release of Domino.Action works.

The Preview pane (the right side of the screen) displays the currently selected document in Preview mode. The first time you open the database in this view, the currently selected document is the SiteCreator Overview. This document explains how SiteCreator works, what will happen during each phase of the site creation process, and what additional steps you must take at the end of the process. You can read the document when it's in this Preview mode, but you must double-click the name of the document in the view to open the document.

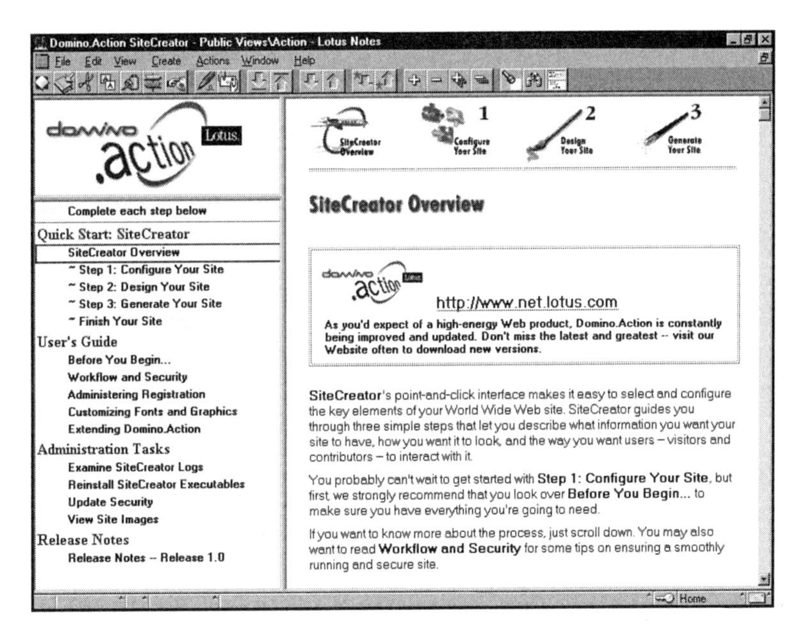

Figure 1.2 The opening screen of the SiteCreator database.

At the bottom of the SiteCreator Overview document is a Launch Step 1 hotspot (see Figure 1.3). After you read the document, click this hotspot, which will return you to the Action view (Figure 1.3) with step 1 in the Preview pane ready. Double-click step 1 to begin the process of creating your Web site.

The Site Creation Process

As you go through the steps involved in creating your site, SiteCreator will offer you suggestions, so you need not have decided ahead of time how you want the site to appear and work. However, you should have goals in mind for what you want to accomplish with your site. Then you should collect any information or graphics you want to include on your Web pages, and you should know where on your system such files are stored.

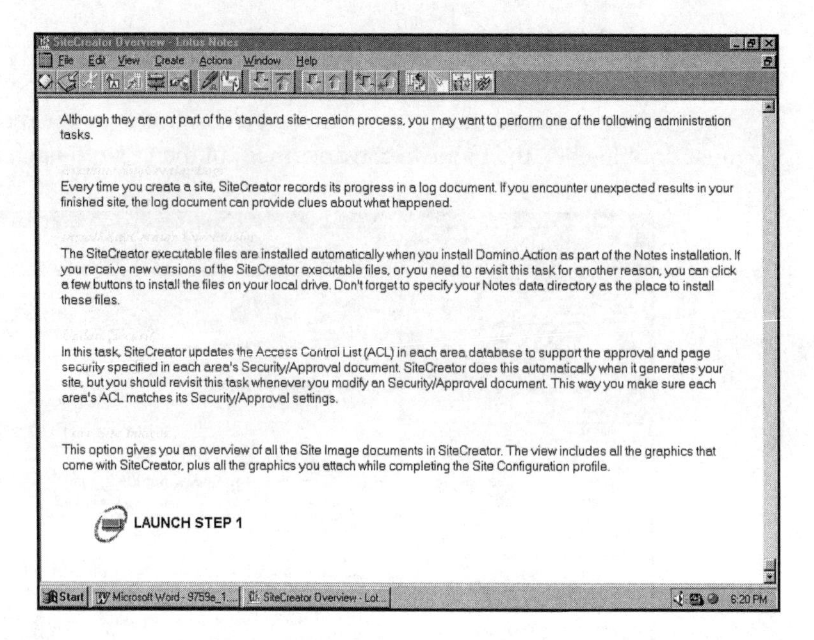

Figure 1.3 The LAUNCH STEP 1 Hotspot.

The site creation process goes through the following steps:

Step 1: Configure Your Site. You supply information about your company, where the Domino.Action Library is located, the name and location of your Web site, who's in charge of your Web site, and so on. You'll also select the *areas* you want to have for your site. An *area* is a portion of the site containing related information, such as descriptions of your services or products. An *area* becomes a separate database when SiteCreator generates the site.

Step 2: Design Your Site. You'll work with a series of documents that control the appearance, organization, and approval settings for each of the areas you've selected for your site. This is where you set the page layout, select background colors or images, choose categories, and specify who is authorized to compose, approve, and read the pages in the area. A Quick Design option lets you reduce your design time by using default settings. You can always edit the design later if you change your mind.

Step 3: Generate Your Site. Using the design decisions you made and the data you included in the configuration information, SiteCreator retrieves the needed design elements from the Library database and creates a new database for each site area you specified in the site configuration.

Step 4: Finish Your Site. After you complete the three important steps toward building your site, including building all the site areas, you should refresh all the documents and establish all the links between the site areas.

In this lesson, you learned what Domino.Action is, how to install it, how the SiteCreator works, and the steps involved in the site creation process. In the next lesson, you'll start at step 1 of configuring your Web site.

Configuring Your Site

In this lesson, you learn how to open the Site Configuration document and what information to include on the form.

Completing the Site Configuration Document

You specify the "backbone" information for your Web site in the Site Configuration document. In this document, you enter data on the name and location of the Library database, the name of your site, who's in charge of the site, what types of information you want included in the site, and information about your company. Much of this information will appear on your home page, as well as in the area databases that you tell Site Creator to make.

To open the Site Configuration document:

1. Open the SiteCreator database.
2. In the SiteCreator Overview document, click the **LAUNCH STEP 1** hotspot as described in the previous lesson. Alternatively, in the Action view (the left side of the screen), double-click **Step 1: Configure Your Site** to open that document (see Figure 2.1). This document briefly explains what will happen in this first step of the process.
3. To continue the process, click **Configure Your Site** at the bottom of the document. This opens the Site Configuration view.
4. The Set up Site Configuration document is automatically selected. Click the **Edit** hotspot on the Preview pane to change the default settings on the Site Configuration form (see Figure 2.2).
5. Complete the fields in the Site Configuration form using the guidelines provided. Then save the form and close it. A check mark appears in front of Step 1 in the Action view to indicate that this step is complete.

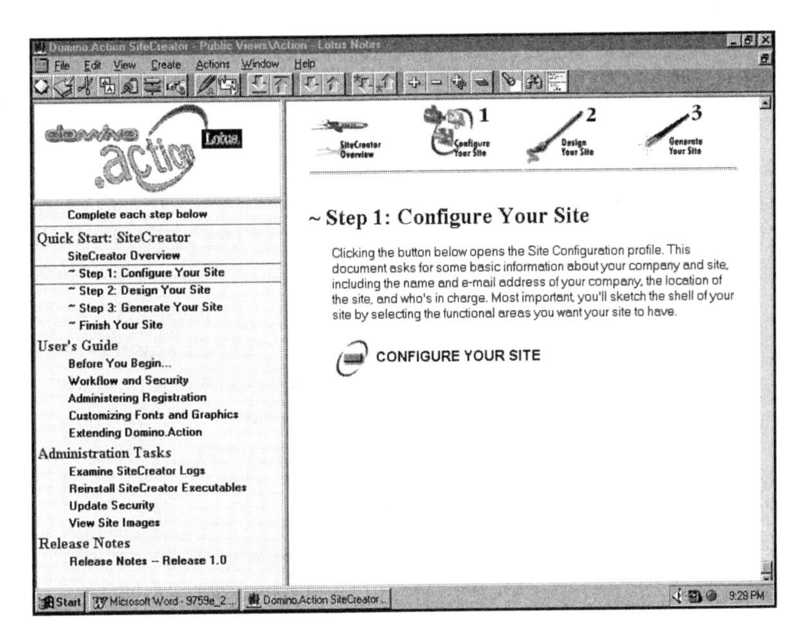

Figure 2.1 The Step 1: Configure Your Site document.

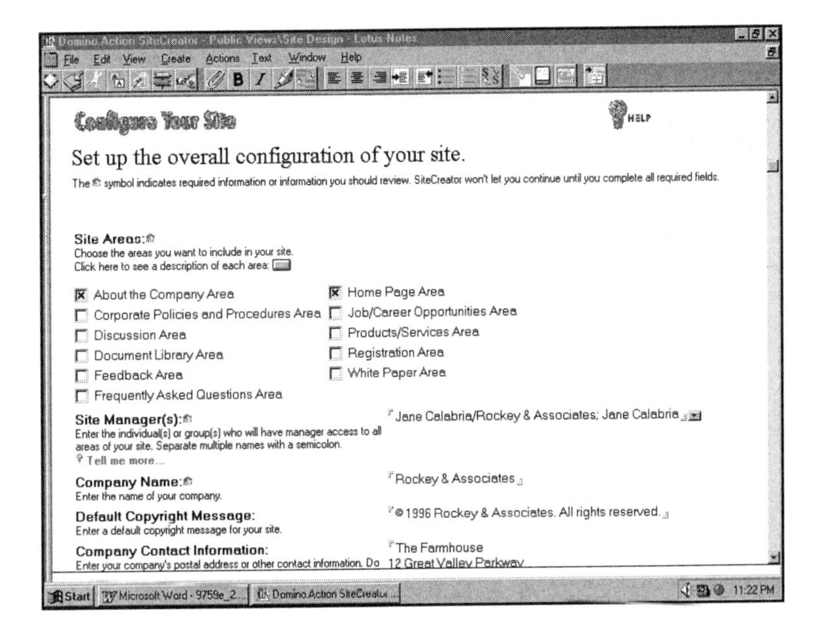

Figure 2.2 The Site Configuration Form.

Fields on the Site Configuration Document

Fill in the fields on the Site Configuration form as follows, making sure to complete all required fields:

Site Areas You can select up to 11 areas, each of which will become a database serving a particular purpose. The choices are explained in Table 2.1.

Site Manager(s) The Site Manager is the person or group who will have Manager access to all areas of your site and is the equivalent of the Webmaster for your site. SiteCreator assumes the person filling in this form will be the Site Manager, but you may enter the names of any person or group that appears in your Public Address Book (click the list button to open a browser that enables you to select people or groups from the Public Address Book). Because the databases you are creating can be accessed from both Notes and the Internet, all names must appear in both hierarchical (Bob Dobbs/Planet Notes) and flat (Bob Dobbs) format. Separate multiple names with semicolons. *This is a required field.* In the group and person documents in the Public Address Book, be sure to enter the flat format name in each person document or for each participant in each group as well as the hierarchical name if applicable.

Company Name The name of the company that the site will serve. *This is a required field.*

Default Copyright Message Enter a copyright notice here that will appear throughout the site. You'll have the opportunity to change this message on specific pages later. If you're working on a private intranet site, you can leave this field blank.

Company Contact Information Enter the company postal address or any other contact information that you want, such as telephone or fax numbers. Don't include the company name, as it gets pulled automatically from the Company Name field.

Company Contact E-Mail Address Enter an e-mail address where you will receive requests for information (see Figure 2.3). *This is a required field.*

Site Image(s) Click the **Attach Image** button to open the Site Design form, with which you can create an image library document. The .GIF and .JPEG images you attach will be available to use as you design your site. See the Attaching a Site Image section for more details.

Site Server Enter the name of the Domino server where you want to create your site. SiteCreator defaults to Local. Leave the selection at Local if the Library database is located on the computer where you are working. *This is a required field.*

Site Directory Enter the directory where you want to create the site. It must be a subdirectory of the \Notes\Data directory, so you need only enter the path relative to that directory. If the directory doesn't exist, SiteCreator will create it for you. The default setting is the \Action subdirectory. *This is a required field.*

Library Server Name The name of the server where the Library database is located. SiteCreator defaults to Local. Leave the selection at Local if the Library database is located on the computer where you are working. Otherwise, enter the name of the server where the Library database is located. *This is a required field.*

Library File Name The path and name of the Library database, relative to the Notes data directory. If you stored the Library file in c:\notes\data, enter just the file name of the Library database. If you stored the Library database in a subdirectory of the Notes data directory, list both the subdirectory in which the Library database is located and the file name of the Library database (for example, \website\ourweb.nsf). *This is a required field.*

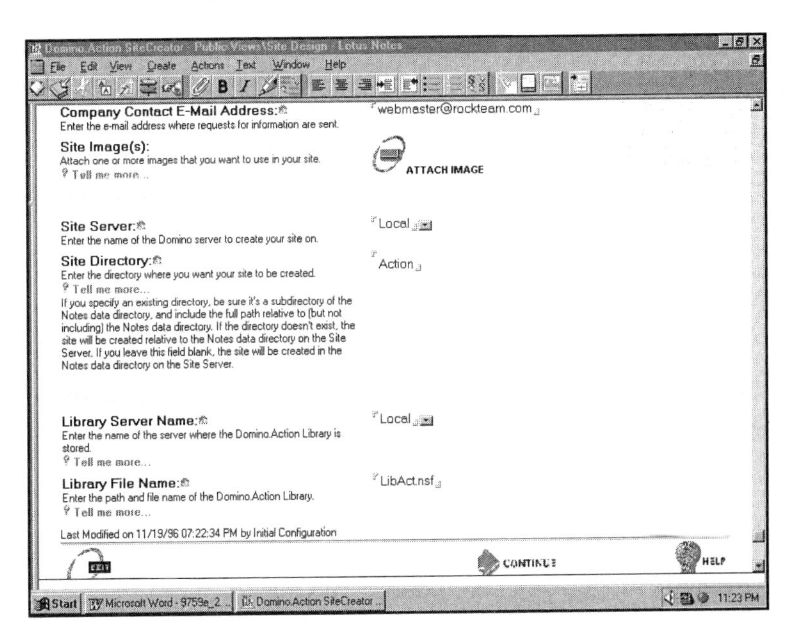

Figure 2.3 The bottom portion of the Site Configuration form.

Table 2.1 Site Areas and Their Purposes

Area	*Purpose*
About the Company	General information about the company and its products and services.
Corporate Policies and Procedures	Policy and procedure guides, employee manuals, and human resources information. This area would be appropriate for a company's internal site.
Discussion	Visitors to this area can exchange information and ideas with one another and with company personnel who moderate the discussion.
Document Library	Store reference documents in this area.
Feedback	Provides a questionnaire that visitors to your site can complete. You define the questions and answer choices that appear in the questionnaire.
Frequently Asked Questions	List of the questions and answers most often handled by customer service, marketing, corporate communications, or technical support personnel.
Home Page	The site home page. The starting point from which users can reach all other areas of the site. This area is automatically selected for you.
Job/Career Opportunities	List of current employment opportunities in your company. This area would be appropriate for a company's internal site.
Product/Services	Descriptions of your products and services and pricing information.
Registration	Visitors to the site can register here.
White Paper	Store white papers in this area.

Attaching a Site Image

A site image is a graphic file that contains a drawing or photograph that you intend to include in your Web pages. This might be your company logo, a photograph of your building, the map showing directions to your store, or a picture of the president of the company or of your product. For each image that you want to include in your site, you have to create a Site Image document (see

Figure 2.4). Here you name the image, describe it, categorize it, and attach a copy of it. A new Site Image document appears when you click the **Attach/ Import Image** button in the Company Image(s) field of the Site Configuration document. Images must be in .GIF or .JPEG format, and you should make them in the size you want to appear on the Web page (so if you want to use your logo in several sizes or colors, make a separate graphic file for each size or color). You can add more Site Image documents later or replace the ones you're adding now (see Lesson 6, "Generating Your Site," for more information).

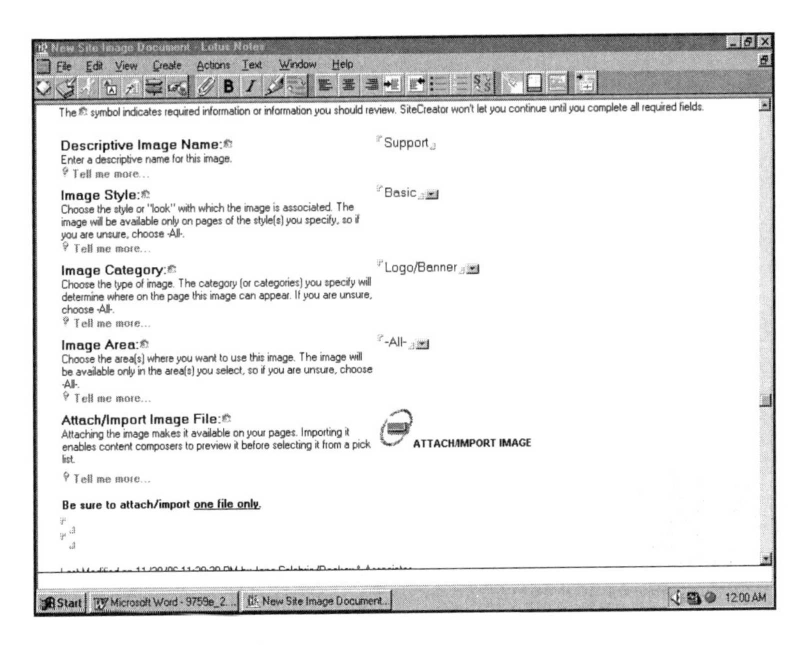

Figure 2.4 The Site Image form.

Complete the fields of the Site Image document as follows:

Descriptive Image Name Enter a brief name to identify the image. This name will appear on the drop-down lists when you select images for your pages.

Image Style Select a "look" with which to associate the image. The choices include All, Basic, Corporate, and Contemporary. If you are not going to mix and match looks in your site, select **All**.

Image Category Select a category from the keyword list. The category determines where the SiteCreator will place the image on your Web pages, as certain types of pages call for specific categories of images. The available categories are:

All An image that fits in any or none of the categories below.

Logo/Banner Your company logo is an important image for your site. Capture your logo in more than one size or have different colored logos for different types of pages. A banner image stretches across the top of a page and identifies the purpose of the page.

Background A background image fills the entire background of a Web page. If your image is not large enough to fill that space, it will be repeated or *tiled* to fill the page. Background images should be light in color with a simple pattern so the text on top can be easily read by a visitor. Typically, backgrounds have a textured look.

Product Image If you've included a product/services area, you may want to include pictures of your products.

Person Image If you want to display photos of employees or company officials in your About Company area or of authors in the White Paper area, place the photos in this category.

Image Area If you want to use an image only in a specific site area, select that area. Otherwise, specify **All**.

Attach/Import Image Click the **Attach/Import Image** button. In the Create Attachments dialog box (see Figure 2.5), select the file you want to attach and then click **Create**. When the Import dialog box appears, select the same file and then click **Import**. Below the Attach/Import Image button, the attachment icon appears in the first available field and then the picture of the image appears in the second available field (see Figure 2.6).

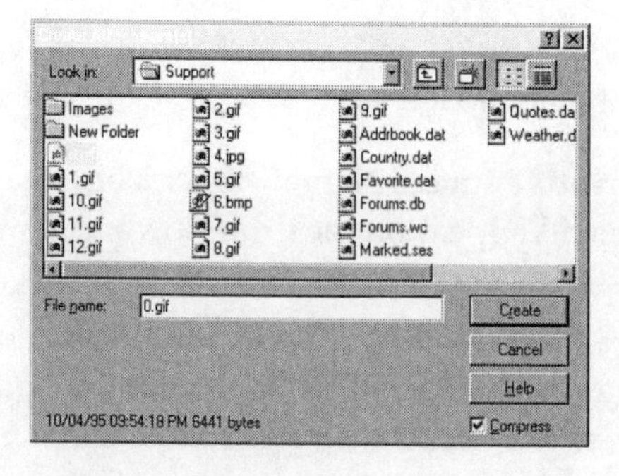

Figure 2.5 The Create Attachments dialog box.

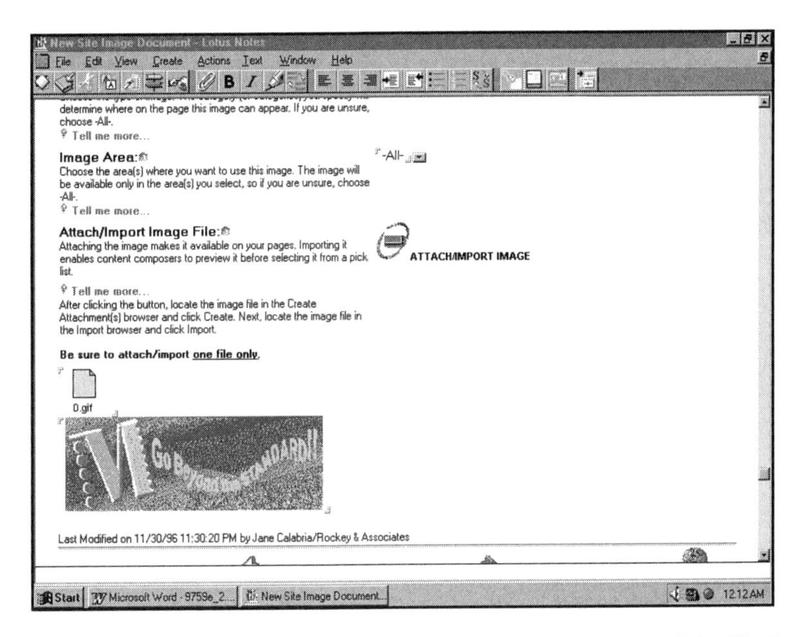

Figure 2.6 The attachment and the imported picture at the bottom of the Site Image document.

My Image Doesn't Show Up or It's Too Big You must save your image in a graphics file format that can be published on the Web, either .GIF or .JPEG. Also, make sure your image is saved in the same size you want it to appear on the Web page. You cannot resize it.

Click **Continue** at the bottom of the Site Image Document to save it and return to the Site Configuration form. If you want to add another image, click the **Attach/Import Image** button on the Site Configuration form again and fill in a Site Image form for each image you need to store for your site.

Closing the Site Configuration Document

After you complete the Site Configuration document, click the **Exit** or **Continue** hotspot at the bottom of the page. Click **Exit** if you do not intend to continue at this time. Click **Continue** if you want to go to step 2 now. This will return you to the Navigator and place a check mark in front of step 1.

In this lesson, you learned how to configure your site by completing the Site Configuration document and store image files using the Site Image document. In the next lesson, you'll learn about designing your site.

Designing Your Site

In this lesson, you learn how to set the appearance, organization, and content-approval options for your site areas by starting with the home page.

Starting with the Site Design View

When you click the **Continue** hotspot at the bottom of the completed Site Configuration document, the SiteCreator returns you to the Action view (see Figure 3.1). From here, follow these steps to continue the site creation process:

1. Click **Step 2: Design Your Site** in the Action View pane (the lower-left of the screen). If that document is not in the Preview Pane as the Design Your Site document explains, this step of the site creation process will lead you through setting the appearance, organization, and content approvals for your pages.
2. You have two options at this point: Click the **Quick Design** hotspot at the bottom of the document to accept the Domino.Action defaults for fast site setup or click the **Custom Design** hotspot if you want to review each document as you go along. If you choose the Quick Design method, you should still review all the documents for fields that have a star in front of them.

If you chose the Custom Design option, the Site Design view appears (see Figure 3.2), where you see listed all the site areas that you selected in the Site Configuration form. For each site area, there are several documents listed that you must complete in order to build your site.

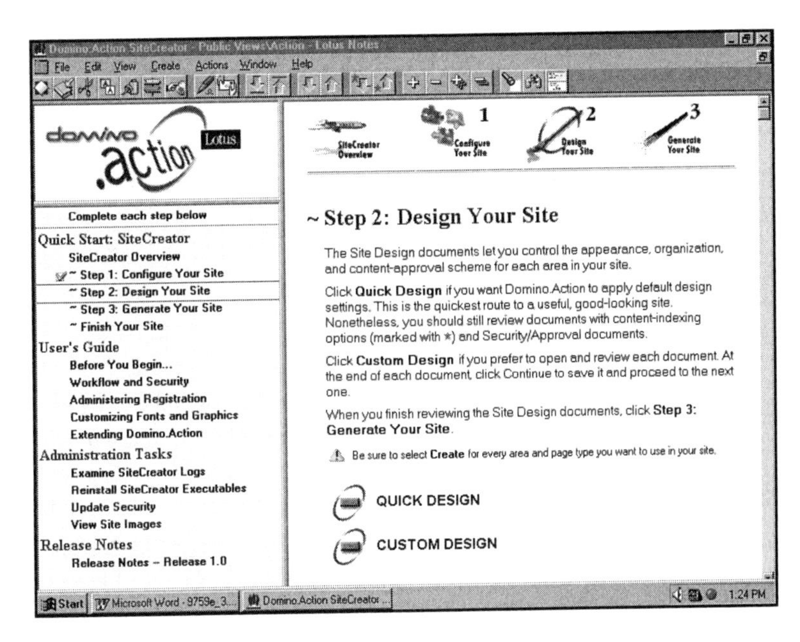

Figure 3.1 Design your site.

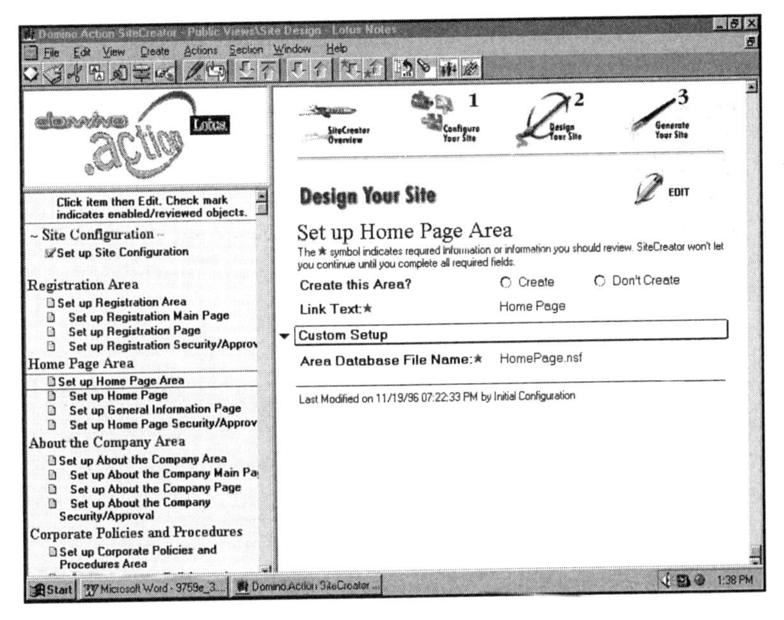

Figure 3.2 The Site Design view with the Set up Home Page Area document in preview.

The most logical procedure is to start with the home page area and then work through the other site areas starting at the top and going down the list.

Setting Up the Home Page Area

The home page is the first page visitors see when they look at your site, so it's important that it be attractive, informative, easy to use, and that it has valid links to your other pages.

1. There are four documents listed under the Home Page Area category in the Site Design view. The first document is Set Up Home Page Area. This document specifies whether the area should be created, what the database is named, and what link text appears on other pages to allow users to return to the home page. Click the **Edit** hotspot in order to make changes.
2. The first field on the form is Create this Area?. In the radio button next to this field, select **Create** so that the SiteCreator will later create a home page area for your site.

CAUTION

Where Is My Home Page? The Create radio button must be selected for every page type you want to use in your site.

3. The second field is Link Text. As visitors to your site view different pages, they may want to return to your home page so they can start in a different direction. On each page you'll want to include a link that visitors might click to return automatically to the home page. Enter the text for the Home Page link in the Link Text field or accept the default text.
4. Click the **Custom Setup** section head to expand the section if you want to enter a name for the database that contains your home page area in the Area Database File Name field, such as HomePage.nsf. If the default file name is acceptable, you don't need to change it.
5. When the Set Up Home Page Area form is complete, click the **Continue** hotspot at the bottom of the page to return to the Site Design view.

Setting Up the Home Page

The Set Up Home Page document automatically appears in the Preview pane once you complete setting up the home page area. Click the **Edit** hotspot to modify the Set Up Home Page document (see Figure 3.3).

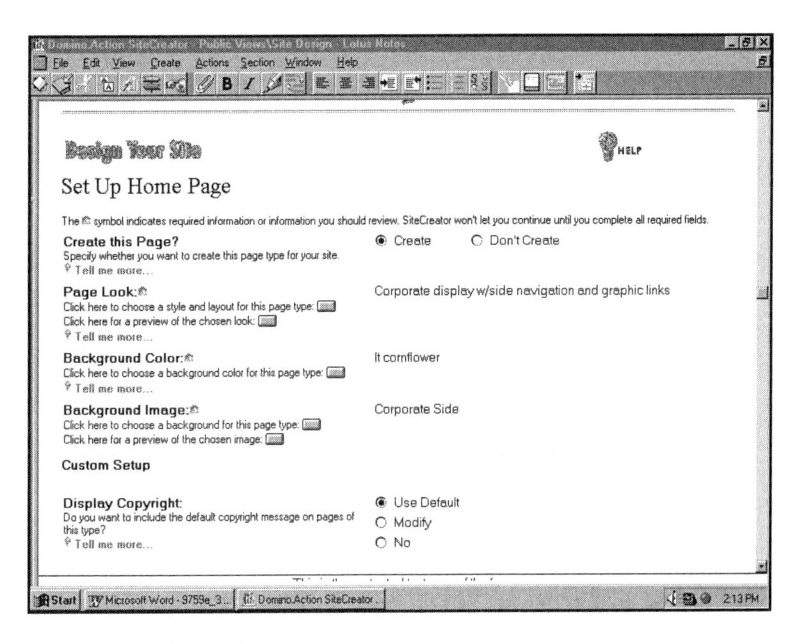

Figure 3.3 Set Up Home Page form.

In this form you will provide information about page layout, background color, background image, and copyright information for the home page. Remember that the home page is the page all visitors to your Web site will see first, so it is important to establish the "look" for your site here. This document actually prepares a home page form in the home page database that you will later use to add your own information for site visitors.

To complete this form:

1. To have the SiteCreator create this page (not now—during step 3), select the **Create** radio button in the Create this Page? field.
2. Click the button next to the Page Look field to select one of the available layouts from the dialog list. This includes Basic, Contemporary, and Corporate layouts, with navigation information in different positions on the page. To gain some idea what any one of these layouts looks like, you can choose it from the list, then click the button labeled **Click here for a preview of the chosen look** immediately below the Page Look field. A screen similar to Figure 3.4 will appear.

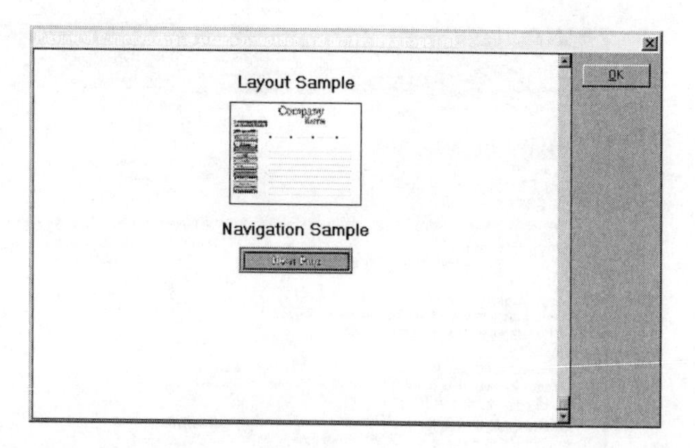

Figure 3.4 Preview of Corporate display with side navigation and graphic links.

3. Click the **Background Color** button and choose a color for your page. Even if you are planning to use a background image, you should still select a color, since quite a few Web browsers offer their users the option to turn off backgrounds.
4. If you plan to use an image in the background (either one you attached in a Site Image document or one Domino.Action provides for you), click the **Background Image** button and select the image name from the dialog list. To see what your selection looks like, click the **preview** button.
5. Click the Custom Setup section to expand it if you want to change the copyright settings you made in the Site Configuration form. There are three choices: **None**, **Use Default** (which uses the one you already specified), or **Modify** (which lets you change the copyright text just for this page).
6. Click the **Continue** hotspot. This returns you to the Site Design view.

Setting Up General Information Pages

You use General Information pages for documents that apply to your entire site, such as extended copyrights, licenses, and legal information. A "By Title" link on the home page gives you access to these documents.

To set up a General Information page:

1. Click **Set Up General Information Page** under the Home Page Area category in the Site Design view (see Figure 3.5).

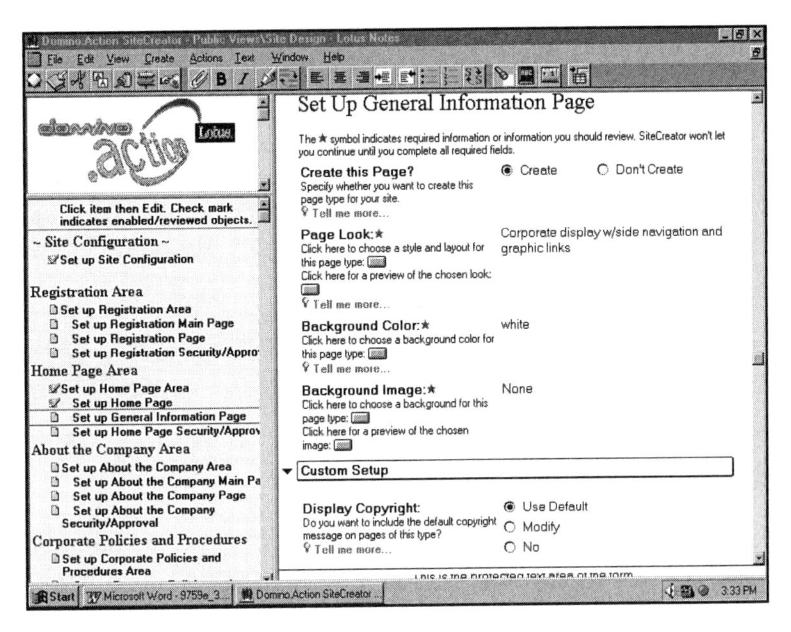

Figure 3.5 The Set Up General Information Page document.

2. Then click the **Edit** hotspot to modify the existing document.
3. Choose the **Create** option under Create This Page?.
4. Select a style and look for the page from the dialog list that appears when you click the button under Page Look. To see what your choice looks like, click the **preview** button.
5. Click the **Background Color** button to choose a color for your page.
6. If you plan to use an image in the background, click the **Background Image** button and select the image name from the dialog list. To see what your selection looks like, click the **preview** button.
7. Click the **Custom Setup** section to expand it if you want to change the copyright settings you made in the Site Configuration form. There are three choices: **None**, **Use Default** (which uses the one you already specified), or **Modify** (which lets you change the copyright text just for this page).
8. Click the **Continue** hotspot. This returns you to the Site Design view.

Setting Up the Home Page Approval Process

On the Set up Home Page Security/Approval page (see Figure 3.6) you specify who will be authorized to compose pages in the Home Page Area, who will be authorized to approve the pages before they become available on the site, and who will be authorized to read pages in this area of the site. Click the **Edit** hotspot to modify the document.

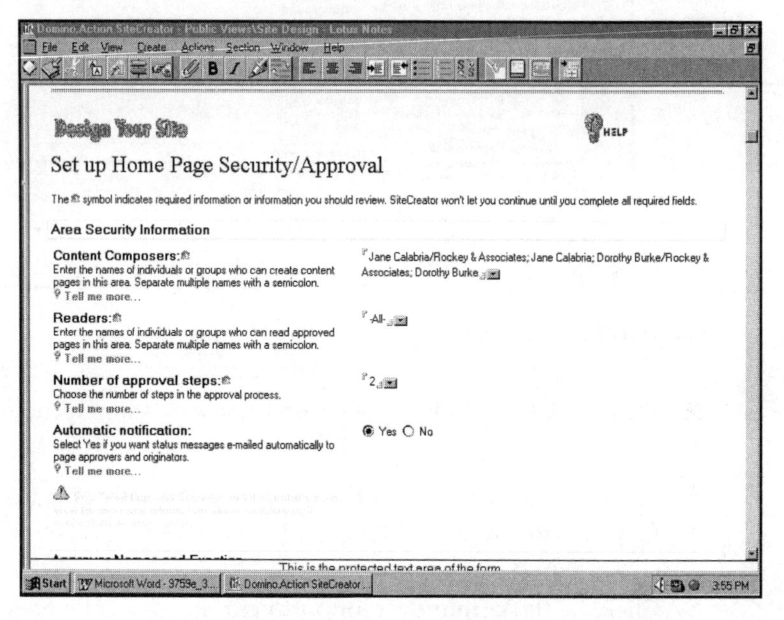

Figure 3.6 The Set up Home Page Security/Approval form.

To complete this document, follow these steps:

1. For the Content Composers field, enter or select the names of the people or groups who may compose pages in this site area. If you click the down arrow, a browser opens that lets you choose names from the Public Address Book. If you leave the field empty, anyone will be able to compose pages in this site area. Multiple names must be separated by semicolons. For each person, both the hierarchical (Jim Harkin/Hamilton-Beaks) and the common name (Jim Harkin) must appear.
2. In the Readers field, specify the people or groups who may read the pages in this site area. The default is **All**, which means everyone will be able to

read the pages. You would not ordinarily limit the readers of your home page; but you may very well limit the readers of pages in other site areas.

3. If you want to establish an approval process where people or groups approve the contents of the page, enter the number of steps (up to five) you want in the Number of Approval Steps field. Otherwise, enter **0** for none. Don't specify more steps than you need, as each step involves a notification and approval process.
4. If you entered a number of approval steps greater than zero, the Automatic Notification field appears. When you select **Yes**, e-mail is automatically sent to the approver alerting him or her that a page needs approval. Likewise, the composer of the page and the Web Master are alerted when the page is accepted or rejected.
5. If you entered a number of approval steps greater than zero, the Approver Names and Functions section appears (see Figure 3.7). Under Approver Names, you'll see fields for Step 1 Approvers, Step 2 Approvers, and so on, depending on the number of steps you specified. In each of these fields, enter or select the names of people or groups who will be involved in that level of approval. Then under Approver Function, you may optionally enter a brief description of what an approver at that level must do. The people or groups you specify must appear in the Public Address Book.

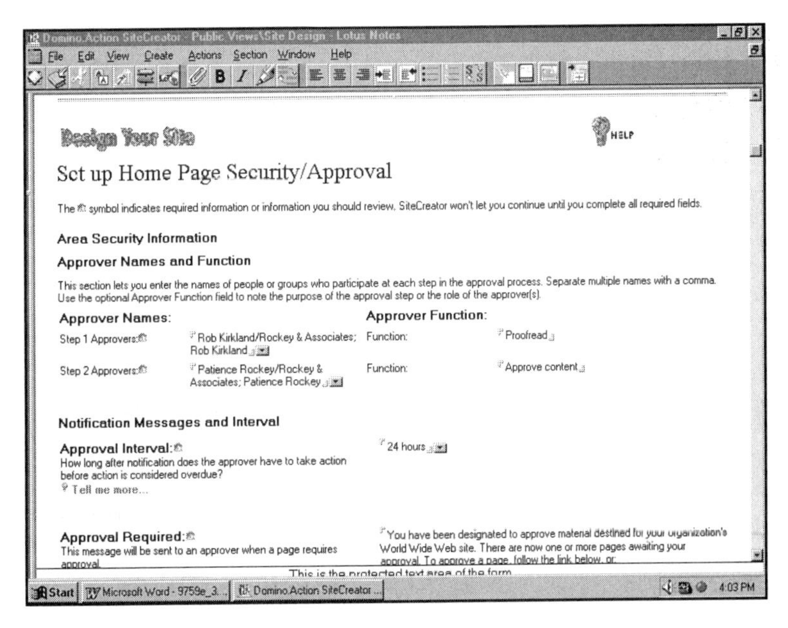

Figure 3.7 The Approver Names and Function section.

6. If you set Notification to **Yes**, the Notification Messages and Interval section appears (see Figure 3.8). You need to enter a time limit in the Approval Interval field to indicate how long after receiving notification the Approver will have to approve or reject. If the Approver does not reply within that time interval, the system sends out an overdue alert to the tardy Approver.

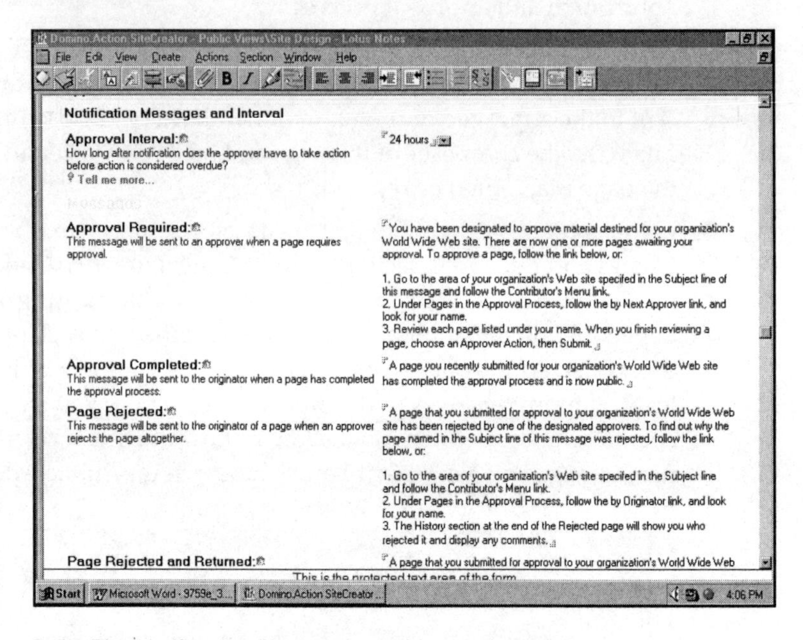

Figure 3.8 The Notification Messages and Interval section.

7. Also in the Notification Messages and Interval section, there are four fields in which appear the text of the messages that will go out to people during the approval process. You may edit the messages. The four fields are: Approval-Required Message, Approval-Completed Message, Page-Rejected, and Page-Rejected and Returned.

8. When you have completed this form, click the **Continue** hotspot to return to the Site Design view.

In this lesson, you learned how to start the design process for your Web site by beginning with the home page. You chose a layout and background for the page and then set an approval process to designate who could compose or read the page or approve its content. In the next lesson, you'll learn how to set up a site area other than the home page.

Setting Up a Site Area

In this lesson, you learn how to set up a site area other than your home page. You create an area main page, choose page layouts, and set approval process options.

Creating the Site Design Document

For each of the areas you selected on the Site Configuration document (e.g., About the Company, Feedback Area, White Paper Area), you'll be setting up a Site Design document. You created a Site Design document for the home page area in the previous lesson. The Site Design document asks if you want to create the site, what link text you want to use to bring visitors to this area of the site, and what name you want to give to the database that SiteCreator will generate for this area.

To complete the Site Design document:

1. From the Site Design view, select the first document under the category heading for the area. For example, if you chose to create an About the Company area, the document is called Set up About the Company Area.
2. Click the **Edit** hotspot in the Preview pane to modify the document.
3. You should now see a screen similar to Figure 4.1. In the Create field, select Create to have the SiteCreator create the site area.
4. When visitors come to your Web site and want to learn about your company, they will click a hyperlink to go immediately to that area of your site. In the Link Text field, enter the text the visitors will click to go to this area. For example, to send a visitor to the About the Company Area, you might enter "Learn more about our company." A link back to the home page is automatically added to your area pages.

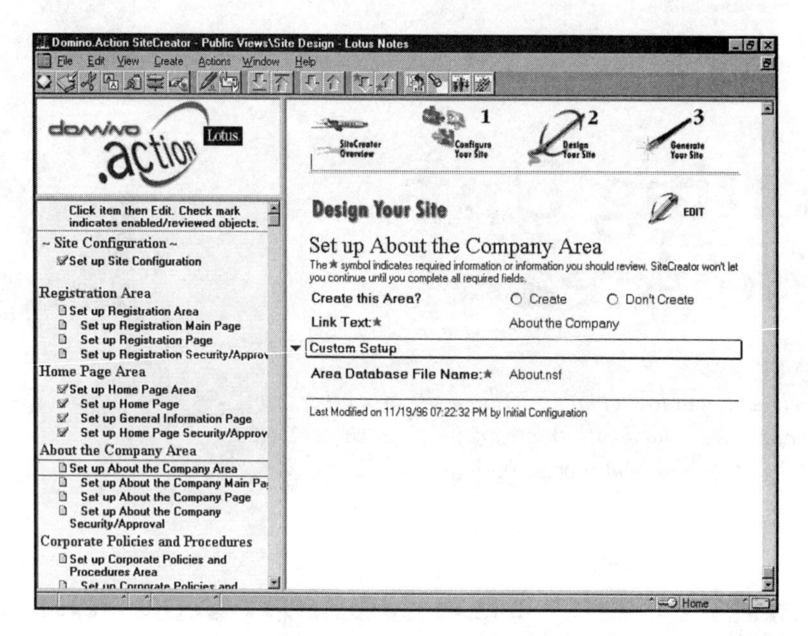

Figure 4.1 The Site Design document for the About the Company Area in the Preview pane.

5. If you want to use another name for this area database other than the default name, click the **Custom Setup** section head and enter the file name in the Area Database File Name field.
6. Click the **Continue** hotspot to save the document and return to the Site Design view.

Creating the Area Main Page

After you set up an area, you need to create an area main page. This is the introductory page users see when they jump to a site area. Normally, this page contains information about the site area plus links to other pages in the area.

To create an area main page:

1. From the Site Design view, select the set up main page document (for example, in the About the Company Area this document is called Set Up About the Company Main Page, as shown in Figure 4.2).

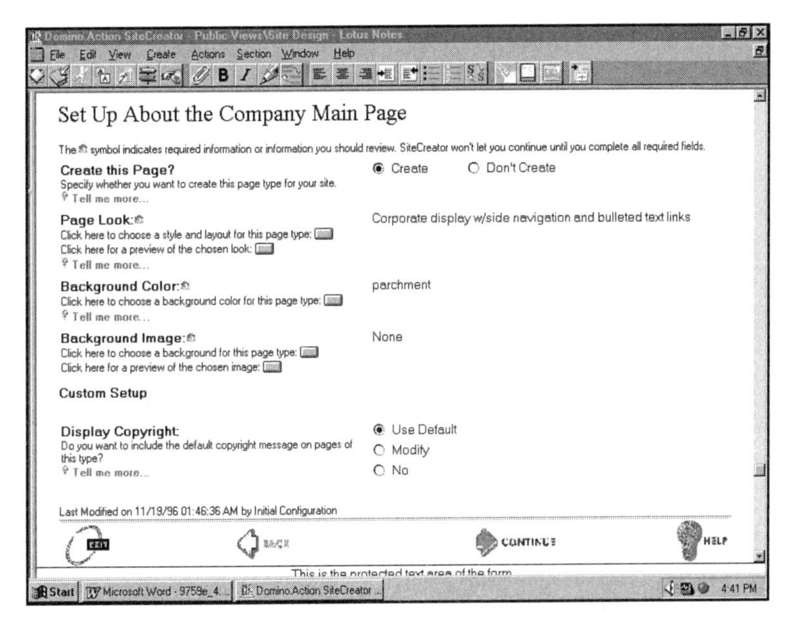

Figure 4.2 The Set Up About the Company Main Page document.

2. To have the SiteCreator create the page, select **Create** in the Create this Page? field.
3. Click the **Page Look** button and select one of the available page layouts. To see what the chosen layout looks like, click the **preview** button (see Figure 4.3).

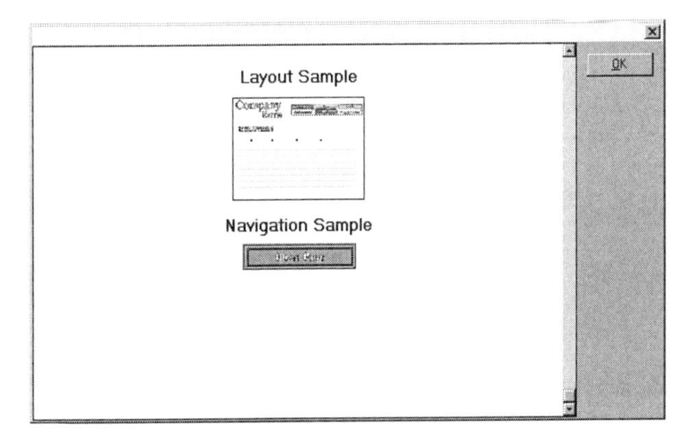

Figure 4.3 A preview of corporate display with top navigation and graphics.

4. Click the **Background Color** button and select a color for the background of the page from the list of colors.
5. If you want to use a **Background Image**, select the name of the background image you attached when you created the Site Configuration document or one of the Domino.Action images provided for you.
6. Click the **Custom Setup** section head if you want to change the copyright or to not use one on this page. From the Display Copyright field, choose **No, Use Default** (the one you set in the Site Configuration document), or **Modify** (which gives you the ability to enter new text or correct the existing copyright).
7. Click the **Continue** hotspot to save the document and return to the Site Design view.

Setting Up a Page

The next step is to set up pages for your site area. These pages can contain a variety of information, but the Set Up document lets you establish categories for the types of pages you make for that particular site area.

To set up pages for the site area:

1. From the Site Design view, select the page set up document to display it in the Preview pane. For the About the Company Area, this document is called Set up About the Company Page (see Figure 4.4).
2. To have the SiteCreator create the page, select **Create** in the Create this Page? field.
3. In the Page Look field, click the button and select one of the available page looks from the dialog list. To see what your choice looks like, click the **preview** button.
4. Click the **Background Color** button and select a color for the background of the page from the list of colors.
5. If you want to use a **Background Image**, select the name of the background image you attached when you created the Site Configuration document or one of the predesigned background images provided by Domino.Action.

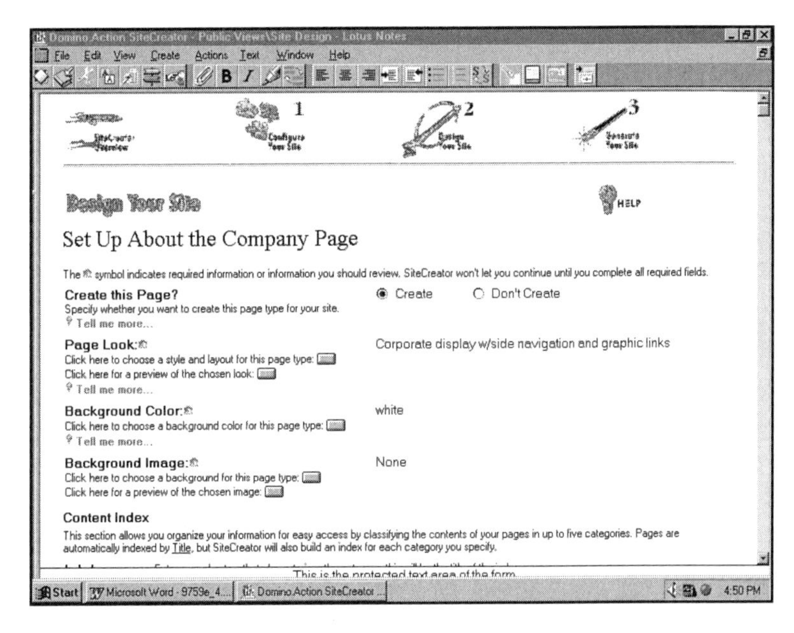

Figure 4.4 The Set Up About the Company Page document.

6. To set up the categories for your pages, click the **Content Index** section head (see Figure 4.5). You can sort your pages into five categories that you specify. For each category, enter a Label (descriptive title) for the category and Choices (set the keywords for the category that a user can select). Then click **Yes** or **No** in the Choices field. If you select No, users will only be able to select from the keywords listed in the Choices field for that category. If you select Yes, users will be able to add keywords other than those in the Choices field for that category.
7. Click the **Custom Setup** section head if you want to eliminate or change the default copyright notice on this page. From the Display Copyright field, choose **No, Use Default** (the one you set in the Site Configuration document), or **Modify** (which gives you the ability to enter new text or correct the existing copyright).
8. Click the **Continue** hotspot to save the document and return to the Site Design view.

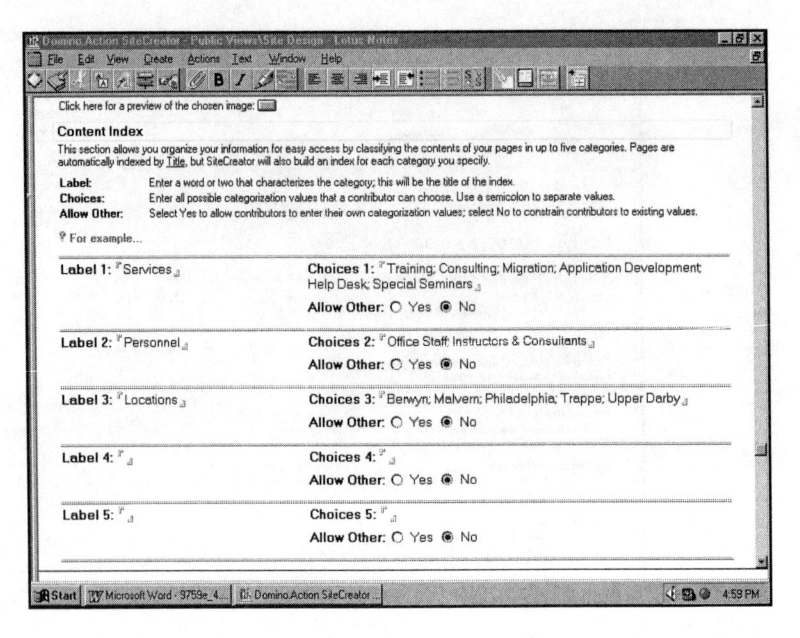

Figure 4.5 The Content Index section.

Specifying the Approval Process

On the Security/Approval page, you specify who will be authorized to compose pages in the area, who will be authorized to approve the pages before they become available on the site, and who will be authorized to read pages in this area of the site. If you enable an approval process, you have to specify the details of how it will work.

To complete the Set Up Security/Approval document:

1. Click the Set Up Security/Approval document to display it in the Preview pane (for example, in the About the Company site area, the document is called Set up About the Company Security/Approval as shown in Figure 4.6).
2. For the Content Composers field, enter or select the names of the people or groups who may compose pages in this site area. If you click the down arrow button to the right of the field, a browser opens that lets you choose names from the Public Address Book. Use semicolons to separate multiple names, and be sure to use both the hierarchical (Joan Blossom/Blossom Fragrance) and common (Joan Blossom) names.

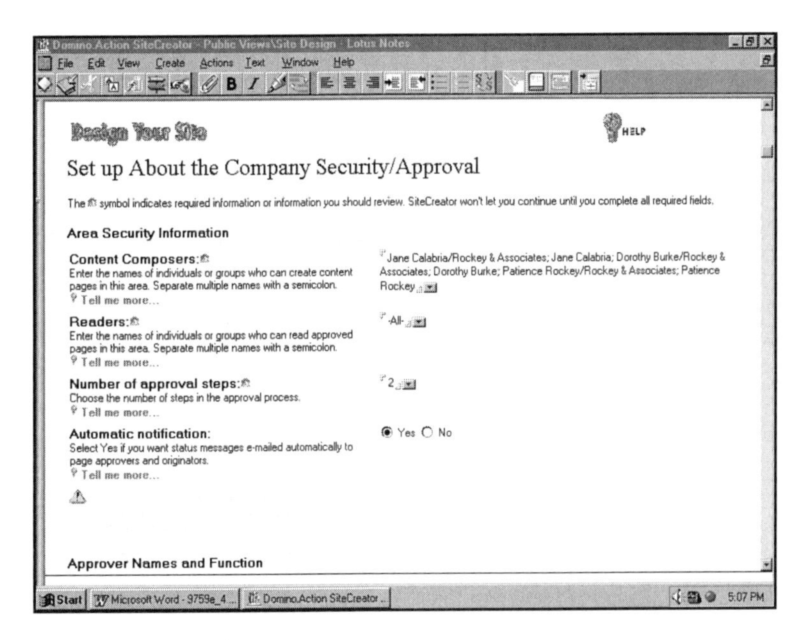

Figure 4.6 The Set up About the Company Security/Approval document.

3. In the Readers field, specify the people or groups who may read the pages in this site area. Leave it set to **All** if you want everyone to read the pages.
4. If you want to establish an approval process where people or groups approve the contents of newly composed pages before they become available to readers, enter the number of steps (between 1 and 5) you want in the Number of Approval Steps field. To disable the approval process, enter **0** for no steps.
5. If you entered a number of approval steps greater than zero, the Automatic Notification field appears. When you select **Yes**, e-mail is automatically sent to the approver alerting him or her that a page needs approval. Likewise, the composer of the page and the Web Master are alerted when the page is accepted or rejected.
6. If you set up approval steps, the Approver Names and Functions section appears (see Figure 4.7). Under Approver Names, you'll see fields for Step 1 Approvers, Step 2 Approvers, and so on, depending on the number of steps you specified. In each of these fields, enter or select the names of people or groups who will be involved in that level of approval. Then under Approver Function, you may optionally enter a brief description of what that level approver must do.

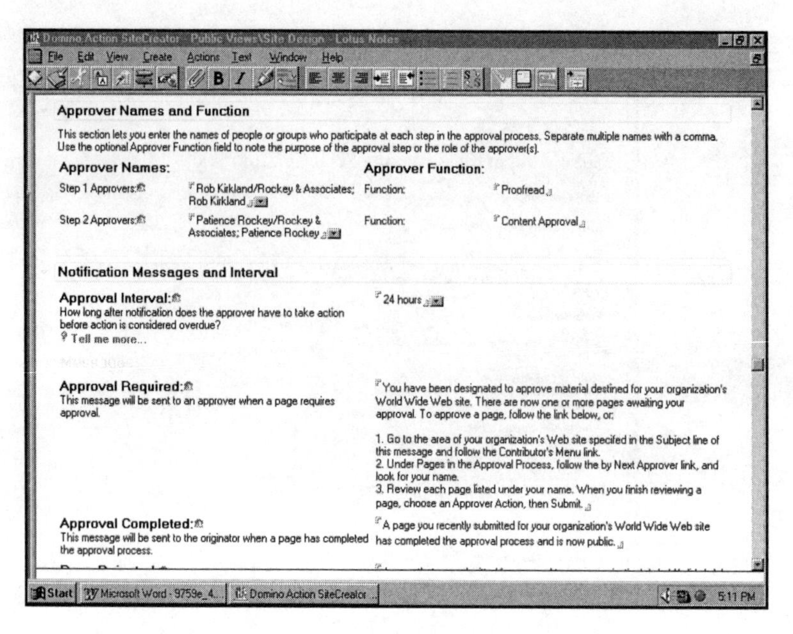

Figure 4.7 The bottom of the approval process document.

7. If you set Notification to Yes, the Notification Messages and Interval section appears (refer to Figure 4.7). You need to enter a time limit in the Approval Interval field to indicate how long after receiving notification does the Approver have to reply. If the Approver does not reply within that time interval, an overdue alert is sent.
8. Also in the Notification Messages and Interval section there are four fields in which appears the text of the messages that will go out to people during the approval process. You may optionally edit the messages. The four fields are: Approval-Required Message, Approval-Completed Message, Page-Rejected, and Page-Rejected and Returned.
9. Once you have completed the form, click the **Continue** hotspot to return to the Site Design view.

In this lesson, you learned how to set up a site area by creating a main page, specifying how you want pages to look within the site area, and setting up the approval process. In the next lesson, you'll see how the various site areas differ in their setup.

Working with Site Areas

In this lesson, you look at the various site areas available in Domino.Action and how their setups differ from the standard setup described in Lesson 4, "Setting Up a Site Area," and the home page setup of Lesson 3, "Designing Your Site."

The About the Company Site

This is a very straightforward site to set up using the procedures outlined in Lesson 4. It provides the visitor to your site with information about the company, its goals, its products and services, its officers, its locations, and so on.

The Corporate Policies and Procedures Site Area

This site area is geared more toward an intranet site rather than an Internet site. It is where users would find an employee manual, benefits information, vacation and sick leave policies, office procedures, and so on. You can easily set it up by using the procedures outlined in Lesson 4.

Discussion

The Discussion area is where users can comment on your company and services, ask questions, make suggestions, complain, and share information with one another. It is a Notes discussion database, but it is available to Web users.

Banners

To make the Discussion area more inviting and identifiable, Domino.Action adds a design feature to this site area main page. In the Set up Discussion Main Topic Page document there is an additional field called Banner where you may specify the banner you want to use on the page by clicking the Banner button and selecting one from the dialog list. A banner is a graphic that usually goes across the top of the page from the left margin to the right margin. Domino.Action has graphics available for you to use, but if you attached an image file as a banner in the Site Configuration document, you may specify the name of that file in the Banner field. You may preview your choice by clicking the **preview** button (see Figure 5.1).

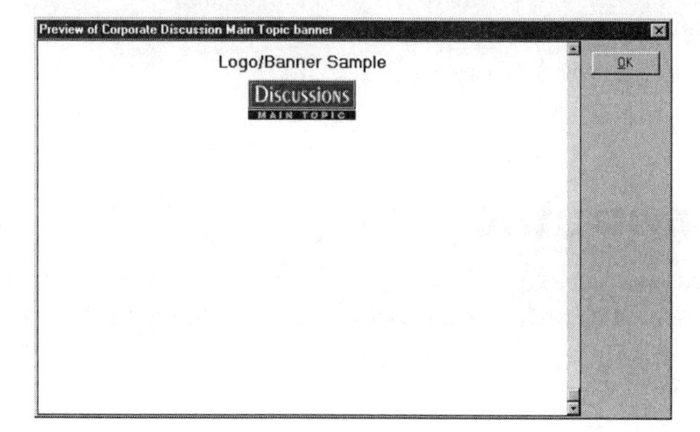

Figure 5.1 Preview of Corporate Discussion Main Topic banner.

Domino.Action also adds a banner to the Main Topic and Response pages in the Discussion site area. Pick a Main Topic banner or a Response banner in the Banners field of the setup document for each of these kinds of pages.

Categorization

Making the discussion area easy to use is important, and one way to do it is to index the pages. Each page in a discussion area is automatically indexed by author, date, and title. The Set Up Discussion Main Topic document has a Content Index collapsible section (see Figure 5.2) that allows you to further index discussions *by category*.

In the Label field, accept the default label of Categories or enter a label that better defines the category. Enter the keywords for the category in the Choices field if you want to narrow the categories to a select few. Select **Yes** under Allow Other if you want the users to be able to add new keywords on their own, in which case any keywords you entered in Choices are just to get the ball rolling. Don't allow other keywords if you want to narrow the areas of discussion. If you don't know where to start, click the **For Example** hotspot to see some suggestions.

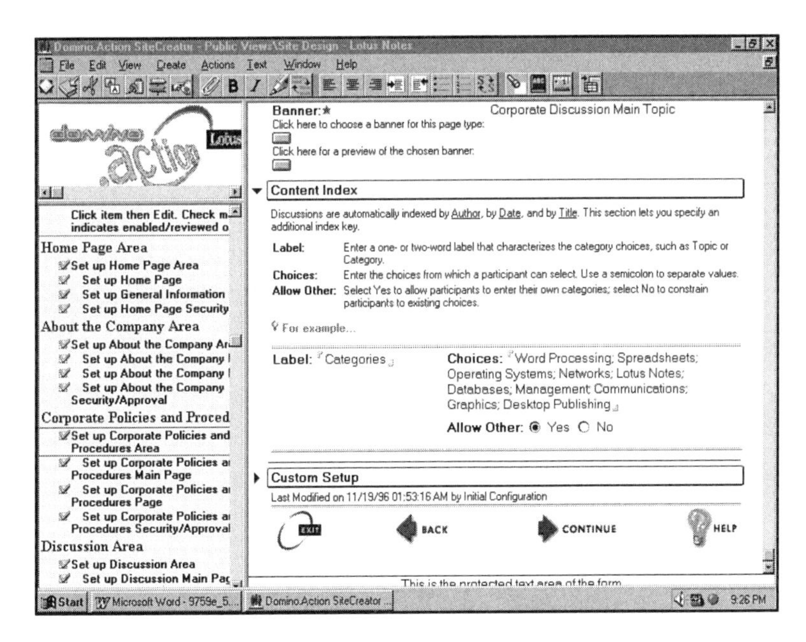

Figure 5.2 The Content Index section of the Set Up Discussion Main Topic Page document.

The Discussion Response Page

The discussion site area provides an additional page type for users to respond to questions or comments posted by others. This page type also features a banner in its design. In all other ways it sets up in the same way as other page types. In usage, as a response document, it inherits information from the document to which it responds.

The Security/Approval Page

There are two additional fields in the Security/Approval page for the Discussion area. If you select **Yes** in the Allow Anonymous Access field, you are permitting any visitor to view the pages in this area without entering a user name or password. Selecting **No** restricts visitation to registered users or specified-names or groups.

Selecting **Yes** in the Allow Anyone to Author field permits any visitor to author documents in this area. However, they will not be able to edit documents, not even the ones they created. Choosing **No** restricts authoring of documents to the individuals and groups specified in the Content Composers field.

Document Library

The Document Library provides an area where you can store documents for shared use or files for downloading. On the Set Up Document Library Page, there is a Content Index section similar to the one in the Discussion site area (see Figure 5.3). Although the pages are automatically categorized by title, you may specify five additional categories.

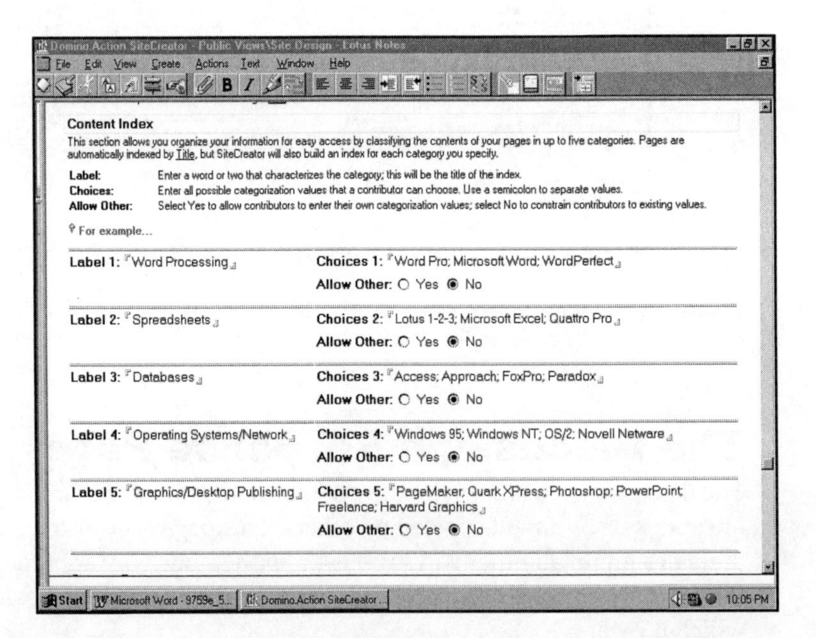

Figure 5.3 The Content Index section of the Set Up Document Library Page document.

In the Label field, enter a label that better defines the categorization choices (such as "Class Manuals"). Enter the categorization keywords in the Choices field if you want to narrow the categories to a select few ("Introductory," "Intermediate," "Advanced," and so on). Select **Yes** under Allow Other if you want the users to be able to add keywords in addition to the ones you entered in the Choices field.

The Feedback Site Area

The Feedback site area provides users with a feedback form to fill out and submit. The Banner choices allow you to set up either a user feedback (for your site) or a customer feedback page, although you can use a banner you attached to the Site Configuration document or no banner to create a different type of feedback page. The unique portion of setting up this site area is the Feedback Custom Questions section of the Set Up Feedback Page document. In this section (see Figure 5.4), you can specify up to five feedback questions to include on the feedback form.

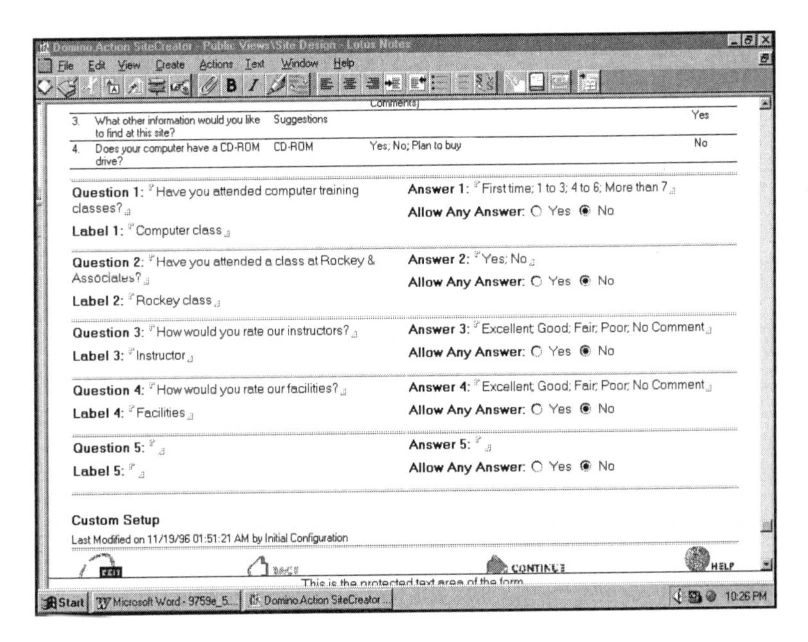

Figure 5.4 The Feedback Custom Questions section.

In the Question field, enter the question you want users to answer (such as "Did you find this site helpful?").

Enter a brief label that characterizes the question in the Label field to help index the database information (such as "Rating"). You don't need to use date, author, or title because Feedback is automatically indexed by those categories (author information is automatically collected, so Feedback pages don't need an author field).

In the Answer field, enter all the possible answers to the question (such as "Extremely," "Somewhat," "Not much," or "Not at all"). Separate multiple entries with a comma or semicolon. Leave the field blank if you want the users to supply their own answers, or choose **Yes** under Allow Any Answer to encourage user comments.

Frequently Asked Questions

You can publish frequently asked questions and their answers in this area of your Web site and save yourself the trouble of answering the same questions over and over again, while providing useful information to visitors to your site. The pages for this site area do not display a banner area, but you do have a choice of page looks.

Like several of the other site areas, the pages in the Frequently Asked Questions area are automatically indexed by title. You may specify one other indexing category in the Content Index section of the Set up FAQs Page document (see Figure 5.5).

Specify an indexing category in the Label field (such as "Company") and then enter keywords in the Choices field ("Directions," "Experience," and so on). If you want users to add their own keywords, select **Yes** in the Allow Other field.

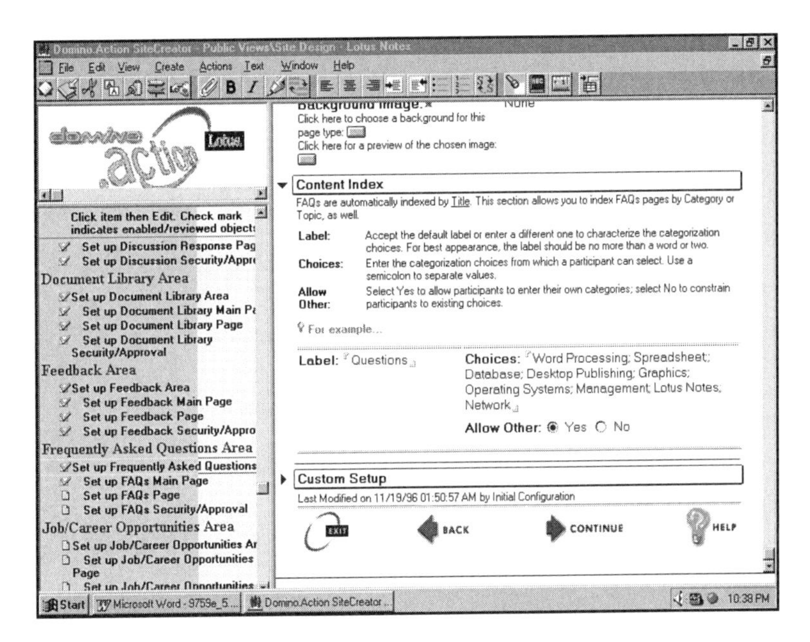

Figure 5.5 Content Index section of the Set up FAQs Page document.

Job/Career Opportunities

Whether you're running an intranet or an Internet site, offering job opportunities will attract many users looking to improve their current positions, make career advancements, or start new jobs. As a company, it gives you an inexpensive way to widely advertise your job openings.

Pages in this site area are automatically indexed by title, but you can specify up to five categories in the Content Index section of the Set Up Job Posting Page document (see Figure 5.6).

Specify an indexing category in the Label field (such as "Administrative Support") and then enter possible keywords in the Choices field ("Secretary," "Data Entry," and so on). If you want users to add their own keywords, select **Yes** in the Allow Other field.

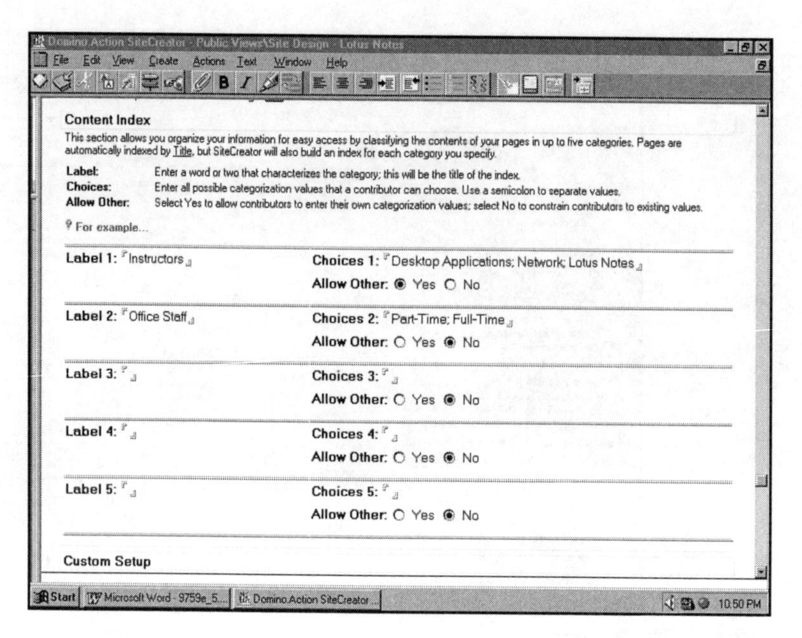

Figure 5.6 Content Index section of the Set Up Job Posting Page document.

Product/Services

The Product/Services area gives you a chance to sell, either by displaying your products or explaining your services. This site involves more than one type of page; Product Information, Product Review, and Product Specifications pages are all included.

Product Information pages are automatically indexed by title, but you may specify five additional categories in the Content Index section of the Set Up Product Information Pages document.

Because the Product Review pages are responses to the Product Information documents, setting up these pages is straightforward and uses no categorization. Instead, these pages inherit the categories from their parent documents (the Product Information pages).

The Product Specifications pages have only the standard fields and no categorization questions, as they inherit their category from their parent documents (the Product Information pages).

Registration

The Registration site area lets you collect information about visitors to your site and store it in a database. Once a visitor is registered, you can allow him greater privileges in your Web site. The registration process automatically adds newly registered users to a *registered users* group. By adding this group to database access control lists, you can give registered users rights different from those accorded to anonymous (non-registered) visitors to your site.

The Set Up Registration Page has some unique fields for you to complete. There are two collapsible sections on this document. The first one is called Registration (see Figure 5.7) and contains the administrative information for collecting and storing information on users.

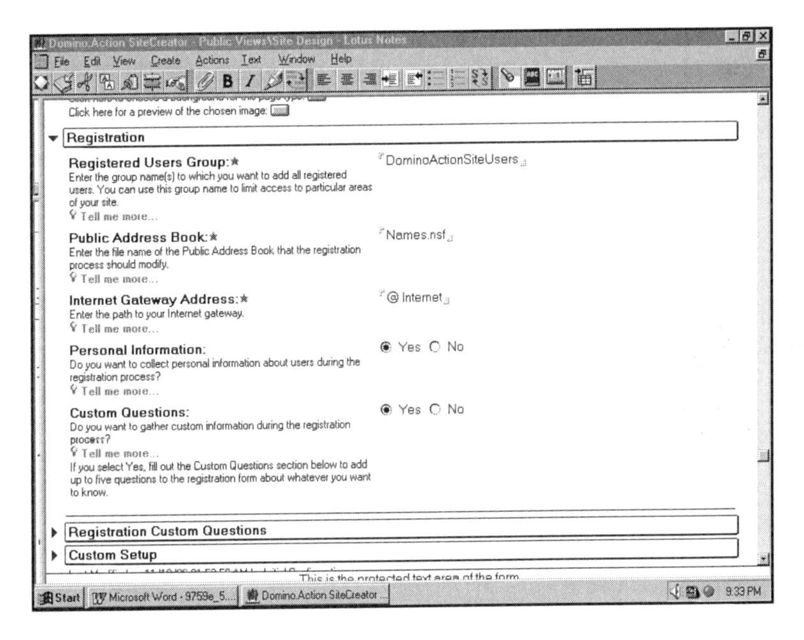

Figure 5.7 The Registration section.

Complete these fields in this section:

Registered Users Group: Enter the name of the group or groups in the Public Address Book to which you want to add all the registered users. If you add more than one group name, users will be added to all the named groups.

Public Address Book: Enter the file name of the address book to which the registration information will be added. Names.nsf is the name of your company's Public Address Book, but you may want to create a new address book for testing purposes. The Public Address Book must reside on the Domino server and be located in the Domino data directory. Always include the path in the file name if the file is located in a subdirectory.

Gateway Address: Enter the address of your Internet mail gateway here. By default, @ Internet appears in this field. If your Domino server has direct access to the Internet gateway domain, use the SMTP gateway domain name. If not, enter all the mail routing hops necessary to get e-mail to your company's Internet gateway domain. Consult your Notes Administrator if you're not sure of the mail-routing path.

Personal Information: Select **Yes** if you want to collect personal information about your users during the registration process, such as company name, address, and phone number.

Custom Questions: Select **Yes** to ask up to five custom questions during the registration process and then fill out the Registration Custom Questions section of the Set Up Registration Pages document.

In the Registration Custom Questions section (see Figure 5.8), you can add up to five specific questions you want users to answer. Enter each question in the Question field and then add a selection of possible answers in the Answer field. If you want users to add their own answers, select **Yes** in the Allow Other field.

Once you have created the Registration site area database, be sure that the default access in the access control list is Author. The Author should have create rights, and not delete rights. Make roles for Readers, Approvers, Composers, and Web Master. Composer and Reader roles should also be given default access. Add the name of the Domino server to the access control list and assign it Manager access.

In the creation process, SiteCreator makes two agents for the Registration site area. The Handle Requests agent processes registration requests and password-change requests submitted by site visitors. Every time a visitor to your site submits a registration request, this agent creates a Person record in the Public Address Book on the server, then adds the person to the registered users group you specified in the Set Up Registration Page document (the default group name is DominoActionSiteUsers). When a password change is requested, the agent replaces the old password with the new password in the existing Person document. The Handle Requests agent must be enabled and set up to run on the Domino server or registration won't work. To set the agent up to run on the Domino server, click the **Schedule** button and select the Domino server's name from the Run only on list box.

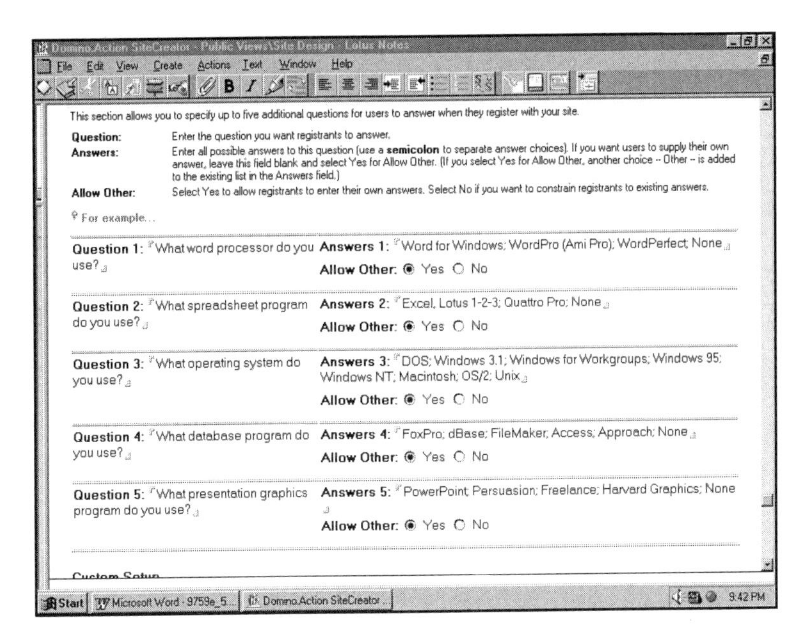

Figure 5.8 The Registration Custom Questions section.

You must also enable the **Send Mail** agent. This agent automatically sends e-mail to users:

- When a registration request has been processed, it sends the message `Thank you for registering with http://siteURL. Your username is username. Please remember that your password is case-sensitive.`
- After processing a password change request, the agent sends the message `Your password has successfully been changed. Your username is username. You may now log in with your new password. Please remember that your password is case-sensitive.`
- If the agent cannot process a registration or password-change request, it sends the message `There was a problem with your registration request. The error returned was: error. Try resubmitting your request. If you get another`

```
error notification, contact the Webmaster. Include the text of this message and
describe the problems you are experiencing.
```

TIP **Neither of the Agents Is Working** Mail-routing must be enabled on the Domino server for these agents to work. The Notes Administrator must set up the necessary Server, Connection, and Domain documents in the Public Address Book. In addition, the Server document in the Public Address Book must be set up to allow the registration agents to populate the Public Address book.

Although the two agents operate automatically, you must enable them by opening the Notes client on the Domino server (using the server ID) and adding the Registration database (Registra.nsf, by default) to the workspace.

1. Click the Registration database icon, and then choose **View**, **Agents**.
2. Check the box in front of Handle Requests.
3. Select the server on which the agent should run (the Domino server) and click **OK**.
4. Select the server where you stored the registration database and then return to the Agents view.
5. Check the box in front of Send Mail.
6. Select the server on which the agent should run (the Domino server) and click **OK**.
7. Select the server where you stored the registration database and then return to the Agents view.

The White Paper Site Area

The White Paper site area lets you store white papers for user reference. The pages are indexed by title, but as with many of the other site areas you can add up to five categories in the Content Index section of the Set Up White Paper Page document. You could skip setting up the White Paper area entirely and include white papers as a category of document in the Document Library area of your site.

In this lesson, you learned how the different site areas are set up and which instructions differ from the general procedures outlined in Lesson 4. In the next lesson, you'll learn how to generate your site.

Generating Your Site

Now that you've set all the parameters to configure your site, you're ready to go ahead and generate the databases. In this lesson, you learn the steps that complete this process.

Generating Your Site

The generation process begins with the AppAssembler, which combines information you entered in SiteCreator with templates and other design elements from the Library to generate the components of your site. These components are Lotus Notes databases that can be used in Notes or they can be published to the Web for viewing from a Web browser.

1. Go to step 3 of the Quick Start Site Creator category: Generate Your Site (see Figure 6.1).
2. Click the **Generate Your Site** hotspot to begin the generation process.
3. When the processing of documents is complete, the Run AppAssembler document appears in the Preview pane (see Figure 6.2).
4. Click the **Run** button to begin assembling the application. The process may pause for you to enter your password before it completes the task. Depending on the number of site areas you set up, the generation could take up to an hour. While the AppAssembler is running, you may run Notes or other applications in the background but do not change any of the SiteCreator documents.
5. When the process is complete, click the **Return to Action View** button.

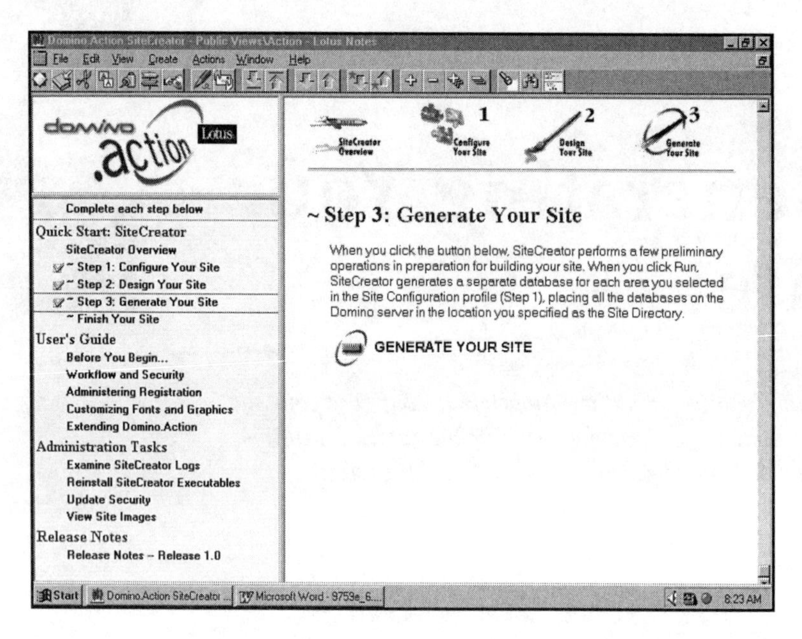

Figure 6.1 The Step 3: Generate Your Site document.

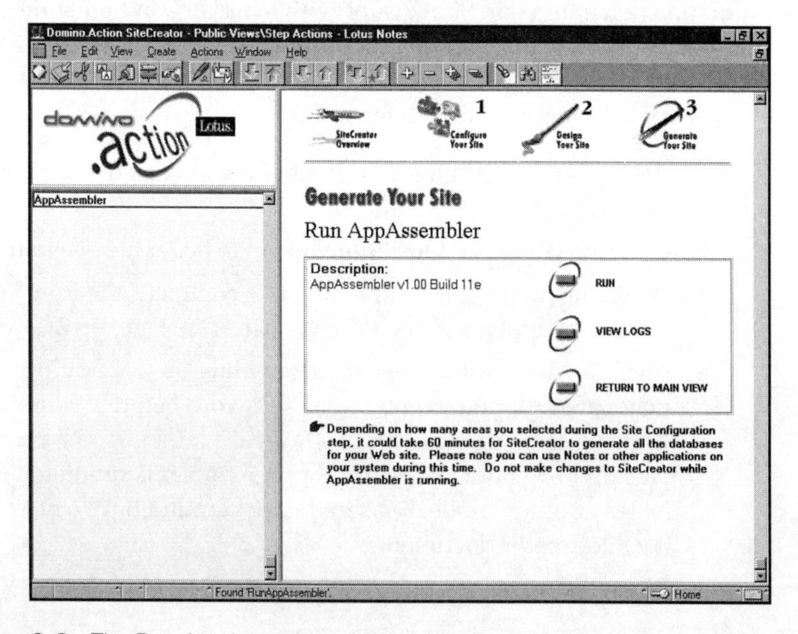

Figure 6.2 The Run AppAssembler document.

Finishing Your Site

The Finish Your Site step in the site creation process refreshes your database documents and establishes all the links between the documents.

1. From the Action view, select the Finish Your Site document (see Figure 6.3).
2. Click the **Finish Your Site** button.

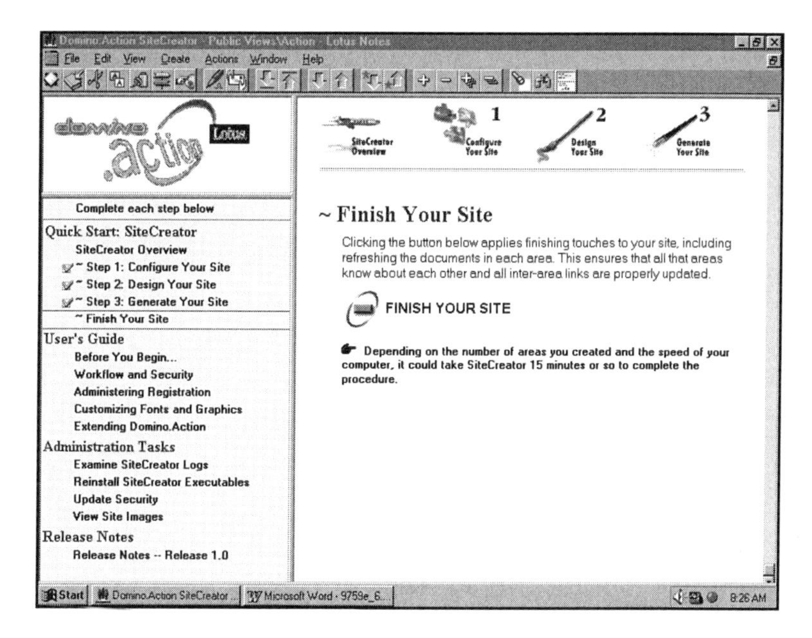

Figure 6.3 The Finish Your Site document.

3. SiteCreator resets all the access control lists for each of the databases you created and updates them. You may want to review them manually once this operation is complete and make sure that the names defined as Content Composer, Site Manager, and Approver are in the Public Address Book and in the same format as in the Security/Approval documents of each database.

Getting Your Site Up and Working

The area databases now exist in the \Notes\Data\Action directory. You can open these databases or add their icons to your workspace. However, before your site is up and running, there are a few finishing touches you must make. Replicate any local databases to your Domino server, making certain that you change the Site Configuration document to specify the location of your databases as being on your Domino server instead of your local computer.

Specify your home page database as the default home page (or have the Notes Administrator do this for you):

1. In the Public Address Book, open the Server document for your Domino server.
2. Under the HTTP section, enter the file name of your home page database (unless you changed it, the file name is Homepage.nsf) in the Default Home Page field.
3. Save and close the Server document.

Add content to your pages (or have the Content Composer do it if you are not the designated Content Composer):

1. Start your Web browser.
2. Go to the specific area to which you want to add content.
3. Click **Edit/Approve This Page**.
4. Add a title and other content to the page.
5. Select **Process**.
6. Click **Submit**.
7. If the Security/Approval profile for the area calls for one or more approval steps, each Approver must accept the content.

To approve the pages:

1. When you are the Approver, you must go to the main page for the site area.
2. From the Contributor's menu, select one of the Approval Process views.
3. Go to the page that needs approval.
4. Click **Edit/Approve This Page**.
5. Review the document.
6. Scroll down to the Approval Section and select an Approver Action.
7. Click **Submit**.

Add content to any other pages needed for the site and get approval.

1. Go to the main page for the site area.
2. From the Contributor's menu, select the page to which you want to add content.
3. Add the title and content.
4. Select **Process**.
5. Click **Submit**.
6. Follow steps 1 through 6 in the previous instructions to approve the pages.

Create a Full Text Index for the area database:

1. From the Notes workspace, select the area database icon.
2. Choose **File, Database, Properties** from the menu or click the database icon with the right mouse button and select **Database Properties**.
3. Click the **Full Text** tab of the Properties Box.
4. Click **Create Index**.
5. Repeat for each area database.

Now your site should be fully functional.

Updating the Site

To change the design of your area databases, make your changes to the area's Site Design documents in SiteCreator and then regenerate the site:

1. **Disable any areas you are not changing**: Select all the Site Design documents in all the unaffected areas by highlighting each one and then pressing the spacebar. After the unaffected documents are all selected, choose **Actions, Public, Disable Creation**.
2. **Regenerate the site**: Run Step 3: Generate Your Site again. Once the generation process is complete, click **Finish Your Site**.
3. **Refresh updated documents**: From the workspace, select each database with changes and then choose **Actions, Update Existing Documents**.

Replacing a Graphic

To replace the graphic from the Web (you must use a Web browser that supports file upload, such as Netscape Navigator), perform the following steps:

1. Go to the main page of the area where you want to replace the graphic.
2. Click the link to the Contributor's menu.
3. Click the File Library's **By Category** link to see a list of all the .GIF files.
4. Click **Edit Page** next to the graphic you want to replace.
5. A File Upload document opens. Scroll down the page and click **Edit This Page**.
6. Place a check mark next to attachments you want to mark for deletion.
7. Click **Submit**.
8. When you see the message `You successfully submitted this page,` click the **Go to** link for the page you just submitted.
9. Click **Edit this page**. Use the **Browse** button to locate the new .GIF file.
10. Click **Submit**.

You must follow these steps for each .GIF file you want to replace, and you must upload a file in each area in which it will be used.

To replace the graphic from Notes, you need to edit the Site Image documents:

1. From the main view of the SiteCreator, open the View Site Images document and click the button.
2. Select the image you want to replace and click the **Edit** icon.
3. Delete the existing .GIF file and image.
4. Click the **Attach/Import Image** button.
5. Use the Browser to locate the new .GIF file and then click **Create**.
6. Locate the image file and then click **Import**.
7. Save and close the document.

TIP **I Can't Edit the Attached Graphic File** After you create or edit a File Upload or Site Image document in Notes, you will not be able to edit the attached file from the Web. If you create a File Upload document from the Web, you won't be able to edit the attached file from Notes.

If you want to use Domino.Action to create another Web site, you must remove the databases from the \Notes\Data\Action directory on your computer. Then make new SiteCreator and Library databases, but give them different file names and titles than your first site. Otherwise, follow the procedures set out for the first site. If you intend to move these databases to your server and run both sites, you will have to consult with the Notes Administrator on how to run multiple sites on the same server. You'll also have to assign different file names to each area database so they aren't confused with the original site files.

In this lesson, you learned how to generate your site and how to finish the site creation process.

Index

A

B

C

D

E

F

G

H

I-J-K

L

O

P-Q

R

V

W-X-Y-Z

Technical Support:

If you cannot get the CD/Disk to install properly, or you need assistance with a particular situation in the book, please feel free to check out the Knowledge Base on our Web site at **http://www.superlibrary.com/general/support**. We have answers to our most Frequently Asked Questions listed there. If you do not find your specific question answered, please contact Macmillan Technical Support at **(317) 581-3833**. We can also be reached by email at **support@mcp.com**.

Complete and Return this Card for a *FREE* Computer Book Catalog

Thank you for purchasing this book! You have purchased a superior computer book written expressly for your needs. To continue to provide the kind of up-to-date, pertinent coverage you've come to expect from us, we need to hear from you. Please take a minute to complete and return this self-addressed, postage-paid form. In return, we'll send you a free catalog of all our computer books on topics ranging from word processing to programming and the internet.

Mr. ☐ Mrs. ☐ Ms. ☐ Dr. ☐

Name (first) ☐☐☐☐☐☐☐☐☐☐☐ (M.I.) ☐ (last) ☐☐☐☐☐☐☐☐☐☐☐☐☐☐☐

Address ☐☐☐☐☐☐☐☐☐☐☐☐☐☐☐☐☐☐☐☐☐☐☐☐☐☐☐☐☐☐☐☐☐☐☐

☐☐☐☐☐☐☐☐☐☐☐☐☐☐☐☐☐☐☐☐☐☐☐☐☐☐☐☐☐☐☐☐☐☐☐

City ☐☐☐☐☐☐☐☐☐☐☐☐☐☐☐ State ☐☐ Zip ☐☐☐☐☐ ☐☐☐☐

Phone ☐☐☐ ☐☐☐ ☐☐☐☐ Fax ☐☐☐ ☐☐☐ ☐☐☐☐

Company Name ☐☐☐☐☐☐☐☐☐☐☐☐☐☐☐☐☐☐☐☐☐☐☐☐☐☐☐☐☐☐☐☐☐

E-mail address ☐☐☐☐☐☐☐☐☐☐☐☐☐☐☐☐☐☐☐☐☐☐☐☐☐☐☐☐☐☐☐☐☐

1. Please check at least (3) influencing factors for purchasing this book.

Front or back cover information on book .... ☐
Special approach to the content .... ☐
Completeness of content .... ☐
Author's reputation .... ☐
Publisher's reputation .... ☐
Book cover design or layout .... ☐
Index or table of contents of book .... ☐
Price of book .... ☐
Special effects, graphics, illustrations .... ☐
Other (Please specify): ________________ ☐

2. How did you first learn about this book?

Saw in Macmillan Computer Publishing catalog .... ☐
Recommended by store personnel .... ☐
Saw the book on bookshelf at store .... ☐
Recommended by a friend .... ☐
Received advertisement in the mail .... ☐
Saw an advertisement in: ________________ ☐
Read book review in: ________________ ☐
Other (Please specify): ________________ ☐

3. How many computer books have you purchased in the last six months?

This book only .... ☐ 3 to 5 books .... ☐
2 books .... ☐ More than 5 .... ☐

4. Where did you purchase this book?

Bookstore .... ☐
Computer Store .... ☐
Consumer Electronics Store .... ☐
Department Store .... ☐
Office Club .... ☐
Warehouse Club .... ☐
Mail Order .... ☐
Direct from Publisher .... ☐
Internet site .... ☐
Other (Please specify): ________________ ☐

5. How long have you been using a computer?

☐ Less than 6 months ☐ 6 months to a year
☐ 1 to 3 years ☐ More than 3 years

6. What is your level of experience with personal computers and with the subject of this book?

	With PCs	With subject of book
New	☐	☐
Casual	☐	☐
Accomplished	☐	☐
Expert	☐	☐

Source Code ISBN: 0-7897-0975-9

7. Which of the following best describes your job title?

- Administrative Assistant ☐
- Coordinator ☐
- Manager/Supervisor ☐
- Director ☐
- Vice President ☐
- President/CEO/COO ☐
- Lawyer/Doctor/Medical Professional ☐
- Teacher/Educator/Trainer ☐
- Engineer/Technician ☐
- Consultant ☐
- Not employed/Student/Retired ☐
- Other (Please specify): ________________ ☐

8. Which of the following best describes the area of the company your job title falls under?

- Accounting ☐
- Engineering ☐
- Manufacturing ☐
- Operations ☐
- Marketing ☐
- Sales ☐
- Other (Please specify): ________________ ☐

9. What is your age?

- Under 20 ☐
- 21-29 ☐
- 30-39 ☐
- 40-49 ☐
- 50-59 ☐
- 60-over ☐

10. Are you:

- Male ☐
- Female ☐

11. Which computer publications do you read regularly? (Please list)

____

Comments: ________________________________

Fold here and scotch-tape to mail.

BUSINESS REPLY MAIL

FIRST-CLASS MAIL PERMIT NO. 9918 INDIANAPOLIS IN

POSTAGE WILL BE PAID BY THE ADDRESSEE

ATTN MARKETING
MACMILLAN COMPUTER PUBLISHING
MACMILLAN PUBLISHING USA
201 W 103RD ST
INDIANAPOLIS IN 46290-9042

NO POSTAGE
NECESSARY
IF MAILED
IN THE
UNITED STATES